A History of

Longmans

And Their Books 1724–1990
Longevity in publishing

A History of

Longmans

AND THEIR BOOKS 1724–1990

Longevity in Publishing

ASA BRIGGS

The British Library
and
Oak Knoll Press

First published 2008 by
The British Library
96 Euston Road
London NW1 2DB
and
Oak Knoll Press
310 Delaware Street
New Castle
DE 19720

A CIP Record for this book is available from both
The British Library and the Library of Congress

ISBN 978 0 7123 4873 7   (The British Library)
ISBN 978 1 584562 34 4   (Oak Knoll Press)

Designed and typeset by Richard Morris
Printed in Hong Kong by Paramount Printing Company

This History is dedicated to the memory
of Cyprian Blagden (1906-1962), historian
of Longmans and of the Stationers'
Company, and to the continuing influence
of Tim Rix, publisher, without whom it
would never have been written.

Contents

Abbreviations

BL	The British Library
BSTJ	*The Bookseller and the Stationery Trades Journal*
BTHGN	*Book Trade History Group Newsletter*
CC	H. Cox and C. Chandler, *The House of Longman* (1925)
CUP	Cambridge University Press
DNB	*Dictionary of National Biography and ODNB*
E	*The Economist*
EHP	A. Briggs (ed.), *Essays in the History of Publishing* (1974)
EHR	*English Historical Review*
ELT	English Language Teaching
ER	*Edinburgh Review*
ESTC	*English Short Title Catalogue*
FM	Fraser's Magazine
GM	*Gentleman's Magazine*
JRSA	*Journal of the Royal Society of Arts*
KP	Charles Knight, *Passages of a Working Life* (1864)
LA	Longman Archive, University of Reading
LSE	London School of Economics
M	Mumby's *Publishing and Bookselling*, 1974 edn. (ed. and revised by I. Norrie)
MLR	*Modern Languages Review*
NQ	*Notes and Queries*
OUP	Oxford University Press
PBSA	Papers of the Bibliographical Society of America
PC	*Publishers' Circular*
PH	*Publishing History*
PRO	Public Record Office [now the National Archives]
PW	Philip Wallis, *At the Sign of the Ship* (1974)
QR	*Quarterly Review*
RSA	Royal Society of Arts
RES	*Review of English Studies*
SOB	Charles Knight, *Shadows of the Old Booksellers* (1927 edn.)
SPCK	Society for Propagating Christian Knowledge
TDPP	C.W. Timperley, *Dictionary of Printers and Printing* (1839)
TL	*The Library*
TLS	*Times Literary Supplement*
UCL	University College of London

Acknowledgements

It is impossible to list all the people inside and outside the House of Longman, unfortunately some no longer alive, who have helped me in innumerable ways during the long preparation of this book, particularly Tim Rix and Annabel Jones whose help has been invaluable. My researches were also assisted and supported at many stages by Susan Hard, and the final text was meticulously handled by Pat Spencer, to whom, as always, I owe a great debt.

I would like to thank Pearson Education for the use of the Longman Portraits and access to the Longman Archive. Jim Edwards and Michael Bott, who were in charge of the Archive at the University of Reading, have been of immense value to what I have always considered to be a project and not a single publication. I am also grateful to Lady Elizabeth Longman, the staff of the British Library, in particular David Way of British Library Publishing, the designer of this book Richard Morris, the London Library, the compilers of the the DNB and ODNB, the Library of the University of London, the National Library of Scotland and Bristol Council and Central Library.

The core members of the Worcester College group on the history of the book, which I organised from 1983 to 1991, included Giles Barber, John Barnard, Alan Bell, Jim Edwards, Simon Eliot, John Feather, David Foxon, Graham C. Greene, David McKitterick, Don McKenzie, Robin Myers, John Sutherland, Michael Turner and Ian Willison. Michael Twyman and James Mosley were drawn in whenever the group dealt with printing. The size of the group was flexible, the discussions were uniformly helpful.

I would also like to acknowledge the help, sometimes substantial, that I have been given at different times and in different ways by Howard B. Abrams, Robin Alston, Verity Andrews, Nicolas Barker, Basil Blackwell, Noël Brack, Johnnie Butler, Charles Chadwyck-Healey, David Daiches, Eric de Bellaigue, Marysa Demoor, Robert Duncan, Pat Gibson, Wendy Gordon, Basil Greenslade, John L. Herkless, Anthony Hobson, Leslie Howsam, John Issitt, Derry Jeffares, Paula Kahn, Benjamin Kaplan, David Lea, Howard Leathlean, Jeremy Lewis, Jane Millgate, Maurice Milne, Dale Morris, Joyce Nairn, Simon Nowell-Smith, Jeremy Osborne, Peter Pitman, Monroe Price, Randolph Quirk, James Raven,   Julian Rea, Maurice Rickards, Willie Shen, Chris Stray, John Trevitt, John Wilson, Robert Woof and Michael Wymer.

I am, of course, solely responsible for the final product. The support of my wife has been indispensable throughout a protracted, often daunting, always absorbing enterprise, dogged by ill health, not only my own, but always characterised by a determination to see the project through.

Illustrations

The sources are placed under the illustrations. We are very grateful to the institutions concerned for allowing us to reproduce them: The British Library; the Bodleian Library, the University of Oxford; Constable & Robinson Ltd.; Hertfordshire Archives and Local Studies; The Guildhall Library, City of London; the National Portrait Gallery, London; The Nuffield Foundation; Pearson Education; The Royal Collection; the Worshipful Company of Stationers and Newspaper Makers. The Longman Archive has provided much of the material for illustrations, including the Jefferays Scrapbooks in Part II of the Archive, but it does not have an extensive range of modern titles and the Library is grateful therefore to the following for the use of copies from their personal collections: the author, and Annabel Jones, Lady Elizabeth Longman, Andrew MacLennan, Lynette Owen, Tim Rix, Michael Rodgers and Roger Watson.

For a newspaper, a magazine, or a book publishing house to survive for over a hundred years, maintaining its name and some recognizable part of its corporate identity is a great feat ... [Yet] all institutions have to be reborn from time to time as the price of survival.

(A.L. Nevins, *The Price of Survival* (1967), published in New York on the 150th anniversary of 'The House of Harper')

An exposure of the causes of the present deteriorated condition of health and diminished duration of human life compared with that which is attainable by nature; being an attempt to deduce from the phenomena of nature such rules of living as may tend to correct the evidence and restore the health of mankind to its pristine strength and vigour forming a code of health and long life, founded on principles fixed and indisputable.

(Title of a new Longman book by Joel Pinney, 1830)

PS Please note that my telegraphic address is Longevity London.

(Letter from the publishing agent A.P. Watt, to Lady Randolph Churchill, 20 January 1898)

We are programmed for survival.

(Tom Kirkwood, BBC Reith Lecturer, 2001)

15

AT THE

QUEEN's HEAD TAVERN in *Pater-Noster-Row*,

On *Thursday*, the 3d of *Febr.* 1725. exactly at *Ten* in the Morning,

(*At one of the Clock the Company will be entertained with a good* DINNER)

The Following COPIES and Parts of COPIES

Of the Late

Mr. W. TAYLOR,

Will be disposed of by AUCTION to the
Highest Bidder, in 88 LOTS.

I. *Those who purchase them, to pay in Ready Money, or give such Security for
Payment thereof in Six Months, as his Executors shall approve of.*

II. *The Copies, and the several Parts and Shares of Copies throughout the whole,
are believed to be true and exact: However, every one is at liberty before the
Sale to satisfy themselves herein.*

III. *If any of the Books are printing, the Expence to be paid by the Purchasers,
over and above the Price of the Copy.*

	Lot			
aWard	1	ART of Speaking, in 12mo.	Half.	11:5:0
		Campbell's Vitruvius, 1st and 2d Volumes, containing 200 Copper-Plates, just going to the Press.	A Sixteenth.	
		Annals of King George, vol. 1, 2, and 3.	One Third.	
		Abridgment of Ashmole's Order of the Garter, 8vo.	A Sixth.	
Osborn & Longman	2	Adventures of Theagenes and Chariclea, 2 vol. 12mo.	A Fourth.	4:0:0
		Art of English Poetry, 3d and 4th vol. 12mo.	Half.	
		Abelardi Epistolæ.	Half.	
aWard	3	Ainsworth's Latin and English Dictionary, 4to, now in the Press, upon which has been advanced about 35 l. for each Tenth Share.	One Tenth, and one Sixtieth.	40:5:0
Pearse & Bickerworth	4	Athenian Oracle, 4 vol. 8vo, out of print and much wanted.	A Fourth.	4:10:0
Kingston	5	――― Ditto.	A Fourth.	4:15:0
Rivington	6	――― Ditto.	A Fourth.	4:3:0
Osborn & Longman	7	――― Ditto.	A Sixth.	5:5:0
	8	Andry of Worms.	The Whole.	
		*Advice to a Son, 12mo.	The Whole.	
		Bridle for the Tongue, by Hooton, something to be paid for the 2d Edition.	A Third.	
Jos Downing	9	Bellcaris's Memoirs of Scotland.	Half.	1:1:0
		Boulton's Surgery, in 8vo.	The Whole.	
		Buchanani Epistolæ, 8vo.	A Third.	
		Boetius, by Preston.	A Fourth.	
		Bellini of Fevers, in English, 8vo.	Half.	
Innys	10	*Boyle's Theological Works abridged, in 3 vol. 8vo.	Half.	4:15:0
		Blackhall's Sermons, 2d vol. 8vo. (except one Sermon.)	100 and 2th	
Osborn Horsdom	11	Boyer's French Dictionary, in 4to and 8vo.	A Sixth.	6:6:0
		Buchanan's History of Scotland, 2 vol. 8vo.	Half.	10:5:0
		Boulton on Witchcraft.	A Sixth.	
ashley	12	Book of Homilies, in Folio, (now in the Press.)	A Sixth.	11:5:0
Bel	13	――― Ditto.		10:0:0
D	14	Blome's Hist. of the Bible, in 4to, 333 in 1500, going to the Press.		
			Lot	118:12:0

1 Prologue: Longevity

I was first drawn to the idea of writing this book, long in preparation, by the longevity of the Longmans as publishers. The time span in itself was attractive. I had already spent almost three decades on the history of broadcasting – radio and television – where the time span was short. Now I could go back to 1724, the year when the first Thomas Longman started selling books in London. I knew that on my way to the twentieth century I would pass through the Victorian years where I felt thoroughly at home. For much of the twentieth century I would be covering the period of my own life.

That was one attraction. I also warmed to the prospect of exploring what was still in the 1970s and 1980s a relatively neglected medium. Books then figured little in communications – or media – studies, which were already in their infancy, and although the term 'communications revolution' had been brought into use, the main emphasis was on television, then the newest medium, a medium frequently compared with print. As an avid reader and collector of books I belonged to what was then (and often before) a self-acknowledged minority. I wished to know more about what happened between the invention of printing and that later communications revolution of my own time. How had evolving 'book trades', best thought of in the plural, dealt with the changing demands for information, education and entertainment, which in the twentieth century became a sacred trinity for British broadcasters?

I had always believed as an historian that the history of words matters profoundly. These particular key words in the trinity – information, education and entertainment – were not regularly employed in 1724. Nor in their modern sense were the three words 'publishing', 'literature' and 'leisure'. Nor indeed the word 'modern' itself. How did these terms acquire their present sense? There were key questions also. How did the relationships between spoken and printed words change or those between printed words and 'images'? What was the role of patronage and of 'the market'? How many books were printed and in what sizes and print runs, and how were they categorised and priced? What was the significance of the word 'genre'? 'How did the history of newspapers and periodicals relate to the history of books? Did 'fiction' reflect or influence? What was the effect on it of 'serialisation'? How did declining reference back to Greek and Roman 'classics', and even to the Bible, alter perspectives in the nineteenth and twentieth centuries? The questions continue to multiply.

Words covering relationships demand historical study as much as the relationships themselves. Yet I was driven to explore also more specific

An example of the trade sale catalogues used by bookseller

The Trade Catalogue List of the 'late Mr. W. Taylor', to be 'disposed of by Auction to the Highest Bidder, in 88 Lots' 3 February, 1725, 'exactly at Ten in the morning, (at one of the Clock the Company will be entertained with a good Dinner)'

BL Cl.7aa.1

[A collection of the catalogues of trade sales of books, books in quires, and copyrights, held on 11 December 1704 and from 3 April 1718 to 15 December 1768]

Longman Archive on permanent loan to the British Library

working relationships within the book trades between papermakers, printers, bookbinders, booksellers, publishers, authors (I was one), and readers (I was one of these too). I knew that they were not just responding to texts; they gave their own meanings to them. Their responses, therefore, demanded analysis as well as description. So too did what came to be called 'the cultures of print'. Interpretation of them involved looking at the role of intermediaries, agents and the study of such relationships. The study of any relationship demands an interdisciplinary approach, incorporating as it had to do psychology, sociology, economics and technology.

There is now a highly sophisticated study of the history of 'the book trade' on both sides of the Channel (France led the way) and on both sides of the Atlantic. I have learnt much from it and I have contributed to it,[1] and while this *History* of one of the great publishing houses does not claim to be a history of 'the trade' it could not have been written without my drawing upon it. The topics that I have selected in the largely chronological chapters that follow reflect not only my own approaches and preoccupations but those of others besides myself. One of them for example, is the formulation of a literary canon, determined at least as much by publishers as by editors. Another, for long more neglected, is the development of the textbook. The activities of the House of Longman should never be studied in isolation. Indeed, they cannot be. Comparison with the activities of other publishers is crucial. So, too, is exploration of 'context', affecting all publishing, as does law, particularly the law relating to 'literary property'. Scholars have increasingly recognised this.

Within the history of the 'book trades' one of the themes on which I focus in this *History* and the theme that gives my book its title is longevity, essentially within this context a preoccupation of my own. In a society that is preoccupied with individual 'ageing', human longevity is now being studied even more intensively than the history of the book trades. Yet within the pattern of these trades institutional ageing and longevity have received little attention. The contemporary remarks that illuminate both stories stand out, like Edward Bulwer Lytton's question posed in 1863, 'Is it a sign of longevity when a man looks younger than he is?' or the first sentences of Nigel Cross's *The Common Writer: Life in nineteenth century Grub Street* (1985): 'Titles that remain in print long after the deaths of their authors are at the top of the hierarchy of books . . . It is these extant books that we are accustomed to think of as literature.'

Since the nineteenth century book lives have shortened while human lives have further lengthened in both cases and though the hierarchies

---

1   I have listed my own connections in Appendix 5, an autobiographical appendix. Appendix 1 deals, necessarily selectively, with bibliographical sources. I have deliberately not included footnotes in this introductory chapter, in Appendix 5 or in my Epilogue which refers back to this Prologue.

have become suspect the significance of the ephemeral has come to be appreciated. A different twentieth-century quotation with very broad implications makes a contrasting point to that of Cross – 'the life of a library is, as a rule, less than half that of a man'. Yet there are institutional libraries that have spanned different generations, even different centuries. Thus, leaving on one side the libraries of Oxford and Cambridge and the British Library, a provincial subscription library in Leeds, founded in 1768, in which members held shares, is still a place of scholarship as well as discussion in the twenty-first century. One of its twentieth-century librarians, Frank Beckwith, wrote learnedly on the range of eighteenth century subscription libraries. Of the London Library, founded in 1840, John Wells wrote in the concluding paragraph of his highly entertaining *Rude Words: A Discursive History of the London Library* (1991) that 'the closer you get to the idea of the London Library, the more it recedes into infinity'.

When I first started to write this *History* I had already planned to give it as a sub-title 'a study in longevity'. That was before the House of Longman ceased to exist as an independent business in 1994, an event which took me by surprise and for which I was not prepared. I knew, however, that as early as 1968, six years before I edited a volume of essays to celebrate the 250th anniversary of the House, Longman had become part of the multi-product Pearson conglomerate, which already included a publishing sector. Neither Longman nor Pearson thought of it then in terms of a conglomerate. In 1994, however, they both did.

There had been no Longmans connected with the House of Longman after the death of seventh-generation Mark (1916–1972), the last of his line, but the Longman Group survived and prospered between 1972 and 1990, the terminal date of my *History*, making many mergers of its own under the aegis of Pearson. One of them was the take-over in 1985 of the well-known British firm of Pitman, founded in the nineteenth century by Isaac Pitman, the great pioneer of shorthand. The last of them in 1988 was that with the American publishing firm of Addison-Wesley, founded in 1942. This was a move that seemed designed to strengthen the Longman Group, but there was a twist to the story. Addison-Wesley survived beyond 1994. The Longman Group did not.

Why the Group did not survive seems as important a question to ask now as my initial question why the House of Longman had survived for 266 years between 1724 and 1990, but to answer it would require a thorough examination not only of the Longman archive during the four years from 1990 to 1994 but of the Pearson archive, including in this case the pre-1994 archive, so far inaccessible. That was one of the reasons that from the start of my venture I decided to stop in 1990, not in 1994. Pearson itself was to change almost totally between 1994 and the present. Yet significantly, if only for marketing reasons, the Longman imprint survived not only Longmans but the end in 1994 of the Longman Group as an identifiable entity.

The imprint has appeared, however – and recently increasingly – on a number of books published after 1994, for example on the cover of a well-designed Pearson Education list of history books on offer on the 275th anniversary of 1724 in 1999 – '275 years of publishing history' – and on the title pages in the *Silver Library*, published in 2000. There were echoes here. The name 'Silver Library' had been used by Longmans, Green and Co. a hundred years before when books in series became increasingly fashionable. The volumes in the first *Silver Library* cost 3s 6d. Four were by Arthur Conan Doyle (1859–1930), four by Richard Jefferies (1848–1887) and four by Andrew Lang (1844–1912), a central figure in Longman history, now largely forgotten.

Publishers' imprints often have a short life, and during the 270 years of its existence Longmans, who from the start drew in other partners, employed no fewer than twenty-eight imprints. The longest of all of them – Longman, Hurst, Rees, Orme, Brown and Green – lasted from 1823 to 1825, and Longman, Rees, Orme, Brown, Green and Longman (two Longmen there) lasted from 1832 to 1838. These were such formidable lists of names that the novelist Sir Walter Scott (1771–1832), for part of his life a Longman author, coined the phrase 'the long firm' to describe the organisation. I even considered making 'The Long Firm' part of my title. From 1838 until 1959, deep into the twentieth century, however, only one other name, that of Green, survived alongside that of Longman.

The names 'Longmans' and 'Green', which appeared together on the title pages, were not always in use together within the limited world of publishing. The single word 'Longmans', which is used for convenience, along with 'Longman', throughout most of this *History*, was already being displayed on the spine of Longman books as early as 1900, and in 1969 the name Longman replaced the name Longmans that had been used only over the previous ten years. 'Nowadays everyone in Longman House correctly refers to the Company as Longman', Noël Brack, a former director of the Company, who kept his own archive including a diary, one of my most valuable sources for some of the later chapters in this *History*, wrote to me on 20 November 1982.

～

Whatever current imprint the House employed at any particular time between 1724 and 1994, the Longman enterprise usually described itself as a 'House', not as a business or a firm or, indeed, as a company. 'House' was an old description for a publisher, but one that was not exclusive to publishing: the House of Commons and the House of Lords place the word within a constitutional context as did the House of Hanover. Within the context of publishing, it has a long history of its own, as has the word 'shop', employed in printing as well as in retailing. It has been used outside publishing too. Philip Clarke wrote a book in 1973 called *The First House in the City: an Excursion into the History of Child & Co. to mark its 300th year of Banking at the same address*, and in the nineteenth century the word 'House' was employed in the fashion business, as I explained in my *Victorian Things* (1988) when I examined the House of Worth. And it still survives in this context.

In the case of Longman, there was at the very beginning a real house in London's Paternoster Row, built after the Great Fire of London in 1666 and purchased by Thomas Longman I (1699–1755) in 1724 along with its household fittings. It bore a sign, the Sign of the Ship, and it later acquired a number, 39. In the nineteenth century the house and the House survived another fire in 1861, started in a nearby tallow maker's premises. It was then lavishly rebuilt, only to be once more destroyed by fire, this time for ever, along with the whole Row, in German air raids over London in December 1940. The Longman archive on which my *History* depends are, therefore, sadly incomplete. They are, however, easily accessible, thanks to an enlightened Longman decision to deposit them in Reading University, taken as long ago as 1974, and there is ample scope for further scholars to work on them. I have explained how they are organised in Appendix 1, largely reserving my footnotes for references to books and periodicals. My *History* will provide, I hope, a framework within which other scholars can pursue their own researches. It does not claim to be a last word.

The two dates 1861 and 1940 are landmarks in the Longman chronology, which sustains that framework, and I have set it out in a third appendix, relating it to other chronologies, not simply the chronologies of other publishing houses. Fittingly, a former inhabitant of the House of Longman, but never one of its owners, Cyprian Blagden, one of the two people to whom this *History* is dedicated, picked out the two landmark dates also. He gave the title *Fire More Than Water* to a series of twentieth-century meditations on the history of the House which he put on paper in 1949. His title was inspired by what he called the 'outlandish' proverb that 'ships fear fire more than water'. The water in the proverb was not the water that put the fires out, but the seas and the oceans that were traversed by ships which amongst their cargoes were carrying books.

Aptly, Longman had a ship as a colophon, an ideographic symbol; and by a coincidence, John Murray I (1745–1793), the founder in 1768 of what when I began writing this *History* was Britain's second oldest surviving 'commercial' publishing house, which was to survive the twentieth century, but only just, published initially from another Sign of the Ship, 32 Fleet Street. That was a street which for generations was at the centre not of the book trade but of the related newspaper industry, until all of that industry has moved east. Meanwhile, the House of Murray itself, which moved west to Albemarle Street as long ago as 1812, was taken over by Hodder Headline in May 1999 and thus made part of the W.H. Smith publishing and bookselling group. The group subsequently sold Hodder Headline and Murray to Hachette Livre in September 2004. The first W.H. Smith (1825–1891), a rich and eminent (some preferred the adjective 'worthy') Victorian, had followed his father in making a fortune by retailing newspapers, but moved into selling books, in the first instance at railway stations. He even published them. In the late-twentieth century W.H. Smith as a company was to change far more than Murray.

Newspapers and books sold by the first Smith travelled by rail, not by sea, although Smith himself, politician as well as businessman, has passed down to history thanks to W.S. Gilbert, Arthur Sullivan's partner, as 'Ruler of the Queen's Navee'. In the changing world of steam, publishing continued to be compared with a voyage, under whatever sign the publisher sailed. Daniel Defoe (1660–1731), author of *Robinson Crusoe* (1719), wrote succinctly that the person who is 'most concerned for the Safety of a Ship' is the man who 'has a Cargo on the Bottom'; and the first published work (1733) of Samuel Johnson (1709–1784) was a translation of Lobo's *Voyage to Abyssinia*. Most appropriately of all, the first book to bear the imprint of T. Longman and his partner J. Osborn in 1726 was Captain George Shelvocke's *A Voyage round the World by way of the Great South Sea*, printed also in Fleet Street for J. Senex and J. Innys at the Globe, a fitting locational name, at the Prince's Arms in St. Paul's Churchyard. When William Wordsworth (1770–1850) and Samuel Taylor Coleridge (1772–1834), both Longman authors, contemplated writing 'The Ancient Mariner' together, the first book to which Wordsworth turned was Shelvocke's.

In the nineteenth century Benjamin Disraeli (1804–1881), who had a close (and lucrative) relationship with the House of Longman, returned to the old metaphor of the ship when after meeting Thomas Norton Longman, then aged 31, to arrange for the publication of his novel *Endymion* he wrote to him in October 1880 that he was glad to see the old ship again and 'trust it may be auspicious of a good voyage'. In the twentieth century, *Essays in the History of Publishing* included a page of reproductions of Longman ship colophons.

The voyage has long served as a metaphor, and we still talk of 'launching' books, but fires have always been facts, not least when phoenixes rise from them. They did not blaze strongly enough, however, even during the Blitz, to destroy the sense of Longman being a 'House'. Indeed, during and after the Second World War the business was still thought of as a House after temporary moves to locations far from Paternoster Row, first to Wimbledon, then to London's West End at the end of 1947, and last, twenty years later in 1967 out of London to one of England's new towns, Harlow. Its headquarters were to be in a new building, designed by Sir Frederick Gibberd, an architect who came to specialise in landscapes, and it was to be proudly named Longman House in 1968. Ironically plans were being made to move the headquarters to another new building being erected nearby when in 1994 Longman ceased to exist as a separate publishing house. Like Gibberd's building, it was just outside Harlow's main railway station. Ironically too, Gibberd figures outside this *History* not for any railway connections, but as the designer of the first airport terminal building at Heathrow.

~

'Dynasty', like 'voyage', another word with both ancient and modern associations – ancient Egypt and modern Texas – is a useful word to employ unmetaphorically when describing book-publishing connections. The Longman dynasty might have come to an end, however, not in 1972 when Mark Longman died at the early age of fifty-six, leaving behind his two daughters but no sons, but in 1755, very near the beginning of the Longman story, for the first Thomas Longman left no children. It was fortunate for the survival of the business that he had a nephew, also called Thomas (1730–1797), who succeeded him, and that this Thomas had no fewer than twelve children. The oldest of his surviving sons Thomas Norton (1771–1842) had seven children – three sons and four daughters.

Such contrasts in family size are part of dynastic history, and dynasties, like voyages, are often compared. Thus, in the context of a very different branch of business from publishing, Arthur Raistrick in his *Dynasty of Ironfounders, the Darbys and Coalbrookdale*, published by Longmans and Green in 1951, traced five generations of the Darby family who followed in the wake of the first Abraham Darby. Abraham lived and worked in Bristol, the first Thomas Longman's birthplace, before moving in 1708 to Coalbrookdale up the River Severn; and his descendants continued in the business until 1851 when the family ceased to be involved.

It was not with business dynasties of bankers, brewers and ironfounders, however, that the Longmans were usually compared but with the royal family, not least in the year 1924, when the House was celebrating its bicentenary. The comparison had been made long before, however, in 1837, when Queen Victoria came to the throne, a year when the *Publishers' Circular and Booksellers' Record*, an invaluable source for historians of publishing, was launched by a group of publishers, among them a Longman, the first of them to be called William (1813–1877). A very different kind of publisher from the Longmans, Charles Knight (1791–1873), a zealous advocate and publisher of cheap books and periodicals, observed that 'the dynasty of LONGMAN, in Paternoster Row, seems to have endured for almost as many generations as the House of Brunswick' and that 'the baptismal name of Thomas has descended in the firm as regularly as that of the four Georges'.

By 1901, the year when Victoria died, the early Longmans had for long been numbered like sovereigns – Thomas I, Thomas II, Thomas (Norton) III and on to Thomas IV (1804–1879). There were too many Longmans at work in Paternoster Row after Thomas IV to make further numbering meaningful, but the sense of dynasty persisted beyond the creation in 1926 of a limited liability public company, Longmans, Green & Co. A non-limited family company had been set up in 1889.

It has always been difficult to generalise about the relationship of family – and dynasty – to institutional longevity, whatever the business, including monarchy, in Britain sometimes known as 'the Firm'. And even in relation to personal longevity, especially what was sometimes called 'ultra-longevity', there was always more room for reflection than for generalisation. That was the point of the immediately popular book by the poet Edward Young (1683–1765), *The Complaint: or Night Thoughts on Life, Death and Immortality*, published in 1742 by Longman and others. Longevity, particularly 'at the top', could no more be taken for granted than immortality. Authors, prose writers as well as poets, were often preoccupied with reflecting on the subject. As far as owners of businesses were concerned, the problems of family succession were always relevant at a time when family business was the norm; and as late as 1950 out of ninety-two public companies studied in a sample, collected by D.F. Channon, fifty were controlled by families.

How 'family' affected patterns of management and enterprise in profit-making was examined at the end of the nineteenth century – at some length – in Alfred Marshall's *Principles of Economics*, the first edition of which, published by Macmillan, appeared in 1891. This was an important volume in publishing history since Frederick Macmillan (1851–1936), nephew of Alexander Macmillan (1818–1896), the founder with his brother Daniel (1813–1857) of another great Victorian publishing house, chose it to test out the landmark Net Book Agreement of 1900 which was devised to maintain a uniform retail price of books on sale in bookshops. Marshall had his doubts. To him, however, it was obvious that the son of a man already established in business began with 'very great advantages over others'; he learnt 'quietly and almost unconsciously about men and manners in his father's trade' and acquired 'a technical knowledge of the processes and machinery of the trade'. He would start with capital and 'establish trade connections'.

Nevertheless, for Marshall, who did not refer to 'the book trade' in this connection or at any other point in his *Principles* – few economists have done – 'the actual state of things' was 'very different'. When a man 'has got together a great business, his descendants often fail, in spite of their great advantages'. When young, they might have been 'left too much to the care of domestic servants', and once placed in business, might not have had their own ambitions stirred. Mere 'assiduity and caution' were never enough. 'When a full generation has passed, when the old traditions are no longer a safe guide, and when the bonds that held together the old staff have been dissolved, then the business almost invariably falls to pieces unless it is practically handed over to the management of new men who have meanwhile risen to partnership in the firm.'

The House of Longman, unlike many other family publishing houses, avoided some of the perils that might have cut its longevity by drawing into partnership in each century people from outside, as Marshall recommended. The first of them was Owen Rees (1770–1837), a man of great ability, who came from a social background very different from that of Thomas Norton III, and, of equal significance, immediately on arriving at Paternoster Row became a partner and not a subordinate, essentially a publishing partner. Other members of the Rees family were drawn into Longman publications also. Booksellers at that time were increasingly being described as publishers, although Thomas Norton III and Rees still called themselves booksellers. Other partners were to be introduced at later dates to deal with different aspects of an expanding business. The first of them, Thomas Hurst (1775–1847), whose name preceded that of Rees in the Longman imprint from 1804 to 1825, was the only partner whose name was extinguished after financial irregularities had been discovered. He had probably been brought in to provide working capital.

The most important of the later partners, J.W. Allen (d.1937), joined the House in 1884 but did not become a partner until 1918 when he inherited a bundle of shares from William Ellerby Green (1836–1918), who had been a partner, like his father before him, since 1862. Allen was largely responsible for building up the educational side of the Longman business, pioneered by others and the key to its future success, and although he had to wait for nearly thirty years before he became a partner, his influence as a business 'strategist', a term not then employed, was never in doubt from the year of his arrival in Paternoster Row. He had been a teacher in Liverpool when he joined the House, and once inside it he not only organised – and travelled – but wrote. His *Junior School Arithmetic* is said to have sold two million copies. He stayed in the business until 1932 and died in 1937.

The best-known later outsider was J.H. (later Sir John) Newsom (1910–1971), who joined the Longman Board in 1957 and became Joint Managing Director. He had been an outstanding Chief Education Officer of Hertfordshire, appointed at the early age of 29, and had established his reputation far outside the county as a pioneer of educational advance, one of the main national and international themes of the 1960s. Six years after he had joined Longman, his name was to be attached to the Newsom Report, *Half Our Future*, drafted by the Central Advisory Council for Education (England). In a special supplement *The Times Educational Supplement*, summarising its recommendations on 18 October 1963, identified pipe-smoking Newsom as joint managing director of Longmans, Green & Co., choosing as its headline 'A longer school life and a longer school day'. In the school context, where there had long been battles about the school leaving age, the word 'longer' had a distinctive force, and Newsom linked it not with institutional longevity but with national survival.

Unlike Rees, Newsom did not come from publishing circles, and also unlike Rees, he was never entirely at home in them. He remained better-known outside publishing than inside it. It was other young new entrants, brought in at a lower level, some through training schemes, who not only kept the affairs of the House of Longman in good shape but converted the business into a global concern. Some of them were born entrepreneurs who expanded the business on the peripheries of empire, an empire which by then was no longer being described as such in official circles. The word 'Commonwealth' had taken over from the word empire, via transitional talk of 'Commonwealth and Empire', as the word 'conglomerate' was soon to take over from the word 'empire' in publishing. Several of the young entrepreneurs working for Longman moved to Harlow to shape policy after 1968.

After seven generations of Longmans, this input from a new generation of young publishers, keen, enthusiastic, and, above, all, professional in their outlook, was essential to the longevity of the business, if not of the House. They opened the way for a period of unprecedented change in the long history of publishing. Tim Rix, born in 1934, was outstanding amongst them and it was because of his remarkable record as a publisher that I chose to end this *History* with his departure from Harlow in 1990. A key decision in recent publishing history was taken, however, by the last of the Longmans, Mark, who turned to S. Pearson and Son in order to protect the Longman Group from being swallowed up by a large American publishing house. As he foresaw, what began as a defensive move on his part had immediate expansionist effects on the Longman business. It not only brought other publishing houses into an extended Longman Group, a new designation, but placed Longman, already international in its range and structure, within a new business context.

It was a non-Longman generation, with extra capital at its disposal, who, as the last chapters of this *History* show, made the most of exciting new opportunities after Mark's death. 'Generation', an old word, is as much of a keyword in the story told in this *History*, therefore, as 'voyage' or 'dynasty'. The phenomenon was a more general one. In his widely-read *Anatomy of Britain Today* (1965), Anthony Sampson, journalist and commentator, who included a chapter on the Press but none on book publishing, referred in his introduction to 'the emergence of a more thrusting and ambitious generation of managers'. Coming from the newspaper world, he also pinpointed the conflict between 'professionals and amateurs'.

~

The word 'publishing' has a long history of its own. In Johnson's great *Dictionary* (1755), which on its title page listed Longman as one of its publishers, the definitions of 'to publish' that he offered his readers were 'to discover to mankind'; 'to make generally and openly known'; and 'to proclaim' and 'to divulge'. They all seemed to suggest 'glad tidings of great joy', and Johnson's second definition of 'a publisher' was 'one who puts out a book into the world'. This came after his first definition 'one who makes publick or generally known', which itself was followed by an example taken again from religion – 'the holy lives, the exemplary sufferings of the publishers of this religion and the surpassing excellence of that doctrine which they published'. In England the Christian religion, whatever form it took, was central to the whole culture just as it had been central everywhere to the early history of printing and bookselling. European criticism of religion, a fundamental aspect of the Enlightenment, was stronger in Scotland than in England.

Now Johnson applied the concept of 'longevity' (length of life) to individuals (and animals) only, and the example that he gave of the use of the word in his *Dictionary* read simply: 'The instances of *longevity* are chiefly amongst the abstemious'. Yet he touched on longevity elsewhere, without using the word, in his Preface to the *Dictionary*. 'When we see men grow old and die ... from century to century, we laugh at the elixir that promises to prolong life to a thousand years.' For Jean-Baptiste de Grainville, the French author of *Le Dernier Homme* (1805), 'an early classic of science fiction' translated into English in 1806, 'the duration of human life was wisely regulated by the omniscient mind of the Almighty, according to the size of the globe and the fecundity of its inhabitants'.

Values changed as significantly as language between 1755 and 1805, as they were to do between 1968 and 1990, when there was far more emphasis on economics than on religion. In the eighteenth century, it was not the business acumen of the first two Thomas Longmans that knowledgeable commentators singled out as their main attributes but their benevolence and integrity. Thomas I was said, for example, to have treated the aged Ephraim Chambers, author of the pioneering *Cyclopaedia of the Arts and Sciences* (1738), 'with the liberality of a prince and the tenderness of a father'. 'His house was ever open to receive him, and when he was there nothing could exceed his care and anxiety over him; ... during his illness jellies and other proper refreshments were industriously left for him at those places where it was least likely he should avoid seeing them.'

Thomas II was described by a younger contemporary, the printer and author John Nichols (1745–1826), as 'a man of the most exemplary character, both in his profession and in his private life, who had followed faithfully in his uncle's 'footsteps' and who was as 'universally esteemed for his benevolence as for his integrity'. Nichols, who was responsible for the *Gentleman's Magazine* from 1792 to 1826 – his son was to follow in his footsteps – did much in this then influential medium to promote the 'culture of the book' which seemed to represent 'civilisation' itself. The *Gentleman's Magazine* had been founded in 1731 by Edward Cave (1691–1754), son of a cobbler, and it was one of a number of periodicals that encouraged the reading of books. When Cave, for whom Johnson wrote, turned in 1734 from books to human beings, he was fully aware of mortality and offered a prize of £50 for the best poem on 'Life, Death, Judgement, Heaven and Hell'.

~

For all such profundities, Cave and Johnson were as deeply interested as I am in the business side of publishing. For example, Johnson wrote in March 1776 to the head of his old Oxford College that it was perhaps not considered 'through how many hands a book often passes before it comes into those of the reader, or what part of the profit each hand must retain, as a motive for transmitting it to the next'. Almost a hundred years later, in 1871, the great French novelist Gustave Flaubert (1821–1880) observed sensibly, with reference to Hippolyte Taine's *History of English Literature*, that it was necessary to dispose of the absurd notion that 'books dropped like meteorites from the sky'.

A generation before Johnson, Defoe had been one of the first people to make use of business procedures – and terms – in a modern sense, carefully explaining, for example, in his *Complete English Tradesman* (1725) how the 'complete tradesman' should frame his business letters. The word 'business' was already beginning to be employed in the late-seventeenth and early-eighteenth centuries to connote a specific sector of economic activity, 'commercial transactions'. But it could still carry with it a sense of uneasiness ('care'), and it did not necessarily imply enterprise. The word 'enterprise', a key word in any modern economic vocabulary, most recently in Thatcherite years, when the noun 'culture', more widely used than ever before, was attached to it, figures only once in Defoe's *Robinson Crusoe*, in the fourth paragraph, in the context of a fatherly warning against the dangers of enterprise rather than as an admonition to pursue it.

Crusoe ignored the warning, but his subsequent adventures were not described by Defoe as 'enterprising', and the full implications of the word were appreciated by publishers only during the years covered in the last chapters of this *History*, and then not all at once or by all publishers. It is late in the story that the description 'entrepreneur' could be easily attached to a publisher. It is interesting to note that no articles on the publishing business appeared in the first thirty years of the specialised journal *Business History*, first published in 1958. Nor was it referred to in general books on current business. There was no reference to it, for example, in G. Turner's journalistic survey *Business in Britain* (1969). Nor had there been in the two-volume Victorian study by H.R. Fox Bourne, *English Merchants, Memoirs in Illustration of the Progress of British Commerce*, (1870).

The story told in this *History* is itself more – and less – than a business case study of the kind, short or extended, that recent business historians, many of them looking to the Harvard Business School, commonly assemble and analyse. The quantitative evidence is inadequate to sustain one, but even if it had been adequate, I would have wanted to broaden the scope of this institutional history to cover 'culture' as well as 'commerce' and, above all, the relationship between them. The history of books, whatever their kind – and they come in many different kinds – has different strands of which the business history strand is only one. Indeed, there are many important books about books which leave out the economics altogether. One large book on books by F. Donaldson, for example, scarcely touches on costs and prices, and sets out to describe the 'history, art, power, glory, infamy and suffering' of books, 'according to their creators, friends and enemies'. On its dust cover it depicts Dr Johnson and his bookseller (not

Longman) in heated discussion. Just before Longman, books themselves were at the centre of the illuminating ancient/modern discussion, one of many such, in Jonathan Swift's unforgettable *The Battle of the Books* (1704).

Perhaps the most remarkable book on books, now rarely read, *The Bibliomania or Book Madness*, written by the bibliophile, the Revd. Thomas Frognall Dibdin (1776–1847), was published by Longman (with illustrations) in 1811. 'If you wish to speculate in books, or to stock a newly-discovered province with what is most excellent and popular [a dubious pairing] in our language', Dibdin advised his readers, 'hire a vessel of 300 tons burthen, and make a contract with Messrs. Longman, Hurst & Co., who are enabled from their stock of quires ... to satisfy all the wants of the most craving bibliomaniacs.' Dibdin, a pioneering book collector who left Rees out, also wrote *Bibliophobia* (1832), and in 1836 published two volumes of sometimes inaccurate reminiscences of his 'literary life'.

Dibdin was the first secretary of the still-active book collectors' club, the Roxburghe, the oldest existing British society of bibliophiles, with strong aristocratic connections. The Roxburghe was founded in 1812 on the day of the sale of the unrivalled collection of Caxtons belonging to John Ker, the third Duke of Roxburghe after whom it was named. Dibdin, who had catalogued Earl Spencer's Library at Althorp, has been rightly described as 'the most prolific chronicler, anecdotist and publicist in the history of bibliophily'.

Book collecting has its own history, with one of the quarterlies devoted to it in the 1930s being called *The New Colophon*, and book making – printing, binding and not least, illustrating – has fascinated as many writers on books as searching for books and buying them has fascinated collectors and librarians. Collectors concern themselves with books as physical products as well as with their price, their content, and their circulation; and their covers have a wider appeal than to historians of design. Longman is said to have used a book jacket as early as 1832 for a *Keepsake Annual*, a then favoured literary genre. Douglas McMurtrie, writing from the viewpoint of the designer and printer, has lovingly described in a book called *The Book* (1943) 'the ambition of the true artist in the bookmaking field' to present 'fine works of literature in a fine format'.

This was the ambition of Thomas Norton Longman IV, if not of all his publishing contemporaries or family successors: he chose Richard Doyle to illustrate his children's books, and in 1863 he sponsored an illustrated imperial quarto edition of the New Testament with fine wood engravings. The edition was limited to 250 copies. (A few years after Thomas Norton IV's death, however, the book was selling in shilling parts.) His eldest son, Thomas Norton (1849–1930), the last of the Thomas Nortons, the partner who dealt with Disraeli in 1880, devoted a chapter in his typewritten *Memories*, a valuable source for the historian, to 'Books, Pictures etc.' in the possession of his family: they included a 'Horn Book' acquired by his father, which he dated at 'around 1725', that is around the time when Longman came into existence. Thomas Norton was relieved when it did not fetch its reserve price at a wartime Red Cross sale at Christie's in April 1917 and was returned to the family.

Throughout its history the House of Longman, which was never involved in printing its own titles, has had its own distinctive place in the story of bookmaking. As early as 1732, Augustin Calmet's *An Historical, Critical, Geographical, Chronological and Etymological Dictionary of the Holy Bible* was illustrated with 'above one hundred and sixty copperplates'. Decades later, the great wood engraver Thomas Bewick (1753–1828) figures frequently in the early nineteenth-century story of the House – his two-volume *History of British Birds* was printed in Newcastle and sold by Longman in London. So too does Owen Jones (1809–1874), author of the magnificent *Grammar of Ornament* (1856), who produced an edition of Gray's *Elegy* in 1846, which he presented to Thomas IV. He also collaborated with Henry Noel Humphreys in the preparation of *Illuminated Books of the Middle Ages* (1844), a fine example of chromolithography, then the most up-to-date, if the most controversial, of techniques.

Another book of typographical interest which Longman published, *The Diary of Lady Willoughby* (1844), a pastiche of a contemporary account of the seventeenth-century Civil War, restored and publicised the elegant typography of the English printer, William Caslon (1692–1766) who made his own types. Longman also produced a photographic frontispiece, the first in the world, for *The Pencil of Nature* by William Henry Fox Talbot (1800–1877) which was published in 1844: the photographs for the book were taken in a Reading studio. It took time for one of the most important inventions of the nineteenth century, photography, revealed to the world in 1839, to transform the publishing of books, newspapers and periodicals, and, with moving pictures, and later with television, to create new visual media.

~

There is, of course, an economic as well as an aesthetic dimension to printing, binding and illustration, as there always had been to sales. It is brought out in detail in the 'Impression Books' kept systematically by Longman, but unfortunately by reason of multiple disasters incomplete: they record the costs of the different elements in publishing a book – printing, paper, the indispensable material, postage, and 'advertising and labels'. They thus constitute essential evidence for historians. Binding too became a key item in the nineteenth century, although in the eighteenth century most publishers' copies were unbound and customers would decide upon their own personal bindings. Nevertheless, as early as 1772 Thomas II wrote to a business correspondent in Boston, Henry Knox, with whom he had regular and friendly dealings, that owing to the rising cost of leather he was binding books in canvas.

The first trade bindings in cloth or half-bound in cloth and leather, were being produced in the 1820s, but it was not until the 1840s that binding of sheets became general and not until 1887 that the House of Longman acquired its own Ship Binding Works, setting up a subsidiary company which at the end of the nineteenth century employed several hundred workers and which bound some books for other publishers. Although the craft of bookbinding had preceded the craft of printing, it was only during the nineteenth century that a new bookbinding industry was created which, in the words (1939) of Douglas Leighton, whose family had been concerned with the production of books for nearly two centuries, 'opened new vistas to adventurers in books, and was of genuine benefit to the reading public'.

Printing no new books themselves, Thomas I and Thomas II employed William Strahan (1715–1785) as one of their main printers, and the first page of Strahan's ledger includes an entry relating to Longman, who had ordered the printing of the last fourteen sheets of *Chambers's Cyclopaedia* No. 1000 at £1.85 a sheet. When Strahan died, leaving a fortune of around £100,000, his third son Andrew, who had no children, took over the business, which in 1819 passed into the hands of his nephews, Andrew and Robert Spottiswoode, the first of whom married the daughter of Thomas Norton Longman III. Family and business history were thus inextricably intertwined. In this story too fire was more than symbolic. A fire in the Spottiswoode warehouse in 1837 destroyed 'various publications in course of issue by Mr. Murray, by Messrs Longman & Co [and] by Mr. Bentley'. Rees watched the fire. So did a reporter (*Morning Chronicle*, 22 March 1837) who noted that after the firemen had obtained 'a plentiful supply of water, they soon began to play upon the flames with considerable effect'.

The Longmans also had close family links with the paper industry which all the time depended on water. One of Thomas II's twelve sons, George, went into partnership with the papermaker John Dickinson, and they traded together, at first under the name of Longman and Dickinson. In 1823 Charles Longman, son of Thomas Norton Longman III, was apprenticed to Dickinson at the age of fourteen. Four years earlier there was another Spottiswoode link when Charles's sister Mary married Andrew Spottiswoode who later became Printer to the Queen.

～

Family history is directly related to both the economic history of books as products to be bought and sold and the history of literature, each of which have been transformed in recent years, just as much as business history has been. It is partly because of the wide range of themes they each encompass that the study of the history of the book in the late-twentieth century focused less on business than on 'culture', a concept with a long and complex history and historiography before and after Matthew Arnold's *Culture and Anarchy* (1869). Robert Darnton, an American pioneer of booktrade history, proposed in 1982 that the world of the book and its history (something more than the history of publishing) should be conceived of as a 'cultural system'. Originally the word 'system' had been more widely used in relation to an 'economic system' than to a 'cultural system'.

The components of any system must be clearly identified not only by historians but by participants in cultural processes, whose personal choices count. This becomes clear when individuals or individual businesses with a long life are studied in detail. There is a critical initial growth stage in every business after early survival; and then over various periods of time the makers of business decisions must be able to identify and 'exploit' markets, old or new, 'mass' or 'niche' (twentieth-century terms). They must be prepared, if necessary, to switch to new products and markets in the light both of demand and of technological and economic change. Adaptability is as necessary in dealing with production as with sales. Awareness of context is crucial. As early as the mid-1950s Longman lent money to two Chinese firms to help set up a printing plant, and in 1957 placed a manager in Hong Kong to operate a production office. This was a decision which had longer-term implications for selling books around the world. Later there was to be a huge potential Chinese market for books at hand. The situation was always changing.

The general state of the economy during the 1970s, 'stagflation', inflation and unemployment together, posed difficult questions for all publishers, but few of them were completely new. In each of the three centuries covered in this *History* there were ups-and-downs in the fortunes of the economy as a whole, cyclical and structural movements, long and short, in employment, incomes and prices, which affected the book trades like other branches of trade, although not always in obvious ways. There were good and bad years, not easily predictable in advance. Sometimes there was the drama of 'crisis' in the story, heightened by commentators, notably in 1826 when the Edinburgh firm of (Archibald) Constable & Company, linked with Longman earlier in the nineteenth century, 'crashed' and Sir Walter Scott, the best-known author of the decade, a Longman as well as a Constable author, crashed with it.

This was a year of many financial crashes outside as well as inside publishing, which revealed fundamental weaknesses in the banking structure even more than in the structures of the book trades. As T.S. Ashton, clear-headed historian of the industrial revolution, put it in 1948, resorting to Voyage metaphor – with this and surrounding years in mind – 'it was through . . . changing seas' that men of commerce and industry 'steered their courses'. The organisational weaknesses in banking were largely remedied in the 1840s when, by law, banking was converted into a system; as was the pattern of transportation – on which the publishing of newspapers even more than that of books increasingly depended.

During this decade, later to be labelled 'the hungry forties', railways, following a speculative 'mania', were beginning to cheapen the movement of freight, and the decade ended with a major reform in the postal service, important at every stage to the book trade. In the longer run, however, capital-intensive 'systems' did not necessarily last any longer than institutions. 'Infrastructures' became obsolescent or difficult to maintain in the twentieth century before, during and after the 'great depression' of 1929–33, when the House of Longman was directly affected and its bankers did not immediately come to its help. During the last thirty years of the twentieth century, when book publishing went through a major reconstruction – some called it 'volcanic' – there was rightly as much argument about banking and transportation (including railways) as there had been during the 1840s.

It was during the last thirty years of the twentieth century, when English literature had become an established university subject – a major structural change in education affecting the choice and survival of books, including textbooks – that there was most talk of the thrust of technology. Indeed it was in the Orwell year, 1984, projected in a best-selling book of 1948, that a range of new communications technologies, the products of advanced developments in microelectronics, dazzled publishers, including Pearson/Longman. Technology must always be brought into the history of books whether it is the fifteenth century, the nineteenth century or the twentieth century that is under review. Yet technology in itself always involves options and is never solely responsible for change. It is economics that influences technological timing and the choice of new technologies, but it is psychology that determines the reactions, often ambivalent or contradictory, to technological advance.

Novelists from Defoe onwards, including writers of science fiction, have often understood economic and cultural processes – and the economics behind them – better than technologists or, indeed, futurologists. Robinson Crusoe knew about choice and risk, but conscious of his solitude – and with no father to guide him – he traced the hand of Providence in all that he did and in all that happened to him. The makers of cultural institutions, seldom in solitude and, recently at least, indifferent to the hand of Providence, have always had to be able and willing, like him, to learn from their own experience if they were to progress. The record is patchy. Mortality rates in publishing have been high. Meanwhile a few makers of publishing houses have left their own stamp on institutions for far longer than others. There was no single individual, however, who conjured up an adjective to describe what he was doing as well as did John Reith, maker of the culturally distinctive early BBC.

There were long-term economic and social forces at work during the quarter of the millennium covered in this *History*. Circumstances changed profoundly with the expansion of population and wealth and from the eighteenth century onwards, with the growth of London and of other cities, and with the opening up of new markets at home and abroad; and in examining them historians must pay attention not only to technology, which could restrain as well as accelerate, but to demography, unprecedented increase in wealth – in the incomes of most social groups – and to the role of law. They must consider also the diffusion of print and of 'literacy' in the process of the development of new educational policies and institutions, including compulsory schooling and the multiplication of libraries, commercial and public, and the 'massing' of what in the twentieth century came to be called the media; the processes were complex. 'Secularisation' is as contentious a word as 'globalisation'.

Of basic interest at every stage was the role of women as authors as well as readers and in the latest stages of the story as managers. 'Women's studies' have transformed the main aspects of book-trade history: they have never been marginal. In the history of Longman Thomas I's widow, Mary, was a partner in 1755. She was, however, the only woman partner in the history of the House. Later in the century and into the nineteenth one outstanding woman spoke with influence and authority in Paternoster Row. Anna Laetitia Barbauld (1743–1825), an Aikin by birth, knew personally different Longmans and their partners and her opinions counted. She published a selection of prose and poetry called *The Female Speaker*. Two other remarkable women of this period, Hannah More and Harriet Martineau, were less important in the history of the House of Longman than Sarah Trimmer (1741–1810), a prolific author of moral tales. It is interesting to compare such women with those described by Paula McDowell in her *The Women of Grub Street: Press Politics and Gender in the London Literary Marketplace, 1678–1830* (1998).

Great though these changes were, there remained three old and still-surviving institutions concerned with books that were already there at the beginning when Thomas I founded the House of Longman and which were still there in 1990. They bear witness to the presence in Britain of the past in the present, and they have all had their historians. The University Presses of Cambridge and Oxford and in London the Stationers' Company, with its buildings not far from Paternoster Row, already had long histories behind them in 1724. Founded in 1557 and granted a Livery three years later, the Company lost its Hall in the Great Fire of London in 1666, but its new Hall, completed in 1670, was to survive (though damaged) the great fires of London in 1940 which destroyed Paternoster Row. This was a fitting subject for Blagden, who wrote the Stationers' Company's history.

The Company did not lose its functions with the lapse of the book licensing system in 1695: many printers and publishers were Freemen of the Company, and after 1710, when what came to be called the world's first Copyright Act became law, all book titles had by law to be registered with the Company. (Large numbers were not.) Although these requirements were relaxed in the eighteenth century and in 1775 the lucrative privilege, shared with the Oxford and Cambridge University Presses, of being the sole printers of almanacs was lost, the Company carried on confidently into the twentieth century. In 1933 it opened its ranks to people concerned with newspapers as well as with books after an amalgamation with the recently formed Newspaper Makers' Company, and it was re-named the Worshipful Company of Stationers and Newspaper Makers. It continued to insist nonetheless that those people seeking its freedom should be associated with one of the traditional guild trades – printing, bookbinding, bookselling and paper-making and merchandising.

When it celebrated its fourth centenary in 1957, seventeen years before Longman's 250th anniversary, the commemorative brochure of the Company began with a sentence that relates directly to this Introduction: 'In these days of change and invention, it is rare to find something that has persisted, with few changes [an over-statement] or interruptions, for four centuries'. The brochure noted with thanks another very special example of continuity – members of the publishing House of Rivington, founded in 1711 by Charles Rivington, the son of a Chesterfield butcher.

Rivington acquired the premises and trade from a deceased bookseller, Richard Chiswell, who had been in business in the Rose and Crown, St. Paul's Churchyard, since 1663. The House was older, therefore, than the House of Longman, and members of the Rivington family served as Clerks of the Stationers' Company for more than 150 years. Their publishing House had been taken over, however, by Longman in 1890 in the most dramatic of all nineteenth-century publishing takeovers, and at the time of the takeover William Ellerby Green, as a Longman partner, acquired the Sign of Bible and Crown, Rivington's historical emblem. Son of a father who had become a Longman partner in 1822 and whose name remained part of the Longman imprint after it became a public company in 1926, Green appreciated from his own family experience just how important continuity was.

~

By 1890 Rivington, like Longman, had already moved for many years towards educational publishing before the takeover, while remaining deeply involved in religion. In the House of Longman, which still published books of many kinds, books for the class-room had become a staple of its own business. The particular concentration on education had a long history. As early as the end of the eighteenth century, when there was a very different balance between competition and co-operation in bookselling and publishing from that in the twentieth century, school books and other children's books figured prominently in the Longman lists, and soon there were separate educational lists covering 'all branches of knowledge'. Some books were described as 'entirely new'. Some were sixth or seventh editions of textbooks, in rare cases sixtieth or seventieth editions.

One of the earliest steps in Longman's long road to becoming an educational publisher had been taken in 1736, when Thomas I (along with Samuel Buckley) acquired by purchase from the Norton family 'the Royal Grant and Privilege of printing' William Lily's sixteenth-century Latin

Grammar. Ironically, in the light of later history, the reprint of this old book, first published in 1509, was a pointer to the future. Lily's friend John Colet, then Dean of St. Paul's, had sent the *Grammar*, the work of a committee, to Erasmus for criticism: the eighteenth-century publishers stated in quite different circumstances that they hoped that their new edition, 'revised and improved', along with a new edition of Lily's *Rules*, would have 'the Approbation and Encouragement of those Gentlemen, who have the Care and Instruction of Youth'. Thomas II was so impressed by the success of this venture that he called one of his sons Thomas Norton, who passed into Longman history as Thomas Norton III.

In 1974, when the Longman business celebrated its 250th anniversary, the periodical *Education*, looking back to the late-nineteenth century rather than further back to the early-eighteenth, suggested over-simply that the secret behind the longevity of the Longman business lay in the 'company's close and continuing association with the world of education', including 'so-called higher education'. This was not, however, how most of the members of the Longman family had viewed their own experiences. Some were drawn to the stage, others to science, some to poetry. Thomas Norton Longman III acquired Wordsworth's and Coleridge's *Lyrical Ballads*, first published in Bristol by Joseph Cottle in 1798, and published in 1800 the edition which passed into history, and the last Thomas Norton Longman considered that the 'most interesting and valuable of his personal possessions' were his Wordsworth manuscripts, which included a long list of *errata* in the 1800 edition.

The last Thomas Norton Longman, always known as Mr Norton, knew well also that the *Lyrical Ballads*, with a strange story surrounding it, was only one of the famous books with which his House had been associated. They included Scott's poem *The Lay of the Last Minstrel* (1805), Disraeli's novels *Lothair* (1870) and *Endymion* (1880), Anthony Trollope's novels *The Warden* (1855) and *Barchester Towers* (1857), Richard Burton's *Personal Narrative* (1855), Matthew Arnold's *Poems* (1853), J.H. Newman's *Apologia pro Vita Sua* (1864), Max Müller's *Lectures on the Science of Language* (1864), Robert Louis Stevenson's *The Very Strange Case of Dr. Jekyll and Mr. Hyde* (1886), *The Collected Works of William Morris* – and, among periodicals, the *Edinburgh Review* (1802), *The Annual Register* (Longman acquired a share in 1805 and became sole publisher in 1890 after the merger with Rivington) and the *English Historical Review* (1887).

All the novels and poems on this list were still being read in 1974. They had passed into 'English Literature', and some of them figured in school curricula, which were themselves to experience many vicissitudes after 1974. Some of the vicissitudes were foreseeable, but that landmark year in the history of the House of Longman provided a better vantage point from which to survey English literature than 'the world of education'. The editor of *Education* was wise, therefore, when he extended his vista beyond education and observed that continuity like that of the House of Longman would have been 'remarkable', he stated, 'in any enterprise': it was all the more so 'in the inspirational and individualistic world of publishing where firms can prosper or plunge with the fortunes of just one book'.

~

Within the House of Longman, which had never found itself in that position, decision-makers had always stressed quality rather than specialisation, not least in the books that were assembled in specialised categories, of which education was only one. As the *British and Colonial Printer & Stationer and Booksellers' Circular* put it in December 1884, when there was already a sizeable educational list:

> For Longmans to be the publishers of any work is a feather in the cap of an author; if his talent be only mediocre, he may never attain such another compliment, but this is a testimonial that he religiously [note the adverb] preserves. It may be safely said, however, that Longmans never publish anything that has not been closely scrutinised and well recorded.

It would be interesting to know whether 'colonial' authors as well as colonial booksellers noted the adverb 'religiously' when they read this article. Such authors were to figure prominently in late-twentieth century lists. At a time when 'colonies' were being disposed of, Longman managers miles away from Harlow were making the most of the legacy of the English language in the new 'nations' that were coming into existence in Africa and Asia. And in the process they were always looking for new authors.

The acronym *ELT* (English Language Teaching) carried with it a continuing sense of mission. In 1989, the year before Rix, who had risen through *ELT*, left the company, the worldwide sales of Longman books had reached more than £160 million, £45 million of which accrued from the United States, and there was a trading profit of £23.1 million. 'Culture' had not always been so happily allied with 'commerce' as it was in Rix's Harlow. This was a period when the business pages of newspapers became as indispensable a source for the historians of publishing as the 'literary' pages.

In such circumstances, longevity, for long a great Longman asset, seemed to matter less than the allure of immediate financial gains. Nevertheless, a plethora of business histories was then appearing not only in newspaper and periodical articles, but in books, including jubilee and centenary histories of particular firms. This was not entirely new. As long ago as 1924 the *Publishers' Weekly*, a specialised source, began its bicentenary article on 'Longmans, Green and Company' with the observation that 'few stories in any field of commercial history could make more interesting reading than that of the House of Longman'.

Thomas Norton III had not chosen to celebrate the centenary of the foundation of the House of Longman in 1824. Centenaries were not then in fashion: Dr. Johnson with all his authority had defined the word 'centenary' as simply as 'the number of a hundred', giving as his example, 'every centenary of years from the Creation'. Yet the mid-Victorians chose to celebrate particular centenaries, focusing, for example, on the tercentenary of Shakespeare's birth in 1864 (the bicentenary had been called a 'jubilee'); and a generation later, when the mood had changed again and so-called new publishers in the 1890s were making the most not only of novels but of novelty, the late-Victorian House of Longman began to celebrate its own age at birthdays and at anniversary celebrations. Conviviality behind the scenes had long been a feature of 'the trade'. Now the conviviality became open when celebrations were reported in the Press by 'new journalists' who made the most of their presence.

Bicentenaries, so much celebrated in the twenty-first century, remained rare, and when in October 1924 Harold Cox, editor of the *Edinburgh Review*, which had been published solely by the House of Longman since 1826, referred back, in his first pages of a long article on the House, to three earlier articles on the House published anonymously in 1860 in *The Critic*, he emphasized not only longevity but change. Since the First World War, 'the Great War', the hold of the past was increasingly suspect in many places, if not at 39 Paternoster Row. Nevertheless, Cox praised above all else the 'hereditary character' of the Longman business -'the detailed experiences of the father can be passed on to the son' – while admitting that criticism of the principle of heredity was 'much in evidence at the present time ... as implying the subjection of present actions to past influences'.

The House of Longman, proud of its pedigree, chose to celebrate its bicentenary – amid congratulations – with a luncheon in London's Stationers' Hall, the right setting, on Wednesday 5 November 1924, when it described itself as the only publishing firm in London that could look so far back in time across two centuries of history. The venue, of course, like the day of the year, suggested even longer vistas. So, too, did the presence at the luncheon of a large number of distinguished historians. Only John Murray represented other publishers.

The historians present included Professor T.F. Tout, pioneer of medieval studies at Manchester University, for whom 'the constitutional history of England in the middle ages came first and all other aspects of history were appendages' – it was he who had introduced one of Longman Green's most effective newcomers, C.S.S. Higham (1890–1958), to the Longman family; G.P. Gooch, whose *History and Historians of the Nineteenth Century* had been published by Longman in 1913; and the then editor of the *English Historical Review*, G.N. (later Sir George) Clark, who was to become Provost of Oriel College, Oxford, in 1947. Mrs. Creighton, the widow of the first editor of the *English Historical Review*, founded in 1886, and her husband's biographer, was also present.

Other guests at the lunch included Longman authors, among them

Conan Doyle, Sidney and Beatrice Webb, somewhat surprisingly established Longman authors, if working on their own terms, by then unusual, and Sir William (later Lord) Beveridge, who was to become a Longman author, never dependent on the House. The archaeologist Sir Arthur Evans, of Knossos fame, was present not only in his own right as a scholar but as a member of the extended Longman family. C.J. Longman had married Harriet, the daughter of John (later Sir John) Evans and Harriet (née Dickinson): Arthur was another of John's children: Joan was his sister. There remained a close connection with the Society of Antiquaries, over which both Arthur and Joan presided, as well as with the paper industry.

Among other speakers in 1924, another Longman author, W.R. Inge, the 'gloomy Dean' of St. Paul's, living in a great house not far from Paternoster Row, expressed the hope that both the House of Longman and the House of Murray would 'outlive all other dynasties, except the British Crown'; and the scientist Sir Joseph Thomson, Master of Trinity College, Cambridge, describing publishers as 'obstetricians with regard to literature', claimed that science owed as much to publishers as it did to scientific societies. Indeed, 'if it had not been for the publisher', he asked, 'how science would have progressed at all'.

The Roman Catholic Archbishop of Westminster, Cardinal Bourne, gave special thanks to the Longmans for encouraging Roman Catholic writers, and William Morris's biographer, J.W. Mackail, while praising the Longmans for standing behind the 'continuity of literature', surprisingly referred not to the Longman edition of the collected works of Morris but to Sir John Herschel's *Treatise on Astronomy* and J.W. Colenso's *Arithmetic*. 'Literature', Mackail claimed, 'is in some respects a science, and the exposition of science may be and has been high literature.' Surprisingly, perhaps, given what were then the Longmans' own personal interests, there was almost as much talk about science at the lunch as there was about history, perhaps the most interesting comment on it being made by Thomson, who observed that from the publishers' point of view science 'suffered too much by changing too quickly'. Herschel (1792–1871) certainly deserved to be singled out, as he has been on many occasions since in histories of scientific thought and influence.

The important toast to the 'Publishing Trade' was proposed not by an historian, but by an old friend of C.J. Longman, Rider Haggard (1865–1925), by then Sir Henry Rider Haggard, author of *King Solomon's Mines* (1885) and *She* (1887), the latter published by Longman. Haggard chose the occasion to use words that might have been uttered by Tout. 'I have an enormous respect', he began, 'for anything which, like the House of Longman, has endured for two whole centuries. It reminds me of the British Constitution.' He did not refer to the fact that on an earlier November 5th more than a century before 1724 the Constitution had been in peril. There was an adventure story there that he might have dwelt upon. His own powers of endurance were then in decline. He did not feel well and, although he gave one more public speech in his life, he died in May 1925.

The main toast at the luncheon was to 'Literature and Science', again seen in combination, and it was proposed by an historian, G.M. Trevelyan (1876–1962), who, like his great uncle and his uncle before him, T.B. Macaulay (1800–1859) and Sir George Otto Trevelyan (1838–1928), was a Longman author. In 1924 he had not yet published his *History of England*, but his *British History in the Nineteenth Century* had already appeared two years earlier, and his *History of England*, which was to sell well, came out in 1926, the year in which Longman became a limited company. That was one year before Trevelyan became Regius Professor at Cambridge.

In proposing his toast, Trevelyan, like Haggard, had constitutional rather than economic themes in mind. 'A great historic publishing house like this', he declared confidently, 'is not a creature of the State, nor of the Church, nor of the Universities, nor of any corporate body. Neither is it the creation of the money-getting impulse ... It stands, indeed, for self-help and the effort of the individual, but it stands also for family tradition, for ideals of public usefulness and assistance to the cause of literature and science, handed on from generation to generation.' There was special warmth in Trevelyan's words, for his relationship with Longman, lucrative in financial terms, had always involved more than money.

In his reply C.J. Longman responded in similar spirit, but spoke more generally, quoting the poet Sir Henry Newbolt and striking an imperial note that must have appealed to Haggard more than to Trevelyan. He regretted that the Poet Laureate (Robert Bridges) and the poet and novelist Thomas Hardy were not present. They were 'the Elder Brethren of Literature in this country'. He also referred to the English language having 'spread to the ends of the earth'. He 'did not know whether in the next two hundred years scientists would establish communication with Mars and Venus', but if they did he 'would expect the English language to extend to them'. More copies of *Robinson Crusoe* had been sold in India during the previous five years than William Taylor, its first publisher, had ever sold. C.J. did not mention textbooks: they were to figure in the future even more than they did before 1924.

C.J. was to live until 1934, and in his later years Trevelyan was to pay many tributes to the House of Longman, both in private and in public, before he died at the age of eighty-six in 1961. His *Social History*, published during the Second World War – first in the United States – and not until 1944 in England (because of paper shortage), was his best-seller and one of theirs. When it appeared in London, it was after a 'doodle bug' rocket attack that he thanked Robert Guy Longman (1882–1971), who had suggested that he should write it, for what over the years the House of Longman had done for him:

Here I sit in Cambridge in perfect safety, while you in London are bearing the weight of the Second Battle of Britain in the last stage of the victorious war ... I have been connected with your firm for forty-five years, and have published fifteen out of my twenty books with you. My Father and Great-Uncle published with you ever since the 1820s. Never once has there been any misunderstanding between the members of my Family and the members of your Firm. Never once have your people failed to produce our books up to the best standards of the time. And now you are producing my latest work [*Social History*] under fire courageously borne by men and women alike.

At that point social and personal, private and public, history met. And so it did more than once for other members of the Trevelyan family. In 1930 Longman had published *William III and the Defence of Holland* by Mary Trevelyan, G.M.'s daughter, and in 1942 two volumes of collected poems and plays by his brother, R.C.

In the aftermath of the Second World War, which depressed Trevelyan more than the War itself, the aged historian paid another tribute to Longman in 1949 following the publication of a book of essays in honour of him and of his work, *Studies in Social History*, which was edited by one of his former pupils, the historian Jack (later Sir John) Plumb. Trevelyan told those present at what by then had become a characteristic Longman celebration that although he had received very high honours 'both from the Crown and the University', this particular honour went 'nearer to my heart'. 'There is nothing in my life as an historian that has been a greater source of pride and advantage to me than my co-operation with Longmans, a tradition in my family of more than a century and a quarter.'

Sadly, when R.C. and G.M. and Longman along with Noël Brack went to Cambridge for Trevelyan's funeral in 1962, their names were not mentioned at all in the newspaper lists of those present, although Brack had handed in a paper with their names written down.

By the time that Longman celebrated its 250th anniversary in 1974, there had been further far-reaching changes not only in publishing but in the study of history, not least social history, again, as in the case of publishing, with greater changes still to come, including a shift from social to cultural history. Yet in Britain, in particular, history had not lost its appeal for general readers, and Longman was still proud of its own history list at the date when this *History* ends. Indeed, its 1989 history brochure was called *Longman History, 1989, A Tradition in its Own Right*. Longman was one of several publishers who continued to produce history books designed to appeal to a broad audience.

Essays in the History of Publishing, which were published as part of the 250th anniversary celebrations, looked to the future as well as the past, and originally they were going to be called *Publishing and Society*. One commentator on them compared the Longmans to John Galsworthy's Forsytes – 'they had branched into property and judicious alliances'. They had done this, of course, long before the Forsytes established themselves and the commentator did not foresee that, like the Forsytes, they were soon to pass into history. It was a history that was to engage the active attention of Rix, who, along with his colleague Roy Yglesias, had been one of the essayists. In 1983, two years after becoming Chairman of the Group, he decided to sponsor a series of seminars on the history of publishing held at Worcester College, Oxford, to which I had moved as Provost in 1976. Rix invited me to chair them, and they were valuable, I believe, in bringing together scholars of many interests and disciplines, along with publishers. Put into context in the first appendix to this *History*, they were instrumental in encouraging the re-shaping of the history of the book trade.

More detailed scholarly research is still necessary to unravel fully the transformation in the history of publishing. Yet, as Trevelyan would have been the first to insist from his own vantage point in Cambridge, where the Cambridge University Press is engaged in producing an ambitious multi-volume *History of the Book in Britain*, it would be sad if either business history or literary history – or for that matter synthetic 'general history' – were to leave out the 'poetry', or, to use as complex a word as 'business', the 'romance' in the story. At the time of the bicentenary of Longman, on 16 October 1924, the liberal newspaper the *Daily Chronicle*, later the *News Chronicle*, held to be a casualty of late-twentieth-century publishing, headed an article on the 'famous publishing firm of Longman, Green and Co.' with the words 'The Romance of Longmans'. 'To delve into the records of this unique House,' it went on, 'is to come into touch with many of the most famous names in British and European literature and with every branch of letters and learning, from poetry to higher mathematics.'

In relation to publishing as a whole, Frank Mumby's forerunner to his invaluable volume *Publishing and Bookselling: A History from the Earliest Times to the Present Day* (1930), kept up-to-date by a bookseller, Ian Norrie, was called *The Romance of Publishing* (1910), and even after the change of title, a reviewer of the new version of Mumby headed his review of it 'The Romance of Book Production'. He reminded Mumby's successors and his readers that the romance of which Mumby had written in 1910 – with particular reference to the eighteenth century – had not been lost in the twentieth-century book trade. 'I am thinking', the reviewer wrote in *The Author* in the winter of 1924, 'of how the young brothers Foyle are said to have founded their immense business with no assets but a few shillings, a hand-barrow, and pluck and vision.'

Sadly, perhaps, the most romantic story of all in relation to Longman, the much-repeated story, that Thomas I, having married his Master's daughter, went on to take on his father-in-law as a partner, is wrong. It was his Master's sister, Mary, whom Thomas I married, and her father, who was not a bookseller, plays little part in the story. Nevertheless, the origins of Thomas I's apprenticeship had elements of romance about them. Thomas was a Bristol orphan who was the first member of his family to be sent to

London to be an apprentice in the book trade, and in her will his mother had left him a necklace of pearl for his future wife to wear. Nor was that the last touch of romance. Later in the story, the last of the Thomas Norton Longmans was handed a ring by his father which had been given to him by Sir Walter Scott.

Entry to the publishing (or the bookselling) business through apprenticeship in the Stationers' Company had little in common with the lead into the publishing business in the twentieth century. Yet the practice of apprenticeship left as marked an imprint on the development of English publishing, at its formative stage when Thomas joined it, as it did on the English economy as a whole. Appropriately, one of the pioneers of business history in Britain, Charles Wilson, Professor of Economic History at Cambridge, who had written a multi-volume history of Unilever and had later entered the field of book history with his *First with the News: the History of W.H. Smith, 1792–1972* (1985), called his social and economic history of England in the seventeenth and early eighteenth centuries *England's Apprenticeship, 1600–1763*. This was a Longman book of 1965, part of a series on social and economic history which I edited. Thomas I completed his own eighteenth-century apprenticeship, described in the next chapter of this History, just forty years before the terminal date of Wilson's still highly readable volume.

JACOBI USSERII ARMACHANI

ANNALIUM

PARS POSTERIOR.

IN QUA,

PRÆTER MACCABAICAM

ET

NOVI TESTAMENTI HISTORIAM,

Imperii Romanorum Cæsarum sub C. Julio & Octaviano
ortus, rerúmque in Asiâ & Ægypto gestarum continetur

CHRONICON:

AB

Antiochi Epiphanis regni exordio, usque ad Imperii
Vespasiani initia atque extremum Templi & Reipublicæ
Judaicæ excidium, deductum.

LONDINI,

Typis *J. Flesher*, impensis *Johannis Crook*: apud quem prostant sub
insigni Navis in Cœmeterio Paulino. M DC LIV.

2 *The Creation of a Business, 1724–1797*

On 4 August 1724, a precise date (old style), Thomas Longman I paid precisely £2,282 9*s.* 6*d.* (also old style) for the bookselling and publishing business of William Taylor, who had traded under The Sign of the Ship in London's Paternoster Row.[1] Taylor had died of 'a violent fever' in May 1724, and Longman, born in Bristol and then 25 years old, bought the business from Taylor's executors, John Osborn(e) and William Innys.[2] He was in a position to do so because four years earlier at the age of 21 he had inherited his father's and some of his mother's West Country properties. He had finished his apprenticeship on 9 June in 1723, and he was to be made a Freeman of the Stationers' Company on 6 October 1724.

'The Row', situated in the parish of St. Gregory, a narrow street, little more than a passage, was then a lively place of activity for booksellers, publishers, authors and, not least, readers. There had already been booksellers there – along with mercers, silk men and lace-makers – in the reign of Queen Elizabeth I.[3] Indeed, even before the invention of movable printing type in the fifteenth century, the first great modern invention in the history of communications, there had been scriveners there, people who wrote on parchment, working alongside the makers and sellers of rosaries.[4] The area

The title page to the second part of Ussher's *Annales* (1650–54) published by John Crook. The volume carries the device of a ship in full sail, its first known use on a title page. James Ussher, a scholar (who also became the Archbishop of Ireland in the Church of Ireland) wrote this monumental work towards the end of his life, his purpose being to give the date of the foundation of the world

Longman Archive Pt II 55/2

---

1   The reformed Gregorian calendar was not adopted in England until 1752. In old style the year was reckoned as beginning on Lady Day, 25 March. 'Give us back our eleven days' was a popular cry of protest at the moment of change. A monetary decimal system was not introduced until February 1971.

2   Taylor was described in *Read's Journal*, 9 May 1724, as 'an eminent bookseller, reputed to be worth between 40 and 50,000 pounds'. Innys, who published at The Sign of the Princes Arms from 1711 to 1732, married Taylor's widow in 1725. (*London Journal*, 16 Jan. 1725.)

3   See J. Stow, *Survey of London* (1598; revised and enlarged edn., 1603). For a seventeenth-century visit to Paternoster Row to buy not a book but a waistcoat, see Samuel Pepys' *Diary*, 21 Nov. 1660. In 1720 John Strype, *A Survey of the Cities of London and Westminster* (Book 3, p.195) in two volumes provided an invaluable supplement to Stow when he discussed old Paternoster Row.

4   W. Harvey, *London Scenes and London People* (1863); 'Aleph', *Paternoster Row and the Chapter Coffee House* (1864); T. Rees and J. Britton, *Reminiscences of Literary London from 1779 to 1853* (1896), Part I, Paternoster Row. For an older, colourful popular description of the early and later history of the Row, with illustrations, see *Pinnock's Guide to Knowledge*, 2 Aug. 1834. For Rees and Britton's association with Longman, see below, p.58.

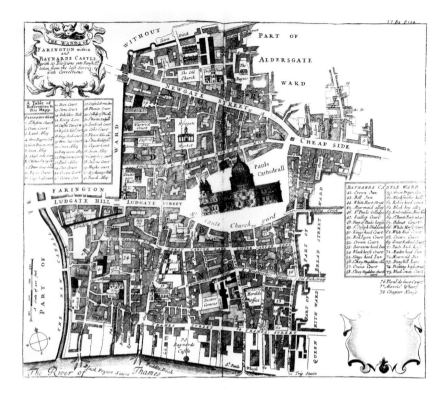

From a map of Farringdon
Within Ward, 1720 by Richard
Blome (fl. 1720–1755)

Guildhall Library, City of London

round St. Paul's Cathedral was not, however, London's only bookselling centre in the late seventeenth century. Two others were located around the Law Courts and in 'Little-Britain', off Smithfields, and there were booksellers operating in other places, including Bishopsgate Street and Tower Hill.

A late-seventeenth-century description of the 'Little-Britain' area by the lawyer and writer Roger North successfully catches the atmosphere of bookselling as it must also have been somewhat later in the Row. What North called 'a mighty trade in books' drew large numbers of people, including 'learned authors', to the bookshops 'as to a market', but buying was not the only activity. There was 'agreeable conversation' there too. 'The booksellers themselves were knowing and conversible men, with whom, for the sake of bookish knowledge, the greatest wits were pleased to converse.'[5]

The adjective 'bookish' at that time had few adverse connotations. And it was books themselves that did much to focus images of the Row that shaped perceptions of both bookselling and booksellers. A characteristic example was W. Harvey's *London Scenes and London People* (1863), which described 'booksellers and publishers of modern times' as 'the best patrons of literature' who rewarded their authors with 'both hands, if their

5   GM, Vol. 50 (1780), p.20.

headwork deserves it'.[6] Folklore clustered. 'The Row [became] legible' as a palimpsest 'not only through … the physical reality of the buildings, but from the remembered and the memorialized'.[7] There was a rich literature on the Row, easy of access in both shops and libraries. 'Bookstalling', exploring the bookstalls, was an agreeable diversion as W.R. Roberts described it in *The Book Hunter in London*. One of his illustrations was Paternoster Row on a Bank Holiday.[8]

The unforgettable Great Fire of London in 1666, chronologically the first of several fires to figure in this *History*, destroyed the Great Hall of the Stationers' Company and huge amounts of neighbouring property, much of it in the hands of leaseholders.[9] It did not obliterate all old boundaries, but it changed the appearance of the area around St. Paul's, destroying along with the old Cathedral St. Gregory's Church which had been attached to its south-west corner.[10] In the new development that followed, the building of Christopher Wren's new cathedral, a protracted process, the cathedral

---

6   Harvey, *op. cit.*, p.214, where he described 'the flight of fashion' from the Row. 'What a changeable world we inhabit … think of beaux and belles resorting thither on foot to purchase their gay clothes'.

7   J. Raven, 'Memorializing a London Bookscape: The Mapping and Reading of Paternoster Row and St. Paul's Churchyard, 1695–1814' in R. Alston (ed.), *Order and Connection* (1997), p.179. Raven has meticulously mapped and analysed details of occupation and ownership, following in the wake of P.W.M. Blayney, *The Bookshops in Paul's Cross Churchyard* (Occasional Papers of the Bibliographical Society, No. 5 (1990) and his work has been continued by Nigel Hall. See also Raven's 'Constructing Bookscapes: Experiments in Mapping the Sites and Activities of the London Book Trades of the Eighteenth Century' in J. Murray (ed.), *Mappa Mundi: Mapping Culture/Mapping the World* (2001), pp.35–39, his 'The Book Trade and the Precinct' in A. Burns and D. Keene (eds.), *The History of St. Paul's Cathedral, 600–2004* (2004), and 'The Book Trades' in I. Rivers (ed.), *Books and their Readers in Eighteenth Century England: New Essays* (2001), pp.1–34.

8   W.R. Roberts, *The Book Hunter in London* (1895), p.209.

9   Pepys described in his diary (26 Sept. 1666) 'the great loss of books in St. Paul's Churchyard and their Hall also': John Evelyn claimed that many businesses survived the Fire without great loss: 'only the poor booksellers have been indeed ill-treated by Vulcan'. Most of the records of the Stationers' Company were preserved.

10   Tom Fuller wrote that St. Paul's may be called the Mother Church, having one babe in her body (St. Faith's in the crypt) and another in her arms (St. Gregory's). For the 'Great Fire' see J. Bedford, *London's Burning* (1966), and for the rebuilding of London and the range of regulations associated with it see T.F. Reddaway, *The Great Fire of London* (1951 edn.) and P.E. Jones and T.F. Reddaway (eds.), *The Survey of Building Sites in the City of London after the Great Fire of 1666 by Peter Mills and J. Oliver*, 5 vols. (1962–7).

dominated the cityscape from the time of the laying of its foundation stone in 1675. The Choir was completed by 1697, and in 1710 the great dome, which stood out above all the buildings around as it was to do until the fierce fires of the Second World War.

It was during the reign of Queen Anne (1702–1714) that the St. Paul's area became 'the greatest book mart in the world', and from the start there was a physical contrast between the open churchyard of the cathedral and the hidden haunts of booksellers and book buyers, the kind of contrast that engenders legend.[11] Each of the houses in the narrow street had its secrets. Many of the houses were small with narrow frontages, but some were surprisingly large. Leasehold was the most common form of property tenure, and there were frequent changes of tenure and of trading. Sometimes books were sold on their own: frequently other items were sold too.[12]

When Thomas acquired his new business in 1724, the substantial purchase price that he paid for what was a successful going concern in the Row covered Taylor's household goods as well as his stock-in-trade, his books 'both bound and in sheets', and his premises, shop and warehouse. Taylor, 'a man of capital, respectability and position',[13] had occupied two adjacent properties with different histories – one at The Sign of the Ship in Paternoster Row and the other at The Sign of the Black Swan, at the corner of Paternoster Row and Ave Maria Lane. Both Signs were to be used by the House of Longman, the former far more frequently.

The property at The Sign of the Ship had been described in a twenty-one-year lease of 1667 as a 'good and sufficient house in accordance with the Act of Parliament for rebuilding the City'.[14] The property at The Sign of the Black Swan had been a separate bookshop until 1719 when Taylor acquired the remaining lease of it from the influential bookseller and publisher Awnsham Churchill after the death of his brother and partner John. Praised as a bookseller 'well furnished for any great undertaking', Awnsham, who never married, was from 1705 to 1710 Member of Parliament for Dorchester, where his father had been a bookseller.[15] Awnsham's brother

11   C.H. Timperley, *A Dictionary of Printers and Printing with the Progress of Literature, Ancient and Modern* (1839) and his *Encyclopaedia of Literary and Typographical Anecdote* (1842), largely a second edition of his earlier work.

12   James Raven, *The Business of Books: Booksellers and the English Book Trade 1450–1850*, (2007) pp.28, 116–7, 177.

13   *The Critic*, 24 March 1860, p.366.

14   Before the Great Fire there had been a building on the site called the 'Cherry Tree' and later the 'Cross Keys'.

15   J. Dunton, *The Life and Errors of John Dunton, Late Citizen of London written by himself in Solitude* (1818 edn.), p.204. For Dunton, a lively but challenging source, see *SOB*, Ch.II, and below, pp.112–3. See also H.R. Plomer, *A Dictionary of the Printers and Booksellers who were at Work in England, Scotland and Ireland from 1668–1725*, Vol. 2, (1922), pp.69–70.

John had acquired the lease of the Black Swan for 21 years in 1714, and on his death it passed into Awnsham's hands. The Churchills were the publishers, *inter alia*, of William Camden's *Britannia* and of John Locke's *Essay Concerning Human Understanding*.

~

The pre-Longman history of 'At The Sign of the Ship' leads back deep into the seventeenth century before the Great Fire. While Thomas Longman was a new recruit to the book trade, the business that he acquired was already old in 1724. Long before the Taylors, 'At The Sign of the Ship' had been seen over a London bookseller's shop in 1640 in the Churchyard of old St. Paul's. The owner, John Crook(e), who had started as a London bookseller in 1638 at The Sign of the Greyhound (not a new sign), also in St. Paul's Churchyard, offered his customers 'all manner of books ... brought from beyond the seas', by which he meant books from across the Irish Sea, not very far away, where he played an important role as a printer.[16]

In 1660 Crook(e) was appointed Printer General in Ireland, with power to print all books and statutes, but he continued to trade in London also, and when his shop was destroyed in the Great Fire, he moved temporarily to Duck Lane, a small street leading out of Smithfield, under a different but related Sign, that of the Anchor.[17] The last book which he published was *The French Gardiner*, 'Englished by John Evelyn'. His finest book, a magnificent folio of Archbishop Ussher's *Annals* (1650–54), incorporated a device of a ship in full sail with a Latin imprint on the woodcut *Sub Insigne Navis in Cemeterio Sancti Pauli*.

After Crook(e) died in 1669, leaving a widow but no will, his former apprentice, Benjamin Tooke, also connected with Ireland, took over his business; and in 1670, during the rebuilding of London after the Great Fire, he moved the Sign of the Ship back to St. Paul's Churchyard. Tooke was a substantial publisher who held shares in many publishing undertakings, including the works of Jonathan Swift, and it was Swift who helped him to secure the title of Printer to the Queen in 1713. Active in the affairs of the Stationers' Company, Tooke died in 1716, leaving his business to his son, also called Benjamin.[18]

In 1687, however, Tooke had sold his Churchyard shop to William Taylor's father, John, who traded there until 1706. The son of a Sherborne clothier, John was described by Dunton as an honest, industrious and

THE FRENCH
GARDINER:
INSTRUCTING
How to Cultivate all forts of
FRUIT-TREES,
AND
HERBS for the GARDEN.
TOGETHER
With Directions to Dry, and Conferve
them in their Natural.
An Accomplifhed Piece,
Written Originally in *French*, and now
Tranflated into *Englifh*.
By *JOHN EVELYN* Efquire,
Fellow of the Royal Society.
The third Edition illuftrated with Sculptures.
Whereunto is annexed, the Englifh Vineyard Vin-
dicated by J. Rofe, now Gardiner to his Majefty : with
a Tract of the making and ordering of Wines in France.
London, Printed by T.R. & N.T. for B. Tooke, and
are to be fold at the Ship in St. Pauls Churchyard. 1675.

The title page of the third edition of *The French Gardiner*, 'Englished by John Evelyn', 1675

BL 1506/225 (1)

---

16   For reference see Plomer, *op. cit.*, Vol. 1, 1641–1667 (1907), p.11.

17   No ships are portrayed in R.B. McKerrow, *Printers' and Publishers' Devices in England and Scotland, 1485–1640* (1913), although there were several anchors.

18   Tooke held many Stationers' Company offices. From 1687 to 1702 he was Warehouse-Keeper of the Company and in 1688/9 Junior Warden. He was Treasurer from 1677 to 1702.

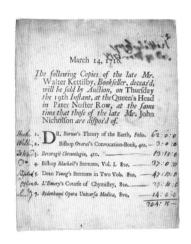

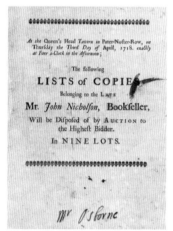

These trade sale catalogues
show how a bookseller could
build up his list at auctions
of the stock and copyrights of
other booksellers

BL Cl.7oaa.1

obliging man with 'moderate principles'.[19] In 1703 he instituted an annual sermon at the Baptist church in Lincoln's Inn Fields to commemorate his escape from death in the great storm of that year. Taylor had previously traded successfully under The Sign of the Globe at the west end of St. Paul's Churchyard, and for a time he worked in partnership with his son William, who had served his apprenticeship with him. The last book of his to bear the Globe imprint was *The Female Advocate, A Poem written by a Lady in Vindication of her Sex* (1686). By a coincidence, the last of his books bearing the Ship imprint was *The Husbandman's Disputation* (1706).

In 1711 William Taylor, who for four or five years had been operating on his own account, moved The Sign of the Ship, by now a ship in full sail, around the corner from St. Paul's Churchyard into the premises in Paternoster Row that Thomas Longman I was to buy. A catalogue of books printed for him 'At the Ship' includes John Donne's poems as well as *Lex Mercatoria: Or the Laws relating to Merchants* and *The Best Way to be Wise and Wealthy: Or the Excellency of Industry and Frugality*. In less serious vein, the list included *The Tunbridge Beau's Love Letter* and *The Epsom Lady's Answer*. The catalogue list was headed with a Ship colophon: the first of his books to bear a Ship colophon had appeared in 1707 while he was still operating from St. Paul's Churchyard. It was an edition of the Book of Common Prayer with paraphrases of the Psalms.

~

These were stirring times, when religion and politics were inextricably intertwined on both sides of the Irish Sea and when there was a brisk demand both for pamphlets and for news concerning both. They were years of strategic importance, therefore, in the history of the periodical and of the newspaper as well as in the history of the book.[20] In 1688 William and Mary had succeeded James II, who fled abroad, and the Battle of the Boyne in Ireland, which was to pass into legend as well as into history, was won by the Protestants in 1690. Religion and politics were intertwined also on European soil during the long War of the Spanish Succession, which began in 1702 and did not end until the Peace of Utrecht in 1713. William died in 1702, and the reign of Queen Anne was shaped not only by foreign conflict but by a 'dreadful Spirit of Division' in Britain itself which also found ready expression in books.

According to Joseph Addison (1672–1719), writing in 1711 in *The Spectator*, a periodical which did much to proclaim the 'civilising culture' of the book (and of the essay), 'as men formerly became eminent in

---

19   Dunton, *op. cit.*, p.207.

20   Dunton (*ibid.*, pp.2110–11) referred to Roper, a former partner of his, who
      printed the *Postbag* and *The Annals of Queen Anne*, and to John Salusbury, 'a
      desperate Hypergorgonic Welshman' who printed *The Flying Post*.

learned Societies by their Parts and Acquisitions, they now distinguish themselves by the Warmth and Violence with which they espouse their respective Parties.'[21] Preceded by *The Tatler*, 1709–11, edited by Richard Steele (1672–1729), it referred to the 'perusing' of a book in its first sentence.[22] This was the first great expansionist phase in the history of the book in times when the 'ubiquity of print' came to be taken for granted.

Expansion had preceded the lapse of the licensing system in 1695, a landmark date. If 'something of a legislative accident', as it has recently been called, since the lapse followed differences between the Commons and the Lords on the wording of any new legislation to replace the old, nevertheless, according to Macaulay, it did more for liberty and for civilisation than the Great Charter or the Bills of Rights'.[23] The licensing system had been in operation (with a break between 1679 and 1685) since 1662 – and had replaced earlier executive decrees going back to 1557, the year when the Stationers' Company was founded. The Company was no longer in full control of the process, although it maintained intact many of its controls, among them its apprenticeship system.[24]

Whatever their background or attributes, all book trades apprentices were required to advance by the same route, learning from practice 'the Mysteries of the Trade'. They also had to follow its 'Customs'. Boys were expected to be fourteen years old when they began their apprenticeship, and Masters had to show that they were Freemen of the City of London as well as the Company. Yet as late as 1757, John Nichols, the source of much of our knowledge of publishing, was apprenticed before he was 'quite thirteen', and Thomas was older than the average.[25] As an orphan too, Thomas was outside the trend. The number of fatherless apprentices fell by forty per cent between the first and the last decades of the century.

By then the business side of 'publishing' was more openly apparent to the world than it had been when Daniel Defoe (1660?–1731), a prolific as well as a perceptive writer, published his treatises, along with pamphlets and a

JOHN NICHOLS,
PRINTER.

Engraving of John Nichols, (1745–1826), author of *Literary Anecdotes of the Eighteenth Century* in nine volumes (1812–15)

Longman Archive

---

21 *The Spectator*, No. 125, 24 July 1711. *The Spectator* was launched in March 1711.

22 Both Steele and Addison were keen social observers as well as readers. T.B. Macaulay believed that if Addison had written a novel it would have been 'superior to any that we possess'. (*Literary Essays* (1923 edn.), p.651.)

23 J. Brewer, *The Pleasures of the Imagination, English Culture in the Eighteenth Century* (1997), p.131; T.B. Macaulay, *The History of England from the Accession of James II*, 2 vols. (1948), Vol. 2, Ch. 21. See also R. Astbury, 'The Renewal of the Licensing Act of 1693 and its Lapse in 1695', in TL, 5th series, Vol. 38 (1978), pp.296–337.

24 Raven, *The Business of Books, op. cit.*, pp.65–8, 85–8, 201–4.

25 J. Nichols, *Literary Anecdotes of the Eighteenth Century*, Vol. VI (1815), p.628. For Nichols see above, p.11.

Frontispiece (which includes
a ship) and the title page of
*The Life and Strange Surprizing
Adventures of Robinson Crusoe
of York, Mariner* by Daniel
Defoe, Taylor's edition (1719)

BL C.30.f.6.

Review as well as fiction. His fiction, Ian Watt observed in his pioneering
study of the English novel in 1957, is the first that presents us with a picture
both of the individual's life in its larger perspective as an historical process
and with a closer view 'which shows the process being acted out against
the background of the most ephemeral thoughts and actions'.[26] Yet Defoe
did not refer to his own works as 'novels' and he denied that he was writing
'fiction'.[27]

A study of him, traveller as well as writer, was to appear in 1856 among
the first fifty volumes of Longman's *Travellers' Library*, an ambitious new

---

26   I. Watt, *The Rise of the Novel* (1957), p.24, subtitled *Studies in Defoe, Richardson
and Fielding*. Subsequently much has been written about eighteenth-century
novels from many different angles. For contemporary comment see I.
Williams (ed.), *Novel and Romance, 1700–1800: A Documentary Record* (1970).
For retrospective narrative and analysis see L. Davis, *Factual Fictions: The
Origins of the English Novel* (1983); G. Day, *From Fiction to the Novel* (1987); M.
McKeon, *The Origins of the English Novel* (1987); and J. Paul Hunter, *Before
Novels* (1990).

27   See E. Zimmerman, *Defoe and the Novel* (1975); J.J. Richetti, *Defoe's Narratives:
Situations and Structures* (1975); P. Earle, *The World of Defoe* (1976); P. Rogers,
Robinson Crusoe (1979); and G.M. Sill, *Defoe and the Idea of Fiction, 1713–1719*
(1983).

venture, marking a further transformation in publishing.[28] It was written
by John Forster, biographer of Dickens, who fully appreciated that Defoe
was the kind of writer who would have been particularly interested in the
kind of property deal that Thomas I made in 1724. In 1831 a former Longman
clerk and agent, Edward Moxon (1801–1858), who became, in his own right,
an important publisher, particularly of poetry, based his *Englishman's
Magazine* on Defoe, and included material signed De Foe, Jr.[29]

~

The signature of Longman I on
a lease for 'The Black Swan'
20 September, 1735

Longman Archive Pt II 55/2

The premises which Thomas I acquired in 1724 consisted of front and back
shops on the ground floor, each dealing in new and second-hand books,
along with a warehouse, kitchen and wash-house; and on the first floor
there were several rooms, including a small parlour, a dining room which
was still in use by Longman descendants in the early-nineteenth century,
and a bedroom over the kitchen. On the second floor were family bedrooms,
and on the top floor bedrooms for apprentices and servants. These too were
used as bedrooms until the fire of 1861.[30]

On 31 August 1724 Thomas had to pay a further £230 18s., a sum
significantly less than the initial £2,282 9s. 6d., for a number of copyrights
that Taylor held, what would later be called his publishing assets. These did
not in most cases carry the right to print or publish a particular book. They
were rights that were shared, as was then customary, with other publishers.
The shares, which could be marketed, provided a given proportion of the
stock of a book when it was printed or reprinted.[31] They also carried with
them the requirement to provide a proportionate share of the costs of such
a reprint.

The Taylor list included several works that were jointly published
with Jacob Tonson and with Bernard Lintot, outstanding among early-

---

28   For the *Travellers' Library*, see below, p.281. Unlike Routledge's *Railway Library*,
      which started three years before, in 1848, Longman's list included no fiction.

29   See below, pp.196 and H.G. Merriam, *Edward Moxon, Publisher of Poets* (1939),
      pp.30–5.

30   An Account by Cyprian Blagden, 'Longmans', written for Hazell, Watson and
      Viney in a *Meet our Customers* series (1951). During the subsequent rebuilding,
      which went on until 1863, the business was carried on temporarily at 14
      Ludgate Hill (LA).

31   See below, p.48.

eighteenth-century publishers, along with nine titles published jointly with John Osborn.[32] Many of them dealt neither with what was then the staple of most publishing, religion, nor with the classics or medicine, other flourishing fields, but with the aftermath of the bursting of the South Sea Bubble in 1720. They included editions of the *Reports of the Commissioners and Trustees for Raising Money on the Estates of the South Sea Company Executors*, published on the order of the House of Commons. The South Sea Bubble was very much a Taylor preoccupation.[33] On the initiative of the Speaker of the House of Commons, he was concerned too, along with Tonson and Lintot, in the recording in print of Parliamentary votes. The printing of debates, a more controversial development, was to follow later in the century. An official record, printed by Messrs Hansard, started in 1774.[34]

One title among Taylor's copyrights that Thomas Longman did not acquire was the most famous and valuable title of them all, already introduced in Chapter One – the *Life and Strange Surprizing Adventures of Robinson Crusoe of York, Mariner*, the first copies of which were sold for five shillings. Taylor is said to have made a profit of £1,000 from it, the envy of other men in the trade. There were three new imprints in 1719 along with a sequel, *The Further Adventures of Robinson Crusoe*, which went through two new editions in 1720 and 1722.[35] It was not until the tenth edition of 1753 that the name of Longman appeared on the title page along with those of eight other publishers after Thomas had at last secured a share in the rights. The edition bore two Longman names, those of

32   The nine included J. Jones, *A Vindication of the former part of the St. Matthew's Gospel* (1719), Solomon Lowe, *A Grammar of the Latin Tongue* (1726), and J. Crawford, *Cursus Medicinae or a Complete Theory of Physic in five parts* (1724). One of Taylor's sole publications was W. Whiston, *The Celebration of Solar Eclipses without Parallaxes*. There had been a total eclipse of the sun on 11 May 1724.

33   See J. Carswell, *The South Sea Bubble* (1960).

34   For Hansard, see below, p.219.

35   See H.C. Hitchins, '*Robinson Crusoe' and its Printings, 1719–31: A Bibliographical Study* (1925). In 1720 Defoe wrote a further related text, *Serious Reflections ... of Robinson Crusoe* which was not a success and was not reprinted until 1925. The various versions have been subject to detailed scholarly research. The first critic of the book, Charles Gildon, believed that Defoe 'drew' Crusoe from the 'consideration' of his own 'mind': 'I have been all my life that Rambling, Inconsistent Creature, which I have made thee'. (*The Life and Strange Surprising Adventures of Mr. D.* (1719), p. x, p. iii.)

Thomas I and Thomas II, the first Longman book to do so.[36]

By then Thomas had already travelled far on his own personal voyage, avoiding 'strange surprising adventures', and, childless, had already drawn his successor, his nephew, Thomas II, into the business. It might have been an omen that on the day in 1753 when his nephew's apprenticeship ended and when he joined Thomas I as a Partner, *The Tempest* was playing at Drury Lane. There was no danger of shipwreck. Thomas had only two years of voyaging ahead of him, and already in 1752 he had purchased from the Dean and Chapter of St. Paul's a piece of land at Friern Barnet, just south of the church, as a burial vault.

~

Thomas's journey had begun in 1699 just before the old century ended, and Bristol, where he spent his boyhood, was a city where many ocean voyages began, if not Crusoe's. In the first instance, however, Thomas's was a journey by land, not by sea, with London as the destination. It was as an orphan that at the age of seventeen he was apprenticed in 1716 to John Osborn, whose business was carried out not in the immediate area of St. Paul's Churchyard but At the Sign of the Oxford Arms in Lombard Street.[37] This was in the heart of what came to be called the City, not far from what was to become another of England's long surviving, but then only recently founded, institutions, the Bank of England, which had been granted its Charter in 1694.[38]

The year 1716 was an interesting time for Thomas to arrive.[39] The River Thames froze, and Lintot was one of the many book retailers who set up a stall on the ice to sell his wares. On 9 June 1716, the day when Longman began his apprenticeship, Lintot was advertising a number of books by John Gay and Alexander Pope, including the second edition of *The Temple of Fame*, the tenth edition of *The Rape of the Lock*, and the first eight books of Pope's version of the *Iliad*. The context within which Pope and other writers pursued their lives has been thoughtfully explored by Howard Erskine Hill in his *Social Milieu of Alexander Pope* (1975). Apprentices were at the heart of it.

Like all new apprentices, Thomas had to promise that he would be

---

36   In the sale of Taylor copyrights on 3 Feb. 1725, the Taylor share of *Robinson Crusoe* was bought by Mears and Woodward, and Woodward sold it to Longman in 1753. *NQ*, 19 April 1890, 'Booksellers' Sales in the Eighteenth Century'.

37   There is a Court Book entry of 19 June 1716, referring to Thomas as the son of Ezekiel Longman and bound to John Osborn. See D.F. McKenzie, *Stationers' Company Apprentices, 1701–1801* (1978), p.255.

38   See J.H. Clapham, *The Bank of England: A History*, 2 vols. (1944).

39   See Appendix 3 *The Longman Family*.

obedient to his new Master and Mistress, 'respectful to their children, kindred and neighbours', and 'neither to know or hear of any treason, murder or felony done, or to be done but you shall forthwith discharge and reveal the same to your Master'. In Dunton's interesting account of apprenticeship this family dimension was especially stressed. 'I would reckon my Master and Mistress as another Father and Mother, and be as tender and loving towards the Children as if they were my Brothers and my Sisters.'[40] Thomas followed the precept faithfully. Indeed, in time, as we have noted, he was to marry his Master's sister.[41]

Another aspect of apprenticeship which was emphasised by all masters was good behaviour. Thomas had to swear that he would not frequent taverns and alehouses, that he would 'wear apparel decent and seemly', that he would use 'fair and gentle words in buying and selling', and that he would not 'play at dice, cards or any other unlawful game'. Finally, he was required to be 'no stealer, loiterer or errant, nor runner away, nor ... enticer of others to do so'. The ideal was that of William Hogarth's 'industrious apprentice', and Thomas was only two years younger than Hogarth, who was himself apprenticed to a silver-engraver. (Hogarth's father, Richard, had produced a school book, published by Taylor.[42]) Obedience was the keynote of such rules of apprenticeship, which emphasised vocation more than enterprise, loyalty more than intelligence, and co-operation more than competition.

We know less of Thomas's feelings and motivations in 1716 or of the home that he left behind him than we do of Crusoe's, for he divulged very little information about himself. We do know, however that his great great grandfather, also a Thomas Longman, was a yeoman in the parish of Winford in Somerset, eight miles from Bristol, and that a third son of this earlier Thomas Longman, also called Thomas, born in 1612, had been apprenticed in 1626 to a very different trade from that of the founder of the House of Longman, that of 'sopemaker', bound to Alderman Robert Rogers in the sum of £50.[43]

---

40 Dunton, *op. cit.*, p.52.

41 See above, p.26.

42 *Grammar Disputations* (1711) consisted of 'an examination of the eight parts of speech by way of question and answer, whereby children in a very little time will learn not only the knowledge of grammar, but likewise to speak and write Latin'. Hogarth added that he had found this out 'by good experience'. William Hogarth was then fourteen years old.

43 *Bristol Apprentice Book* 04352 5(a), fo. 12. No detailed evidence concerning Winford survives. By a coincidence, the living of the parish was in the hands of Worcester College, Oxford, where I carried out much of the research on this *History*. In the 1980s the parish included a sizeable proportion of people involved in information technology.

Engraving of a Frost Fair on the frozen River Thames. It was described as 'A wonderfull Fair or a Fair of Wonders, ... in the time of the Frost December 1684 till 4 February.' Originally published in [1685]

BL Maps K Top 28.38.2

In 1633, having finished his apprenticeship, this Thomas Longman is described as giving a free dinner to the 'Company of Sope-making' 'according to Ancient Custome' on Quarter Day;[44] and a year later he is recorded as contributing 20 shillings towards a fund raised by his Company for 'the Defence of our Trade' against soapmakers setting up at Lambeth, London. Thomas obviously prospered, whatever the competition, and later he married Anne, the daughter of Ezekiel Wallis, Alderman and one-time Mayor of Bristol. His youngest son, also called Ezekiel (1638–1665), was described on the Bristol Burgess and Apprentices Roll as a 'sopeboyler' – was this a leap in status? – and he too married the daughter-in-law of a Bristol Mayor, William Crabb. She died in childbirth at the age of 22 in 1662, and a year later he married again, this time the daughter of a merchant.[45]

---

44 *Transactions of the Bristol Records Society*, Vol. X (1940), p.194.

45 Her name – Mary – appeared on a monument in the Temple Church to William Crabb, who died in 1702 at the age of 87. This information was given to Thomas Longman IV in a letter of 20 Jan. 1844 by William Tyson, a member of the Society of Antiquaries, who was on the staff of the *Bristol Mirror*. He had been approached by the Longman family to provide information about Ezekiel. Tyson established the connection between the families of Longman and Crabb, and pointed out also that there had been a 'large mural monument' to Ezekiel in St. Thomas's Church before it was taken down and rebuilt 'about the year 1793'. In his will, dated 1654, with a 1658 codicil, this seventeenth-century Thomas, who died in 1658, refers to his brother William's land in Winford and to land of his own in Winford as well as to Bristol properties that he had purchased. (LA Part II/251/1)

Ezekiel, a name much favoured by future Longmans, was not the first Old Testament name to figure in the family record. Thomas Longman of Winford's second son was called Moses. He figures as a Bristol mercer in 1655 in an argument about the behaviour of one of his apprentices who had broken apprenticeship rules by boasting to a fellow apprentice that his master had promised his father that he 'would send him beyond the seas in a short time'.[46]

Bristol was renowned for its soap and its sugar as well as its ships in the seventeenth century; and in 1633, the year when Thomas 'the sopemaker' became a freeman, Bristol soap emerged triumphantly from a whiter-than-white test when, in the presence of witnesses, it was compared with other soaps:

> The saide napkins washed with Bristoll soape weare alltogether as white washed and as sweete or rather sweter than the other yett in the washinge of the said Napkins. There was not Alltogether soe much soape expended of the said Bristoll Soape as there was of the other Soape. Soe that it Appered to All them present, That the said Bristoll Soape was as good or rather better than the said other soape.[47]

This was powerful testimony. Nevertheless, it was not through soap, even cultural soap, not then thought of, that the Longmans of the future were to thrive. Moreover, while four soap makers were Mayors of Bristol between 1702 and 1729, thereafter there were none.

Another of Thomas's sons, James, followed a very different career from Ezekiel. Apprenticeship played no part in his life, just as it played no part in the life of many future Longmans or, indeed, of most of the authors on whom eighteenth-century publishers were to depend.[48] James was educated at New College, Oxford, where he became Chaplain, and in 1643 he moved to the parish of Aynhoe. 'Ejected by the Puritans', he moved to Churchill, Somerset, but was restored to his living after the Restoration.

---

46 Record of 23 July 1655 printed in *Transactions of the Bristol Records Society*, Vol. XIX (1955), pp.20–1.

47 *Loc. cit.*, Vol. X (1940), p. 194. J. Matthews, the writer of an early-nineteenth century *Bristol Guide* (1825), p.95, quoted Malachy Postlethwaite's *Universal Dictionary of Trade and Commerce* (1751) in which it was stated that the first manufacture of soap in England was in Bristol. Two hundred years before Thomas Longman I went to London, Bristol was already supplying the capital with 'the best grey speckled soap, and with white also'.

48 There had been a link between clergymen fathers and publishing apprentices in the seventeenth century. In the eighteenth century, however, there was a stronger link between lawyer fathers and publishing apprentices. (C. Blagden, 'The Stationers' Company in the Eighteenth Century', in *Guildhall Library Miscellany*, Vol. I (1952–9), pp. 36ff.)

A bachelor, he died in 1677 and was buried at Aynhoe.[49]

One of Ezekiel's sons, another Ezekiel (1662–1708), Thomas I's father, married twice as his father had done. When he married for the first time in 1682, he was described as a merchant. In 1697, however, when he married again, he was described as 'Gent'. He produced through his first marriage yet a third Ezekiel (1684–1738), who was apprenticed to a linen draper and became 'immensely rich', and through his second marriage the founder of the House of Longman. There was another son, Henry, born in 1701, who was apprenticed to Thomas Warren, a Bristol vintner. He moved to London – when is not known – and his son Thomas, born in 1730, was to succeed the childless Thomas I in charge of the bookselling business.[50]

In 1694, when the Printing and Licensing Act of 1662 was allowed to lapse, the Common Council of Bristol had been unique in resolving that 'a printing house would be useful in several respects' and had invited William Bonny, who had begun business in London, where he was employed by Dunton, to establish a business even though he was not a Freeman of the City. Although during the Civil War the King's portable printing press had been moved to Bristol, there was no established local tradition of provincial printing, and there seem to have been no connections between the Longman family and Bonny, who went on to start the *Post Boy*, the city's first short-lived news and advertisement sheet, in 1702. John Wesley's first open-air sermon, *Free Grace*, delivered in Bristol, was printed by Felix Farley, a local printer, who along with Peter Pine, was responsible for many of Wesley's later publications.[51]

When Ezekiel died in 1708, leaving the future Thomas I an orphan at the age of nine, the boy was placed in the care of guardians, who were instructed in his father's lengthy will, drawn up when Thomas was only six, to ensure that he was 'well and handsomely bred and educated according to his fortune'; and it was his guardians who sent him to London in 1716 to join John Osborn as an apprentice. Whether or not he had the slightest choice in the matter is unknown. Despite the injunction in his father's will, Thomas may have felt uneasy, as Crusoe was in the novel, about 'the state wherein God and nature' had placed him, for by the time that he left Bristol for London his half-brother, Ezekiel, fifteen years older than he was,

---

49 A.G. Matthews, *Walker Revised, being a version of John Walker's Sufferings of the Clergy during the Grand Rebellion, 1642–60* (1948), p.282. In his will, proved on 3 Nov. 1677, James described himself as 'by the mercy of Jesus Christ and the calling of the Church of England, Priest, Rector of Aynhoe'.

50 (LA/Part II/251/1)

51 J. Feather, *The Provincial Book Trade in Eighteenth-Century England* (1983), p. 118. Another Bristol printer, Nathanial Biggs, figures prominently in later chapters of this history, see below pp.151, 200.

was already on the way to making his fortune. Clearly Thomas faced strong family competition.[52]

~

We know nothing about why the first Longman ever to move into bookselling and publishing was apprenticed to John Osborn, who was to play such a big part in his life. There are several Osborn(e)s in the Stationers' Company records; and there are more awkward problems in placing them in history than there are in placing the Longmans.[53] Neither family was metropolitan by origin. Thomas's West Country background left its influence on the House of Longman: the Osborn family's background was in Derbyshire, 'Ashbourne in the Peak'. John Osborn's father, also called John, lived longer than his son, and has often been identified as Thomas I's master, but despite many statements to the contrary, passed on, usually without acknowledgement, from one author to another, there is no evidence that the father, who may have dealt in property, was ever involved in the book trade.

A discourse by the then Rector of Ashbourne, John Boydell, *The Church Organ: or a Vindication of Grave and Solemn Musick in Divine Service*, printed by the author, was to be sold by J. Osborn and T. Longman in 1727, and later in the eighteenth century by a coincidence Ashbourne was to figure in Samuel Johnson's life. His friend, Dr John Taylor, lived there, another coincidence in names, and Johnson visited him on several occasions. The fact that the friend was called Taylor was again a coincidence: there was no family connection with the William Taylor mentioned previously. And there were other coincidences. The Irish poet Tom Moore (1779–1852), a favourite and favoured Longman author in the nineteenth century, had a house in Ashbourne, Mayfield Cottage, a 'scribbling retreat'. 'I could not possibly have a more rural or secluded corner to court the Muses in'.[54]

The younger Osborn to whom Thomas was apprenticed in 1716 was to play an active part in the affairs of the Stationers' Company, serving as

---

52   Other Longmans figure in late-seventeenth-century and early-eighteenth-century Bristol records. The executors of James Longman, a mercer, were referred to in documents concerning seals in 1693, 1695 and 1699. Thomas Longman, a Virginia merchant, signed a leaflet printed by Christopher Penn, a local bookseller, in 1724, the year Thomas I started his business in London: it dealt with the measurement of sugar, a basic item in Bristol trade. This Longman died in 1753. (*Felix Farley's Bristol Journal*, 1 Dec. 1753.)

53   The point is remarked upon by T. Belanger, 'A Directory of the London Book Trade, 1766' (PH, Vol. I, 1977). 'Care must be taken in keeping straight the several Osborn(e)s.' Cf. PC, 13 Aug. 1892, which notes four Osborns in the early eighteenth-century book trade.

54   Letter to James Corry, 1 July 1813 (LA/Part II/64). For Moore see below, pp.187ff.

Under Warden from 1731 to 1733 and attending a meeting of the Court in the week before his death. In London's first daily newspaper, the *Daily Courant*, 23 Oct. 1724, there had been an advertisement for a new book in Latin, *Oratio Anniversaria Harveiana*, to be obtained from W. and J. Innys at the West End of St. Paul's and J. Osborn at the Oxford Arms in Lombard Street.[55] In 1725 he joined Thomas as a partner and he died without issue in 1733. In his will he was described simply as a 'stationer': his father was described as a 'gentleman'.

The younger Osborn's sister Mary married Thomas not at the time when his son Osborn and Thomas became partners, as legend has it, but much later on 27 January 1731 (old style). Mary was then forty years old, and Thomas was fully settled in his business. The place of their marriage was St. Paul's Cathedral, and they had a special licence from the Bishop of London.[56] It was only after Thomas's death in 1755 that Mary, having been left the main share of her family's stock, briefly became a partner in the business, senior partner with Thomas's nephew, Thomas II, who had been left almost a half.[57]

If scattered and patchy records dispel legend, as they do in so many business histories, there are genuinely fascinating links at the beginning of the story of the Longman business when it is considered within a broader context.[58] Thomas's new partner of 1725, the younger John Osborn, only ten years older than himself, had been apprenticed on 6 September in 1703, at the customary age of fourteen, to Thomas Guy, the founder of Guy's Hospital, then fifty-nine years old and a bookseller who had himself been apprenticed to John Clarke, a bookseller, in 1660.[59] There is a firm link, therefore, as has been noted, between the history of the House of Longman and the history of another of Britain's old institutions, Guy's Hospital, founded in 1726, itself to be threatened with mortality in the

---

55   The advertisement was repeated on 13 November.

56   J.W. Clay (ed.), *The Registers of St. Paul's Cathedral* (1899), 27 Jan. 1731.

57   See below, p.55.

58   The legends – and this was not the only one – are often couched in confident language and embroidered with rich detail. For example, Francis Espinasse in *The Critic*, 24 March 1860, observed that while Thomas was still an apprentice, Osborn's daughter, Mary, 'discovered that one of these days she would have no objection to become Dame Mary Longman, and the young apprentice began to suspect that he had found a fit, fair, and, best of all, a willing recipient for "his mother's necklace of pearl!"'. For the Espinasse articles see below, p.243ff.

59   Plomer, *op. cit.*, Vol. 2, pp.136–8. He later made his peace with the Stationers' Company, and in 1718 he provided sums of money for 'poor members'. He was the senior living member of the Court when Osborn, who had risen at a rapid rate within the Company, was elected an Assistant in 1723.

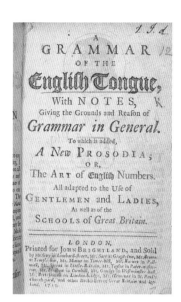

The title page of *A Grammar of the English Tongue*, 1711, a book adapted for 'the use of Gentlemen and Ladies, as well as of the Schools of Great Britain' and whose imprint carried, amongst many others, the names of Osborn & Varnam

BL 121 2.h.1.

last decade of the twentieth century. Defoe in his *Tour Through England and Wales* had made a brief reference to the new hospital created by 'the charitable act and single endowment of one person': 'considerable progress had been made [on the venture] while these sheets were in the press'. 'It was only when this gentleman died that the world was told that it was to be a separate hospital.'[60]

Through Guy there is a fascinating link too, not with the history of the hospital but with the history of the Oxford University Press, for Guy, the son of a coal-heaver and lighterman, a Baptist, during a significant period of his life had dealt in 'Oxford Bibles' that were printed abroad; and from 1678 to 1691, before the lapse of the Licensing Act, he printed Bibles in the Sheldonian Theatre in Oxford, having been invited to do so by the formidable Dr John Fell, Dean of Christ Church and Head of the Delegates of the Oxford University Press.

Dunton described Guy in 1705 as 'a man of strong reason, [who] can talk on any subject you will purpose'.[61] He had acquired at least some of his riches out of his early career as a publisher. His first book was a history of Barbados (1673). Five years earlier he had opened London premises, the Oxford Arms, at the corner of Lombard Street and Cornhill, where he was joined in 1675 by his brother John. The first of his books to bear the imprint At the Oxford Arms was the fifth edition of *The Complete English Scholar in Spelling, Reading and Writing* (1682), and his last recorded book to be published under his own imprint was in 1707.[62]

It was under the Oxford Arms Sign, directly associated with education and indirectly with religion, that Osborn also traded – in partnership with Guy's nephew, Thomas Varnam, the son of a Tamworth mercer and of Guy's sister, Anne. In his will, proved in 1709, Guy, who owned land in Tamworth, a frugal man for all his wealth, left bequests to Thomas's children and to several Osborns whom he described as heirs of 'my aunt Osborn'. There was a bequest of £1,000 too to John Osborn, who was also left £100 for serving as his executor. In addition to 'Oxford Bibles', Osborn and Varnam also published grammars and dictionaries along with books of instruction,

---

60   *Tour Through England and Wales* (Everyman edn., 2 vols., 1962). See also H.C. Cameron, *Mr. Guy's Hospital, 1726–1948* (1954).

61   Dunton later reviled him in *An Essay on Deathbed Charity Exemplified in the Life of Thomas Guy, late Bookseller in Lombard Street* (1728). For Charles Knight, Guy, 'though claimed by booksellers as one of their body', had acquired his property by stockjobbing rather than by literature.

62   There were to be other Guy-Longman links. In 1826 Longman was to publish an address on anti-slavery delivered 'to the students at Guy's Hospital at the close of the lectures on experimental philosophy'. It was printed by A. and R. Spottiswoode. Later in the nineteenth century all the editors of *Gray's Anatomy*, published by Longman (see below, p.288), came from Guy's Hospital.

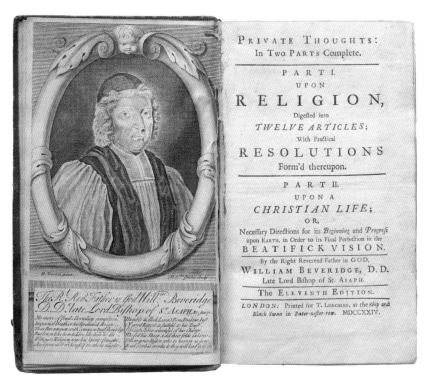

PRIVATE THOUGHTS:
In Two PARTS Complete.

PART I.
UPON
RELIGION,
Digested into
TWELVE ARTICLES;
With Practical
RESOLUTIONS
Form'd thereupon.

PART II.
UPON A
CHRISTIAN LIFE;
OR,
Necessary Directions for its *Beginning* and *Progress*
upon EARTH, in Order to its Final Perfection in the
BEATIFICK VISION.

By the Right Reverend Father in GOD,
WILLIAM BEVERIDGE, D.D.
Late Lord Bishop of St. ASAPH.

The ELEVENTH EDITION.

LONDON: Printed for T. LONGMAN, at the *Ship* and
Black Swan in *Pater-noster-row*. MDCCXXIV.

The frontispiece and title
page of *Private Thoughts
... upon a Christian Life*, by
William Beveridge, 1724.
'One of Longman's earliest
publications, it was advertised
in Wilford's Monthly Catalogue
of September 1724 and in the
Daily Courant of Wednesday
September 2nd, 1724, as "this
day" published.' (Henry R.
Plomer, *Note on some Longman
Publications*, 9th January, 1909)

Personal Collection

branches of publishing in which the House of Longman was eventually to
specialise. Varnam died in 1714.

The first book published with an Osborn and Varnam joint imprint
(and that of many other publishers) was *A Grammar of the English Tongue*
(1711). Religion also figured prominently in their lists, and when Thomas
I purchased Taylor's copyrights in 1724, a large proportion of them were
devoted to religion. After he became a publisher in his own right and moved
to Paternoster Row, Thomas followed carefully in Taylor's footsteps: one of
the first title pages to bear the name of Longman, along with the names of
others, was the eleventh edition of *Private Thoughts upon a Christian Life* by
the Revd. Dr William Beveridge (1637–1708). This appeared on 2 September
1724, less than one month after Longman's purchase of the business. On
that day, readers were told in the *Daily Courant* to go to Thomas Longman's
at The Ship and Black Swan in Paternoster Row to obtain it along with
Beveridge's other publications, including a folio copy of two volumes of his
sermons.[63] His *Private Thoughts* had first appeared posthumously in 1709.

Dr Fell had enjoyed a long-standing relationship with Beveridge also.
In 1668 he 'set his heart' on printing the synodical canons of the Eastern

---

63   *Daily Courant*, 2 Sept. 1724. The Beveridge volume was also advertised in
     Wilford's Monthly Catalogue, Sept. 1724.

Church, and Beveridge was appointed to edit them. When they appeared in 1672 in two folio volumes of 1,588 pages of Greek, Latin and Arabic, they were regarded as a remarkable work of scholarship. Even more remarkable was the feat of printing involved. Compositors capable of setting up Greek were hired in France and types too were acquired from abroad.[64]

Longman's name appeared on several other volumes of Beveridge, including his *Great Necessity of Public Prayer and Frequent Communion* and his *Worthy Communicant, with Meditations before and after the Sacrament.* Beveridge did not become a bishop until 1704, although he had been offered Bath and Wells in 1691. As Bishop of St. Asaph from 1704 to his death in 1708, he took a keen interest in the Welsh language. The subtitle of his *Private Thoughts* ran 'Necessary directions for its beginning and progress [of the Christian Life] upon Earth in order to [reach] its final perfection in the beautiful vision.' That was a different kind of voyage, a spiritual one, from that on which Thomas I was to embark fourteen years later.[65]

~

Thomas's own religious views are not known. What is known, and what he himself well knew, is that religion played a major role in eighteenth-century publishing. 'As to *Religion*', a bookseller told the *Gentleman's Magazine* in 1734, 'if we take a view of our *Stock*, our *Copies*, or our *Accounts*, we find ourselves indebted to it for so great a Proportion of our *Income* as three Parts in Four. Not to mention Bibles and Common Prayers, Expositions and Manuals which are a staple source. There are larger Articles which have been Estates to the Proprietors, as *Barrow's, Beveridge's, Tillotson's* Sermons; and other eminent Writings of great Variety for and against Christianity.'[66] The 'fors' predominated.

Thomas added at once to the shares in books which Taylor possessed, non-religious as much as religious, some shares for 'the whole' or 'a half', some down to 'a sixth'.[67] These were recorded by the Stationers' Company which before naming book titles ruled off a column to denote the size of share held – halves, twelfths, eighths, twenty-fourths, and sixty-fourths. A memorable day for Thomas was 3 February 1725 when at a Paternoster Row sale at ten o'clock in the morning he bought many shares. This was before

---

64 N. Barker, *The Oxford University Press and the Spread of Learning* (1978), p.20; P. Sutcliffe, *The Oxford University Press, an Informal History* (1978), p.xx.

65 One of Beveridge's critics complained in 1711 that he delighted in 'jiggle and quibbling, affects a tune and rhyme in all he says, and rests arguments on nothing but words and sounds'. (A. Whitby, *Short View of Dr. Beveridge's Writings* (1711).)

66 GM, Vol.4, May 1734, p.259.

67 See C.J. Longman, *The House of Longman 1724–1800: A Bibliographical History* (1936).

the booksellers present, an exclusive company, summoned by invitation, were entertained at twelve o'clock to 'a good dinner'.[68] This mode of buying with a celebration of the transaction was more than a matter of ritual. It raised necessary capital at a time when liquid capital was short and it spread risks.

A few months earlier, in October 1724, Thomas had turned from theology to science in his new publications, and his name figured in a prospectus for 'printing by subscription' several volumes of the complete works of the chemist Robert Boyle (1627–1691), already prepared for the printer. Each subscriber was 'to lay down fifteen shillings and the Remainder on the delivery of the Book in Sheets', promised by 10 December. The volumes were to be printed 'on good paper ... for W. and J. Innys at the West End of St. Paul's Church-yard, J. Osborne, at The Oxford Arms in Lombard Street, and T. Longman, at The Ship and Black Swan in Pater-Noster Row'.[69]

The voluminous works of Boyle (seventh son of the Earl of Cork), a pioneer chemist and a founder and Fellow of the Royal Society, covered many subjects besides chemistry and were edited by Dr Peter Shaw (1694–1763), Thomas Longman's doctor, who helped Thomas's wife through a serious illness in 1739.[70] Born in Lichfield, an important city on the eighteenth-century cultural map of England, Shaw was the son of the Master of Lichfield Grammar School, and in retrospect won the praises of Nichols (and others) as a highly effective communicator of knowledge.[71] His lectures in London and in the spa town of Scarborough between 1731 and 1733 won him a fashionable audience which included doctors, and it was by following this route that he became a highly successful doctor himself. He did not become a Fellow of the Royal College of Physicians until 1754, having been appointed two years earlier Physician Extraordinary to King George II. He attended the King on most of his visits to Hanover.

General Instructions, DIVINE, MORAL, HISTO-RICAL, FIGURATIVE, &c. SHEWING The Progress of RELIGION from the CREATION to this TIME, and to the END of the WORLD; And tending to confirm the TRUTH of the Christian Religion.

By THEOPHILUS GARENCIERES, Vicar of Scarbrough, and Chaplain to his Grace PEREGRINE DUKE of ANCASTER.

ACTS xvii. 11, 12.

YORK, Printed by J. White, at the Sign of The Printing Press in Stonegate, for the Author; and sold by Francis Hildyard in York; T. Ryles in Hull; J. Osburn and T. Longman in Pater-Noster-Row; James and J. Knapton in St. Paul's Church-Yard; Th. Osborne at Grey's Inn, and N. Moody within Lincolns-Inn-Gate, London, M.DCC.XXVIII.

In 1728 'J. Osburn and T Longman in Pater-noster Row' were named as one of four London booksellers who 'sold' the *General Instructions, Divine, Moral, Historical, Figurative etc.* Two booksellers came from York and Hull

Longman Archive

---

68 The highest priced shares at the first Taylor sale were a tenth and a sixteenth in Ainsworth's *Latin and English Dictionary*, then in the press. They fetched £40 5s. 6d. Longman did not acquire a share until 1728.

69 J. Wilford, *Proposals for Printing by Subscription* (1724). Many of Boyle's works in his lifetime had been published by William Taylor's father, John. His *The Martyrdom of Theodora* (1687) raised basic questions about the relationship between 'romance' and 'history'. He also wrote *General Heads for the Natural History of a Country ... for the Use of Travellers and Navigators* (1692). In order to pursue his scriptural studies Boyle also learned Hebrew and Syriac.

70 Shaw's edition of Boyle divided, 'abridged and methodized' Boyle's works into Physics, Statics, Natural History, Chemistry and Medicine. In 1745 Shaw published with Longman and Shewell *A new Practice of Physic; wherein the various diseases incident to the human body are described.*

71 Nichols, *op. cit.*, Vol. IX, p.764.

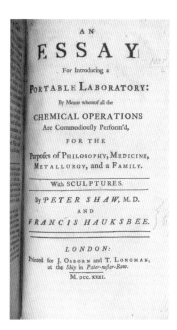

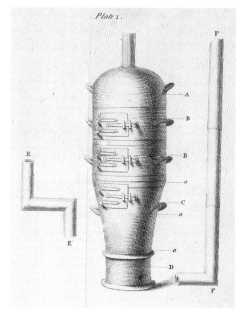

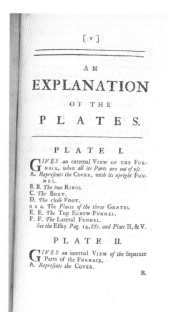

An engraving from *An Essay
for introducing a Portable
Laboratory: by means whereof
all the Chemical Operations are
Commodiously Perform'd for the
Purposes of Philosophy, Medicine,
Metallurgy, and a Family* by
Peter Shaw, MD and Francis
Hauksbee

BL 1035K7 (2)

In 1750, when Thomas published anonymously an octavo volume
written by Shaw called *The Reflector*, 'representing human affairs as they
are and may be improved', Thomas told him in a letter that 'no author that
I know of has wrote more usefully than yourself; or shewn a greater regard
to the welfare of mankind'.[72] Shaw was, indeed, a dedicated 'improver', and
appropriately one of his publications was a three-volume edition of the works
of Francis Bacon, the seventeenth-century prophet of scientific and social
advancement. Thomas also published in 1761 *The Tablet, or Picture of Real
Life, justly representing as in a Looking-Glass, the Virtues and Vices, Fopperies
and Fooleries, Masks and Mummeries of the Age* and in 1763, two years before
his death, a book with a very different title, *Essays for the Improvement of
Arts, Manufactures and Commerce, by means of Chemistry* which, like Boyle,
he thought of as a 'universal' as well as a practical science.[73]

One of the most remarkable publishing achievements associated
with Thomas and Shaw related not to Bacon or to Boyle but to an early work
of Shaw himself, a very practical work, *An Essay for Introducing a Portable
Laboratory by Means whereof all the Chemical Operations are Commodiously
Perform'd for the Purposes of Philosophy, Medicine, Metallurgy and a Family*.
The title itself stands out, particularly the references to 'Philosophy' and
to 'a Family', but it is the superb illustrations, a series of plates of an

---

72   Quoted in Blagden, *Fire More than Water*, p. 17.

73   See J. Golinski, *Science as Public Culture: Chemistry and Enlightenment in
Britain, 1760–1820* (1992), p.33. Shaw had published in 1721 *The Dispensary of
the Royal College of Physicians*.

exceptionally high quality, which invite the reader not only to read but to experiment. Shaw had a collaborator for this book, Francis Hawksbee, and it was published as early as 1731, the year of his first London lecture, with an Osborn and Longman imprint. Shaw offered the laboratory for sale at his lectures, an offer which depended on his partnership with Hawksbee who was an instrument maker.

~

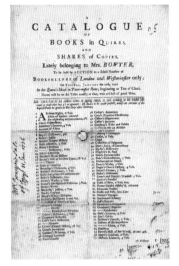

A month after associating himself with Boyle's *Works* in 1724, Thomas acquired a one-third share in the Delphin *Virgil*, an edition of French origin, hitherto the property in England of Jacob Tonson junior, the nephew and successor of Jacob Tonson I (1656–1737), the publisher of the poet John Dryden;[74] and four years after that he paid £40 for a one-twentieth share in Ainsworth's *Latin and English Dictionary*, a valuable property in which, for whatever reason, he had not secured a share at Taylor's sale of copyrights in February 1725. In the same year, his name appeared among the publishers of Nathan Bailey's *An Universal Etymological English Dictionary*, many 'improved' editions of which were to be brought out between its first publication in 1721 and 1802. Some of them included illustrations.

Bailey, who died in 1742, kept a boarding school in Stepney, and some of his 'definitions' are as memorable as Johnson's were to be. He defined 'mouse', for example, as 'an animal well-known' and 'cat' as 'a domestic creature that kills mice'. He provided some etymologies and indicated primary stress in pronunciation. In 1730 he brought out a folio volume, *Dictionarium Britannicum: or a more Compleat Universal Etymological English Dictionary than any Extant*. Johnson possessed an interleaved copy. Bailey, who was a Baptist, died in 1742, five years before the prospectus for Johnson's *A Plan of a Dictionary* was published.

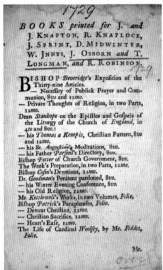

Thomas I's name was attached to this prospectus, along with those of a number of other publishers, including T. Shewell, Osborn's former apprentice and for the brief period from 1745 to 1748 Thomas's partner, John and Paul Knapton, C. Hitch and Andrew Millar.[75] Johnson, who like Shaw was born in Lichfield, recalled that the idea had 'grown up in his [own] mind insensibly'.[76] The words to be listed in the *Dictionary* were to be 'deduced

Two trade sale catalogues from the BL/Longman collection

BL C1.70aa.1

---

74 See G.F. Papoli, *Jacob Tonson, Publisher* (1968). The Delphin editions were dedicated to the French Dauphin, *ad usum serenissimi Delphini*. Other shareholders in the edition of Virgil included W. Innys, J. and P. Knapton and C. Hitch.

75 *The Plan of a Dictionary of the English Language* (1747). (See J.L. Clifford, *Young Samuel Johnson* (1955), p. 178.)

76 G.B. Hill (ed.), *Boswell's Life of Johnson*, Vol. I (1934), p. 182. See B. Redford, *The Letters of Samuel Johnson*, Vol. I (1992), for his letter to Charles Burney, musician and friend, 8 April 1755.

from their originals' and 'illustrated in their different significances'. 'One great end of this undertaking', Johnson maintained, was 'to fix the English language', including orthography, pronunciation and accent. All words that for any reason were unworthy were to be rejected.

Yet he had other ends in mind too, which he specified. Speaking with authority, he wished to examine the general fabric of the language, tracing the usual 'modes of derivation and inflection' of each word in order 'to mark the progress of its meaning', a purpose appreciated by many, if not all, of his first reviewers. One of them, a Whig, Thomas Edwards, dismissed the *Dictionary* as 'nothing but a booksellers' job'.[77] Johnson himself used the sea metaphor described above in Chapter 1: 'I have sailed a long and difficult voyage round the world of the English language.'[78]

Samuel Johnson's famous *Dictionary*, showing its title page. First published in two volumes, Thomas I died in June 1755, soon after the *Dictionary* was published, on the day on which the issue in weekly parts was announced in the newspapers

BL 701.1.12

---

77   *London Chronicle*, 12–14 April 1755; GM, Vol. LIV, April 1755; and *Monthly Review*, April 1755, which largely devoted its space to quoting Johnson himself. A letter by W.S. (William Strahan) to the GM, Feb. 1749, served as 'a puff'. For other critical reactions see G.E. Noyes, 'The Critical Reception of Johnson's Dictionary in the Later Eighteenth Century' in *Modern Philology*, Vol. LII (1955). For 'the need for an English dictionary' see R.W. Wells, *Dictionaries and the Authoritarian Tradition* (1973).

78   Quoted in TDPP, p. 695, on the same page as he referred to the death of Thomas I. For fictional voyages see P.P. Gove, *The Imaginary Voyages in prose Fiction: ... with an Annotated Check List of 215 Imaginary Voyages from 1700–1800* (1941).

Johnson's idea of a *Dictionary* was not a new one, but it was only after his 'Plan' had been drafted in 1746, and agreement had been reached with the publishers in June of that year, that he began his labours, with the overall sum of £1,575 in his pocket. His one surviving letter to Thomas Longman suggested that there might be a breakfast at which he and the publishers would sign the contract, but on this occasion such customary conviviality was not deemed necessary: one of the publishers, Paul Knapton, could not attend. The signing, therefore, was done separately on 18 June 1746. As C.J. Longman was to point out in his *Bibliographical History*, Johnson at that time was still Mr Johnson. He did not receive his Master of Arts degree by diploma from Oxford University until 20 February 1755 and his first doctorate from Trinity College, Dublin until 1765.

The first volume of the *Dictionary* was completed in the spring of 1753, and, with Strahan named as the printer (not so named on the title page), the two long-awaited folio volumes, priced at £4 10s. a set, weighing 25 pounds, finally appeared on 15 April 1755, to be followed by new editions in 1755 (published in 165 sixpenny weekly numbers), 1765, 1773, revised by Johnson himself, 1784, and 1786.[79] An octavo edition cost only ten shillings. In his impressive preface to the first edition Johnson 'told the world' eloquently and movingly how he had carried through his long labours through sickness and sorrow, through distress and inconvenience, 'not lulled in the soft obscurities of retirement', or under the shelter of 'academic bowers' and with 'little assistance' from 'the learned' and 'without the *patronage* of the great'.

The last of these comments endows the *Dictionary* with a particular significance in the history of eighteenth-century publishing. The point was made eloquently, if too generally, by Macaulay in a review of James Boswell's *Life of Johnson*, first published in 1741: 'It was a dark night between two sunny days. The age of patronage had passed away. The age of general curiosity and intelligence had not arrived.'[80] Macaulay did not touch on pricing. In fact, the price of the *Dictionary* represented nearly two months' wages for Johnson's own amanuenses.

Originally Johnson had thought of Lord Chesterfield as a patron and had dedicated his 'Plan' to him. Thereafter, however, it was Chesterfield about whom Johnson complained most, remarking that he had not granted

A painting of Samuel Johnson (1709–1784) by Sir Joshua Reynolds, soon after the *Dictionary* was published

The National Portrait Gallery, London no. 1597

---

79   For the compilation of the Dictionary see J.H. Sledd and G.J. Kolb, *Dr. Johnson's Dictionary: Essays in the Biography of a Book* (1955) and A. Reddick, *The Making of Johnson's Dictionary, 1746–1773* (1990). For Strahan's expenditure as printer, £1,239 11s. 6d., of which in 1775 £441 11s. 6d. was still owed to him by the partners, see R.A. Austen-Leigh, *The Story of a Printing House* (2nd edn., 1912), p.25. Two thousand copies of the *Dictionary* were printed. See also J.L. Clifford, *Dictionary Johnson: Samuel Johnson's Middle Years* (1979).

80   *Lord Macaulay's Essays and Lays of Ancient Rome* (authorized 1885 edn., published by Longman, Green and Co.), p. 178.

him even one 'act of assistance'. 'Is not a patron one who looks with unconcern on a Man struggling for Life in the Water and when he had reached ground encumbers him with help?', he was to ask Chesterfield in a remarkable and much quoted letter, dated 7 February 1755, written just after Chesterfield had commended the *Dictionary* in Robert Dodsley's *The World*.[81] 'The notice which you have been pleased to take of my labours, had it been early, had it been kind ... but it had been delayed until it was of no value.' Johnson's voyage completed (note the metaphor again), Chesterfield was now offering 'to send out his cock-boat to tow me into harbour'.[82]

'I hope it is no very cinical [sic] asperity not to confess obligation', he concluded, 'where no benefit has been received, or to be unwilling that the Public should consider me as owing that to a Patron, which Providence has enabled me to do for myself.'[83] Under the entry 'Patron' in his *Dictionary* Johnson had written 'commonly a wretch who supports with insolence, and is paid with flattery'. According to Boswell, Johnson substituted the word 'patron' for 'garret' in a line in his *The Vanity of Human Wishes* – 'Toil, envy, want, the garret and the jail'.[84] Nevertheless, he amiably called Dodsley 'my patron, Doddy'.

Johnson had mixed judgements to make on his publishers, as they had on him. While he was preparing the *Dictionary* he tried to stay clear of them until his labours were over. 'My Resolution has long been, and is *not* now altered', he wrote in November 1751, 'that I shall *not* see the Gentlemen Partners till the first volume is in the press.'[85] Long after he had finished his work, he described Andrew Millar (1706–1767) as 'the Maecenas of the age' and congratulated him for 'raising the price of literature'. Yet, according to Boswell, Millar is said to have remarked when he received the copy of the last sheet of the *Dictionary*, 'Thank God I have done with him'. 'I am glad that he thanks God for anything' had been Johnson's riposte.[86]

There is no Longman comment on Johnson – or the other way round.

---

81 Reddick, *op. cit.*, pp.95–7; *The World*, 28 Nov., 5 Dec. 1754. Chesterfield had complained with some exaggeration in 1752 that 'though we have ten thousand Greek and Latin grammars and dictionaries, we have not a single one in English'. (Letter to the Bishop of Clonfort, printed in B. Dobrée (ed.), *The Letters of Philip Dormer Stanhope, 4th Earl of Chesterfield*, Vol. V (1932).

82 TDPP, p.695.

83 The Yale manuscript gives 'the World' for 'the Public'.

84 Boswell, *Life*, Vol. I, p.264. In 1800 Thomas Norton Longman and his partner Owen Rees were to be joint publishers of Chesterfield's *Letters*.

85 Letter to Strahan, 1 Nov. 1751. (Reddick, *op. cit.*, p.50.) The first volume of the *Dictionary* was not finished until April 1753.

86 Hill, *op. cit.*, Vol. I, pp.287-8. Nicols considered that Jacob Tonson and Andrew Millar were in their time 'the best *patrons* of literature'.

Sadly, indeed, Thomas I died on 18 June 1755, only two months after the *Dictionary* appeared, by a coincidence on the ninth anniversary day of the signing of the original agreement.[87] Paul Knapton died too in the same summer, and in a letter to Thomas Warton, his Oxford friend, Johnson had to explain why he could not go to Oxford until he and his publishers could 'recover from our confusion': 'two of our partners are dead'.[88]

Unlike the prospectus, the published *Dictionary* bore two Longman names, those of Thomas I and his nephew, to be known later as Thomas II: he had become a partner in 1753 after a seven-year apprenticeship. The son of Thomas I's younger brother Henry, who lived in Silver Street, only five hundred yards away from Paternoster Row in the adjacent parish of St. Olave,[89] he was provided by Thomas I with £2,000 to acquire his share. At the same time the business was capitalised by Thomas I on the basis of a £5,000 figure, and Thomas II, as he soon became, was promised that on his aunt Mary's decease her share would pass over to him. Thomas I also mentioned specifically Thomas II's patent right to Lily's *Grammar*.

In his will, which faithfully followed guidance set out in one of the early books published by Longman and Osborn in 1728, Thomas Wentworth's *The Office and Duty of Executors: or a Treatise directing Testators to form, and Executors to perform their Wills and Testaments according to Law*, Thomas I left an annuity of £20 to his widow, and £1,500, along with £10 for mourning to his sister Sarah Longman. Mary, his widow, was sole executrix. Thomas did not forget Dr Peter Shaw, who was left a ring – as he himself had been.

The strong family sense that bound kinship and business through changing times had been demonstrated in the family burial vault acquired by Thomas I in 1752. The first name recorded there was that of Martha Osborn, Thomas's mother-in-law, who died in that year. Eventually there

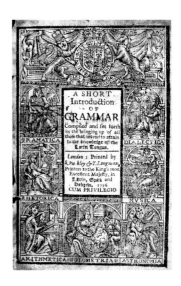

Title page to Lily's *Latin Grammar*, 1736 edition

Longman Archive

---

87 A new folio edition of 'the Dictionary originally compiled' by Bailey, called *A New Universal Etymological Dictionary*, also appeared in 1755 with a preface by J.N. Scott. It was printed for T. Osborne and J. Shipton, J. Hodges, R. Baldwin, W. Johnson and J. Ward, and was obviously designed to compete with Johnson. The two dictionaries were advertised in parallel. See P.B. Gove, 'Notes on Serialisation and Competitive Publishing: Johnson's and Bailey's Dictionaries', in the Oxford Bibliographical Society, *Proceedings and Papers*, Vol. V (1940) and DeWitt Starnes and G.E. Noyes, *The English Dictionary from Cawdrey to Johnson* (1946), Ch. XXII.

88 Letter of 24 June 1755 printed in Reddick, *op. cit.*, p.110. Warton, who had found Johnson's preface 'noble', was afraid that because of 'his contempt for patronage' it would 'disgust' his critics. (J. Wooll, *Biographical Memoirs of the Rev. Joseph Warton* (1806), p.232.)

89 Henry also had two daughters. There is a reference in the Longman Archive (Part III/B) to a family note in a 1686 Prayer Book kept by Henry's wife, another Mary, to her own, her husband's, and her son's and daughter's birthdays.

were to be nineteen names in all in the Longman vault, the last of them that of Louisa Longman who died more than a century later in 1870. The name of Mary Longman, as has been noted, the only woman partner in the long history of Longman, appeared, along with that of Thomas II, on the title page of Johnson's Proposals for an edition, 'printed by subscription', of *The Dramatick Works of William Shakespeare*, a multi-volume edition which Johnson had first proposed in 1745 when Tonson claimed the copyright.[90] Yet four years before Mary died on 16 January 1762 she had already passed over all control of the business to Thomas II. He was to remain head of the House until his death in 1797.

The bi-centenary of Johnson's own death on 13 December 1784 was to be fittingly celebrated by the House of Longman, privileged to be the only survivor among the first publishers of the *Dictionary*. It was organised, appropriately, in the Stationers' Hall. At the same time Longman published a superb facsimile of the first folio edition of the *Dictionary*, which had remained in its possession,[91] and it also commissioned two scholarly papers on its history.[92] Other bi-centenary works included D. Greene, *Samuel Johnson* (1980) and K.K. Yung (ed.), *Samuel Johnson, 1709–1784: A Bicentenary Exhibition* (1984), the catalogue of an Arts Council Exhibition.

Few books, including *Lyrical Ballads*, have been the subject of more papers, scholarly and unscholarly, than Johnson's *Dictionary*; and several of his biographers have pointed out correctly that the *Dictionary* served readers and writers not only as a 'wordbank' but as 'an encyclopedia, transmitting knowledge and values to its users'.[93] It is necessary reading for an understanding not only of Johnson – or of publishing – but of a

---

90 In his preface Johnson expressed his intention 'to correct what is corrupt and to explain what is obscure'. The first volume was published in 1758, but the last of his eight volumes did not appear until 1765, after some of the subscribers to the series had complained of the long delay. In the interval Johnson wrote a novel, *Rasselas* (1759), which he did not describe as such – he called it a 'book' and a 'work' – and he launched his periodical *The Idler* (1758–60).

91 A facsimile two-folio reprint of the fourth edition (with an introduction by J.L. Clifford) had been published by the Librairie de Liban in the Lebanon in 1978. (Letter from Miss Anne Webster, the Staffordshire Bookshop, to the author, 19 June 1984.) 'Owing to the trouble in that country', she added, 'it is extremely difficult to obtain … but I do have a few copies.' For the Librairie de Liban see below, p.421.

92 J.D. Fleeman, 'The Genesis of Johnson's Dictionary' and B. O'Kill, 'The Lexicographic Achievement of Johnson' (1984). Fleeman also prepared for the Oxford Bibliographical Society *A Preliminary Handlist of Copies of Books associated with Dr. Samuel Johnson* (1984).

93 R. DeMaria, 'The Politics of Johnson's Dictionary' in the *Publications of the Modern Languages Association of America*, No. 104 (1989). See also DeMaria's *Johnson's Dictionary and the Language of Learning* (1986).

whole age to which Johnson's name has often been attached, for example by Sir A.W. Ward and A.R. Waller in their volume in the *Cambridge History of English Literature* (1913), subtitled *The Age of Johnson*.

~

Even before Johnson started to assemble his *Dictionary*, Thomas I had been involved in other far less well remembered large-scale encyclopaedic enterprises with cultural ramifications that were as wide as those of the *Dictionary* itself. One of the earliest was the publishing of Ephraim Chambers's *Cyclopaedia* (1728), a remarkable pioneering work, dedicated to the King and published by subscription. It was described later, when other encyclopaedias had been published, as 'the original of [all] the multitudinous omnigatherums'. Its formidable subtitle ran

> An universal dictionary of arts and sciences, containing an explication of the terms and an account of the things signified thereby in the several arts, liberal and mechanical, and the several sciences, human and divine, compiled from the best authors.

Not surprisingly, an elaborate system of cross references was required.

Thomas I supported Chambers at every stage, by 1740 becoming the biggest shareholder in the *Cyclopaedia*, and he made him an *ex gratia* gift of £500 after Chambers's ambitious venture had proved successful. He then held eleven out of the sixty-four shares. Millar held three and Rivington one. When Chambers was ill during the late 1730s, Thomas is said to have made sure that 'jellies and other proper refreshments were industriously left for him at those places where it was least likely that [Chambers] should avoid seeing them'.[94] Chambers himself, born in Kendal, the son of a dissenting farmer, had made no claim to be a pioneer.[95] In his Preface he stated modestly that he was the heir of 'a large patrimony gradually acquired by the industry and endeavours of a long race of ancestors': he had conceived of his project while apprenticed to 'Mr. Senex the Globe maker', a printer whose shop was in Fleet Street. He had worked also in association with Innys, Osborn and Thomas Longman in the publication in 1726 of Shelvocke's *A Voyage Round the World*. When Chambers began to prepare his *Cyclopaedia*, he left the Senex shop for quiet rooms in Gray's Inn Lane.

The one English name that Chambers mentioned among the 'long

Title page of *Cyclopaedia or, An Universal Dictionary of Arts and Sciences ...* Compiled from the best authors...by E. Chambers [with engraved plates] 1728 published in two volumes. John Osborne and T. Longman were named amongst the subscribers

BL 122144.bb.3.

---

94 The story was told anonymously (by Espinasse) in *The Critic, loc. cit.*, March 1860. Espinasse also wrote the not entirely accurate article on Chambers for the first DNB.

95 Johnson had spelt 'pioneer' in the first edition of the *Dictionary* as 'pionier', using the French form, but in his second edition, 1755–6, he changed it to 'pioneer'.

race of ancestors', still a neglected name, although it was known to Mark Roget when he prepared his *Thesaurus*, was that of a London clergyman, Dr John Harris (1666–1719), the author of the *Lexicon Technicum or an English Dictionary of Arts and Sciences*, a folio work which had been published by subscription in 1704 with Isaac Newton as one of the subscribers (and authors). Harris delivered the seventh series of Boyle lectures at St. Paul's in 1698, and served briefly as Secretary of the Royal Society in 1710, but he was later dismissed from his post.

The folio two-volume Chambers *Cyclopaedia* cost four guineas, and a year later its editor was elected a Fellow of the Royal Society. He died in 1740 and was buried in the cloisters of Westminster Abbey. By 1746, his *magnum opus* had gone through five editions, and in 1753 a supplement was prepared by D. Hill and G.L. Scott and published in two folio volumes. Later in the century Thomas II began a difficult search for the right man to update it, and eventually settled on Abraham Rees (1743–1825), the son of a Welsh independent minister. Rees was to become the editor of an 'improved', if unpaginated, Folio edition issued in numbers, the first number of which was published in 1778. Costing sixpence, some of the numbers sold as many as 5,000 copies.[96] Thomas II's son, Thomas Norton III, went on to invite Rees to edit a well-illustrated *New Cyclopaedia, or Universal Dictionary of Arts and Sciences* of his own, details of which were set out in a prospectus of 1801. There was a characteristic continuity in this. Rees, born in 1743, lived on until 1825.

The desire to tabulate details of every branch of human knowledge was strong in the eighteenth century on both sides of the Channel in what Daniel Mornet called '*un siècle encyclopédique*';[97] and a French translation of Chambers encouraged Diderot and D'Alembert to produce the *Encyclopédie* (1777), the great work of the Enlightenment, preparations for which began in 1751.[98] Meanwhile, Chambers *Cyclopaedia* had been a useful source for Johnson also: indeed, he told Boswell that he had 'formed his style' partly on the basis of what Chambers had written. One of Johnson's amanuenses, Alexander Macbean, 'a man of great learning' – all but one of

---

96 J. Britton, *Autobiography* (1850), p. 267. In 1779 Rees, who was mathematics tutor at a London dissenting academy, published *The Obligation and Importance of Searching the Scriptures* and in 1790 *The Doctrine of Christ, the only eternal remedy against the fear of death; and the union of good men in the future world*.

97 *Revue d'histoire littéraire de la France*, Vol. XVII (1917). Subsequent French scholarship has made more of other tendencies in eighteenth-century thought. See F. Furet *et al.*, *Livre et Société dans la France du XVIIIe siècle*, 2 vols., (1965, 1970) and J. Lough, *Essays on the Encyclopédie of Diderot and d'Alembert* (1968).

98 See R. Darnton, *The Business of Enlightenment, a publishing history of the Encyclopédie, 1775–1800* (1979).

the amanuenses were Scots – had worked with Chambers.[99]

It was Johnson who used the phrase 'this age of dictionaries' in a letter written to the novelist and publisher Samuel Richardson (1689–1761) in 1754. A number of other English (en)cyclopaedias, a word for which Chambers found it necessary to be apologetic, were published after Chambers, among them Barrow's two-volume *Dictionary of Arts and Sciences* (1751), a three-volume *Dictionary of Arts and Sciences* (1763), and, above all, the three-volume *Encyclopaedia Britannica*, the first edition in a long sequence of editions, published in Edinburgh in 1773.[100]

~

There was encyclopaedic knowledge in another great eighteenth-century publishing venture to which Thomas I was to contribute two years before his death. In 1729 a group of eight publishers nurtured the publication through subscription and in instalments of *An Universal History*, the first instalment of which appeared in 1736 and the first five folio volumes in 1740, to be followed by a sixth in 1742 and a seventh in 1744.[101] The volumes stopped short of 'modern times', however, and twelve years elapsed between the publication of a prospectus relating to further volumes in 1747 and the publication of the first additional volume in 1759. By then Thomas I was dead and the volume bore the imprint of Thomas II.

In 1751, the first Thomas had acquired a one-third share in the project for the further volumes at a sale of the stock of John Osborn, another Paternoster Row publisher, one of the several Osborns who was not a relative of Thomas's former partner, and he refunded to Osborn a sum to cover moneys which Osborn had already spent on work on the modern history.

The *Universal History* was important both in the history of history and in the history of publishing. It provided details of remote peoples who had not figured in any previous universal histories, and it had a comparative dimension. It appealed, therefore, both to innovatory scholars and to curious readers. It was to be extolled by Thomas Jefferson (1743–1826) and studied by the young John Stuart Mill (1806–1873); and if Edward Gibbon (1737–1794) found its style 'plodding' and Jefferson called it 'very plain, but perspicuous', Mill, who read it 'incessantly', was assiduous enough as a

---

99 Hill, *op. cit.*, Vol.I. p.187; Clifford, *op. cit.*, pp.52–3; and Sledd and Kolb, *op. cit.*, pp.19–25.

100 See also below, pp.223 for Samuel Taylor Coleridge's interest in producing a definitive encyclopaedia of a different kind.

101 *An Universal History from the Earliest Account of Time to the Present compiled from Original Authors: and illustrated with Maps, Cuts, Notes, Chronological and other Tables* (1736–1744). The complete set of seven volumes cost fourteen guineas.

A bookshelf containing a row of the *Universal History*, showing the multi-volume nature of the work, published between 1736 and 1765

Longman Archive Pt III

boy to write a 'compendium' of the sections on the *Ancient Past* which he called an 'abridgement'. 'I had my head full of historical details concerning the obscurest ancient peoples', he wrote in his posthumously published *Autobiography*, published by Longman in 1873.[102]

In the history of publishing, the *Universal History* was the kind of work that was almost immediately translated into foreign languages, the first of them, published in Holland, in French in 1731. This was pirated in 1764 and 1765 by two Irish publishers who were described by the English publishers, who had invested so much money in the venture, as 'base interlopers in a neighbouring kingdom'.[103] The fact that the pirated editions had appeared in octavo, not folio, impelled the English publishers to produce their own cheaper octavo edition, protected by the grant of a Royal Licence. The set of six volumes of the new edition cost only six guineas.

Proposals for 'the Modern Part of the Universal History', printed in 1758, bore along with the name of Thomas II those of T. Osborne, C. Hitch, L. Hawes, A. Millar, J. Rivington, and four other publishers; and early in 1759 the price of the first eight octavo volumes was announced at £2, 'one of the cheapest [such] works ever offered to the public'. That was not the only edge to the proposal. Previous universal histories were now sweepingly described as 'enormous heaps of waste paper'. It was a bold description, but, viewed historiographically, the new volumes were significant in that

---

102 See below, p.246.

103 The reference to 'interlopers' appeared in the preface to an English octavo volume, which was registered by the Stationers' Company in January 1747. A German translation, begun at Halle in 1745, played a part in the development of a seminal German school of history. For the record of these and other translations see Abbattista, *loc. cit.*

they hailed in what would now be called 'Eurocentric' fashion the advance of Europe over other continents and the 'wild unpolished spirit of liberty' which had enabled it with 'irresistible impetuosity' to forge ahead of the rest of the world. The authors of the *Universal History*, like the contributors to Rees's *Cyclopaedia*, were all anonymous.

At first sight surprisingly, there were no references in the volumes to the history of England before the third edition of the work appeared in 1784. Meanwhile, the novelist Tobias Smollett (1721 1771), who was actively involved in the preparation of the *Universal History*, published in instalments his own *History of England* (1757–8), and David Hume's six-volume *History of England* (1754, 1757), was reprinted in octavo volumes in 1762.[104] There was little in common between Hume (1711–1776) and Smollett as historians except that they were both born in Scotland. Smollett's history is largely forgotten, Hume's survived, although Smollett's miscellaneous works are still widely read – and enjoyed. An active reviewer as well as a picaresque novelist, a skilful translator and an ambitious historian, Smollett was both a scourge to those of his contemporaries whom he chose to single out for condemnation and a profitable investment for consortia of publishers.

Thomas II was one of the latter, but it was not until 1783 that along with G. and J. Robinson he published the third edition of the novelist's *Humphry Clinker* (1771). George Robinson (1737–1801), who had begun work as an assistant to John Rivington, worked closely with Longman, who helped to set up his highly successful independent business. It was so successful, indeed, that he became known as 'the King of booksellers'. William West, a bookseller neighbour in Paternoster Row, considered him as 'the Prince, nay the King'.[105]

Engraving of David Hume (1711–70), a frontispiece from a painting by Allan Ramsey, 1776

Longman Archive Pt II Scrapbooks Vol.7

~

A number of other publishing ventures on which Thomas I embarked, some of them continued by his nephew, deserve to be singled out. While his partner, John Osborn, was still alive, the two of them published a new edition of Joseph Warder's *The True Amazons, or the Monarchy of Bees* in 1726 and John Horsley's *Britannia Romana or the Roman Antiquities of Britain* in 1732. Natural history and human history, which could be almost equally fanciful, then co-existed in apparent harmony. A third edition of *The True Amazons* had appeared in 1716, and a further edition appeared as late as 1749 with T. Astley's name on the title page along with that of T. Longman. It was 'sold by R. Baldwin'. Warder, looking for constitutional lessons, wrote of the King Bee, not the Queen Bee, and it was not until a supplement was added to Chambers *Encyclopaedia* in 1753 that the true role of the Queen in the hive, as

104 An eight-volume edition with plates and his account of his life was printed for Cadell and sold by Longman in 1791.

105 W. West, *Fifty Years' Reflections of an Old Bookseller* (Cork, 1837), p.92.

observed in France and Holland, was properly acknowledged.[106]

In a different field of scientific study, *A Course of Experimental Philosophy by J.T. Desaguliers* followed in 1734 (John Senex was another partner). As early as 1727, Thomas had published in quarto Herman Boerhaave's *A New Method of Chemistry*, said in a manuscript list, undated and handwritten but from internal evidence prepared in the eighteenth century, to have been translated by Shaw and Ephraim Chambers,[107] and, a year later (along with J. Tonson), Fontenelle's *Eulogium of Sir Isaac Newton*. Longman and Osborn also figured, as did Tonson, on the title page of Newton's *The Chronology of Ancient Kingdoms Amended* (1728). In 1730 George Ernst Stahl's *Philosophical Principles of Human Chemistry* had been on Thomas's list: it was a digest by Peter Shaw. John Quincy's *Lexicon physico-medium* and *Pharmacopaeia officinalis et extemporanea* appeared (with Thomas I as sole publisher) in 1726, and later editions followed in 1730, 1742 and 1749.

Thomas I had inherited from his partner Osborn his half-share of the patent of 'printer to the King in Latin, Greek and Hebrew' after John Osborn the younger's will had been proved in 1733, and a year later Thomas went on to acquire some of Osborn's titles.[108] There was continuity in these purchases also. In 1725 he and his partner had been responsible for the eighth edition of John Locke's *Some Thoughts Concerning Education*, first published in 1693; and in 1751 he bought a share in the fifth edition of Locke's complete works, the first edition of which had appeared in 1714 under a Churchill imprint at The Black Swan. Thomas II had a share also in the 1765 edition of Locke's *Letters Concerning Toleration*. Already Thomas I had published (with others) a volume of David Hume's *Treatise of Human Nature*, having been introduced in 1739 to Hume's work, at first published,

---

106 See K. Thomas, *Man and the Natural World* (1983), p.62.

107 The list, which is not given an archive reference, was one of a number of lists and catalogues, including *Books printed for J. Osborn and T. Longman at the Ship and Black Swan in Paternoster Row*, which was published in 1736.

108 John Osborn the younger, whose will was drafted in September 1731 and proved in March 1733, left to his parents land in Ashbourne and to his wife, Shirley, his holding of English stock in the Stationers' Company. Osborn left £20 to the Company and £10 to Sir Sampson Salt. John Osborn senior, whose will was drawn up in March 1733, immediately after his son's death, left almost the whole of his estate to 'my dear and loving son-in-law Thomas Longman and daughter and *only child* Mary Longman and their heirs'. He also appointed them executors.

anonymously, by the 'common sense' philosopher Francis Hutcheson (1694–1744).[109]

There were many other early Longman links in Scotland at a time when Scotland, constitutionally united with England since 1709, had far more connections with the European Enlightenment than England had. It also had its own publishing history, although, like Ireland, there were links with England.[110] Taking one example, Alexander Monro's *The Anatomy of Human Bones* (1726), printed in Edinburgh for William Monro, was sold by Longman and Osborn in London, while Monro sold for them Newton's *The Chronology of Ancient Kingdoms* in Scotland, as did Smith and Bruce in Ireland. Almost fifty years later, in 1774, Longman was to be one of the six London publishers of Adam Smith's *The Theory of Moral Sentiments*. Such links proved increasingly important in the history of the European Enlightenment, but it was in France that Diderot and d'Alembert provided in 1751 what later came to be considered a manifesto, their 'preliminary discourse' on their *Encyclopédie*.[111] In 1799 Longman was to publish Diderot's novel *The Natural Son* in two volumes.

There were always several titles relating to philosophy, broadly interpreted, on the Longman lists, as there were to science and history, including antiquarian as well as philosophical history. Thus, Thomas and his partner were involved in 1730 in the publication of the second edition of Sir William Dugdale's *The Antiquities of Warwickshire*, 'illustrated with maps, prospects and portraitures ... from the original copper plates'. It remains an important book in the history of local history, and Dugdale's name was to be perpetuated through a Dugdale Society. Antiquarian studies never lost their appeal. Nor were they incompatible with scientific studies. Yet so long as Thomas I was alive and, indeed, long afterwards,

---

109 Letter from Hume to Hutcheson, 16 March 1740, printed in J. Burton, *The Life and Correspondence of David Hume*, 2 vols. (1846). Hume told Hutcheson that he would like him to approach Longman to test the practices of publishers. ' 'Tis in order to have some check upon my bookseller, that I would willingly engage with another; and I doubt not your recommendation would be very serviceable to me, even though you be not personally acquainted with him.' Hume had been drawn into both philosophy and history by what he called in his sketch of his 'own life' 'a passion for literature ... the ruling passion of my life'. *Of the Passions* was the title of the second volume of his *Dissertations* (1757). For Locke see J.L. Axtell (ed.), *The Educational Writings of John Locke: A Critical Edition* (1968).

110 In 1799 the Revd. Marshal Ebenezer's *The History of the Union of Scotland and England ... and the advantages resulting from it to the Scots* was one of the first books appearing in the Longman/Rees list. It was printed in Edinburgh for Peter Hill and Longman & Rees.

111 See R.N. Schuab (ed.), *Preliminary Discourse to the Encyclopaedia of Diderot and d'Alembert* (1963), p.xi.

theology and related works – often overlapping – remained predominant. Out of 161 Longman titles, including reprints, published during the 1750s and recorded in the *English Short-Titles Catalogue* (ESTC), as many as forty-five were concerned with religion.[112]

~

When in 1734 the bookseller writing in the *Gentleman's Magazine* described the 'indebtedness' of publishers to religion, he had gone on to ask what would happen to publishing if the 'Scheme of *Infidelity*' should generally prevail. Would men buy books 'relating to *Religion* when they think it a cheat or a Matter not worth their Concern'? Since so many other 'Parts of *Learning*' would be affected by 'the Decay of Religion', he answered, 'if *Religion* fails we may shut up our Shops'.[113] Thomas I's response to the predominance of theology was to perpetuate it, although his was a far more broadly based theology than the 'Church and King' theology of the Rivingtons, whose Anglican orthodoxy led to their being made publishers for the Society for Propagation of the Gospel, founded in 1702.

Nevertheless, different Rivingtons did not all follow the same pattern, and, like the Longmans, they held shares in the works of the great dissenting hymn writer Isaac Watts (1674–1748), who was to be accorded a monument in Westminster Abbey. The Longmans took the lead in publishing Watts, and their imprint appeared on seventeen Watts reprints during the last decades of the eighteenth century.[114] Unlike Watts's nephew, James Brackstone, whose name had appeared on the title pages of four of Watts's volumes in 1743 and 1745,[115] the Longmans, like Samuel Johnson,

---

112   Analysis based on the British Library Catalogue. It lists 207 Longman titles, but of these forty-two are reprints and new editions and four are duplicates. The lists, which may be incomplete, have to be treated with great care.

113   GM, Vol. 4, May 1734, p. 259. In 1797 John Evans wrote a pamphlet, 'printed by T.N. Longman and sold by J. Cottle, Bristol', *An Attempt to account for the infidelity of the late Edward Gibbon Esq.* For Thomas Norton Longman's association with Cottle, see below, Chapter 4.

114   I. Watts, *Hymns and Spiritual Songs* appeared in three volumes in 1740. The other names on the imprint included D. Midwinter, A. Ward, R. Hett, C. Hitch, J. Hodges and J. Davidson.

115   I. Watts, *A Guide to Prayer* (1743), *The Improvement of the Mind* (1743), *The Knowledge of the Heavens and the Universe* (1745) (first pub. 1726) – this volume also bore the name of T. Shewell – and *The World to Come* (1745).

put their trust in his immortality, remaining Watts's main publisher even after his copyrights expired.[116]

As the writer of some of the most famous hymns in the English language, such as 'Jesus Shall Reign', 'When I Survey the Wondrous Cross', 'There is a Land of Pure Delight' and 'O God our Help in Ages Past', still sung as lustily in the twenty-first century as in the eighteenth, Watts was one of the most influential of Longman authors, but he was far more than a hymn writer. His posthumous book *The Improvement of the Mind or a Supplement to the Art of Logic* (1782) was among Johnson's favourites and inspired him to include Watts, about whose life he confessed that he knew little, in his *Lives of the Poets*: his name, he said, 'has been long held by me in veneration'.[117] Watts also wrote *Logic or the Right Use of Reason in the Enquiry after Truth* (1725) which drew him far closer to Locke than has usually been recognised, and, at a different level, *The Knowledge of the Heavens and the Earth Made Easy or the first principles of astronomy and geography*. Both books were published by Longman.

Watts's hymns were in the 'learned' rather than in the 'popular' tradition; and although some of those that he devised specially for children were to be satirised in the mid-nineteenth century, they were satirised just because by that time they were extremely well known in schools as well as churches and chapels.[118] Charles Wesley's magnificent hymns were in a different tradition, and Watts, of small size and nervous disposition, was a very different kind of person from Wesley: lambs were his favourite animals, as important to him as they were to William Blake, yet he was convinced that dogs as well as children were evil if they were not taught to be better. He had a gift for memorable phrases, such as 'innocent play', and in *The Improvement of the Mind*, he used the term 'useful knowledge' which was to acquire a special aura in the nineteenth century.[119] His *Divine Songs Attempted in Easy Language for the Use of Children* (1715) included a hymn of 'praise to God for learning to read'.

THE
IMPROVEMENT
OF THE
MIND:
OR, A
SUPPLEMENT
TO THE
ART of LOGICK:
Containing a Variety of
REMARKS and RULES
FOR THE
ATTAINMENT and COMMUNICATION
of useful Knowledge, in Religion, in
the Sciences, and in common Life.
By I. WATTS, D.D.
The SECOND EDITION.
LONDON:
Printed for J. BRACKSTONE, at the *Globe* in
Cornhill; and T. LONGMAN, at the *Ship* in
Pater-noster-Row. MDCCXLIII.

The title page to *The Improvement of the Mind*, by Isaac Watts (1674–1724). The first edition was published in 1714. The only two publishers shown in this second edition are Blackstone at the Globe and Longman at The Ship

Longman Archive Pt III G

116 Walter Jeffery, letter to W.A. Kelk, 30 Nov. 1936 described how when he had told C.J. Longman the story of Brackstone 'damning and cursing' Watts he found it funny. For Watts, who deserves a major biography, see G. Burder (ed.), *Works of the Reverend and Beloved Isaac Watts D.D.*, 6 Vols. (1810), a revision of an older publication by D. Jennings and P. Doddridge (1753).

117 Letter to W. Sharp, 7 July 1771, quoted in Redford, *op. cit.,* Vol.III, p. 38.

118 For the two traditions see L. Adey, *Class and Idol in the English Hymn* (1988), p.22. See also E. Routley, *Hymns and Human Life* (1952); and B.L. Manning, *The Hymns of Wesley and Watts* (1942). Matthew Arnold praised 'When I Survey' as a movingly powerful hymn. For the sales and influence of *Divine Songs* see Adey, *op. cit.,* Ch.7, 'Nurseling and the Infant Scholar' and A. Richardson, *Literature, Education and Romanticism* (1994), Ch. 3.

119 See below, p.280.

The title page of *A Plain and Serious Address to the Master of a Family on the Important Subject of Family Religion*, 1761 by Philip Doddridge (1702–1751)

BL 4406.bb.14

If Watts provided consolation as well as inspiration, so too did Philip Doddridge (1702–1751), a dissenting hymn-writer in the Watts tradition, who prepared the posthumously published text of *The Improvement of the Mind* from one of Watts's manuscripts. His own *Hymns founded on various Texts in the Holy Scriptures* was to be edited by another dissenter, Job Orton (1717–1783), and published posthumously by a consortium.[120] Longman was one of the twelve publishers of Doddridge's *A Plain and Serious Address to the Master of a Family, on the Important Subject of Family Religion*, 'printed by assignment from the author's widow' in 1761. The home was always as much in mind as the school.[121]

Directly in line with Watts's *Divine Songs* – and Doddridge's hymns – was another Longman publication, Elizabeth Hill's *The Poetical Monitor* (1796), subtitled 'Pieces Select and Original, for the Improvement of the Young in Virtue and Piety'. Intended at first for charity-school children, it could be bought from J. Johnson, C. Dilly and other booksellers as well as from the particular charity with which Hill was connected – Shakespeare's Walk Protestant Dissenters' Charity School, founded in 1712 and originally located in the parish of St. Paul, Shadwell. There were 144 'pieces', including five from Watts, nine from Doddridge and a hymn by Charles Wesley. In a selection of epitaphs there was an anonymous 'Address on a Lady's Scull, placed on a Piller [*sic*] Near the Former'. This was a fitting complement to lines from Watts 'Enjoy the day of mirth, but know there is a day of judgement too'.[122]

Hill's particular charity did not figure in *Sequel to the Poetical Monitor*, published by Longman, Hurst, Rees and Orme in 1815, which included several Longman authors – the poet James Montgomery (1771–1854), who also wrote hymns and poems relating to the voyages of Christian missionaries,[123] Amelia Opie (1769–1853), whose poem *Fathers*

120 Orton himself had printed in Shrewsbury in 1769 a book which was sold in London by two booksellers, Longman and J. Buckland – *Religious Exercises Recommended; or discourses on secret* [a surprising adjective] *family worship, and the religious observation of the Lord's Day.*

121 See D. Vincent, 'The Domestic and the Official Curriculum in Nineteenth-Century England' in M. Hilton *et al.* (eds.), *Opening the Nursery Door: Reading, Writing and Childhood, 1600–1900* (1997).

122 See R. Tsurumi, 'Between hymnbook and textbook' in *Paradigm*, Vol. II, Issue 1, Jan. 2000, pp.24–9.

123 In 1826 Longman published in two volumes *The Poetical Works of James Montgomery, Collected by Himself*. The second volume included his *The World Before the Flood* (1813) which by 1826 had appeared separately in several editions. Montgomery was a poet who sold well as the Longman Impression Books show (LA/Part I/137-276). No fewer than 3,500 copies of *The World Before the Flood* sold in its first year. He also wrote hymns and psalms and collections of poems about the *West Indies* (1810), *Greenland* (1819) and *Australia* (1827).

and Daughters, A Tale went through six editions between 1804 and 1810, and Anna Laetitia Barbauld, sister of John Aikin, who was as prolific as she was.[124] Active Unitarians, their father, also called John, divinity tutor at the famous Dissenting Academy in Warrington, had been a member of what has been described as the first English reading society, founded at Leicester around 1740.

While establishing personal publishing relationships with such moralising authors, as future Longmans were to do – and they are described more fully in Chapter 4 – Thomas Longman I and Thomas II never neglected 'entertainment', which figured as prominently in their eighteenth-century lists as 'improvement' or 'instruction'. In this line of publishing they worked mainly through consortia, making the most, for example, of *Arabian Nights* or *Thousand and One Nights*, 'one thousand and one stories told by the Sultaness of the Indies', said to have been translated from Arabic into French and from French into English in 1706. The book was featured on the Longman list as early as 1725 before Watts entered it, remaining there under different titles throughout the century and going through eight editions.[125]

There were other translations from the French too, from the 1720s onwards, including Ambrose Philips's translation of *The Persian Tales*, the third edition of which was advertised by Longman and Osborn in 1728, and, a year earlier, a translation of the Abbé de Bellegarde's *Reflexions upon Ridicule; or what it is that makes a man ridiculous*.[126] One of the best-selling books of the eighteenth century, *Don Quixote* by Cervantes, which appeared in translation in 1712, continued to be published in several versions, long before Cervantes became a key figure in literary and linguistic scholarship,[127] and Longman had a share in the 1749 edition 'translated by several hands' and published by 'the late Mr. Motteux', and in a new edition, translated by Smollett, which was printed in 1770 'for W. Strahan, J. and F. Rivington, W. Johnston, R. Baldwin, T. Longman' and eleven other publishers. It included 'twenty-eight new copper plates, elegantly engraved'.[128]

The words 'printed for' figure prominently on Longman title pages,

Title page of *Arabian Nights Entertainments:* Vol.IV 13th edition, 1772

Longman Archive Pt III G

---

124 See A.L. Le Breton, *Memoir of Mrs Barbauld, Including Letters and Notices of Her Families and Friends* (1874).

125 C.C. Mish, 'Early Eighteenth-Century Best Sellers in English Prose Fiction', in PBSA, Vol. 75 (1981).

126 J.E. Chandler (ed.), *The House of Longman: Bibliographic History* (1936), pp.290–1.

127 For Cervantes in literature see A. Flores and J.J. Bernadete (eds.), *Cervantes Across the Centuries* (1947) and A. Close, *The Romantic Approach to Don Quixote: a Critical History of the Romantic Tradition* (1978).

128 For *Don Quixote* as a best seller see Mish, *loc .cit.* In 1761 Longman also had a share in the new Smollett translation of *Gil Blas*.

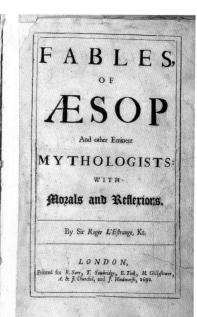

The frontispiece, title page and illustration (detail) from Roger L'Estrange's translation of *Fables of Aesop* in 1692. It appears in the 'Catalogue of J.O.&T.L in 1726'

Longman Archive Pt III G

as in the editions of Watts. Sometimes, however, books were described as being 'printed for the author' and 'sold by' T. Longman and other booksellers. Interpreting the words in imprints – and their order – is a more intricate process than analysing the balance between risks and profits in the 'book trade'. The success of a particular book is easier to identify. Books like *Don Quixote*, for example, were a profitable long-term investment for booksellers as were rights in a number of far older books like *The Fables of Aesop and Others*, shares in which were eagerly sought and widely purchased. Thus, a new version of *The Fables*, translated into English by Samuel Croxall DD, 'with instructive applications, and a print before each fable', was 'printed for' seventeen booksellers, headed by J.F. and C. Rivington with T. Longman next: they included J. Johnson, J. Robinson and C. Dilly.

Likewise a six-volume edition of Plutarch's Lives, published in 1795, a year of war, had the names of eight booksellers on its imprint. Ten publishers including Thomas Norton, G.G. and J. Robinson and the Rivingtons sponsored a 1798 edition in Latin of the complete works of Sallust (86–34 BC).[129] A longer list of booksellers figured, however, in the imprint of a new twelve-volume edition of *The Works of Samuel Johnson*

---

129 A year later Sallust's History of the *Wars of Catiline and Jugurtha* was printed and sold in 'free translation' by Robert Raikes in Gloucester. It was sold in London by Thomas Norton and the Rivingtons.

(1796) with 'an essay on his life and genius', also printed separately, by Arthur Murphy. There were no fewer than fifty-two shareholders, headed in this case by T. Longman.

Johnson did not edit *The Works of the English Poets . . . with Prefaces Biographical and Critical by Samuel Johnson* (1779–81), which appeared, attributed to him, in seventy-five volumes, re-named *The Works of the Most Eminent English Poets* and published in four octavo volumes in 1780. This was an anthology mainly of eighteenth-century authors, the copyrights in whose work belonged to metropolitan publishers. No poet writing before Milton was included, so that a canon leading back to Chaucer if no further was not offered to the reading public. Very soon after first publication individual volumes were sold separately from the whole set. As Goldsmith had predicted, the legal decision in 1774 to open up copyright did not inspire the London booksellers to take advantage of new opportunities of influencing the reading public.

The Plays of William Shakespeare (1786–1790) was printed for thirty-two booksellers. Rivington came first on the list, as his name also did on two editions of Milton's *Paradise Lost* (1790), one of them 'printed from the text of Tonson's correct edition of 1711' and the other, 'the ninth edition, with notes of various authors'. T. Longman's name figured on both as it did on a further edition of 1793 – 'illustrated with texts of scripture'. The name of Rivington did not figure on the title page of this edition, which was printed for twenty-four booksellers.

~

Thomas I and Thomas II did not concentrate on shares of a 'literary' kind, profitable though many of them were. Guide books of various kinds could run through regular new editions, and in at least one early venture Thomas I and Osborn were shrewd enough to hold the whole share. This was in the fourth edition of W.W. Gibson's *The Farrier's New Guide, containing first the Anatomy of a Horse* (1725), the first Osborn/Longman (that order) book to show a ship on its title page; and a year later they had printed for them the second edition of Gibson's *The Farrier's Dispensatory* and the first edition of his *The True Method of Dieting Horses*. In the age of the horse, which continued until the advent of the automobile, there was an obvious demand for such guides, as there was to be later for guides to gardening and cookery. The first and second editions of *The Farrier's New Guide* were 'printed for William Taylor'. They included 'figures previously engrav'd on copper plates'. The fifth edition of *The Farrier's Dispensatory* (1741) was described as 'corrected'.

Guides always had to be kept up-to-date. A new edition of Batty Langley's *The Builder's Jewel . . . and Workman's Remembrancer* with 100 plates was printed for T. Longman and five other booksellers, including the Robinsons in 1797: Langley had died in 1751. Philip Miller's *The Gardeners' Kalendar; directing what works are necessary to be performed every month in the kitchen,*

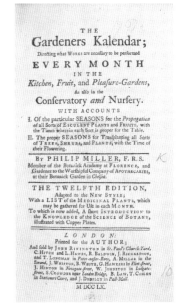

The title page to *The Gardener's Kalendar*, 1760 by Philip Miller (showing fourteen other subscribing booksellers). The eleventh edition was 'adapted to the new style; with a list of the medicinal plants, which may be gathered in each month'... The twelfth edition included a short introduction to the 'science of botany'

BL 449 d.4

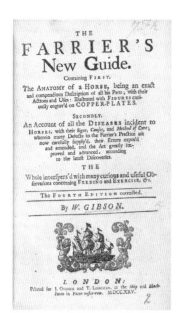

By this date Longman was also a publisher of guides and books for professionals.

The title page and fold-out frontispiece to W. W. Gibson's *The Farrier's New Guide*, 1725 (showing the ship). This was the fourth edition, of which there were to be many more

BL 779.f.4

fruit and pleasure gardens, as also in the conservatory and nursery appeared in 1760 with fourteen other publishers involved as booksellers for a work which was 'printed for the author'; and eleven years later Thomas Hitt's *The Modern Gardener: or Universal Kalendar, containing monthly directions for all the operations of gardening* was published. John Abercrombie's *Everyman his own Gardener*, 'a new and much more complete gardeners' calendar ... than any one hitherto published' was to appear in 1794 in other editions. In 1796 *A treatise on the culture of the pineapple and the management of the hot-house* by William Speechley was 'printed for the author' at Welbeck in Nottinghamshire and sold by T.N. Longman and two other booksellers, one of them John Debrett (*c.* 1750–1822).[130]

Hannah Glasse's *The Art of Cookery Made Plain and Easy* (1770), which went through several editions, had no fewer than twenty-eight publishers' names attached to it, and Eliza Melroe's *An Economical and New Method of Cookery, describing upwards of eighty cheap, wholesome and*

---

130 Debrett's *Peerage of England, Scotland and Ireland* first appeared in 1802 and his *Baronetage* in 1808.

nourishing dishes (1798) was 'printed and published for the author' and 'sold also by T.N. Longman and all other booksellers in town and country'. This comprehensive designation was frequently employed in imprints on works of reference. Thus, in the previous year, an anonymous Edinburgh pamphlet on brewing, printed for P. Hill and T.N. Longman and reprinted in 1798, eschewed guidance for the public and castigated (part of the title) 'the extreme impolicy of renewing the impost of two pennies Scots per Scot's pint, on malt liquors, brewed within certain towns in Scotland'.

Magistrates and clergymen were felt to be in need of particular guidance on such subjects, and Patrick Colquhoun's *Observations and Facts relative to Public Houses: interesting to magistrates in every part of Great Britain, to the clergy and parochial officers, and generally to brewers, distillers, proprietors and occupiers of licensed ale houses; as well as to the public at large* (1798) was a practical work, written by 'a magistrate, acting for the counties of Middlesex, Surrey, Kent and Essex'. It was 'sold by Sewell, Longman, Debrett and J. and A. Arch', the last of whom were to figure in the intricate history of the *Lyrical Ballads*.[131] Patrick Colquhoun (1743–1820) was a metropolitan magistrate who wrote pamphlets on many subjects, collecting relevant statistics to illustrate them.

Professionals were in particular need of guides at a time when professional qualifications were in increasing demand; and usually in co-operation with other publishers, Thomas produced a wide range of guides for professional readers, such as William Bohun's *The Practising Attorney; or Lawyer's Office. Comprehending the Business of an Attorney in all its Branches* (1732)[132] and Henry Crouch's *A Complete View of the English Customs* (1745), printed by Thomas Baskett. Crouch died in 1732. A second edition in 1764 was 'printed for Thomas Longman and Thomas Shewell'. Practical arithmetic was never neglected. John Smart's *Tables of Interest, discount, annuities, &c*, which first appeared in 1724, was 'revised, enlarged and improved' by Charles Brand in 1780 and printed for Thomas II, T. Cadell and N. Conant with an appendix containing 'some observations on the general probability of life'.

Isaac Keay's *The Practical Measurer, his Pocket Companion* appeared in 1730, while Osborn (described on the title page as J. Osbourne) was still a Longman partner; and in 1727 the two of them were sole proprietors of Brigadier-General Douglas James's *The Surveyor's utmost desire fulfilled; or the art of planometry, longemetry and altemetry*. In 1772 Thomas II was a part owner, along with six others, of William Leybourn's *Panarithmologia*, a popular ready reckoner. In 1799 William Traill's *Elements of Algebra*, a

The title page to Eliza Melroe's *An Economical and New Method of Cookery*, 1728, describing 'upwards of eighty...dishes...and above forty soups;... with new and useful observations, etc'

BL 1037.h.16 (1)

---

131 See below, p.199ff.

132 An early 'Everyman' book of guidance for non-professionals in the law was J. Giles, *Every Man his own Lawyer; or a Summary of the Laws of England in a new and instructive Method* (1740).

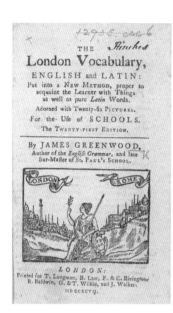

The appetite for education was reflected in the success of James Greenwood's *The London Vocabulary, English and Latin*, 1797. The first edition had been published in 1700. Greenwood, a master at St. Paul's School, 'put into a new method, proper to acquaint the learner with things as well as pure Latin words. Adorned with twenty-six pictures for use of schools.'

BL 109.a.31

Scottish work, written 'for the use of students in universities', bore the imprint of Thomas II and T. Cadell.

Medicine, which could attract non-medical as well as medical readers, was an early speciality. A work of Hippocrates was published in Latin solely by Longman and Osborn in 1727 – several other books in Latin figured then and later in the century in Longman lists – and Thomas Morgan's *Philosophical Principles of Medicine* (their own full copyright), and William Cheselden's *The Anatomy of the Human Body* (with several publishers involved) appeared in 1730. An equally important investment in Latin and English was publishing for the Royal College of Physicians, where Shaw's Fellowship may have assisted co-operation: its 'dispensatory', *Pharmacopoeia*, was published by Longman in both languages in 1747 and 1748, with J. Nourse the other publisher involved. John Latham's *On Rheumatism and Gout* (1796) was printed for T.N. Longman alone.

Works on medicine were mainly for young adults, but both Thomas I and Thomas II were equally interested in works for schools, particularly texts of grammars, and this was an interest which was to persist throughout the history of the House. Lily, the main text, was used at Eton, buttressed by royal command, and in other schools and was often known as the 'common grammar'. Yet Longman also published books in Latin designed for the boys of Westminster School, and another school mentioned by name in its lists was the Free School at Colchester.[133] The twelfth edition of William Turner's *Exercises to the accidence and grammar: or, an exemplification of the several moods and tenses, and of the principal rules of construction* appeared in 1770. This edition of Turner, a master at the school, like his thirteenth edition in 1774, was 'printed for E. Ballard and T. Longman', the sole names mentioned on the title page. A year later, Longman shared in the sixteenth edition of James Greenwood's *The London Vocabulary, English and Latin ... for the use of schools*. Greenwood had died in 1737.

Given that there was no central direction of classical studies, there could be bitter argument then and even more in the nineteenth century about the relative merits of different approaches to Latin and Greek grammar and syntax, influenced at times but not always by continental European scholarship.[134]

Meanwhile, English grammar, often studied via classical grammar,

133   In 1760 William Camden's *Institutio Graecae Grammatices Compendaria* was published by Longman and Buckley *in usum regiae scholae Westmonasteriensis*.

134   For a wide-ranging survey, see C. Stray, 'The Smell of Latin Grammar: Contrary Imaginings in English Classrooms', in *Bulletin of the John Rylands University Library of Manchester*, Vol. 76, No. 3, Autumn 1994 and 'Printers, Publishing and Politics in the Classical Textbooks of Benjamin Hall Kennedy', in PBSA, Vol. 40, No. 4, pp.451–74 (1996). See also M.L. Clarke, *Classical Education in Britain, 1500–1900* (1959), pp.74–97 and *passim*.

raised less bitterness, and in this field Longman, when he acquired the copyrights in 1798, published the highly successful grammars of Lindley Murray (1745–1826) which ran into many editions. Sometimes dubbed 'the Father of Grammar', Murray, a Quaker, was born in colonial America, but moved to Britain, where he made York, not London, his headquarters.[135] He was a prolific author, whose titles, offering graded education at all levels, spoke for themselves, and by 1839 his *English Spelling Book* had reached what was called its fortieth edition and his abridged *English Grammar* its one hundred and twenty-fifth. Murray always paid close attention to 'levels' to the interchange between teacher and learner and to what he called 'propriety' and 'effect'. The full version of his *English Grammar* was described as 'adapted to the different classes of learners with an appendix containing rules and observations for assisting the more advanced students to write with perspicacity and accuracy'. The abridged version included 'exercises in syntax designed for the use of the younger class of learners'.

Successful on both sides of the Atlantic, Murray's best-known book in America was not a grammar but an anthology, his *The English Reader*, 'a collection of humourless set passages', 250 of them, described by an American admirer, who had learnt many of them by heart, as 'the very embodiment of the highest wisdom and virtue'.[136] It first appeared in England in 1799, printed at York for Longman and Rees, the new partnership.[137] Murray also wrote and published with Longman *The Power of Education on the Mind in Retirement, Affliction and at the Approach of Death*. It appeared in their 1807 list.

A now better-remembered Longman author than Murray, Mrs Sarah Trimmer, raised, as he did, ethical as well as pedagogical issues. Her book *An Attempt to Familiarize the Catechism of the Church of England* (1791) was described as 'for the use of teachers in schools and families': it bore the names of five publishers, including Longman and Rees and J.F. and C. Rivington. With a formidable list of publications under her name, Mrs Trimmer, who from 1788–89 edited for the *Family Magazine*, popularised religious education as a prop to the social order not only in charity schools, the special concern of Hannah More (not a Longman author), but in Sunday

Mrs Sarah Trimmer, engraving from a painting by Henry Howard *c*.1798

Longman Archive Pt II Scrapbooks

---

135 For his American background see C. Monaghan, *The Murrays of Murray Hill* (1998).

136 'An Old School Book', in the *Magazine of American History*, Vol. 10, July–Dec. 1883, pp.111–114. Murray was discussed at a Textbook Colloquium held appropriately at York on the 150th anniversary of his birth. See *Paradigm*, the Journal of the Colloquium, Vol. 2, Oct. 2000, and the paper on him by Frances Austin *Paradigm* Vol.2, Dec. 2003.

137 See below, Chapter 4.

Schools, new institutions in the late eighteenth century.

In her *Sunday-School Catechist* (1788) she warned her readers about 'persons who can read setting themselves up above the station in life it hath pleased GOD to place them'. 'Who made all mankind?' she asked. 'Who made some rich and some poor?' 'We should consider that it is the wish of God that there should be ranks among mankind.' Mrs Trimmer's more appealing side was revealed in books like her *Fabulous Histories Designed for the Instruction of Children respecting their Treatment of Animals* (1786), but there was a condescending note in many of her titles like *A Friendly Remonstrance concerning the Christian Covenant and the Sabbath Day; intended for the Good of the Poor* (1792).[138]

~

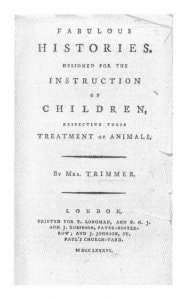

The title page of *Fabulous Histories* by Mrs Trimmer, first edition 1786

BL 780/31. (2)

The ability of Thomas II to promote writers as different as Mrs Trimmer and Daniel Paterson (1739–1825), author of *A new and accurate description of all the direct and principal cross roads in England and Wales* (1792), which went through eighteen editions by 1829, displays his skills (and his tolerance) as a publisher. It seems inadequate, at the least, therefore, to describe the years from 1758 to 1797, when he died, simply as 'a period of consolidation' in the history of Longman.[139] The description is, indeed, misleading, for during these late-eighteenth-century years there were significant developments in the organisation, range and power of publishing, if not in its underlying technology, and Thomas II had his own distinctive contribution to make. He was active to the last. He even published along with Debrett, although for less than one year, from September 1795 to April 1796, an eight-page periodical, *The Sylph*, at first twice a week then once, in which the articles, all unsigned, showed considerable imagination. In the absence of other evidence, it has been suggested that he or his son was the writer as well as the publisher.[140]

Ariel, *The Sylph* proclaimed, has 'returned to earth in order that we may by our advice, authority and influence bring about a reformation of morals and manners, so much wanted in the degeneracy of the present time. It is our desire not only to make men good (or as far as we can) amiable'.[141] The advice, not unique to *The Sylph*, covered literature more

---

138 See M.G. Jones, *Hannah More* (1952) for the prolific writer of *Cheap Repository Tracts*, and for Robert Raikes, founder of Sunday Schools, A. Briggs, *The Age of Improvement* (2000 edn.), pp. 14–15. See also S. Trimmer, *Reflections upon the Education of Children in Charity Schools of Every Denomination* (1792).

139 PW, p.12.

140 See G.S. Marr, *The Periodical Essayists of the Eighteenth Century* (1923), pp.238–40.

141 *The Sylph*, 20 Sept. 1795, p.12.

than politics. 'No novel in future [should] be published with a preface (since the preface contains the only moral and beneficial part). [*The Sylph*] will thus strip novels of their false colours.'[142] This was difficult advice to follow. No publisher, not even Thomas II, had he so wished, could have handled the miscellaneous novels of the time quite in this way. Nor could Thomas I have done.

Prefatory matter, like the Preface by Samuel Richardson (1689–1761) to *Clarissa* (1748), often left out in subsequent editions, was essential reading at the time; and Richardson, who like Pope, commanded large sums for his copyrights, did not need Thomas I to publish him in his lifetime. He introduced a fictitious Mr Longman into his *Pamela* (1740), which in its author's words, borrowed 'none of its Excellencies from the romantic Flights of unnatural Fancy'. The novelist with whom Richardson has so often been compared, as he was at the time, Henry Fielding (1707–1754), was published by Thomas II only posthumously and then mainly through consortia. There were ten members in a consortium which produced a two-volume edition of his *Joseph Andrews* (1742) in 1769 and thirteen in a consortium which produced a three-volume edition in 1781. Later there were six members of a consortium which in 1792 produced an edition of *Tom Jones*. Twelve volumes of a collected Fielding, along with the life of the author had appeared in 1783 through a consortium of twenty-three, including Strahan and the Rivingtons.

Some of the other novels published by Longman during the 1790s were written by authors whose names are seldom remembered, among them Mary Robinson (1758–1800) and (Mrs) Jane West (1758–1852). The latter, author of *A Gossip's Story* (1799), also produced a three-volume *Tale of the Times* (1799), *Advantages of Education*. Mary Robinson and Jane West were far more contrasting characters than Richardson and Fielding. Mrs Robinson, an actress, known as Perdita, had been a mistress of the Prince of Wales, the future George IV. Mrs West, pious, married and didactic, wrote verse and plays as well as 'conduct' novels. She was versatile too. In the same year as Longman published her *A Gossip's Tale* (1797), they also produced her *Elegy on the Death of the Right Honourable Edmund Burke*. The Longman Impression Books reveal that 4,500 copies of her *Letters to a Young Man* (1801) and 4,500 copies of her *Letters to a Young Woman* (1806) were sold in various editions.

The number as well as the range of Longman titles impressed contemporaries, among them Henry Dell, a bookseller himself, who in a poem, *The Booksellers* (1766), referred to Thomas II as 'the first, and of the whole, the best' of 'the Paternoster Tribe': 'tho' rich, a man of worth

---

142 *Ibid.*, No. 19, quoted in A. Sullivan (ed.), *British Literary Magazines, The Romantic Age* (1983), p.399.

Portrait of Thomas Harris
(1742–1820) painted by John
Opie. Harris was Proprietor and
Manager of Covent Garden and
the brother of Elizabeth Harris
(1740–1808), who married
Thomas Longman II. This
connection with the theatre
must have given added interest
for Longman II and his son,
who were the publishers of
many plays. Thomas Longman
V wrote in his *Memories* (1921)
that Harris's reign of office
at Covent Garden ran from
1774–1802 and from then on to
1809 with John Philip Kemble,
'at which date he retired into
private life and died in 1820.'

Pearson Education

he stands confest'.[143] Thomas I's name had figured as a 'bookseller' in the Row in the first edition of a *Complete Guide to London's Streets and Occupiers* (1740), placed between the names of Stephen Theodore Janssen, occupation unspecified, and Isaac Therond, 'Merchant'. Other neighbours were Thomas Walters, 'Silkman', Thomas Hayne, 'African Director', and W. Selwin, 'City Receiver'. All three of these names had appeared, as Thomas's name did not, in Kent's *Directory* for 1738. A bookseller, Arthur Bettesworth & Co., headed both lists: his sign was The Red Lion.

The appearance of the Row changed in 1770 when by Act of Parliament all outdoor signs had to be removed or placed flat against the wall. From then on, therefore, the address of the House of Longman was 39 to 41 Paternoster Row, with Number 39 as the main entrance.[144] Sometimes the words 'at Amen Corner' were added. Number 38 remained a stationers' shop, under new ownership after the death of John Bloss, who had occupied it for forty years from 1713 to 1753, but in a *Guide* of 1785 Number 43 was described as a tallow factory (the factory where the fire was to start in 1861). Number 47, The Rose, was occupied from 1760 by Richard Baldwin II, one of a large family of booksellers of different generations who occupied different premises. He remained there for the rest of the century.

One institution in Paternoster Row stayed under its own name, the Chapter Coffee House, founded before Thomas I arrived in the Row. With its club atmosphere, it was described just before the time of Thomas I's death not only as a copyrights mart but as a favourite meeting place for booksellers and 'the literati': 'when they say a good book, they do not mean to praise the style or sentiment, but the quick and extensive sale of it'.[145]

Thomas II was the first Longman to live outside 'the House' in

143 H. Dell, *The Booksellers, A Poem* (1766). Nicols dismissed Dell's poem as 'a wretched, rhyming list of booksellers in London and Westminster' (*Notes and Queries*, 10 March 1904).

144 See A. Heal, 'The Numbering of Houses in London Streets', *Notes and Queries*, Vol. CLXXXIII (1942), pp.100–101.

145 *The Connoisseur*, 31 Jan. 1754.

Paternoster Row. In 1792 he moved to Greenhill House, Mount Grove, Hampstead, a pleasant eighteenth-century house with a sloping garden, pulled down during the 1870s to make way for a Wesleyan chapel. It was a home, however, not an office, and it was from Number 39, also lived in, that his expanding business, both provincial and international, was carried out. Thomas II, called to the Court of the Stationers' Company from 1778 to 1782, was directly involved in both branches of 'the trade' and in the sale of second-hand as well as new books. He had an eye for new openings, outside as well as inside his business: for example, he actively supported the establishment of *The Times* newspaper in 1788, in retrospect one of the most significant of the new developments.[146] He also used *The Times* for advertising purposes.

~

There was a close connection in the late eighteenth century between the press and the theatre. Indeed, they were mutually dependent. Different newspapers (or periodicals) praised different plays and, even more, sided with the different performers – and managers. Where the impulse to publish plays came from is not always certain, although they had an obvious practical use. In the case of Longman it may have been family links, not neighbourliness, that drew the House of Longman for the first time into the world of the theatre, for in 1760 Thomas II married Elizabeth Harris, then only twenty years old, the sister of Thomas Harris who in 1767 became proprietor of Covent Garden, which, along with Drury Lane, had the monopoly of staging spoken drama in London.

On the surface, at least, the marriage was an odd match, for while Harris (d. 1820), who in the words of his biographer in the DNB, 'came of a respectable family', which made its money, as several Longmans did, out of soap-making, his own life was far from respectable. Known in his prime as the 'King of Clubs', with, for a time, a mistress, Jane Lessingham, who was known as the 'Queen of Clubs', he had several illegitimate children. He also had a much-publicised quarrel from 1768 to 1774 with George Colman about the management of Covent Garden. The Longman family inherited his portrait by Opie and a number of Harris documents, including mortgages taken out with Thomas II. Harris built up a substantial collection of

---

146 Charles Wentworth Dilke, *Diary*, 4 Jan. 1788: 'Mr. Longman wrote to me desiring my support to a periodical paper called *The Times*.' For the early story of *The Times* see *The History of the Times*, Vol. I, 1785–1841 (1935). John Walter I, the founder of *The Times* (1738–1812), who had lost his capital in a Lloyds debacle, had moved into printing in 1784. For a Strahan connection, see *ibid.*, p. 4. *The Times*, priced at 2½d., was first called the *Daily Universal Register*. In 1789 it cost 4d.

theatrical paintings, including several Gainsboroughs.[147]

Thomas II published many plays, although even in this line of business his uncle had led the way. In 1757 as a member of a consortium he had brought out Nathaniel Lee's *The Rival Queens or the Death of Alexander the Great*, and in 1765 he was one of eleven booksellers, including Rivington, who published *Love's Last Shift* by Colley Cibber (1671–1757). In 1777 he was one of the seven publishers of Cibber's *Dramatic Works*, and in the same year he shared also in the publishing of Cibber's *The Double Gallant*, 'marked with variations of the manager's book at the Theatre Royal in Drury Lane'.[148] There was a similar addendum – also in that year – to James Miller's *Mahomet the Inspector*.

Interest in publishing plays was to be maintained by Thomas II's son Thomas Norton III, who in the years from 1793 to 1795 published no fewer than five plays by John O'Keeffe (1747–1833), among them *Sprigs of Laurel* (1793), *Wild Oats* (1794) and in 1795 *Life's Vagaries* and *The Irish Mimic or Blunders at Brighton*, the last of them said to have been received 'with universal applause'. In 1793 he had also published a comic opera by O'Keeffe, *The Castle of Andalusia* and in 1795 and 1796 'airs, duets, glees and choruses' from O'Keeffe's opera *Merry Sherwood* and *The Lad of the Hills* (in County Wicklow). In 1798 he was joined by other publishers in producing four volumes of O'Keeffe's collected works, 'published under the gracious patronage of the Prince of Wales'.

Other playwrights favoured by Thomas Norton included William McCready, author of the two-act farce *The Irishman in London: or the Happy African* (1793) and the five-act comedy *The Bank Note or Lessons for Ladies* (1795), William Pearce, composer (among other works) of *Windsor Castle or the Fair Maid of Kent* (1795), performed at Covent Garden in honour of the marriage of the Prince of Wales and Caroline, Frederick Reynolds, author of *How to Grow Rich* (1793) and in the same year *Notoriety*, both 'comedies', and Prince Hoare, whose *Lock and Key*, 'as performed at the Theatre Royal, Covent Garden in 1797, was described as being correctly taken from the prompt book'. In 1806 he was to launch a series of plays which had been

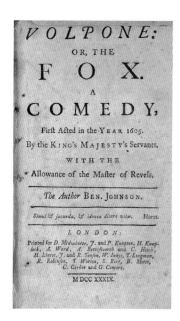

Title page to *Volpone*; this edition was 'printed for' fourteen booksellers, including Longman, in 1739

Longman Archive Pt III

---

147 See *The History of the Theatres of London and Dublin by Mr. Victor* (1761); *A Letter from T. Harris to G. Colman, on the Affairs of Covent Garden* (1768); G. Colman, *T. Harris Dissected* (1768). For Richard Brinsley Sheridan, proprietor of Drury Lane, as completely different in temperament as in politics, see L. Kelly, *Richard Brinsley Sheridan* (1997). Some of his theatrical paintings are now in the Garrick Club in London.

148 Cibber's *An Apology for the Life of Mr. Colley Cibber* (1740) gives basic autobiographical details. It is also an illuminating history of Cibber's own time.

acted at Drury Lane and Covent Garden.[149]

These plays too were 'printed under the authority of and by permission of the managers from the prompt books – with biographical and critical remarks by Mrs. Inchbald'. Playwright as well as actress, Elizabeth Inchbald could be highly critical: thus, she 'objected' strongly in 1807 to the fact that a dramatist could not speak of national concerns 'except in one dull round of panegyrick'.[150] The role of Harris in the Longman story, which continued through the first years of Longman and Rees, is unclear. He lived on until 1820, dying at Wimbledon, which coincidentally was to figure in twentieth-century Longman history.[151]

~

The Longmans' interest in the theatre was a metropolitan interest. It could also be reflected, however, in shared provincial publications. Thus, in 1795 Thomas Norton sold copies of *The Seaman's Return or the Unexpected Marriage*, an 'operatic farce' by John Price of Worcester which had been performed in Worcester, Ludlow, Wolverhampton and Shrewsbury. It was printed by H. Procter of Worcester and sold by J. Eddowes of Shrewsbury. Procter also printed *An Historical and Topographical Account of Leominster* in 1795 and a *Ludlow Guide* in 1797, both sold by Longman and the former by J. Barrow of Leominster, D. Walker and J. Allen in Hereford, and Hall and Co. in Worcester.

It is remarkable how diverse the local links of Longman became, particularly during the last decades of the century when a provincial bookselling network was built up. The 1760s lists already revealed some of the links. They were of different kinds. Sometimes Longman was the bookseller of books printed in the provinces. Sometimes the names of provincial booksellers were given on the title page of books which Longman published in London. Sometimes the initiative for co-operation came from Longman, sometimes from an enterprising provincial printer or entrepreneur. There were 'local interests' too in the provincial publishing network. Thus, T.A. Knight's *A Treatise on the culture of the apple and pear and on the manufacture of cider and perry*, printed by Procter and sold by booksellers in Hereford, Leominster and other western towns, was said to be sold in London by T.N. Longman, the only metropolitan bookseller named on the imprint.

---

149 Drury Lane and Covent Garden, which had together received royal patents under Charles II, had a monopoly in 'legitimate drama' until 1843. For the King's Theatre, centre of Italian opera, which was under the control of Drury Lane and Covent Garden from 1778 see C. Price, J. Milhouse and R.D. Hume, *Italian Opera in Late Eighteenth-Century London*, Vol. I, 1778–1791 (1993).

150 'On the Abuse and Use of Novel-Writing', in *The Artist*, 13 June 1807, p.18.

151 See below, pp.401ff.

Shrewsbury was prominent in the growing networks linked with Longman, including religious networks, with J. and W. Eddowes the local personalities involved.[152] J. Eddowes published *Religious Exercises Recommended* (1769) by the dissenter Job Orton (1717–1783) who had ministered at Shrewsbury before joining Doddridge in Northampton. He went on to publish Orton's *A Short and Plain Exposition of the Old Testament* (1787), which was sold by Longman in London. The Eddowes, who feature also in the history of retailing as makers of 'aperient pills', shared with two other Shrewsbury booksellers the sale of T. Rowley's *The Frolicks of Fancy* (1785), 'a familiar epistle, characteristic of *Tristram Shandy*'. Edmund John Eyre's comedy *Consequences* (1794), performed in Shrewsbury, Wolverhampton and Worcester, was 'printed and sold by Thomas Norton Longman', and by Eddowes and two other Shrewsbury booksellers, by J. Tynos, W. Smart, E. Andrews and J. Baskerfield in Worcester, by W. Smart in Wolverhampton and by Nicholson far away in Cambridge.

One book printed even further away in Glasgow 'for the author', Thomas Moore's *The Psalm Singers' Delightful Pocket Companion*, was sold exclusively in London by Longman and in Shropshire by Eddowes, who also printed *A discourse on the influence of religious practice upon our inquiries after truth*. The British Library copy is bound up with the half-title for *A Discourse on the Death of [Richard] Price*, delivered at Hackney in 1791 by the Birmingham Unitarian, Joseph Priestley.

It was not only dissent that depended on networks, and in 1794 Eddowes also printed and sold Joseph Plymley's *Charge given at the visitation of the Archdeaconry of Salop in the diocese of Hereford* with Rivingtons among the other names listed on the imprint, along with Longman and Cadell. It was also sold by Merrill in Cambridge and Fletcher in Oxford. Likewise, sermons preached by John Plumptre, Dean of Gloucester, were printed by G. Gower in Kidderminster and sold in London by Longman, the Rivingtons and G. and J. Robinson, while a sermon delivered in Stourbridge by Robert Foley, Rector of Old Swinford, entitled *A Defence of the Church of England*, was printed and sold by J. Rollason of Coventry and bore the names of J. Allen of Hereford, Hall and Co. of Worcester, T. Pearson of Birmingham as well as those of Thomas Norton and the Rivingtons.[153]

Thomas II and Thomas Norton could make wider contacts, however,

---

152 For Shrewsbury as a town in change see A. McInnes, 'The Emergence of a Leisure Town: Shrewsbury, 1660–1760', in *Past and Present*, No. 120 (1988), pp.53-87.

153 Gower also printed and sold in Kidderminster Robert Gentleman's *Plain and affectionate addresses to youth* (1792) and *The Young English Scholar's complete pocket companion ... in six parts, selected from the best of writers, divided into short lessons, and adapted to the capacities of children* (1797). In London they were both sold by Longman and by G.G. and J. Robinson.

than the Rivingtons. In Cambridge J. Merril(l)'s name was linked with
Thomas's in several imprints. There were two Cambridge Merrills, father
and son: the latter played a part in the debates on the role of national
and provincial booksellers during the 1770s.[154] A sermon delivered in
Cambridge in 1790 by Abraham Rees, who was to edit the updated edition
of Chambers's *Cyclopaedia* was 'printed by H. Goldney' for T. Cadell, J.
Johnson, C. Dilly and J. Bowtell. It was delivered in memory of the Revd.
Robert Robinson who died at Birmingham, and was entitled *The doctrine
of Christ, the only effectual remedy against the fear of death.*[155] What was 'the
doctrine of Christ'? One of the most conspicuous Longman books of
1790, printed for W. Charnley of Newcastle-upon-Tyne and T. Longman,
J. Johnson, R. Fisher and S. Hodgson of London was *A Book of Common
Prayer of the Church of England, reformed upon Unitarian principles.* It was
to be presented to the Bishop of Llandaff.

One of the most interesting items related to Birmingham in earlier
Longman lists was John Baskerville's *Vocabulary or Pocket Dictionary,* printed
by Baskerville (1706–1775) in Birmingham and sold by eight booksellers in
London of whom Longman was one. Another item in the previous year's
list was Richard Harvey's *The Farmers' and Corn-buyers' Assistant,* printed
in Norwich 'by the author' and sold by three London booksellers, Longman,
Crowder, and Wilson and Fell, and by other booksellers in Bury, Braintree,
Colchester, Hadleigh, Ipswich and Yarmouth. J. Shave of Ipswich also sold
it along with other books on Longman lists. In 1785 P. Hamilton's *Remarks
on the means of obviating the fatal effects of a mad dog* was printed by Shave
and Jackson, and sold by him 'and all the booksellers in Suffolk, Norfolk
and Essex'.

~

The development of overseas markets in what has come to be called 'the
Atlantic world', which included the Caribbean, can have been no more
complicated than the maintenance of provincial connections,[156] and
Thomas II's interest in overseas markets, real but not unique, is reflected

John Baskerville's *Vocabulary
or Pocket Dictionary,* 1765
was printed by Baskerville
in Birmingham, and sold by
eight booksellers in London,
including Longman

BL 1568/4137

154 Feather, *op. cit.,* pp.5, 8–10, 62.

155 In 1798 Thomas Norton with three other booksellers, Cadell, G.G. and J.
Robinson and W. Davies, published Rees's sermon, printed by A. Hamilton,
*The privileges of Britain delivered at the meeting held in Old Jewry on a day
appointed for a General Thanksgiving.* Thomas Norton also sold another
thanksgiving sermon delivered on the same occasion in 1798, 'printed for
the author' by M. Brown of Newcastle-upon-Tyne and sold by W. Charnley of
Newcastle, L. Pennington of Durham, and J. Graham of Sunderland.

156 See C.N. Davidson (ed.), *Reading in America* (1989) and J. Raven, *London
Booksellers and American Customers* (Charleston, 2002) and 'The Export of
Books to Colonial North America', in PH, Vol. 41 (1997).

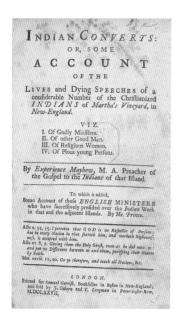

Longman already had links
with the overseas trade; the
Anglo-American link is
illustrated in this pamphlet on
the Indian Converts, published
by Samuel Garrish in Boston in
1727, and sold by T. Osborn and
T. Longman as booksellers in
London

BL 493.g.14

in his transatlantic correspondence, already mentioned, with Henry Knox of Boston, which has fortunately survived the vicissitudes of fire and water. It dates back to January 1772 when Longman thanked Knox for the 'kind present of three pair of ducks': 'unfortunately all but two ducks died in passage'.[157]

In the summer of that year Longman described the importance of selling books that he sent him at a fair price, avoiding 'underselling', a future major preoccupation. He promised to send books 'as fast as possible': they were now 'usually retailed in London according to the printed catalogue sent you'.[158] Longman also referred to the communication of magazines and periodicals which had an American as well as a British readership.[159] In April 1773 he had sent among other periodicals twenty copies of the *Gentleman's Magazine*, eighty of the *London Magazine*, and four of the *Monthly Review* and the *Critical Review*.[160]

The personal friendship between the two men survived the American War of Independence during which Knox became a General. Another Knox correspondent before the War of Independence had been James Rivington, who for personal reasons had moved to American soil and tried to persuade Knox into book piracy, but broke with him after they took different sides in the War.[161] When the War was over, Knox was punctilious in paying his debts to Longman in Dutch guilder bills of exchange, the first instalment in 1793, the last in 1805. In a letter of 1793 he thanked Thomas for his 'forebearance and liberality' while pointing out the 'extreme inconvenience' to himself: he was no more responsible for the earlier destruction of books in transit for which he was called upon to pay than he was for the War itself. 'May you, Sir,' he concluded, 'experience all possible happiness in this life, in the earnest and sincere desire of your most humble servant.'[162]

157 This letter was written on 18 January 1772. The originals of the letters are in the possession of the Massachusetts Historical Society, and I express my thanks to them for allowing me to quote from them in this *History*. There are copies in the Bodleian Library.

158 Letters of 21 July 1772, 18 Feb. 1773.

159 Letter of 5 Oct. 1772.

160 Letter of 20 April 1773. In October a consignment in 'brown paper parcels' was held up at Cowes for a month. (Letter of 4 Oct. 1773.)

161 Tebbel, *op. cit.*, p. 87. Rivington later served as a double agent. See J. Bakeless, *Turncoats, Traitors and Heroes* (1959), p. 228. *The Bookseller*, 6 June 1890, reprinted a colourful account of James's activities which it had first printed in December 1859.

162 Letter of 15 Dec. 1793. It was unfortunate that 1,000 guilder bills produced only £902 15s. 11d. (Letter of Longman to Knox, 4 March 1794). The first surviving letter from Longman to Knox is dated 13 Aug. 1790.

Before there had been any thought of war, indeed before Thomas I had acquired Taylor's books and premises, there had already been an Anglo-American connection in the Longman prehistory. One of the books bearing an Osborn-Varnam imprint was *Psalms, Hymns and Spiritual Songs of the Old and New Testament for the Use, Edification and Comfort of the Saints in Public and Private, especially in New England*. Even more remarkably, another book published in Boston in 1727 by Samuel Gerrish bore the names of J. Osborn and T. Longman as its sole salesmen in London – *Indian Converts: or, some Account of the Lives and Dying Speeches of a considerable number of the Christianized Indians of Martha's Vineyard in New England* (1727).

How far this early-eighteenth-century history was known to Thomas II is not clear. It was certainly not known to his successors. For the most part, Thomas II was bound to the present. In the words of William West, who saw Thomas II 'almost daily' during the years from 1785 to 1787 in order to discuss 'books for country orders' and who also accompanied him to the theatre to see 'the flower of the stage', Thomas continued in the last years of his life 'to pursue the calm even tenour of his way; and with a fine, mild placid disposition, his business always appeared more a source of amusement to him than of anxiety'.[163] In fact, with a large family to care for, he often faced family crises. Only one of his five daughters married, and of his sons, two died in infancy and one, his eldest, Edward, was drowned when he fell overboard off an East India ship far away in the Indian Ocean. This accident, reported in *The Times* on 11 August 1796, took place only a few months before Thomas's own death at Hampstead on 5 February 1797.

Thomas, aged sixty-six, and described appropriately but modestly in the Press as 'a very considerable Bookseller', had asked for a simple burial – 'I hate the foolish parade of pompous funerals' – and he left all his substantial estate to his widow and surviving children – £20,000 to Elizabeth, and £5,000 each to his sons and daughters. His business now passed into the hands of his oldest surviving son, Thomas Norton Longman, while his second son, George, five years younger, went into partnership with John Dickinson (1782–1869), the papermaker. The partnership traded as Longman and Dickinson, and in 1809 it leased a London office in the Old Bailey. Another more important acquisition was a new paper mill at Apsley. Dickinson, who patented a papermaking machine, had as strong a family sense as Thomas I had had.[164] And in the nineteenth century the

---

163 West, *op. cit.* (1835), and *The Aldine Magazine*, 29 Dec. 1838, 'Letter to my son at Rome', 22 Dec. 1838. The same impression of Thomas's state of mind is conveyed in a portrait of his wife by the school of Zoffany. It was one of a pair: the second was that of her Covent Garden brother.

164 See J. Evans, *The Endless Web: John Dickinson & Co. Ltd, 1804–1954* (1955), Chs. I and II.

two families were to become even more closely interconnected.[165]

Of Thomas II's legacy to his wife, a half was to be held in the Bank of England and the other half was to be invested in Government 'or other good stock'. Thomas also left £320 in the English Stock of the Stationers' Company. This stock, set up by letters patent in 1603 and managed by a Stock Board under the direction of the Court of the Company, had more than held its value in a century when the role of the Company in the bookselling business had drastically changed: dividends were 12.5 per cent per annum.[166] Yet the dynamic of late-eighteenth-century publishing

---

165 See below, p.168.

166 See below, p.108.

derived not from the administration of the Company but from the talents of individual publishers like Thomas II.

For all the tributes paid to Thomas II for his 'placid disposition' and the 'even tenour' of his ways, few of his contemporaries had been so dogged by personal circumstances in rapidly changing times. Indeed, when Thomas Norton III wrote to Knox telling him of the death of his father, 'your old correspondent', after a long illness, he explained that Thomas had been 'incapable of attending to any businesses for near a twelvemonth past'. And he ended by sending Knox 'the best wishes of our family' and a PS 'My mother, my uncle, and myself are appointed executors.'[167] Thomas Norton showed that he was a true father's son, however, when in the same letter he wrote that he had observed in his father's papers a letter from Knox promising him that the balance on his old account would be duly settled '£658 7s. 7d. according to my father's ledger'. 'I have no doubt', he added, 'that you will have the goodness to comply with your promise.'

~

By the time that Thomas Norton III wrote this letter, he had been persuaded or perhaps driven to give active support to William Pitt's government which in confronting revolutionary France after 1793 was deeply concerned about radical subversion in Britain itself. Already a year earlier Thomas II had published John Bowles's *A Protest against T. Paine's Rights of Man*, and Thomas Norton went on to publish two essays by a clergyman, Fitzjohn Brand, extolling the merits of John Reeves's 'loyal associations'. He also published successive editions of John Gifford's *A Short Address to Members of the Loyal Association on the Present State of Public Affairs, containing a brief exposition of the designs of the French upon this country.*[168]

John Gifford was a pen-name: Gifford's real name was John Richards Green. He had started the *Anti-Jacobin Review* in July 1798, not to be confused with the earlier *Anti-Jacobin*, associated with George Canning (1770–1827), which under the editorship of William Gifford, a very real name, lasted from November 1797 to July 1798. The *Anti-Jacobin Review* survived until 1821 with Green as its editor until 1818. The last volumes were published from various publishers' addresses in Paternoster Row.[169]

There is other evidence of pressure on the Longmans and, indeed, of collaboration. Buried away in secret, official archives, deliberately kept

Thomas Norton Longman III and his family, painted *c*. 1812 by John Downman ARA

The family portrait shows Mr and Mrs Longman (neé Slater (1773–1842); Sarah Longman (1810–60) is on her lap, Mary (arranging flowers) who married Andrew Spottiswoode, Printer to the Queen; the little boy with his arm in his father's is Thomas Longman IV (1804–79), the boy in front is Charles Longman (1809–73) who went on to provide the Dickinson connection, and the daughter sewing is Louisa (1803–70). The youngest child, William (1815–77) was not born until after the picture was painted

Personal collection

---

167 Letter of 27 Feb. 1797.

168 For the Loyal Associations see R.R. Dozier, *For King, Constitution and Country* (1983). Longman was one of the six publishers of the papers of the Association for Preserving Liberty and Property against Republicans and Levellers, 'addressed to all the loyal associations', in 1793.

169 See H. Ellis, 'The Anti-Jacobin Review', in A. Sullivan (ed.), *British Literary Magazines, The Romantic Age, 1789–1836* (1983), pp.12–21.

'A peep into the Cave of Jacobinism', Britannia firing flaming bolts at a French revolutionary creature

Frontispiece from John Gifford's Anti-Jacobin Review, published from 1798-1821. Cartoon by James Gillray, September 1798

BL P.P.3596

incomplete, are details relating not only to Green but to Thomas II's brother-in-law Thomas Harris. The Government was then spending in secret funds almost £5,000 a year on the Press. Newspapers had small circulations and some editors had no scruples about accepting public funds. In one official record of subsidies paid to the Press in the early 1790s, unearthed by the indefatigable Professor Arthur Aspinall, we read 'Mr. Harris for Mr. Longman, to be divided between the editors of *The Ledger, Saint James's* [*Chronicle*] and *London Evening* [*Post*] £300'. There were then nine newspapers, including these three, which were being regularly subsidised to the extent of £2,500.[170]

*A peep into the Cave of Jacobinism.*___"Magna est Veritas et prævalebit."

---

170 A Aspinall, *Politics and the Press, 1780–1850* (1949), p. 176n and p. 68. See also S. Koss, *The Rise and Fall of the Political Press in Britain*, Vol. I (1981), Ch. 2, pp.30–44. The last editor of the *Anti-Jacobin Review*, un-named and unknown, claimed that the only public reward Greene himself had received was to be made a Police Magistrate. 'Magnificent Boon'. (Quoted in Ellis, *loc. cit.*, p. 19.) As John Gifford, Greene also published a six-volume political life of William Pitt in 1809.

St Paul's, near Paternoster Row, where the four publishers were among those gathered to hear Thomas Bowen's sermon on 22 July 1798

BL Maps Crace 19 no. 61

Newspapers and books have separate but related histories. Sometimes, as in this cryptic note, they converge. Yet there were common motivations in publishing that had little to do with money. In 1798 Thomas Norton was joined by John Murray II and Joseph Highley as well as the Rivingtons in the publication of a sermon delivered in nearby St. Paul's 'before the Temple Bar and St. Paul's Military Association' by Thomas Bowen on 'The Duty of Loving our Country' on Sunday 22 July.

THE
RELIGION
OF
NATURE
DELINEATED.

Ἔνιοι φεύγοντες τὴν Δεισιδαιμονίαν ἐμπίπτοσιν εἰς Ἀθεότητα τραχεῖαν καὶ ἀντίτυπον, ὑπερπηδήσαντες ΕΝ ΜΕΣΩ κειμένην τὴν Εὐσέβειαν. Plutarch.

Χαίρειν ἂν ἐάσας τὰς Τιμὰς τὰς τῶν πολλῶν ἀνθρώπων, τὴν ΑΛΗΘΕΙΑΝ σκοπῶν, πειράσομαι τῷ ὄντι ὡς ἂν δύνωμαι βέλτιςος ὢν καὶ ζῆν, καὶ ἐπειδὰν ἀποθνήσκω, ἀποθνήσκειν. Plato.

LONDON:

Printed *by* Samuel Palmer, *in* Bartholomew-Close,
And Sold by B. LINTOT, W. and J. INNYS, J. OSBORN and
T. LONGMAN, and J. BATLEY. 1726.

3   *The Dynamics of Growth*

The last chapter focused on individual people and on particular books, all of them directly or indirectly linked with the history of Longman. Attempting to deal more generally, if briefly, with the dynamics of the eighteenth-century book trades as a whole is a necessary supplementary task. The Longmans, however many people were involved in the affairs of their House, were always part of a bigger scenario. This was not only a 'bookscape', to use Raven's term, for as he himself points out, booksellers often sold products other than books and booksellers' shops could be quickly converted into mercers' shops or butchers' shops.[1] An earlier bibliographer/ historian, Graham Pollard, rightly insisted in 1959 in his Sandars Lectures on 'The English Market for Printed Books', that book trade history cannot be handled effectively within narrow limits or studied in isolation from other trades.[2] Nevertheless, without placing the Longmans themselves within the bookscape and within a larger culture of print, their distinctive achievements can neither be understood nor explained.

The Religion of Nature was published in 1726, showing B.Lintot, and J. Innys, J. Osborn and T. Longman and J. Batley as booksellers, with an engraving of a printing house

Longman Archive

In the eighteenth century, when book production and book selling changed significantly, printing and bookselling, already largely separated from each other, were both highly personalised; and just as the range of publications and formats widened so too did different kinds of publishing personalities emerge, with some of them eventually calling themselves not booksellers but publishers. There was no standard type. Some publishers were 'catch-penny opportunists', others missionaries of change. Most kept their secrets to themselves: some were self-publicists. A small group of metropolitan booksellers, many of them located in Paternoster Row, worked closely together. The first and second Thomas Longmans were members of the group as were their successors who stayed in Paternoster Row as neighbours came and went. Their economic position strengthened during the course of their lifetimes.

The processes of change were protracted and had relatively little to do with the technology of production. Emergent publishers were not usually

---

1   J. Raven, 'Constructing Bookscapes', in J. Murray (ed.), *Mappa Mundi* (2001),pp.35–9.

2   PH, Vol. IV (1978), p.9. Pollard's Sandars Lectures, delivered in Cambridge, were not published at the time, but an accessible, unrevised and uncorrected text, published in PH after his death in 1976, clearly reveals his intent and his methodology. See also *Studies in the Book Trade in Honour of Graham Pollard* (1975).

A true Representation of a Printing House with the Men at Work. Engraved for the New Universal Magazine, *1752*

St Bride's Printing Library

printers or bookbinders. Nor ultimately were they retail booksellers or general wholesalers, although the Longmans remained so for longer than their competitors and collaborators. Like them, they arranged for the manufacture of books usually at their own expense (although they might publish on commission) and, just as important, they secured their distribution. By the end of the century a new definition of publisher was current. The situation was radically different from that in 1724 when Thomas Longman I acquired 39 Paternoster Row, although to the time of his death he, like his nephew after him, called himself a bookseller, not a publisher.

'Technology', a new eighteenth-century word which did not figure in Johnson's *Dictionary*, had no effect on such definitions of bookselling and publishing, but there was a marked absence of significant technological change in the production of books. And that in a century when there were wide-ranging changes in the production of metals, of textiles and of coal, changes to which the label 'industrial revolution' was to be attached in the nineteenth century.[3] Even when water power was still being extensively employed, not least in textiles, and the steam engine was being hailed as the greatest invention since printing, 'hand print' persisted. The steam

---

3   See G.N. Clark, 'The Idea of the Industrial Revolution', David Murray Lecture, University of Glasgow, 15 Oct. 1953.

engine was applied to brewing as well as to textiles in the late-eighteenth century before being applied to printing.[4]

In the history of change in movable-type printing, which was considered as a craft – some thought of it as an art – the key date – and it was more than symbolic – came after the end of the eighteenth century. In 1814 the proprietor of *The Times*, John Walter II (1776–1847) introduced Friedrich Koenig's two-cylinder steam-powered press which was hailed by *The Times* itself as 'the greatest improvement connected with printing since the discovery of the art itself'. 'A system of machinery almost organic has been devised and arranged, which, while it relieves the human frame of its most laborious efforts in printing, far exceeds all human powers in rapidity and dispatch.'[5] A screw press driven by steam had been built by Andrew Baver before Koenig constructed his Cylinder Printing Machine in 1812, and a sheet of *The Annual Register* for 1811 had been printed on Baver's press in that year. Yet it was Koenig, who in 1816 worked with Baver on a Perfecting Machine which printed on both sides of the paper in one operation, who has passed into history. He left *The Times* and England in 1817.

Left: The Stanhope Press. Engraving from *Typographia* by T.H. Carson, 1825

BL 619.K.26

Right: The Koenig Press erected in the office of *The Times* in 1814

BL 011851.K.37

---

4   For the context and consequences of steam power see A. Briggs, *The Power of Steam* (1982) and G.N. von Tunzelman, *Steam Power and British Industrialisation to 1860* (1978).

5   *The Times*, 29 Nov. 1814. In the same newspaper (8 Dec. 1814) Koenig, who had arrived in Britain in 1806, described his experiences as an inventor, attributing his success to the British patent system which provided 'an inducement for individual enterprise'. A Fleet Street book printer, Thomas Bentley, who fully appreciated the significance of the invention, had already negotiated with him about its employment.

Some of the techniques followed in early industrialisation, like 'rolling' and the use of cylinders, were to influence the production of books as well as newspapers, but the full implications of William Nicholson's 1790 patent for a printing machine embodying the cylinder principle, which ultimately doomed the hand press, were not immediately apparent. Nicholson himself died in a debtor's prison. Meanwhile, the substitution of iron for wood in the printing press – Stanhope's iron hand press – was a straightforward technical 'advance', and the first Stanhope iron press was built for the Oxford University Press shortly after 1800. Labour costs were high: printing-house compositors were the highest paid skilled workers in London.[6] They composed characters into words, lines, paragraphs and other groupings. Proof readers were the final arbiters of spelling and punctuation.

Turning from printing to paper, the basic raw material and, as surviving Longman Ledger Books show, the main element in costs, economic historians have explained the fact that the paper industry in the eighteenth century did not grow like the cotton industry 'for the good reason that the demand for paper was quite unlike the demand for textiles. It was neither so large nor so elastic': in an age when limited literacy set limits to the demand for paper, there was not the same stimulus to invention.[7] But economic historians have also recognised, as contemporaries always did, that there was an increase in the production of paper in England and Scotland and that this was limited also by a formidable pressure of taxation.

Paper was made by hand, sheet by sheet, and imported paper was taxed throughout the eighteenth century – at an increasing rate. Home-made paper was taxed from 1711, at first at 15 per cent, but the excise tax increased sharply later in the century, doubling between 1793 and 1801. The only rebate ('drawback') was allowed to university presses on paper used for printing books in Latin, Greek and other 'learned languages'. This had nothing to do with innovation.

The struggle to abolish the paper tax, deemed a 'tax on knowledge', was

6   It was doubtless with labour costs in mind that Andrew Spottiswoode purchased in 1819 a Maudslay steam engine at a cost of £782 in 1819 along with a perfecting machine, then patented, for £1,200. (*The Story of a Printing House, being an account of the Strahans and Spottiswoodes* [2nd edn., 1912], p.36.)

7   D.C. Coleman, *The British Paper Industry, 1495–1860* (1958), p.333; A.G. Thomson, *The Paper Industry in Scotland, 1590–1861* (1974); A.M. Shorter, *Water Paper Mills in England* (1966); R.H. Clapperton, *The Paper-making Machine – Its Invention, Evolution and Development* (1967) and J. Grant, J.H. Young and B.G. Watson, *Paper and Board Manufacture, a General Account of its History, Processes and Applications* (1978).

to be a major political campaign in the nineteenth century.[8] The duties were to be halved in 1837 and abolished in 1861.[9] In the course of campaigning revealing statements were sometimes published expounding the effect of taxes on costs, like one set out in 1831 with reference to an octavo volume of 500 pages printed on 'respectable paper' to be sold retail for twelve shillings a copy. Taxes then amounted to one-fifth of costs, as an *Edinburgh Review* table demonstrated.

FOR 500 COPIES	COST £.s.d	TAX £.s.d
Printing and corrections	88.18.0	–
Paper	38.10.0	8.12.10
Boarding	10.0.0	3.3.8
Advertising	40.0.0	20.0.0
Total	177.8.0	31.16.6
11 copies to libraries 14 copies to author		

FOR 750 COPIES	COST £.s.d	TAX £.s.d
Printing and corrections	95.6.0	
Paper	57.15.0	12.19.4
Boarding	15.0.0	4.15.7
Advertising	50.0.0	25.0.0
Total	218.1.0	42.14.11
11 copies to libraries 14 copies to author		

Figures were also set out for 1,000 copies, but it was noted that a run of 750 copies was 'average'. If all 475 copies of the 500 available for sale were sold, the profit to the publisher and author would be only £22 9s. 11d.: on 725 copies it would be £305 9s. 5d. 'Were an attempt made to treat the dealers

---

8   In an interesting article in the ER, Vol. 53, 1831, pp.427-37, the tax was described as a 'tax on literature': 'nothing ever called more strongly for immediate revision and amendment'. J.R. McCulloch, a Longman author, in his *Dictionary of Commerce* (1844), p.160, called the paper tax a 'tax on literature', and like related taxes, 'at once impolitic, oppressive, and unjust'. Abolition ultimately became the target, as it already was for radicals.

9   See C.D. Collet, *History of the Taxes on Knowledge: Their Origin and Repeal*, 2 vols. (1899) is a basic text. See also P. Hollis, *The Pauper Press* (1970) and J.H. Wiener, *The War of the Unstamped* (1969).

George Longman M.P.
(1776–1822) married into the
Dickinson family, where he
became an important investor
in the new methods of paper
manufacture, as well as MP for
Maidstone. This portrait was
by James Northcote (1746–1831),
a well-known painter who had
been apprenticed to Reynolds

Pearson Education

in blacking, coffee, tea or sugar, as authors and publishers are treated', the compiler of the figures said, 'the whole country would be in flames.'[10]

Even without detailed statistics, the effects on costs of paper duties and of another of the taxes on knowledge – that on advertising – were obvious. Publishers had to pay for their taxed paper as their initial outlay before they concerned themselves with printing and binding, the costs of which were already being reduced by technical changes before the repeal of the paper tax. Small print runs were a central feature of the eighteenth-century book trade and this in itself necessarily implied high book prices. The struggle to secure cheaper books involved more than a pressure to reduce costs and particularly taxes: it raised particular questions concerning the way publishers fixed the prices of books in relation to costs and general questions concerning social (and educational) consequences. Prices provide 'an index of accessibility'.

Technical changes were faster in the first decades of the nineteenth century than at any point in the eighteenth century, and entrepreneurs appeared comparable in their motivation and achievement to those in other trades. One of them – in printing – was William Clowes (1779–1847), who accelerated the shift from hand operations to steam power and whose workshops became one of the great sights of London. He had arrived in London in 1802 where he became a compositor. Setting up his own business as a printer in 1803, by 1837 he was using twenty steam presses at his works in Duke Street, 'throwing off at the rate of 750 sheets, printed on both sides per hour'.[11] Clowes's first sizeable outside order came from Longman and Rees.[12] As an impressive example of continuity the firm of Clowes was still printing for Longman at the time of its 250th anniversary.

Leaving on one side protracted changes in the technology of book

10   ER, Vol.53, p.433.

11   Note by William Collins, the Glasgow publisher, quoted in D. Keir, *The House of Collins* (1953), p.122. For Clowes see W.B. Clowes, *Family Business, 1803–1953* (1953). In 1829 the Cambridge University Press approached Clowes to give advice, and his main assistant, J.W. Parker, was appointed Printer to the Press in 1836 and stayed in the post until 1854. (Sutcliffe, *op. cit.,* pp.136, 151-2.) There is a Clowes Printing Museum at Beccles, Suffolk.

12   Clowes, *op. cit.,* pp.7, 12. See also M. Plant, *The English Book Trade: An Economic History of the Making and Sale of Books* (1939).

production, including the use of stereotyped plates and the introduction of book cloth, largely associated with the nineteenth rather than the eighteenth century,[13] there were other changes in book distribution in the eighteenth century which marked the beginning of what came to be called in retrospect 'a communications revolution'. Thus road building and improved postal services directly influenced the fortunes of publishers, particularly of newspapers, during the last decades of the eighteenth century, as they also did the fortunes of dealers in other commodities.[14] And long before that in the late seventeenth century and early eighteenth century there had been significant changes in the organisation of bookselling during what Defoe called 'a Projecting Age'.

It was then that the world of print, including job printing, began to concentrate on the topical, on what was happening at the time and just beyond it.[15] Novels and newspapers went together, sustaining each other, part of the same preoccupation, although some novels turned, as fiction always had done, to a world of romance far removed from the world as it was[16] and some 'newsmongers' were so concerned at a 'dearth' of news that they fell back on non-news sources. Thus, the printer of the *Leicester Journal* was once so short of news that he reprinted passages from the Old Testament each week, getting half way through *Exodus* before foreign news came in by mail. By the end of the eighteenth century editors, novelists and poets were involved in 'discourse' with their readers by means of the printed page. What Q.D. Leavis called in 1939 'the reading public', highly

---

13   For the early history of stereotyping, earlier in France and in Scotland than in England, see J. Carter, 'William Ged and the invention of Stereotype', in TL, Vol. 15 (1960) and M.L. Turner, 'Andrew Wilson: Lord Stanhope's Stereotype Printer', in the *Journal of the Printing Historical Society* (1975). For bookbinding D. Leighton, *Modern Bookbinding* (1935), p.19; L. Darley, *Bookbinding Then and Now* (1959), which describes the first bookbinding machine William Burn's rolling press (pre-1827); and J. Carter, *Publishers' Cloth, an outline history of publishers' binding in England 1820–1900* (1935). Bookbinders' cloth was first classified in Kelly's *Directory* in 1841. Miniature editions of Dante and Tasso were bound in cloth in 1822 ('Bookbinding' in QR, July 1898, p.210).

14   See M. Plant, op.cit. (3rd edn. 1974).

15   Defoe's *An Essay upon Projects* (1697) was the first work publicly acknowledged by him. His Preface was signed D.F. His *Essay upon Literature* (1726) was more concerned with the making of books than with the writing of them. Printing (p.114) had made possible 'the spreading of useful Knowledge in the World, making the Accession to it cheap and easy'. See M. Twyman, *Printing 1770–1970: an illustrated history of its development and uses in England* (2nd edn. 1998).

16   When Walter Scott turned from poems to novels, he was to describe his *Ivanhoe* (1819) as 'a Romance'.

From the left:

John Dunton (1659–1733)

Samuel Richardson
(1689–1761), from a picture
by Chamberlin

Edward Cave (1691–1754),
founder of the *Gentleman's
Magazine*

Thomas Cadell (1742–1802)

James Lackington (1746–1816)

Andrew Donaldson from an
etching by Kay, 1789

Thomas Longman III
(1771–1842)

All these – curiously
memorable – illustrations
are taken from *A History of
Booksellers, the old and the new ...
With portraits and illustrations,*
by Henry Curwen, 1873

BL 2308.aa.4.

stratified, had come into existence.[17] Much reading, however, was carried on 'aloud': those people who could not read would gather around a person who could.[18]

~

It is impossible to investigate the changing dynamics of the book trade, including crucial relationships between authors and readers, without examining the intricate networks of individuals and families who – through co-operation, competition and various blends of the two – were responsible for what came to be thought of as publishing. Some of them were mentioned in the last chapter. Many of them took risks, whatever their origins or experiences, with their reputations as well as their fortunes at stake. A few of them, named from the start as 'gentlemen', were pillars of established society. Others did not try to be. And for all of them there were risks, particularly the risk of disaster by fire, like a fire in 1770 in Paternoster Row which destroyed the premises of three publishers and a printer.

One of the publishers was the Unitarian Joseph Johnson (1738–1809), the poet William Cowper's publisher. A radical bookseller, who had moved to 8 Paternoster Row in 1765, Johnson knew the meaning of political as well as economic risks. He was imprisoned in 1797, along with other publishers, for selling Part I of Tom Paine's *Rights of Man*. Among his other authors were William Godwin and Mary Wollstonecraft.[19] In the cheerful words of a committed Cambridge Unitarian formally expelled by the University for his views in 1793, William Frend, Johnson was responsible for providing 'an Heretical Shelf or two at a Bookseller here'.[20]

~

Looking back at the eighteenth century, in the absence of oral history, although now in the presence of computers, we have to begin by turning back to accounts written at the time – or within memory – of what was happening to the trade, what had just happened to it, and sometimes, if the author of the account was so minded, what he felt would happen next. There was conviviality then, but there was also ample gossip and

---

17   Q.D. Leavis, *Fiction and the Reading Public* (1939).

18   See G.A. Cranfield, *The Press and Society: from Caxton to Northcliffe* (1978), pp.89-97, for William Cobbett's references to listening to his *Political Register* read aloud and for organised 'readings' in Victorian times see P. Collins, 'Reading Aloud' (The Tennyson Society, 1972).

19   See L.P. Chard, 'Bookseller to Publisher: Joseph Johnson and the English Book Trade, 1760-1810', in TL, 5th series, Vol. 32 (1977), pp.138–54, G.P. Tyson, *Joseph Johnson, A Liberal Publisher* (Iowa City, 1979).

20   Quoted in Feather, *op. cit.*, p.117.

occasional warfare, and just because of the gossipiness, what was written by contemporary participants or observers always must be studied critically. Some of their comments were, in effect, coded.

The sense of scene always rests on impressions rather than 'facts'. When *The Dunciad* by Alexander Pope was published anonymously in 1729, 'a crowd of authors' were said to have 'besieged the shop' and 'entreaties, advices, threats of law and battery, nay cries of treason, were all employed to hinder the coming out of *The Dunciad*. On the other side the booksellers and hawkers made as great an effort to procure it.'[21] The clatter was almost as great as the clatter in the poem, which at the time, as in retrospect, was a conservative manifesto. Pope disdained 'the new'.

Moments like this were always reported, as was the imprisonment of Johnson or in a totally different context the 'crisis in the book trade' in 1826.[22] Routines were not so reported; and in the relative absence of sources

---

21   Quoted in SOB, p.110.

22   See below, p.145.

there remains, even in the best of early studies of the book trade, a strong anecdotal element, often imbued with nostalgic sentiment, sometimes with foreboding. Most of the studies were written in retrospect, like Henry Curwen's *A History of Booksellers* (1873), a book published by a new nineteenth-century publisher, Chatto and Windus.[23] Curwen, born in 1845, was editor of *The Times of India*. He died in 1892. His curious illustrations are as memorable as his text. What publishers, old and young, looked like seemed to matter to him, and they often looked very strange.

The testimony of such books – and of articles in nineteenth-century periodicals – is invaluable, for none of the Longmans were great raconteurs or, indeed, tellers of stories concerning their trade. Nor were the Rivingtons, whose 'Bible and Crown' business was founded in 1711.[24] Among eighteenth-century booksellers who became publishers only one of them left behind him revealing personal testimony – John Murray I from Scotland, the ambitious newcomer who bought a bookshop in Fleet Street in 1768. There is much to be learnt of the routines of the book trade and, indeed, of what business decisions had to be taken in Murray's papers, fortunately, unlike the Longman papers, intact. The only comparable set of papers are those of the printer/publisher William Strahan.[25]

Murray was franker than Strahan in dealing with both fellow publishers and authors, their motivations and their fortunes. 'Many blockheads in the trade are making fortunes', he told a friend, the Revd. William Falconer, whom he would have liked to have taken with him to London as a partner, 'and did we not succeed as well as these, I think it must be imputed only to ourselves'.[26] Murray had to be tough, however, in dealing with consortia of more established booksellers, for he depended on them for many of his own undertakings, lacking, as he did, the capital to back all his ventures: nearly forty per cent of the 1,000 titles with Murray's name in the imprint included the names of other London booksellers.

Individual authors came into Murray's picture, however, as they did into Thomas Longman I's and II's, being paid outright for their products or sharing profits with them. Murray concluded,

> A Bookseller in a Purchase looks to the probability of the sale and seizes hold of the manuscript of an author already well and successfully known to the Public in preference to another ... perhaps better, written by an author whose reputation is not so well established.[27]

---

23   See O. Warner, *Chatto and Windus* (1973).

24   See above, p.19.

25   See below, p.102.

26   Quoted in W. Zachs, *The First John Murray and the Late Eighteenth-Century Book Trade* (1998), p.24.

27   *Ibid.*, pp.77, 63.

For a writer of 1747, setting out to describe 'all [London's] trades, professions, arts, both liberal and mechanic', 'a mere Title-Monger' could 'never make anything but a Bungler'.[28] There was no guarantee that they would make money, whether or not they financed their own books, but as a result of their experiences they became more conscious of their own role. Many of them had their works turned down often quickly and often by more than one publisher.

They were as diverse a group as the publishers themselves, some being linked together as 'men of letters', a term that was to survive with different meanings in different circumstances, given that the profession of letters (or literature) was not like the old 'learned professions' of the Church and the Law. There was no formal training and there were no formal qualifications. Some authors thought of themselves as 'hacks' not as 'men of letters', and the word Grub Street, the name of a real street near Moorfields in London, often came to be attached to them.[29] Yet in some respects 'scribblers' and 'translators', who needed to be paid for their labours, were the harbingers of the future. Their co-existence with writers who neither needed nor expected to be paid establishes the proposition that far from there being one single eighteenth-century trend leading up to the 'emergence of *the* author', as the first scholars to explore 'the Augustan age of literature' claimed,[30] it was through intermittent and scattered discussions about the nature of authorship and, above all, through contractual relationships with publishers that changes of attitudes took place.[31]

~

28   R. Campbell, *The London Tradesman Being a Compendious View of All the Trades, Professions, Arts, both Liberal and Mechanic ... Practised in the Metropolis* (1747), pp.134–5, 128. Campbell scorned publishers of 'Trifles', who loaded 'the Public with the Rubbish of the Press'.

29   See P. Rogers, *Grub Street: Studies in a Subculture* (1972). Yet the name had a mythical quality. See K. Macdermott, 'Literature and the Grub Street Myth', in P. Humm, P. Stigant and P. Widdowson (eds.), *Popular Fictions, Essays in Literature and History* (1986), pp.16–28.

30   See A. Belljame, *Men of Letters and the English Public in the Eighteenth Century, 1660–1744* (1948); A.S. Collins, *Authorship in the Days of Johnson; being a study of the relation between author, patron, publisher, and public, 1726–1780* (1929); R.W. Chapman, 'Authors and Booksellers', in A.S. Turberville (ed.), *Johnson's England* (1938); and J. Saunders, *The Profession of English Letters* (1964).

31   See M. Ezell, *Social Authorship and the Advent of Print* (1999), pp.181–194; D. Griffin, 'Fictions of Eighteenth-Century Authorship' in *Essays in Criticism*, Vol. 43 (1993); and I. Hunter, 'Lessons from the "Literatory": How to Historicize Authorship' in *Critical Inquiry*, Vol. 17 (1991), pp.479–509.

At every point in the story of eighteenth-century publishing a gallery of characters has to be introduced, each with his (or her) own history.[32] The 'her' is important. Some of the characters were authors; some were publishers; some of them, like Pope himself and Richardson, were both. Their histories were sometimes colourful. Thus, Robert Dodsley (1703–1764), a friend of Pope and one of his publishers, who never completed his seven-year apprentice's indenture in the Stationers' Company, was a footman before he became a bookseller – in Pall Mall. The range of his publications, all selected by himself, was exceptionally wide, including, as it did, *The World* (1753) and *The Annual Register* (1758) in which the House of Longman was to acquire a share in 1805.

Dodsley was also the first publisher of Gray's *Elegy*, and from its foundation in 1754 a member of the Society for the Encouragement of Arts, Manufactures and Commerce, familiar with new 'inventions' of many kinds and their effects on production and distribution. By the time of his death in 1764 his name had appeared on the imprints of 468 titles, on 233 of them as sole sponsor.[33] His brother James, rich and innovatory, carried on the business until 1797, associated with many new consortia, but in 1790 selling *The Annual Register* to the Rivingtons. For his authors Dodsley had great respect: Nichols described him as 'a man who never learned to consider the author as an underagent to the publisher'.[34]

Another member of the consortium to which Dodsley belonged, was Andrew Millar, the publisher who won Johnson's praises.[35] He had set up his bookshop in the 1740s in the Shakespeare Head, the house which he renamed (after a fellow-Scot) Buchanan's Head. It had belonged to the eldest Tonson, first of three Jacobs in a row, an innovator in his formats and in his titles. It was Tonson, in Michael Treadwell's phrase, who 'made the classics English and the English classics'.[36] Like Dodsley, Tonson was a leading member of the Kit-Cat Club, one of the first and certainly the most famous of eighteenth-century literary clubs, which brought together in the

---

32   See *inter alia* C. Turner, *Living by the Pen: Women Writing in the 18th Century* (1992); C. Gallagher, *Nobody's Story: The Vanishing Act of Women Writers in the Marketplace, 1670–1820* (1994); and P. McDowell, *The Women of Grub Street: Press, Politics and Gender in the London Literary Marketplace, 1688–1730* (1997).

33   J.E. Tierney, 'R. Dodsley, R. and J. Dodsley and J. Dodsley' in J.K. Bracken and J. Silver (eds.), *The British Literary Book Trade, 1700-1820* (1984), p.114 and *The Correspondence of Robert Dodsley* (1988); and H.M. Solomon, *The Rise of Robert Dodsley: Creating the New Age of Print* (1996).

34   Nichols, *op. cit.*, Vol. I (1812), p.298.

35   See above, p.54.

36   M. Treadwell, 'London Trade Publishers, 1675-1750' in TL 6th Series, 4 (1982), pp.99–134.

early eighteenth century Whig 'wits', including Steele and Addison, and Whig aristocrats. These were the men who in the judgement of Horace Walpole, writing half a century later, were 'the patriots that saved Britain' in the long wars between 1688 and 1714.[37]

For Samuel Johnson, also writing later in the century, when new collected editions of Steele and Addison were proving highly lucrative for publishers, Addison and Steele through their periodicals *The Tatler and The Spectator* had employed 'wit in the cause of truth' and made 'elegance subservient to piety'.[38] Addison himself wrote in *The Spectator* of 'endeavouring as much as possible to establish a taste of polite writing'. He would avoid, he said, all 'fashionable Touches of Infidelity'. It was not until 1776 that Longman became a partner in a three-volume edition of *The Miscellaneous Works of Addison*, along with W. Strahan, J.F. and C. Rivington, T. Caslon, T. Cadell and others. Thomas II had shared for the first time in such an anthology in 1753, *The Beauties of the Spectators, Tatlers and Guardians, collected and digested under alphabetical heads*. The names of J. and R. Tonson, J. and P. Knapton, W. Innys and others were also noted on this imprint. *The Beauties* was one of the books, tied in a red handkerchief, that was given by Bob to Maggie Tulliver in George Eliot's *The Mill on the Floss* (1860).

The Tonson family maintained a strong position in the mid-eighteenth-century book trade through their ownership of valuable 'copies',[39] and the traditions of the Kit-Cat Club lived on in circles in which Thomas I did not move.[40] Thomas II belonged, however, to a Literary Club of Booksellers who met first at the Devil's Tavern, Temple Bar and later at a monthly dinner at the Shakespeare Tavern at which they discussed together 'the germ of many a valuable production'. The productions included *The Lives of the Most Eminent English Poets* (1779–80), attributed to

---

37 The third chapter of SOB refers to Ned Ward's *The Secret History of Clubs* (1709) and to Sir Godfrey Kneller's painting of Kit-Cat Club members. See R.J. Allen, *The Clubs of Augustan London* (1933). See also K.M. Lynch, *Jacob Tonson: Kit-Kat Publisher* (Knoxville, 1971).

38 G.A. Hill and L.F. Powell (eds.), *Boswell: Life of Johnson* (1934 edn.), Vol.2, p.303.

39 See G. Papali, *Jacob Tonson, Publisher* (Auckland, 1968) and H.M. Geduld, *Prince of Publishers, a Study of the Work and Career of Jacob Tonson* (Bloomington, 1969).

40 Brewer, *op. cit.*, p.43.

Samuel Johnson, a commercial venture worked out behind closed doors.[41] Thomas II also acquired many rights in earlier authors whom Tonson had published, including Milton, in 1760 and 1765,[42] and he belonged to a consortium which in 1768 published the letters of Jonathan Swift: the volume bore the inscription 'printed for C. Bathurst', and the consortium included W. Strahan, R. Baldwin, E. Johnston and J. and F. Rivington, a highly disparate group of publishers.

Such disparities were not uncommon. Financial considerations were paramount. Yet Strahan (1715–1785), who was also the King's Printer, keeping that part of his business separate, straddled all groups. Edinburgh-born and apprenticed in Edinburgh, he set up as a printer in 1729, and, as we have seen, he figured prominently in 1755 as a partner in the production of Johnson's *Dictionary*. He printed many books for Thomas II – and for John Murray I. With no bookshop of his own in times when these were becoming common, he published many books himself, frequently not declaring his interest. A close friend of Millar, he printed for him the first volume of Edward Gibbon's *The History of the Decline and Fall of the Roman Empire* in what still stands out as the landmark year of 1776 along with Adam Smith's *An Inquiry into the Nature and Causes of the Wealth of Nations*.

For this volume the words 'printed for W. Strahan' appeared on the title page along with the words 'and T. Cadell in the Strand'. Thomas Cadell (1742–1802), Millar's former apprentice, had emerged from Bristol as Thomas I had done and had come into prominence after Millar's death in 1768. His highly successful career was a result of all three of Millar's children having died in infancy. His name appeared on more imprints, over 4,000, than any other publisher of his time.

Strahan himself was Master of the Stationers' Company in 1774, an important year in the history of the Company and the trade, when he also became a Member of Parliament, speaking there only when book trade interests seemed under threat. His portrait was painted by Sir Joshua Reynolds.[43] A great letter writer, he described cogently and memorably the

---

41   Curwen, *op. cit.*, pp.86–7; E. Marston, *Sketches of Booksellers at the Time of Dr. Johnson* (1902), pp.94–6. Alexander Chalmers produced a fuller Scottish edition in 1820. See R. Terry, *Poetry and the Making of the English Literary Past* (2001) which, however, does not examine the publishers' commercial role in establishing what became a literary canon.

42   In 1760 the names, among others, of J. and R. Tonson and T. Longman appeared on the title page of an edition of Milton's *Paradise Regain'd* and *Samson Agonistes*, and in 1765, again with J. and R. Tonson and others, on an edition of *Paradise Lost*. There were twenty-two names, including that of T. Longman, on late-eighteenth-century editions of Alexander Pope's translations of the *Iliad* and the *Odyssey*.

43   See J.A. Cochrane, *Dr Johnson's Printer: The Life of William Strahan* (1964).

Very neceſſary for all Printers, Bookſellers, Stationers, &c.
Likewiſe for all Lottery-Office-Keepers, Shopkeepers, and
others, who have Occaſion to advertiſe in any of the Newſpapers in *England, Scotland,* or *Ireland.*

LONDON, JUNE 7, 1784.
This Day is publiſhed, Price only 4 d.
P E N D R E D's
Liſt of the Maſter Printers
I N
London, Weſtminſter, and *Southwark*
With the Number of each Houſe, and their Situation.
Alſo a Liſt of thoſe reſiding in the ſeveral Towns of
England, Scotland, and *Ireland,*
With the Number of Miles each Town is diſtant from *London.*
N. B. Thoſe who print Newſpapers are particularly diſtinguiſhed.
To be had at the RED HART, (No. 21,) *Shoe-Lane, Fleet-Street.*
. Hair-Dreſſers Bills for Lanthorns may alſo be had, Price Three-Halfpence.

PENDRED'S HANDBILL OF 1784 (See p. xvi)

Pendred's Handbill, advertising the List of the Master Printers in London and Country Printers.

The earliest directory of the book trade by John Pendred, 1784 (edited with an introduction, and an appendix, by Graham Pollard, 1955)

BL 2719.X.13234

range of internal balances within the book trade, playing down profits and stressing 'the multiplicity of concerns' in which he himself was involved. The trade, he declared, required 'great Industry, Economy, Perseverance and Address to make any great figure in it'. He himself had paid special attention to 'Bookwork' and had become a 'Proprietor of about 200 books' in all, each one of which required 'some Attention', and a 'separate and distinct Account'. His ledgers, held in the British Library, reveal more about printing and publishing than any other source, including Murray.[44] Thomas II figures in them.

~

While Strahan was the last printer who demands such a long-term obituary, there were other eighteenth-century printers whose careers were memorable, like Henry Sampson Woodfall (1739–1805), who set up shop in Paternoster Row in 1748: he had read Homer to Pope at the age of five. In partnership with his son George between 1767 and 1793, he printed *The Public Advertiser*, and in 1797 he was Master of the Stationers' Company. He printed several books for Thomas II, and his name as printer appears with that of A. Strahan on Sir John Comyns's six-volume *A Digest of the Laws of England*, published by Thomas II and eleven other publishers in 1792. There are several other printers whose surviving ledgers have been

---

44 See *The Story of a Printing House* (1911), privately printed and written (with no name on the title page) by Richard Arthur Austen-Leigh. See also Leigh's 'William Strahan and his Ledgers', in TL, Vol. III (1922–3), p.286 and P. Gaskell, 'The Strahan Papers' in the *TLS*, Oct. 1956, p.592.

subjected to elaborate scrutiny – among them a father and son, William Bowyer the older (1663–1737) and William Bowyer the younger (1699–1771), and Charles Ackers, whose name did not appear in the first edition of the *Dictionary of National Biography*.[45] The first directory setting out names of printers, preceded by a handbill devoted not only to printers but to the book trade as a whole, was John Pendred's deliberately selective *The London and Country Printers, Booksellers and Stationers' Vade Mecum* of 1785. Its list of country booksellers was of practical value to the London trade.

The only surviving copy – edited by the bibliographer Graham Pollard in 1955[46] – had been acquired by the Bodleian Library in 1895. According to Pendred, in 1785 there were 124 printers, 151 booksellers, 164 stationers, 48 engravers and 17 bookbinders in London. He also listed 49 country newspapers and their London agents.[47] For John Feather, who among his other researches made a detailed study of the provincial trade, the latter were 'the key to understanding' Pendred.[48] They needed practical information about the London book trade for their daily use. The handbill stated that for each provincial town the number of miles from London would be set out, and places where newspapers were printed would be identified. What Pollard considered to be omissions in Pendred were 'qualitative judgements' on Pendred's part.

It is interesting to compare the limited information that Pendred provided with the information, more comprehensive in scope, that was provided in Leigh's new edition of *The Picture of London*, the last edition

---

45   For the Bowyers see K.I.D. Maslen and J. Lancaster, *The Bowyer Ledgers: The Printing Accounts of William Bowyer, Father and Son* (Bibliographical Society & Bibliographical Society of America, 1991). For Ackers see D.F. McKenzie and J. Rodd (eds.), 'A Ledger of Charles Ackers', *Oxford Bibliographical Society*, new series, Vol. 15 (1968), pp.249–52. Ackers charged Thomas Longman £54 3s. in 1737 for printing 28½ sheets of Chambers's *Dictionary*. In 1740 he charged Longman and Messrs Rivington £18 4s. for printing Mr. Bedford's *Sermons*. Longman and Rivington paid their debts in cash nine months later.

46   G. Pollard (ed.), 'The Earliest Directory of the Book Trade', Supplement to the *Transactions of the Bibliographical Society*, Vol. 14 (1955), pp.xi–xvi.

47   Eight years before its printing, a *Manuel* [later *Almanach*] *de l'auteur et du libraire*, a duodecimo booklet of 118 numbered pages, has claims to be the first major European trade directory. See G. Barber, 'Pendred abroad: a view of the late eighteenth-century book trade in Europe' in *Studies in the Book Trade in Honour of Graham Pollard* (1975), pp.231–57. Barber prints a complete translation of an article on the book trade written by a German authority, J.G. Krünitz, for the *Oeconomische Encyclopaedie* (Berlin, Leipzig, 1776, Part 7, pp.190–210. Krünitz was well-informed about what was happening to the trade in London as well as in Leipzig and Paris.

48   J. Feather, *The Provincial Book Trade in Eighteenth-Century England* (1985).

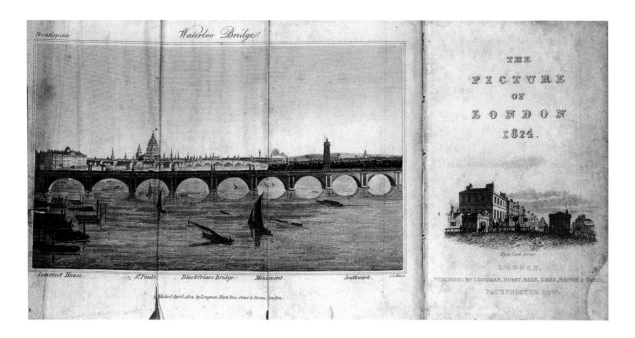

of which appeared in 1830. [49] It had a completely different purpose from Pendred, describing itself as 'a brief and luminous guide to the Stranger, on all subjects concerned with general information, business and amusement' in the Metropolis. In it Leigh distinguished between ten sub-divisions of booksellers. Seven of them, including Thomas Norton, supplied the town and country trade with books of every description, including their own publications, and executed foreign orders; two of them, one John Murray II, confined themselves largely to their own publications; ten were wholesale booksellers; and forty-two were retail booksellers and publishers.[50]

In the successive editions of an older *Picture of London* (1802), printed by Lewis and Company, Paternoster Row for Sir Richard Phillips (1767–1840), a new section was introduced in 1815 on 'the English Booksellers' which included the names of 'publishers' who were not also 'general dealers'; and three years later separate lists were printed of 41 publishers and wholesale booksellers, 32 dealers in second-hand books, 32 'dealers in modern books, chiefly by retail', 5 medical booksellers, 4 law booksellers, 24 circulating libraries and 6 juvenile libraries. The balance continued to

Frontispiece and title page from the new edition of Samuel Leigh's *Picture of London*, 1824 published by Longman, Hurst, Rees, Orme, Browne & Green

Longman Archive

---

49   The *Picture* set out to be 'a correct guide ... for the use of Strangers, Foreigners and all Persons who are not intimately connected with the British Metropolis'.

50   Quoted in Pollard, *loc. cit.*, p.36.

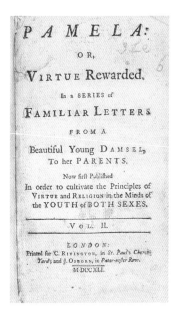

Title page to Richardson's
Pamela, 1741,Vol.II

BL C 71.cc.8

change as it was to do in printing and bookbinding also.[51]

Phillips himself, who was to sell many of his titles to Thomas Norton, was knighted in 1808 when he was Sheriff of London, and he worked for many years through a retail bookseller, Benjamin Tabart, who ran a Juvenile Library in New Bond Street.[52] He produced an *Encyclopaedia* as well as a magazine, and wrote many books, including *Millions of Facts* and a *Morning's Walk from London to Kew* (1816), describing a journey pursued in very different fashion by late-twentieth-century users of The National Archives.[53] Some of his contemporaries were as interested in his advocacy of a 'vegetarian diet', what the poet Tom Moore called his 'Pythagorean diet', as they were in his writing, while others attacked his 'jacobinical record'.

~

In both the nineteenth and twentieth centuries most writers on the eighteenth-century book trade, whether dealing in statistics or not, chose 'growth' not 'balance' as their main theme. The nature of that growth is perhaps best illuminated not by breaking up the century into shorter periods but by focusing on particular manifestations of growth that continued throughout the century – for example, the rise of the 'reading public', drawn to circulating libraries as well as to bookshops; the emergence of newspapers alongside books, sermons, pamphlets and ballads, their fortunes inter-related; and the particular appeal of novels as a genre. The last of these is the subject of an immense literature, raising the tantalising question 'When did the novel "really" begin?'[54]

Just as interesting, however, if less tantalising, is the use of the adjective 'circulating' and of the noun 'circulation'. Defoe had referred positively, proudly and generally to the 'circulation of trade within ourselves, where all the several manufacturers move in a just rotation from

---

51 D. McKitterick, *A History of Cambridge University Press*, Vol. II *Scholarship and Commerce 1698–1872* (1998). For bookbinding see C. Ramsden, *London Bookbinders, 1780–1840* (1954). A Masters' Association, founded in 1794, did not disappear until 1824, to be refounded in 1837. A Journeymen's Association, carefully studied by E. Howe, left excellent records kept in order by John Jaffray, a member of the union (TL, new series, Vol. 25, 1944–45, pp.185–6). See E. Howe, *Society of London Bookbinders, 1780–1951* (1952). For unionisation of the compositors through the London General Trade Society of Compositors, founded in 1826, a portentous phenomenon, see Plant, *op. cit.*, p.382.

52 There is a useful entry on Phillips in the DNB which points to the 'far from entirely trustworthy *Memoirs of the Public and Private Life of Sir R. Phillips* (1808). See also J. Issitt, 'Introducing Sir Richard Phillips' in *Paradigm*, Vol. 1 No. 26 (1998), pp.25–9.

53 For a note on him see PC, 6 Jan. 1916.

54 See above, p.36.

the several countries where they are made', to the city of *London*, by far the largest city in the kingdom, 'as the blood in the body of the heart'. He was not thinking exclusively of commodity trade. He knew that ideas circulated as well as goods, and that money and credit moved along with them. He believed too, however, that the centrality of London to the system was beyond criticism.

Towards the end of the century Arthur Young (1741–1820), a writer almost as prolific as Defoe, took up similar themes. More concerned with the rotation of crops than the diffusion of books and with the spread of innovative agricultural rather than of innovative industrial techniques, Young nevertheless had books in mind when he compared England and France in the decade of the French Revolution, drawing attention to what he called 'the circulation of intelligence' in England. Anticipating more modern metaphors, he leapt beyond steam power to talk of 'electric sensibility'.[55]

In considering such references, it is necessary, as has already been stressed, to lengthen time spans rather than to shorten them. Late-seventeenth-century changes led directly into the eighteenth century, as eighteenth-century changes led directly into the nineteenth century. Each publishing house had its own chronology, which it could never completely control. There were two eighteenth-century dates, however, which stood out for all London's booksellers – 1710, when a law came into effect in England establishing intellectual 'property rights',[56] sometimes called 'The Queen Anne Act', and 1774, when the House of Lords ruled judicially that perpetual copyright had been illegal in England since 1710.

Between the two events, which will be considered in more detail later in this chapter, the markets for books continued to be dominated by metropolitan interests. They had a grip on the book trade, with the main challenge coming from Ireland and from Scotland, the latter a country chafing at their control. Scotland had its own literary scene well-known to some people in London, among them Strahan, who always exploited his Scots connections, for example, printing and publishing Johnson's *A Journey to the Western Islands of Scotland*. In 1762 he had acquired a half share in the so-called Ossian's *Fingal*, a book which acquired a reputation throughout Europe.

Only just in the background of the bookselling and printing houses of London, the Stationers' Company changed its historic role during the course of the eighteenth century, but, nevertheless, retained its prestige

---

55 A. Young, *Travels in France during the Years 1787, 1788 and 1789* (ed. J. Kaplow, 1969), p.160. The Defoe passage is quoted in M. Byrd, *London Transformed: Images of the City in the Eighteenth Century* (1785), p.15. Both are referred to in an American study by J.P. Klancher, *The Making of English Reading Audiences, 1790–1832* (1987).

56 See below, p.124.

The Golden Primer, published in 1819 by William Darton (1755–1819). Darton was an example of a house which specialised in children's titles, as well as other types of literature. Darton was an important publisher of juvenile literature early in the nineteenth century. He had started his firm in the late 1780s and the business, which also branched out into other fields, was continued by his two sons

Bodleian Library, University of Oxford, Opie Collection G59

and, even more important, its substantial corporate assets. The number of Liverymen of the Company reached what was then an all-time high of 517 in 1810.[57] There was still no dissociation between guild and trade as there already was in many other ancient Liveries. It is true that important new publishers emerged, like John Murray I, who had not served an apprenticeship or become a Freeman, but his family successors were all Liverymen,[58] as were the most important new printers of the century.

The Company maintained its twice-yearly dividend on its 'English Stock' for the whole of the century except in two bad years, 1779 and 1780, and the rate of return on it was far higher than that on government securities. By 1800 the holding was double in value what it had been in 1729. Unlike the stock-in-trade of individual publishers, who might hold 'English Stock', as Thomas II did,[59] the revenues accruing to the Company had never been derived from all kinds of books. What would now be called printed ephemera never formed part of it, although almanacs, lucratively

---

57   R. Myers (ed.), *The Stationers' Company: A History of the Later Years, 1800–2000* (2001), p.35.

58   Zachs, *op. cit.*, p.22. Murray I was not exceptional in his debut. Out of the forty-six partners whose names appeared on the title page of the 1792 edition of the *Works* of Johnson, fewer than half were members of the Stationers' Company.

59   See above, p.84.

Stationer's Hall 1750.
An etching by R. Cole,
reproduced in Curwen's
History of Booksellers, 1753

BL 2308.aa.4

linked to each successive year, always did until the landmark year, 1774. The
Company's monopoly in them was then lost, but half a million almanacs
produced by the Company were still being sold at the beginning of the
nineteenth century.

Among the categories of publications which did not figure on the list of
'English Stock' were books concerned with controversial theology, partisan
political writing, and 'news', all in great demand, not least during the first
and last decades of the eighteenth century. It was through these categories,
however, that individual booksellers whose business was expanding, along
with other kinds of trade in print, including advertisements, secured their
profits. They depended, however, before and after 1774 on a characteristic
eighteenth-century combination, not unique to the book trades, of
competition and co-operation and of secrecy and conviviality. It was a
common adage that 'there are "secrets in all trades"', and it was well-known
that within what Defoe called 'the cant of trade' every craft and calling had
'its particular customs, privileges and technicalities of language.'[60]

The 'particular customs' of the book trade, many of them in retrospect
perverse, clustered around sharing in the ownership of 'copies' both in

---

60 For the structures of economic organization T.S. Ashton, *The 18th Century*
    (1955) is still the best synthesis. See also his shorter study, admirably concise
    and compact, *The Industrial Revolution* (1948). 'In the eighteenth century the
    characteristic instrument of social purpose was not the individual nor the
    State but the club' (p.187).

A later agreement of 1853 but showing the use still made by publishers of the eighteenth-century Chapter Coffee House. In this case 'the Partners' agreed the cost and that William Clowes should print 1500 copies of the *London Latin Vocabulary*

Longman Archive

new publications and in old titles. As was shown in Chapter 2, a large undertaking, like *Biographia Britannica* (1747–48), described as being 'in the manner of Mr. Bayle's Historical and Critical Dictionary', might have more than twenty, even more than thirty, publishers' names attached to the publication.[61] At that time, Thomas I was in short-lived partnership with Shewell, and their names came tenth on the list of publishers of the *Biographia*, with Innys first, Tonson nineteenth, and Rivington twenty-second. Even more booksellers (twenty-six) had been associated with the second English edition of Bayle's *Dictionary*, which appeared in five folio volumes between 1734 and 1737. A rival version, which continued to be published until 1741, bore the names of thirteen booksellers. No single publisher had a share in both ventures.

There was a formal sequence of publishing procedures. An initiating publisher – or 'undertaker' – on the production of a 'plan' or 'prospectus', usually bearing the names of the several publishers, who would take a share in the venture, would seek to raise enough funds to enable him to meet paper, printing and other costs. The biggest shares were halves, the smallest one-hundred-and-twenty-eighths. Holding a fractional share signified a willingness to join in the subsequent production of reprints or new editions, and when a reprint or new edition appeared, shares in titles might be acquired by other booksellers.

In this sharing of risks and rewards there was an obvious element of competition as well as co-operation, but the fact that the sales, like the holdings in Stationers' Company stock or other book sales, were open only to members of 'the trade' closed 'the system'. It ensured that books in demand were distributed wholesale only by a small number of London booksellers, what would later be called an oligopoly. Admission to trade sales was strictly limited – by catalogue only. Advance details were given concerning place and time; descriptions of the property to be sold; and

---

61   *A General Description of All Trades, Digested in Alphabetical Order* (1747), p.28.

terms, including credit facilities, an essential requirement. A cash deposit, with three or six months' credit for the balance, was the usual mode of settlement. When a copyright owner died, or left the book trade, his copyrights were offered to the other booksellers at a sale. Widows were accepted as property holders.

The developing use of the word 'copyright', already introduced, and still very much in use in the twenty-first century, always demands detailed examination.[62] The use of an older, long since dead word, 'conger', now, however, demands immediate explanation. It was already in use before Thomas I started his apprenticeship to describe 'a particular Society of Booksellers who put in Joynt Stocks for the Buying and Printing of Copies, and Trading for their Common Advantage'[63] – the arrangement preceded the word – and there was nothing really new about the so-called 'new conger' which Thomas I joined. The Rivingtons were members too. It was called the Chapter, named after the Chapter Coffee House, located on a profitable site next to St. Paul's Ally and a crossing to Ivy Lane. Meetings were held to trade copyrights. Thomas had been quickly accepted as a dealer at the heart of the London book trade.

The names of the Rivingtons as well as that of Thomas II figured in 1772 at the head of the list of publishers of *Two Letters to One of the Associations at the Chapter Coffee-house in London, in which are contained Free Thoughts on the Revival of a Bounty for encouraging the Exportation of Corn*. The adjective 'free' in this thoroughly protectionist title looks strange in the light of the nineteenth-century gospel of free trade. Such combinations of booksellers were to be frowned upon in many quarters in the mid-nineteenth century, but many of the so-called 'Chapter books' which were dealt in at the Chapter House were still selling when Curwen wrote in 1873.[64]

As has been noted, substantial profits could be made out of the system which involved high prices for books and small print runs. Publishers besides Thomas II who left more than £60,000 at their deaths included James Dodsley, Robert's brother, who took over the business in 1759, and Charles Dilly. Charles and Edward Dilly, nonconformist in religion and drawn into close relations with American writers and booksellers, were James Boswell's publishers, described by him as 'my worthy booksellers and friends': at their 'hospitable and well covered table' he had seen 'a greater number of literary men' than at any other London table except that of Sir

---

62   See below, p.124.

63   See Pollard, *The English Market for Printed Books*, pp.26–7; N. Hodgson and C. Blagden, *The Notebook of Thomas Bennet and Henry Clements, 1688–1719* (1956), pp.67–70. Curwen, *op. cit.*, p.297, suggested that the term might have been derived from the conger eel and implied that 'the association, collectively, would swallow up all smaller fish'.

64   Curwen, *op. cit.*, p.67.

Joshua Reynolds.[65] Edward Dilly is said to have 'literally talked himself to death' in 1779: it was at one of his parties in the Poultry that he introduced Johnson to the radical John Wilkes.

Raising subscriptions from outside the trade – and these could be organised by authors of books, often with publishers acting as collecting agents – were designed to secure the same purpose as congers, and while this method was by no means obsolete at the end of the century, there was more willingness now on the part of individual producers to accept their own risks. Moreover, as banking and transport facilities improved (country banks; better roads; more speedy postal services) and as the 'reading public' – and the population as a whole – surged, the most established of them had generated sufficient capital to embark on further ventures.[66] Yet joint publication did not disappear. The consortium that produced Johnson's *Dictionary* was first widened at the time of the publication of the fourth edition in 1773, when the imprint now carried the names of twenty-five shareholding booksellers: in 1799 the number was twenty-eight, increasing to forty-one in 1806.[67] As late as 1851, no fewer than fifty-six publishers held shares in Gibbon's *Decline and Fall of the Roman Empire*.[68]

~

That was long after the period focused on in this chapter ends. Before the period began, in 1705, nineteen years before Thomas I set up shop, John Dunton (1659–1733) published his *Life and Errors*, described by him as a 'vindication', which opened up the first publishing scenario. Long used as a source of information, it has seldom been regarded as completely reliable, either about individuals involved in the book trade or about the practices of the trade, including the 'conger', a word that he used. Most recently it has

---

65   Quoted in SOB, p.226. Boswell wrote an ode to Charles Dilly (GM, Vol. 61, 1791, p.367).

66   See 'The Relish for Reading', in P.J. Korshin (ed.), *The Widening Circle, Essays on the Circulation of Literature in Eighteenth-Century Europe* (1976) and 'Middle-Class Literacy in Eighteenth-century England', in R.F. Brissenden (ed.), *Studies in the Eighteenth Century* (1968).

67   J.H. Skedd and G.J. Kolb, *Dr Johnson's Dictionary. Essays in the Biography of a Book* (1955), pp.126–33. Lists of names, like sales figures, should be treated with caution. C.J. Longman noted that of the twenty-nine booksellers named on the title page of Vol. 1 of Bishop Gibson's *Preservative against Popery* (1738) nine were no longer in business and most of them were dead (CC, pp.9–10). See for Murray lists, Zachs, *op. cit.*, p.81

68   C. Blagden, 'Publishing, An Historical Survey', in the *National Provincial Bank Review*, No. 1 (1960), p.12.

been turned to for Dunton's judgements on the 'mentalities' of his time.[69]

Not the least interesting feature of his adventurous life was that already in 1690, five years before the lapse of censorship, he had launched a pioneering twice-weekly magazine, *The Athenian Gazette*, which lasted for nearly six years and set out 'to satisfie all *ingenious and* curious *Enquirers* into *Speculations*, Divine, Moral and National, &c'.[70] Answers to readers' queries were provided by what Dunton called the 'Athenian Society', number one was devoted entirely to love, one (13) devoted entirely to love and marriage. The *Gazette*, which spawned a host of early-eighteenth-century derivatives using the word 'Athenian', like the *Athenian Catechism* (1704), the *Athenian Spy* (1704, 1709 and 1720) and the *Athenian Sport* (1707), not to mention the *Athenian Oracle* (1710), prepared the way for much that was to come in a striking diversity of eighteenth-century forms of communications – not only novels and newspapers, but essays, periodicals, 'correspondence columns' and prints and caricatures.[71]

Dunton quite deliberately broke with tradition, prizing everything that was new:

We are all tainted with the Athenian Itch
News, and new Things do the whole World Bewitch.[72]

Yet if Dunton himself was bewitched, traditionalists – and they were an articulate group – were not, and the tensions between them, well captured by Swift, themselves stimulated many new modes of writing. Their very diversity was an expression of the powerful drives behind 'modern literature'.

~

In a later publishing scenario, publishers very different from the Dodsleys,

---

69 The beginning of the long full title of Dunton's book, *The life and errors of J.D. Late Citizen of London Written by himself in solitude,* should be compared with the title of *Robinson Crusoe,* ending as it does with the words 'in solitude'. A new American reprint of Dunton was published in 1969. See Hunter, *op. cit.,* esp. pp.99–106.

70 The *Athenian Gazette,* No. 1, 16 March 1690. The second number, proceeding, like the first, by question and answer, was called the *Athenian Mercury* 'to oblige Authority'. See for studies of Dunton G.D. McEwen, *The Oracle of the Coffee House* (1972), and S. Parks, *John Dunton and the English Book Trade* (1976). Dunton spent a brief time peddling books across the Atlantic in New England in the 1680s. He once said that if he had been able to start his life again he would never have kept a shop.

71 Among the shares in the titles that Thomas I bought from Taylor in 1724 were four volumes of the *Athenian Oracle,* and *Athenian Sports,* sub-titled *2000 Paradoxes.*

72   The couplet, quoted in many places by Dunton, was written by Robert Wilde in *Poems on Several Occasions* (1683), p.83.

the Tonsons and the Longmans were the Newberys, who later in the century kept off the street and out of the debtors' prison the novelist and dramatist Oliver Goldsmith (1728–1774), a writer who was suspicious of most metropolitan booksellers and publishers. The Newberys identified new market opportunities, opening up access to books as Dunton had done, and had the organisation and the drive to exploit them. One of the reasons for briefly tracing their history is that their success depended on their approaching children's publishing at a time when the role of children in society was changing significantly.[73] Thomas I and Thomas II had much to learn from them.

Both their growth and their decline were directly related to the context in which they operated. John Newbery I (1713–1767) specialised in children's books and patent medicines, making much of his fortune, as many booksellers did, not out of the former but the latter, moving his premises from the Bible and Crown bookshop near Temple Bar to the Bible and Sun in St. Paul's Churchyard. His *A Little Pretty Pocket-Book* of 1744, price 6*d*. (or 8*d*. for an edition which included a bell and pin-cushion), was a landmark. Intended for 'the instruction and amusement of little Master Tommy and pretty Miss Polly', it set the tone.[74]

Twenty-one years later Goldsmith supplied one of Newbery's most famous titles, *The History of Little Goody Two-Shoes* (1765), said to be the first children's novel, which ran through twenty-nine 'editions' between 1765 and 1800. It was dedicated 'to all young gentlemen and ladies who are good or who intend to be good'. *The Lilliputian Magazine* (1751), costing 3*d*., was certainly the first children's magazine, and was picked out by the politician George Canning and the poet and essayist Leigh Hunt (1784–1859) as a formative influence on the encouragement of the reading habit. 'These sort of publications must be confessed to have greatly contributed to lay the foundation of that literary taste and thirst for knowledge which now pervades all classes.'[75]

Newbery enjoyed his success without waiting for the verdicts of posterity. In *The Twelfth Year Gift*, published in the last year of his life, he exclaimed 'Trade and Plumb-cake, for ever. Huzza!'. After his death,

---

73   See J.H. Plumb, 'The New World of Children in Eighteenth-Century England', in *Past and Present*, Vol. 67 (1975), pp.64–93; M.F. Thwaite, *From Primer to Pleasure, an Introduction to the History of Children's Books in England, from the Invention of Printing to 1900* (1966); F.J.H. Darton, *Children's Books in England* (3rd edn., revised B. Alderson, 1982); G. Avery and J. Briggs, *Children and Their Books* (1989); M.V. Jackson, *Engines of Instruction, Mischief and Magic: Children's Literature in its Beginnings to 1839* (1989); and J.C. Steward, *The New Child: British Art and the Origins of Modern Childhood*, Berkeley (1995).

74   *Penny Morning Post*, 18 June 1744.

75   TDPP, p.838.

his son Francis (1765–1781) set up business in Paternoster Row (No. 15), at first in partnership with Thomas Carman, his step-brother, who broke the Stationers' Company monopoly of almanacs in 1774. His cousin, also called Francis, was a publisher too.[76] All the Newberys, 'ingenious advertisers', were willing and able to quote poets like Dryden and Pope in selling their wares:

> 'Children, like tender Oziers, take the bow,
> And as they first are fashioned, alway grow'

or

> 'Just as the twig is bent the tree's inclined;
> 'Tis education forms the vulgar mind.'

The Newberys in their different generations also produced an impressive range of 'serious' books, such as a seven-volume *The Circle of the Sciences* (1746-7), the first children's encyclopaedia, which included volumes on grammar, arithmetic, rhetoric, poetry, logic, geography and chronology 'made easy'.

The Ladies' Complete Pocket Book (1772) sold 4,000 copies in three days, and Goldsmith's play *She Stoops to Conquer* (1773) is a play still performed. New editions of Daniel Paterson's *A New and Accurate Description of all the Direct and Principal Cross Roads in Great Britain* (1771) which the Newberys first published were later to be published by Longman.[77] It was a valuable property which Francis Newbery and Carman were prepared to protect through the law. The case they brought to establish their copyright was an important one, if only because bookselling, as we have seen, depended on improved communications, the Paterson theme.

The Longmans had other Newbery links besides Paterson. They had no link, however, with publishers such as Francis Noble, who with his brothers built up in parallel a flourishing and many-sided business which involved publishing fiction (the Nobles were once called 'novel manufacturers'[78]), bookselling (including the sale of second-hand books and the unsold stock of neighbours and competitors), and 'library lending'. Francis Noble's library premises, located in Covent Garden, specialised in current publications, and it seems appropriate in the light of mid-twentieth-century social history that later in the eighteenth century, another Noble,

Catalogue of Francis Noble's Circulating Library consisting of above 20,000 volumes – at Otway's Head, Gray's-Inn Gate, Holborn (c.1737)

Bodleian Library, University of Oxford: John Johnson Collection

---

76 See C. Welsh, *A Bookseller of the Last Century, Being Some Account of the Life of John Newbery and the Books he Published with a Notice of the Life of Later Newberys* (1885); S. Roscoe, *John Newbery and His Successors, 1740–1814: A Bibliography* (1973); and J.R. Townsend, *John Newbery and His Books* (1995).

77 There were two Paterson publications – *A New and Accurate Description* and *A Travelling Dictionary: or Alphabetical Tables of the Distance of all the Principal Cities, Borough, Market and Sea-port Towns in Great Britain, from Each Other*.

78 See Nichols, *op. cit.*, Vol. 3, p.648 and J. Raven, 'The Noble Brothers and Popular Publishing', in TL, 6th series, Vol. 12/14 (1990), pp.293-365.

his brother Samuel, managed a circulating library, located far away from Paternoster Row in Carnaby Street, fashion centre two hundred years later.

Fashion counted for far more in the Nobles' eighteenth-century publishing business than it did in the Longman business, although Noble in one of his advertisements, casting 'novelty' aside, was at pains to note how 'fully sensible' the public were to 'obnoxious innovations of any kind'. Before the decade when Samuel Noble flourished, Thomas II had already established himself, in Dell's words, as 'on the whole the best of the *Paternoster* tribe',[79] a tribe that included the dissenter Joseph Johnson, before and after he was sent to gaol, who was accused of supporting 'obnoxious innovations' both of an intellectual and religious kind, Ralph Griffiths (1720–1803), who published *Fanny Hill* and later the *Monthly Review*, and George Robinson, who acquired the *Lady's Magazine* in 1771 and entertained in his shop ladies as different as Mrs. Thrale, Mrs. Inchbald and Mrs. Radcliffe.

~

A very different figure from all three, James Lackington (1746–1815), who never belonged to any tribe but who sold many of Johnson's and even more of Longman's books, is still famous, like Dunton before him, for what he wrote as well as for what he said. He was not on intimate terms with any publisher or author, but it was he who wrote the most famous of all eighteenth-century bookselling autobiographies, set out, like Richardson's *Clarissa*, in the form of letters to a friend, with verses cited at their headings. The autobiography appeared in what was called its tenth edition in 1810.[80] There is a realistic strain, if also a touch of fantasy, in Lackington's self-assessment of his own career, 'Cobbler turned Bookseller', for his career had an exceptional dynamic of its own. There was ample evidence of competitiveness and ambition in almost every letter that he wrote. Born in 1746, the son of bookless parents in Wellington, Somerset, he arrived in London and set up shop in 1774, already identified as a critical year in

79 See J. Raven, *British Fiction, 1750–1770, with a chronological Check-list of Prose Fiction Printed in Britain and Ireland* (1987). As well as publishing novels, the Nobles bought up the unused stock of their competitors.

80 J. Lackington, *Memoirs of the Forty-Five First Years of the Life of James Lackington, Bookseller* (printed for the author, 1791). It has been suggested that for not uncommon promotional reasons Lackington moved straight from the third to the seventh edition (1794). See 'Small Profits do Great Things: James Lackington and Eighteenth-century Bookselling' in *Studies in Eighteenth-century Culture*, Vol. 5 (1976); and F.M. Honour, 'James Lackington, Proprietor, Temple of Muses' in *The Journal of Literary History* (1967). In 1804 Lackington also published *The Confessions of J. Lackington, Late Bookseller, at the Temple of Muses*. In his preface to the second and later editions of his *Memoirs* he noted that would-be readers could not buy the book from other booksellers, who called it 'waste paper'.

the history of the book trade. From the start he was a bookseller, not a publisher;[81] and in 1793 he opened a huge new bookstore at one of the corners of Finsbury Square which he called the 'Temple of the Muses'.

With its dome, flag and bold sign over the entrance, 'Cheapest Booksellers in the World', an adjective that never stirred Longman's ambitions, the Temple of the Muses was designed with a great staircase, circular galleries and a series of 'lounging rooms'. Women were prominent among Lackington's customers. Every book on offer – and they were all catalogued and given numbers – was sold at the lowest possible price. Lackington allowed no credit, and attributed his success to his ready-money mode of business and to the cheapness of his prices. His carriage bore the motto 'Small profits do great things'.[82] The main sources of Lackington's

Contemporary engraving of *The Temple of the Muses* in Finsbury Square (opened in 1793), from *The Repository of Arts, Literature, Commons, Manufactures, Fashions and Politics*, 1809–15

Charles Knight remembered the Temple having an 'imposing frontage. A dome rises from the centre on the top of which a flag is flying...Over the principal entrance is inscribed "Cheapest Booksellers in the World, where above Half a Million of Volumes are constantly on Sale" *Shadows of the Old Booksellers*, Charles Knight 1865

BL 119.f.1 plate opposite p.251

---

81   There was a class of books which at first he would not sell, books written by 'free thinkers': 'I would neither read them myself, nor sell them to others.' 'Such', he wrote later, 'was my ignorance, bigotry, superstition, or what you please.' Lackington had become a Methodist when young, but left Methodism later, quoting a Bristol sermon of John Wesley, which he had heard, that he could 'never keep a bookseller six months in his flock'. (SOB, p.257). In his last years Lackington returned to Wesleyan Methodism and built and endowed three chapels.

82   *Ibid*, p.260.

cheap books were publishers' private sales of remainders: at one single afternoon's sale he claimed to have purchased books worth £5,000. He had been willing, however, to break with the convention, which he called 'a kind of standing order amongst the trade', that 'in case any one was known to sell articles under the publication price', such a person was to be excluded from future sales. (In America Knox had been given this warning by Thomas II.)

Owners of 'rights in copies' might object to Lackington's methods, which were to be frowned upon by mainstream publishers in the nineteenth century, but he himself took pride in having been 'highly instrumental in diffusing that general desire for READING, now so prevalent among the inferior orders of society'.[83] If only for this reason, he considered himself a *great man*, acknowledging a debt, almost in the vein of Dunton, to 'Messrs ENVY, DETRACTION and co' for his 'present prosperity', the only debt that he was not prepared to pay.[84] The inscription under his portrait in the frontispiece in his *Memoirs* notes that 'a few years since' he 'began business with five pounds' and now sold 'One Hundred Thousand volumes yearly'. At no time would the Longmans ever have boasted of either their circulations or their wealth in this way.

Writing about publishers of new books, Lackington used the word 'publisher' in a way, already described, that it would never have been used in the early century. In seeking to maintain a balance when judging their intentions as publishers and the efforts of their authors, he observed that it was 'owing to the encouragement of booksellers that the public [a word that mattered to him] is possessed of that valuable work Johnson's Dictionary'. The 'same liberality to the doctor', he added, had been shown when he produced 'his edition of Shakespeare, and the English Poets':[85] it would always 'reflect honour on the parties'; and 'so sensible was the doctor of this' that he once asserted – although he was never consistent in all this – that booksellers were the best Maecenae.[86] Lackington also referred to the generosity shown to Ephraim Chambers by his publisher, although he did not mention Longman by name. Lackington maintained:

---

83 *Memoirs*, Letter XXXV. In the same letter he described how he had been 'initiated into the various manoeuvres practised by booksellers and that he had been to many trade sales. In Letter XXXVII he noted that 'the sale of books in general has increased prodigiously within the last twenty years', and he referred to book clubs as well as bookshops and (in later editions) to circulating libraries and Sunday Schools.

84 Letter XXXII.

85 See above, p.69, for the very limited role of Johnson himself in producing these editions.

86 Letter XXVI.

Frequently the money which is paid for the copy is but trifling compared with the expense of printing, paper, advertising &c, and hundreds of instances may be adduced of publishers having sustained great losses, and many have been made bankrupts, through their liberality in purchasing manuscripts and publishing them; and on the other hand it must be acknowledged that some publishers have made great fortunes by their copy-rights, but their number is comparatively small.

He added that while, on the one hand, some authors had been paid too little, 'on the other hand' many books had been published that 'were not worth the expenses of paper and printing'.[87]

~

Longman books inevitably made their way to the Temple of Muses: at one time Lackington claimed to have had 'TEN THOUSAND COPIES of Watts Psalms' in his shop. In another place he mentioned Abraham Rees's *Dictionary*, noting that before Rees was engaged to revise and improve Chambers's *Dictionary* 'very large sums for that purpose had from time to time been obtained from the proprietors by persons who have never fulfilled their engagements'. Rees did.[88] Such judgements are revealing, but to learn more fully how Thomas II as a major publisher fitted into a bigger picture it is necessary to turn to other less dramatic sets of reminiscences than Lackington's, notably those of William West, already drawn upon.[89]

West's account of his own life began with the start of his apprenticeship. Fresh from his village, he had crossed Blackfriars Bridge on his way to No. 54 Paternoster Row to work with Thomas Evans (1739–1803), a prosperous bookseller, whose own first job had been as a porter to the Ludgate Street booksellers, W. Johnston. West could only just descry St. Paul's 'with its dome towering amid the smoke and fog that surrounded it', and in order to reach Evans's shop he had to approach it through 'a dark and narrow entry'. Appropriately, memories of *Robinson Crusoe* came back to him, for none of the London landmarks meant much to him. 'I had no more idea of the features and character of the plans in the interior of a man-of-war', he reminisced, 'or of Robinson Crusoe's island'.[90]

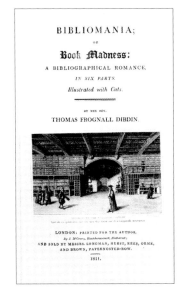

Bibliomania; or Book Madness: A bibliographical romance in six parts. Illustrated with cuts. By the Rev.Thomas Frognall Dibdin (1776–1847) printed by J. M'creery 'and sold by Messrs. Longman, Hurst, Rees, Orme and Brown, Paternoster Row'. This was the 1811 edition, first published in 1809 with many further editions

Longman Archive

---

87 *Ibid.*

88 See above, p.58.

89 The full title of West's *Fifty Years' Recollections of an old Bookseller* (Cork, 1835) continued *consisting of Anecdotes, Characteristic Sketches, and Original Traits and Eccentricities of Authors, Artists, Actors, Books, Booksellers, and of the Periodical Press for the Last Half Century*. West included in his book a long letter to him from Rees (pp.253–77).

90 *Fifty Years' Recollections*, p.250.

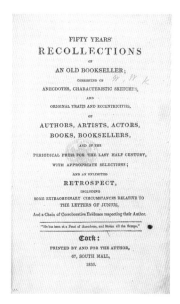

Title page of *Fifty Years'*
Recollections of an old Bookseller,
1835

'Fifty years' recollections of
an old bookseller; consisting
of anecdotes, characteristic
sketches, and original
traits and eccentricities of
Authors, Artists, Actors,
Books, Booksellers, and of the
Periodical Press for the last
half century ... including some
extraordinary circumstances
relative to the letters of Junius,
and a chain of corroborative
evidence respecting their
Author ... and an unlimited
retrospect, etc. ' [The preface
signed: W. W., i.e. William
West.]

Cork: printed by and for the
author, 1835.

BL 819.g.39

Robinson Crusoe was established by then as 'one of those novels which
may [be] read not only with pleasure, but also with profit' by children, often
in shortened form, at a time when abridgements were frowned upon or
even forbidden as anthologies had been in the seventeenth century.[91] West
seemed to have learnt from the text. He described his own state of mind,
Crusoe-like, in a manner that Thomas I never described his. On the day
when West first arrived in Paternoster Row, he was 'pervaded with a kind
of awe at the gloomy appearance of the stores of literature before me'.
West remained apprehensive about what he might find in the bookselling
district of London, 'the great mart of bustle and gay confusion', but he was
happy to be 'snugly fixed in the field of literature'.

He was apprenticed not to Thomas Evans, who succeeded to the
business of Howes, Clark and Collins at No. 32 Paternoster Row and
who belonged to the Musicians' Company, but to Robert Colley, who was
a Freeman and Liveryman of the Stationers' Company.[92] It was the then
Master of the Stationers' Company, Alderman Thomas Wright, in the
same year Lord Mayor of London, who presented West with the customary
Bible.[93] After his initiation West sat at the head of the table as a 'prenticed
king' at a formal dinner. He wore a cocked hat, and for the first time in
his life was confronted with 'ardent spirits'. There was nothing gloomy
about this. The conviviality had begun. Whatever else was happening to
the Stationers' Company, it was abandoning few of its ancient rituals at its
initiation ceremonies, and West approved of them. He was proud too of the
place of the Company in the corporate life of the City of London.

West went on to give a lively account of Thomas Evans, for whom he
worked after becoming a Liveryman, describing him as the 'third bookseller
in England': the House of Longman, where one of his nephews was a clerk,
came first. For West, Evans was 'a man of the most regular habits' with
diverse interests, including the proprietorship of a newspaper, the *Morning
Chronicle*, launched in 1769,[94] which kept him in touch with topicality as

---

91   TDPP, p.618.

92   West states *en passant* that his elder brother had been bound as an apprentice
to Evans 'about 1778' and that it was after his brother left Evans that he himself
joined the Evans household.

93   Wright, a wholesale stationer working in partnership with Alderman Gill in
Abchurch Lane, presented the Company with a large silver tea urn in 1786, and
when he died twelve years later bequeathed £2,000 for another ornament. He
left £300,000 in his will.

94   Nichols, *op. cit.,* Vol. III, pp.720–1. In 1790 Evans's only son married a daughter
of the second Archibald Hamilton, a printer, whose father had worked with
Strahan. Along with Smollett, Hamilton established the *Critical Review* in 1756.
Hamilton was a friend of John Murray I, who occasionally wrote reviews in the
Critical Review.

did the reports of Select Committees of the House of Commons, some of them deemed secret, which he also published. His 'extreme punctuality', West observed, a quality that he particularly admired, 'procured him the best and the most select customers in England, Ireland and Scotland'. Yet Evans was also responsible for the *Antiquarian Repertory*, and religion figured prominently in his list.

An increasing interest in antiquity remained topical, and there were few counties which did not acquire their own histories: 'the clergy now-a-days study all history but that of the Bible', an observer claimed in 1767.[95] Nevertheless, religion and politics converged at the end of the eighteenth century as they had done at the beginning, if in a somewhat different pattern. 'At present', a reviewer wrote in 1792 to Ralph Griffiths, then known for his ownership of the highly successful *Monthly Review*, 'I see nothing to expect but either the horrors of civil commotions, or the dead calm of terror, produced by inquisitorial oppression.'[96]

Among the anonymous books of 1789 marked as 'sold by Longman' and, in this case, one Norwich bookseller, was *An Alarm to the Public, and a Bounty Promised to Every Loyal Subject Who Will Come Forward to Repel the Enemy*. It was printed in Yarmouth. Norwich had been the first provincial city in England to launch a newspaper, the *Norwich Post*, in 1701. One named Evans author, Richard Watson, Bishop of Llandaff (1737–1816), whose widely read *Apology for Christianity* appeared in 1776, was to be drawn deep into his own time when in 1796, in the wake of the French Revolution, he wrote *An Apology for the Bible*, a one-volume 'answer' to Tom Paine's *Rights of Man*, itself an 'answer' to Edmund Burke's *Reflections on the Revolution in France* (1790).

Burke's response, which went through eleven editions, has passed into history. So has the poet Wordsworth's open *Letter to the Bishop of Llandaff*. Watson's has not. Paine reached a new readership when the price of his *Rights of Man* fell. Sales of Paine's Part 1, a pamphlet priced at three shillings and sixpence, the same as Burke's *Reflections*, were estimated at 50,000, but an inexpensive second edition (1792), priced at sixpence, sold between 200,000 and 500,000. Paine had sensibly refused to dispose of the copyright for a thousand guineas.[97] Few copyrights were worth so much.

An Alarm to the Public and a Bounty Promised to Every Loyal Subject who will come Forward to Repel the Enemy. Arms and Accoutrements provided for every man gratis. Printed and sold by F Bush in Yarmouth, sold also by T. N. Longman in London and J. March in Norwich, 1789

BL 8135.d.81 (2)

95 Quoted in Paul Langford, *A Polite and Commercial People, England, 1727–1783* (1989), p.97.

96 Quoted in Roper, *op. cit.*, p.172.

97 See M.D. Conway (ed.), *The Writings of Thomas Paine* (1895), Vol. 3, p.64. The extent of working-class readership – the range of estimates is extraordinarily wide – is covered in R.K. Webb, *The British Working Class Reader, 1790–1848* (1955). For the background see A. Cobban (ed.), *The Debate on the French Revolution, 1789–1800* (2nd edn., 1960). For British radicalism see A. Briggs, *The Age of Improvement* (2001 edn.), p.115 and A. Goodwin, *The Friends of Liberty* (1979).

In a passage describing his own place in the Evans business West did not for the most part pick out such highlights in publishing history. Instead he drew lessons from them, recording, perhaps more usefully for the historian, some of the routine duties that he was required to discharge. On almost all weekdays between 1785 and 1787 he would go round to Longman to collect 'various books for the country orders', and for that reason he was called, 'as in all wholesaler booksellers' shops, a collector'. 'In this department', he explained, 'almost every apprentice is at first very properly initiated in the rudiments of his business by purchasing such books as his employer may not have in his establishment for the supplying of country orders. By this means he readily acquires a knowledge of the stock, habits, manners and connexions of most other houses; of the value of books; and becomes fitted for a future active in the in-door department.'[98] Thomas II had made his own children follow this career pattern by starting with book sales.

Every Sunday West and his fellow employees went over the Evans accounts which were kept with the Bank of England, noting meticulously 'upon a large sheet of parchment' every penny 'undercharged or overcharged to a country correspondent ... to be corrected in the next invoice'. The most exciting regular time in the month for both Evans and West was 'Magazine Night', usually held on the last and first days of each month, for it was then, working until one or two o'clock in the morning, that the bookseller and his assistant packed their country orders including the periodicals on which the fortunes of many books depended.[99] Already there was a monthly and even a seasonal pattern, although Christmas did not yet figure prominently as it was to do less than a century later.

There was the same excitement nearby at 39 Paternoster Row, where West got to know well Christopher Brown, an employee 'nursed in the cradle of the wholesale book trade', who had left Evans to serve Thomas II until his death and after him Thomas Norton Longman until he was too old to do so. Evans offered to advance money to Brown to set up his own business, but 'he constantly refused, saying he could not think of

---

98   *The Aldine Magazine of Biography, Bibliography, Criticism and the Arts,* Letters to my Son at Rome, Letter V, 22 Dec. 1838. The address on the letter was given as 'Aldine Chambers, Paternoster Row', where it was 'published for the proprietors by Simpkin, Marshall & Company'. The Aldine Chambers were built on the site gutted by fire in 1770. Patrons of the Magazine included Cosmo Orme and Thomas Brown, future partners in the Longman business (see below, Chapter 4). Its editors acknowledged a debt to their 'brethren of the Press, metropolitan and provincial'.

99   For later accounts of Magazine Night or Magazine Day, see one by Charles Knight (KP, pp.263–4), quoting Coleridge, 'There is no bustle to our minds half so agreeable as the bustle of Paternoster Row on the last day of the month'.

leaving Mr. Longman: nor did he ever attempt to do so'.[100] By the end of the eighteenth century, with the 'vast extension of the wholesale foreign and domestic trade, and a new general system of publishing modern works', there were new connections, provincial and international. Before moving to Longman, Brown had succeeded John Harris as Evans's chief assistant after Harris had moved to work with Murray. Harris had left Evans earlier in his life in order to start business as a bookseller on his own account at Bury St Edmunds, in West's words, 'one of the most respectable concerns, in its way, in the Kingdom'.

Not surprisingly, West noted with pride how by the time that he wrote his autobiography in early-Victorian England several of the youths who had worked with Evans had become 'the ornaments of the profession'. And, without mentioning technical change, he generalised sensibly about progress in publishing:

> Numerous changes have taken place in the publishing and printing business since I first haunted Paternoster Row. Paper, type, ink, compositorship, and press work, have advanced from almost the lowest to nearly the highest degree of perfection.[101]

Ink was a significant item in this cluster: machines did not figure in it at all.[102]

West lived long enough to put things into perspective – or to try to do so. Griffiths, whose own life, as we have seen, spanned years of contrasting experiences, referred as early as 1766 to the increasing tendency of booksellers to become publishers.[103] 'We seem to live in an age when retailers of every kind of ware aspire to be original manufacturers, and particularly in literature'. It was not – and is not – easy, however, to fit Thomas II or his near-neighbours the Rivingtons into the categories of booksellers that Griffiths outlined.[104] They remained wholesale booksellers as well as publishers. Old style retailers did not fit in either. Nor did the maligned chapmen or chapwomen who had distributed books

When Longman II died in 1797, he left £300 to his 'faithful servant' Christopher Brown, described by West as 'a valued assistant'. Brown has also been described as a 'shopman' and he played an important part in the management of Longman's overseas business. In 1803 he was left a large fortune by a great friend and bookseller of forty years, Thomas Evans. Brown died in 1807, and his son, Thomas was apprenticed to the House in 1793. This engraving is taken from West's *Years of an Old Bookseller* 1837

Longman Archive

---

100 When Evans died in 1803, he bequeathed the bulk of his fortune to Brown. Seeking a modest funeral, as Thomas II did, he asked to be buried without a coffin or shroud and that the whole of his funeral expenses should not exceed forty shillings (Nichols, *op. cit.*, Vol. II, p.721).

101 *Fifty Years' Recollections*, p.251.

102 See Professor G. Wilson, 'Paper, Pen and Ink: An Excursion in Technology', in *Macmillans Magazine*, Vol. I (1859), pp.31–9. Cf. J. Alden, 'Pills and Publishing: Some Notes on the English Book Trade, 1660–1775' in TL, 5th series, Vol. VII (1952), pp.21–35.

103 See above, p.116.

104 *Monthly Review*, Vol. 34, June 1766.

that the poor could afford to buy were losing ground, as pedlars, hawkers and 'flying stationers' had done.[105] West drew attention not only to well-remembered publishers like the Rivingtons, George Robinson, who had been an assistant with the Rivingtons, and Phillips, but to new publishers, often operating in established bookselling premises, like John Harrison, John Cook(e) and Alexander Hogg.

The first of these dealt in periodical publications, as Griffiths did, and like the second, in cheap reprints of novels, among them *Robinson Crusoe*, and plays, a profitable line of business, and the third, who lived next door to Cook(e) in Paternoster Row, in religious works issued in weekly sixpenny parts. Harrison, West noted, published not only *The Novelist's Magazine*, in a hundred illustrated volumes, but also the *Sacred Classics*, the *Musical Magazine*, the *British Magazine*, the *Wits' Magazine*, the *Pocket Magazine* and the *Lady's Pocket Magazine*, the last of which included engravings by J.W.M. Turner. Thomas Dibdin was one of his contributors. Cook(e) produced cheap weekly serial publications 'adorned with cuts', one of them Hume's *History of England*, which he published after the copyright shared by Cadell and Longman had expired.

All three publishers – and some others – took full advantage of the House of Lords judgement in 1774, declaring perpetual copyright illegal. One of the others, John Bow, a cheap reprint publisher, moved his premises to Paternoster Row. There was now a more open market as book prices fell. So, too, did the size of books. It became feasible to publish abridgements and adaptations of texts as well as anthologies. Among these was Roach's *Beauties* [and 'beauties' was a favourite word for anthologists] *of the Poets of Great Britain* (1793), sold in twenty-four illustrated parts, each priced at sixpence. It listed the names of twenty-four authors in its title and was 'printed by and for J. Roach, Russell Court, opposite to the Pitt Door of the New Theatre Royal, Drury Lane'. Cooke's 'cheap and elegant pocket editions' of 'the most esteemed works in the English Language' were advertised not only for their low prices but because they were 'superbly embellished'.

~

By the last decades of the eighteenth century use of the word 'copyright' had come into general use. It was a new word with abstruse connotations, but with practical implications for all publishers whether they were initiating new titles or dealing in reprints. Once used, it appeared thereafter in all publishing history.[106] Significantly, the word itself had not figured in

---

105 See M. Spufford, *Small Books and Pleasant Histories* (1985) and D. Vincent, *Literature and Popular Culture in England* (1989). There is ample evidence of reading by the poor before Tom Paine.

106 The legal niceties were explored brilliantly, if not definitively, before the end of the nineteenth century by the essayist Augustine Birrell in *Seven Lectures on the Law and History of Copyright in Books* (1899).

what later came to be called the world's first Copyright Act of 1710, which 'vested' the 'sole liberty' of printing and reprinting 'copy' (a word that dated back to the fifteenth century) for a term of fourteen years from the date of publication and for a further fourteen years if the author were then still alive. A term of twenty-one years was set for old books whose authors were dead. This meant that 'the sole liberty' to publish them would expire in 1731. The length of the terms set out in the Act was short, echoing patent provision.

The word 'right' did not appear in the 1710 Act, which referred to 'liberty' in what was then a resonant traditional sense, and the word 'copy' was used only in its old, though still current, sense to describe 'a document which is to be copied'.[107] In the first draft of the legislation there had been a reference to books as 'the undoubted property' of their authors, but at the committee stage, after pressure from the metropolitan book trade, this reference, to be of fundamental importance in the future, was omitted. Moreover, the authority of the Stationers' Company was re-affirmed. The Company's Register was to validate the record of copy ownership.[108]

Pope, who, like Defoe, knew a great deal about the Act, which directly affected him and which came into effect in April 1710, used the word 'copyright' in a letter of 1732,[109] but Johnson did not include it in his *Dictionary*. The *Oxford English Dictionary* gives no example of the use of the word 'copyright' before 1735, but quotes William Blackstone's employment of it in his *Commentaries* (1767). It was not until the nineteenth century that copyright could be defined concisely, but in the late-eighteenth century, when the word was new, authors were already beginning to think of their writings as literary property. 'Surely if there be *Degrees of Right*', wrote a pamphleteer in 1788, 'that of Authors seemeth to have the Advantage over most others: their property being, in the truest sense, their own, as acquired by a long and painful Exercise of that very Faculty which denominateth us MEN'.[110]

Owners of other forms of cultural capital were treated similarly

---

107 The Act referred to 'the sole liberty of printing and reprinting', not to copyright. This was left open to any person, author or publisher. See M. Rose, *Authors and Owners, the Invention of Copyright* (1993) and B. Kaplan, *An Unhurried View of Copyright* (1967).

108 For the tangled politics behind the Act see J. Feather, 'The Book Trade in Politics: the Making of the Copyright Act of 1710', in PH, Vol. VIII (1980), pp.19–44.

109 See D. Foxon, *Pope and the Early Eighteenth-Century Book Trade* (1991) and the review of it by P. Rogers, 'The Business of Poetry', in *TLS*, 26 April 1991.

110 W. Warburton, *A Letter from an Author to a Member of Parliament* in his collected *Works*, Vol. 7 (1788), p.925. William Warburton (1798-1779), a friend and executor of Pope, was a prolific writer and fierce controversialist. In 1759 he became Bishop of Gloucester.

too. Thus, in 1734 copyright protection of engravings was introduced, with copyright in sculpture to follow in 1797, in lectures (a major mode of communication) in 1835, and in sheet music and musical compositions in 1842, the year of an important new Copyright Act. Under the system other forms of protection were upheld through what later would come to be regarded as 'restrictive practices'. Demarcation lines were insisted upon by publishers. Injunctions were sought to prevent rebel publishers from publishing even ancient texts. In the long run, with authors rather than publishers in mind, the *Oxford English Dictionary* was to define copyright straightforwardly in the twentieth century as 'the exclusive right given by law for a certain term of years to an author, composer (or his assignee) to print, publish and sell copies of his original work'.[111]

The Act of 1710 employed quite different terminology, and although it is right to consider it as 'a response' to 'the intreaties of those whose interests were concerned', the metropolitan publishers, it was described at the time as an act for the 'encouragement of learning'; and it contained pertinent clauses, later to prove highly contentious, stating that nine copies of every new book or revised edition should be delivered to the Warehouse Keeper of the Stationers' Company to be forwarded to the Royal Library, the two English and the four Scottish universities, the Faculty of Advocates and Sion College. In this respect the privileges of the Stationers' Company were reaffirmed. Indeed, it was now made the agent of distribution as well as of registration and of the 'policing' of the Act. There was one novel element in the Act which was to be dropped in 1739. On appeal the price of a book was to be controlled. There is no evidence that it ever was.

In these circumstances, booksellers continued to act after 1710 as they had done before the passing of the Act, for example, trading in shares in old books, not only individual books but collections of books, on the assumption that they would not lose their value. In 1731, led by Tonson II, they were willing to go to law if necessary, to support their claims to old titles like Shakespeare's plays and Milton's poems, and they believed that the law would back them. A generation later, Lord Camden was to interpret their entitlements quite differently, entirely in terms of interest, not of cultural patronage: 'their property consisted of all the literature of the Kingdom, for they had contrived to get all the copies into their own hands'.[112]

To protect their interests, booksellers did not hesitate between 1710 and 1774 to turn to the Court of Chancery for protection against any publisher who in practice challenged their monopoly, while at the same time petitioning Parliament, critics said, 'with tears in their eyes', for a longer exclusive term of literary ownership. They were careful in doing so

---

111   See I. Parsons, 'Copyright and Society' in EHP, p.31.

112   Quoted in Kaplan, *op. cit.*, p.6.

to avoid open talk of 'perpetual copyright' which now aroused immediate opposition outside the book trade. Under increasingly bitter attack inside and outside Parliament for their 'monopoly', they were more successful in the Courts than in Parliament, for after two bills (which they had helped to draft) were passed by the House of Commons in 1735 and in 1737, they were both shelved in the House of Lords.[113]

No new copyright legislation emerged, therefore, in the eighteenth century, and the London booksellers, the most powerful of interest groups in the book trade, campaigned successfully for protection against importers of books, including 'pirated' editions of their own books printed in Scotland and Ireland, neither of which had figured in the 1710 legislation. An Act of 1739, to be renewed every seven years, forbade the import into England and Wales of foreign reprints.[114] Thereafter, although not for the first time, the issue of copyright, now beginning to be identified as such, became entangled with the question of 'piracy', a highly emotive concept, emotive in the year when this *History* begins and still emotive in the year when it ends.[115]

What has been called 'the battle for literary property' continued until 1774, with the trade doing its utmost to ensure that the 1739 Act was enforced, and in 1759, a year of resolute organised booksellers' action, as the year 1774 was to be, Thomas Longman II showed where his sympathies – and his interests – lay. He joined most of his fellow booksellers in seeking to curb Irish imports, contributing £100 to a fund raised in April 1759. This was the same size of sum contributed by the Rivingtons, Baldwin, Dodsley, Johnson and Newbery. Tonson subscribed £500, Millar £300.[116]

The views of the trade were set out in a letter signed by John Whiston after a 'general meeting' had been held of 'all the considerable booksellers':

---

113 The common law never developed any law of copyright before 1709. See Patterson, *op. cit.* and H.B. Abrams, 'The Historic Foundation of American Copyright Law: Exploding the Myth of Common Law Copyright' in the *Wayne Law Review*, Vol. 29, No.3 (1983).

114 See J. Feather, 'The Publishers and the Pirates; British Copyright Law in Theory and Practice, 1710–1775', in PH, Vol. XXII (1987), pp.5–26 and his book *Publishing, Piracy and Politics: An Historical Study of Copyright in Britain* (1994). The Court of the Stationers' Company resolved to petition Parliament on this issue in 1731.

115 See The Campaign Against Book Piracy, *Anti-Piracy Kit* (n.d. [1983?]). Copyright remained alive too. See J. Phillips, *The Economic Importance of Copyright* (1989), published by the Common Law Institute of Intellectual Property Ltd.

116 G. Walters, 'The Booksellers in 1759 and 1774: the battle for Literary Property', in TL, Vol. XXIX (1974), pp.287–31.

> No one, *after the first day of May next*, shall sell any Scotch or Irish
> editions of books first printed in England, *classics excepted*; or shall
> purchase or take in exchange, or bring in by any means whatsoever,
> such Scotch or Irish books ... Any bookseller or printer knowing of
> any person bringing in or selling such editions, or piratical editions
> shall give immediate notice to one of the committee who shall
> directly order a prosecution against such offender, to be paid out of
> a common fund.

The Committee chosen consisted of Tonson, Millar, Hitch, John and James
Rivington, John Ward, and William Johnson. Thomas II figured among
the 'wholesale-dealers' whom the Committee represented.[117]

This powerful combination of booksellers authorised resort to
legal action, and to begin with this was successful. The first major case,
Millar v. Taylor, went in their favour in 1763. Millar, tough and litigious,
claimed perpetual copyright in James Thomson's *The Seasons* after a rival
publisher, Robert Taylor, had brought out an edition of his own. Significantly,
however, the judgment in *Millar v. Taylor* was not unanimous, and was
based not on publishers' rights but on authors' rights to rewards from the
act of 'creation'. In the words of the eminent judge Lord Mansfield (1705-
1793), whose family name coincidentally was Murray, it was 'just that an
author should reap the pecuniary profits of his own ingenuity and labours. It
is just that another should not use his name without his consent.'

Millar's victory was short-lived. When on his death his estate was
disposed of and *The Seasons*, the words of which were to be used by Haydn
in his oratorio with that name, was bought by a syndicate of printers, a rebel
Edinburgh printer and bookseller, Alexander Donaldson, who published
an unauthorised edition of his own, refused to accept a new Chancery
decision of 1774 based on *Millar v. Taylor*. Pitting Scotland, from which
Millar had originally come, against London, where he had exercised great
power, Donaldson claimed in a petition to Parliament that between 1763
and 1774, he 'had had to struggle with the united forces of almost all the
eminent booksellers of London and Westminster'.

Appealing to the House of Lords in 1774, he won his case (*Donaldson
v. Beckett*), and this proved to be a lasting victory. Henceforth there was to
be no talk of perpetual copyright.[118] Nevertheless, not all Scots booksellers
were on Donaldson's side. In a letter from Aberdeen to Dilly, Dr Beatty,
who did not need to identify himself, wrote that he had been 'very glad
to hear' that 'the Booksellers of London' intended to apply for a new Act
of Parliament 'to counteract in some Measure' the decision 'in relation

---

117   The letter is quoted in Pollard, *loc. cit.*, PH, Vol. IV, pp.30–1.

118   See A. Gray, 'Alexander Donaldson and the Fight for Cheap Books', in the
Juridical Review, Vol. 38 (1926).

to Literary Property, a Decision which must otherwise, in my humble opinion, be attended with bad consequences not to Booksellers only but to authors also and Literature in general'. 'The Inconveniences to Booksellers from this Decision are obvious and if we only believe the Newspapers, were foreseen and admitted even by Mr. Donaldson's Counsel'. The effect on printing too would be disastrous, Beatty considered: 'we may bid adieu to all correctness and elegance in that Art'. As for 'Authors' – and he mentioned Johnson and Blackstone – 'could it be said that when a man has employed his best days in composing a useful Book, the profits of a precarious sale for fourteen years are a sufficient reward for his labour'?[119]

Victory in the House of Lords, while conclusive, had, in fact, been a narrow one. Among the eleven judges whom the Lords asked for non-binding advice, there was a majority of only one in favour of Donaldson's appeal. And there may have been miscounting.[120] Yet the most powerful speech by Lord Camden (1713–1793) had denied the case for perpetual copyright in such vehement language that his words were to echo down the years. The case rested, he argued, on 'patents, privileges, Star-chamber decrees, and the bye-laws of the Stationers' Company: all of them the effects of the grossest tyranny and usurpation, the very last places in which I should have dreamt of finding the least trace of the common law'.[121]

Without pressing for new legislation, the London booksellers had been taking steps – by combinations – to maintain their authority, seeking in effect to insure themselves against the decision even before it was reached. They remained in a strong position to do so. For Goldsmith, an embittered observer, the House of Lords decision in 1774, which the booksellers deeply resented, in no way destroyed their fortunes. 'The London booksellers talk of ruin', he wrote – and we may assume that Longman was one of them – 'but they know better. In fact, that species of trade which they possess by occupancy will still continue to be theirs in great measure ... that aid which they have hitherto given and continue to give each other will sufficiently place them above compassion, without any assistance from Parliament.'[122]

---

119 Letter of 29 March 1774 (Longman ArchivePart II 16/6).

120 See Abrams, *loc. cit.*, pp.1158–71. For other studies, each with its own twists and nuances, see M. Woodmansee, 'The Genius and the Copyright: Economic and Legal Conditions of the Emergence of the Author', in *Eighteenth-Century Studies*, Vol. 17 (1984), pp.425–48; D. Saunders, *Authors and Copyright* (1992); and M. Woodmansee and P. Jaszi (eds.), *The Construction of Authorship: Textual Appropriation in Law and Literature* (1994). Authors' perspectives are discussed in D. Griffiths, *Literary Patronage in England, 1650–1800* (1996), an illuminating re-assessment.

121 *Parliamentary History of England*, 953, 992 (House of Lords, 1774).

122 For Goldsmith see K.C. Balderstone (ed.), *The Collected Letters of Oliver Goldsmith* (1928) and G.S. Rousseau (ed.), *Goldsmith: The Critical Heritage* (1974).

Pushed increasingly towards publishing rather than bookselling – but not immediately – they looked increasingly to themselves.

Goldsmith's comment was fair, and a quarter of a century later Longman, almost as active a litigant as Millar had been, in a sequence of cases, not all of them concerned with copyright, succeeded in a Court case of 1809 (*Longman* v. *Winchester*) in maintaining his copyright in annual calendars of which Winchester had incorporated sections in an 'Imperial Calendars' of their own. Lord Eldon (1715–1828), Lord Chancellor, a conservative lawyer – and politician – who paid no attention to the examples either of Mansfield or Camden, accepted the case of Longman as plaintiff that in so far as the defendant leaned on the plaintiff's labour he was an infringer. He did not raise the question, as Mansfield would have done, as to whether it mattered that the defendant had altered the form of presentation of the copyright material. Nor, indeed, did he comment on any special characteristics of the calendar as a product.

Already there had been 'legal perversities' in judgments in a number of cases, dealing with the evolving road pattern, in one of which, *Cary* v. *Longman* (1801), Longman was not plaintiff but defendant; and Thomas Norton Longman and Owen Rees, his new partner, were both supporters in 1808 when the statutory copyright period was extended to twenty-eight years in all circumstances and, six years later, when the period was extended to cover the life of the author. Even before a major new Copyright Act was passed in 1842 'an indulgent attitude towards using other people's works seemed increasingly out of keeping with the realities of the market'.[123] The politics behind the 1842 Act is unravelled in a later chapter.[124] So, too, is the rhetoric. And it was two-sided. The sub-title of a book entitled *Copyright and Patents for Inventions*, published in Edinburgh, the obvious location, in 1879, ran 'Pleas and plans for cheaper books and greater industrial freedom, with due regard to international relations, the claims of talent, the demands of trade and the work of the people'.[125]

~

Meanwhile, outside the Courts, different sections of a divided 'publishing interest' were taking different views about how to operate within an expanding market or, to use what was then more familiar language, how to relate to 'their public' within which there were different 'publics'. One immediate consequence of the 1774 judgment had been that John Bell (1745–1831), a Scot who set up his own shop in London, launched a famous

---

123 Kaplan, *op. cit.*, p.22.

124 See below, pp.214ff.

125 The author was R.A. Macfie of Dreghorn. Two American publishers were listed on the title page after T. & T. Clark of Edinburgh – Scribner and Welford in New York and Henry Carey, Baird & Company in Philadelphia.

109-volume series of *Poets of Great Britain Complete from Chaucer to Churchill* (1782, 1777–83) at 1s. 6d. a volume and a similarly priced *British Theatre* in twenty-one volumes (1776–1778), both series quickly reissued. Described by his biographer as 'the most resourceful and inventive bookseller of his generation',[126] Bell, treated by established London publishers as an interloper, proclaimed the glories of 'British classics', organising his Apollo Press as a British counterpart to the old Dutch publisher Elzevier.

In retrospect, we can trace two publishing trajectories even before the wars against revolutionary France began. One, as we have seen, was to produce cheap, often pocket, editions of books at lower prices than ever before; the other was to stand by 'old customs', publishing a limited number of copies for a cultivated but limited audience. In time, successful authors were to benefit from cheaper reprints of their works published by Houses such as Longman which had never put their trust in 'cheapness' as such. So, too, were readers, who could thereby buy books that they wanted to buy and possess, not borrow, at prices that they could afford.

There were some people, however, who were not prepared to wait, with Charles Knight leading the way forward – from Windsor, at first sight ironically, as his first home base.[127] He subsequently divided his life into three 'epochs',[128] with pioneers like himself, some of them active in the Society for the Diffusion of Useful Knowledge, founded in 1827, setting out from the start to plan 'the commerce of book production' on 'broad foundations', in his plan integrating text and pictures, and publishing and selling magazines and encyclopaedias as well as books.[129] From 1833 to 1844 Clowes, who became Knight's printer, became involved in both trajectories. So did Archibald Constable, who from his Edinburgh base not only reached out to London first to Longman, then to Murray, but dreamed of reducing prices and selling more copies of his books.

During the revolutionary and Napoleonic wars there seemed to be a logic, economic, social and cultural, about the course of change, above all, changes in communications, as population grew and with it a larger 'reading public' emerged. Yet change did not always come about easily. For example, while the numbers of people unable to read and write (the

An engraving, from a photograph, of Charles Knight (1791–1873), a leading pioneer of cheap publications

BL 10856.f.5

---

126 See S. Morrison, *John Bell* (1930).

127 The family connections of Knight are said to have been royal, although he never seems to have made the point. His father, born in 1750, was said to have been a natural son of Frederick, Prince of Wales, and Charles was said to have been with a guardian in Yorkshire (W.B. Clowes, *op. cit.*, p.28.)

128 Knight hoped (11 Nov. 1863) that his choice of the word 'passages' in his title of *Passages of a Working Life during half a Century* would keep him from 'many of the usual faults of Autobiography' (Preface, p.xi). The phrases in quotation marks are from *ibid.*, p.263.

129 KP, p.183.

two activities were sometimes separated) had declined during the course of the eighteenth century, illiteracy, linked to poverty, was still restricting the growth of the reading public in the early-nineteenth century. There was still some confusion about the meaning of the adjectives 'literate' and 'literary', even about the nouns 'literacy' and 'literature'.[130]

Other nouns were employed in different ways, not necessarily for reasons of clarity. Thus, in the early-eighteenth century, in an age that was becoming dependent on print in everyday life, Defoe had given a more dynamic definition of the noun 'circulation', which became one of the key words of the time along with 'copyright', than Johnson did when he defined 'circulation' in what now seems to be a curiously limited way, taking one of his illustrative quotations from Swift: 'God, the ordinary ruler of nature, permits this continual circulation of human beings'.[131]

In 1758 Johnson was to note in his periodical *The Idler* how 'almost every large town has its weekly historian, who regularly circulates his periodical intelligence',[132] and later in the century a writer referred specifically to the book trade when he extolled 'the circulation of Learning by catalogues of books with the prices affixed'.[133] This was at a time when Fanny Burney (1752–1840), the daughter of Charles Burney, a friend of Johnson, could described herself as a 'humble novelist', working within

Samuel Richardson (1689–1781), portrait by Joseph Highmore in the Stationers' Company. Richardson was Master in 1754. A successful printer as well as author, he printed the *Journals* of the House of Commons before they were printed by Luke Hansard (1752–1828)

The Master and Wardens of the Worshipful Company of Stationers and Newspaper Makers

130   The subject of literacy, which has a bearing on the development of urbanisation and of industrialisation, remains controversial. See R. Schofield 'The Measurement of Literacy in Pre-industrial England' in J. Goody (ed.), *Literacy in Traditional Societies* (1968) and 'Dimensions of Literacy, 1750–1830', in *Explorations in Economic History*, Vol. X (1972–3); T. Laqueur, 'The Cultural Origins of Popular Literacy in England, 1500–1850', in the *Oxford Review of Education*, Vol. 2 (1976) and *Religion and Responsibility: Sunday Schools and Working Class Culture, 1780–1850* (1976); D. Cressy, *Literacy and the Social Order* (1980); H. Graff (ed.), *Literacy and Development in the West* (1981) and *The Legacies of Literacy: Continuities and Contradictions in Western Culture and Society* (1987); and, above all, D. Vincent, *Literacy and Popular Culture, England, 1750–1914* (1989).

131   Likewise, there was nothing dynamic in Johnson's definition of 'revolution' as 'motion in a circle; a course in which the motion tends to the point from which it began' and 'a series in which the same order is always observed, and things always return to the same state'. That was a definition that could never have been considered adequate or accurate after the French Revolution of 1789.

132   W.J. Bate, J.M. Bullitt and L.F. Powell (eds.), *The Tatler and The Rambler* (1963), p.94. Johnson's *Idler* essays appeared in the *Universal Chronicle, or Weekly Gazette*. *The Idler* did not appear until the second number of the *Chronicle* and disappeared before its demise in 1760.

133   As late as 1839 West wrote in the *Aldine Magazine* how deeply it was to be regretted 'that we have not a general catalogue in England that combines the advantage of names, dates, price and publishers' names', and even some of the catalogues of individual Houses did not give all these details.

'the republic of letters', a term that preceded the creation of the French republic. A different word was province.

~

Henry Fielding once referred to himself as 'the founder of a new Province of Writing'.[134] Samuel Richardson (whose *Pamela* had been published by Thomas I's old partner in the acquisition of Lily, Samuel Buckley) became a bookseller and publisher himself as well as an author and editor. He was employing three printers and a staff of forty in the decade when Thomas I died. In 1753, like Thomas I before him, he was Upper Warden of the Stationers' Company. A bi-centennial celebration of him, sponsored by Longmans, was held in the Stationers' Hall in 1989 and included an exhibition and two lectures, one by Michael Treadwell on 'Richardson, Citizen and Stationer'.

~

The reputation of novelists depended in part, at least, on notices in the reviews, many of them demanding detailed attention.[135] In the wake of Cave's *Gentleman's Magazine*, other reviews, some of them already briefly mentioned, quickly followed. They need to be considered as a group. They circulated information about texts, using direct quotation as well as making summaries and sometimes critical judgements. They also confronted each other. The *Monthly Review*, founded in 1749, faced a genuine rival in 1756 when the *Critical Review* was launched by another novelist, Tobias Smollett. A further rival was the *European Magazine*, founded in 1782 and edited at first by James Perry, who in 1789 became editor of the *Morning Chronicle*. The *Magazine* survived major changes in Europe, revolution in France and the rise and fall of a Napoleonic empire.[136]

Many of the reviews included news, as well as notices of books, and some, including the *Gentleman's Magazine*, reported from Parliament. As their numbers increased, the reviews incorporated both 'intelligence' and

Invitation to Stationers' Hall, 1989, to celebrate the tercentenary of Richardson's birth, showing the traditional devices of Longman and that of the Stationers' Company

Personal Collection

---

134 I. Williams, *The Criticism of Henry Fielding* (1970), p.63.

135 For a detailed study based on a close reading of Defoe, Richardson, Fielding and Sterne, which concentrates on the role novelists gave to readers, but completely leaves out the publishers of their books, see J. Preston, *The Created Self, The Reader's Role in Eighteenth-Century Fiction* (1970).

136 The first series of the *European Magazine* lasted until 1825. A new series, conceived on different lines from the original, lasted for only one year.

entertainment.[137] They always included long and short notices of books that had recently appeared. So, too, did the *English Review*, founded by John Murray I in 1783 and merged in 1793 with the *Analytical Review* after John Johnson, its publisher, had been sent to gaol. Longman was later to have a limited interest in it. In 1793 a group of churchmen founded the *British Critic*, backed by funds from William Pitt's secret service.[138] Francis and Charles Rivington secured a third share in it.

The sales figures for the various reviews in 1797, as given by Timperley, a rare instance of immediate computation, were the *Monthly Magazine* and the *Monthly Review* 5,000 each, the *Gentleman's Magazine* 4,550, *The Critical Review* and the *British Critic* 3,500 each, the *Universal Magazine* 1,750 and *The Analytical Review* 1,500.[139] The *European Magazine* had a circulation of 3,250.[140] These are estimates which in an age of computerisation are still taken as reasonably reliable. They point both to the still limited size of a growing 'reading public' and the obvious interest in keeping up-to-date in a changing society.

Some twentieth-century historians of literature, less concerned with statistics than with the changing relationships between authors, readers, critics and publishers, dismissed eighteenth-century reviews and reviewers for their 'dependence' on booksellers who financed the reviews in order to advertise ('puff') the books that they printed and sold;[141] and at the very end of the nineteenth century Lewis E. Gates described them as 'merely booksellers' organs ... written for the most part by drudges and penny-a-liners, who worked under the orders of the bookseller like slaves under the lash'.[142]

This was a caricature, although there was never any shortage of 'puffing'. Apart from their value in encouraging publishers to produce

---

137 See W. Graham, *English Literary Periodicals* (1935); M. Morris, 'Periodicals and the Book Trade' in R. Myers and N. Harris (eds.) *Development of the English Book Trade* (1981); A Forster, 'Review Journals', Isabel Rivers (ed.), *Books and Readers in eighteenth-century England* (2nd edn. 2001); D. Roper, *Reviewing Before the Edinburgh* (1978); and J. Klancher, *The Making of English Reading Audiences, 1790–1832* (Madison, 1987).

138 *British Critic*, 'A Proposal for the Reformation of Principles', p.265. For the role of government see B. Porter, *Plots and Paranoia: A History of Political Espionage in Britain* (1989).

139 TDPP, p.795.

140 Roper, *op. cit*, p.22.

141 J. Clive, *Scotch Reviewers: The Edinburgh Review, 1802–1815* (1957), p.32. The same judgement had been made more strongly by A.R.D. Elliott in the *Cambridge History of English Literature*, Vol. XII (1915), p.141. He referred to 'the spurious criticism of periodicals, notoriously kept alive by publishers to promote the sale of their own books'.

142 L.E. Gates, *Three Studies in Literature* (1899), pp.46–51.

readable catalogues, reviews cannot be quickly disposed of on literary grounds. Not all the people who wrote for them were 'hacks', any more than all those booksellers who dealt in new books rather than in old copies were 'semi-piratical figures', as some early historians of the relationship between publishers and authors were to suggest. Readers, often addressed directly in a variety of modes, with the 'gentle' usually to the fore, were treated quite differently and in different language not only by different authors but by different critics. There was no perpetual, no ineradicable, antagonism between publishers and authors. The poet John Campbell was not typical when he compared publishers with ravens feasting on their victims and when he sent one publisher a Bible in which the phrase 'Now Barabbas was a thief' was changed to 'Now Barabbas was a publisher'.

There were some London publishers who never put a penny into reviews or derived any profit from them, but an active minority were willing to acquire reviews by purchase or to start new ones, following the example of Richard Griffiths whose *Monthly Review* cost £2 and proved both successful and illuminating.[143] Thomas Longman II was involved in more than one side venture in reviewing, before Thomas Norton Longman forged links with Archibald Constable who opened his own bookshop in Edinburgh in 1795. Turning to periodicals and books, he launched the *Farmers' Magazine* in 1800 and became proprietor of the *Scots Magazine* in 1801.

It was Constable's initiative and drive which lay behind the *Edinburgh Review* (1802) in which he and Thomas Norton Longman III held part ownership. Innovatory in content, it renounced any intention of covering comprehensively all books published, seeking instead to be distinguished 'rather for the selection than for the number of its [unsigned] articles'.[144] This was a decisive move, for the *Edinburgh*, vigorous from the start, went on to set new standards of both writing and interpreting in an age when Thomas Norton, having lost and regained his stake in the *Review*, was to show a genuine competitive interest in acquiring new titles with the capital to do so.[145]

The *Edinburgh Review* did not have a monopoly. The *Critical Review* continued to be published until 1817, the *Monthly* until 1845, and the *British Critic* in various forms until 1847. Meanwhile, in a competitive situation two other new journals, in particular, affected the whole dynamics of reviewing – the Tory *Quarterly Review*, launched in 1809, and *Blackwood's*

---

143 See B.C. Nangle, *The Monthly Review, First Series, 1749–1789* (1934), pp.xix–xx. Seen in perspective this was the first of the type of periodical which was to become supreme in literary interest and taste in the nineteenth century. See W. Graham, *English Literary Periodicals* (1935), pp.208–9.

144 Quoted by Clive, *op. cit.*, p.35.

145 For Longmans and Constable, see below, pp.175ff.

Magazine ('Maga'), also Tory in outlook, launched in 1817. First called the *Edinburgh Monthly Magazine*, it was to survive until 1980.

~

Impossible as it is even with computerisation to measure the impact of reviews, it has become possible for the first time to produce, if not to establish, fuller estimates of the number of books produced and their sales. Before 1700 the annual increase in the production of books and pamphlets probably never rose by more than 1 per cent each year: the average increase between 1700 and 1800 was around 2.3 per cent.[146] Concomitantly, over the eighteenth century as a whole the amount spent on books increased more than tenfold. Different publics – those for novels, for example, and those for school books – each had its own tempo and dynamics. There were regional differences also in the appeal of different genres. Changes in their classification must always be examined.

Given the high prices of books, which put them outside the range of most of the population, not all the spending on books was on buying them. Before the end of the eighteenth century large numbers of circulating libraries, some non-profit making proprietary institutions, many attached to bookshops, had come into existence. The former were sometimes associated with local 'literary and philosophical societies'. The latter advertised 'books lent to be read or chang'd for others'. The business was becoming so organised that by 1791 William Lane, founder of the Minerva Press in 1770, who published books in exceptionally large quantities, was advertising for sale to provincial retailers 'complete CIRCULATING LIBRARIES ... from One Hundred to Ten Thousand Volumes' for sale to provincial retailers.[147] By the end of the eighteenth century there were at least 250 circulating libraries in the provinces.[148]

It was in the provinces, indeed, where reviews provided invaluable information about new titles, that the earliest expansion had taken place – in spas such as Scarborough and Bath. There was ample scope for enterprise. Thus, when Caesar Ward and Richard Chandler, both London booksellers, opened a shop in Scarborough (c. 1734), they advertised 'raffles for books'. They also sold newspapers. At Bath, a town with a very different history from Bristol, the premises of the bookseller James Leake, Samuel Richardson's brother-in-law, included what was described in 1740 as a 'Library

An eighteenth-century trade card: Caesar Ward's and Richard Chandler's advertisement as booksellers in London, York and Scarborough

Bodleian Library, University of Oxford: John Johnson Collection [Booktrade London C]

---

146 J. Raven, *Judging New Wealth: Popular Publishing and Responses to Commerce in England, 1750–1800* (1992).

147 D. Blakey, *The Minerva Press, 1790–1820* (1939), p.114.

148 P. Kaufman, 'The Community Library; a chapter in English social history', in *Transactions of the American Philosophical Society*, new series, Vol. 57 (1967), pp.12–13. See also his *Libraries and their Users* (1969) and A.D. McKillop, 'British Circulating Libraries, 1725–30', in TL, 4th series, Vol. XIV (1934), pp.477–85.

appealing to 'Best Persons of Quality': he charged a guinea subscription. Defoe in his *Tour Thro' the Whole Island* called his shop 'one of the finest booksellers' shops in Europe'. Later in the century, as Brighton developed from Brighthelmstone, several circulating libraries were opened, one serving as the local post office. Another, 'Miss Widgett', dealt in millinery as well as books. It subsequently was acquired by a London librarian, to be followed by two 'librarians' one of whom demolished the building in 1795 and created imposing new premises. There was said to be more talking there than there was reading, 'unless it be the newspaper'.[149]

Other large towns soon followed the example of the resorts. So, too, did London, where Thomas Wright's 'Entertaining Library', renamed the Universal Circulating Library, said to have been founded in 1741, specialised in novels. He had competitors, moreover, including the Noble brothers, who unashamedly called their library 'the original Circulating Library'.[150] Birmingham acquired its first library in 1751: Liverpool in 1757, Bristol in 1772, and Exeter in 1783. A 1797 pamphlet, now in the Bodleian Library at Oxford, gave instructions to would-be organisers of libraries, *The Use of Circulating Libraries Considered: with Instruction for Opening and Conducting a Library either upon a large or small Plan*. Such advice was not always necessary. At Lewes in Sussex a group of sixty subscribers were able to create a library of a thousand volumes between 1786 and 1794.[151] Earlier in the century a Lewes bookseller had sold books in Brighton 'during the season'. There was still more of a season in taking the waters than in reading books.

The fact that women patronised late-eighteenth-century circulating libraries, frequently reading books written by women authors, was a favourite topic dwelt on by observers of manners and fashions. Reading with all its dangers was felt by many – we do not know how many – to be too temptingly accessible. Popular literacy, in particular, was suspect in many quarters, and Sarah Trimmer was not alone in fearing 'a conspiracy against Christianity and all Social Order'.[152] One writer in the *Gentleman's Magazine* wrote of the 'debauching' influence of libraries, and in Richard

Gye's Premises, 1819, Printer and Stationer, Market Place, Bath

Longman Archive

149   *The Royal Pavilion Review*, Dec. 2004, p.11.

150   *Whitehall Evening Post*, 11 Nov. 1749. For the Nobles, see above, p.115. They separated in 1752. TDPP called Wright's shop the first circulating library in London. Benjamin Franklin had made a private arrangement to borrow books from it (W. Macdonald (ed.), *The Autobiography of Benjamin Franklin* (1905), p.52). After Wright retired (c. 1750), his business was re-established by William Bathoe and in various guises continued into the nineteenth century.

151   GM, Vol. 64 (1794), p.47.

152   For Trimmer, see above, p.73; H.C. Barnard, *A History of English Education from 1763* (2nd edn. 1961); B. Simon, *Studies in the History of Education, 1780–1870* (1960); and R. O'Day, *Education and Society, 1500–1800: the social foundations of education in early modern Britain* (1982).

Sheridan's play *The Rivals* (1775) Mrs. Malaprop in one of the subsequently most quoted passages in English literature spoke of them as 'vile places',[153] and Sir Anthony Absolute described a circulating library in a town as 'an evergreen tree of diabolical knowledge'. 'Those who are so fond of handling the leaves will long for the fruit at last.'[154]

Many novels, including those which Sydney Smith, who figures prominently in the next chapter of this *History*, called 'the brick and mortar novels of the Minerva Press', were published to be bought by libraries, not by individuals. Ordered by number from a catalogue rather than available on open access, many of them were designed according to formula. As Fanny Burney wrote in 1782, 'the last page in any novel in Mr. Noble's circulating library may serve for the last page of mine, since a marriage, a reconciliation, and some sudden expedient for great riches, concludes them all alike'.[155] Four years earlier in the preface to her own 'epistolary' novel, *Evelina*, published anonymously, she had observed that 'were it possible to effect the total extirpation of novels our young ladies in general, and boarding-school damsels in particular, might profit from their annihilation; but since the distemper they have spread seems incurable ... to contribute to the number of those which may be read, if not without advantages, at least without injury, ought rather to be encouraged, than condemned.'

~

The Longman business, as we have seen, had been less dependent on fashion than most other publishing businesses throughout the eighteenth century, but, as we have also seen, it too had grown in range as well as in size before the 1790s.[156] It published plays at one end of the spectrum and books of guidance of various kinds at the other, becoming specialists in both. And it paid special attention to education as it was to do increasingly in the nineteenth and twentieth centuries. In 1796 and 1797, to take illustrative examples from only two years, it published three versions of Hoare Prince's *Lock and Key*, 'a musical entertainment in two acts, as performed at the Theatre Royal, Covent Garden', 'correctly taken from the prompt book', and a book by a schoolmaster, John Mair, *Book Keeping Modernized, or Merchant Accounts by Double Entry, according to the Italian Form.*

---

153 GM, Vol. 58, 1788. See also H.M. Hamlyn, 'Eighteenth-century Circulating Libraries' in TL, fifth series, Vol. 7 (1947).

154 See R.B. Sheridan, *The Rivals* (1775), Act 1, Scene 2.

155 *Diary and Letters*, Vol. II, 6 April 1782, quoted *ibid.*.

156 For the role of fashion in the eighteenth century, see N. McKendrick, J. Brewer and J.H. Plumb (eds.), *The Birth of a Consumer Society* (1982); J.H. Plumb, 'The Commercialisation of Leisure in Eighteenth-century England' (The Stenton Lecture, 1972).

The young were never out of sight. Thus, a year later, in 1798, a topical book, co-published with Newbery, Elizabeth Helme's two-volume *Instructive Rambles in London, and the Adjacent Villages*, was 'designed to amuse the mind and improve the understanding of youth'.

There are no fewer than 168 extant sales catalogues covering the period from 1718 to 1768, the earliest of them kept by John Osborn and preserved until the twentieth century within the House of Longman,[157] and from them it is possible to trace the changing attractiveness to publishers of particular titles and to discover just how much publishers were prepared to pay for a share in them before the French Revolution and the advent of the 'romantics' who were read far more widely in the later nineteenth century than they were in their own lifetimes.[158] The Longman titles of the eighteenth century were often as long as the prices were high, and only a few achieved the succinct brevity of *Sermons on Several Subjects* (1790). One short title of 1792 introduced a difficult word – *A Dissertation on the Querulousness of Statesmen*. It was published jointly by Murray, Longman and Debrett. One particular Longman title, a favourite with successive generations, James Thomson's *The Seasons*, was priced at only 2s.: it was produced by new stereotype technology and sold 6,000 copies. Longman and Rees also published five editions of Robert Bloomfield's *The Farmer's Boy* between 1800 and 1802, selling around 20,100 copies.

Imprints require as much investigation as titles. By a 1681 Ordinance of the Stationers' Company, every piece of printing had to 'bear the name either of the printer or of a bookseller with a shop in London or the suburbs';[159] and imprints on the title page of books or on advertisements set out bare details of the publishers responsible not only for new books but for an old or new edition. They were of different kinds, with the fullest of them giving the name of the place of printing (London lost its monopoly after

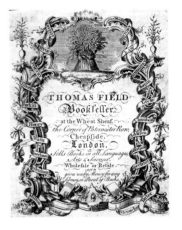

Tradecard for Thomas Field, Bookseller at the Wheat Sheaf, the corner of Paternoster Row, Cheapside, London

Bodleian Library, University of Oxford: John Johnson Collection [Booktrade Trade Cards 4]

157 See C. Blagden, 'Booksellers' Trade Sales, 1718–1768' in TL, 5th series, Vol. V (1951) and T. Belanger, 'Booksellers' Trade Sales, 1718–1768' in TL, 5th series, Vol. XXX (1975). Other major sources of information on trade book practice include the Ward catalogues in the John Johnson Collection of the Bodleian Library, and the John Murray catalogues in the Murray archive. All but one of the fifty-nine catalogues in the Longman archive covering the period from 1718 to 1752, the year before Thomas I's death, are duplicated in the Ward set, which includes more than sixty catalogues not held in the Longman archive.

158 See, for the example of Wordsworth, S. Gill, *Wordsworth and the Victorians* (1998). Cf. N. Rowe, *Wordsworth and Coleridge: the Radical Years* (1987).

159 Blagden, *The Stationers' Company* (1960), p.163. As far as newspapers and broadsides were concerned, the obligation was incorporated by statute in the Stamp Act of 1712.

From *The Ramble of Philo, and his man Sturdy* 2 Vols. 1788 (containing advertisements for Freeman printer, bookseller, and a leaf of conditions for Fuller's Circulating Library)

BL 1154.g.9

1695[160]); 'printed by', followed by the name of the printer; 'for', followed by the name of the bookseller or booksellers who held the copyright of the book; and 'sold by' the name or names of other booksellers. A less full imprint was simple – name of place; 'printed by'; 'sold by'; and where. A third was simplest of all. Only the name of the publisher – and his address – were given. When a date appeared it was not always reliable.

The phrase 'sold by' figures prominently in ESTC imprints. It could relate to the selling of books that were published privately at the author's expense. An interesting Longman example was Thomas Whiting's *The London Gentleman's and Schoolmaster's Assistant*, 'containing an easy and very comprehensive system of practical arithmetic, ... an abstract of chronology ... an extensive geographical table ... and a number of original questions as exercises'. It was 'printed for the author' in 1787 and 'sold by T. Longman'. Another example was a second Whiting book, *The Mental Accountant* (1788), 'containing rules for performing the computations which usually occur in business without a pen'. The notice about it added that the book was obtainable 'not only from Longman' but from 'the booksellers in Westminster'.

Imprints on the title page of the names of the publisher or publishers gain both in interest and importance after the decline in authority of the Stationers' Company and the unprecedented eighteenth-century advance in provincial printing. For various reasons, however, the imprints must be examined critically, for sometimes not all names were listed and sometimes an old name survived on an imprint even though the particular person named was dead. The order of names in the early eighteenth century was based usually not on the size of the particular publisher's share but on seniority in the Stationers' Company, and the order of names would change, therefore, with the years. Yet it was not always the case that the publishers with the oldest share came first.

Sometimes the form of an imprint is of corroborative importance historically, as it is in showing that John Osborn I, Thomas Longman's father-in-law, was not his partner and that it was his son John Osborn II who figured in the 1724 imprint of *Stanhope's Kempis*. Their names appeared separately according to Stationers' Company rules of seniority. From the start Longman title pages presented a great variety of imprints. In a small number of cases T. Longman and partner were sole publishers – for example, of the lucrative *The Farrier's Dispensary* (1741), already mentioned, which in that case bore only T. Longman's name, as did John

160 There is now a wealth of material (with gaps) relating to provincial printing. See, for example, J. Oldfield, *Printers, Booksellers and Libraries in Hampshire, 1750–1800* (Hampshire Papers, 1993) and I. Maxted *Books with Devon Imprints* (1989). A British Library Exhibition was held in 1983 on *The English Provincial Printer, 1700–1800*.

AT

Hargrove's Circulating-Library,

IN THE

HIGH-STREET, *KNARESBRO'*,

BOOKS IN

HISTORY,	ANATOMY,
ANTIQUITIES,	ARTS,
VOYAGES,	SCIENCES,
TRAVELS,	PLAYS,
LIVES,	POETRY,
MEMOIRS,	HUSBANDRY,
PHILOSOPHY,	TRADE,
NOVELS,	GARDENING,
ROMANCES,	DIVINITY,
PHYSIC,	And SURGERY,

Are lent to read by the day, week, month,
or year.

N. B. Gives the full value for any library,
or parcel of books.

A

CATALOGUE

OF

HARGROVE's

CIRCULATING LIBRARY,

AT

HARROGATE.

CONTAINING UPWARDS OF

ONE THOUSAND FIVE HUNDRED VOLUMES,

WHICH ARE LENT OUT TO

READ AGREEABLE TO THE CONDITIONS,

SPECIFIED IN THE FOLLOWING PAGE.

*N. B. The Subscription to this Library entitles the
SUBSCRIBER, (only) to the perusal of either
Books or Newspapers.*

York:

PRINTED BY W. BLANCHARD.

1801.

Quincy's *Lexicon physico-medicum* (1749), a school edition in Greek of *Aeschylus* (1773) and a translation of Demosthenes (1777). Thomas I, as we have seen, was in a special relationship with the scientific author Peter Shaw, yet Shaw's *Essays for the Improvement of the Arts, Manufacturers and Commerce* (1761) bore the dual imprint, T. Longman and R. and J. Dodsley.

The imprints of the 1790s are particularly interesting for the light they throw on Thomas II, Thomas Norton Longman and the first non-Longman partner, Owen Rees. Thomas II ruled over all the 1792 imprints, including John Bowles's *A Protest against T. Paine's Rights of Man*, and his name was still there in 1796 with eleven other names on the title page of *Entick's New Spelling Dictionary*. Thomas Norton figured in the imprint of John O'Keeffe's play *Sprigs of Laurel*, printed by H.S. Woodfall as early as 1793, and of Frederick Reynolds's *How to Grow Rich* and *Notoriety*. Thomas

Hargrove's Catalogue for books in Knaresborough and Harrogate, printed in York by W. Blanchard, 1801

BL 1430.b.19.(2)

An eighteenth-century tradecard for John Comyn, Stationer at the Lamb in Grace Church Street

Norton and Owen Rees appeared together on the imprint of Clara Reeves's novel *Destination* in 1799. John Evans of Islington's *An Attempt to account for the Infidelity of the late Edward Gibbon* (1797) was 'printed for T.N. Longman and sold by J. Cottle, Bristol'.

Bristol will figure prominently in the next chapter which covers the partnership between T.N. Longman and Rees. The connections preceded their partnership, however: Robert Southey's *Joan of Arc* (1798) was 'printed by N. Biggs for T.N. Longman, London and Joseph Cottle, Bristol', the second volume of his *Poems* (1799) was printed by Biggs and Cottle for T.N. Longman and O. Rees as was his *Letters written during a short residence in Spain and Portugal* (also 1799). Thomas Norton, like Thomas II, had links with Bristol, Bath and the West Country apart from those with Rees, Cottle and Biggs. A small proportion of eighteenth-century Longman imprints had West Country associations, direct and indirect. They included Cornelius Bayley's *The Swedenborgian Doctrine of a Trinity* (1785), which was published in the North of England, but sold by T. Longman in London and W. Bulgin in Bristol. Bayley's *An Entrance into the Sacred Languages* (1782) was printed for the author by R. Hindmarsh and sold by T. Longman in London and T. Mills in Bristol. There were fifteen Longman links with Bath. A 1782 volume printed in Bath and sold in London by Longman was *The Glory of the Heavenly City*' by a 'Young Lady of Bristol'. *Bath, A Poem* (1748) had been 'printed for Messrs Longman and Shewell: London; Bath: J. Leake; Bristol: M. Lewis'.

~

The development of networks in the eighteenth-century provincial book trade has been studied intensively[161] – and in Chapter 2 an account was given of Longman networks outside the West of England – yet more remains to be discovered about the trade representatives who served several London publishers in the provinces. There were cross-regional connections as well as connections between provincial centres and London, where in order to make money every provincial printer or bookseller had to have an agent to supply not only the London trade but to maintain contact with other provincial booksellers who depended on London agents for supplies.

One of the men who developed the wholesale trade in books was Benjamin Crosby, who travelled throughout 'the length and breadth of the land' soliciting orders. His two assistants, William Simpkin and Richard Marshall, took over his business in 1814.[162] Their subsequent history as wholesalers, operating as part of their business as London agents for regional clients – and they also published some books of their own – was at the heart

---

161 See Feather in *The Provincial Book Trade*, 1985 and I. Maxted, *The British Book Trades 1731–1787* (The Exeter Working Papers in British Book Trade History).

162 J. Wolfreys, 'Simpkin and Marshall', in Brocket and Silver, *op. cit.*, pp.250–2.

of the nineteenth and early-twentieth-century processes of publishing. Their warehousing business, with its headquarters in Paternoster Row, near to the Longmans, did not depend on advertising, increasingly important though that was in the retail trade and in the local and national newspaper trade in scale and in range. Advertising sheets, heralds of both a national and a provincial eighteenth-century press and book trade, had appeared long before steam power was applied to printing production.

As far as the eighteenth-century book trade was concerned, it remained important that it was difficult to buy good new books outside London, as Lackington, a good judge, noted on a trip in 1787 to Edinburgh, an important city on the map of publishing. There was nothing but 'trash' to be found in Manchester, Preston and Carlisle, he reported, and only in York and Leeds were there 'a few' 'good books'. According to Samuel Johnson, country booksellers could not make a living from good books. In Ireland, however, where English copyright did not hold, there was, as we have seen, an active and growing printing and publishing trade as well as a bookselling market. Thomas I was involved there from the very start of the Longman story, and one of his books, already mentioned, Francis Hutcheson's *An Inquiry into the Original of our Ideas of Beauty and Virtue* (1725), a book of importance in the history of 'taste', bore the curious imprint 'London: printed by J. Darby for Wil. and John Smith in Dublin; sold by W. and I. Innys, J. Osborn and T. Longman and J. Chandler, 1725'.[163]

Hutcheson's *An Essay on the Nature and Conduct of the Passions* (1728) bore the equally curious imprint 'London: printed by J. Darby and T. Browne for John Smith and William Bruce, booksellers in Dublin, and sold by J. Osborn and T. Longman and S. Chandler, 1728'.[164] Twelve years later, John Abernethy's *Discourses concerning the Being and Natural Properties of God* was sold in Dublin by Smith, who also specialised in continental literature, and in London by Longman, Smith's chief contact in London. It was 'printed for the Author'.[165]

~

Statistics concerning both imprints and titles remain hazardous evidence, but with great effort it would now be possible to compare all Longman titles with those of other bookseller/publishers, particularly Rivington and Murray. According to John Sutherland, by the 1820s a broader Longman

---

163 See above, p.107.

164 Both titles were entered in the records of the Stationers' Company. (See Pollard, *op. cit.*, p.94). Parts of the works had appeared in the *Dublin Weekly Journal* in which John Smith had an interest. As early as 1726, Smith, an Irish Presbyterian, published *A Catalogue of Books newly arrived from England, Holland and France.*

165 For the relations of authors with Ireland see R.C. Cole, *Irish Booksellers and English Writers, 1740–1800* (1986).

from 12 s. to 13 s. Beans from 10 s. to 18. s. Oats from 8 s. to 10 s. Malt from 22 s. to 24 s.

Advertisement.

GEORGE BARTON, of Huntingdon, Bookseller, Sells the following Things at his Shops in Peterborough, at St. Ives, and at St. Neots, every Market Day, viz. All sorts of bound Books New and Old, at reasonable Rates. Any Gentleman may have Books sent for from London every Week. Likewise Maps and Pictures, Wholesale or Retale; Music-Books of all sorts, Violins, Hoit-boys, Flutes, Mock-Trumpets, Flagelets, Reeds for Hoit-boys, Fiddle-Bows, and Bridges, Fiddle-Pinns, Nuts, and Fiddle-strings; Books and Paper Rul'd, or Unrul'd; Writing, Blew and Marble Paper, Quils, Penknifes, Pens, Pen-Cases, and the best of Red, Shining, Japan, and Indian Inks, Ink-stands, and Pencil-Books to Write with a Brass Pen, and rub out; Demy-Royal, and Super-Royal Paper, and Paper for Hanging of Rooms, Wax, Wafers, Pencils, and Pocket-Books, Cards, Slates, and Slate-Pencils, Spectacles and Cases, Parchment, Stamp'd, or Unstamp'd, Vellom for Drum-Heads, or for Lac'd-Patterns, either Green or White, Sand, Snuff, and Snuff-Boxes, Plays, or any other Books to let out to Read by the Week, and Copy-Books for Children to Write in, or Printed Copy-Books, and Leaf Gold. Likewise ready Mony for any Library, or Parcel of Old Books, and Old Books new Bound, at Reasonable Rates, by George Barton, aforesaid, at the House late Mr. Lovewell's by the Corn-Market. N. B. At the same Places you may have Daffy's and Stoughton's Elixir, Bateman's true Spirits of Scurvy-Grass, Golden and Plain, the Natural Balsam of Chili, so often mention'd in the Advertisements, and Sugar Plumbs for the Worms in Children.

George Barton of Huntingdon's Advertisement

Bodleian Library, University of Oxford: John Johnson Collection

HOPE.8.871(20)P12

partnership, which now included more non-Longmans than Longmans, described in the next chapter, was responsible for no fewer than 12.6 per cent of all books published in England between 1824 and 1827. Murray's share was only 3.2 per cent, Rivington's 3.8. Taking a longer time span, according to Cox and Chandler, between 1724 and 1800 the Longmans published on their own or with others a total of at least 2,797 books.

Older statistical evidence, collected by Blagden, relates to Longmans' 'investment' (outlay) in printing, and paper for, books from 1806 to 1808. Blagden went on to compare them with statistics relating to 1856 to 1858.

Clearly outlay on books published through consortia in which the House of Longman held a share, a significantly high share in 1806, declined sharply between the early and the mid-nineteenth century, with outlay on Longman's own books rising sharply.[166]

---

166 See CC, p.x. C. Blagden, 'Publishing – An Historical Survey' in the *National Provincial Bank Review*, Nov. 1960, Table II p.15.

Longman Outlay, 1806–58 (£s)

YEAR	TOTAL INVESTMENT	INVESTMENT IN SHARE BOOKS	INVESTMENT IN BOOKS OF LONGMAN'S COPYRIGHT
1806	21,209	13,292	7,917
1807	34,820	11,684	23,136
1808	14,662	14,662	27,862
1856	36,233	2,005	34,228
1857	32,809	913	31,896
1858	42,591	871	41,720

The significance of mid-nineteenth century figures is examined in Chapter 5 of this *History*. For the long term the statistics have been meticulously analysed by Simon Eliot, who shows that with the increase in the number and range of titles there was always increasing scope for specialisation, with publishing becoming a far more diverse enterprise between the 1790s and the 1850s, indeed between the 1790s and the 1820s, an awkward decade in the fortunes of the book trades.[167]

Sutherland has demonstrated that the extent of the crash of 1826, coming in the middle of the decade, has been exaggerated, as it was at the time. So has its impact on publishing patterns. There was no great 'purge' of publishers: in fact, there were more who were active in 1826 (162) than in 1824 and 1845 (148, 141) or in 1827 (156). The number of books published in 1826 (887) was smaller than those published in 1824 and 1825 (916; 942) and 1827 (995), but larger numbers of cheap books, priced at six shillings and under, were published in 1826 than in the other years.

Sutherland does not attempt to look at the 'crash' comparatively. Whatever its effects on the book trade, the year 1826, following a financial crash in December 1825, was a critical year in the economy when large numbers of country banks stopped payment. The absence of an adequate banking system, therefore, along with arguments about how to respond to it, should be noted in any assessment of the situation in 1825-6. The use of accommodation bills by printers and booksellers was related to it. By a controversial Act of 1819, known from its initiator, Sir Robert Peel, as Peel's Act, private 'country banks' were no longer able to issue currency and sustain local credit. Sir Walter Scott, a victim of the 'crash', opposed the extension of the Act to Scotland in his

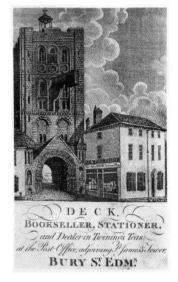

Trade card for John Deck, Bookseller, Stationer, Bury St Edmunds

Bodleian Library, University of Oxford: John Johnson Collection [Booktrade Suffolk temp sequence Subject. Bury St Edmunds]

---

167 S. Eliot, 'Some Patterns and Trends in British Publishing, 1800–1919', *Occasional Papers of the Bibliographical Society*, Vol. 8 (1994).

A
CATALOGUE
O F
B O O K S,
To be Sold, or Lent to Read, by

R O B E R T   T A Y L O R,

Bookseller, Printer and Stationer, High-Street,
BERWICK upon TWEED.

Where Gentlemen may be furnished with all Sorts of Books new
and old; Plays, Pamphlets, and all the monthly and weekly
Publications; all Sorts of Shop and Paper-Books; Ivory Leaf
Books; Maps; Prints; Sea Charts; Writing Paper of all
Sorts, gilt and plain; Mourning Paper; Red and Black
Ink; Ink-Powder; Indian-Ink; Japan-Ink; Ink-Standishes;
Slates for accompts; Mogul Cards; Common-place-books;
Ass-skin and other Memorandum Books and Letter-Cases; with
all Sorts of stationary Ware, Wholesale and Retale, at rea-
sonable Rates; likewise Dr. Hill's and other Medicines; Gold-
Beater's Leaf; and Blacking-Ball.

A L S O

Books neatly bound, gilt, and lettered, after the
best Manner, and most reasonable Prices.

A N D

All Manner of PRINTING performed after the
neatest Manner.

BERWICK, Printed by R. TAYLOR. 1771.

A catalogue of Robert Taylor's
Books, Berwick upon Tweed,
1771

Bodleian Library, University of Oxford:
John Johnson Collection [Provincial
Library labels etc.]

Letters of Malachi Malagrowther (1826).[168]
Like other writers on publishing, Sutherland turns from the statistics to the dramatis personae, re-evaluating two publishers who prospered during the most challenging year. Thomas Tegg (1776–1845), who had opened a shop in Cheapside in 1805, faced problems like other booksellers in 1826, but after 1826 bought the liquidated stock of other publishers, to be described in the future as 'remainders', and prospered as a result. Henry Colburn (1784/5–1855), described by his contemporaries as 'a small bustling bundle of energy with no scruples whatever', even as a 'guttersnipe ... wholly indifferent to book-design and workmanship' and 'lacking in literary taste', also displayed 'sheer topical ingenuity'. He accounted for 2.8 per cent of the trade in 1826.[169]

Between 1823 and 1829 Colburn increased his production of fiction in what Sutherland describes as 'meteoric' fashion and had not only picked out a number of new novelists 'of the future', among them Edward Bulwer Lytton, Frederick Marryat and Disraeli, but established a 'three-decker' mode of publication, pricing his three post-octavo volumes at 31s. 6d. In the process, however, he over-extended himself, always a possibility in publishing, never a problem for Longman/Rees, and in 1829 he was forced into an 'ill-fated' partnership with Richard Bentley, who was to leave a more lasting mark on publishing than Colburn did.[170]

Such changing fortunes are seen in longer-

168 Longman, Rees, Orme, Brown and Green – as they now were – published at the time several topical works on banking and on the financial crisis of 1826, for example, *A Treatise on the Currency* [author described as Britannicus]: *in which the principle of uniformity is advocated and observations on the Proceedings of County Bankers during the last thirty years, and on their Communications with Government together with a Remedy proposed against the alarming consequences arising from the circulation of Promissory Notes*. It is fascinating to trace the deletion of the name of Hurst from the ESTC Longman list of 1826.

169 J. Sutherland, 'Henry Colburn Publisher', in PH, Vol. XIX (1986), pp.59–85. Sutherland rightly notes that Colburn's 'tenacious hold on Pepys, Evelyn and Garrick material argues more literary taste than most critics have granted him' (p.81).

170 See below, p.233.

term perspective in the next chapter of this *History* which returns directly to the House of Longman in what in retrospect at least was its golden age. In general terms, the whole age has been described as the romantic age or 'era' just as the early eighteenth century has been described as 'the Augustan age'. Whatever the dangers in such labelling– and there were many[171] – Longman/Rees as publishers and the other partners associated with them were intimately involved in the fortunes of the canonical group of British writers subsequently deemed 'romantic' at home and abroad. There was to be more than one generation of 'romantics', but the fact that the first generation was particularly closely connected with Bristol from which both Thomas Longman I and Owen Rees had come adds particular point to the theme of 'romanticism' in the Longman story.

171 See A. Briggs and P. Clavin, *Modern Europe, 1789–Present* (2nd edn., 2003), p.149. 'The main difficulty in placing romanticism in history is ... less that of finding a definition than of finding one's way through the mass of definitions that have already been put forward'. See also H.R. Furst, *Romanticism and Revolt* (1967); M. Butler, *Romantics, Rebels and Reactionaries, English Literature and its Background* (1981); K.R. Johnston, G. Chaitin, K. Hanson and H. Marks, *Romantic Revolution: Criticism and Theory* (1990); W.G. Rowland, *Literature and the Market Place; Romantic Writers and their Audiences in Great Britain and the United States* (Lincoln, Nebraska, 1996) and W. St Clair, *The Reading Nation and the Romantic Period* (2004).

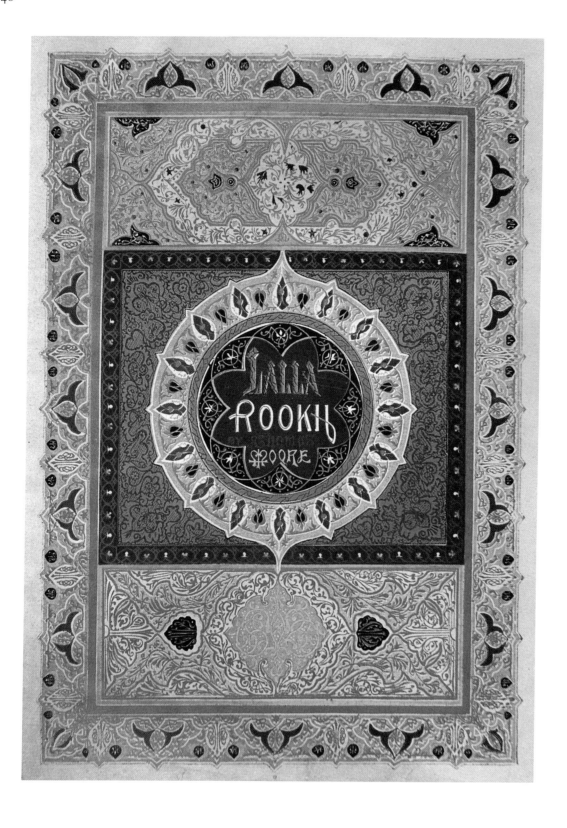

4 *Publisher, Authors and Readers, 1797–1842*

The first of the major turning points in the House of Longman as a business came in the late 1790s, the decade when Thomas Longman II died, for it was then that the first outsider to the Longman family, Owen Rees, emerging from a Welsh dissenting background and still only in his twenties, arrived at Paternoster Row. The exact date of his arrival is not known. According to all previously accepted accounts he was brought into the House before, not after, Thomas II's death; but from imprints there is no evidence that this was so. The name of Rees as a bookseller still figured separately in Bristol street records as late as 1798.[1]

The Bristol in which Rees had served a local apprenticeship was very different from the Bristol that Thomas Longman I had left nearly a century before. Now with twice as large a population, 62,400, it was something of a 'metropolis of the west'. It was also passing through a particularly interesting, if brief, phase in its history. The centre of anti-radical rioting in 1797, in the preceding decades it had already been a centre of what came to be called the 'romantic movement'.[2] Thomas Chatterton (1752–1770), 'the marvellous boy' who professed to have discovered ancient poems, became an early hero of the 'movement' when he committed suicide after spending the last four months of his life in London, not in Bristol; and by a coincidence that was the year when William Wordsworth was born.

In 1801 Longman/Rees published, more accidentally than deliberately, what came to be considered one of the main manifestos of 'the romantic

Tom Moore's *Lalla Rookh*, an oriental romance, was published by Longman in 1817 in a magnificent binding, and proved to be a major success. Moore sold 'his poem' to Longman before publication, for 'three thousand pounds!' It went on to be reprinted six times in its first year

Longman Archive Pt III

---

1 Unfortunately the date of the T.N. Longman/Rees partnership is not given on the list of partners, recorded in Paternoster Row probably by the Head of the Binding Department of the House in the nineteenth century, where T.N. Longman's partnership date (1793) is given retrospectively. Wallis, who refers to this list, describes Rees as 'active from 1797' (PW, p.4), but offers no evidence to this effect. The first T.N. Longman and O. Rees imprints date back to 1799. Rees's obituaries do not give the date of the partnership, but the ESTC throws up separately the names of Rees and T.N. Longman as sellers of J.A. Rose's *An Impartial History of the Late Disturbances in Bristol* (1793), Rees in Bristol, Longman in London.

2 See W.E. Minchinton, 'Bristol – Metropolis of the West in the Eighteenth Century' in *The Transactions of the Royal Historical Society*, Vol. 4, 5th series (1954), p.86. Bath had a life of its own, linked less to Bristol than to the great metropolis in London.

movement', Wordsworth's preface to the *Lyrical Ballads*, poems by himelf and Samuel Taylor Coleridge, and early in 1803 they published Joseph Cottle and Robert Southey's edition of *The Works of Thomas Chatterton* in two volumes. At the same time, they presented Chatterton's sister, Mrs. Newton, with fifty copies of the work and a reversionary interest in any future edition.[3]

There were many continuities and several coincidences in the Bristol story. Wine Street, from which Owen Rees carried on his trade in books, had long been known for its bookshops. Indeed, it was only four years after Thomas I launched his London business in Paternoster Row that a Bristol bookseller, Thomas Sendall, opened a new circulating library there, informing would-be customers that he had begun 'a method of furnishing curious lovers of reading with a great variety of books to read'.[4] Later in the century, when the number of Bristol booksellers had grown significantly, an undated local broadsheet referred in verse to another Bristol circulating library at No. 10 Wine Street, kept by Isaac James.[5]

The versifier was confident that 'those who come once will come again'. His doggerel verses referred to *Robinson Crusoe* 'and other books like it' (were there any?) as being in general demand:

> *Books*, did you say? Where are they sold?
> At *James's* Shop: both New and Old . . .
> Did *Crusoe* please your early Years
> Here in *my* Book *the Truth* appears:
> How *Selkirk* from the World secluded
> Led such a Life as very few did.

Certainly the James list was comprehensive:

> If you whole Volumes will not buy
> At once; for Numbers pray apply:
> *Geographies* or *Martyrologies*;
> *Encyclopædias*, where all Knowledge is;
> *Hist'ries of England*, how we go on;
> All kinds of *Magazines*; and so on.

---

3   E.H.W. Meyerstein, *A Life of Thomas Chatterton* (1948), p.495. See also L. Kelly, *The Marvellous Boy* (1971). Chatterton claimed to have found his Rowley poems in the loft of St Mary Redcliffe. See I. Haywood, 'The Making of History' in *Literature and History*, Vol. 9, No. 2, 1983, pp.139–51 and for a scholarly bi-centennial edition of Chatterton D. Taylor (ed.), *Complete Works*, 2 vols. (1971).

4   *Felix Farley's Bristol Journal*, 30 March 1728.

5   There is a full record of books borrowed from the Bristol Library, including those borrowed by Southey and Coleridge. See P. Kaufmann, *Borrowings from the Bristol Library Society, 1771–1784* (1960), pp.121–8. Significantly, the book borrowed most often was Hawkesworth's *Voyages*. Geography, including travel, was in the lead among the subjects covered in books borrowed. *Belles lettres* came second, and theology and ecclesiastical history third.

The broadsheet, now in the Bodleian Library, was headed 'Isaac James, Bookseller, Tea-Dealer, Glover and Undertaker'.

There is no evidence as to what particular Longman books were then on sale or whether Rees himself sold such articles as candles (a complementary product), snuff (possibly complementary), and scientific instruments, including spectacles. What is known is that next door to his shop the writer and future Poet Laureate, Robert Southey (1774–1843), the son of a draper, had been born. Joseph Cottle (1770–1853), co-editor with him of *The Works of Chatterton*, will figure many times later in this *History* as it moves in and out of Bristol up the Wye Valley and before long into the Lake District and Scotland. A poet himself, as was his brother Amos, Cottle was more than an intermediary in what proves to be not so much one story as a series of linked stories. He was an initiator, and, almost as important, he was also an extremely generous man.

If he and his printer, Nathaniel Biggs, (fl. 1795–1801) had not been in serious financial difficulties in 1798, the *Lyrical Ballads* would never have made their way to Paternoster Row. Indeed, it was Cottle's remarkable generosity to Southey and other poets then living in Bristol, offering them lucrative terms and sometimes paying them in full in advance, that had made him financially vulnerable, with his printer becoming vulnerable with him. A 1798 playbill of the Theatre Royal in Bristol describes a benefit evening for Biggs at which he gave a farewell address. The evening opened with *A Cure for the Heartache* and concluded with a specially requested rendition of the 'Epilogue Song'.

The events set out in this chapter of my *History* constitute a prelude, not an epilogue, with the French Revolution in the background as it was to be throughout the life of Owen Rees, who died in 1837, less than three months after the accession of Queen Victoria. That was a year that saw also the publication of Thomas Carlyle's *French Revolution*, a great work that could be compared at the time with Aeschylus and Isaiah. Carlyle might have been a Longman author. When he had travelled to London in the spring of 1831, carrying with him the unfinished manuscript of *Sartor Resartus*, he hoped, following advice given to him by the editor of *The Edinburgh Review*, to submit it to Murray, but unfamiliar with 'the usual custom of publishers', offered it also to Longman and Rees who, after having kept his manuscript for two days, turned it down. By then English attitudes towards the French Revolution had changed more than once since 1798 or, indeed, 1815, and they were to change again between 1831 and 1837.[6]

For John Stuart Mill, who was to become a Longman author, Carlyle's

Thomas Norton III (1771–1842) painted c.1830 by Thomas Phillips RA (1770–1845) *The Oxford Dictionary of National Biography* records that Phillips painted over 700 portraits including Byron, Moore and other 'Romantics', as well as scientists and other 'men of letters'. This was painted when Longman was probably fifty-nine. Phillips is listed as one of the many contributors to Rees's *Cyclopaedia*

Longman Archive

---

6   For some of the changes see G. Lewis, *The French Revolution: rethinking the debate* (1993).

Bristol in 1817. Painting
attributed to S. Anstie.

BL Maps K Top 37.37e.

French Revolution was not so much a history as an epic poem.[7] The taste
for 'epics' was a feature of the 1790s, as the taste for ballads had been in the
late seventeenth century and, indeed, still was; and Coleridge (1772–1834),
who spent a long spell in Germany in 1798–9, planned an epic on evil that
would take him twenty years to produce – ten years to collect materials; five
to compose the text; and five to correct. It would incorporate mathematics,
'fossilism', medicine, and 'the minds of men'.

~

The story of how Longman and Rees became intimately involved with
the fortunes of 'romanticism' began in June 1794 with a chance meeting
between Southey, then an undergraduate at Oxford, and Coleridge, then
an undergraduate at Cambridge.[8] Together they moved to Bristol, and the

---

7   See R.L. Stein, *Victoria's Year: English Literature and Culture, 1837–8* (1987).
     Mill was writing in the *Westminster Review*, Vol. 27 (1837), p.17.

8   While there, Coleridge read Wordsworth's *Descriptive Sketches*, published in
     January 1793 along with 'An Evening Walk', by Joseph Johnson, remarking
     later in *Biographia Literaria* (1817) that 'seldom, if ever, was the emergence of
     an original poetic genius above the literary horizon more evidently announced'
     (1907 edn., ed. J. Shawcross, Vol. I, p.56).

following year Southey was to claim in romantic fashion that it was destiny not choice that had determined their actions. 'Our names are written in the book of destiny on the same page.' So, too, was that of Cottle, who had by then moved from Bristol's High Street to Wine Street, not far from Rees, who was now publishing books as well as selling them. They included *The Mad Gallop or Trip to Devizes*, described on its frontispiece as being sold in London by T.N. Longman (and J. Parsons),[9] two editions in Welsh (1788) of works by John Bunyan, including his *Holy City*, and an exposition of the first ten chapters of *Genesis*.[10]

Both Southey and Coleridge were published by Cottle, as was Wordsworth, who had his own Bristol connection through his friendship with the son of a rich Bristol sugar merchant, J.P. Pinney.[11] Not surprisingly, therefore, Cottle liked to quote a remark of Southey that Bristol deserved 'panegyric instead of satire': he knew of 'no mercantile place so literary'.[12] Charles Lamb (1775–1834) also figured in Cottle's Bristol scene. A school friend of Coleridge, he entered Cottle's life in June 1797, when he met Coleridge and Wordsworth at Nether Stowey, in the countryside not far from Bristol.

At this stage in the writers' lives they were all radicals, as was Cottle himself; and in 1794 and 1795 Southey and Coleridge shared the dream of escaping from 'Oppression's Temple', crossing the Atlantic, and starting a new 'Pantisocratic' community in Pennsylvania where all things would be shared in common. Not surprisingly, the settlement would be equipped with 'a good library of books', and Bristol, where they could see ships all ready to take them, would be the starting point of their voyage. The two friends were already writing their own books. In 1794 Southey had written *Wat Tyler*, which was to be maliciously published years later, in 1817, after he had completely changed his political perspectives.[13] Also in 1794 the two

Frontispiece from J. Cottle *Early Recollections: chiefly relating to the Late Samuel Taylor Coleridge during his residence in Bristol* 2 vols. Longman, Rees & Co, & Hamilton Adams & Co 1837

BL 1164.h.19

---

9   In 1800 Rees and Longman published 'The Pleasures of Retirement' by 'John Jefferys of Bristol'. It was printed in Bristol by Biggs and Cottle.

10   For the Welsh background of Rees's publishing see E. Rees, *The Welsh Book Trade before 1820* (1988).

11   It was at Pinney's house that Coleridge first met Wordsworth. (See S. Gill, *William Wordsworth, A Life* (1989), p.92.) In a letter to a friend Wordsworth said that he went to Bristol 'to see those two extraordinary young men, Southey and Coleridge'.

12   J. Cottle, *Early Recollections; chiefly Relating to the Late Samuel Taylor Coleridge, during his Long Residence in Bristol* 2 vols., (Longman, Rees and Co.; Hamilton, Adams & Co., 1837), Vol. II, p.6. For his part, Southey pressed Cottle to write a history of Bristol. J. Latimer's multi-volume *Annals of Bristol* did not appear until 1906, but J. Morgan published *A Brief Historical Sketch of Bristol* in 1851.

13   See G. Carnall, *Robert Southey and his Age: The Development of a Conservative Mind* (1960).

men published together through Cottle the highly topical historical drama *The Fall of Robespierre*.

Southey and Coleridge had their own local circle, political as well as literary, and one of their converts to Pantisocracy was a young poet, Robert Lovell, who died young in 1796, as Chatterton had done before him. Southey, Coleridge and Lovell married three sisters, the high-spirited Fricker girls, whose widowed mother kept a dress shop in Bristol. Coleridge married Sara Fricker on 4 October 1795, and when Southey secretly married Edith Fricker the following month, Cottle paid for the ring and the marriage fees. Meanwhile, Wordsworth had also came into Cottle's vision, and while he was staying at the Pinneys, Cottle immediately offered him ten guineas in advance for an unfinished poem. Wordsworth was awaiting his sister Dorothy, with whom he planned to set up home at the Pinneys' country house, Racedown, Dorset.

When in 1796 Cottle published *Poems on Various Subjects* by 'S.T. Coleridge, late of Jesus College, Cambridge', for the copyright of which he paid thirty guineas, Southey and Coleridge in defiance of their early philosophy and close friendship were already falling apart.[14] There were temperamental differences between them, and their personal experiences – and reading – began to diverge. As an author, Southey, who after his marriage made a journey to Portugal to explore its politics more than its scenery, delivered what he promised: Coleridge, just as ambitious, but with more genius, as Dorothy Wordsworth immediately recognised, did not.[15]

It was entirely in character that in 1799 Southey edited not for Cottle but for Longman and Rees their *Annual Anthology*, attracting among his contributors the young scientist and occasional poet Humphry Davy (1788–1829), who at the age of twenty had arrived in Bristol to superintend Dr Thomas Beddoes's Pneumatic Institution at Clifton, set up in 1798, in order to study the 'medical powers' of 'airs and gases'. Later to be knighted (1812), Davy was to be taken up by many publishers, including Constable.[16] Science and poetry then went together, not least for Wordsworth, and Davy's first poem (1795) was called 'The Sons of Genius'.

Beddoes (1760–1808) had lectured on Chemistry at Oxford University, and in 1799 his *Essay on the causes, early signs and prevention of pulmonary consumption for the use of parents and preceptors* bore a Longman imprint. Southey noted how Beddoes had invented 'a new pleasure', 'laughing gas'. For Coleridge another 'pleasure', laudanum, was to have a dangerous effect

---

14   See G. Whalley, 'Coleridge and Southey in Bristol' in RES, new series, Vol. 1, No. 4 (1950), pp.340–45.

15   E. de Selincourt (ed.), *The Letters of William and Dorothy Wordsworth* (1935–7), Vol. I, p.196.

16   See K. Curry, 'The Contributions to The Annual Anthology', in PBSA, Vol. 42 (1948), pp.50–65.

on his life. He began to take it in 1796, influenced by Beddoes's important translation from the elegant Latin of Dr John Brown's *Elements of Medicine* (1795). The addictive properties of opium were not understood until the second half of the nineteenth century.[17]

The trail of consequences was fully concealed from Cottle's view when, under intense financial pressure, in 1799, he sold over a hundred of his copyrights to Longman/Rees for £210. They included J.P. Estlin's *Discourse at the Chapel in Lewin's Mead, Bristol, on the Nature and the Causes of Atheism*[18] and a work reputed to be by a Persian scholar, *Poems, containing the Plaints, Consolations and Delights of Achmed Ardebeili, a Persian exile, with notes historical and explanatory*. (They were, in fact, poems by Charles Fox (1764–1809). There was also a medical lecture by Beddoes.)

Ironically, in retrospect, but for what seemed good reasons at the time, Thomas Norton and Rees did not take over the copyright of the *Lyrical Ballads* which had been left off Cottle's list of literary assets. The poet thought of these early poems as 'experimental', and it was only after the text had been returned free by Cottle to Wordsworth in October 1799 that Wordsworth in turn had sold it directly to Longman and Rees in 1800, along with an additional volume. The title *Lyrical Ballads* had been deleted from a list of all the copyrights that Longman acquired from Cottle. When Cottle's 1798 edition of the *Ballads* appeared anonymously, as Sir Walter Scott's early Waverley Novels were to do, and many other novels already did, Southey wrote 'an anonymous review on the basis of insider knowledge', calling the 'Ancient Mariner' 'a Dutch attempt at German sublimity' with an 'absurd and unintelligible' story. A reply by Lamb in the *Critical Review* enthusiastically took up the cudgels, claiming that the 'Ancient Mariner' was 'a right English attempt, and a successful one, to dethrone German sublimity'.[19]

A young Macaulay, who was to write so critically of Southey's prose, read the poem with delight, picking it out in the bookshelves of his godmother, Hannah More (1745–1833), pre-eminently successful Evangelical tract and

---

17   According to Beddoes, who wrote a biographical preface to Brown's *Elements of Medicine* (2 vols. 1795), the opinions of Brown (1735–1788), an Edinburgh doctor, had been so widely 'diffused by oral communications as to affect the whole practice of medicine in Great Britain'. Brown criticised other physicians for prescribing opium to bring on sleep. It was, he claimed, 'the most powerful body of all others in producing and keeping up the watching state'.

18   Estlin was a well-known Unitarian minister and schoolmaster whose views influenced Coleridge's planned lectures in Bristol *On Revealed Religion, its Corruption, and its Political Views*.

19   *Critical Review*, 2 Nov. 1798.

The title page of Robert Southey's *Joan of Arc* (1796) published by Joseph Cottle of Wine Street, Bristol

BL 433.i.l (2)

fable writer.[20] Cottle had given her what proved to be a very rare copy of the first Bristol edition of *Lyrical Ballads*.[21]

What became the famous Preface to the *Ballads*, which appeared in the first Longman/Rees edition, was to be described years later as 'what almost amounts to a systematic theory of poetic art', a manifesto of 'romanticism'.[22] Yet the poems continued to be read without the preface, with neither Southey nor Coleridge complaining that readers did so. It was Southey not Coleridge or Wordsworth who most impressed Longman and Rees as a poet, and they continued to provide him with a regular living after he had abandoned all his early political views. His *Joan of Arc* (1796), which had been acquired by Cottle for fifty guineas – Cottle also gave him fifty copies – appeared in a Longman edition in 1800, with a further edition of 1805.[23] Longman and Rees gave him £115 for his poem *Thalaba the Destroyer (a metrical romance)*, which appeared in four editions between 1801 and 1821. Southey called it a 'metrical romance' not an epic, and for Marilyn Butler, who has brilliantly charted the history of romanticism, the poem was a 'cunning cultural palimpsest', no less so than Coleridge's 'The Ancient Mariner'.[24]

Before Southey had sent *Thalaba* to Longman and Rees, he had contemplated publishing it himself, but had been advised realistically by Coleridge to finish the poem at once, sell it to Longman and Rees, and get £100 for it.[25] The 'most prudent' course an author could follow, Coleridge generalised later, was 'to sell the copyright, at least of one or

20   A. Cruse, *The Victorians and Their Books* (1935), p.42.

21   Cottle, *Reminiscences*, p.260.

22   G.M. Harper, *William Wordsworth, His Life, Works and Influence*, 2 vols. (1916), Vol. I, pp.424–5. For other pre-1980 judgements – and there were many – see A.D. Harvey, *English Poetry in a Changing Society, 1780–1825* (1980), Ch.3, pp.58–77.

23   Sir Herbert Croft, a dubious character, detested by Chatterton's surviving sister, Mrs Newton, said memorably of Southey's *Joan of Arc* if unfairly, 'He writes prose somewhat like bad poetry and poetry somewhat like bad prose'. (Quoted in Meyerstein, *op. cit.*, pp.493–4.) In an unsigned critique in the *Monthly Review* (April 1796), the book was warmly praised and the allusions to *Pilgrim's Progress* described as 'particularly happy'. (Quoted in L. Hadden (ed.), *Robert Southey: A Critical Heritage* (1972), pp.41–2.) This comment would have appealed both to Cottle and to Rees.

24   M. Butler, 'Romanticism without Wordsworth', in K.R. Johnston, G. Chattin, K. Hanson and H. Marks (eds.), *Romantic Revolutions: Criticism and Theory* (1990), p.142.

25   Letter from Coleridge to Southey, 24 Dec. 1799 (E.L. Griggs (ed.), *Unpublished Letters of Samuel Taylor Coleridge* (1933), Vol. II, p.137). See also L. Hanson, *Life of Coleridge, Early Years* (1938), pp.402–3.

more editions for the most that the trade will offer'.[26] Coleridge's own private comments on *Thalaba* were more scathing even than Southey's on 'The Ancient Mariner': it had 'as much relation to poetry as dumb-bells have to music'.

    Thalaba was attacked in the *Edinburgh Review* in a fashion that Southey described as 'Thalabicide', and the poem sold only slowly: 500 copies, half the edition, were left in 1804. Yet Longman and Rees published not only a second heavily revised edition in 1809 but another long Southey poem *Madoc* (1805), priced exceptionally highly at 42s. Its price shocked Southey, who received only £3 17s. 1d. as his own income from the first year's sale.[27] It was only the somewhat surprising sales success of Southey's last epic poem *Roderick the Last of the Goths* (1814), heavily annotated, which went through five editions between 1814 and 1818 and was praised (privately) by Byron as 'one of the finest poems he had ever read', that enabled him to clear his debts with the House.[28] It was through income derived not from his poems but from his prose, including his lives of Wesley and of Nelson, not published by Longman and Rees, that Southey, who was appointed Poet Laureate in 1813, flourished.[29] His *Life of Nelson*, published by John Murray, for whom Southey had become a main reviewer in Murray's *Quarterly Review*, appeared in that year.

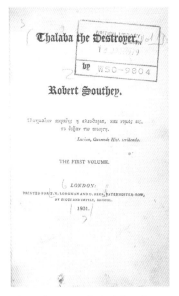

The title page of *Thalaba: the Destroyer* Vol. 1. by Robert Southey, published by T. N. Longman & O. Rees, 1801

BL W50/9804

26 In *Biographia Literaria* (1907 edn.), Vol. I, p.152, Coleridge exhorted those 'who in early life feel themselves disposed to become authors NEVER [to] PURSUE LITERATURE AS A TRADE'. Yet throughout his writings he dwelt frequently on the rules of the trade. Thus, sure that there were insuperable difficulties in trying 'to unite the functions of author and publisher', he noted realistically the cash-flow problem in publishing – paying for paper and printing before receiving sales revenue.

27 See Hadden, *op. cit.*, pp.24–6, which deals with Southey's finances. His father had failed in business and he was supported at Oxford by his uncle. Cottle's father, Robert, a Bristol tailor and woollen-draper, had confronted even greater financial problems than his son was to do. He was involved in several bankruptcies, the first of them in 1779, the second in 1790 (*Felix Farley's Journal*, 1 Jan. 1791). For Southey's comments on the price of *Madoc* see his statement in C.C. Southey, *The Life and Correspondence of the Late Robert Southey* (1850), Vol. II, p.322. 'Not that it is dear compared with other books [it was], but it is too much money; and I vehemently suspect that in consequence, the sale will be just sufficient for the publisher not to lose anything, and for me not to gain anything.'

28 E.H. Coleridge (ed.), *The Poetical Works of Lord Byron* (1898–1904), Vol. III, p.496. Coleridge, who praised Southey's poetry, despite his criticisms of *Thalaba*, wrote of *Roderick* that 'while retaining all his former excellencies of a poet eminently inventive and picturesque, he surpassed himself in language and metre, in the construction of the whole, and in the splendour of particular passages' (*Biographia Literaria*, Vol. I, p.46).

29 J.W. Warter, *Selections from the Letters of Robert Southey* (1856), Vol. II, pp.223–3 and Vol. III, p.46. Longman paid Southey in advance, as Cottle had done, and in 1822 he noted that his account with them was now producing him about £200 a year.

~

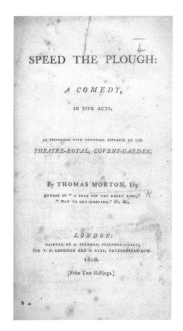

Title page to the comedy
Speed the Plough by Thomas
Morton (1764-1838) printed for
T.N.Longman and O.Rees, 1800

BL 11779.ddd.2 (4)

From the start of his London partnership Rees was directly involved in the overall conduct of the Longman book trade, and his name until 1804 appeared only with that of Longman on the House's imprints. He showed conspicuous enterprise. Within the organisation – and even more so after 1804, when with more partners there was now greater specialisation of duties within the House – he adapted himself to new requirements, inevitably involving greater complexity. There were more new book titles each year and more competition among publishers to secure them.

During the year 1800, when Rees was already established in Paternoster Row, no fewer than ninety titles were published by Longman and himself. The most topical title of the year was *Reflections on the Political State of Society at the Commencement of the Year 1800*, whose author, John Bowles (1751–1819), had produced other topical titles for Thomas II, usually his sole publisher. They had included *The Dangers of Premature Peace* (1795) and in 1793, the year when Britain went to war, *Dialogues on the Rights of Britons, between a Farmer, a Sailor and a Manufacturer*.[30]

In retrospect, the most interesting author's name in the Longman/ Rees list of 1800 was that of Cesare Mussolini, whose *Italian Exercises* was 'printed for the author': then in its second edition, it was said to be 'entirely free from those errors that were in the first'. Two other publications had titles which were to become particularly apposite in the twentieth century – *Management*, a comedy in five acts by Frederick Reynolds (1764–1841), and another comedy *Speed the Plough*, by Thomas Morton (1764?–1838). No fewer than eight Longman/Rees versions of the latter, which introduced Mrs. Grundy, embodiment of respectability, into the dialogue, though not into the action, incorporated into the title page the phrase 'as performed with universal applause at the Theatre Royal, Covent Garden'.[31] Rees shared in the applause: in its obituary of him *The Times* singled out the fact that he had been 'a warm patron of the drama and an acute and excellent dramatic critic'.[32]

Yet, while London was at the centre of both Rees's and Thomas Norton's world, the provincial periphery – and Scotland as well as Wales – were never neglected. Both men travelled frequently outside London,

---

30 His pamphlets, along with John Reeves, have been described as 'vulgar conservatism' by M. Philp in EHR Vol. 110, 1995.

31 Morton's play *Zorinski* was also listed, but only once. So, too, was a second play by Reynolds, *Speculation*. Reynolds, whose first plays (1786) were based on Goethe's *Werther* and Rousseau's *La Nouvelle Héloïse*, wrote nearly a hundred comedies and tragedies.

32 *The Times*, 12 Sept. 1837. The obituary records that before he retired, 'above' forty of his 'oldest friends and associates' assembled 'an entertainment', provided for him 'as a tribute to his integrity and gentlemanly conduct'.

occasionally together, as the provincial book trade grew in importance, Rees the more frequently of the two, making acquaintances and sometimes friends not only in the English provinces and in Scotland, but in Ireland. 'Mr. Rees left us last night on his usual Irish and Scotch journey', we read in the draft of a letter of 1821.[33]

Relations with their provincial contacts, scattered as they were, demanded patience and care, and Rees was as much concerned with them as Thomas Norton. 'When there were often angry contentions between the booksellers and the authors', wrote John Britton, a Longman author, one year younger than Rees and one of the best-informed, if least critical, of Rees's judges, Rees had always been 'eager and anxious to reconcile differences, to soothe irritated feelings and endeavour to urge authors to industry and perseverance, and his colleagues to forebearance and generosity'. 'At my own humble home I never saw him with a frown on his benignant countenance, nor heard a harsh, ungenerous sentiment from his lips.' 'Never was there a man who more fully and totally acted the part of 'Harmony' on the great stage of the world.'[34]

Such judgements make Rees sound like a paragon. It was not so much his temperament or his moral qualities that most helped him to direct an expanded and complex business, however, but the fact that his background was quite different from that of the Longmans. The family from which he came was a 'remarkable' one and had several different branches.[35] His father, Josiah Rees, was a distinguished Unitarian minister, born in 1744 at Llanfair-ar-y-bryan in Carmarthenshire, the son of another outstanding preacher, Owen Rees, 'one of the most respectable dissenting ministers of his time', who died in 1768, leaving a widow who lived on to be a hundred.[36]

Unitarianism was seldom a settled religion, and from his base at Gellig-ron, near Pontardwe, Josiah played an important part in Welsh religious history when he became a major influence in the conversion of

---

33   Letter to Sir E. Brydges, 30 June 1821.

34   J. Britton and T. Rees, *Reminiscences of Literary London* (1896), p.44. Britton, born in 1771, was entertained at Richmond in 1845 by a number of admirers who formed a Britton Club, which raised a subscription of £1,000 to enable him to write his autobiography, the first part of which appeared in 1850. He died in 1857.

35   See W.J. Phillips, 'Iolo Morganwg and the Rees family of Gellig-ron', in the *Journal of the National Library of Wales*, Vol. 14 (1965–6), pp.227–36. Iolo Morganwyg, Edward Williams, 'the Welsh bard', was given some financial assistance both by Owen Rees and Thomas Norton Longman during the first decade of the nineteenth century. For the Welsh background see R.H. Jones and E. Rees (eds.), *A Nation and its Books* (1998).

36   Manuscript Record, 'Rees Family of Gellig-ron' (National Library of Wales).

a group of Welsh Presbyterians into Unitarians. He was the first preacher at the opening assembly of the Welsh Unitarian Association in 1803. He married twice and died in 1804 at the age of sixty, having revealed a deep interest in Welsh history and literature as well as religious politics. This was expressed in his launching in 1770 of a pioneering fortnightly magazine in Welsh, *Eurgrawn Cymraeg*.[37] Richard Morris, a Churchman, chose the word *Eurgrawn* in the title in place of *Magazin*, which had been originally suggested, describing 'Magazin' as 'an abominable word to be introduced in a new work in the language'. In its English context it had been introduced into the language in its modern meaning by Edward Cave.

Of the ten children by Josiah's second marriage, Owen was the oldest, and when he was apprenticed to Arthur Browne, a Bristol bookseller, his father paid £5 for the privilege. Another of Josiah's sons, Thomas, might have become a publisher also and was employed as a reader by Longman and Rees. He also took over the editorship of the *Annual Review* from Arthur Aikin. In 1808 he met Coleridge 'for an hour or two' to discuss Wordsworth's *The White Doe of Rylstone*.[38] Thomas made his reputation, however, as an author in his own right and as a Unitarian minister, for a brief time serving at his father's chapel. While Owen was working with Longman after leaving Bristol, Thomas was in charge of various Unitarian chapels in or near London. In the *Dictionary of Welsh Biography* Owen Rees figures only in a paragraph devoted to the life of his brother Thomas, who was to be upset by scandal in the 1850s, when he fled to Spain to avoid a possible prison sentence: he died at Brighton in 1864. Keenly interested in antiquities, Thomas was a Fellow of the Society of Arts, and in 1819 he acquired a doctorate of Glasgow University. He was also a contributor to the *Monthly Repository* and in 1815 published *The Beauties of South Wales*, with Britton as his co-author.[39]

Josiah's second son, also called Josiah, spent much of his time trading abroad in places as far apart as Hamburg and Martinique. He was married in Malta, where Coleridge had spent fifteen months in 1804 and 1805, 'in many

---

37 Another title of the magazine was *Trysorfa Gwybodaeth*. For its significance see D.R. Phillips, 'The *Eurgrawn Cymraeg* of 1770', in the *Journal of the Welsh Bibliographical Society*, Vol. V (1937–42).

38 Letter of 23 May 1808 from Coleridge to Thomas Norton Longman in Griggs, *op. cit.*, Vol. I, p.424. Coleridge had suggested changes to the text, maintaining generally at the same time that 'a Publisher had an undoubted *Right* (in the *equity* between man & man, as well as in the vulgar sense of the word) to have the means of some distinct Information concerning [the] nature [of a text submitted to him] and the probability of it's [*sic*] immediate sale'. In another trenchant judgement the ER was to describe the *White Doe* as the very worst poem we ever saw imprinted in a quarto volume' (quoted in Lord John Russell, *Memoirs, Journal, and Correspondence of Thomas Moore* (1853), p.272).

39 Britton and Rees, *op. cit.*, p.45; *Dictionary of Welsh Biography* (1959), pp.826–7. The Society of Arts was not granted a Royal Charter until 1847.

respects, the most memorable and instructive period of his life';[40] and for a time he served as British Consul in Smyrna. One of his sons, George Owen, who was to be the chief beneficiary in Owen Rees's will, started practising medicine in London in the year before his uncle died. He was to act for a time as Principal Medical Officer of the New Model Prison at Pentonville, and later as Assistant Physician at Guy's Hospital. There is no evidence to suggest that he knew of Thomas Guy's connection with Thomas Longman I.

Through his own family history Owen Rees had just the right kind of personal experience to form a creative partnership with Thomas Norton. His Welsh connections meant a great deal to him, and it was to Wales that he was to return, all too briefly, when he retired from Longman at midsummer in 1837. By then he had become a rich man, a tangible reward for his own industry and perseverance. He had always worked hard, but his decision to return to his own property, 'the place of his nativity', Gellig-ron, where his father had lived and had once kept a school, came too late. According to family records, by then 'his unremitting attention to business had undermined his constitution'.[41] Britton had written to him three weeks before his death that 'if there is anything I can do for you either in town or elsewhere do not hesitate to ask anything quite *unreservedly*'. Old friendships, he stated, were 'invaluable'; after the age of sixty, new friendships were difficult to make: indeed it was incompatible with the natural relations of life to make them.

Rees died on 5 September 1837, one month after returning from London to Wales, and was buried in the family grave at Gellig-ron, where a tablet was prepared to commemorate him. 'The loss to this neighbourhood of so worthy and excellent man is irreparable', wrote the *Cambrian*, which printed discourses delivered at his funeral in both Welsh and English. 'By none will his loss be more sincerely deplored than by the necessitous poor and indigent who never applied to him in vain.'[42] No fewer than three hundred people attended his funeral service in the small Unitarian Chapel.

The *Gentleman's Magazine* noted on his death how '[Tom] Moore's Works, Scott's Works, and indeed a number of the Works of the principal authors of his age', all of them described later in this chapter, bore 'testimony to the important share Mr. Rees had in bringing forward their productions, and of the friendly intercourse which subsisted between them and him'.[43] *The Times* too made the same point: 'Few men in the metropolis ever had larger opportunities of cultivating the acquaintance and intimacy of men distinguished in all the walks of literature, and in bringing forward their productions.'[44]

Owen Rees (1770–1837). Thomas Longman V, commenting on his family's pictures, in his *Memories* of 1921, wrote that this was 'generally pronounced to be a "good picture"' but the artist is unknown.

Thomas Clarkson (1760–1846), the abolitionist, wrote to Longman from his home, Playford Hall, on 16 November 1837 that 'I have been very much affected ... by the Death of your late worthy Partner, Mr Rees, a gentleman of such Kindness and Goodness of Heart, ... such affability of manners, such Readiness to serve any one who applied to him, that all who knew him could not but deeply and sincerely feel his loss.'

Longman Archive

40   R. Holmes, *Coleridge: Darker Reflections* (1998 edn.), pp.17–50.

41   Manuscript Record, 'Rees Family of Gellig-ron' (National Library of Wales).

42   The *Cambrian*, 16 Sept. 1837.

43   GM (1837), p.430.

44   *The Times*, 12 Sept. 1837.

For Rees relatives counted as much as authors, even the most distinguished of them, and on his death in 1837 he was able to make generous provision for them since he had no children of his own. He left his property at Gellig-ron 'and other lands in Glamorgan' to his brother Josiah, along with £5,000. Thomas and Richard Rees were each bequeathed £5,000, and Susannah and Sarah Rees £3,000 each. Owen also left £1,000 to be divided between the children and grandchildren of his late half-sister, Mary. Whatever radical political economists, some of them well-known to Rees, might think of the economic consequences of inherited wealth, Rees was clearly thinking, as Thomas Norton was, of his own family's future.

It was not a relative, however, but a close friend, 'Miss Jenkins of Swansea', who wrote a poem in his memory and had it printed in the *Cambrian*. It included the lines:

> No widow'd heart is left for him to mourn,
> No orphan from a tender parent torn.

The author went on to apostrophise 'genius' – as Rees himself might well have done in writing of others, including his authors:

> . . . Lament for him whose fostering care,
> Thy children too were ever wont to share,
> His hand oft led them to the shrine of Fame,
> And would extend to aid the humblest claim.

A deep trust in 'genius', which scholars have identified as one of the expressions of 'romanticism', was often expressed in literary circles throughout Rees's lifetime – and later.[45] For Curwen, 'at the time of Thomas Norton Longman's accession to the chiefdom of the Paternoster Row firm, the literary world was undergoing a seething revolution. Genius was again let loose upon the earth to charm all men by her beauty, and to scare them for a while by her utter contempt for precedent.'[46]

~

One of the witnesses to Rees's will was a later Longman Partner, Thomas Brown (1778–1869), who had joined the House as an apprentice in 1792 at the age of 14 before Thomas II died. He was the son of Christopher Brown, who had worked devotedly for Thomas II and had been admitted to the Stationers' Company in 1804, five years after Rees. He brought in capital too (via Thomas Evans) when he became a Partner in 1811. His continuing presence in Paternoster Row was in itself testimony to the

---

45 See *Biographia Literaria* (1907 edn.), Vol. 2, pp.24–6.

46 Curwen, *op. cit.*, p.89. Scott, who refused to flatter Byron, nevertheless described *Childe Harold IV* in an unsigned review as an 'extraordinary poem' that deserved 'the full praise that genius in its happiest effects can demand of us'. (QR, Vol. XIX, April 1818.) For extracts from the review, with commentary, see T. Redpath (ed.), *The Young Romantics and Critical Opinion, 1807–1824* (1973).

enlarged business of 'the long firm', and it was one of his duties to look after new apprentices. He lived in No. 39 and became known as 'the Nestor of the Row'. He was Under-Warden of the Stationers' Company in 1856 and Upper Warden in 1857/8.

When he retired in 1859, he left £100,000 to charities, including £5,000 to the Stationers' Company, £5,000 to the Company's School, £3,000 to the Royal Literary Fund and £10,000 to the Bookseller's Provident Retreat. He also left £500 to his godchild, F.W. Longman (1846–1908), an invalid for most of his life following a riding accident, £1,550 to be shared between twenty-three members of Longman staff, and the residue of his estate to the grandchildren of his 'friend and former partner, Thomas Norton Longman'. Just before his death he gave £1,500 to the Dean and Chapter of St Paul's for the new great West Window.[47] This, like 39 Paternoster Row, was to be destroyed during the Blitz of 1940.

By contrast, the career of another early partner, Thomas Hurst, served as a warning. Having also brought in capital much earlier in 1804, when along with Cosmo Orme (1780–1859), he became a new partner, his name preceded that of Rees on the House's imprint and continued to do so until 1826. He and Orme had previously been joint partners with a bookseller called Lee in a bookselling business at 32 Paternoster Row, where Orme, born in Scotland, joined him. Orme had been a clerk with Longman and Rees and he joined Hurst after his brother, who had returned from India with a fortune, advanced him £1,000. Orme, who had been approached by Constable to act as a London distributor of his books,[48] never married and retired from Longman in 1841, a year after the closing of the Longman Old (second-hand) Book department where he and Hurst had worked together. Hurst had been forced out as a partner after being caught up through his brother John in the ramifications of the financial 'crash' of 1826.[49] His name appeared on the imprints of the first books published in 1826, and then disappeared for ever.

When the year began, he had been living in an 'elegant but unostentatious style, with a carriage and good establishment, on the brow of Highgate Hill', a man of substance and reputation. When the year ended, he was a ruined man unable to regain credit. One of the accommodation bills he signed in the Longman name – without telling his partners – provided what Curwen, writing half a century later, called 'a lesson and warning' both to speculators and also 'to generous-hearted persons, who

Thomas Brown (1778–1869). In 1811 he became the Partner in charge of the Cash Department at Longman. His obituary in *The Bookseller* commented that 'for many years there has not been any instance of a gentleman who, by life-long industry and integrity, had accumulated [such] a large fortune.' 'The Retreat' was a group of houses at Abbots Langley for the retirement of people in the trade (which still exists)

Longman Archive

47   Blagden, *Fire More Than Water*, p.22.

48   J. Millgate, 'Archibald Constable and the Problem of London: "Quite the connection we have been looking for"', in TL, 6th series, Vol. 18, No. 2, June 1966, p.115.

49   See below, p.165.

Cosmo Orme (1780–1859).
Orme entered the Partnership
in 1804 with Thomas Hurst
(1775–1847), who had built up
the large wholesale country
business. In 1807 Bevis Green
became Hurst's apprentice.
Orme left around £20,000 in
his will

Longman Archive

are susceptible of being imposed on by the seductions of the cunning
and the crafty'.[50] 'Speculators' was a term much used in publishing in
the 1820s as was, outside as well as inside the book trades, the word
'speculation', not carefully distinguished from 'investment' even by
knowledgeable observers.

Hurst could not claim ignorance as an excuse. Common though the
practice of using post-dated bills was, it was condemned by the leaders
of the book trade as strongly as 'underselling', disposing of books below
the publisher's price. Thus, as early as 1811, in a letter to the Ballantynes,
Edinburgh printers with whom Scott was in undisclosed partnership,
Thomas Norton had made it clear, as John Murray II was to do, that it was
a practice of the House not to grant 'any sort of accommodation bills, as
it renders our names too common with bankers, with whom, of course,
we are always desirous of remaining in the most respectable light'.[51]
Accommodation bills were exclusively paper transactions, costly to transact,
through which participants in business transactions reached a 'mutual
accommodation' involving promissory notes that could be converted into
cash only at deeply discounted rates.

Bankers themselves, on whom conversion depended, were in trouble
in 1826, particularly country bankers who depended on back-up from
London bankers,[52] and the full extent of Hurst's (and his bank's) dealings
was not known until after the business of Hurst and Robinson (Hurst was
Thomas's brother) had gone bankrupt. Before that Thomas Hurst had
received large sums from Thomas Norton and Rees as well as the return
of the capital that he had invested in the House, but it was not Hurst but
the House's bankers, 'Sir Peter Pole Bt and others', who ran an extensive
country banks agency, who found themselves in court in 1828.[53] Having
been the House's bankers for twenty-five years, they had brought down
forty-three corresponding country bankers and they now faced legal action
initiated by Thomas Norton and Rees. The sums involved were huge, and
one of the bills that Hurst discounted – for £2,500 – was not to his brother
but to his wine merchant.

Longman/Rees, Orme, Brown and Green as they were now called,
were represented in the case by top counsel – Sir James Scarlett (1769–1844),

---

50   Curwen, *op. cit.*, p.45.

51   Letter of 7 Feb. 1811. LA.

52   For the country banks see L.S. Pressnell, *Country Banking in the Industrial
Revolution* (1956) and for the City D. Kynaston, *The City of London*, Vol. I,
1815–1890 (1994), esp. Part I, Ch. 6, 'Curst be the Bubbles'.

53   The Pole partners included Henry Sykes Thornton who was connected with
the Evangelical 'Clapham Sect' to which Macaulay's father Zachary belonged.
Marianne Thornton wrote a vivid letter on the 'panic' to Hannah More. The
Governor of the Bank of England was connected by marriage to Pole.

later the first Baron Abinger, who appeared for them in other cases, Henry (later Lord) Brougham (1778–1868), ambitious Whig politician, and John Campbell (1779–1861), a future Lord Chancellor, who was to figure in a different capacity in Longman history as an 'umpire' in a book trade dispute about underselling in 1852.[54] It took the jury only ten minutes to find for the defendants (the bankers). Clearly the Longman cashier for eighteen years had been an unconvincing witness when he had stated that he had not thought that it was necessary for a second partner to sign when Hurst drew bills. Both he and a clearing clerk at Pole's Bank had not entered items in their registers.

The defence case in 1828 was that Brown, described as 'the super-intendent of the Cash Department' at Longmans, should have kept a check.[55] But when the case was lost, it was Hurst, and not the bankers – or Brown – who suffered. His loss of reputation was so complete that during his last years he was dependent on the charity of others.[56] Meanwhile, it was ironic that Orme, with whom he had first been a partner, should go on to serve as the first President of the Booksellers' Provident Institution.

From 1810 onwards, before and after Hurst, regular Partners' meetings were held at 39 Paternoster Row and they were to continue into the twentieth century, each partner having specialised tasks to perform. Within this framework Brown, blamed in court, had been from the start in charge of cash and authors' accounts, and for a time Orme received authors who called at Paternoster Row, while Hurst was in charge of the country department.[57] In 1813 a four-page folio catalogue described in detail rare old books on sale, including Lyson's *Environs of London* (£250), *Biographia Britannica* (£225) and Walton's *Compleat Angler* (£70).[58] In 1815, when the partners abandoned the wholesale business, 'elegant and commodious Retail Rooms' were opened and 'an unprecedented Collection of the Rarities and Curiosities of Literature was placed on display'. 'Often books were bought for their outside merely.' When John Keats required a copy of Chapman's *Homer* to replace Benjamin Haydon's copy which he had lost, he wrote 'I must get one [and it would be a second-hand copy] at Longmans'.[59]

---

54 Campbell, an author of several books, some of them very sharply criticised, wrote *Lives of the Lord Chancellors* (1845–7), the first volume of which was highly praised.

55 *The Times*, 27 Oct. 1828.

56 For an obituary see GM, Vol. 28 (1847), p.105.

57 He is frequently referred to in diaries. For a memoir of him see the *Bookseller*, Aug. 1859, p.1169.

58 PC, 13 Jan. 1906.

59 Quoted in CC, pp.6–7. The second-hand book trade continued until 1849, the retail department until 1886.

Bevis Ellerby Green (1793–1869)
was the son of a farmer
near Doncaster. He came to
London at thirteen and was
apprenticed to Hurst, becoming
a Partner in the 'long firm'
when Hurst retired, and did
not retire himself until 1864.
John Blackwood described him
as 'almost the only decent-
looking Christian' in a crowd
of booksellers and publishers,
and he made generous bequests
in his will, according to *The
Bookseller* for 1st April 1869,
the total of which made up
£200,000

Longman Archive

A few years later Hurst and Orme further augmented the stock of the Old Book Department with the acquisition of 'a large collection of scarce and curious books on old Poetry and Drama' from the collection of Thomas Hill, a catalogue of which, *Bibliotheca Anglo-Poetica*, was prepared by a Longman clerk. The author of *The Book Hunter in London* described Hill as a bibliomaniac rather than a bibliophile, 'devoid of intellectual endowments', but he was a friend of Barnes, the editor of *The Times*.[60]

On Orme's retirement, another clerk, Thomas Reader (1818–1905), took over the running of the country department. He had arrived in Paternoster Row in 1834, and in 1865 he too was to become a partner. Long before then Bevis Ellerby Green, born in 1793, the first Green to figure in Longman imprints, who had become a partner in 1822, was given charge both of the country and of the foreign departments. He did not retire from the business until 1864, and when he died in 1869, he was succeeded by his son William. Bevis left £200,000 in his will, and among his charitable gifts were three pavilioned shelters for London cabbies in Paddington and South Kensington.

Reader, Orme and Green do not seem to have had nicknames. Yet nicknames or soubriquets, such as 'Nestor of the Row', were common in the early-nineteenth-century trade which remained highly personal in character despite the entry of newcomers. Until his fall, Constable, a portly man, was known as the 'Czar of Muscovy', Murray as 'the Emperor of the West', and Thomas Norton and his string of partners, as 'the Divan'. One day, when Thomas Norton was dining with Constable, he had congratulated him on the fine swans, still a Longman symbol, on his pond. 'Swans', Constable had replied, 'They are only geese, and their names are Longman, Hurst, Rees, Orme and Brown.' It was a joke that did not go down well at 39 Paternoster Row.[61]

~

Contented and secure in his Hampstead residence, far away from his Divan, Thomas Norton III had no wish to emulate Constable or Murray nor to win such popular acclaim as Rees received in 1837. He had been given the name Norton for family reasons: as has been noted, Thomas I had acquired the lucrative Royal Grant and privilege of printing Lily's Latin

---

60   See *The Book Hunter in London*, p.78.

61   Curwen, *op. cit.*, p.131.

Grammar from the Norton family[62], and through his marriage he had acquired new dynastic 'connections' that were both political and religious. His wife, another Mary in the Longman story, whom he had married in 1798, was the daughter of William Slater of Horsham and a cousin of the Revd. Sydney Smith (1771–1845). Born in the same year as Thomas Norton, Smith, an Anglican clergyman with all the right connections, was as renowned in his lifetime and since for his wit as for his Whiggery. His connection with Longman has not been mentioned, however, by most of his biographers.

Thomas Norton and Mary had seven children, three sons and four daughters, the first Longman children in the direct line since Thomas I had arrived in London. They were christened not in St Gregory by St Paul's but in Hampstead Parish Church. Through his children, Thomas Norton III's connections were of a different kind from those of Smith: some

'A few Bookish People'

McLean's Monthly Sheet of Caricatures No 24 or 'The Looking Glass' Vol. 2nd Dec 1st 1831

Longman Archive

---

62   See above, p.72.

William Slater of Horsham
(n.d), painted by Thomas
Phillips RA

Thomas III married Slater's
daughter and he was thus
father-in-law to Thomas Norton
Longman III. William Slater
was also a cousin of Sydney
Smith's, who used to frequent
Mrs Longman's parties in
Hampstead

Pearson Education

of them had a business as well as a social dimension. His son Charles, following in the wake of his uncle George, was apprenticed in 1823, at the age of fourteen, to John Dickinson, the papermaker, who still provided the Longman business with most of its paper; and after his marriage he moved to Nash House, an agreeable stuccoed residence (with portico and pediment) that adjoined Dickinson's mills in Hertfordshire.[63]

Things could not be kept entirely within the family, however, and Thomas Norton as a large-scale user of hand-made paper, who insisted on the highest quality, often had to look beyond Hertfordshire. One of his other suppliers was William Balston, Chairman of London's Master Paper Makers, operating at Springhill Mill in Kent, a perfectionist who was disappointed when Longman/Rees found fault with the colour or weight of the deliveries.[64] Meanwhile there was a further Longman family link with the printing trade, for in 1819 Thomas Norton III's daughter Mary married Andrew Spottiswoode (1787–1866), a grandson of William Strahan, who was to be in sole control of the printing business until 1848–9.

Like his grandfather and uncle Andrew before him, Andrew Spottiswoode was for a time a Member of Parliament – first for Saltash and then for Colchester – and, important in the politics of the trade, he chaired a committee of the Association of Master Printers opposed to changes in copyright law. Both he and John Dickinson were active in the affairs of the Stationers' Company, and in 1859 Dickinson was to propose and Spottiswoode to second a Company resolution, which was lost, to liquidate the English Stock of the Stationers' Company by paying a bonus of 150 per cent.[65] It was not until 1961 that the Stock was wound up, but one of the most famous almanacs that then sustained its income, *Old Moore's*, was disposed of in 1927 as no longer 'considered to enhance the reputation or dignity of the Company'.[66]

~

During the years covered in this chapter, the Company maintained without difficulty or loss of reputation and dignity its great social functions, but in this respect the individual publishing Houses, now responsible for the daily operations of the book trades, were just as active in pursuing a social side, now more open than in the days of Thomas Longman II. From the

---

63   See J. Evans, *The Endless Web. John Dickinson & Co, 1804–1954* (1955).

64   T. Balston, *William Balston, Paper-Maker, 1759–1849* (1955), p.111.

65   C. Blagden, *The Stationers' Company* (1960), p.267. Blagden was one of the first scholars to trace movements over time in the price and ownership of stock.

66   An anonymous pamphlet of 1871 attacking the Company survives, appropriately, in the Company's archives – *Entered at Stationers' Hall: A Sketch of the History and privileges of the Company of Stationers.*

start Thomas Norton and Rees appreciated the importance of establishing a social presence in London. However much they travelled, this was always their base. The parties that they gave together in London soon became famous. Some were at Greenhill House in Hampstead, others in Paternoster Row. Many descriptions of them have been recorded, perhaps the most famous of them that of the American author, Washington Irving (1783–1859), who has been described as the first American man of letters. 'The two ends [of the table] were occupied by the two partners of the House', Irving wrote. Rees was 'the laughing partner' and Longman 'the caring partner who attends to the joints'.[67]

In fact, both men cared, and both men could laugh. Irving, who was actively involved, sometimes in a commercial way, in the promotion of American books, also noted more revealingly that there were certain 'geographical boundaries in the land of literature' ruled over by Longman and Rees. 'An author crosses the port line about the third edition and gets into claret: When he has reached the sixth or seventh he may revel in champagne and burgundy.' 'Dined with Messrs Longman and Co. at one of their literary parties', Henry Crabb Robinson (1775–1867), the Unitarian foreign editor of *The Times*, one of the founders of the Athenaeum Club and, above all, a committed and informative diarist, wrote in 1812. 'I had heard much of these literary parties. ... Longman himself is a quiet gentlemanly man.'[68] His own accounts of the parties were always lively, even inspired. And Orme, frequently mentioned by Crabb Robinson, seems to have served as a go-between.

At their parties Thomas Norton III and Rees were surrounded not only by newcomers but by regularly invited guests who constituted what was described at the time as a 'circle'. As early as 1804, Southey told Coleridge to go to 'one of [Longman's] Saturday evenings: you will see a coxcomb or two, and a dull fellow or two; but you will, perhaps, meet Turner and Duppa, and Duppa is worth knowing'.[69] Wordsworth was less

---

67 Irving's account of his British experiences in *The Sketch Book of Geoffrey Crayon, Gent* (1819–20) established his reputation on both sides of the Atlantic where there were many signs of Anglo-American animosity. 'In all the four corners of the globe', Sydney Smith had asked, 'who reads an American book?' Irving, who attended Murray's parties as appreciatively as those of Longman and Rees, for the first time on 16 August 1817, was to prove that this was a foolish question. Murray became Irving's English publisher and had his portrait painted and hung next to Byron's in the drawing room at 50 Albemarle Street. See B.H. McClary (ed.), *Washington Irving and the House of Murray* (Knoxville, 1969).

68 E.J. Morley (ed.), *Henry Crabb Robinson on Books and Their Writers*, Vol. I (1938), p.67. Robinson's diary refers several times to Orme who took him Longman books to read at home (e.g. *ibid.*, p.184).

69 Quoted in Curwen, *op. cit.*, p.99.

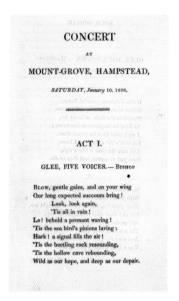

A glee from a Concert
Programme at Mount Grove,
Hampstead, January 10, 1818

Longman Archive

sure. 'At Longman's I dined once', he wrote to Scott in 1808. 'Some curious
fishes were present'. They included Sharon Turner (1768–1847), lawyer and
historian – and friend of Murray – who was introduced to Thomas Norton
by Crabb Robinson, and 'a log of literature, a dry-salter of the name of Hill,
a *proprietor* of a periodical publication of which probably you never heard,
entitled the *Monthly Mirror* ... The head of the table was illuminated by the
splendid countenance of that sun of Literature, Artaxerxes Longimanus,
and in opposition were exhibited the milder glories of a sister planet, Rees
I believe being the name which he bears among mortals – Upon the whole
it was but a dull business, saving that we had some good haranguing, talk
I cannot call it, from Coleridge.'[70]

Years later, when the two hosts had grown older together, Henry
Vizetelly (1820–1894), himself a publisher with a long and colourful
history, recalled the day when as a young man he had paid a visit to the
Longman office in Paternoster Row to see William Longman, Thomas
Norton's younger son. He also met there, he said, Thomas Norton, whom,
he had heard, 'was supposed to stand a great deal on his own dignity'. 'He
condescendingly murmured a few words to me', Vizetelly remembered, 'as
he sat bolt upright in his armchair, gravely munching an apple. He was
treated by his sons ... with all the old-fashioned filial respect which parents
exacted from their children in the last [the eighteenth] century.'[71]

Rees, who was dead by the time that Vizetelly visited Paternoster Row,
had often entertained authors on his own at weekly literary gatherings in
the premises, again usually on Saturday evenings, occasions which may
have been less formal than the Longman Hampstead dinners and which
could be compared with the lunches and dinners that authors gave for
each other. Samuel Rogers (1763–1855), banker and poet, who had made
his reputation with his poem written in 'heroic couplets' *Pleasures of
Memory* (1792), which had taken nine years to perfect,[72] was famous for
such hospitality. So, too, was Richard Monckton Milnes (1809–1885), later
(1863) Lord Houghton, an ineffective poet but an influential figure in the
book world, including the European world of erotica. Crabb Robinson was
as welcome at these tables as he was at Longman's, Rees's or Murray's,
and left his full and illuminating notes on them which until 1938 were not
published – and then only in a selection. Appropriately one of Rogers's later
collections of poems was called *Human Life* (1819).

---

70   Wordsworth to Scott, 14 May 1808, printed in E. De Selincourt, *The Letters of
William and Dorothy Wordsworth* (2nd edn., 1969), pp.237–8.

71   H. Vizetelly, *Glances Back Through Seventy Years* (1893), Vol. I, p.203. The
recollection may well have been faulty. Vizetelly's dates do not fit. None the less,
Vizetelly, who launched the *Pictorial Times* in 1843, was conveying an impression
which others may have shared.

72   A. Dyer (ed.). *S. Rogers, Table Talk* (1856), p.18.

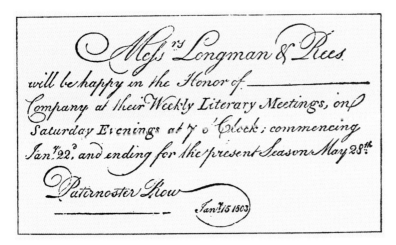

Invitation to a Longman soirée

Longman Archive

One very early nineteenth-century account of a social gathering, sent to a Welsh author living in Cambridge who was about to visit London, concentrated on the gossip which could be picked up there. 'Longman and Rees have established a *converzatione* every Saturday at their house where when you make your appearance in London you will meet with all sort[s] of curious gossip. This is an example for you of individuals who acquire money in trade employing it with a spirit that is not to be found ... among those who have it put in their pocket by others without any exertion of their own. Yes, we have a President of the Royal Society who, to be sure, does so, but we have also one of the Antiquarian Society who never expended a sixpence to forward diffusion of learning or of anything else but what centres in egotism.'[73]

~

Dynastic marriages as well as social skills strengthened the business power of Thomas Norton, but it was entirely appropriate that the bust to his memory in Hampstead Parish Church, where his children had been married as well as baptised, should be presented by 'literary friends'. Their support had been mobilised by a prominent political economist, J.R. McCulloch (1789–1864), a man who cared less about dynasty than about enterprise. Born in Galloway in 1789 and educated at Edinburgh University, McCulloch had become in 1818 the leading writer on political economy for the *Edinburgh Review*: the first book that he reviewed was David Ricardo's *Principles of Political Economy*. He also edited for Longman *A Dictionary, Practical, Theoretical, and Historical, of Commerce and Commercial Navigation*, first published in 1832, to which he contributed an informative chapter on the book trade.

---

73   Letter from Owen Pughe to Edward Williams, 21 April 1803 (National Library of Wales).

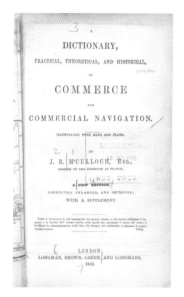

Title page to J.R. McCulloch
*A Dictionary, Practical,
Theoretical, and Historical, of
Commerce and Commercial
Navigation*, Longman, 1832,
New Edition 1852

BL W32/2843

For all the strength of his Whig connections, as historically important to the business as those of Thomas Norton, McCulloch, pamphleteer as well as reviewer, never called himself a Whig. His main asset was his shrewd business sense. He edited *The Scotsman* from 1818 to 1820 and was Professor of Political Economy at University College London from 1828 to 1837. In 1825 he had published his book *The Principles of Political Economy*. A leading spokesman of what came to be called 'classical' economics, he delivered the Ricardo Memorial Lectures in 1824. He showed independence and judgement as Comptroller of the Stationery Office, a post which he occupied from 1838 to 1864, where he often had to face both Whig and radical opposition. He died in office.[74]

A twentieth-century writer on the history of the *Edinburgh Review* from 1802 to 1832, looking back at the Scottish Enlightenment and at the subsequent careers of men such as McCulloch, calls his book *Rethinking the Politics of Commercial Society*.[75] That was the kind of society in which Thomas Norton felt most at home. Nevertheless, many of the public and private tributes paid to him on his death focused, as eighteenth-century tributes to his ancestors would have done, not on his business qualities but on his kindness to his social inferiors, particularly those who had 'grown gray in his service'. He was 'almost adored by his domestics'.

Thomas Norton's death was by accident, and inspired a different poetical response from that of Rees. He liked to travel down the hill from Hampstead to Paternoster Row on horseback, and it was on one of his regular journeys in August 1842 that he fell off his horse – with fatal consequences. He was passing the Smallpox Hospital at St Pancras when the accident took place, and was carried back to Hampstead. He died five days later. 'I see by today's paper the death of poor Longman', wrote the poet Thomas Hood (1799–1845), 'another proof that two legs are better than four'[76]: one of three poems by Hood included by Christopher Ricks in his *New Oxford Book of Victorian Verse* (1987) concerned 'Miss Kilmansegg and her precious leg'.

Hood's was a comment in character, made to Colburn, the publisher from whom he separated a year later, and while he benefited from the editorial responsibility which Colburn afforded him, Hood believed that authors had received far too little official recognition. They should rank

---

74   See P.M. Handover, *The London Gazette, 1665–1965* (1965), pp.72–6.

75   B. Fontana, *Rethinking the Politics of Commercial Society, the Edinburgh Review, 1802–1832* (1985). See also D.N. Winch, *Adam Smith's Politics, an Essay in Historiographic Revision* (1978). There is only one passing reference to publishing and to Longman in Fontana's volume which concentrates on the 'content' of the *Review*.

76   Hood to Colburn, 30 Aug. 1842 in P.F. Morgan (ed.), *The Letters of Thomas Hood* (1973), pp.492–3.

above soldiers and lawyers, who were 'equivocal blessings to humanity', but far too often they were the victims of publishers, whom he described in 'an emendation of the Gospel' as 'Publishers and Sinners'.[77] Reflecting on his dealings on contentious questions of copyright with the next Longman, Thomas Norton IV – and these reached a new stage in 1842 with the passing of a new Copyright Act – Hood told Charles Dickens that he felt that Longman had 'shown himself deficient not only in the courtesy of a gentleman, but the common civility of a Tradesman'.[78]

This was a condescending comment from a comic writer of genius, whose puns were notorious. Hood had little to do with Thomas Norton III, although, through Charles Lamb, Rees published Hood's *Plea of the Midsummer Fairies* in 1827, which included a poem 'Hero and Leander' which he dedicated to Coleridge.[79] It was *Punch*, however, a new periodical launched in 1841, which in 1843 printed Hood's most famous poem 'The Song of the Shirt' which dealt with a far more terrible plight than that of even the most exploited authors. Seamstresses, sometimes in direct contact with their clients, suffered pain as well as exploitation.

Two of Hood's most memorable other verses related to John Pyke Hullah (1812–1884), a Longman author, who was to become the government's Inspector of Music in Training Schools in 1872. In as many capacities as he could and over many years Hullah publicised his musical sight-reading system for 'the millions', based on the tonic sol-fa. (This echoed Constable who had talked of 'literature for the millions'.) One of Hood's verses included as a refrain the word 'Hullah-buloo':[80] he made fun of claims that Hullah's sight readers numbered 'millions, billions and quadrillions, not to name quintillions'. 'Music for the millions', like 'literature for the millions', was a mid-Victorian slogan. Yet the millions were never again approached with such fun as Hood was prepared to devote to them. Nor was Hullah. An 1877 Longman catalogue listed the second edition of Hullah's *The History of Modern Music, A Course of Lectures Delivered at the Royal Institution* (8s. 6d.) and a *2nd Course of Lectures* covering the period from the beginning of the seventeenth century to the middle of the eighteenth (10s. 6d.).[81]

Title page of Thomas Hood's *The Plea of the Midsummer Fairies* (1827)

BL 993.f.25

---

77 Hood to Dickens, May 1843, in Morgan, *op. cit.*, p.535.

78 Letter from Hood to Dickens, May 1843, in *ibid.*, p.537. On occasion Dickens accepted Longman invitations to dinner. There is no evidence that Hood did.

79 'I have not heard from Mr. Rees', Hood wrote to Edward Moxon, then employed by Longman and Rees '& think that people noted for dilatoriness ought to be protested'. Letter of 27 July 1827, *ibid.*, p.81.

80 See P.B. Scholes, *Mirror of Music, 1844–1944*, 3 vols. (1947), pp.11–13. 'The Hullah Movement'.

81 General List of Works Published by Messrs Longmans, Green & Co., March 1877, p.13.

~

Cartoon of Sydney Smith
(1771–1845), a lithograph by
Daniel Maclise, 1838

The National Portrait Gallery, London
no. D6786

Sydney Smith, a very different character from Hood, was even more famous
for his sayings than Hood for his puns. Some of them were topical quips,
some, like 'I never read a book before reviewing it: it prejudices a man so',
survive among the best-known quotations in English literature.[82] There are
no fewer than fifty-two Smith quotations in the second edition of the *Oxford
Dictionary of Quotations*, although the total stands far behind the number of
quotations from Johnson who supplied more than 350. Smith, like Johnson,
had been forced to make his own way in life: his father did not leave him
a penny. He was sent to school at Winchester, however, where Joseph
Warton, Johnson's friend, was headmaster, and from there to Oxford.

Ordained in 1794, Smith spent critical years in Edinburgh, 'the Athens
of the North', before becoming a famous London preacher and an habitué
of Holland House, the home of Lord Holland, one of the great aristocratic
Whig leaders, where he was always a welcome guest.[83] Thomas Norton
was sufficiently impressed with his own personal connection with Smith
to choose to give the unusual name 'Smith' to his own youngest daughter
(with the name Sarah prudently added). Another of his daughters, Louisa,
held salons in Hampstead, complete with music, although not on the scale
of the magnificent aristocratic soirées in Holland House.

The biggest publishing link between Thomas Norton and Smith
related to the *Edinburgh Review*. Smith was the most important of its
intellectual co-founders, co-operating enthusiastically with Francis (later
Lord) Jeffrey (1773–1850) and a number of young Edinburgh University
graduates, all except Smith, who was thirty-one, under thirty years old. They
were working with speed as well as enthusiasm to capture a readership
dissatisfied with reading journals 'in their dotage'.[84] Leaving aside
questions of commerce, the *Review* had behind it not only the intellectual

82   Quoted in H. Pearson, *The Smith of Smiths* (1934), p.54. Cf. Southey's comment:
       'I look upon the invention of reviews to be the worst injury which literature
       has received since its revival' (C.C. Southey (ed.), *The Life and Correspondence
       of the Late Robert Southey*, Vol. II (1849), p.276.

83   For Holland House, see Lady Holland, *Memoir* (1855); J. Clive, *Thomas Babington
       Macaulay* (1973), pp.208ff; and L. Davidoff, *The Best Circles: Society, Etiquette and
       The Season* (1973). For Smith see S.J. Reid, *The Life and Times of Sydney Smith*
       (1896); H. Pearson, *op. cit.*; A. Bell, *Sydney Smith, A Biography* (1980); P. Virgin,
       Sydney Smith (1994); and C. Nowell Smith (ed.), *The Letters of Sydney Smith*, 2
       vols. (1953).

84   There had been an earlier *Edinburgh Review*, with Adam Smith as one of its
       editors, which lasted for one year from 1755 to 1756, but it was Sydney Smith's
       Edinburgh, not Adam Smith's, that was to leave its mark. It was to survive until
       1929. See J. Clive, 'The *Edinburgh Review*: The Life and Death of a Periodical'
       in EHP, pp.115–40.

traditions of the University of Edinburgh, brilliantly established during the 'Age of Enlightenment', but the 'irrepressible passion for discussion which succeeded the fall of old systems at the beginning of the French Revolution'.[85]

With Brougham as one of its most prolific unnamed writers and with Jeffrey himself contributing no fewer than seventy-nine articles during the first six years of the life of the *Review*, it had impeccable Whig credentials. The first number, which appeared on 10 October 1802, costing 5 shillings, had a blue and buff (saffron) cover, the colours of the coat and waistcoat of the Whig leader, Charles James Fox. The 750 copies printed were sold out in less than a month, and within a year a total of 2,000 copies were sold in Edinburgh alone. The Whiggery of the *Review* was 'philosophical', however, stopping short of 'philosophical radicalism', which was not to find a review outlet until much later, 1824, when the *Westminster Review* was launched by the utilitarian sage Jeremy Bentham (1748–1832) and his close friend and disciple, James Mill (1773–1837).[86] Surprisingly, Longman had been approached to be its first publisher and would have accepted if James Mill had not launched an attack on the *Edinburgh Review* in the first article that he wrote. Thomas Norton then withdrew.[87] It was left to his son to draw in James Mill's son, John Stuart Mill (1806–1873) as a Longman author.

From the vantage point of the mid-Victorian years Walter Bagehot (1826–1877), from 1860 to his death the Editor of the *Economist*, a new publication of 1842, was to attribute the business success of the *Edinburgh* to Jeffrey, its 'great editor', who, if 'he might not know his subject ... knew his readers'. He also knew his contributors. Bagehot said of Jeffrey, memorably but with exaggeration, that 'he invented the trade of editorship. Before him an editor was a booksellers' drudge: he is now a distinguished functionary.'[88]

~

Neither Thomas Norton nor Rees had ever been tempted to treat Jeffrey as a 'bookseller's drudge', but they had had changing feelings about Constable, the pioneering Scottish publisher behind the *Review*, who had risen very quickly to fame: in the words of the Scottish Whig judge Lord Cockburn,

---

85   H. Cockburn, *Life of Jeffrey, with a Selection from his Correspondence*, Vol. I (1852), pp.125–6. In 1802 Britain was for a brief spell at peace with Napoleonic France.

86   See G.L. Nesbitt, *Benthamite Reviewing: The First Twelve Years of the Westminster Review* (1934). See also W.E.S. Thomas, *The Philosophic Radicals: Nine Studies in Theory and Practice, 1817–1841* (1979).

87   *Ibid.*, pp.34–5.

88   W. Bagehot, 'The First Edinburgh Reviewers' in the *National Review*, Vol. 1 (1855), reprinted by N. St John Stevas in *Literary Essays*, Vol. I (1965), p.332, and 'Lord Jeffrey', *ibid.*, p.346, where the same words were repeated. Bagehot also wrote an essay on Scott.

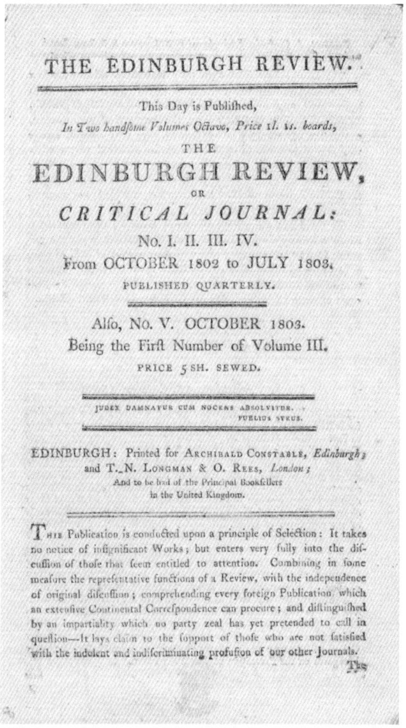

THE EDINBURGH REVIEW.

This Day is Publiſhed,
In Two handſome Volumes Octavo, Price 1l. 1s. boards,
THE
EDINBURGH REVIEW,
OR
CRITICAL JOURNAL:
No. I. II. III. IV.
From OCTOBER 1802 to JULY 1803,
PUBLISHED QUARTERLY.

Alſo, No. V. OCTOBER 1803.
Being the Firſt Number of Volume III.
PRICE 5 SH. SEWED.

JUDEX DAMNATUR CUM NOCENS ABSOLVITUR.
PUBLIUS SYRUS.

EDINBURGH: Printed for ARCHIBALD CONSTABLE, *Edinburgh*; and T. N. LONGMAN & O. REES, *London*;
And to be had of the Principal Bookſellers in the United Kingdom.

THIS Publication is conducted upon a principle of Selection: It takes no notice of inſignificant Works; but enters very fully into the diſcuſſion of thoſe that ſeem entitled to attention. Combining in ſome meaſure the repreſentative functions of a Review, with the independence of original diſcuſſion; comprehending every foreign Publication which an extenſive Continental Correſpondence can procure; and diſtinguiſhed by an impartiality which no party zeal has yet pretended to call in queſtion—It lays claim to the ſupport of thoſe who are not ſatisfied with the indolent and indiſcriminating profuſion of our other Journals.
The

Rates of Payment to Contributors to the E

Macaulay	£25 per sheet
Stephen	£20 & 21
Empson	the same
Senior	the same
Hayward	the same
Mr. Jno. Mill. India House	£20
J. A. Roebuck MP	£20
Charles Buller MP	£20
Revd. Henry Rogers	£20
Lord Monteagle	£20
Mr. G. C. Lewis	£20
Henry Rich MP	£18
H. Merivale	18 gs
Thomas Galloway	£18
George Moir Edinb	£18 gs
J. H. Burton Esq do	16 gs
Prof. Spalding St. Andrews	£18
Peacock, Dean of Ely	£20

The Edinburgh Review

Publicity for 'two handsome volumes' of *The Review*

BL pp 6/99h

A page from the Editor's notebook showing the rate of payment to contributors of *The Review* in 1847

Longman Archive

he 'had hardly set up for himself when he reached the pinnacle of his business'.[89] When he visited London for the first time in 1795 and met Thomas Norton, not then in sole charge of the House, the initial prospects for collaboration between the two of them seemed promising. Nor was it based solely on the *Edinburgh Review*. In 1802, the year of its founding, when Longman/Rees took a half share in it, Longman/Rees also acquired shares in the copyright of Scott's two-volume *Minstrelsy of the Scottish Border*, an immediately successful combination of epic and ballad, which sold 21,300 copies in five years,[90] and Constable was allotted a fourth part of them.

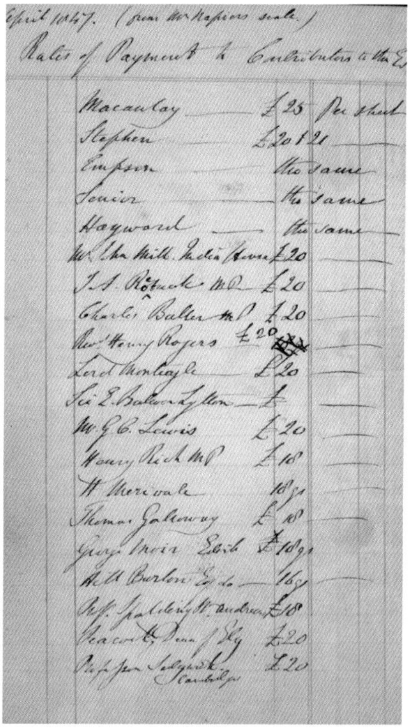

After a visit to Scotland in 1802, Thomas Norton told Constable that he recognised him as 'a real man of business, of honourable mind, and of universally acknowledged talents in your profession';[91] and in 1803 he congratulated Constable on a new partnership that he had formed with Alexander Gibson Hunter. It would be a partnership, Thomas Norton added, that would 'command all that is valuable in the literature of Scotland',

89 H. Cockburn, *Memorials of His Time* (1856), pp.168–9.

90 J.G. Lockhart, *Memories of the Life of Sir Walter Scott* (1837), Vol. I, p.35.

91 In a postscript he asked very practically for a Scottish article on 'Atmosphere' for the Rees *Encyclopaedia*.

going on to conclude that 'we shall doubtless do the same in England'. 'By a liberal exchange of copyright, and thus promoting and combining our interests, we shall infallibly raise our fortunes and our names infinitely higher and to a more important station than has yet been known in the annals of our profession.'[92]

Such cheerful talk implied that there would be a continuing complementarity of interests between Constable and Co. and Longman and Rees. In fact, there were soon signs of conflict, and it was ominous that when Hunter's younger brother was sent to London to be instructed in the mysteries of bookselling, he was directed not to Longman, who nevertheless received him with kindness, but to John Murray II. On one of Thomas Norton's visits to Scotland in 1804, when he had been taken ill, Hunter had told Constable that 'these Englishers will never do in our country. They eat a great deal too much and drink too little.'[93] Murray, who had been only fifteen years old when his father died in 1793, could claim, if it suited him, to be not English, but Scots – his father had been called McMurray before he changed his name to Murray – and soon it was his turn to travel to Scotland, where he and his father had both been born.[94]

Archibald Constable (1774–1827) by Sir Henry Raeburn c. 1820. The *Edinburgh Review* was founded in 1802

Constable & Robinson Ltd.

Murray, leaving his mother briefly in possession, with Highley, whom he had inherited from his father, in charge of day-to-day business, felt shackled by this co-partnership, describing Highley as 'a drone of a partner' in 1795; and he felt himself to be 'emancipated', a word that Thomas Norton would never have used, when his partnership with Highley was dissolved in 1803. Murray was now free to make the most of his family links with Edinburgh and its civic institutions. Yet an open breach between Longman/Rees and Constable did not come until November 1805, the year of Trafalgar, when in a stormy season Thomas Norton, not Constable, formally intimated his wish to break the connection, a break which Hunter's aggressive behaviour had made inevitable. A connection between Murray and Constable now took its place, for Constable knew how important it was to retain and, indeed, extend his links with London.[95] Bitter words were exchanged by Rees and Hunter, in particular, before and after Longman and Rees, never shy about litigation, began legal proceedings to protect their rights in the *Review* by

---

92 Longman to Constable, 31 Dec. 1803; T. Constable, *Archibald Constable and his Literary Correspondents: A Memorial*, 3 vols. (1873), Vol. I, p.19. The letters that follow to and from Constable are all taken from this volume which was edited by Archibald's son. In 1890 his grandson, also called Archibald, formed a new Archibald Constable and Company.

93 Letter to Constable, 3 Oct 1804.

94 Smiles, *op. cit.*, Vol. I, pp.32–3.

95 Millgate, 'Archibald Constable and the Problem of London', pp.110–23.

John Murray II (1778–1843),
known as 'young Murray',
mezzotint, after unknown artist

The National Portrait Gallery, London
no. D4653

injunction.[96] Under the original agreement with Constable in 1802, they were entitled to a half share of the revenues derived from the periodical so long as it was published under that title, and their assent was required to any re-arrangement with a different publisher.

With high hopes of profiting from his new relationship with Constable, Murray played his hand well, proving both prudent and clever in seeking to cool the temperature while pursuing his own interests.[97] He told Constable that both Thomas Norton and Rees were upset by the break: 'it is one of the misfortunes of our nature that disputes are always the more bitter in proportion to former intimacy'. Yet he warned him also 'that the extensive connexions between your House and Longman's cannot be severed all at once without mutual inconvenience, and perhaps, mutual disadvantages ... When persons have been intimate, they have discovered each other's vulnerable points; it therefore shows no great talent to direct at them shafts of resentment: it is easy both to write and to say ill-natured, harsh and cutting things of each other; but remember that this power is *mutual.*'

The words implied that 'mutuality', a noun in favour, should become the basis of Murray's own relationship with Constable: 'As for myself, you will find me exceedingly assiduous to promote your views, which I shall enter with feelings higher than those of mere interest; indeed, linked as our houses are at present, we have a natural tendency to mutual understanding.'[98] Murray was soon to be as unassured about the stability of any relationship with Constable as Longman and Rees had been, but he continued to be associated with the *Edinburgh Review* until 1809. It was not pressure on Murray's part, however, that had led Thomas Norton and Rees to give way to Constable in 1805 and decide not to go to Court.

---

96 Rees had not saved the relationship between Longman and Constable when he visited Edinburgh in September 1804. A matter of contention was Constable's *Medical Journal* in which Longman claimed a half share. Constable grumbled also that Longman had interests that conflicted with his through shares in the *Annual Review* and in the *Eclectic Review*. The position of Orme may have been raised too after he became a partner of Thomas Norton and Rees.

97 There is an informative note from Sharon Turner to Jeffrey about the ownership of the ER, dated 4 April 1807 (NLS MS 331, fols 364–5).

98 Letters from Murray to Constable, 7, 14 Dec. 1805.

The key figure behind the decision was not Constable but Jeffrey, who after becoming editor of the *Review*, had quickly taken full charge of its operations, immediately introducing regular (and generous) rates of pay for the contributors, whose first motto had been *tenui musam meditamur avena* ('we cultivate literature upon a little oatmeal').[99]

Thomas Norton and Rees, who had been little involved in the editorial side of the *Review*, had been responsible for its English and foreign sales from its second number onwards, but Jeffrey now told Murray unequivocally that:

> neither I nor any of the original and regular writers in the *Review* will ever contribute a syllable to a work belonging to booksellers. It is proper ... to announce to you directly that you may have no fear of hardship or disappointment in the event of Mr. Longman succeeding in his claim to the property of this work. If that claim be not speedily rejected or abandoned, it is our fixed resolution to withdraw entirely from the *Edinburgh Review*.[100]

Jeffrey, as proud as Constable, believed at that point that Constable should start a *New Edinburgh Review*, and it was only after Thomas Norton and Rees, faced by his ultimatum, agreed to accept £1,000 from Constable for their claim to property rights in the title that No. 22 of the *Review* appeared under Constable and Murray's auspices in 1807.

Under Murray sales increased, with 5,000 of the next 7,000 copies printed in Edinburgh being sold by Murray in London.[101] That seemed to Constable and Murray just what it ought to be. Yet before long there were financial and political complications. For all his bold initiatives – and he always had the next initiative in mind – Constable was 'never possessed of much free capital'. He drew heavily on Murray, therefore, for operational finance through accommodation bills, as he was to do with other partners or agents later[102] and when he could not cover the first third of the £1,000 due to Thomas Norton and Rees, Murray sent his first warning signals, going on to tell Constable in 1808 that such behaviour was 'not reconcilable with friendship or business'.

At the end of that year Constable and Hunter responded by setting up a London branch of their own House, for the sale in London of the *Edinburgh* and of books published by Constable, but this proved to be a

---

99 The basic rate was fixed at sixteen guineas per sheet, with a higher rate up to twenty-five guineas a sheet: Jeffrey had the power to decide which rate to offer.

100 Letter of 1 June 1807.

101 *Ibid.*, p.80.

102 Curwen, *op. cit.*, p.129.

short-term response, and the company which managed it lasted only until 1811. Hunter, having inherited a fortune, retired from the Constable business, including the *Review*, and a rich Scot, Robert Cathcart, took his place, bringing in as partner his ambitious brother-in-law Robert Cadell (1788–1849), a former clerk with Constable, who was to marry Constable's daughter.

Characteristically Constable used the new partnership not to consolidate his finances, but to make a further leap forward. In 1812 he acquired from the trustees of the former proprietor of the *Encyclopaedia Britannica*, Andrew Bell, an incomplete new fifth edition along with plates for engravings and the stock of its unbound printed sheets of the first five of fifteen volumes. He planned to incorporate a prestigious new Supplement written by the philosopher Dugald Stewart and other authors of acknowledged repute, including Scott and Humphry Davy, and he offered lavish terms to secure their acceptance. In response Scott contributed articles on 'Chivalry' and 'Romance'.

The leap might have justified itself financially from the start had not Cathcart died suddenly, 'the groundwork', as Cadell put it, of subsequent 'losses and deficiencies'.[103] In consequence, Cadell and Constable apportioned between them Cathcart's shares, with no prospect then of additional new capital. To secure ready cash in order to re-finance debts and in order to seek to reap the expected returns from the *Britannica* Constable turned first to London – and again to Thomas Norton – and then in November to Leeds, persuading Robinson & Son, booksellers there and sellers of other products besides books, to purchase large quantities not only of the *Encyclopaedia* but of other Constable books. It was a momentous move, taken hastily, for the Robinsons were interested in far more than in selling the *Encyclopaedia* and in 1818 J.O. Robinson in partnership with John Hurst of Wakefield, brother of the Longman/Rees partner Thomas Hurst, eager to expand their trade, moved to 19 Cheapside, London.

Meanwhile, Constable's relationship with Thomas Norton and Rees had improved, but with their own encyclopaedia to promote, they (Thomas Norton and Rees) were not interested in acquiring another. They did buy back their old share of rights in the *Edinburgh Review*, however, in 1814, although there had been a far bigger change in review publishing in 1809 with long-term political as well as publishing implications[104]. Murray, confident that he could attract ample writing talent, including talent from Scotland, without relying on Constable to discover it, contemplated and brought to life a review of his own, the *Quarterly*, completely different in tone from the *Edinburgh*, Tory not Whig in its political complexion. He could move with almost as much confidence as Constable had done in

---

103 Quoted in Millgate, *loc. cit.*, p.117.

104 In 1808–9 Leigh and John Hunt had founded a radical weekly *The Examiner*.

1802, for he had the blessing both of Scott and George Canning. He had also secured as its first editor William Gifford (1756–1826), who had edited the *Anti-Jacobin*, Canning's political journal. Since 1808 he had been a reader for Murray.

Gifford had no difficulty in finding reviewers, and when he was prevented from carrying out his editorial duties by illnesses, which dogged him throughout his editorship, Southey and J.W. Croker (1780–1857), a Tory with a record stretching back before the French Revolution, were never slow to give advice.[105] He was succeeded as editor in 1825 (after a short interval) by Scott's son-in-law and future biographer, John Gibson Lockhart (1794–1854). Canning died in the same year as Gifford, 1827, but Lockhart, who did not win immediate support from all the writers for the *Quarterly*, continued to edit it with great success until 1853. He died in 1854, four years after Jeffrey.[106]

The open rivalry between the *Edinburgh* and the *Quarterly* added, as has been noted, to the prosperity of both. And Thomas Norton and Rees began to share in the benefits when in 1814 under financial pressure Constable offered them their old rights in the publication of the *Edinburgh Review* on payment of £4,500. This was four times the sum that had been paid to Longman/Rees when they reluctantly gave them up in 1807. Circulation of the *Edinburgh* had by then risen from 7,000 to 13,000, and the price had been raised to six shillings. The *Quarterly* reached a circulation of 17,000 in 1817.

Southey considered the *Quarterly* the 'greatest of all Murray's works', but in the highly informed opinion of Scott, who was sometimes subjected to unfavourable reviews in it, Constable 'knew more of the business of a bookseller in planning and executing popular works than any man of his time', including Murray, and whatever the vicissitudes of his business, he would always remain 'the prince of publishers'.[107] It was not lack of acumen and certainly not lack of vision that brought him down in 1826, but failure to cope with his finances in exceptionally difficult circumstances. Scott had been present in 1825 when Constable set out details of a vast project, which appealed to Jeffrey and to Murray, to publish a 'Miscellany of Original and Selected Publications, designed to provide cheap, various, useful, and agreeable knowledge in the departments of Literature, Science, and the

The Quarterly Review for February and May, 1809. Published by John Murray, it was a Tory, not a Whig quarterly. This is the second edition, of Volume 1, published in 1810

BL PP5989ab

---

105 Gifford was bitterly attacked in William Hazlitt's *The Spirit of the Age* (1825): 'he has all his life been a follower in the train of wealth and power'. For Gifford and his contributors see H. and S. Shine, *The QR under Gifford: Identification of Contributors, 1809–1824* (1949).

106 See A. Lang, *Life of John Gibson Lockhart*, 2 vols. (1897). Lang made no use of Lockhart's letter to Murray or to Croker.

107 W.E.K. Anderson (ed.), *The Journal of Sir Walter Scott*, (1972 edn.), pp.331–2. Murray was himself described also as 'the prince of publishers'.

Arts'. They would be published in cheap cloth covers. Given such vision, Constable had been sure that he could retrieve his financial situation late in 1825 – and told Scott that he could do so – but his business collapsed a year later in a dramatic manner. Indeed, his fall in 1826 was even more rapid than his ascent.[108]

He had made a serious mistake when he put his trust in Robinson & Son. Their financial practices were not dissimilar from Constable's own, but they speculated heavily in concerns, such as hops, which were well outside the book trade, and when they went bankrupt in the financial crash of January 1826 they brought down Constable with them. Another Scottish business was directly involved. The firm of Ballantyne and Company, in which Scott was an unacknowledged partner, inevitably followed, and, in the absence of limited liability, Scott found himself responsible not only for his own debts but also those of the Ballantynes, James and John. And since Scott had also backed many of the accommodation bills through which the firm of Constable obtained operating capital, he was held liable also for some of that company's debts.[109]

Scott believed at first that he himself had made enough money out of his books published by Constable to escape personal financial disaster, but he could not avoid the ramifications of the collapse of Hurst Robinson, of Constable and of Ballantyne and Co. The ramifications were, indeed, wide. Even 'Longman people' were said to be in 'great difficulty, and involved a good deal through Hurst's brothers', Scott reported to Blackwood. He was wrong. The Longmans, who had themselves used Ballantyne and Co. among their printers, were not in great difficulty in 1826: Murray for a variety of reasons was. He had long dreamed of owning and managing a newspaper, but *The Representative*, the first number of which appeared on 25 January 1826, was a disastrous failure. He lost £26,000 on the venture in which a young and ambitious Benjamin Disraeli had promised to take up a half share.[110]

Although themselves escaping ruin, the Longmans were as plainly involved in the consequences of Constable's fall as they had been in those of his rise. Only Constable's partner, Robert Cadell, who had married Constable's daughter, emerged successfully from the wreckage after having initially gone bankrupt too. By cleverly distancing himself from

---

108 For a full account of the general banking and credit crisis of 1825–6 see A.D. Gayer, W.W. Rostow and A.J. Schwartz, *The Growth and Fluctuations of the British Economy, 1790–1850*, Vol. I (1953), pp.180–210.

109 Scott's financial involvement with James Ballantyne went back to 1802, and in 1809 he had also supplied the capital for the short-lived publishing firm of John Ballantyne and Co., which had been wound up in 1813 amid what Lockhart called 'losses and embarrassments'.

110 There is a lively account of the venture in R. Blake, *Disraeli* (1967), pp.27–43.

his father-in-law, who went bankrupt in 1826, and working through a completely new firm of Cadell and Company, formed in June 1826, he not only saved himself but Scott as well. Scott himself had refused to follow the bankruptcy route and worked out an honourable arrangement to pay off his own and the Ballantyne debts through trustees. He then went on to join with Cadell in a determined effort to achieve this goal by writing new works and exploiting to the full the value of the copyrights of those works already published. As part of the strategy Scott's trustees and Cadell jointly purchased the copyrights of the Waverley Novels for £8,500. They also bought back Longman's shares in Scott's poems, together with a large quantity of printed stock. Cadell's skill in marketing both the old stock and the new collected editions enabled Scott's heirs to pay off his remaining debts, and Cadell, having gained control of all the Scott copyrights, himself died a very rich man.[111]

Between the fall and death of Constable and the end of the decade, while Cadell and particularly Scott were labouring hard, the former re-grouping his business, the latter writing his novels, the country suffered from a prolonged period of economic depression, usually described simply by contemporaries as 'distress'; and this was followed by a major political change in 1830. After years in the political wilderness the Whigs returned to power, albeit in coalition, under the prime ministership of the supremely aristocratic Earl Grey. This gave a political twist to the story of the *Edinburgh* and the *Quarterly*. Sydney Smith, a friend of Grey, secured no new political preferment, but one of the best known and most ambitious of the first *Edinburgh* reviewers, Brougham, a leading exponent of the case for 'cheap and useful knowledge', became Lord Chancellor and Jeffrey Lord Advocate. In consequence the *Edinburgh* was now an even more prestigious asset than ever for the House of Longman.

A number of pamphlets and books published by Longmans in 1830 dealt with topical political circumstances. They included *Observations on the State of the Country, and on the Proper Policy of the Administration, Parties and Factions in England at the Accession of William IV* and *The Result of the General Election or What has the Duke of Wellington gained from the Dissolution*. Meanwhile, all the periodicals which dealt with such issues, including *Blackwood's*, continued to have competitors. One particularly lively newcomer was *Fraser's Magazine*, launched in 1830 and edited by William Maginn (1793–1842), which included as one of its main features a 'Gallery of Literary Characters'. It survived until 1882, gaining in reputation in the 1840s. In 1863 it was to pass into the hands of the Longmans as a result of the take-over of J.W. Parker.[112]

The perspicacious and productive novelist Edward Bulwer Lytton

Buy a BROOM ? !!

'Buy a BROOM?!!'

Cartoon of Henry Brougham (1778–1868) by George Cruickshank (1792–1878), published by George Humphrey 1825

The National Portrait Gallery, London no. D16762

---

111   J. Millgate, *Scott's Last Edition: A Study in Publishing History* (1987).

112   See below, p.269.

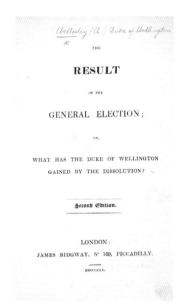

RESULT

or the

GENERAL ELECTION;

or,

WHAT HAS THE DUKE OF WELLINGTON
GAINED BY THE DISSOLUTION?

Second Edition.

LONDON:
JAMES RIDGWAY, N° 169, PICCADILLY.

MDCCCXXX.

The Result of the General Election of 1830. The first edition of the pamphlet was published by Longman and thereafter by other publishers

BL 8135.bb.77

(1803–1873), later the Earl of Lytton, who warned authors of the effects on their prose of writing too much for periodicals, now in increasing demand, complained as early as 1833, using the favourite Longman metaphor, that since literary works, 'in the magnificent thought of Bacon, are "the Ships of Time"', too much precious cargo was being wasted on 'vessels which sink for ever in a three months' voyage'.[113] Bulwer Lytton dedicated the fourth book of his volume to Isaac D'Israeli, who died in 1848. D'Israeli's son, Benjamin, largely ignored by the *Quarterly* between his contretemps with Murray II in 1826 and his father's death, chose a different metaphor derived from transport when he was writing about periodicals a generation after Bulwer Lytton.

Now professing admiration for both the *Edinburgh* and the *Quarterly*, he compared them with post horses, which in the age of the stage coach had done a 'roaring trade' but which in the age of railway had lost all touch with 'progress': 'Instead of that intense competition and mutual vindictiveness which before distinguished them, they suddenly quite agree. The boots of the "Blue Boar" and the Chambermaid of the "Red Lion" embrace and are quite in accord ... in denouncing [the] infamy of railroads'.[114] It was a witty but inaccurate judgement. By the 1850s there was such a wide range of periodicals, some of them weeklies rather than quarterlies or annuals, some of them well illustrated, that another far less distinguished commentator than Bulwer Lytton or Disraeli could choose an older metaphor, claiming that 'there were [now] more magazines in the wretched field than there were blades of grass to support them'.[115] Their particular histories often remain obscure, as do the shifts in their publishers. Their influence, however, was often beyond doubt. Thus, the *Saturday Review*, founded by Beresford Hope in 1858 and edited by J.D. Cook, attracted many outstanding contributors, including Leslie Stephen, future editor of the *Dictionary of National Biography*, the lawyer Sir Henry Maine, John Morley, Froude and Lord Robert Cecil, later, as Marquis of Salisbury, Britain's last Victorian Prime Minister.

~

One of the early writers in the *Edinburgh Review* spans the decades. Thomas Babington (later Lord) Macaulay (1800–1859), whose father Zachary was a member of the 'Clapham Sect' and whose mother was born in Bristol,

---

113   E. Bulwer Lytton, *England and the English*, 2 vols. (1874 edn.), p.228.

114   Quoted in W.F. Moneypenny and G.E. Buckle, *The Life of Benjamin Disraeli* (1929 edn.,), Vol. II, p.291.

115   William Tinsley, a publisher of novels, quoted in R.D. Altick, *The English Common Reader* (1957), p.359. Tinsley launched *Tinsley's Magazine* in 1867.

wrote his first essay for the *Edinburgh* (on 'The West Indies') in 1825;[116] and in 1830, when Jeffrey, who was greatly impressed by Macaulay's talents, retired from the editorship to take up political office, he hoped that Macaulay would succeed him. Although he did not, Macaulay continued to write for the review, thereby establishing his reputation as an essayist before he left England for India in 1833 and before he became renowned as an historian. In time he established himself as Longman's favourite author. His puns, most of them bad, were as prolific as Hood's or Thackeray's. He and his sister once made *The Mysteries of Udolpho* the prize in a bet as to who could make most puns in conversation in a period of two hours. Macaulay won with two hundred.[117]

Macaulay's first writings had appeared not in the *Edinburgh Review* but in a magazine published by Charles Knight, who admired Constable's efforts to publish for the millions. Macaulay did not fully share Knight's vision, however, and even in his essays written for Knight, he had dealt not with history but with classical subjects. When he assembled his essays for the first time in 1846 he did not include an essay on history which he wrote in 1828 in which he compared the role of historians and novelists.[118] As a young man he had written poetry as well as prose. *The Lays of Ancient Rome*, published by Longman in 1842, were conceived of in 1835 when he was re-reading Livy and reading for the first time B.G. Niebuhr's *The History of Rome*.

Each of his own 'Lays' was set in its historical context, and in his Preface, even more relevant to an understanding of his work than the Preface to *Lyrical Ballads* is to an understanding of Wordsworth's, he emphasized how interesting a subject history could be to general readers. 'All human beings, not utterly savage, long for some information about past times, and are delighted by narratives which paint pictures to the mind.'[119] By 1875, more than 100,000 copies of *The Lays* had been sold, and some of them, particularly 'Horatius', were well-known to schoolchildren, among them children who were taught no classics at school.[120] Doubtless many of the *Lays* were learnt by heart. It seems entirely appropriate that the national monument to Macaulay is placed in Poets' Corner in Westminster Abbey.

L A Y S

OF

A N C I E N T   R O M E.

BY

THOMAS BABINGTON MACAULAY.

LONDON:
LONGMAN, BROWN, GREEN, AND LONGMANS,
PATERNOSTER-ROW.
1842.

The title page of Macaulay's *Lays of Ancient Rome*, published by Longman 1842

BL 1466.e.11

---

116   ER, Vol. XLI (1825). It included (p.476) a magnificent comment which had nothing to do with the West Indies. 'If Henry VIII had been a private man, he might have torn off his wife's ruff and kicked her lap-dogs. He was a King and he cut off her head.' See J. Millgate, 'Father and Son: Macaulay's *Edinburgh* Debut' in the RES, Vol. XXI (1970).

117   G.O. Trevelyan, *The Life and Letters of Lord Macaulay* (1976), Vol. I, p.170.

118   *Miscellaneous Writings of Lord Macaulay* (1860), Vol. I., p.240.

119   T.B. Macaulay, *The Lays of Ancient Rome* (1842), p.9.

120   Trevelyan, *op. cit.*,p.426.

It was in July 1838 that Macaulay, four years before the publication of his *Lays*, wrote to Macvey Napier, Jeffrey's successor as editor of the *Edinburgh Review*, telling him of his plans for a *History of England* which would provide 'an entire view of all the transactions which took place between the [1688] revolution, which brought the Crown into harmony with the Parliament and the revolution [1832] which brought Parliament into harmony with the Nation.'[121] His full plans were never achieved, however, and the last volume in the five volumes of his *History* that were published by Longmans had to be prepared for publication after his death by his sister. It reinforced his reputation.[122] The 'spirit of the age' had changed dramatically between the 1830s and the 1850s, a decade beyond the range of this chapter, which began with the Great Exhibition in the Crystal Palace. Yet as early as 1830 Macaulay was already confident about the 'progress' of the nation, which he identified with increased national wealth when he reviewed anonymously and at length Southey's *Sir Thomas More, or Colloquies on the Progress and Prospects of Society* (1829).

Southey compared, as many other writers, notably Carlyle, also did,[123] pre-industrial and industrial society, past and present, finding the outcome deeply disturbing. By contrast, Macaulay looked hopefully to the future, presenting a picture of what the state of affairs might be not in the year 1860 but in the year 1930. England would then have a population of fifty millions, 'better fed, better clad and better lodged than the English of our time'. 'Machines, constructed on principles yet undiscovered, will be in every house.' 'There will be no highways but rail-roads, no travelling but by steam.' 'Our debt, vast as it seems to us, will appear to our great grandchildren a trifling encumbrance.' Only Macaulay's last optimistic paragraph ended with the past. 'It is not by the intermeddling of Mr. Southey's idol – the omniscient and omnipotent State – but by the prudence and energy of the people, that England has hitherto been carried forward in civilization.'

Wordsworth is said to have listened to Southey reading him every page of his *Colloquies*, but he professed to be unable to judge 'its effect as a whole'.[124] He made no judgement on Macaulay, who worked closely at different stages in his career with more than one member of the

---

121 BL Add MSS 34,619 M. Napier (ed.), *Selections from the Correspondence of the late Macvey Napier Esq* (1879), p.265.

122 See J. Clive, *Macaulay: The Shaping of the Historian* (1973).

123 His 'Signs of the Times', however, appeared in the ER in 1827. See J.A. Froude, *Thomas Carlyle, A History of the First Forty Years of His Life*, Vol. II (1882), p.76.

124 De Selincourt, *op. cit.*, p.380; K. Curry (ed.), *New Letters of Robert Southey*, Vol. 2 (1965), pp.195–6. See also Curry's 'Robert Southey', in C.W. Houtchens and L.H. Houtchens, *The English Romantic Poets and Essayists: A Review of Research and Criticism* (revised edn., 1966).

Longman family. Indeed, his relationship with the House became as close as it had been with the *Edinburgh Review*. One eighty-page historical work commissioned by Longman that Macaulay never published in final book form in his lifetime was a substantial, if incomplete, account of the French Revolution of 1830. This was to be part of a Longman series edited by the Revd. Dionysius Lardner, the *Cabinet Encyclopaedia*, described more fully at the end of this chapter.[125] A carefully bound copy of 'rough pulls' (March 1830) made its way into the library of C.J. Longman, to be treasured as 'a literary curiosity of striking interest'.[126] Years later, in 1977, a published edition of it was to appear.[127]

~

How did Macaulay's relationship with the House compare with that of other Longman authors? It is an important question given that one of the central themes of this particular period in the history of literature was the development of new relationships between individual authors, not least poets, novelists and historians, and the publishers on whom their fortunes depended.

For some authors, at least, the relationship seemed to be characterised by poverty on the one side and wealth on the other, the most familiar of national contrasts in the years between 1815 and 1850. Thus, for the journalist William Jerdan (1782–1869), Editor and in 1843 Proprietor of the *Literary Gazette*, and one of the founders of the Royal Society of Literature in 1821, most authors had for a third of a century been 'steeped in poverty'. Only a few had 'barely contrived to exist'. 'Not one in a hundred, who were without private and extrinsic resources to fall back upon', had succeeded 'to the realisation of a moderate independence.'[128] Yet it is difficult to generalise. Like publishers, authors had their 'good' and 'bad' times. Some, like Samuel Rogers, were rich enough to assist other authors as well as themselves.

One of the most famous Longman authors, the Irish poet Tom Moore (1779–1852), a man who could be particularly demanding, was certainly not exploited by his publishers. Yet his relationship with Longman and Rees did not begin particularly well, as Macaulay's had done. In 1812, for example, he described receiving 'a most submissive and apologizing letter from the insolent bibliopolist of Paternoster Row', and in 1814 he complained

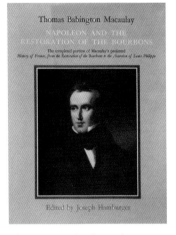

The cover to the first edition of Macaulay's *Napoleon and the Restoration of the Bourbons*, published by Longman in 1977

Longman Archive

---

125 See below, pp.222ff.

126 T.N. Longman V, *Memories*, p.181. See also G.O. Trevelyan, *op. cit.*, p.412.

127 J. Hamburger (ed), *T.B. Macaulay, Napoleon and the Restoration of the Bourbons* (1977).

128 W. Jerdan, *Autobiography*, Vol. II (1853), pp.37–8. His autobiography is in four volumes. See also his *Men I Have Known* (1866).

about the formality of a letter he had just received which bore in place of a Longman signature the name of the House. By the 1830s, however, the relationship was already close. All Moore's letters to Longman began 'Dear Tom', and on Thomas Norton's death in 1842 Moore wrote to his son asking him to be treated as a sharer in the family's loss 'as far as anyone not related to him *can* be'.[129]

It was long before that – in December 1814, indeed – that Moore was paid £3,000 by Thomas Norton for a poem *Lalla Rookh*, an 'oriental romance', which he had still not yet begun to write, and this was the largest sum ever paid in advance for a poem, comparable with the sum of £20,000 paid later to Macaulay for his *History*.[130] As late as 1810, Moore had been contemplating handing over the text of a poem to Murray, with whom his relationship was always to be more complex – and more difficult – than his relationship with the Longmans, and it was only in the year of his marriage, 1811, that he told Thomas Norton, with what might have been more than a touch of exaggeration, that 'at last' he had 'come to a determination to bind myself' to Longman's 'service', 'if you hold the same favourable dispositions toward me as at our last conversation upon business'.

Moore was then a member of a group formed around Lord Moira and the Prince Regent, and he added characteristically to his letter that while he would be glad 'to be allowed half an hour's conversation' with Thomas Norton, he could not reach his house before four o'clock since he would be 'up all night at Carlton House', the residence of the Prince of Wales.[131] After the Prince Regent broke away from his Whig friends, Moore drew close to the young Whig aristocrat and future Prime Minister, Lord John Russell (1792–1878), who had early dreams of being a poet himself and over time had his own complex relationship with Longman and Rees.

The relationship began more promisingly than Moore's. In 1820 Longmans published Russell's *Essays and Sketches of Life and Character by a Gentleman who has left his Lodgings*, which included essays on 'The Love of Fame', 'Society in London' and 'The World'. And that was ten years before as a Whig minister in Grey's new administration of 1830 he was given a place on the small committee that prepared the first Reform Bill. When Russell became leader of the Whigs in the House of Commons in 1841 he immediately secured a pension for Moore, and backed Moore throughout his life, standing by him in a number of personal financial crises. When Moore died in 1852 he edited his papers and handed the

---

129 Letters of 19 May 1812, 30 Aug. 1842 (LA Part II 26/8).

130 Letter from Thomas Norton Longman to Moore, 5 Aug. 1814; Letter from Moore to Longman, 17 Dec. 1814.

131 Quoted in CC, p.223.

proceeds to Moore's widow.[132]

Russell was not the initial intermediary in the *Lalla Rookh* transaction. The man who was, James Perry (1756–1821), the radical editor of the *Morning Chronicle*, was as useful to Moore at this decisive point in his literary life as an early twentieth-century agent would have been. He told Thomas Norton in the summer of 1814 of the poem that Moore was writing;[133] and when, according to Perry, the publisher began by asking to see the text before deciding whether or not to publish (he pledged himself to show it to no one else), Perry questioned him on the somewhat surprising grounds that he was not sure whether Thomas Norton had what he called 'a Bookseller's knack', the power to judge whether or not a poem would attract a large audience. Very soon, however, Thomas Norton was pressing Moore to enter into a 'conclusive arrangement' with him, adding that he should rest assured that 'we shall not be disposed to be behind in the amount of our offer'. He kept his word.

Few of the financial arrangements that Longman and Rees made with their authors were as acceptable to them as those with Moore who was already a 'literary lion' when Perry acted as his intermediary, and once the deal was made, Moore remained for decades a favourite and a profitable author on the Longman list. *Lalla Rookh*, now largely forgotten, first printed in quarto, was an immediate success, which generated a transatlantic readership and was reprinted six times, the last four in octavo, in its first year. An American correspondent, who wrote to Moore in 1828 asking him for his autograph (and for good measure those of Byron, Scott and the Duke of Wellington as well) told him that it was thanks to men like himself and them

Portrait of Thomas Moore (1779–1852) by Thomas Phillips, RA. One of the Longman collection of portraits, Longman V in 1921 wrote that he believed it was 'the best portrait there is of the well-known Poet, ... the marked intimacy and friendship which existed between author and publisher is sufficient to account for its being handed down to the present owner.'

Pearson Education

---

132 S. Walpole, *The Life of Lord John Russell*, Vol. I (1889), p.112; and J. Prest, *Lord John Russell* (1972), p.19. Russell (ed) *Thomas Moore, Memoirs, Journal and Correspondence of Thomas Moore*, 8 Vols. (1856).

133 Perry's usefulness to Moore as an intermediary may have been exaggerated. Jeffrey admired Moore's talents and his principles, and in asking him to write for the *Review* he gave him details of the sums paid to its writers (Letter of 30 March 1814). Moore considered reviewing to be 'a sort of hedge-firing and ambuscade warfare which is not quite the thing for my disposition'. The last Editor of the *Morning Chronicle* was J.D. Cook.

that 'we attribute the gradual but permanent disappearance of the inveterate prejudice which has so greatly pervaded this country *vis-à-vis* Britain'.[134]

Once the *Lalla Rookh* deal was made, Moore wrote with delight to his friend, Rogers, to whom he was to dedicate it, that he had 'just sold my Poem ... for three thousand pounds!' Thomas Norton and Rees did not know, Moore added, what they were buying, but he did not fear any *considerable* diminution of the sum if they were not eventually offered 'the same quantum of poetry they have bargained for (5,000 lines)'.[135] A few months later, Moore was describing the Longmans as *patres nostri*,[136] although his poem was not published until 1817. When eventually it appeared, he wrote to his mother in one of his regular weekly letters that everything was 'going famously' and that a second edition was being prepared 'so that my conscience as to the Publishers' pockets is now quite at rest'.[137]

Soon Moore was referring other would-be authors to 'Messrs. Longman'. In 1818, for example, he directed Sheridan's sister Alice Lefanu there, adding that he would lose no time in preparing them to receive the manuscript of a life of Elizabeth Sheridan of which they would be the 'ultimate judges'.[138] In the same year, Longman published on half-and-half terms his *The Fudge Family in Paris*.

Meanwhile, Thomas Norton and Rees had pushed *Lalla Rookh* almost beyond the limits of their powers. They attempted, for example, to have it publicised in the *Quarterly Review* after writing to a man whom they hoped would review it:

> As we are deeply interested in the success of Moore's *Lalla Rookh*, & as we have some reason to think that were a good spirited Review of the work sent through a pertinent channel to the Editor of the Quarterly Rev. it wd be adopted by him. We shall feel particularly obliged if you could write a pretty full review of the work, for we know no one so competent of the undertaking; and we shall be most

---

134   Letter from Samuel J. Carr, n.d. Moore had transatlantic contacts himself, one of them with Joseph Dennie (1768–1812), who edited *The Portfolio* in Philadelphia and was responsible for 'puffing' Wordsworth's works in that periodical.

135   Letter from Moore to Rogers, 22 May 1815. Moore wrote to his mother (6 March 1817) from Ashbourne that 'the way I have managed my money matters with Longman is satisfactory and convenient to them, and I should hope safe for myself'. All the Moore letters are in LA Part II/268/1. They were transcribed largely in 1981 and should be collated with earlier collections made by Lord John Russell and W.S. Dowden (ed.) *The Letters of Thomas Moore* (1964) and *The Journal of Thomas Moore*, 6 Vols. (1983–1991).

136   Letter from Moore to James Perry, 1 July 1816.

137   Letter to his mother, 30 May 1817.

138   Letter from Moore to Mrs Lefanu, 21 Dec. 1818.

happy to remunerate you liberally. You must have in mind the politics of that Review. Pray do not refuse us. Of course the matter must be entirely *entre nous*.[139]

'Longman & Co', the signatory to this letter, were writing very much as publishers, not as booksellers, and they told the Revd. W. Shepherd, a Unitarian minister, the man they hoped would review it, to buy his copy of *Lalla Rookh* 'from Robinsons or any other bookseller on our [account]'. Shepherd did not write one and no review of *Lalla Rookh* appeared in the *Quarterly Review*.

Moore himself was encouraged by his publishers to turn to prose as well as poetry, and over a long lifetime as a writer he produced so many biographies, including a much praised two-volume *Memoirs of the Life of Sheridan* (1825), that it was suggested that he should go on to produce a volume called *The Cat* which would contain nine lives.[140] It was ironical that he had once remarked that he found writing biography difficult: it was 'like dot engraving, made up of little minute points which have to be attended to or the effect is lost'.[141]

When Moore ran into difficulties with John Murray II in the 1820s about his projected *Letters and Journals of Lord Byron*, Thomas Norton and Rees gave him the same kind of sensible advice as Murray had offered Constable in 1805,[142] and they went to help him to draft an agreement. Moore always found it more difficult to deal with Murray, who had published Byron's *Childe Harold*, than with 'Messrs Longman', for Murray knew that Longman and Rees were Moore's established and well-entrenched

---

139 'Longman & Co' (as they described themselves) to the Revd W. Shepherd, 17 Nov, 29 Dec. 1817. Shepherd, educated at Hackney College in its prime, had other Longman connections. His manuscript papers are in Harris Manchester College, Oxford. Longman & Co. had, of course, many Unitarian connections.

140 Rees and Britten, *op. cit.*, p.99. The *Life* had gone into a fourth edition by the end of the year.

141 Letter from Moore to S. Rogers, 21 April 1828.

142 Letter from Rees to Moore, 29 Sept. 1826. Murray was anxious for Moore to write this book partly in order to divert attention from Leigh Hunt's *Recollections of Lord Byron and his Contemporaries* which appeared in 1828. Murray's biographer, Samuel Smiles, called Hunt's book 'a scandalous attack on his old patron and benefactor'. (Smiles, *op. cit.*, Vol. II, p.306.) Hazlitt, who praised Hunt, had a low opinion of Moore as a poet. 'He can write verses, not a poem'. 'If *Irish Melodies* do indeed express the soul of impassioned feeling in his countrymen, the case of Ireland is hopeless.'

publishers.[143] For all the element of competition in seeking and finding authors, Longman and Murray always respected each other's business dealings. They also co-operated with each other in many matters relating to publishing.

Nevertheless, there was more than an element of irony (a word which, along with the related adjective and adverb, it is impossible to keep out of this *History*) in the quadrilateral Moore/Byron/Longman/Murray relationship, and more than a touch of drama. Longman and Rees, not Murray, might have been Byron's first publisher of *Childe Harold* had not they turned down Byron's *English Bards and Scotch Reviewers* in 1809, before Byron became famous, on the grounds that it involved an onslaught not only on the *Edinburgh Review* but on Wordsworth and Scott, poets whom they published.

Byron's critique of the *Edinburgh*, first published anonymously through a minor publisher, he himself came to regard later as 'pert, petulant and shallow'.[144] It was initiated by a review in it of his first published poems, *Hours of Idleness* (1807), which he mistakenly thought was written by Jeffrey: 'the poesy of this young Lord belongs to the class which neither Gods nor Men are said to permit'. In fact, the author was Brougham. It was Jeffrey, however, whom Byron described in a lashing postscript to *English Bards* as 'the great anthropophagus': the 'anonymous writers in the *Edinburgh*', he went on, were 'his dirty pack, who feed by "lying and slandering" and slake their thirst by "evil speaking".' Ironically, Byron's style on this occasion bore some resemblance to the style of the reviewers. Byron praised two other poets, Samuel Rogers and the Scot Thomas Campbell, never a friend of the Longmans (or Wordsworth), but besides attacking the Lake poets ('Pond poets') he also attacked Moore who was to become his friend. Again ironically, the *Edinburgh* was a sharp critic of Wordsworth also – and this time it really was Jeffrey who was responsible.[145]

Much happened to Byron, Moore – and to the world – between 1809, when Byron's book appeared anonymously, and the publication of Moore's *Life, Letters and Journals of Lord Byron*, what he called 'Thoughts and Adventures', in 1830. When in exile in 1821, Byron handed over his memoirs to Moore, then in debt and facing a debtor's prison, who was visiting him in Italy, and it was to Murray, not Longman, that Moore contemplated selling them. This was partly because a prudent Longman

---

143 According to Moore, Longman thought it 'a subject of regret that they were not themselves the publishers of the *Life of Byron*, but they recognised Murray's claim (Moore, *Diary*, 8 Feb. 1828).

144 L.A. Marchand (ed.), *Byron, Letters and Journals* (1973–1994), Vol. IV, p.563n.

145 It was Southey, not Wordsworth, who was Byron's main target. For the source of the quarrel between Wordsworth and Byron see R. Woof, *William Wordsworth, the Critical Heritage, 1793–1820* (2001), pp.829–30, 896–7.

was not anxious to acquire them, but mainly because as long ago as
1811 Murray had established a close personal relation with Byron, being
sometimes addressed by him in verse:

> Strahan, Tonson, Lintot of *The Times*,
> Patron and publisher of rhymes.[146]

In all, Byron is said to have earned £20,000 from Murray, and while
there were times when Byron was irritated by him, once calling him 'the
most timid of God's booksellers', their relationship continued throughout
Byron's life.

After Byron's death in 1824 Murray expressed to his executors his
desire to publish a complete edition of his poems. 'The public', he told
Byron's solicitor, 'are absolutely indignant at not being able to obtain
a complete edition of [his] works.'[147] Murray bought such of the Byron
copyrights that he did not possess at an auction in 1828, after Thomas
Norton had told Byron's friend and executor J.C. Hobhouse that he 'would
be likely to obtain more by a private treaty with [Murray] than by any private
or public competition among Publishers'. Given such preliminaries,
it seems at first sight strange that it was in Murray's house that it was
decided that the precious memoirs should be burned, and with Moore
protesting – the manuscript was cast into the fire. What has subsequently
often been called 'literary vandalism' was pressed for by Byron's family
and executors.[148] Gifford came into the picture too: he thought, like
Hobhouse, whose politics were very different from his own, that they were
not fit for publication. They were fit only for a brothel. Moore immediately
reported what had happened to T.N. Longman and to Rees, but he went
on to produce his volume of Byron's letters and journals which eventually
appeared in 1830.

Its publication did not simplify relations between Moore and Murray,
and after one contretemps about money in 1831 Murray found it necessary
to write to Moore that he was occasioning him 'a degree of distress which
I can hardly describe to you. You forget that Longman are your publishers,
have made large sums by your writings and are therefore your natural
bankers.'[149] They were, and very generous bankers too. Thomas Norton
always gave Moore financial backing when he was in difficulties, a not

---

146 Quoted in Curwen, *op. cit.*, p.184.

147 Smiles, *op. cit.*, p.305.

148 Marchand, *op. cit*, Vol. III, pp.1245–51.

149 Letter from Murray to Moore, 11 Nov. 1831. In February 1832 Longman had to tell
Moore that they were in a situation *vis-à-vis* Murray 'which precludes us from
advising you ... You know you can depend upon *our* indulgence and our regard
for your Pocket.' (Letter of 25 Feb. 1832.)

unusual situation. 'We are sorry you should allow our account to haunt you', Rees had written to Moore in 1821, 'for, God knows, nothing has been further from our minds than that it should for a moment render you uncomfortable.' Their only hope was to see him 'in smooth waters with a fair wind'.[150]

When Russell set up a fund in 1826 for the use of Moore's son, the properly named John Russell Moore, Thomas Norton assisted in the raising of money, and two years later congratulated Moore on getting £3,000 from Murray which enabled him to meet sums that he owed to Longman/Rees.[151] He also invited Moore to his parties, one of them, in 1831, well described by Sydney Smith, a fellow guest. 'The road up to Longman's being rather awkward, they told the coachman to wait for them at the bottom.' 'It would never do', Smith explained to Moore, if 'when your memoirs come to be written' that it would be said, 'he went out to dine at the house of the respectable publishers, Longman & Co., and on his way back was crushed to death by a large clergyman.'[152]

The memoirs did not come to be written in Moore's lifetime, but in 1852, after his death, the House of Longman, then in different Longman hands, purchased his papers on condition that Russell would prepare an edition of Moore's *Diary and Correspondence*. He did so, producing a botched and hurried piece of work, published when he was in the thick of national politics. One book which Moore had not written for Longman, although they agreed on the project, was a life of Sydney Smith.[153]

The correspondence between Thomas Norton, Rees and Moore throws considerable light on the organisation of publishing in the early nineteenth century, revealing in particular how reprints and new editions, including collected works, their size, their prices and their lay-out, were handled. For example, Thomas Norton ordered illustrations by Richard Westall for the first copies of *Lalla Rookh*, and in 1836 suggested a handsome new edition of *Lalla Rookh* 'with some very good engravings in the shape of the best of Heath's annuals'.[154] (Charles Heath, engraver and publisher

---

150   Letters from Rees to Moore, 29 Dec. 1821; 11 July 1823.

151   Letters of 26 Feb., 6 July 1826 from Russell to Longman and Co.; Diary note, 8 Feb. 1828; Letter of Moore to Murray, 30 March 1828, authorising him to pay the money.

152   Quoted in Pearson, *op. cit.*, p.261. This was a dinner also attended by two noted entomologists, and Smith suggested to Mrs Longman a 'suitable menu' which would have included earthworms on toast and caterpillars in cream.

153   Letter from Moore to Thomas Longman, 9 May 1845; memorandum of Agreement, 28 June 1845; Letters from G.A. Smith to Thomas Longman (dealing with access to materials), 28 April, 8 Aug. 1845.

154   Letter from Rees to Moore, 8 July 1836.

of illustrated *Annuals*, a popular and profitable genre at this time, executed small plates for popular English classics.) The result was an expensive edition, published in 1839, of 3,000 copies which cost £1,853 6s. 4d.; and three years later in the 'bad year', 1842, another 1,500 copies of it were printed, with a further 1,500 to follow in 1845.

Thomas Norton never failed to recognise the importance of the visual dimension to books, apparent in bindings as well as illustrations.[155] And he doubtless enjoyed also a sense of patronage in commissioning artists. It was his son, however, who employed new technology in an 1851 octavo edition of *Lalla Rookh* printed on stereotype plates. Stereotypes were of great importance in the economics of publishing. Once a stereotype had been made – and at first such making was resisted – there was no more need for movable type. The stereotypes could be stored, and this eliminated the need for new editing and proof reading. Texts were thereby stabilised.

There was cross-reference also in the Longman/Rees/Moore correspondence to music publishing, expanding in range and circulation in the nineteenth century. Longman, who had published some musical scores in the eighteenth century, continued to do so in the nineteenth, putting an increased emphasis on education as in Auguste Bertini's *New System for Learning and Acquiring extraordinary Facility on all Musical Instruments, particularly the Pianoforte, Harp and Violin (as well as in Singing) in a very Short Space of Time, with a new and easy Mode of marking the Fingering of all Wind Instruments* (1830). They did not own Moore's musical copy, however: his *Irish Melodies*, in various editions which enjoyed enormous success, particularly 'The Last Rose of Summer', were set to music by Sir John Stevenson and published by James Diffy.[156] There were other Longmans who were 'music sellers' in London, not related to the Longmans of Paternoster Row, among them Longman, Lokey and Company and Longman, Broderip and Clementi. The various Longmans have sometimes been confused with each other as the various Osbornes had been.

In one place in the correspondence between Rees and Moore there is an interesting reference to *The Times*, not as a newspaper but as an advertising medium. Rees told Moore in 1825 to write to Thomas Barnes, its editor, to thank him for printing the first notice of his *Life of Sheridan*. Barnes had been sent the sheets by Rees, and the notice appeared on the day of publication.[157] The letters bring out the carefully cultivated personal relationship between Moore and his publishers. 'You may draw upon us

---

155 For the importance of pictorial illustration, with particular reference to Knight and cheap publications, see P.J. Anderson, *The Printed Image and the Transformation of Popular Culture* (1991); and W.H. Ivins, *Prints and Visual Communication* (1953).

156 See H.M. Jones, *The Harp That Once - A Chronicle* (Harvard 1937).

157 Letter from Rees to Moore, 8 Oct. 1825.

Now all the world is sleeping, love,
But the Sage, his star-watch keeping, love,
        And I, whose star,
        More glorious far,
Is the eye from that casement peeping, love.
Then awake!—till rise of sun, my dear,
The Sage's glass we'll shun, my dear,
        Or, in watching the flight
        Of bodies of light,
He might happen to take thee for one, my dear.

A page from Moore's *Irish Melodies* showing the high quality of engraving

Longman Archive

from the £100 as you suggest', Rees tells Moore in 1834, adding that 'Mr. Longman requests me to solicit the favour of your company at Hampstead to dinner on *Thursday the 31st*. And I request the same favour for Owen Rees, Monday the 4th August at ½ past 6.'[158]

On one occasion in 1836 an effort was made to lure Moore away from Longman, when he was offered £1,000 for an edition of his 'works, prose and poetical complete', 8,000 copies of which were to be printed in monthly numbers, with 'Turner embellishments', described as 'the best style of Illustrations'. 'To obviate any delicacy on the point of leaving the Longmans', Moore's correspondent, E.J. Moran, adduced 'the precedent of Wordsworth, who is at this moment doing similarly with Moxon'.[159]

Lines cross, as this chapter so completely demonstrates, and any full account of Wordsworth's experiences with Edward Moxon (1801–1858), who was employed by Longman and Rees 'in the country line' from 1821 to 1828, must lead back to the Bristol of the 1790s, and to the Rees connection with Cottle. Any account of experience recollected must always refer back to experience forged and looking back appealed not only to Cottle but to Wordsworth himself. 'Lines composed a few miles above Tintern Abbey' were reflections on a return. And there were to be many returns, not all of them in tranquillity or, as in Samuel Rogers's poem of 1792, linked through 'the pleasure of memory'.

Moxon, close to Lamb, whose adopted daughter Emma Isola he was to marry in 1833, is interesting not only in relation to Lamb or to an ageing Wordsworth but in his own right. A publisher of poets, he was a poet himself, as Cottle had been. As early as 1826 the House of Longman had published a volume of verses of his own, *The Prospect and Other Poems*, and in 1829 he had followed this with *Christmas*, dedicated to Lamb. He prepared a number of editions of his sonnets, the first of them in 1837, the last in 1843. His edition of the first volume of Coventry Patmore's poems appeared in 1834, and he was one of the first publishers to appreciate Robert Browning's 'domestic romances and lyrics'.[160]

---

158 Letter from Rees to Moore, 23 July 1834.

159 Letter from E. Moran to Moore, 30 July 1836.

160 See H.G. Merriam, *Moxon: Publisher of Poetry* (1939), p.164 and E. Gosse, *Robert Browning: Personalia* (1895).

Moxon died in 1858, having published Shelley's poems and letters, the latter with an introduction by Browning. He was tried for blasphemy for publishing Shelley's *Queen Mab* and died while E.J. Trelawny's *Recollection of the Last Days of Byron and Shelley* was in the press.[161] Longman and Rees had turned down Shelley's *Laon and Cythna*, later called *The Revolt of Islam*, in 1818, and Shelley had gone on to print and advertise it at his own expense. None of Shelley's poems had been produced commercially in his lifetime.[162]

Moxon's first introduction to Wordsworth in 1826 had come through Lamb. 'The bearer of this note', Lamb told Wordsworth, 'is my young friend MOXON, a young lad with a Yorkshire head, and a heart that would do honour to a more Southern county: no offence in Westmoreland. He is one of Longman's best hands, and can give you the best account of The Trade as 'tis now going; or stopping … Moxon is but a tradesman in the bud yet, and retains his virgin honesty.' Lamb also told Wordsworth that once or twice a week Moxon 'lugged' from Longman to Lamb's a cargo of the new books, including novels.[163]

Ten years later, by agreement, the publishing of all Wordsworth's poems was transferred from Longman and Rees to Moxon. Yet a new Wordsworth volume *Yarrow Revisited and Other Poems*, published in 1835, which sold well, bore the joint imprint of Moxon and Longman and Rees. While Wordsworth's relationship with Moxon was subject to some of the same strains as his relationship with Longman and Rees had been, it was a more personal one. Wordsworth came to like Moxon, and stayed with him in London in 1845 when he was presented to the Queen as Poet Laureate, on the same visit meeting Tennyson on the invitation of Lord John Russell. More lines were connecting. By then, Moxon had become Tennyson's regular publisher, beginning with his *Poems, chiefly Lyrical* of 1833, 'resplendent with lilac colours'.[164] Moxon's death was a severe blow to Tennyson: thereafter he never felt the same about any publisher.

Meanwhile, Cottle, who had published Wordsworth, Southey and Coleridge when they were all young,[165] had written two books of reminiscences recalling the very different age of publishing described in the first pages of this chapter, the first of them jointly published by Longman and Rees. Cottle died only five years before Moxon, although he

---

161 Merriam, *op. cit.*, pp.114–21.

162 See his letter to an unnamed publisher in F.L. James (ed.), *The Letters of Percy Bysshe Shelley* (1964), p.563.

163 Merriam, *op. cit.*, Ch. 10, 'Moxon and Wordsworth', pp.130–49.

164 R.B. Martin, *Tennyson, the Unquiet Heart* (1980), p.160. The *Poems* were reviewed crushingly in the QR, but were strongly defended by Rogers, who called him the most promising genius of the day.

165 See above, p.153.

Joseph Cottle (1770–1853)
c 1800 by Robert Hancock
pencil and wash

In *The Annals of Bristol in the
Eighteenth Century*, 1893, John
Latimer, wrote that 'The dreams
of the youthful philosophers
[Southey, Coleridge and their
friends] were soon roughly
disturbed by an encounter
with the harsher realities of
life ... Cottle's liberality to the
enthusiasts will be remembered
long after his prosy poetry is
forgotten.'

The National Portrait Gallery, London
no. 5723

had long ceased to be a publisher, and his *Early Recollections* had
been criticised, often unfairly, as 'the refuse of advertisements
and handbills, the sweepings of a shop, the shreds of a ledger
and the rank residuum of a life of gossip'.[166] In addition, some
reviewers obviously believed that Cottle had revealed too much
of the young Coleridge and his addiction to laudanum. Cottle
did not apologise. He claimed, as most modern biographers
would claim, that 'in order to redeem its character, [biography
must present] an undisguised portrait of the man rather than a
stream of undeviating eulogy' and that 'every incident connected
with the lives of literary men, especially at the commencement
of their career, always excites interest'. He described himself as
'fighting the Battle of the Public'.[167]

In 1828 he wrote to Wordsworth after what he called 'a
mutual epistolatory interruption of thirty years',[168] and thereafter,
they were to remain in contact. When on 29 April 1837 Cottle
sent Wordsworth a copy of his *Early Recollections*, he added that
'you and I are rapidly advancing in life. It becomes us to look well at our
foundations.' Ten years later he expressed the same thought in a letter of
24 April 1847. 'We are *birds of passage*, and may meet next in a better world',
and in June 1850 he wrote to Wordsworth's widow 'Now the *last* of my early
friends is gone!'

When another early friend, Southey, had died earlier in 1843, Cottle
had written to a large number of people, soliciting support for a memorial to
Southey in Bristol. They included Wordsworth, Brougham, the Archbishop of
Canterbury and the Prime Minister, Sir Robert Peel. Few of his respondents
promised money, although Jeffrey gave £10, describing Southey as 'one of
the best writers and most excellent men of our generation'.[169] The Bishop of
Gloucester sent £5. 'Longmans' sent nothing, stating that they had already
subscribed £5 for a 'Tablet in the North'.

Southey had never forgotten or forgiven the crushing attacks on his
poetry and on that of 'the Lake School' in the *Edinburgh Review*. Jeffrey

---

166 QR, Vol. LIX (1837).

167 *Early Recollections*, Vol. I, pp.17–18, p.xxv; Letter from Cottle to T. Poole, 15 June
1836. Many of the criticisms of *Early Recollections* were unfair, for example, the
sweeping condemnation of the first volume in the QR. Longman did not share
in the condemnation, but a second Cottle volume, *Reminiscences of Samuel Taylor
Coleridge and Robert Southey*, which appeared in 1847, six years before Cottle's
death, was published not by Longman but by Houlston and Stoneman.

168 G. Lamoine, 'Letters from Joseph Cottle to William Wordsworth, 1828–1850' in
Ariel, Vol. 3 (1972), p.80.

169 Letter from Cottle to Wordsworth, giving full details, March 1844, cited in
Lamoine, *loc. cit.*, pp.90–2.

did not use the term,[170] but in a later review of Wordsworth's *Poems in Two Volumes* (1807) he generalised disparagingly about 'a certain brotherhood of poets, who have haunted for some years about the Lakes of Cumberland',[171] and seven years later, when he reviewed Wordsworth's long poem *The Excursion*, he bitterly condemned 'the Lakers'.[172] Nevertheless, his first comment on the 'little volume of poems called *Lyrical Ballads* ... without any author's name' was that he was 'enchanted' by it.[173]

~

Having briefly spanned half-a-century of nineteenth-century literary criticism, more must be said in this chapter about the *Lyrical Ballads* and about Scott's relations with Longman and Rees, if only because so much was to be written about Wordsworth and Scott from so many different angles during the course of the twentieth century. In the case of the *Lyrical Ballads* the writings have covered such diverse topics as the history of the use of each of the words 'lyrical' and 'ballads', the examinations of imprints, the paper and even paper watermarks; detailed textual criticism; biography; and, to a limited extent, an analysis of the economics of publishing.[174] In the case of Scott, they have covered his attitudes towards history, the relationship

These drawings of 1798 are all described as being 'in the possession of Mr. Cottle', and are reproduced in Cottle's *Early Recollections*, Longman, 1837

Left to right
Charles Lamb, Robert Southey, Samuel Taylor Coleridge, and William Wordsworth

BL 1164.h.19

---

170 See the important article by P.A. Cook, 'Chronology of the "Lake School" Argument: Some Revisions', in the RES, Vol.28 (1977) and S. Gill, *Wordsworth and the Victorians* (1998), pp.17–18. As J.O. Hayden noted in his book *The Romantic Reviewers* (1969), the *Monthly Mirror* used the phrase in June 1801, adding that it was a school 'which we do not altogether admire'. The phrase had been used too by a reviewer of Coleridge's translation of Schiller's *Wallenstein* in the *Critical Review* in Oct. 1800.

171 ER, Vol. XI (1807).

172 *ibid*., Vol. XXIV (1814).

173 C. Morehead (ed.), *Memories of the Life and Writings of Charles Morehead DD* (1875), p.102.

174 For the most beautifully illustrated, stimulating introduction to Wordsworth's poems see R. and P. Woof, *Towards Tintern Abbey* (1998).

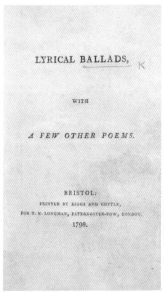

Lyrical Ballads published by
J&A Arch 1798

BL C121.a.15

Lyrical Ballads printed by Biggs
and Cottle for T. N Longman,
London 1798

BL 58.c.12

between his poetry and his prose, and his changing literary reputation, which went through quite different phases from Wordsworth's.[175] Through much of this writing the role of Longman in changing times has been more brightly illuminated than it has in any other place.

The first two volumes of Scott's *Minstrelsy of the Border* were published two years after the *Lyrical Ballads*, to be followed in 1805 by the *Lay of the Last Minstrel* and in 1807 by *Marmion*. Longman and Rees were directly associated with all three, all of them first printed in quarto, as was *The Lady of the Lake* (1810) which was exceptionally highly priced at 42 shillings. In a letter of 1802 Wordsworth had described the readers of quartos as 'gentlemen, persons of fortune, professional men, ladies, persons who can afford to buy, or can easily procure, books of half-a-guinea price [all the Scotts cost more], hot pressed and printed on super fine paper'.[176] By then Wordsworth had his experiences of the *Lyrical Ballads* in mind. Soon, however, he was to be published, by his own choice, at high prices himself. *The Excursion* (1814) had a print run of only 500 and had sold, as Scott's *The Lady of the Lake* (and Southey's *Madoc*) at 42 shillings.

The idea behind the *Lyrical Ballads* and the title, contents and typography had been discussed at a dinner in the country given by Coleridge at Nether Stowey in late May 1798 which was attended by the Wordsworths, brother and sister. Cottle, also present, hoped for two volumes of poems, but received only one, which was published anonymously. The first edition of 500 copies (210 pages, bound in paper boards) had appeared in September 1798 – there is a mystery about the exact date of publication – while the Wordsworths, along with Coleridge, were on a visit to Germany, planned for three months. In the case of Coleridge, it was to last for ten.

Only four poems out of the twenty-three were by Coleridge, and neither he nor Cottle had prepared the advertisement for the volume. Only Wordsworth, to whom Cottle paid thirty guineas, stressed that the poems should be 'considered as experiments'. Coleridge discerned 'an interpolation of heterogeneous matter' in it:[177] Wordsworth himself, however, had been most disturbed by the fact that 'no one seemed to understand' Coleridge's 'The Rime of the Ancient Mariner' which he considered 'an injury to the

---

175 See W.B. Todd and A. Bowden, *Sir Walter Scott, A Bibliographical History, 1796–1832* (Oak Knoll, Del., 1998) and J. Millgate, *Walter Scott, the Making of the Novelist (1984)* and *Scott's Last Edition, a Study in Publishing History*. For Scott as an historian see *inter alia* his *The Tales of a Grandfather* (with introduction by F.W. Farrar, 1911); J. Anderson, 'Sir Walter Scott as a Historical Novelist', in *Studies in Scottish Literature*, Vol. 4 (1967); and D. Brown, *Walter Scott and the Historical Imagination* (1979).

176 De Selincourt, *op. cit.*, p.295.

177 S.T. Coleridge, *Biographia Literaria* (1907 edn.), Vol. 2, Ch. XVII, pp. 28–43 lists Coleridge's differences in approach compared with Wordsworth's.

volume',[178] adding that if the volume should 'come to a second edition', he would put in its place 'some little things which would be more likely to suit the public taste'.[179] Coleridge kept a sense of perspective. As he put it later, the 'Ancient Mariner' represented an endeavour to introduce into the collection of poems 'persons and characters supernatural, or at least romantic'.[180] The use of the last adjective now stands out sharply.

Coleridge, by then familiar with Longman as well as with Cottle, claimed that Thomas Norton had told him in 1800, before the Longman edition of the *Lyrical Ballads* appeared, that booksellers did not like anonymous books – they wanted authors' names – and had added 'acutely' that 'booksellers scarcely pretend to judge the merits of the book': they knew 'the saleableness of the name!' They bought most books 'on the calculation of a first edition of a thousand copies [and] they are seldom much mistaken'. On the basis of the name they could send a book to all 'the Gentlemen in Great Britain and the Colonies, from whom they have standing orders for new books of reputation.'[181]

There were, in fact, some favourable reviews of the first Cottle edition of the *Lyrical Ballads*, including one attributed to Francis Wrangham, a clergyman and classical scholar, in the *British Critic*. The reviewer, most likely John Stoddart, a young lawyer and a friend of Coleridge and of Scott, praised the volume for its 'energy of thought', considering that 'even the most unadorned tale' in the volume was preferable to 'all the meretricious frippery of current taste'. He approved strongly of 'the endeavour to recall our poetry from ... excess of refinement to simplicity and nature'.[182]

Whatever was said about the subject later, the Cottle edition was sold before publication to J. and A. Arch of Gracechurch Street, London, who went on to produce a new imprint bearing their own name, which appeared and was advertised on 4 October 1798. Meanwhile, on learning of Cottle's financial problems, Wordsworth had asked him to transfer his (Wordsworth's) rights in the *Lyrical Ballads* to his previous publisher, Joseph Johnson, who in 1793 had published his *An Evening Walk* and his

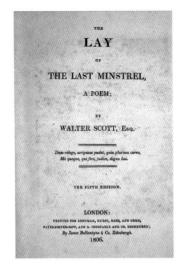

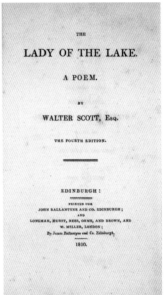

The title page to *The Lay of the Last Minstrel*, 1806

Longman Archive

The title page to *The Lady of the Lake*, 1810 4th edition

Longman Archive

---

178 Letter to Cottle, 24 June 1799, in De Selincourt, *op. cit.*, Vol. I, pp.226–27.

179 Quoted in Hanson, *op. cit.*, p.365.

180 *Ibid.*

181 Undated letter to Southey, written early in 1800, printed in E.L. Griggs (ed.), *Collected Letters of S.T. Coleridge*, 6 vols. (1895), Vol. 1. Dennie's first American edition of the *Lyrical Ballads* was printed in 1802.

182 *British Critic*, Oct. 1799.

Descriptive Sketches.[183] Instead, they were returned directly to Wordsworth by Cottle, before deletion of the title had set down their value as nil in the list of titles offered to Longman.[184] When, however, a two-volume edition, substantially revised, but printed, like the first edition, by Biggs and Cottle, was published in 1801, it appeared under the London imprint T.N. Longman and O. Rees. They had offered Wordsworth £80 for the rights.[185] This was the edition which contained Wordsworth's famous Preface. *The Ancient Mariner* was still there, but its position in the collection was changed, and there was no place for Coleridge's later long poem *Christabel* which he had not been able to complete in time to Wordsworth's satisfaction. Wordsworth had been forced to work frantically to complete *Michael* to take its place.[186]

Coleridge, who considered this edition 'greatly superior to the first',[187] had by then experienced difficulties of his own with Thomas Norton. He had been paid £50 in advance for a verse translation of Schiller's new play *Wallenstein* and had completed the translation in six weeks, but the book 'fell dead', as he had forecast, and money was lost.[188] He had also promised Thomas Norton an essay on Schiller, and not having finished this as promised, he was in debt to Longman and Rees while their edition of the *Lyrical Ballads* was being prepared. 'I am sure that Longman never thinks of me, but *Wallenstein* and the ghosts of his departed genius dance an ugly waltz round my idea', he wrote to a friend in 1802.[189]

Nonetheless, Coleridge and Wordsworth together, not Cottle or Thomas Norton, had decided on the idea of sending complimentary copies

---

183 Letter of 15 Sept. 1798. The letter, which is lost, was referred to in a later Wordsworth letter of May 1799 (De Selincourt, *op. cit.*, p.224). Cottle noted that he could not have made this transfer since he had already reached his arrangement with Arch.

184 Cottle claimed wrongly in his *Reminiscences* that sales had been slow and most reviews hostile, to such an extent that the 'progress to oblivion' of the poems 'seemed ordained to be as rapid as it was certain', 'notwithstanding the merit' which he himself was quite sure they possessed.

185 Coleridge had no rights in the *Lyrical Ballads* (Cottle, *Early Recollections*, Vol. II, pp.26–7), yet Wordsworth gave Coleridge £30 either as an ex-gratia payment or a loan.

186 R. and P. Woof, *op. cit.*, pp.77–8. Both Wordsworth and Coleridge gave different reasons at different times for the non-inclusion of *Christabel*, one of Coleridge's most original metrical experiments. Dorothy Wordsworth's reaction was terse. She wrote in her famous *Journal* on 6 Oct. 1800, 'Determined not to print *Christabel* with the LB'.

187 Letter to Longman and Rees, 15 Dec. 1800 (LA Part II 67/3). Coleridge ended this letter by presenting 'his best respects to Mrs Longman'.

188 R. Holmes, *Coleridge, Early Visions* (1989), p.257.

189 Quoted in Griggs, *Letters*, Vol. 1.

of the *Lyrical Ballads*, along with flattering letters, to 'different people of eminence', including Charles James Fox, the Duchess of Devonshire (each of them great Whig names), and William Wilberforce, who supported Fox's rival William Pitt.[190] Their idea was to 'push the sale'. Coleridge added in a letter to Thomas Norton that he had written letters 'to all my acquaintances whose voices I think likely to have any influence'.[191] Ironically, it was some of the people who did not receive complimentary copies who were most appreciative of the merits of the poems, and it was John Stoddart, the friend who had probably written the review attributed to Wrangham, who wrote a favourable review of the new edition in the *British Critic*. He also read aloud to Scott Coleridge's poem *Christabel*.[192] Privately, Lamb on this occasion was witty but disloyal. 'So you don't think there's a Word's-worth of good poetry in the great L.B.?' he wrote to a friend. 'Between you and me the L. Ballads are but drowsy performances.'[193]

When Longman and Rees published Wordsworth's 1807 *Poems* in two volumes, they bore the inscription on the title page 'William Wordsworth, Author of the Lyrical Ballads'. One thousand copies were produced, but they sold less well than the *Lyrical Ballads* themselves, and in 1814 no fewer than 230 copies were still in stock. It was the fiercely critical reception given to these poems rather than the critical reaction to the *Lyrical Ballads* themselves which reduced Wordsworth to despondency, although in an essay of 1815 he linked the *Lyrical Ballads* with the 1807 *Poems* as sources of 'unremitting hostility'.[194] There had been new admirers, however, one of them the young Thomas De Quincey (1785–1859) who wrote to Wordsworth via Longman/Rees, describing the 1807 poems as 'enchanting'. He met Coleridge and Wordsworth for the first time in that year.

The subsequent fortunes of Wordsworth's reputation as a poet, with which his financial fortunes were directly linked, have been traced in detail,

---

190 The letter to Fox, written by Wordsworth, was peculiarly obsequious: 'In company with the whole English People I have observed in your public character a constant predominance of sensibility of heart ... This habit cannot but have made you dear to Poets'. The Queen is said to have bought a copy and given it as a present.

191 Letter of 15 Dec. 1800 in Griggs, *op. cit.*, Vol. 1, p.164.

192 See Harvey, *op. cit.*, p.98, where he discusses claims that Scott had plagiarised Coleridge (*London Courier*, 15 Sept. 1810).

193 See R. Woof, 'John Stoddart, "Michael", and "Lyrical Ballads"', in *Ariel 1* (1970), pp.7–22.

194 The title of the 1815 edition, *Poems by William Wordsworth*, went on 'including *Lyrical Ballads and the Miscellaneous Pieces of the Author with a new Preface, and a Supplementary Essay*'.

and so, too, have his sometimes tetchy reactions to them.[195] For example, he was irritated that the first quarto edition of *The Excursion*, published in 1814, a poem to which he attached special importance, had sold only 413 copies by 1834: the remaining thirty-six copies were divided between Wordsworth and the publishers. Priced at 42s. before binding and at over 45s. bound, it was an exceptionally expensive book, and Wordsworth had to wait for six years before it appeared in octavo.

Of a later octavo edition of the poem, which cost twelve shillings, Lamb wrote verses in the *London Magazine* thanking 'Messrs Longman, Hurst, Rees, Orme and Brown for enabling me upon my humble shelf to see *The Excursion* in octavo'. The quarto volume had been forbidding not only because of its price but because of its 'cumbrous shape':

> ... books which one is only able
> To read – by spreading on a table
> Seldom invite inspection.[196]

Of this later edition, which cost two guineas and would be accessible only to the 'fashionable and wealthy', Wordsworth himself claimed that he had 'no anxiety about the fate of *The Excursion* beyond the sale of the first edition'.

Longman and Rees continued to be Wordsworth's publisher until 1836, but their relationship was never comfortable, largely because his poems sold slowly, and Wordsworth blamed his publishers for this. As early as 1825 he told Thomas Norton that one reason why he was not making enough money out of his poetry was because of the advertising costs of the House, adding that he would look for a different publisher. He went on to ask Samuel Rogers to serve as an intermediary (as Moore had done), seeking a publisher with 'more liberalty [*sic*] than Longmans, more enterprise, and more skill in managing the sale of works charactered [*sic*] and circumstanced as mine'. Meanwhile, he wrote to Murray from whom he did not receive an immediate reply; and finding it necessary to write again twice, Wordsworth eventually learned the truth: Murray did not wish to publish him.[197] In a revealing letter from Lockhart, the editor of the *Quarterly Review*, Murray had been told that:

> In regard to Wordsworth I certainly cannot doubt it must be creditable
> to any publisher to publish the works of one who is and must continue

---

195 W.J.B. Owen, 'Costs, Sales and Profits of Longman's Editions of Wordsworth', in TL, 5th series, Vol.IX (1954), pp.93–107. For an earlier discussion, in this case not based on statistics, see also H. House, 'Wordsworth's Fame', in *All in Due Time* (1948), pp.37–45.

196 Quoted in B. Dobell, *Sidelights on Charles Lamb* (1903), pp.89–91.

197 Letters of 21 Jan., 19 Feb., 21 March 1825. See P.W. Clayden, *Rogers and His Contemporaries*, Vol. I (1889), pp.40 ff.

Tintern Abbey in moonlight by John 'Warwick' Smith, 1779

The National Library of Wales, Aberystwyth

to be a classic Poet of England. Your adventure with Crabbe [which had cost Murray a substantial amount in losses], however, ought to be a lesson of much caution. ... Everything, I should humbly say, depends on the terms proposed by the great Laker, whose vanity, be it whispered, is nearly as remarkable as his genius.[198]

In his letter to Murray Wordsworth had not mentioned Longman, but he did mention – and it was an interesting connection in this year of the crash – that twelve months earlier his poems were to have been put into the hands of Robinson and Hurst, whose business had subsequently failed calamitously.[199]

When Wordsworth received no satisfactory reply from Murray, he concluded (wrongly) that he, Murray, was 'too great a Personage for anyone but a Count, an Aristocratic or most fashionable Author to deal with', and he next considered Constable, whose bankruptcy following that of Robinson and Hurst ruled out any possibilities there. Wordsworth's timing was appalling. He stayed with Longman, therefore, making new arrangements, and a new edition of his *Poetical Works*, published in five volumes in 1827, was at last a financial success. The 750 copies printed (along with an extra 250 of his poem *The Excursion*), were quickly 'exhausted', and Wordsworth made a net profit on them of £422 10s. 8d. Clearly his reputation was rising again.

Dorothy Wordsworth explained some of her brother's publishing preoccupations in a letter to Crabb Robinson in 1829. Wordsworth was

---

198 Letter of 9 July 1826, quoted in Smiles, *op. cit.*, Vol. II, p.245. This is the only reference to Wordsworth in Smiles's volumes.

199 See above, p.164.

preparing a volume of poems for the press, she told him, but had not 'yet even fixed upon a Publisher'. 'He has had so little profit in his engagement with Longman, that he is inclined to try another', a dubious conclusion since he had at times colluded with Longman and Rees in keeping the prices of his books high. Not surprisingly, Thomas Norton assured him that he and Rees should not think themselves 'unhandsomely used if he applied elsewhere'. If they were to part they would part on friendly terms. 'I wish he had made up his mind', Dorothy concluded sensibly, 'and for my part, am sorry that he has ever entertained a thought of change; for his works are not likely to be much aided in the sale by exertions even of the most active publishers.'[200]

William himself complained in 1833 that Cumberland booksellers had not sold a copy of his poems 'though Cumberland is my native county'.[201] Scott (and Byron) did sell there, however, although Wordsworth's financial preoccupations, which were to goad him into struggling for national copyright legislation in the interests of his family, came to seem small-scale when compared with those of Scott, all of which, Wordsworth believed, were related to his desire to be actively involved, not least financially, in publishing. 'Poor Sir Walter Scott', Wordsworth wrote to his sister when he heard the news of the collapse of Constable and of the Ballantynes, 'how could he so enter into trade as to be involved in this way. He a baronet! A literary man! A lawyer! I wish very much for particulars.'[202]

~

Scott's involvement with Constable and the Ballantyne brothers, James and John, already briefly described, had survived, if at times awkwardly, his changing business with them. He and James Ballantyne had been friends since their schooldays in Kelso, and Constable's imprint appeared, not always alone, on the front page of virtually all of Scott's works, poetry and prose, from the *Minstrelsy of the Scottish Border* in 1802 to *Woodstock*, published in 1826, the year of Constable's crash. Meanwhile, Constable's own dealings with the Ballantyne brothers had gone through many changes after 1814, the memorable year when Scott abandoned poetry for prose and published his novel *Waverley* anonymously. For some literary historians *Kenilworth* (1821) marked the birth of the not yet named three-decker novel.[203]

---

200 Letter from Dorothy Wordsworth to Crabb Robinson, 2 July 1825, printed in E. Hartley (ed.), *The Correspondence of Dorothy Wordsworth with Henry Crabb Robinson*, Vol. I. (1927), pp.139–40

201 Letter to Moxon, 10 Aug. 1833.

202 Hartley, *op. cit.*

203 See D.C. Ewing, 'The Three Volume Novel', in PBSA, Vol. 61, Third Quarter, 1967, p.204.

Longman and Rees were always part of the story, involved as they themselves were in a continuous relationship with Scott which survived all the changes in national politics and in Scott's literary and financial circumstances. Their business relationship had gone back to Thomas Norton's visit to Scotland in 1802 when he reached the arrangement with Constable that led to the inauguration of the *Edinburgh Review,* and on the same visit he also called on Scott to negotiate with him for the third volume of his poems, *Minstrelsy of the Border,* for which Scott was to write an interesting new introduction when his collected *Poetical Works* were re-published, without Longman and Rees being involved, in 1832. In 1804 Rees also had met Scott for the first time to settle terms for his *Lay of the Last Minstrel* (1805), when Scott accepted a half-profits arrangement with Constable and Longman, but later sold the copyright for £500 to Longman and Rees.

Marmion followed in 1808, even more popular than *The Lay,* but this time it was not Longman and Rees who were joint publishers with Constable, but Murray, who through a deal with them acquired a fourth share in the profits. Again, however, there were to be complications, literary and financial. Scott had been introduced to Murray by his fellow Scot, the poet Thomas Campbell (1777–1844), born in Glasgow, who had been planning a series of *Specimens of the British Poets,* which appeared in 1819. Campbell, author of *The Pleasures of Hope* (1799), which included the line 'Tis distance lends enchantment to the view', took pride in the fact, as he put it, that he owed nothing to 'the Row'. From 1820 to 1831 he was editor of *The New Monthly Magazine.* 'Murray', he told Scott, was 'the only gentleman in the trade except Constable', adding gratuitously that 'Longman and Rees and a few of the great booksellers have literally monopolized the trade and the business of literature is getting a dreadful one indeed'.[204]

The word monopoly was also used by Harriet Martineau (1802–1876), who described the period covered in this chapter as 'days of bookselling monopoly', when 'the Byrons, the Moores, the Campbells and Scotts [she left out the writers of the Lake District, where she acquired a house in 1844] were the clients of the Murrays, the Longmans, the Constables'. The days were, she added, 'a rather short transitional stage, when the patrons [i.e. the booksellers] learned, perforce through interest, the taste which had not been formed by education'. 'The publisher decided what the reading public should have to read and at what price.'[205]

MINSTRELSY

OF THE

SCOTTISH BORDER:

CONSISTING OF

HISTORICAL AND ROMANTIC BALLADS,

COLLECTED

IN THE SOUTHERN COUNTIES OF SCOTLAND; WITH A FEW OF MODERN DATE, FOUNDED UPON LOCAL TRADITION.

IN THREE VOLUMES.

VOL. III.

THIRD EDITION.

EDINBURGH:

Printed by James Ballantyne and Co.

FOR LONGMAN, HURST, REES, AND ORME, PATERNOSTER-ROW, LONDON; AND A. CONSTABLE AND CO. EDINBURGH.

1806.

Scott's *Minstrelsy of the Scottish Border* Vol. III 1st Edition. The imprint shows Longman's collaboration with Constable. Longman wrote in 1802 from Edinburgh to Rees in London 'As you mention the *Border Minstrelsy,* I tell you I have secured the second edition for us. Walter Scott is a very first rate man.'

BL 1609/2711

---

204 Letter to Scott, quoted in Smiles, *op. cit.,* Vol. I, p.326.

205 H. Martineau, *Biographical Sketches* (1858), 'Samuel Rogers', p.52. See also her *Miscellanies* (1836), Vol. I, p.30, where as a moralist rather than a businesswoman she claimed that Scott had done more for the 'morals of our society' than all the divines and moral teachers of the past century. His influence was only 'just beginning its course of a thousand years'.

This was at best a partial judgement which did not do full justice either to the Longmans and Murrays or to the Constables or to the Blackwoods. Yet it has been echoed many times since. William Blackwood deemed it completely wrong. 'When I consider the books you have published and are to publish', he told Murray, 'you have the happiness of making it [publishing] a liberal profession and not a mere matter of pence. This I consider one of the greatest privileges we have in our business.'[206]

Doubtless Thomas Norton and Rees felt it a privilege to deal with Scott whom they had helped financially when he turned to 'castle-building' and founded a territorial family home, Abbotsford, in the Border Country near Melrose, an expensive commitment which was very dear to him. 'Messrs. Longman and Company' demonstrated 'unsolicited kindness', Scott recalled, when they added an extra £100 to the £500 they had paid him for the copyright of *The Lay*, 'in consequence of the uncommon success of the work'. It was 'to supply the loss of a fine horse, which broke down suddenly while the author was riding, with [Rees] one of the worthy publishers.'[207] In 1814 Scott yet again committed himself to Longman and Rees for a new novel, *Guy Mannering; or the Astrologer*, 'a tale of private life in Galloway', which was the first novel to appear under the name of 'the author of *Waverley*'.[208]

Longman/Rees were financially involved in the main series of Waverley Novels which made an international reputation for Scott even before his name was openly attached to them, and the publisher who took over Scott's publishing affairs after the crash, Constable's former partner, Robert Cadell, disliked Longman and Rees precisely because they had dealt solely or jointly in so many Scott titles. 'Longman Co. are a damned shabby set', Cadell wrote to his traveller in London in 1828.[209] After Scott's death Cadell was to publish in forty-eight volumes the whole set of the Waverley Novels, originally planned by Constable. When they appeared, however, they were not printed on fine paper or handsomely bound but in monthly parts, appealing to an even wider British public than Scott had previously attracted. It was an impressive achievement, but many of the novels, neatly arranged as they often were – and still sometimes are – in parlour bookcases, may have been more admired than read even in the

---

206 Quoted in Smiles, *op. cit.*, p.456.

207 Letter from Abbotsford, April 1820, quoted in H. Cox, 'The House of Longman', in ER, Vol. 240 (1924), p.222.

208 J. Millgate, *Walter Scott, The Making of the Novelist*, pp.64–7. There had been an argument with Longman about the attribution (and format) of *Ivanhoe* (1819) which centred on the supply of paper: See J. Millgate, 'Making it New: Scott, Ballantyne and the Publication of *Ivanhoe*' in *Studies in English Literature: the Nineteenth Century*, Vol. 34, No. 4, Autumn 1994,

209 J. Millgate, *Scott's Last Edition*, p.9.

nineteenth century. At the end of the century it may be that they were not being read at all. 'Will our posterity understand at least why he [Scott] was once a luminary of the first magnitude?', Leslie Stephen asked as early as 1871.[210]

~

To concentrate only on major romantic authors, whose names have passed into all chronicles of literary history, would be to misrepresent the feel of the publishing business in the age of Thomas Norton and Rees and to ignore interesting influences and relationships within literary history itself. So too would exclusive concentration on the *Edinburgh Review*, which could occasionally generate a sense of intrigue. Thus, when Murray once accused J.W. Croker of being involved in secret talks with Longman about taking over the editorship of the *Edinburgh Review*, Croker told him 'You are either mad, or you must think Messrs Longman and I are in that unhappy condition.'[211]

In 1806 Longman and Rees published part of Volume 2 of the first series of the *Eclectic Review*, nonconformist in its origins and approach, which had been founded in January 1805, and they continued to publish it until June 1813.[212] Another of their ventures, an *Annual Review*, first published in 1803 and last appearing in 1810, was 'intended to comprise in one large volume an account of the entire English literature of each year', was edited, at least in its first five years, by Aikin and included an article by Scott on 'Ancient Romance'. (Thomas Rees may have edited it in 1808.)

In 1819 Longman acquired a one-third share in the *Literary Gazette*, founded in 1817, and five years later Dorothy Wordsworth was irritated when it published two hostile reviews of her brother's *Ecclesiastical Sketches* and *Memorials of a Tour on the Continent*. 'We should not otherwise have given

---

210 Quoted by J.H. Raleigh in 'What Scott meant to the Victorians', *Victorian Studies*, Vol. VII, No.1, Sept. 1963, p.7.

211 M.W. Brightfield, *John Wilson Croker* (1940), p.197. 'When other folks have a bilious attack', Croker went on, 'they sometimes see objects yellow. You, it seems, see them blue and yellow.'

212 Publication was then taken over by Longmans' neighbours in Paternoster Row, Gale, Curtis and Fenner. The *Review* survived deep into the 1860s. Edward Paxton Hood, its last editor from 1861 to 1868, was one of the first people to use the adjective 'Victorian' in *The Age and its Architects* (1851).

it a thought', she explained, had it not been for the Longman 'connection'.[213] Such publishers' 'connections' were common, and Thomas Norton was later to acquire a share in *The Athenaeum*, founded in 1828 and taken over, with Longman support, by Charles Wentworth Dilke in 1830.

Many authors had far less to do with reviewing or with journalism during these years than their publishers, who could be eclectic in their range both of fiction and of non-fiction. It is less surprising than it appears at first glance, therefore, to note that in his pioneering study of the Gothic novel, *The Gothic Quest*, Montague Summers picked out Longman and Rees as 'a well-known house purveying Gothic romances'. He gave as an example 'one of the most famous of all Gothic robber-romances', the three-volume *History of Rinaldo Rinaldini*, translated into English from German by John Hinckley, which appeared in 1800: its author Christian August Vulvius, librarian at Weimar, was the brother-in-law of Goethe. Summers also referred to the Longman/Rees seventh edition of Ann Radcliffe's *Romance of the Forest* (1808), the sixth edition of which had first been published in 1791, her *Mysteries of Udolpho*, first published in 1796, and Francis Lathom's *The Castle of the Tuileries* (1803), a translation from the French.

Another Gothic novel published by Longman and Rees in 1806, *Zofloya; or the Moor: A Romance of the Fifteenth Century*, written by Charlotte Dacre, influenced Byron, while he was still an undergraduate at Cambridge, and Shelley, while he was still a boy at Eton.[214] Shelley's novel *Zastrozzi* (1810), described as a 'romance', was written under its spell. It had itself been strongly influenced both by Matthew G. Lewis's *The Monk* (1796) and by Mary Wollstonecraft's *Vindications of the Rights of Women* (1792) and *The Wrongs of Women*, published posthumously in 1798. It tells the story of the descent of Victoria, the anti-heroine, through all 'the stormy passions of the soul' and of the many transgressions she committed under the impact of Zofloya, the Moor, who at the end of the novel reveals himself as Satan.

Lewis, born in 1775, himself published *Romantic Tales* in four volumes with Longman in 1808. The first of them included *Mistrust*, 'a feudal romance', the second a short poem *The Dying Bride*, and the fourth 'a ballad first related to me by my friend Walter Scott'. Lewis had been encouraged by Thomas Harris, proprietor and manager of Covent Garden

---

213 Letter from Dorothy Wordsworth to Crabb Robinson, 21 April 1822, printed in Hartley, *op. cit.*, Vol. I, p.118. An anonymous reviewer (*Literary Gazette*, 30 March, 6 April 1822) described one of Wordsworth's sonnets as 'particularly absurd' and another as 'maudlin nonsense'. According to the Longman Impression Book (LA Part I/146), 500 copies of *Ecclesiastical Sketches* were printed, but sales, which totalled £55 8s. 4d., failed to cover costs (£50 3s. 3d.) plus advertising (£15). *Memorials of a Tour* was equally unsuccessful: Wordsworth had returned to him sixty-two copies. See Owen, *op. cit.*

214 See M. Summers, *The Gothic Quest* (1938), pp.234–6.

and a Longman relative,[215] to write Gothic plays as well as Gothic tales: *Adelgitha*, frequently revived, was a great success of 1807. Set in 1080, in Otranto, a Gothic name with a history behind it, it had as one of its main characters Lothair, a name to enter Longman history through Disraeli's novel with that title in 1870.[216]

An interesting link with later 'tales of terror' was John William Polidori's *Ernestus Berchtold; or the Modern Œdipus*, published by Longman in 1819. Polidori was employed as Byron's travelling physician in 1816 and was present at the Villa Diodati on the shore of Lake Geneva when at Byron's suggestion the members of the party, which included the Shelleys, each agreed to write a ghost story. The most lasting result was Mary Wollstonecraft Shelley's *Frankenstein* (1818). Polidori's own contribution to terror tales was *The Vampyre* (1819) which was not published by Longman. Nor was *Frankenstein*. *The Vampyre*, which influenced later writing on the subject (and at least one opera) was widely attributed to Byron, who had conceived of a vampire story to set alongside *Frankenstein* in 1816. Polidori's own life ended in horror. He committed suicide in 1821 taking such a large dose of prussic acid that, according to Byron, it would 'have killed fifty Miltiades'.[217]

Mary Wollstonecraft Shelley, a correspondent of the Longmans about her own work and that of her father William Godwin, lived on until 1851, two years before the death of another Longman woman author, Amelia Opie, whom she had met during the 1790s. The well-educated daughter of a Norwich doctor, Amelia married the painter John Opie in 1798. Much praised in her own time, she had published a novel, not her first, *Adeline Mowbray*, in 1804, which pivoted on the relationship between Godwin and Mary

POPULAR NOVELS
PUBLISHED BY
LONGMAN, HURST, REES, ORME, AND BROWN,
Paternoster-row.

THE MYSTERIES OF UDOLPHO. A Romance; interspersed with some Pieces of Poetry. By ANN RADCLIFFE. The 6th Edit. In 4 Vols. 12mo. Price 1l. 4s. Bds.]
A SICILIAN ROMANCE. By ANN RADCLIFFE. The 4th Edition. In 2 Vols. 12mo. Price 8s. Boards.
THE CASTLES OF ATHLIN AND DUNBAYNE. A Highland Story. By ANN RADCLIFFE. The 4th Edition. 12mo. Price 5s. 6d. Boards.
VALENTINE'S EVE. A Novel. By Mrs. OPIE. In 3 Vols. 12mo. Price 1l. 1s. Boards.
VARIETIES OF LIFE; OR, CONDUCT AND CONSEQUENCES. A Novel. By the Author of " Sketches of Character." In 3 Vols. 12mo. Price 18s. Boards.
GUY MANNERING; OR, THE ASTROLOGER. By the Author of " Waverley." 3d Edition. In 3 Vols. 12mo. Price 1l. 1s. Boards.
DISCIPLINE; a Novel. By the Author of " Self-Control." 3d Edit. In 3 Vols. Post 8vo. Price 1l. 4s. Bds.
THE RECLUSE OF NORWAY. By Miss ANNA MARIA PORTER. 2d Edition. In 4 Vols. 12mo. Price 1l. 4s. Boards.
CHRISTABELLE, THE MAID OF ROUEN. A Novel, founded on Facts. By Mrs. HANWAY, Author of " Ellinor," " Andrew Stuart," and " Falconbridge Abbey." In 4 Vols. 12mo. Price 1l. 4s. Boards.
ALICIA DE LACY, a Historical Romance. By the Author of the " Loyalists," &c. &c. In 4 Vols. 12mo. Price 1l. 8s.
DUTY, a Novel. By the late Mrs. ROBERTS, Author of " Rose and Emily." Interspersed with Poetry, and preceded by a Character of the Author. By Mrs. OPIE. In 3 Vols. 12mo. Price 12s. Boards.
WAVERLEY; or, 'TIS SIXTY YEARS SINCE. A Novel. The 3d Edition. With a Preface by the Author. In 3 Vols. 12mo. Price 1l. 1s. Boards.
THE WANDERER; OR, FEMALE DIFFICULTIES. By the Author of " Evelina," " Cecilia," and " Camilla." The 2d Edition. In 5 Vols. 12mo. Price 2l. 2s. Boards.

An advertisement for 'popular novels' published by Longman, Hurst, Rees, Orme and Brown.

Longman Archive

---

215 See above, p.77.

216 See below, p.256. Horace Walpole's *The Castle of Otranto*, generally regarded as the first Gothic novel, appeared in 1764. The story of the genre, which had many twists and turns, has most recently been explored by E.J. Clery in a brilliant monograph *The Rise of Supernatural Fiction, 1762-1800* (1995); in C.A. Howells *Love, Mystery and Misery*, Feeling in Gothic Fiction (1978) and in J. Watt *Contrasting the Gothic: Fiction, Genre and Cultural Conflict* (1999).

217 See R. Woof, *Shelley, an Ineffectual Angel?* (The Wordsworth Trust, 1992), p.32. Polidori was approached by Murray to write an account of his tour with Byron in 1816.

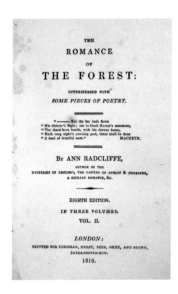

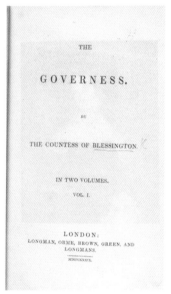

Title page of *The Romance of the Forest; interspersed with some pieces of poetry Vol.II*, by Ann Radcliffe, 1816

Longman Archive

Title page of *The Governess* by The Countess of Blessington, 1839

BL N.1920.

Wollstonecraft, drawing conclusions from it that neither of them would have done.[218] For the most part Amelia Opie avoided 'the public, the picturesque, the Gothic and the comic', concentrating on domestic themes involving the fortunes of women in a male world. Titles like *Single Tales* (1806), *Tales of Real Life* (1813), *Temper or Domestic Scenes: A Tale* (1812) and *Tales of the Heart* (1820) speak for themselves.[219] In 1825 she joined the Society of Friends and thereafter abandoned fiction.[220]

Longman and Rees did not abandon it. Indeed, as tastes in the novel changed, they responded to new tastes. Among their other women authors were Jane Porter (1776–1850), whose *Thaddeus of Warsaw* (1803) gave her a European reputation, and Mary Brunton (1778–1818), born in Orkney, author of *Self-Control* (1812) and *Discipline* (1814), whose books were published in conjunction with a Scottish publisher. (*Self-Control* was to be broadcast as a serial on the BBC Radio *Woman's Hour* in 2003.) In a letter to her Scottish publishers, Manners & Miller in 1811, 'Longman & Co.' described 'the demand for the book' as being 'great'. 'The book is very much admired on the whole, though some complain of the later part of the work. We have not seen Mrs. Barbauld or heard her opinion.'[221] In the same year Mrs Barbauld, a Unitarian, had written a controversial poem *1811* predicting the end of Britain's mercantile supremacy and a return to pastoralism.

A later distinctive and very different woman novelist, Marguerite, Countess of Blessington, born in Tipperary in 1789, was a friend of Byron through her husband, the Earl of Blessington, who died in Paris in 1829. Byron, who visited her salon, wrote one of his last poems for her. Lady Blessington stayed in Paris during the revolution of 1830 before moving to Mayfair in 1831, where, according to the painter Benjamin Robert Haydon, she was a great social success: she attracted 'everybody' (including Crabb Robinson) to her parties.

It was to raise money that Lady Blessington turned to writing, first for annuals and magazines, re-publishing in book form in 1834 an article

218 See M. Butler, *Jane Austen and the War of Ideas* (1975), who claimed (p.121) that the novel 'demonstrates how fully liberals [and Mrs Opie had been one] now came back into the conformist fold'. (Ch. 4 'The Anti-Jacobins'). For a recent Longman author, G. Kelly, Opie's *forte* was domestic heroism (*English Fiction of the Romantic Period, 1789–1830* (1989), pp.84–6).

219 See G. Kelly, 'Amelia Opie, Lady Caroline Lamb, and Maria Edgeworth: Official and Unofficial Ideology', in *Ariel*, Vol.12 (1981).

220 C.L. Brightwell, *Memories of the Life of Amelia Opie* (1854). 'Who now remembers Amelia Opie?' Marilyn Butler asks in her *Peacock Displayed* (1979), p.19. Butler reminds us (p.52) that Thomas Love Peacock had Opie in mind when he called one of his novelists Philomela Poppyseed.

221 Letter of 12 June 1811.

on 'Conversations with Lord Byron' that she had written for the *New Monthly*. A chain of so-called 'silver fork' novels followed, registering yet another change in fashion.[222] The focus was now on the aristocracy and on social behaviour. Some, like *The Governess* (1839), were published by Longman, others by Colburn and Bentley. Lady Blessington had published non-fiction with Longman as early as 1822, *The Magic Lantern or Sketches of Scenes in the Metropolis* was an example. Another was *Gems of Beauty Displayed* (1836). One of Lady Blessington's last journalistic activities was writing for the recently launched *Daily News* in 1846, then edited by Dickens.

~

Better remembered than any of the novelists published by Thomas Norton and his partners was Thomas Bowdler, 'purifier' of Shakespeare – and other books – for 'family reading'. Born in 1754, he studied medicine and travelled widely before producing for Longman and Rees the ten volumes of his *Family Shakespeare*, which appeared in a complete edition in 1818.[223] Bowdler had predecessors to whom he acknowledged his debts, but it was not until 1836, eleven years after his death, that the verb 'to bowdlerise' was coined, one year before Queen Victoria came to the throne. Bowdler's *Shakespeare* omitted all those 'words and expressions ... which cannot with propriety be read aloud in a family': thus, large parts of the opening scenes of *Romeo and Juliet*, *Othello* and *King Lear* totally disappeared.

Within his lifetime Bowdler met with some criticism, particularly from *Blackwood's* and the *British Critic*, but the more that he was criticised the more he insisted that any words which excited an 'impression of obscenity' had no place in literature. Perhaps surprisingly, he had the support of the *Edinburgh Review* which described all other editions of Shakespeare as 'now being obsolete': 'As what cannot be pronounced in decent company cannot well afford much pleasure in the closet [always a dubious proposition], we think it is better, every way, that what cannot be

Title page of *The Belle of a Season A poem* by The Countess of Blessington, 1840

BL 789.e.9

---

222 'A new class of novels has lately sprung up which has attained a very great celebrity [an interesting use of a word with a future]: we allude to those which relate to fashionable life written by persons of rank and fortune.' (*The Star*, 11 May 1826.)

223 The first edition had appeared, anonymously, in 1807, and the first named Bowdler edition in 1809. According to D. Daiches, 'Presenting Shakespeare' in EHP, pp.63–112, Bowdler's sister Harriet appears to have been 'the real, if unacknowledged editor' of the *Family Shakespeare*.

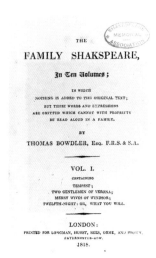

Title page to *Bowdler's Family Shakespeare*, 1818

Longman Archive

spoken, and ought not to have been written, should cease to be printed.'[224] This was 'Victorianism before Victoria'.[225] Yet the Victorian age was well advanced when, with the *Family Shakespeare* selling well and being regularly reprinted, the poet Swinburne claimed that 'no man ever did better service to Shakespeare' than Bowdler.

As Bowdler's sales figures recorded in the Impression Books show, sales were maintained in the 1880s and 1890 with 1885 and 1886, years when the economy was thought to be depressed, peak years for the Bowdler family. Swinburne's opinion was shared by a still later poet, this time a Poet Laureate, Robert Bridges, who introduced the idea of radio into his poetry and during the First World War prepared an anthology of poetry and prose, *The Spirit of Man* (1916), designed, in the poet's words, to bring fortitude and peace of mind to his countrymen in wartime.

~

Thomas Norton and Rees did well financially out of Bowdler, as did their successors in the business, but in the pursuit of knowledge, if not of virtue, they confronted difficulties in assessing profit and loss. Giving evidence to a House of Commons Select Committee of 1818 – not the only time that he appeared as a witness – Rees cited *Dr Rees's Encyclopaedia*, a major financial commitment, which had cost £200,000 in ten to twelve years as one of his main examples. So far it had earned nothing.[226] But as Andrew Spottiswoode told a later Select Committee in 1831 – Rees was also a witness before it – 'Some books pay better than others; it is the general run of books, which form the profit ... The supposed profit on a particular book [difficult to calculate] would not give a view of the real profit in any degree.'[227]

As early as 1802 Rees had informed a Parliamentary Committee that since the most recent increase in the paper duties, the demand for new books had 'much diminished': during the ten months from April 1801 he had put aside 'one-third less paper for printing new Works than he did for the ten months immediately antecedent'.[228] Costing was an aspect of

---

224 ER, Vol. XXXVI (1821), p.54.

225 For the concept, the context and the stress on propriety within the family see M.J. Quinlan, *Victorian Prelude* (1941).

226 Yet in 1820 'Longman & Co' were to give Dr Rees a gratuity of 300 guineas on behalf of the partners when 'a portion of books is now ready for delivery'.

227 *Parliamentary Papers* (1831), *Select Committee on King's Printers' Patents*, Minutes of Evidence, 2 March 1831, p.24.

228 *Ibid.* (1802), *Select Committee on Copyright*. Among others to give evidence to this Select Committee were Richard Phillips, Luke Hansard and William Cobbett. Only Cobbett dissented from the view that 'a repeal or alteration in the duty per weight on printing paper was indispensable to the support or recovery' of the book trade.

publishing on which he always spoke with authority. Sixteen years later, in
two days of cross questioning by the House of Commons Select Committee
on Copyrights, he gave evidence that during the previous twelve months
the House of Longman had spent the very precise figure of £4,638 7s. 8d.
on newspaper advertising, of which £1,500, he hastened to add, had gone
in stamp duties to the government.

At that time Rees was facing hostile questioning about one of the
provisions of a new Copyright Act of 1814 which extended copyright by
fourteen years and laid upon publishers the obligation to supply eleven
copies of every book published to a number of libraries, including the British
Museum and the Universities of Oxford and Cambridge. The subsequent
cost to Longman/Rees had been around £3,000. Rees's questioners several
times referred back in pointed fashion to the evidence that Thomas Norton
III had given to the earlier Parliamentary Committee of 1813 before the Act
came into effect.

What Thomas Norton III had said then – and it was comprehensive
in scope – was that as both a bookseller *and* a publisher he expected a 5
per cent profit on his trade. Moneys were slow to come in, however, and he
allowed 2½ per cent for bad debts. His 'considerable export' to the United
States was already declining before the 1812 war and had subsequently
ceased, and he had 'but a little export' inside Europe (then largely under
the control of Napoleon). Even before Napoleon he had never been 'in the
habit of exporting much to the Continent'.

In 1813 Rees claimed that 'probably no firm dealt more largely in
copyrights' than his. For new books a run of 250 was 'very small', 500 'very
moderate', 750 the average. It was not always easy, even in relation to 'small
editions', to ascertain 'pretty well' before-hand which books would sell. In
the case of small editions the profit was not as large as in that of 'large
editions', but the printing of small editions was 'conducive to the diffusion
of literature': books would reach the public which would never have reached
it if the large edition had been called for. 'Literature' was 'benefited'.

At home, even though the book trade was 'rather depressed' in 1813, as
it was in 1817 and 1831, the sale of books had increased during the previous
ten years, and there was 'a greater variety of publications'. There were
complaints about the high price of books both from 'literary men' and the
public, but publishers' costs had risen, and this meant that despite the overall
increase in the number of books published each year many books which in
earlier years would have been published now had not been.[229] In retrospect,
as at the time, critics associated this reduction with 'monopoly'.[230]

The economics had not changed. Costs were still split up under various

---

229 *Ibid.* (1813). See also *City Press*, Aug. 1813, which reported the replies given to the
    Committee of 1813.

230 See Altick, *op. cit.*, pp.310–12.

headings – 'paper, printing, engraving, printing the engravings, editorship or authorship, advertising'.[231] When a book was projected, it was the cost of the paper required that had to be calculated first and covered [as we have seen], followed by the cost of printing and illustrating. A profit was then added to each of these items. Other costs would be taken into account, including advertising, before a selling price for the books was set, determined largely by 'the quantity expected to be sold'. On average, 'the actual cost' of a book was 'nearly one half of the advertised retail price', and 25 per cent of the retail price usually went to the bookseller:[232] the wholesale price was about 'one half more' than 'the prime cost'. Most books did not 'sell off': only one in ten did. Asked why, Thomas Norton replied that everything depended 'on the character of the book'. Yet the chances were not possible to predict. Some books sold 'after lying some years without a demand'. 'When the French invaded Egypt, books of travel in Egypt sold immediately'.

The sale of Bibles, for which Longmans served as agents to the King's Printers, was a special case since selling prices were regulated by the King's Printers who enjoyed deliberately conferred monopoly rights (Rivingtons served as parallel agents for books produced by the Cambridge University Press), and Rees believed that 'no books were sold cheaper than them'.[233] Other books were less certain of sales, but among those books that did not sell in the shops not one in a hundred was disposed of as waste: nine out of ten were sold at auctions, often held in coffee houses, where the price fetched would always be above waste paper price and 'frequently very near to the full trade price'. Such auctions, still 'quite unknown to the public', were 'confined to the trade' as they had been in the eighteenth century, and prices varied 'very much'.

If the retail price of books were to increase by 5 per cent, Rees went on, there would 'sometimes' be a fall in demand, but it was difficult to generalise about this. Thomas Norton chose to be more discursive. Asked whether some elements in cost were high because of the standards which publishers set in the use of quality paper and the design of 'handsome' formats (what the questioner called 'the publisher's taste'), he replied concisely, if loftily, 'we are always influenced by what we consider the taste of the public'. He welcomed the growth of circulating and subscription libraries: they had 'diffused a taste for reading': 'having read a book, you have a desire to possess it in many cases'.

---

231 Engraving costs, in particular, were higher, probably twice as high as in France. The print trade with Europe had been hit, therefore, even more than the book trade. Books of prints were often in colour and were particularly expensive. Sometimes prints were published separately.

232 In his evidence to the Select Committee on King's Printers' Patents, Thomas Norton gave the figure as 'from 25 to 30 per cent'.

233 Select Committee on King's Printers' Evidence, p.232.

In the evidence that he gave in 1818 Rees stated that he agreed with his partner on this point, emphasising that these books were bought from the publisher and not delivered free as they were to the copyright libraries. He also went on to confirm the existence of many of the customary trade practices that Thomas Norton had set out to describe, for instance, a 26 per cent difference between the price paid by booksellers for a book and its retail price. Rees made a number of points of his own, however, noting, for example, that publishers supplied their authors with a number of copies 'to present to their friends and others, who have granted them the use of books and manuscripts to assist them in bringing forward and completing their works'.

~

The official committees to which Thomas Norton and Rees gave evidence were concerned with the production and distribution of books, not with the vicissitudes of authors. Nor did they deal at any length with bookselling, old and new, which remained of great importance to Longman and Rees, far more than it did to John Murray II. An article in *The Bookseller*, published in 1859, pointed to the fact that during the first decade of the nineteenth century Longman and Rees had 'assumed the first position in the trade, a position they have kept ever since'.[234] As has been noted, the taking in of Hurst and Orme in 1804 had strengthened this side of the business.[235] You could buy first editions of Tasso as well as first editions of Scott.

One favoured 'bibliopolist', Sir Egerton Brydges (1762–1837), a barrister and Member of Parliament for Maidstone from 1812 to 1818, not only bought rare books at Paternoster Row, but gave advice to Longman and Rees on copyright, a subject of great interest to him.[236] He also had books privately printed for him bearing a Longman imprint 'Private Press'. The printer was T. Davison. The works included *Censura Literaria* (1815), 'containing titles, abstracts and opinions of old books' and *Clavis Calendaria or a Compendious Analysis of the Calendar*. Egerton claimed comprehensively that the publication of the *Censura* did far more in promoting 'a taste for old English bibliography than all the other works that were ever published'. Unfortunately however, the number of collectors was 'considerably reduced'.[237]

That was certainly so, but it was the fate of new titles, not of old

---

234 'The House of Longman & Co.', in *The Bookseller*, 25 Aug. 1859, p.1152.

235 See above, p.163.

236 Sir Egerton Brydges, Bart, MP, *Reasons for a Further Amendment of the Act 54 George III, c.156 being an Act to Amend the Copyright Act of Queen Anne*.

237 Note of 2 Dec. 1824 (LA Part II/29/1).

collections, that interested Thomas Norton and his partners most. They never favoured, however, the kind of extension of copyright for authors of new titles which was pressed for by Sergeant (later Sir) Thomas Noon Talfourd (1795–1854), first elected in 1835 as Member of Parliament for Reading, who was an author (and playwright) himself, a friend and biographer of Lamb and an executor of his estate: Moxon was the publisher of his *Final Memorials of Charles Lamb* (1849).

In the *Aldine Magazine*, published in 1839 – the proprietors were Simpkin Marshall & Co., and there were two Longman partners, Orme and Brown – the author of an article on copyright, close to Orme, wrote of the 'fraudulent' and 'disgusting' aspects of Talfourd's second attempt at legislation in 1838:

> 'The establishment of Longman and a few other great publishers [there was another *Aldine Magazine* article on Murray] must feel that it is their bounden duty to protect themselves and others against such a monstrous encroachment and innovation as was meditated upon private property.'[238]

The publishers, whose journal covered 'biography, bibliography, criticism and the arts', had the support of at least one Longman author. Macaulay described copyright as a monopoly and clinched his argument with the words 'there was no copyright at Athens or Rome', and he opposed Talfourd on the floor of the House in 1838.[239] The *Aldine Magazine* claimed the support too of its 'Brethren of the Press, Metropolitan and Provincial'.[240]

Talfourd lost his seat in Parliament in 1841 and was not responsible for the compromise settlement embodied in the Copyright Act of 1842, a settlement which won the support of Macaulay. It lasted just because it was a compromise. Introduced by Lord Mahon, son of Lord Stanhope, hero of the printing press, it increased the basic term of copyright to the author's lifetime plus seven years after his death or forty-two years from publication if forty-two years had not elapsed seven years after the author

---

238 *Aldine Magazine*, Vol. I (1839), Letter S, pp.69–70. The *Magazine* covered improvements in communications on which the distribution of books depended – 'steam carriages and Rail-Roads' and 'the reduction of postage'.

239 *The Complete Works of T.B. Macaulay*, Vol. VIII, pp.198, 213.

240 *Aldine Magazine* (1939), p.i.

died.[241] Talfourd, who had been reluctant to make any compromises in face of largely radical criticism, had argued for a post-mortem term of sixty years, not forty-two, and had won the support of Wordsworth and other authors, but Macaulay rightly described his proposal as 'a tax on readers for the purpose of giving a bounty to writers'.[242]

In their lifetimes authors of new books fared very differently financially after 1842 than they had done before the Act was passed. In the absence of a royalty system, which developed later in the century, they had various choices, not all open to them, in relation to payment for their books. They could sell their copyrights outright in return for a lump-sum payment; they could share profits with the publisher, sometimes on a 50/50 basis, after printing and other costs, including advertising, had been met; or they could publish on a commission basis with the publisher which usually amounted to ten per cent or more.

Outright sale of copyright was the most common arrangement, sometimes on the initiative of the author, sometimes on that of the publisher. 'We beg to offer you One Hundred Pounds for the copy-right of a volume of Poems of 360 pages containing a selection of your best poems', Coleridge had been told in 1811. 'Twenty pounds would be paid on demand, £20 when the manuscript was delivered, and the rest on the day of publication.'[243] In the same year, Coleridge, who did not receive a penny for his translation of *Amatanda*, a fairy tale, talked of 'being betrayed into the unwise adoption of literature as a profession'.[244]

Details of such arrangements were often described in publishers' letters or authors' letters to them, with Lackington commenting that 'many works never sold well whilst the author retained the copyright, which sold

---

241 See for a comprehensive survey for the long period down to 1842, extending his earlier articles, J. Feather, *Publishing, Piracy and Politics: An Historical Study of Copyright in Britain* (1994) and for future as well as past trends W.J. Gordon, *An Inquiry into the Merits of Copyright: The Challenges of Consistency, Consent and Encouragement Theory*, reprinted from the *Stanford Law Review*, Vol. 41, No. 6, July 1989, pp.1343–1469. Gordon begins by quoting a speech by Macaulay in the House of Commons, 5 Feb. 1841. See also A. Ryan, *Property and Political Theory* (1984).

242 Hansard, 3rd series, Vol. 561, cols.341–60.

243 Letter to Coleridge, 2 May 1811 (Longman Ledger, Vol. I, No.67).

244 Note by Crabb Robinson of a conversation with him, described in Morley, *op. cit.*, Vol. I, p.26.

rapidly after the copyright was sold to the trade'.[245] Publishers' records were not fully standardised even after editions of titles began to be called 'standard', an interesting development to set alongside the establishment of three-decker novels, collected editions and serialisation. In the case of Longman and Rees, details of costs were tabulated in their Impression Books, their profit sharing arrangements in their Divide Ledgers, and commission deals in their Commission Ledgers, one of them called the Gentleman's Ledger. There was, however, no systematic registry of sales.

The accounting year ran from midsummer to midsummer. A correspondent was told, 'We account for the Books at what we Term the trade sale price & charge a commission of 10 per cent on the amount of Sales, when we undertake Books, on these terms'.

> We pursue the same plan of publication as we do with Works which are intirely our own property, subscribing them to the Trade [and] keeping them constantly in our Trade Catalogue &c &c. The advertising & carriage of course would be charged to you. The trade sale price of a volume that sells for 12/- in boards is 8/- in quires.[246]

In tracing Wordsworth's development as a poet, W.J.B. Owen made admirable use of surviving Longman records to analyse costs, sales and profits.[247] The paper costs (25 reams) for the first edition of the first volume of the *Lyrical Ballads* (1801), as recorded in the Impression Book, amounted to £31 5s. and of the second volume (31 reams) to £38 15s. The cost per ream in each case was 25s. Hot pressing cost £3 18s. for the first volume and £4 7s. for the second. The printing costs paid to Nathaniel Biggs were £20 13s. for the first volume and £20 6s. for the second. 'Copy to print from and Postages' came to 13s. for the first volume and to £90 10s. for the second (including £80 for Copy). Postage for this volume amounted to 10s. 8d. 'Advertising and labels' for Volume I of the *Lyrical Ballads* was set down as £10 10s.

Another kind of information revealed in the Ledgers reflects indirectly how the fortunes of the trade fluctuated. Thus, in 1811, a 'bad year', business was described as 'so very dull' that it was not possible to offer a place in the House of Longman to the son of the learned Dr Richard Valpy (1754–1836), Headmaster of Reading School, one of their authors,

---

245 *Memoirs* (1791), Letter XXXVI. Lackington shared Coleridge's view that authors who became publishers would not do well: they would not know how to sell. Nor could they expect a bookseller 'to promote the sale of a work in which he is deprived of his usual profits' (Letter XXXV). See also R. Landon, 'Small Profites do Great Things': James Lackington and Eighteenth-Century Bookselling' in *Studies in Eighteenth-Century Culture*, Vol. 5 (1976).

246 Letter to Mr Fitzpatrick, Dublin, 25 March 1811 (Longman Ledger).

247 See above, p.204.

although Longman was 'well disposed to both of them'. Other booksellers were said to be 'to a certain extent similarly situated [as] ourselves'.[248] Talfourd knew the circumstances: he had been one of Dr Valpy's pupils. It was in another 'bad year', 1837, that after long negotiations which had been started in a boom year, 1836, Valpy's copyrights were to be acquired by Longman, as those of Cadell, an older business, were to be acquired eight years later after only a few days of negotiation.[249] That was nine years after Thomas Cadell's death.

The carefully listed Cadell copyrights included Abercrombie's *Gardening and Gardeners' Companion* (half-share); Forsyth's *Fruit Trees* (half-share); Bridge's *Algebra, Equations, Conic Sections and Trigonometry* (whole share); Dawson's *Greek Lexicon* (one thirty-second share); Paley's *Works* (three thirty-second shares); *Walker's Dictionary* (one-third share); and *Debrett's Peerage* (three thirty-second shares). The total cost to Longmans was £8,400, slightly more than the sum (£8,000) paid for Valpy's properties in 1837. These included shares in Greek and Latin works then very much in demand, editions of Sophocles, Demosthenes, Xenophon and Plato.[250]

Longman already held a share in some of the copyrights on the Cadell list, for example, Jeremiah Joyce's *A System of Practical Arithmetic*, originally published by Richard Phillips in 1808.[251] Joyce, a Unitarian, who had been employed by Stanhope as a tutor to his son Lord Mahon, wrote books under different names with different publishers. He was as active an author with Phillips as he had been earlier with Joseph Johnson and as he was to be later with Longman and Rees. Indeed, his connection with Longman and Rees went back to major work which he carried out on fellow-Unitarian Abraham Rees's *Cyclopaedia*.[252] One of his most successful publications, transferred

---

248 Letter to Dr Valpy, 4 May 1811 (LA).

249 See T. Besterman (ed.), *The Publishing Firm of Cadell and Davies: Select Correspondence and Documents, 1793-1836* (1938), pp.viii–ix, and 'The End of the Firm of Cadell', in the *TLS*, 27 April 1951.

250 See 'Remarks by Thomas Turner on A.J. Valpy's Copyrights', Oct. 1837 (LA Part II 25/37); 'Messrs Longman & Co.'s bought of the executors of the late Thos deceased', 2 June 1845; Note by W. Elliott Oliver, 26 April 1845.

251 The full title was *A System of Practical Arithmetic Applicable to the Present State of Trade and Money Transactions, Illustrated by Numerous Examples Under Each Rule for the Use of Schools*. The book was accompanied by *A Key to Joyce's Arithmetic Containing Solutions and Answers*. The two books could be used in schools or at home.

252 From 1791 to 1816 Joyce was Secretary of the Unitarian Society. Tried for treason and found guilty in the notorious trials of 1794, he was quickly released from prison and kept a low political profile after 1794, concentrating on educational writing.

to Longman from Phillips, was *An Easy Grammar of General Geography* (1st edition, 1803). This was published under the name J. Goldsmith.[253]

Phillips had mixed memories of Longman/Rees, as most of his acquaintances had of him. He had an acrimonious dispute with them in 1809, when he declared himself bankrupt, and in 1813 he complained that he had been kept waiting in Thomas Norton's office for two hours until 'Longman was at leisure for an interview'. 'I think the conduct of Mr. Longman and Mr. Rees very ungracious, to say the least', he added, 'and I feel that it will only be possible to treat with them at arm's length'.[254] He tried to do so, disposing in stages of his bundle of shares, which included many educational books. They were usually valued formally by outsiders, including Charles Rivington.[255]

As Longman and Rees acquired most of Phillips's educational books, ranging from spelling books to catechisms on chemistry and political economy, life proved easier for Phillips. He prided himself on the fact that his 'interrogative system of education' had given 'new impulses to the intelligence of society', a description which never appealed to Thomas Norton. The word 'conversation' was often heard, however, in Paternoster Row. It was used, for example, by the highly successful Longman's author of 'conversations' on subjects as different as chemistry and political economy. Mrs. (Jane) Marcet (1769–1858), wife of a physician and lecturer in chemistry at Guy's Hospital, who was praised by Macaulay for her *Conversations on Political Economy* (1816), was able to appeal confidently to young readers. Her *Conversations on Chemistry* (1806) were to go through sixteen editions in forty-six years. Elizabeth Helme, the author of *The History of England* 'related in Familiar Conversations by a Father to his Children interspersed with moral and instructive Remarks', 1804, described her book as 'designed for the Perusal of Youth'.[256]

~

Not every subject lent itself to 'conversations' or to 'catechisms', and Longman and Rees consistently put their trust in encyclopaedias, contributors to which were protected specifically by the Copyright Act

---

253 Joyce also published under the same name *Geography under a Popular Plan* and under the name of the Revd D. Blair *An Easy Grammar of Natural and Experimental Philosophy for the Use of Schools.*

254 Letter written to Cadell and Davies from Paternoster Row and quoted in E. Marston, 'Publishers and Publishing a Hundred Years ago', in PC, 6 Jan. 1906, p.16.

255 There are two volumes of Phillips's Purchase Ledgers in the surviving Longman Archives, Part I 54, 55.

256 'Established School Books printed for Longman, Hurst, Rees, Orme and Brown', July 1813. The first item on the list (LA Part II/60/19) was Lindley Murray's *First Book for Children*, 6th edn., 'price 6d.'

of 1842. For publishers, they were costly as well as ambitious ventures, but committed editors and knowledgeable contributors could make them succeed. The encyclopaedic drive was as strong in the early nineteenth century as it had been fifty years before, although Coleridge, who considered encyclopaedias not as collections of separate articles, but as vehicles for enabling readers to think methodically, 'present[ing] the circle of knowledge in its harmony', believed that by the time of his death 'a strange abuse' was being made of the word (en)cyclopaedia itself'. (He invented the word 'sikky paddy' to cover it.) An *Encyclopaedia Metropolitana* (1817–1845) was planned along the lines he deemed necessary, although he withdrew from the enterprise in 1819, leaving only his *Treatise on Method* (1817) as testimony to his purpose.[257]

Abraham Rees's commercially competitive *Cyclopaedia*, which competed with the *Encyclopaedia Britannica*, ran to forty-five quarto volumes and was completed with the help of 'a phalanx of contributors in art, literature and science' over a period of seven years. It cost £300,000. They included far better known names than the contributors to the earlier Chambers's *Cyclopaedia*, among them Davy, Brougham, John Flaxman and Sharon Turner. One of the lasting features of the *Cyclopaedia* was its biographies, still useful to historians in the twenty-first century. Yet the entries on science, a field of study which was never neglected by Longman or either of his two Rees associates, were stronger than those on history and literature.

When congratulated by a friend on his achievement, Abraham, 'the other Rees', himself a committed Unitarian, having received his gratuity, put science on one side and expressed thanks that after working on it for so long he had 'been spared to publish … four volumes of sermons'. His own funeral sermon was preached by Owen Rees's brother Thomas, close to his brother and to Thomas Norton, but a further promised memoir of Abraham Rees never appeared. Because of its Unitarian connections, the *Cyclopaedia* had been attacked in the *Anti-Jacobin Review* as a 'new vehicle of infidelity'.[258]

The *Cyclopaedia*, to which the committed Unitarian Jeremiah Joyce was one of the contributors, came out in parts or half volumes at regular intervals, and in order to speed their work the contributors met regularly not only in day-time in the Longman office but at soirées described by Britton as 'novelties in England' and, he believed, in Europe.[259] Britton added that 'in such company' as he met at the soirées he not only felt 'elated and proud', but 'substantially benefited, both mentally and morally'.

257 See R.L. Collinson, *Encyclopaedias, Their History Throughout the Ages* (2nd edn., 1966), which includes a reprint of the *Treatise*. For the role of the encyclopaedia as Coleridge saw it, see also R. Holmes, *Coleridge, Darker Reflections*, esp., pp.461–2. Coleridge's project was abandoned in 1819.

258 *Anti-Jacobin Review*, June 1812, p.182.

259 Britton, *op. cit.*, pp.51–2.

Almost as important as the text of the *Cyclopaedia* were the illustrations: T. Phillips, who wrote articles on painting, provided some of them, but so too did Landseer and Opie.

There had been even more of a radical air to another venture, *The British Encyclopaedia or Dictionary of Arts and Sciences* (1809), published by a consortium which included the names of Johnson and Phillips as well as Thomas Norton and Rees, who held 40 per cent of the shares. The name of William Nicholson (1753–1815) appeared on the title page, and the work was completed in eighteen months, but it was Joyce, who had worked unbelievably long hours, who played the leading editorial part. Arranged alphabetically, the *British Encyclopaedia* was in direct competition with George Gregory's *Dictionary of Arts and Sciences*, launched by Phillips as sole publisher in 1805 in two large and heavily illustrated volumes.

Nevertheless, things were not what they seemed to be. Joyce seems to have played the leading part in both ventures. Gregory, an Anglican, Prebendary of St Paul's and Chaplain to the Bishop of Llandaff, acknowledged in his Preface that Joyce had been an assistant. Not surprisingly then, a large part of the text of the *Dictionary* to which Gregory's name was attached, was duplicated in Nicholson. Joyce depended on his friends, including Shepherd,[260] to produce each issue of Nicholson's *Encyclopaedia*, which appeared in complete form in 1809.

An even more famous encyclopaedia, although of a completely different kind, published solely by Longman and Rees, *The Cabinet Cyclopaedia* (1829–1846), ran to 133 octavo volumes, each with its own author and its own title. The volumes were priced at six shillings, the price printed on the spine, a triumph of publishing. Its named editor was Dionysius Lardner (1793–1859), son of an Irish solicitor, who had chosen what was to be exactly the right first name for him. In 1827 he was appointed first Professor of Natural Philosophy and Astronomy at the new University College in Gower Street, 'the godless institution' already mentioned in this chapter, an alternative institution to collegiate Oxford and Cambridge, sponsored by many of the people involved in the *Edinburgh Review*, notably Brougham, whose *Practical Observations upon the Education of the People, Addressed to the Working Classes and their Employers* had been published anonymously by Longman in 1825.[261]

Almost as renowned a lecturer as Brougham was, Lardner, a friend of the actor William Charles Macready (1792–1873), was a populariser who could describe equally well Watt's steam engine and Babbage's calculating machine. He believed consistently in the possibility of explaining in such a way that listeners or readers could understand. Above all, he had no hesitation in approaching knowledgeable people to write for his

---

260 See above, p.223.

261 See H. Hale Bellot, *University College, London, 1826–1926* (1928)

Encyclopaedia, including authors with an established reputation, such as Southey, Wordsworth, Scott, Macaulay and the scientist Sir John Herschel (1792–1871), son of a distinguished astronomer. Herschel, just the right person for Lardner to have approached, believed as strongly as Lardner did in communicating scientific knowledge to a multitude of readers. He also believed in the power of books to inspire or console just as much as to inform. 'Nothing unites people like companionship in intellectual enjoyment'.[262]

There is no definitive account of Lardner's own relationship with his publishers. Southey, who hated attacks on himself, attacked him strongly not only as 'Tyrant and Pedagogue' but as 'Cabinet Maker to Messrs Longman',[263] but it is clear not only that 'Messrs Longman' found Lardner an effective editor but that they shared his belief in the importance of wide access to scientific communication. The title pages of his volumes were differentiated from each other, with some of them focusing on the subject of the volume and others on the whole series and its editor. Often there was a title page with an engraved portrait. Sometimes Lardner's name was left out completely.

The last years of Lardner's life were uneasy and unhappy because of marital scandals which took him to court, even to Parliament, but some of his works and those he sponsored are still read long after his name has been forgotten.[264] His vision, too, was shared in an age before the argument

View of Paternoster Row, 1854 by Thomas Hosmer Shepherd (1793–1864)

BL (The Crace Collection)

262 Quoted in Altick, *op. cit.*, p.96.

263 R. Austin, 'Letters of Thomas Dudley Fosbroke' *Transactions of the Bristol and Gloucestershire Archaeological Society*, Vol. 37 (1914), p.172.

264 See J.N. Hays, 'The Rise and Fall of Dionysius Lardner', in *Annals of Science*, Vol. 38 (1981), pp.527–42.

between 'two cultures', arts and science, had opened up, with Lardner, like many of his contemporaries, taking pride in the fact that science, 'no longer a lifeless abstraction floating above the heads of the multitude', had 'descended to earth' and 'mingled with men'. 'It enters our workshops. It speaks along the iron courses of the rail.'[265] It was closely associated with technology, therefore, a word little used in the age of steam. At last technology was influencing publishing production. Another writer on factory production, Andrew Ure (1778–1857), singled out for satire by Karl Marx as 'the Pindar of the automatic factory', was to be published by the House of Longman. His multi-volume *Dictionary of Arts, Manufactures and Mines* appeared in 1853.[266]

Lardner himself liked to see machines at work with or without steam, and one of the workshops that he visited in the company of Charles Babbage (1791–1871) was the London printing works of William Clowes (1779–1847), where new printing technology was being applied. The House of Longman was to remain associated with the firm of Clowes throughout the whole period covered in this *History,* but during the 1830s it was the novelty of the Clowes establishment, not its likely longevity, that captured the imagination of contemporaries. Its 'great steam presses, the type and stereotype foundry, the paper warehouse and the apartments for compositors, readers &c' fascinated all visitors.

They were encouraged to pay attention to the workers as well as the machines. The compositors, wearing 'easy slippers', remained standing to carry out their work: 'young aspiring devils' (a printing term) rushed around sweeping the frames. Yet 'steadiness, coolness and attention' were deemed more valuable attributes than 'eagerness and haste'. 'All bear in their countenances the appearance of men of considerable intelligence and education.' Almost the only sedentary occupation inside the Clowes factory was that of 'the reader': 'indeed, the galley-slave can scarcely be more closely bound to his oar than is a reader to his stool, a man competent

---

265 M. A. Garvey, *The Silent Revolution: Or the Future Effects of Steam and Electricity Upon the Condition of Mankind* (1852), p.3. See also J. Topham, 'Scientific Publishing and the Reading of Science in Early Nineteenth-Century Britain: An Historical Survey and Guide to the Sources', in *Studies in the History and Philosophy of Science*, Vol. 31 (2000).

266 K. Marx, *Capital*, Vol. I (European Edn., 1930), p.447. Marx cited on several occasions Ure's *The Philosophy of Manufactures* (1835). Longman and Rees published a number of books on industrial technology, some of them with surprisingly detailed titles like J. Farey, *Machinery: Metal Plating Processes* (1818).

to correct not only the press, but the author.'[267] (Oliver Goldsmith had once been employed in the task.)

Babbage, a founder of the Statistical Society of London in 1834, in his fascinating book *On the Economy of Machinery and Manufactures*, published by Knight in 1832, also at a price of six shillings, invited his readers to inspect the book they were holding and went on to offer them a breakdown of publishing costs – paper, printing, binding, author's and publisher's share of the receipts. How many responded can never be known They did respond, however, to the cheap publications of Robert Chambers (1802–1871), beginning with Chambers's *Edinburgh Journal* (1832), which he published along with his brother William, and the 'People's Editions' of books, costing 1s 6d, such as Smith's *Wealth of Nations* and Hume's *History of England*, which began to appear in 1835. They responded too to the (sensational) book that Robert wrote anonymously, *Vestiges of the Natural History of Creation* (1844), published by John Churchill in London. The history of this book reveals as much about the changing history of the book trade as about the history of science.[268]

Bound in red cloth, *Vestiges* was a small book, as were the volumes of the *Cabinet Encyclopaedia*, a point of selling (and producing) importance that had been seized upon earlier by Dibdin in his *Bibliophobia* (1832). Quartos and folios were now in the doldrums, but 'a whole array of Lilliputians, headed by Dr Lardner, was making glorious progress in a Republic of Literature'.[269] The place of science in that republic was to become a source of controversy during the mid-Victorian years, one of the themes of the next chapter of this *History*, as we move from Lilliputians to Leviathans. Of course the size of books was not the only factor that counted. Dibdin had misled when he claimed that 'the dwarf had vanquished the giant.'[270]

---

267 QR, Vol. 165, Dec. 1839, pp.1–30. The author, reviewing Knight's *The Printer* and an article in the *Penny Magazine*, No. 369, 'Printing in the Fifteenth and the Nineteenth Centuries', was addressing 'our literary congregation'. An interesting monthly publication launched by Knight in 1834 was *The Printing Machine: A Review for the Many*. As part of its heading, it showed the steam printing press on which the *Review* had been printed.

268 See J. Secord, *Victorian Sensation, The Extraordinary Publication, Reception and Secret Authorship of Vestiges of the Natural History of Creation* (2000). *Vestiges*, which was to appear in many editions, had a sensational impact. Its author, who compared his anonymity with that of Scott when he wrote *Waverley*, was explicitly influenced by Scott; and Tennyson in turn was influenced by *Vestiges* (Secord, *op. cit.*, pp.9–10).

269 T. Dibdin, *Bibliophobia* (1832), p.18. See also M. Peckham, 'Dr Lardner's "Cabinet Cyclopaedia"' (PBSA, Vol. 45 (1954), pp.37–58.)

270 Dibdin, *op. cit.*, p.3. By one of many coincidences the flagship that escorted the convoy on which Coleridge travelled to the Mediterranean in 1804 was called HMS *Leviathan*.

FIG. 203.—Bones of the Left Hand. Palmar Surface.

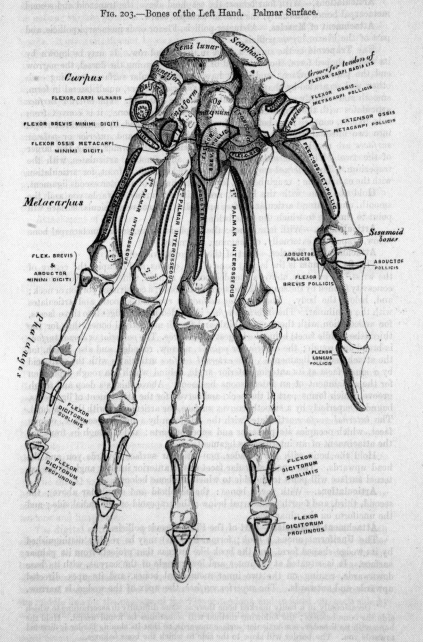

5   *Leviathan, 1842–1879*

Writing briefly and selectively about Longman history in 1949 on the occasion of the 225th anniversary of the founding of the House, Cyprian Blagden felt that he had to end his story with the death of Thomas Norton III in 1842. 'Those who have controlled the business during the last 107 years', he claimed, 'have provided no *new* answers; the interesting thing is that, in themselves, and in their policies, they have provided the old answers over again under new conditions and with changing problems.'[1]

For all his knowledge of publishing in the seventeenth and eighteenth centuries, Blagden's perspective was too short. There were such significant changes in publishing as a whole between 1842 and 1901 – and in perceptions of it – of both books and newspapers – that Longmans could not be left untouched. Nor was that the end of the story. In the twentieth century, many new and quite different answers were to be given within the House of Longman in the years after Blagden had written his brief and, in most respects, perceptive historical account. There was a bigger gulf between Blagden and Rix, however, than there was between Blagden and the two leading Longmans of the mid-Victorian years, Thomas Norton IV (1804–1879) and William (1813–1877), both sons of Thomas Norton III.

When they took over, the two men were blessed by Sydney Smith, who on becoming a Residentiary Canon of St. Paul's in 1831, lived only a few yards away from Paternoster Row in a Canon's residence in Amen Court. Almost the first letter they received after their father's death contained good advice:[2]

> You and your brother are arrived at years of maturity and are quite capable of conducting your own business ... I expect you to live together upon the strictest terms of friendship and to be ready to make mutual concessions; a good deal of your future prosperity will depend upon this.[3]

Thomas Norton was then almost forty years old and William just over thirty. Smith, representing an older generation than either, for once

A page from *Gray's Anatomy* by Henry Gray (1825–1861). The first edition was published by John W. Parker in 1858

Longman Archive

---

1   C. Blagden, *Fire More than Water* (1949), p.29.

2   Smith had expected a bishopric after the Whigs returned to power in 1830. Indeed, Grey, for a long time a friend, is reported to have said 'Now I shall be able to do something for Sydney Smith'.

3   S.J. Reid, *A Sketch of the Life and Times of Sydney Smith* (1884).

William Longman (1813–77)
with his favourite greyhound

Mrs William Longman
(née Emma Pratt-Barlow)
(1818–1848) with her son,
Frederick William Longman,
(1846–1908), by Anthony
Salomé, c.1848

Pearson Education

was not trying to be witty. He lived on, increasingly unwell, increasingly conservative, until 1845: his own eldest son, Douglas, had died in 1829. 'The fact is it is time for me to die', he told the poet Tom Moore, still a favourite Longman author, in 1843.[4]

As before, a rule of seniority prevailed among the Longman partners, as it was to do long into the twentieth century.[5] It was William, however, who was the more able and determined of the two men, and it was he also who usually represented the House in the high politics of the world of publishing. Five years before his father's death he had been one of the founders of the invaluable publication, *The Publishers' Circular*, which provided a weekly list of new books and was soon, while acquiring a rival, to become a publishers' standby. In 1855 he started *Notes on Books*, a House

---

4   Quoted in P. Virgin, *Sydney Smith* (1994), p.284. 'Can you ask of the Dead Oak to put forth of its leaves?' he had asked a friend two years earlier. 'Or the breathless Lion to roar?' Nonetheless, the last chapter of Hesketh Pearson's *The Smith of Smiths* is called 'Growing old Merrily'.

5   The first DNB printed William's biography before that of Thomas IV in an article which began with Thomas Longman I. It barely referred to William's publishing activities except to the fact that he prepared anonymously *A Catalogue of Works in all Departments of English Literature*. The new ODNB (2003) includes an entry on seven generations of Longmans.

The Meet at Farnborough: Thomas Longman IV and his family, 1855

Painting by Abraham Cooper RA (1787–1868), a well-known artist whose subjects often included horses

journal which recorded every Longman publication after 1855.[6] In 1852 he proved an effective Chairman of the Booksellers' Association when the controversial issue of 'free trade in books' came to a head.

William and Thomas Norton IV were rich men – through marriage as well as through inheritance. In 1843 William married Emma, the daughter of Frederick Pratt-Barlow, who had made a fortune out of railways – and wine. Five years earlier, Thomas had married Georgiana Bates, the daughter of Henry Bates, a major in the Royal Artillery. William and Emma moved out to Chorleywood after living at first in Hyde Park Square, and later to Ashlyns, Great Berkhamsted. Thomas and Georgiana moved out in the opposite direction from Sussex Gardens to an imposing new mansion, which replaced that of an older house, Windmill Hill. It was built to order for them at Farnborough Hill. Its architect, Henry Edward Kendall, had carried out substantial alterations to Alexander Pope's villa at Twickenham and to Knebworth, the seat of Bulwer Lytton.

Famous for its rhododendrons, Farnborough Hill, to which they moved in 1863, was far more than a private home. Described a century later as 'a gabled monument to Victorian opulence', it was an impressive edifice, its external frieze adorned with palms, ships and swans, a feature that delighted its next occupant after Thomas Norton, the exiled Empress of France, Eugénie, who bought the property through a solicitor in 1881 and lived there (and elsewhere) until 1920. She kept Thomas Norton's bailiff of the Home Farm, Douglas McLaurie, who died in 1888, enlarged the house and added an abbey with a mausoleum where her husband's and son's bodies were buried.[7]

In Thomas Norton IV's time there were no religious associations, but there was an active social life. The clergyman novelist – and Professor of History at Cambridge from 1860 to 1869 – Charles Kingsley (1819–1875), who lived not far away, was never a Longman author, but he visited Farnborough Hill regularly, as did Henry Reeve (1813–1895), who was known to Thomas Norton as Foreign Editor of *The Times* and editor of the *Greville Memoirs* as well as Editor for forty years of the *Edinburgh Review*. The historian J.A. Froude (1818–1894), married to Kingsley's sister-in-law, was another near-neighbour, prominent on the visiting list. Kingsley (a Macmillan author) was to drive John Henry Newman (1801–1890) to write his *Apologia pro Vita Sua* (1864), a Longman book.[8] Reeve was to disturb Queen Victoria with his *Greville Memoirs* which appeared in 1865.

Thomas Longman and Georgiana themselves lived on a lavish scale. A family painting shows them at a meeting of a hunt: Thomas and all the gentlemen in the picture are top-hatted. A pack of harriers was kept, and they organised fishing expeditions. At Christmas they staged a mumming play in the front hall. One of the huntsmen in the picture was a third Longman brother, Charles, who was involved in the management of the Dickinson paper business and who lived in equal style at a house built for his family on the Shendish estate at Apsley in Hertfordshire, near the Nash Mills which were owned by the Dickinsons. There was also a new Dickinson link with the Longmans through William's wife, Emma: her brother, Frederick William Pratt-Barlow, married John Dickinson's daughter, and both he and his two sons were Partners in the Dickinson business. Once again dynasties had converged. At McLaurie's funeral at Farnborough Thomas Norton IV and George Longman were present as were two Miss Longmans. The Empress sent a wreath. The whole way from McLaurie's house to St Peter's Church blinds were drawn.

~

The greatest prestige of the Longman dynasty derived, as that of their parents had done, from their literary connections, and during the mid-Victorian years, which are covered in this chapter, when 'Literature in its various branches' was not only being written and read but toasted confidently and eloquently at Lord Mayors' Banquets. The publishing world in which the

Portrait of Charles Longman (1809–73), c 1858, painted by Sir Frances Grant FRA. Charles Longman was apprenticed to John Dickinson in 1823, at fourteen, shortly after the death of his uncle, George Longman. He subsequently moved to Nash House in Hertfordshire which became part of Dickinson's offices and then bought the Shendish Estate at Apsley, where he built the house which was to stay in the family until 1930

Pearson Education

7   See H. Kurtz, *The Empress Eugénie* (1964), p.354 and D. Duff, *Eugénie and Napoleon III* (1978), pp.265ff.

8   See below, p.274.

Longmans moved was seldom static, but it was dominated throughout by a small group of publishing 'leviathans', named after the giant mythical creatures. Other newer Houses, like Smith, Elder & Company, played a more innovatory role in literary history, as had Richard Bentley (1794–1871), than the House of Longman, but the word 'House' was applied less often to them than it was to the older House. Moreover, the House of Longman survived both Smith, Elder and Bentley. What remained of the Bentley list was acquired by a new mid-Victorian publisher, the House of Macmillan, in 1898, thought of as a House from the start, and the final Smith, Elder list was taken over by the well-established House of Murray in 1917. Both were very much family concerns.

Bentley's independent business had been launched in 1832 when his partnership with Colburn broke down.[9] He had been born in Paternoster Row, and in 1837 had launched *Bentley's Miscellany* with Dickens as first editor.[10] Smith, Elder & Company, founded in 1816, had been galvanized under the individualistic leadership of George Murray Smith, second son of its co-founder, who published Charlotte Brontë, W.M. Thackeray, John Ruskin and Mrs. Gaskell.[11] The first George Smith, born in Scotland in Morayshire, in 1789, had worked for both Rivington, the oldest House of all, and for Murray before joining up with Alexander Elder, another Scot. Three years after taking over, George Murray Smith discovered that a third partner in the firm, Patrick Stewart, banker as well as publisher, had embezzled £30,000 from the business, a far more serious crime than any committed by Hurst. Smith pulled the business round, but gave it a new sense of direction.

In 1859, a remarkable year for Smith, he launched the *Cornhill* magazine. It appeared in December in order to catch the Christmas trade, of increasing importance in the seasonal round of all publishing, although it was dated January 1860. Smith had long-term objectives in mind, however, believing that 'the existing magazines were few, and when not high-priced' were 'narrow in literary range'; and even before the launching of the *Cornhill* he devoted all his impressive powers to making it a financial as well as a literary success.[12]

The year 1859 had been a remarkable year also for John Murray III

---

9   See above, p.146.

10 R.A. Gettman, *A Victorian Publisher, A Study of the Bentley Papers* (1960), p.153.

11 See J. Glynn, *Prince of Publishers: A Biography of the Great Victorian Publisher, George Smith* (1986).

12 A. Sullivan, *British Literary Magazines, the Victorian and Edwardian Age, 1837–1913* (1984); S.L. Eddy, *The Founding of the Cornhill Magazine* (1970); and P. Smith, 'The Cornhill Magazine, Number 1', in the *Review of English Literature*, Vol. 4 (1963), pp.23–4.

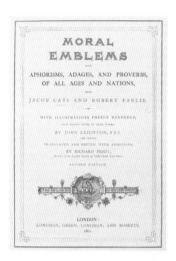

*Moral Emblems, with aphorisms,
adages, and proverbs, of all ages
and nations, from Jacob Cats and
Robert Farlie. With illustrations
... from designs found in their
works, by John Leighton, F.S.A.
The whole translated and edited,
with additions, by Richard Pigot,
The first edition was published
in 1859 and the second in 1862*

The title page shows the 1726
Longman Ship with the moral
  'A good book is a true friend
  A wise author a public
    benefactor'

BL 1347.i.21

(1808–1892), who had succeeded his father in 1843 and who published on
the same day, 24 November, *The Origin of Species* by Charles Darwin and
Self-Help by Samuel Smiles. A distinguished twentieth-century historian
of literature and of Darwin's place in it, Gillian Beer, noted an element
of irony in the conjunction. Darwin, she pointed out, had no 'developed
vocabulary of self help'.[13] She might have added, however, that Smiles, on
whom she did not focus, had 'no developed vocabulary' of 'evolution' or
'development'. Nor did she note in this context that it was to Smiles, a
lucrative Murray author, that a later Murray turned when he wanted to have
published a two-volume life of his father. Darwin is recorded as reading
Self-Help in 1860.[14]

By a further ironical twist of fortune C.J. Longman wrote to Murray
in 1896 offering to sell *Self-Help* in India if Murray would supply copy 'in
quires at a very low price': 'the sale we are looking to is mainly among
the native population who are exceedingly poor and cannot pay much
for books'.[15] Murray agreed, but problems arose later when, despite the
arrangements, Murray tried to sell copies direct on its own account.
During the eighteenth century Murray II had been more active in India
than Longman, and in the early-nineteenth century it had been Murray
who had tried to follow a low-pricing policy.

Thomas Norton IV and his younger brother William, who were in
charge of the affairs of the House of Longman after 1842, were in regular
contact with Murray and they were never disturbed by the manifold
signs of Smith's enterprise even when in 1865 he added to his periodical
publications the *Pall Mall Gazette*, an evening newspaper with eight folio
pages, priced at twopence. Indeed, Thomas Norton, who knew of the
vicissitudes of the *Cornhill*, did no more than ask Smith 'sympathetically'
whether the *Gazette* had ever sold more than 500 copies.[16] The House of
Longman took its time. It waited for sixteen years before launching its own
magazine, having acquired *Fraser's Magazine*, then past its peak, as part of
the Parker take-over.[17]

C.J. Longman, son of William, edited *Fraser's* for a time, in succession
to Froude, and when he went on to edit the new *Longmans Magazine* in 1882
he did not conceive of it as a rival or even as a successor to the *Cornhill*.[18]

The interesting prospectus of his new magazine was adapted to the

13   G. Beer, *Darwin's Plots* (1983), p.23.

14   S. Smiles, *A Publisher and His Friends* (1891).

15   Letter of C.J. Longman to John Murray, 3 March 1896. (LA)

16   Quoted in J.W. Robertson Scott, *The Story of the Pall Mall Gazette* (1950), p.140.

17   For the earlier history of *Fraser's* see above, p.183. For the Parker take-over see
     below, p.269.

18   H. Paul, *The Life of Froude* (1905), editor of *Fraser's* before C. J. Longman, p.140.

needs of the time, and was priced at sixpence, half the price of the first *Cornhill*. It included serial instalments of Margaret Oliphant's novel *The Lady's Walk* and of James Payn's novel *Thicker than Water*, an article on 'The Photographic Eyes of Science', and 'A Chat about Cricket'.[19] Payn (1830–1898) had succeeded his college friend Leslie Stephen as editor of the *Cornhill* in 1883: Mrs. Oliphant (1828–1897) went on to write the history of the House of Blackwood.

The first editor of the *Cornhill*, W.M. Thackeray (1811–1863), who had published his novel *The Virginians* in 1859, had not been Smith's first choice: Smith preferred Thomas Hughes, author of *Tom Brown's Schooldays* (1858). Nevertheless, determined as he was 'to make the new magazine the best periodical yet known to English literature', he was fully aware that 'a shilling magazine which contained, in addition to other first-class matter, a serial novel by Thackeray must command a large sale'.[20] And when Thackeray as editor decided instead to launch a serialized novel by Anthony Trollope, *Framley Parsonage*, Smith had his own views about what

Mrs Thomas Longman, wife of Thomas Longman IV (1815–1890), watercolour by George Richmond c.1845

Mrs William Longman, wife of William Longman (1818–1884), by Anthony Salomé c.1852

Pearson Education

---

19   For Payn see his *Some Literary Recollections* (1884), *Gleams of Memory* (1894) and *The Backwater of Life* (posthumous, 1899). He had contributed regularly to *Household Words* and *Chambers Journal*, and had been one of Smith, Elder's readers.

20   See G.N. Ray, *Thackeray, The Age of Wisdom, 1847–1863* (1958).

kind of novel it should be. It should deal with the Church which Smith regarded as Trollope's own 'peculiar subject'.[21]

Trollope had hoped to send an Irish novel that he was already writing to the *Cornhill*; instead, however, he changed his mind, when he learned of the financial terms that Smith would offer him for *Framley Parsonage*, £1,000, double the sum which Trollope had himself suggested for the Irish novel. This impressed him. He had not been impressed with the qualities of the House of Longman when he overheard one of its members complain that a different novelist 'had spawned upon them three novels a year'. The language, he thought, was more appropriate to the herring than to the Muses.[22]

~

What makes Trollope's comments on writing and publishing particularly interesting then and, indeed, both earlier and later, is that they deal over the years with both the literary and economic relations of authors and publishers. Moreover, in the case of *The Warden, Barchester Towers* and *The Three Clerks*, they deal also with the role of publishers' readers, paid by publishers to comment on a text submitted by an author for publication. In this *History* Trollope's comments are of special significance since Longmans were the first publishers whom he approached in 1855 through the Longman author and ancient historian Charles Merivale.

With a text in front of him, that of *The Warden*, first called *The Precentor*, William Longman turned at once to Joseph Cauvin, a minor author and translator, as a professional reader. Sensibly Cauvin persuaded William to read the novel himself: 'the characters are well drawn and happily distinguished; and the whole story [is] pervaded by a vein of quiet humour and (good natured) satire which will make the work acceptable to all Low Churchmen and dissenters'.[23]

William must have approved of what he read, and the novel was published on a half-profit basis in 1855. In fact, sales proved disappointing, and Trollope, who was offered no advance, received only £9 8s. 8d. in the

Anthony Trollope (1815–82) by Samuel Lawrence c. 1864

The National Portrait Gallery, London no. 1680

In his *Autobiography* Trollope wrote: 'The novel-reading world did not go mad about *The Warden* but I soon felt that it had not failed ... Mr Longman was complimentary and after a while informed me that there would be profits to divide. At the end of 1855 I received a cheque for £9 8s. 8d, which was the first money I had ever earned by literary work; ...'

---

21 *Ibid.*, p.142.

22 A. Trollope, *An Autobiography* (1950 edn., ed. F. Page), p.110. In 1879 Trollope was to write a book on Thackeray for the Macmillan *English Men of Letters* series. Alexander and Daniel Macmillan had launched their own magazine in 1859. There were other interesting connections. Smiles began his autobiography, published after his death, after reading Trollope's.

23 Cauvin to William Longman, 13 Oct. 1854, printed in N.J. Hall (ed.), *The Letters of Anthony Trollope*, Vol. I (1983), pp.38–9. Joseph Cauvin (d. 1875), a member of the Corporation of the Royal Literary Fund from 1852, held a doctorate from the University of Göttingen. He had been the assistant editor of W.T. Brandes, *Dictionary of Science, Literature and Art* (1842).

first year after publication and £10 15s. 0d. in the second.[24] The sequel that he wrote, *Barchester Towers*, which he had contemplated from the start, was put in abeyance, therefore, and a very different novel, *The New Zealander*, was written instead. Cauvin did not like it. Making a strange comparison, he considered it inferior to Carlyle's *Latter-Day Pamphlets* 'both in style and substance': it was 'loose, illogical and rhapsodical', adjectives seldom applied to Trollope's fiction. Trollope's object, Cauvin said, was to show how England might be saved from ruin, which would have been the 'realisation of Macaulay's famous prophecy of the New Zealander standing on the ruins of London Bridge'.[25]

Longmans duly turned down *The New Zealander*, therefore, and later in life Trollope came to believe that Cauvin was right.[26] The novel was not published until 1972 in a complete new American edition of the works of Trollope. When he received the text of *Barchester Towers*, Cauvin considered that novel 'unequal in execution' too. The 'old characters' were there, but of plot there was none. Nevertheless, he found the text 'not uninteresting', 'whatever its defects': 'there was hardly a "lady" or "gentleman" among the characters'.[27] He suggested also that it would be 'quite possible to compress the three volumes [on offer] into one without much detriment to the whole'.[28]

When William proposed a two-volume edition to Trollope, the novelist gave a *carte blanche* to a close friend in the Post Office, John (later Sir John) Tilley (and later his brother-in-law), as an intermediary, a non-professional agent, to respond to William, and Tilley objected both to reducing it and to deleting from it what Cauvin, supported by William, had described as 'indecencies'. Trollope objected also to William Longman's refusal to offer him a cash advance of £100. Soon afterwards, again working on a half-profits basis, he secured what he had asked for, and publication in three volumes went ahead, with Trollope making a number of changes, not all of them the ones that Cauvin had suggested.[29]

This unsatisfactory episode marked almost the end of Trollope's brief

---

24 Hall, *op. cit.*, Vol. II, p.910, Letter from Trollope to H.C. Merivale, which indicates the care that Trollope took with the recording of his financial affairs. In 1856 he began a diary recording how many pages he had written in a day (*Autobiography*, p.119).

25 *Ibid.*, Vol. I, p.42, Letter from Cauvin to William Longman, 2 April 1855.

26 N.J. Hall, *Trollope, A Biography* (1993 edn.), pp.139–40.

27 *Ibid.*, p.145.

28 *Ibid.*, pp.45–6, Letter from Cauvin to William Longman, 8 Dec. 1856.

29 *Ibid.*, pp.32–3, Letters from Trollope to William Longman, 1 Feb. 1857, 3 March 1857. In the former he stated that some 'patch work would not be an improvement on the original composition'.

but revealing business relationship with the Longmans, for when William refused him a £200 advance on his next three-volume novel, *The Three Clerks*, he took the manuscript instead to Bentley, who offered him an advance of £250.[30] 'I am sure', Trollope had told William before doing so, 'that you do not regard £100 as an adequate payment for a 3 vol. novel. Of course, an unsuccessful novel may be worth much less – worth indeed less than nothing. And it may be likely that I cannot write a successful novel, but if I cannot obtain moderate success I will give over, and leave the business alone. I certainly will not willingly go on working at such a rate of pay.'[31]

William tried to persuade Trollope to stick to Longmans on the grounds that he should consider carefully whether 'our names on your title page are not worth more to you than the increased payment'.[32] He did not understand Trollope's interest in money. 'I did think much of Messrs Longman's name', he wrote, 'but I like it best at the bottom of a cheque.'[33] Trollope continued to regard William as a friend as well as a publisher, and after eventually signing up with Bentley, who had by then established his House as 'kings of the three-decker novel', he told William that he knew that this would not 'break any bones between you and me'.[34] It did not. Nor did the fact that Trollope, who believed that William was uninterested in publishing fiction, became for a time a Director of Chapman and Hall, who published several of his novels, beginning with *Doctor Thorne* (1858), for which he received an advance of £400.

Meanwhile, William followed his own path. In 1864, when Charles Edward Mudie (1818–1890) converted his library business into a limited liability company, Bentley took shares in it, as did Murray. William did not, although one of his Partners, Bevis Ellerby Green, held a £500 block of shares.[35] And William, while certainly not primarily interested in novels, was sometimes prepared to try out publishing schemes which surprised Trollope, who had much to say about the book trade in his *Autobiography*, published by John Blackwood, with whom he corresponded regularly. Thus, just before he died, he told Blackwood that he was surprised that a new novel by Margaret Oliphant, with whom he had corresponded about her novel *The Three Brothers*, serialised in the monthly *St. Paul's Magazine*,

---

30   Letter from Trollope to Richard Bentley, 5 Nov. 1857, telling him that he had not disposed of the copyright of *Barchester Towers* to Messrs Longman, *ibid*, p.60.

31   Letter from Trollope to William Longman, 29 Aug. 1857, *ibid.*, p.59.

32   *Autobiography*, p.109.

33   Hall, *A Biography*, p.154.

34   Letter from Trollope to William Longman, 18 Oct. 1857 in Hall, *op. cit.*, Vol. I, p.60.

35   Detail from the Partners' Share Records, 28 July 1864. (LA)

The Party in the Great Hall for Mudie's opening, 1860

BL 2719.X.9577

edited by him in 1869, had been brought out by Longmans in 1882 at the remarkably low price of 12s. 6d. for three volumes. 'What do you think of this?' he asked Blackwood, her main publisher. 'Answer this question.'[36]

    This was a rare example of Longman experimenting in cheap pricing, in the words of the *Spectator* offering as low a price as any publisher could reasonably be expected to do for a three-decker novel. There was consequently an element of irony in the fact, already noted, that Mrs. Oliphant was to go on to write a two-volume history of Blackwood and Sons on the invitation of one of the sons.[37] Yet the Oliphant novel in question, *In Trust*, the *Saturday Review* claimed, was no more likely to sell at 12s. 6d. than at the usual price of 31s. 6d. that publishers charged: 'no private house can find room for the fiction of voluminous authors'.[38] Only Mudie's Library could. And Mudie's did so until the 1890s.

~

36   Letter from Trollope to John Blackwood, 28 Jan. 1882 in Hall, *op. cit.*, Vol. II, p.944. A regular novel writer for *Blackwood's Magazine*, Mrs. Oliphant focused not on the church but on the chapel. Her *Salem Chapel* (1863) was one of her four *Chronicles of Carlingford*.

37   Margaret Oliphant, *William Blackwood and his Sons, Annals of a Publishing House* (1897). See her *Autobiography* (1899), republished with a new foreword by Laurie Langbauer in 1988.

38   *Saturday Review*, 25 Feb. 1882.

The golden age of Mudie's had been the 1860s, and it was of more than symbolic importance that from the start of the *Cornhill* Mudie's had stocked copies of it in its book boxes. 'Mr. Mudie's readers' were for many observers *the* public – although they represented only relatively upper strata within it. Founded by Charles Edward Mudie in Bloomsbury in 1840, the Library had its origins in a small newspaper and stationery shop owned by Mudie's father in Cheyne Walk, Chelsea. It was in Bloomsbury, however, that Charles Edward built up his first 'circulating library' while publishing some books as well as lending them. His shop thrived, however, and in 1852 bigger premises were acquired at the end of New Oxford Street. Like the great publishers, the company itself was becoming a leviathan.

Eight years later, the premises were further expanded and a handsome new hall was opened in 1860 when a huge party to celebrate its opening was attended by 'nearly all the best names in literature and the trade'.[39] Trollope called it Mudie's 'great flare up'.[40] More was involved, however, than festive celebration. For one of the men who worked there, 'to be engaged at Mudie's was regarded ... as practically equal to being in a government position, with the additional advantage that all worked together as one big and happy family under a control that was almost parental'.[41] Yet there were some authors – and critics – who condemned Mudie's 'almost parental attitudes' when selecting books to lend.

Through its purchasing power the Library already exerted a substantial influence on the plots, prices, dates of issue, formats, and even the bindings, of novels; and, although it dealt in non-fiction as well as in novels – and had a large collection of German books – both contemporaries and historians concentrated on the manner in which it dictated the pattern of the British three-decker novel for more than a generation. One of the critics of Mudie's underwriting of the three-decker novel, easy to borrow, expensive to buy, was the eccentric and outspoken novelist Charles Reade (1814–1884), author of *The Cloister and the Hearth* (1861), writing in 1853, before the great new premises were opened. For him the 'three-decker' was an 'intellectual blot on our Nation ... the last relic of our forefathers' prolixity', it was 'the remnant of a past age [which] could no more stand before the increasing intelligence of this age than an old six horse coach can compete with a train whirled past by a single engine'.[42]

---

39   'The Opening of Mr. Mudie's New Hall' in the *Illustrated London News*, 29 Dec. 1860, quoted in G.L. Griest, *Mudie's Circulating Library and the Victorian Novel* (1970), p.21.

40   B.A. Booth (ed.), *The Letters of Anthony Trollope* (1951), p.83.

41   A.A. Stevens, *The Recollections of a Bookman* (1933), p.19.

42   Letter to Richard Bentley, quoted in Griest, *op. cit.*, p.95. See M. Elwin, *Charles Reade* (1911). Reade, a Fellow of Magdalen College, Oxford, lived a bohemian life in London and was highly litigious. See his autobiographical *The Eighth Commandment* (1860).

Mudie resented any suggestion that he himself was 'a remnant of the past'. Indeed it had been by taking advantage of 'modern legislation' (the Limited Liability Act of 1861) that he had been able in 1864 to convert his library from a private concern into a limited liability company with a capital of £100,000, half of which he retained (with an income as manager, a term not used, of £1,000 per annum) and with the rest in the hands of publishers. With or without shares, publishers benefited from their dealings with the Library which stocked not only novels but many of the history books and biographies to which contemporaries attached special importance; and for the most part the selection of these was unlikely to stir up criticism of the Library's selection criteria.

There was something impressive about the care with which the Library handled its clients: it not only loaned books but offered individual advice. Charles Edward's personality was judged 'quiet yet pleasingly dynamic', and although his influence 'stabilised' central features of Victorian publishing, his customers had no quarrel with him about that. Nor had they with his son, Arthur Oliver, described by a 'bookman' as a 'fine English gentleman of the old school' with a soul that 'soared high above money'.[43]

~

Novels were often treated during the mid-Victorian years as 'the vital offspring of modern wants and tendencies', and a Longman author, the northern mill owner W.R. Greg, who also wrote for the *Edinburgh Review*, observed in 1868 that it was 'not easy to over-estimate the importance of novels, whether we regard the influence they exercise upon an age, or the indications they afford of its characteristic ... features.[44] Not surprisingly, the mid-Victorian years have sometimes been called 'The Age of the Novel' or, with particular authors in mind, 'The Age of Trollope' or more often 'The Age of Dickens'. (Trollope died in 1882, Dickens in 1870.) It was a single American novel, however, which most extraordinarily caught the imagination of publishers and readers alike: in a single fortnight in October 1852 Harriet Beecher Stowe's *Uncle Tom's Cabin* appeared in ten editions. Within a year it may have sold over a million copies.[45]

There were other 'vital offsprings of modern wants and tendencies', however, besides novels, and it was Macaulay, who never wrote a novel, who was the great Longman author. Interest in history was one 'vital offspring', and Macaulay's *History of England*, the first volume of which appeared in 1848, was one of the major contributions to Victorian culture. The financial arrangements were very favourable to the author, for in

Uncle Tom's Cabin –first edition. Title page, published in London in 1852

BL 7953.a.57 (2)

43   Stevens, *op. cit.*, pp.28, 19.

44   *Prospective Review*, Vol. 6 (1850), p.495; W.R. Greg, *Literary and Social Judgements* (1868), p.99.

45   C. Gordes, *American Literature in Nineteenth Century England* (1944), pp.29–31.

Thomas Babington Macaulay,
1849, portrait painted by Eden
Upton Eddis (1812–1901)

Pearson Education

September 1848 Longmans had agreed that on the basis of a sale of 6,000 copies Macaulay would be paid £500 a year for five years starting in January 1849, and that if that number of copies were sold before the end of that period Macaulay would be paid two-thirds of the profits on all subsequent volumes. The 6,000 mark was quickly reached and passed, and as early as January 1849 it was necessary to print a third edition.

Before the *History* came the *Essays*, and the idea of publishing these in book form had been in Macaulay's mind before his *Critical and Historical Essays* appeared in three volumes in 1846. William Longman secured his reluctant acceptance to have them published, however, only after a badly edited, unauthorised American edition, sponsored by Henry Vizetelly, had appeared: 'Longman has earnestly pressed me to consent to the republication of some of my reviews', Macaulay wrote to MacVey Napier before he took the decision in 1844 to stop writing for the *Edinburgh Review*. 'To keep out the American copies by legal pressure, and yet to refuse to publish an edition here, would be an odious course, and in the very spirit of dog in the manger. I am, therefore, strongly inclined to accede to Longman's proposition. And if the thing is to be done, the sooner the better.'[46] It was.

The *History* followed, and Macaulay could compare his sale of 3,000 copies of the first edition in the first ten days after publication with sales of 2,000 copies of Scott's *Marmion* in a month.[47] According to the then publisher of Scott's novels, Adam Black, whose name appeared between 1826 and 1891 on the title page of the *Edinburgh Review* as the agent in Scotland for its distribution,[48] there had been 'no such sale since the days of *Waverley*'. This was a comparison that would have pleased Thackeray as a novelist as much as it pleased Macaulay as an historian, for Thackeray greatly admired the historian's style and the depth of his research. He claimed memorably that Macaulay had read twenty books to write a

46 G.O. Trevelyan, *Life and Letters of Lord Macaulay* (1876), p.427, claimed that 'the market for them in the native country is so steady, and apparently so inexhaustible, that it is hardly too much to say that the demand for Macaulay varies with the demand for coal'. A paperback edition of the *Essays* with an introduction by Hugh Trevor-Roper appeared in 1963, published by Fontana Books.

47 Quoted in W. Thomas, *The Quarrel of Macaulay and Croker* (2000), p.285. Scott's *Lay of the Last Minstrel* had sold 2,250 copies in the first year.

48 In 1891 the practice ceased when A. and C. Black, founded in 1801, moved their premises from Edinburgh to London, where they had set up an office in 1889. They became a private limited company in 1914.

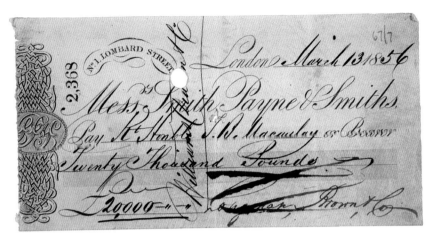

The famous cheque: Macaulay wrote to Thornton of Williams's Bank that it was 'a tolerable sum to have cleared in less than three months.'

Longman Archive

The first two volumes of Lord Macaulay's *History of England* were very well received. But the success of the next two volumes was phenomenal. Published on 17 December, 1855 by the end of February 1856 Macaulay recorded that 25,000 copies had been sold. He noted in his diary:-

'March 7th. Longman came with a very pleasant announcement. He and his partners find that they are over-flowing with money, and think that they cannot invest it better than by advancing to me, on the usual terms of course, part of what will be due to me in December. We agreed that they shall pay Twenty thousand pounds into Williams's Bank next week. What a sum to be gained by one edition of a book!'

sentence and travelled a hundred miles 'to make a line of description'.[49]

The second version of the first volume of the *History*, which appeared in January 1849, was out of print almost as soon as it appeared, and before the end of the month Macaulay was told that only 1,600 copies of a third reprint of 5,000 were left and that 10,000 more copies would have to be printed. They were, and these too were quickly sold. Volume II was equally successful, and it was after Volumes III and IV had appeared in December 1855 that Macaulay was sent in March 1856 the famous cheque for £20,000, described as the largest sum that Longman had ever paid to an author. It is a cheque which has passed into publishing history.

Mudie's had ordered 2,500 copies of the third and fourth volumes in 1855, an impressive order which caused consternation as well as delight in Paternoster Row. Fifteen thousand copies had by then been printed. The third and fourth volumes weighed about seven pounds, thus making a total weight of almost eight tons, and Longman had to ask Mudie's to fetch the volumes themselves.[50]

~

Macaulay, with the prospectus of the new *Cornhill* on his desk, died one year before a number of anonymous articles on the great publishing Houses appeared in *The Critic*, a weekly.[51] They were written by Francis Espinasse

49 Quoted in A. Nevins, 'Literary Aspects of History', in *The Gateway to History* (1938), p.342.

50 Quoted in Griest, *op. cit.*, p.20.

51 *The Critic*, 7 April 1860. *The Critic of Literature, Art, Science and Drama* first appeared as a separate periodical in December 1843. Espinasse used at least three pseudonyms, he described himself as 'its chief, or at least, its most copious contributor'. The last two articles in May 1860 were on Charles Knight. The first three were on 'The House of Longman' [sic], 24 March, 7, 21 April 1860.

(1823–1897), 'a Scot of Gascon descent', born in Edinburgh, described in his *Times* obituary as 'the Nestor of English journalists'.[52] Proclaiming *en passant* that 'we [now] live in an age of competition',[53] Espinasse chose the House of Longman for his main article in *The Critic*, with articles on Murray and Blackwood to follow.[54] Longmans came first because of the age of the House. Seniority counted as much for Espinasse as did output – or even reputation. Yet he mentioned longevity as such only indirectly, when he noted that Longman, one of the original publishers mentioned on the title page of Johnson's *Dictionary*, was now preparing a new edition for publication. Espinasse dwelt less on chronology than on the wide range – and variety – of famous books that had borne the Longman imprint.

At several points in his articles Espinasse touched briefly on economics, referring to the importance of capital in publishing – and of Longman's access to it – but he gave no precise financial details either of the Longman business or those of the other businesses which concerned him. This was not entirely his fault: Partners' ledgers would never have been made available to him, and information about how the prices of books were computed, in particular or in general, would have been difficult to collect quickly. (He could have collected some material, however, from wills.) In general he showed little curiosity about the different ways that publishers handled financial matters, ignoring, for example, the forceful claim of the determined publisher John Chapman, no friend of Longmans, that as a matter of principle 'it was the right of the public to obtain goods at the lowest possible price at which they could be produced and sold'.[55]

Chapman and Hall, Dickens's first publishers (*Pickwick Papers* (1836)), founded in 1830,[56] had set out to provide cheaper novels as early as 1845. At the same time, challenging the convention of the three-decker novel,

---

52   T.H.S. Escott, *Masters of English Journalism* (1911), p.286; *The Times*, 4 Jan. 1897. Espinasse was 'perhaps the last survivor of the generation who could say that they had seen Sir Walter Scott', and in the first number of The *Bookman*, Sept. 1891, he wrote an article called 'Recollections of the Carlyles and their Circle'. Both Wordsworth and Jeffreys warned Espinasse against taking up a literary life, and Espinasse spent his last years as a Poor Brother at the Charterhouse, an institution for 'literary men' memorably described in Cross, *op. cit.*, p.81. See also F. Espinasse, *Literary Recollections and Sketches* (1893).

53   *The Critic*, 7 April 1860.

54   Espinasse also contributed a number of entries to *The Dictionary of National Biography*, the first volume of which appeared in 1885, a project that he was reputed to have conceived.

55   *Morning Chronicle*, 18 May 1852.

56   On the death of William Hall in 1847 the firm became Chapman and Chapman. The novelist George Meredith, whose novel *The Ordeal of Richard Feverel* appeared in the annus mirabilis, 1859, was for thirty years its literary adviser.

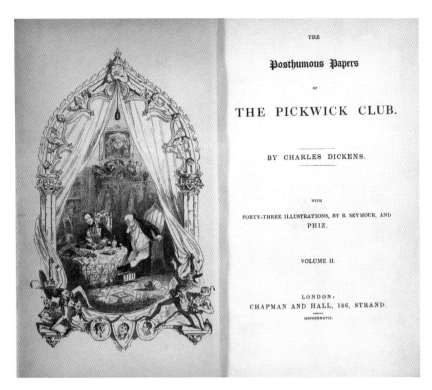

THE

𝔓𝔬𝔰𝔱𝔥𝔲𝔪𝔬𝔲𝔰 𝔓𝔞𝔭𝔢𝔯𝔰

OF

THE PICKWICK CLUB.

BY CHARLES DICKENS.

WITH

FORTY-THREE ILLUSTRATIONS, BY R. SEYMOUR, AND
PHIZ.

VOLUME II.

LONDON:
CHAPMAN AND HALL, 186, STRAND.

MDCCCXXXVII.

Frontispiece to *The Posthumous Papers of the Pickwick Club* Vol. II., 1837

The first monthly numbers appeared in 1836

BL c.59.c.23

they had won the valuable approval of the *Athenaeum* magazine, founded in 1828, not only for providing 'works of imagination in a cheaper form', but for delivering the author from 'an incubus which has borne heavily on his fancy'.[57] Publishing new fiction in four monthly parts, each priced at three shillings, was no more a success, however, than John Murray II's had been, nor were other experiments in pricing. In retrospect, indeed, it has been argued that the three-volume novel was 'not only stable in itself but a source of general stability'.[58]

Irrespective of format or content, there were, as we have seen, economic and other forces bearing on the book trade. The repeal of the paper duties in 1861 cheapened the price of more than one of the major items in the cost of a book. The continuing growth of literacy stimulated demand as in the past. Nevertheless it was restrained by the low incomes of wage-earners. The Press, with the low-price *Daily Telegraph* (1855) in the lead, reflected the impact of the same forces, gaining in circulation. It was *The Times*, however, that gloried most in the prestige of a 'fourth estate'. However, as far as books themselves were concerned, more of them were now being published than ever before, with an increasing number of

---

57   *Athenaeum*, 1 April 1845.

58   J.A. Sutherland, *Victorian Novelists and Publishers* (1976), p.13.

Spy cartoon of John Stuart
Mill 'A Feminine Philosopher',
Vanity Fair, 29 March 1873

Longman Archive Scrapbooks Vol.7

reprints in various formats. Whatever might be said about the fortunes of individual publishers, some of whom could still go bankrupt, the economics of the book trade in years when there were financial and cyclical crises in the whole economy seemed as secure as the British Constitution – or the price of consols.[59]

There were many individual authors of undoubted quality who welcomed the reduction in the price of their own works when they were issued in popular editions. One of them was the economist, philosopher and politician, John Stuart Mill, after his move from J.W. Parker to Longman. Cheaper versions of his earlier books gave him access to a wider public in which he put his trust politically;[60] and in his *Autobiography*, which Longmans published posthumously in 1873, Mill applauded the advice they had given him that 'People's Editions' of his works would be 'most likely to find readers among the working classes' if he gave up the half share of the profits due to him in order that they might be published cheaply.

> To the credit of Messrs Longman, they fixed, unasked, a certain number of years after which the copyright and stereotypes were to revert to me, and a certain number of copies after the sale of which I should receive half of any further profit. The number of copies (which in the case of *Political Economy* was 10,000), has for some time been exceeded, and the People's Editions have begun to yield me a small but unexpected pecuniary return, though very far from an equivalent for the disbursement of profit from the Library editions.[61]

Six-shilling reprints served the same purpose, but much depended on the time interval between the publication of first expensive editions and reprints.

Espinasse, not always in the know, left out all considerations of this kind. He never attempted to probe. Nor did he note that in a publishing world of leviathans there were minnows too, real not mythical fish, or that there were as sharp contrasts among the bigger fish as among the minnows, some of whom would never have wished to describe themselves as leviathans. Some of the most successful business houses – far from minnows – were seeking to attract 'an unknown public' for cheap literature that was outside the range of the Longmans, the Murrays, the Blackwoods, and the Macmillans.

---

59   For contemporary accounts of crises see D.M. Evans, *The History of the Commercial Crisis, 1857-8* (1859), *Facts, Failures and Frauds* (1859) and *Speculative Notes and Notes on Speculation* (1864). J.R. McCulloch wrote critically of limited liability in *Considerations on Partnerships with Limited Liability* (1856).

60   See above, pp.59–60.

61   *Autobiography* (New American Library of World Literature 1964 edn., for which I wrote a foreword), p.196.

~

It was a novelist, not a journalist or a publisher, who brought to public notice, if not for the first time, the presence of the 'unknown public'. Wilkie Collins (1824-1889), writing in Charles Dickens's *Household Words* in 1858, sought to dispel the illusion that 'the great bulk of the reading public of England' were like the readers of *Household Words*, mainly middle-class, Dickens's 'great public'. Instead, they were reading 'penny-novel journals', publications that 'filled the shop windows of tobacconists and stationers'. Five such journals alone had a combined weekly circulation of half-a-million copies. And this was twelve years before the passing of the National Education Act of 1870 which brought into existence public elementary schools.[62]

The early Victorians, as Hood had noted satirically before the word 'Victorian' had come into use as a noun or an adjective, loved to use the word 'million' or 'millions'. And leaving aside 'sensational' novels, another category to which the adjective 'unwholesome' was often attached, cheap publications offered short stories and serial stories, very different from those that appeared in *Blackwoods* or the *Cornhill*, along with 'snippets of information' – 'trivia', household hints, and riddles. There was always a market for these, and it was to grow during the last decades of the nineteenth century[63]. George Newnes (1851–1910) was claiming too much when he described his *Tit-Bits*, launched in 1881, as the *first* 'snippets paper'. More to the point, it was selling 350,000 copies a week seven weeks later.

Wilkie Collins, like John Stuart Mill, was not pessimistic about the long-term prospect:

> The Unknown Public is in a literary sense hardly beginning, as yet, to learn to read. The members of it are, evidently, in the mass [another word in increasing use[64]], from no fault of theirs, still ignorant of almost everything which is generally known and understood among readers whom circumstances have placed, socially and intellectually, in the rank above them ... The future of English fiction may rest with this Unknown Public, which is now waiting to be taught the difference between a good book and a book. It is probably a question of time only. The largest audience for periodical literature, in this age of periodicals, must obey the universal law of progress, and must, sooner or later, learn to discriminate.

---

62 *Household Words*, No. 18, 21 Aug. 1858, pp.217–24. For a not dissimilar treatment of the subject see *Blackwood's Magazine*, Vol. LXXXII (1858), pp.200–16.

63 Altick, *op. cit.*, pp.287ff.

64 See A. Briggs, The Language of "Mass" and "Masses" in Nineteenth-Century England', reprinted in *The Collected Essays of Asa Briggs*, Vol. I (1985), pp.34–54.

Was there a touch of irony in the phrase 'the universal law of progress'? Collins, familiar with all the problems associated with serial and joint publication – through his verdict on *Household Words* the relationship between Dickens and himself was as complicated as the relationship between any author and any publisher – was a shrewd judge of all publishing issues as well as a creative writer of exceptional talent.[65]

As it was, many observers shared neither Collins's nor Mill's optimism in forecasting the future.[66] Matthew Arnold (1822-1888), son of Arnold of Rugby who was to influence profoundly the future academic development of English literature as a 'subject' taught in schools and universities, thought (and felt) quite differently.[67] No one, however, could dispute the existence of Collins's 'unknown public', for him 'impenetrable'. It was not a new phenomenon, but it became increasingly important with the continuing rise of literacy, which was apparent to contemporaries long before the belated advent of universal elementary school education.[68] Equally relevant was 'the rise of leisure', first for the middle classes, later for the working classes.[69] Reading, 'good' and 'bad', was one of the ways of filling it, and it figured purposefully in the titles of magazines such as *Leisure Hour*. J.S. Mill, quoted by Greg, pitted the 'Evangel of Leisure' against Carlyle's 'Evangel of Work'.[70]

The history of education and of leisure converged in the history of public libraries, first conceived of as the history of 'a public library *movement*', part of a bigger movement which incorporated the campaign to repeal the 'duties on knowledge'. The Public Libraries Act of 1850, passed twenty years before the National Education Act, was in retrospect as much

---

65 See *inter alia* J. Meakier, *Hidden Rivalries in Victorian Fiction: Dickens, Realism and Revaluation* (1987) and L. Nayder, *Unequal Partners, Charles Dickens, Wilkie Collins and Victorian Authorship* (2002).

66 See J. McAleer, *Popular Reading and Publishing in Britain, 1914–1950* (1992) which reaches back in time well before 1914.

67 See the important introduction by G. Sutherland to *Matthew Arnold on Education, a collection* (1973), which includes reprints of Arnold's Inspectors' Reports for 1852, 1869 and 1880. For influential later books in a similar Arnoldian tradition see Q.D. Leavis, *Fiction and the Reading Public* (1932), and D. Thompson, *Reading and Discrimination* (1934). Oxford did not have an English Honours School until 1893 and Cambridge did not have a Professor of English until 1911 (see J. McMurty, *English Language, English Literature: The Creation of an Academic Discipline* (1985)).

68 See D. Vincent, *Literacy and Popular Culture: England, 1750–1914* (1989).

69 See J. Walvin, *Leisure and Society, 1830–1950* (1978) and J. Lowerson and J. Myerscough, *Time to Spare in Victorian England* (1977).

70 Greg, *op. cit.*, p.83, quoting an article by Mill in *Fraser's*. See also V.E. Newberg, *Popular Literature: A History and Guide*.

of a landmark as the Education Act, but it has been far more neglected. Both pieces of legislation are best conceived of as part of a process, the beginnings of which preceded the Acts and which were never completed with their passing.[71] The Mechanics' Institutes, for example, set up in the period covered in the last chapter, with the encouragement of Brougham, all had libraries: university extension and the development of extra-mural education followed the Acts.

The history of museums and galleries was also part of the process. In Birmingham, for example, a room in the Free Library was devoted to a small collection of pictures in 1867 fourteen years before the opening of a new Art Gallery.[72] As a centre of the glass industry, invigorated by the final abolition of the window tax in 1851, enlightened Birmingham manufacturers were aware of 'intimate' connections between industry and the aims and purposes of libraries and galleries. 'By the gains of industry we promote art.' Gas played its part as well as glass in the cultural story of Birmingham, and nationally as well as locally the extension over time of gas lighting directly influenced the history of reading, although the association of books with candlelight was to persist into the twentieth century.

Between 1847 and 1886 public libraries were being established at the rate of three or four a year: in the period from 1887 to 1900 the average was sixteen or seventeen. The requirement to secure the support of a majority of the ratepayers before opening a public library was an obstacle in many places, and if only for that reason the locational distribution of libraries is as interesting as that of private circulation libraries in the eighteenth century. As late as 1887, the year of the Queen's Jubilee, only two parishes in the whole of metropolitan London had rate-supported libraries, and places as different as Bath, Hastings, Huddersfield and Glasgow were without them.[73] The halfpenny rate of 1850 had been raised to a penny in 1855, but the increase had only limited effect.[74]

The chronology, as interesting as the geography, can only be

71 See T. Kelly, *History of Public Libraries in Great Britain, 1845–1965* (1965) and the perceptive review of it by Maurice Bruce in *Adult Education*, Vol. 46, No. 61 (1965), pp.422–4, and J. Minihan, *The Nationalization of Culture* (1977). For a contemporary statement see D. Chadwick, 'On Free Public Libraries and Museums', in *Transactions of the National Association for the Promotion of Social Science* (1857).

72 See A. Capel Shaw, 'The Birmingham Free Libraries' and W.Wallis, 'The Museum and Art Gallery' in J.H. Muirhead, *Birmingham Institutions* (1911), pp.401–43 and 477–521.

73 T. Greenwood, *Public Libraries: A History of the Movement and a Manual... for Rate Supported Libraries* (1891), pp.291–2.

74 C. Welch, 'The Public Library Movement in London' in TL, Vol. VI (1895), pp.95–101.

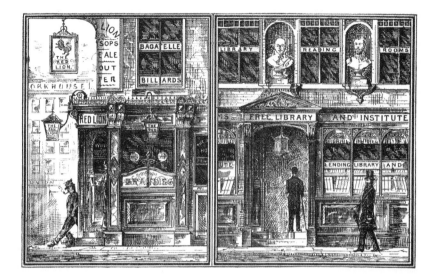

'The Rivals: Which shall it be?'
Frontispiece from Thomas
Greenwood's *Free Public
Libraries*, 1886

BL 2719.x.91631

fully explained in the light of detailed local and regional history, and it
incorporates the history of juvenile libraries, 'local collections', the use of
newspapers and periodicals.[75] Reading was largely 'conditioned by what
was available', though everywhere 'fiction was overwhelmingly the first
choice'. At Liverpool in 1853-4 one 'labouring man' had read in the second
year of the Library, Macaulay's *History* and two others had read 'Moore
and Scott's Poetical Works. Thirty years later, Leeds experimented with
the creation of public libraries in schools.[76] The development of a public
library *service* took decades to mature, although the First World War, like
the Second, gave a great fillip to it.[77] An important twentieth-century date
was 1919 when a new Public Libraries Act abolished the penny rate limit
set in 1855: it also removed the limit on funds that could be spent from the
rates on museums. By then – and it was far ahead – what had begun as a
movement had developed into a system which was to be further perfected
between 1919 and 1930.

   There was often a moral cast to the story which spans this and the
next chapter:

---

75   The periodicals in the late 1850s and 1860s included *All the Year Round,
Blackwoods', Chambers Journal, Cornhill Magazine, Edinburgh Review,
Fortnightly Review, Illustrated London News, Punch, Graphic* and *Good Words*
(Kelly, *op. cit.* p.81).

76   P. Cowell, *Liverpool Public Libraries* (1903), p.50. See also for a later period T.W.
Hand, *A Brief Account of the Public Libraries in the City of Leeds, 1870–1920*
(1920).

77   See *The Times*, 'Reading in Time of War', 13 April 1915, and 'Reading and War
Worry', 12 April 1917.

The public-house is the ante-room of the gaol, while the library is the door-way of knowledge which is power – power for success, for prosperity, and for honour. The public-house is the high-road to perdition; the library the wicket of truth.'[78]

As early as 1802, James Sends had described free libraries as 'temples erected by Literature to attract the votaries of Bacchus.[79] Sir John Lubbock (1834–1913), later Lord Avebury, chose more romantic imagery when he described a Public Library as 'a true fairyland, a very palace of delight'.[80] Lubbock, Vice-Chancellor of London University from 1872 to 1880 and a Longman author, was responsible for major legislative changes in the public approach to leisure, notably the Bank Holidays Act of 1872 and the Shop Hours Act of 1889.[81] He also assembled lists of key books which he recommended 'the public' to read. With him all things connect.

~

William Longman, who had little to say about public libraries, although they all included Longman books, was to take advantage in his business operations both of increasing literacy and of increasing leisure, but he approached the social and cultural issues, including the religious issues that underlay both of them, in a thoughtful rather than a rhetorical fashion. For high-minded statements of the moral purposes of publishing it is necessary to turn elsewhere, in particular to the new Victorian publisher about whom Espinasse did not write, the House of Macmillan, which had – and was to have – as interesting a history, with as many turns of fortune, as those of the three publishers he chose.[82]

Within the context of mid-Victorian Britain no other publisher's declaration of moral purpose was as eloquent, as oratorical, or, indeed, as 'traditional', as the unforgettable declaration of Daniel Macmillan (1813–1857). Born on the Isle of Arran, he had a strong sense of mission:

We booksellers, if we are faithful to our task, are trying to destroy, and are helping to destroy, all kinds of confusion, and are aiding our great Taskmaster to reduce the world into order, and beauty and harmony

---

78 Kelly, (op. cit., p.113) took this quotation from the *Middlesex Courier*. It was quoted earlier by Greenwood in the third edition of his *Free Public Libraries* (1891), p.213.

79 'A General Defence of Modern Novels', quoted in J.T. Taylor, *Early Opposition to the English Novel: the Popular Reaction from 1760–1830* (1943), p.49.

80 Quoted in Kelly, *op. cit.*, p.113.

81 For Lubbock as a Longman author on anthropology, see below, p.284.

82 Macmillans were not selected either in two articles that followed in the wake of Espinasse in an American version of *The Critic*, 8,13 Sept. 1883.

... At the same time, it is our duty to manage our affairs wisely, keep our minds easy, and not trade beyond our means.[83]

This was a declaration that should be compared with the declaration in one of Mudie's catalogues:

The purpose for which the Library was originally established – to create a more general taste for the higher literature, and to meet the increased demand which has thus arisen – is still kept steadily in view, and great care continues to be taken that every work of merit and general interest shall be introduced as soon as published.[84]

Mudie dealt in new books, Daniel Macmillan tried to discover 'books that would last'.

Macmillan and his younger brother Alexander could pass on to other publishers manuscripts that they themselves did not want to publish: Mudie, who used paid readers to judge the merits of new publications, as did most publishers, including Longman, could keep new books out. Yet in the case both of publisher and librarian – and public librarians, gaining in importance during the late-Victorian years, could be as 'selective' on moral grounds as Mudie – more than censorship was involved. One publisher's reader, Geraldine Jewsbury, stated candidly that 'the *author* must ... understand that the *reader* and the public are *company* and require a certain amount of ceremony and politeness to be observed before them'.[85] Not all authors were prepared to meet such a requirement, but many resorted to various forms of self-censorship.

The Macmillans, who began to publish educational works in 1843, were to become Longman's chief competitors in this field for much of the twentieth century. The story might have been different, however, had Daniel been interviewed in 1833 by Thomas Norton III before going to Cambridge, where he and his brother set up a bookselling business. Daniel had arrived from Scotland with a flattering letter to Thomas Norton III, but had been told by a knowledgeable friend that there was 'no vacancy at Longmans'. This did not hold him back from going down in person to 39 Paternoster Row, where Green asked him to leave his address and 'a specimen of your penmanship'. Thomas Norton would not be back until Friday, he said. Again Daniel persisted after Green had added that there was 'small chance' of his being found a place. This time, he saw young Thomas Norton IV, who explained that he was very busy – it was Magazine Day – and asked him to

---

83   T. Hughes, *Memoir of Daniel Macmillan* (1882), p.116.

84   Quoted in Griest, *op. cit.*, p.135.

85   Quoted *ibid.*, p.140.

come back the following Monday. Daniel had no more time to wait.[86] He and his brother soon moved from Cambridge to London, where it seemed a happy coincidence that their first premises were in Aldersgate Street, which had figured dramatically in the life of John Wesley.

Daniel died at Cambridge in 1857; Alexander lived on until 1896, thirty-nine years after Daniel's death, by which time the conditions of publishing had totally changed; and, like the Longmans, he played a major part in its politics. It was of great importance too, both to him and to his House, that in 1863 he was appointed Publisher to the University of Oxford, a post he held until 1880. John Murray III had been offered the post first but refused It was the post of an agent, not a partner.[87] A later Macmillan, Frederick, was as independent as any of the Murrays, but at the end of the century he in his turn was to lay down the conditions for twentieth-century publishing as a whole.

As early as 1882, Trollope had included Macmillans, along with Longman, Murray and Blackwood, Espinasse's trio of leviathans, among 'the eight to ten firms who offered any prospects of a business career' to new entrants to publishing, adding prudentially and characteristically that while the firms all 'might have openings' none of them offered much chance of success.[88] Without family connections luck counted for more than talent. There were new Longman Partners, however, drawn into the House by Thomas Norton IV, who himself had become a Partner as long ago as 1832, the year of the Great Reform Bill, at the age of twenty-eight, and William, who did not become a Partner until 1839. Both worked together as family Partners in a longer lasting partnership than that of the first Macmillans.

~

The first of the new Partners taken in by Thomas Norton IV and William in 1856 was Thomas Roberts (1810–1865), who had been apprenticed to Thomas Brown in 1825 at the age of fifteen and had made his way upwards inside the business, from 1828 representing the firm in the country trade until he became a Partner in 1856.[89] He then succeeded Brown in charge of accounts, having been his assistant since 1854. When he died on Whitsuntide Tuesday in 1865, Roberts was succeeded by Thomas Reader (1818–1905), who had been offered a Partnership in a rival firm before joining Longman in 1834 and who stayed at Paternoster Row for fifty-five years.

Roberts, said to have been a 'gentle and kindly man', left £500 in his

---

86   C. Morgan, *The House of Macmillan* (1943), p.16; FM, p.258.

87   See P. Sutcliffe, *The Oxford University Press, An Informal History* (1978), pp.17–18.

88   Letter of 2 Jan. 1882, printed in Hall, *op. cit.*, Vol. II (1983), p.937.

89   For the 'country trade' see above, pp.104–5.

will to Commercial Travellers' Schools. He also 'acquired some distinction in private life as a numismatist'.[90] Reader's career was different.[91] He worked on his own account as well as for Longman, selling second-hand law books. He was not the only Reader to work with Longman. His father, Charles, had served in Longman's second-hand book department, where he remembered Sir Walter Scott as a customer.[92] One of Thomas Reader's three sons was to be disappointed in not being allowed to follow in his father's footsteps.

Another new Partner of 1865 was Robert Dyer (1817–1884), who, like Roberts, had begun his Longman career as an apprentice. His name remained on the House's imprints until 1889, five years after his death, the year when the Longman business was registered as a private company and its imprint was changed to Longmans, Green and Co., an imprint which lasted until 1926. William Ellerby Green, the longest lasting Partner, was also second in a line of succession: his father, Bevis Green, had trained him in the intricacies of the country and export business, and he became a partner in 1862. After the death of William Longman in 1877 and of Thomas Norton IV in 1879 he was the senior Partner in the business, although never in charge of it.

However hard-working and socially active the various partners were, it was still left to Thomas Norton and William Longman to correspond with and talk to authors and would-be authors about their publications, and this they could do either in Paternoster Row or at home or sometimes in their authors' homes. The biggest changes at Paternoster Row came a year after Espinasse wrote. A fire, which started in neighbouring premises, led to a complete restructuring of the premises which were now given an imposing new façade. How serious the fire was at the time it is difficult to judge: *The Times* described it as 'comparatively trifling', and reported that while one of the houses was destroyed, it was covered by insurance. Nevertheless, many of the early records of the House, which would have made it possible to explore earlier economic history in a way that Espinasse did not attempt to do, were lost in the blaze, and the event stands out as a landmark date in Longman history. At the time the motto was 'Business as Usual'.[93]

'Business as usual' involved the sale of periodicals and magazines as

---

90 Curwen, *op. cit.*, p.94. Roberts was also a Governor of Christ's Hospital, his school, and of St Bartholomew's Hospital.

91 See below, p.278.

92 Letter of 12 July 1950 from Frank Eldridge to Cyprian Blagden giving family details (*Personal Papers*). Eldridge was Thomas Reader's grandson. Charles had been press ganged into the Navy during the Napoleonic Wars and was a member of the crew of a ship that fought under Nelson at the Battle of the Nile.

93 *The Times*, 6 Sept. 1861.

After the fire of 1861, which destroyed a number of buildings, the new Longman building was planned with Blackwood's so that both buildings formed part of one design. Opened in 1863, the keystone of the central entrance represented Literature supported by Arts, Science and Education. The spandrels carried half-size copies of the Ship and the Swan, the two medallions of the old buildings, saved from the fire. *The Builder* described the building as 'Renaissance' in style, 'not wanting in ornament and whilst somewhat grandiose in character, as befits the domicile of the chief of the publishing firms of England, it carries distinctly the aspect of a commercial building'

Longman Archive

well as books. It was from the Paternoster Row address, not an Edinburgh address, that the *Edinburgh Review*, controlled by Longman, had been published since 1847, the year of Napier's death. Under the editorship of Henry Reeve, as we have noted a regular visitor to Farnborough Hill, who took it over in 1855 and remained Editor for forty years, it became an organ of 'liberal and moderate opinions', including Broad Church opinions. It was only rarely that it offended politicians, but it did offend Russell in 1855 when it described him as 'suffering under the unhappy delusion ... to suppose that no Liberal Government can be formed without his headship'; and when Russell wrote to Thomas Norton condemning it, William pledged that the offensive number would not be republished.[94]

Between Napier and Reeve there had been two intervening Editors who for different reasons did not last long. The first of them, William Empson (1791–1852), appointed Editor in 1847, was Professor of the Polity and Laws of England at Haileybury and was married to Jeffrey's only daughter. When he died suddenly after five years his successor was a politician, Sir George Cornewall Lewis (1806–1863), recently Financial Secretary to the Treasury under Russell, who resigned as Editor when Palmerston appointed him Chancellor of the Exchequer in 1855.

The *Quarterly Review*, still controlled by Murray, had a less distinguished editor than Reeve after Lockhart gave way in 1854 to a country parson, the

---

94   Clive, *loc. cit.* in EHP, p.131. For Reeve see J.K. Laughton (ed.), *Memories of the Life and Correspondence of Henry Reeve*, 2 vols. (1898).

Reverend Whitwell Elvin, who stayed in the office until 1861, while *Blackwood's Magazine,* Maga, the third great nineteenth-century review, continued to provide, far more quietly than in its early years, a different kind of Tory Church-and-State alternative to the *Quarterly.* It was now read as much for the fiction it published as for its politics or religion, and it provided a home for George Eliot's *Scenes from Clerical Life* and in serial form *Adam Bede,* another of the new books of 1859. Two successive Blackwoods conceived of Maga as 'an unprecedented phenomenon in the world of letters', forming 'alas! the only remaining link between the Periodical Press and the enduring literature of Great Britain'. The concept of 'enduring literature' appealed to the mid-Victorians.

John Blackwood (1818–1879), who was Chairman of Blackwoods from 1852 to 1879, was wrong, however, in claiming a proprietary right to the advancement of literature. There were many interesting articles in the *Edinburgh Review* on poetry and prose, British and foreign, among them a review by Richard Monckton Milnes of Disraeli's novels which Robert Blake described in 1966 as 'to this day the best statement for the preservation of Disraeli's novels'. The review and the comment are of special interest in that during the period described in this chapter Disraeli the novelist became a favourite Longman author.[95]

Thomas Norton's greatest success, like that of his son after him, was to come much later, with the Tory Disraeli. He arranged for the publication of Disraeli's novel *Lothair,* paying £2,000 for it. A novel written by an ex-Prime Minister, was a unique event, and from Disraeli's point of view it was an important event in that it provided him with hard cash at a time when he was in opposition. By the time that he returned to Downing Street in 1876, the novel had earned him more than £6,000 in royalties, the first time he had been paid in that way, along with £1,500 from American sales. He had either leased his copyright on his earlier novels or had them published on a half-profits basis.

The immediate demand for the novel in 1870, the year of Dickens's death and of the Franco-Prussian War, was well described in a light-hearted letter from Thomas Norton to Disraeli:

> There has been a run upon your bankers in Paternoster Row, and our last thousand is nearly gone. We shall have another thousand in hand on Wednesday next. This will be the sixth thousand, and I do not feel quite certain we shall not be broken before Wednesday! I am not sure that it would not do good, now we have nearly 5,000 in circulation. On Monday morning Mr. Mudie's house was, I am told,

---

95 R. Blake, *Disraeli* (1966), p.206. Milnes was a regular contributor on literature. Dickens, who published no novels with Longman, promised to write articles for the ER but failed to do so. (P.A.W. Collins, *Dickens and Education* (1963), p.21.)

in a state of siege. At an early hour his supply was sent in two carts. But real subscribers and representative footmen, in large numbers were there before them.

Clearly Thomas Norton, who had won Disraeli's complete trust, was as excited as the author. He had read the text himself, and he praised its 'grace and refinement': 'the atmosphere of cultivated mind and manner pervades the whole story'.[96]

The most famous Murray author, who had joined that House's galaxy of new writers, was Charles Darwin. Nevertheless, the relationship between Murray III and Darwin was more complicated than that between Thomas Norton and Disraeli and Darwin did not mention publishers in his *Autobiography*, which was published by Murray in 1887. At first Darwin had not been a favourite Murray author: he had joined their list in an unusual way, not through science but through travel, a Murray speciality. Their famous travel handbooks, which became an institution, had first begun to be produced in 1836 and in 1845 Murray bought the remaindered sheets of Darwin's *The Voyage of the Beagle* (1839) from Colburn for £150, and re-published it. It may be a sign of Murray's uneasiness that he placed the letters M.A. after Darwin's name on the title page. These seemed to add authority.

Murray was doubtful about both the content and title of *The Origin of Species* which was recommended to him by the eminent geologist Sir Charles Lyell (1797–1875), and he placed it sixth in his winter list of thirty-two books; moreover it was a lawyer friend, George Collock, not a scientist, who persuaded him to print 1,000 rather than 500 copies. In fact 1,250 were printed, priced at 15 shillings, and they were all sold a few days before publication day.[97] By the time that Darwin's more controversial *The Descent of Man* appeared in 1871, his name was known throughout the world, and within a year the book went into three editions.

Meanwhile, William Longman's greatest success, involving no uncertainties or surprises, was with Macaulay. He knew just how to handle him as an established author from the moment when Macaulay's *Lays of Ancient Rome* arrived at Paternoster Row soon after Thomas III's death. It was Thomas Norton, however, who in 1853 was approached by Matthew Arnold, who became as well-known for his prose as for his poems, when he was thirty-one years old. Arnold wrote to him after meeting him at a party to ask whether he might publish through him a volume of poems in his

---

96 The letters quoted, from Longman, and those below, are in the Hughenden Papers, now kept in the Bodleian Library. Disraeli's letters are in LA Part II 64.

97 The best account of the publication is in G. Himmelfarb, *Darwin and the Darwinian Revolution* (1959), pp.207–9, where she makes good use of G. Paston (pseudonym for E.M. Symonds), *At John Murray's* (1952). See also N. Barlow (ed.), *The Autobiography of Charles Darwin* (1958) and A. Desmond and J. Moore, *Darwin* (Penguin edn., 1991).

own name. He had already published two volumes of poems anonymously in 1849 and 1852.

'I really think that such a volume as I now propose to form would sell', Arnold told Thomas Norton characteristically, 'if brought out by you and published in my name.' He added that while Froude, not then a Longman author, had promised to review it in the *Westminster Review* and that would help sales, 'a volume of poems is a hazardous undertaking' and he would not be surprised if Longman declined to take his own poems at the publisher's risk. He would be prepared, therefore, to have it published at his own expense.

A deal was struck on Arnold's terms for 750 copies to be printed and priced at five shillings, and *Poems, A New Edition* appeared in November 1853 with a provocative preface by Arnold which has been quoted by all scholars writing about him. By a coincidence, Arnold's letter to Longman was printed in the edition of his collected letters next to a letter to Rosella Pitman, sister of Isaac Pitman, pioneer of shorthand and head of a family business whose future Longmans would take over more than a century later. A writer in the *Spectator*, Arnold noted in his preface, had claimed recently that 'the poet who would really fix the public attention must leave the exhausted past, and draw his subjects from matters of present import, and *therefore* both of interest and novelty'. This was advice that he refused to follow. Defying reviews and fellow poets alike, he insisted that 'the date of an action' 'signifies nothing'. It was 'the action itself, its selection and construction' that was 'all important'. The 'present age', about which Arnold was to say so much in prose, was so 'confused' that it was inimical to poetry.[98] Yet Arnold did not make money out of his Longman connection either with his poetry or his prose. After the House had published in 1861 *The Popular Education of France*, interesting in the comparative history of education, he wrote to his sister in December 1862 that 'we have been rather a ruined couple this last month or two owing to a horrible bill I had to pay Longmans for my French report'.[99] Arnold was by then an inspector of schools.

~

Longmans had a very special position in relation to the supply of books for elementary schools, although it faced increasing competition after the passing of the Education Act of 1870. The two main voluntary societies concerned with elementary education – the British and Foreign Bible

---

98 See S.M.B. Coulling, *Matthew Arnold's Preface: Its Origin and After*, VS, Vol. VII, March, 1964.

99 *Ibid.*, Vol. 2, p.170. In the same month, again by a coincidence, he finished an article on the highly controversial clergyman and writer, J.W. Colenso (1814–1883), a Longman author: 'the man is really such a goose that it is difficult not to say sharp things about him'.

Society, founded in 1807, which included both Anglican churchmen and Nonconformists, and the National Society, exclusively Anglican – received no government grants until 1833, and disputes between the two held back progress in the 1840s. The Secretary to the Committee of the Privy Council set up to administer the grants, James (later Sir James) Kay Shuttleworth (1804-1877), respected by Arnold, was a strenuous advocate of government action, and in 1839 inspectors appointed by the Committee of Council were asked to enquire into the funds at the disposal of schools for books, and to enumerate the books in use under specific headings reading, arithmetic, geography, English history, grammar, etymology, vocal music, linear drawing and land surveying.

No grants for books were, in fact, provided until 1847,[100] but in 1848 the House of Longman was appointed as agent to the Council for the distribution of textbooks. (Satchels were also to be provided.) Eighty-three textbooks, almost fifty of them costing less than a shilling, were subsequently scheduled, with reading lesson books accounting for forty-three and arithmetic for fourteen. Many subjects were left out, but the Committee was satisfied that the list of books and capitation grants were of assistance to school managers and teachers. There were arguments, however, first about the use of cheap Irish textbooks in English schools and second, after 1860, about the size of grants. The arguments centred not only on the size of grants, but on whether or not the government should have control over the choice of books to be used in grant-aided schools.[101]

Despite its privileged position, the House of Longman worked closely with the House of Murray, both of them being required to show great patience; and it did not help that the politician most involved, Lord John Russell, while well-known to them both, had personal links with Longman. Also involved was a Trevelyan, Sir Charles Trevelyan at the Treasury, who was to make his name with the Trevelyan/Northcote report on the Civil Service in 1854.

The case opened not with an article in the press, but with a letter, no longer extant, from Longman and Murray to Trevelyan, written in March 1848, which was followed up in December 1849 with three further letters signed by both Longman and Murray, the first of them referring explicitly to corn. The repeal of the Corn Laws in 1846 had been a main point of reference not for Murray and Longman but for their opponents in the Booksellers' Association case.[102] The Longman/Murray textbook thesis, which they now

---

100 Committee of Council, *Minutes 1847-8*, Vol. I, p.56.

101 Extract from Alec Ellis, 'Influence on the Growth of Literacy in Working Class Children' (*Phd Thesis, Liverpool 1970*). (LA Part II/33/1)

102 The basic documents are reprinted with a valuable commentary in J.M. Goldstrom, *The Correspondence between Lord John Russell and the Publishing Trade*, in PH, Vol. XX (1986), pp.5–59.

reiterated in every letter and which they believed should appeal to a Whig government, was that 'Government should act by literature as it acts by other things; that is, that it should leave the manufacture and the choice of books to private competition and the opinion of the public'.[103]

The saga went back to 1831 when an earlier Whig government, concerned about the condition of Ireland, appointed Commissioners of National Education in Ireland charged with providing day-school education at government expense for Irish children of all denominations. Looking for suitable 'integrated' textbooks, cheap in price, which would antagonise neither Protestants nor Roman Catholics, the Commissioners decided to by-pass commercial publishers and produce textbooks under their own imprint. Their initiative was so successful that when in 1847 the first government grant was made for English and Welsh schools, Kay-Shuttleworth devised his own scheme for publishing and distributing school textbooks on the same lines.

With England and Wales, not Ireland, in mind, Kay-Shuttleworth, a former Assistant Poor Law Commissioner under Edwin Chadwick, shared the Irish Commissioners' view that 'cheap and good books are absolutely essential in carrying out a great scheme of National Education. The children of the poor have not the means to purchase expensive works ...'. Quite consistently, therefore, he approved of the Dublin Commissioners going on the offensive, stating boldly that they 'regard[ed] our four thousand five hundred National Schools as *Manufactories of future Readers*'.[104]

Pondering less on a long-term acquisition of millions of new readers, willing to purchase their books, than on an immediate massive loss of trade in school books, Longman and Murray suggested to Russell from the start that 'a proceeding of this sort' (and they referred only to Ireland, and to Irish textbooks in use in England) was 'an unjust and impolitic interference with private enterprise'.[105] On this occasion, they claimed, it was the government, not the book trade, which seemed to be favouring monopoly, having used free trade, indeed laissez-faire, arguments during the late 1840s to defend itself from taking action to deal with Ireland's catastrophic famine. Russell himself had backed Trevelyan's 'Scrooge-like rhetoric' and had presented a deputation demanding state relief with a copy of Adam Smith. In October 1846 he had stated tersely that 'we

---

103 Letter of 20 Feb. 1851, reprinted *ibid.*, p.16.

104 'Statement of the Commissioners of National Education in Ireland relative to the Compilation, Printing, Publication and Sale of National School Books', 17 May 1851, quoted *ibid.*, pp.22, 29.

105 Letter of 7 Dec. 1849, reprinted *ibid.*, p.7.

cannot feed the people'.[106]

Faced with feeding the mind not the body, Russell procrastinated. He did not reply officially to Longman and Murray until May 1851, although he was in touch with Thomas Norton on other publishing matters, and he wrote now as an adjudicator between them and the Commissioners rather than as a believer in their case. He distinguished between Ireland and England and Wales. In Ireland 'were the principle of free trade invoked by you to be fully carried into effect, I think you must admit that it would be subversive of the whole system of national Education in Ireland'. In England and Wales, however, the Committee of the Council on Education, responsible for government grants, after careful deliberation, had decided neither to edit books of their own nor 'to make a store of books in the schools assisted by them'. Russell pointed out that the Council had employed Longman as their agents since 1848, being paid £1,000 for this service, and that through Longman contracts had been made with twenty-seven publishers.

Russell's was nevertheless a dubious as well as a belated adjudication, for one of the twenty-seven publishers was the Commissioners for National Education in Ireland. Russell himself admitted that a quarter of books used in England and Wales were published by them. He did, however, make one substantive concession. Books should be charged for at a competitive and not a subsidised price.[107] The adjudication was not implemented, and two years later no satisfactory agreement had been reached with the Treasury about what constituted a 'reasonable price'. This led Thomas Norton to write a letter to *The Times* on the subject in May 1853 when memories of the role of *The Times* in the Booksellers' Association case were still fresh.

It was 'utterly impossible', he claimed, for an independent person to compete with government bookselling concerns. Only competition between independent firms could reduce the price of books in the long run, and if the government was selling books to schools at a price below their costs it was defying competition. If the government was doing so for educational reasons, why not extend their 'largesse' to 'poor passengers on the road' or open bookshops under its own control? Thomas Norton took the opportunity of this letter to raise again the issue of international copyright.[108] He did not refer to the fact that the Irish textbooks were used

106 T. Hoppen, *Ireland Since 1800: Conflict and Conformity* (1989), pp.53–8, and G.L. Bernstein, 'Liberals, the Irish Famine and the Role of the State' in *Irish Historical Studies*, Vol. 29 (1995), pp.513–36.

107 Communication of 17 May 1851, reprinted in PH, Vol. XX, pp.33–5.

108 *The Times*, 26 May 1853.

in large quantities in Australia until late in the century.[109]

It was not until 1858 that the Commissioners of Education in Ireland, who still retained a large share of the books used in English and Welsh schools, terminated their book production and distribution activities, leaving the way open for the competition in educational provision that Longman and Murray had demanded in all kinds of schools.[110] This was a victory after years of struggle, but Longman, without Murray, had to return to it in the twentieth century when African governments set out to produce and distribute their own books in what seemed to Longman to be collusion with Macmillan, who in Longman perspectives were benefiting from the fact that Harold Macmillan was the British Prime Minister.[111]

~

In approaching the political economy of the mid-Victorian book trades more can probably be learnt from a study of the attitudes, publicly expressed, of Thomas Norton and William (and of Murray) towards 'free trade in books' and copyright than from the tables derived from the partners' ledgers or from the Espinasse articles in *The Critic*. When it came to determining publishing policy, a term that was not then used, letters exchanged between William and Thomas Norton and John Murray III are particularly relevant. On most issues they were on the same side.

In 1842, the year when this chapter begins, the Copyright Act, introduced, as we have noted, by Lord Mahon, was passed extending the term of copyright to forty-two years or seven years after the author's death. Thereafter, authors as much as publishers were concerned not so much with domestic as with international copyright. Indeed, in 1842 itself, on an American tour, Dickens, the author most roused by the failure of the Americans to legislate, cited Sir Walter Scott in his support as he was drawn into a deeply disturbing debate on 'piracy' which, whether he deliberately sought it or not, he could not avoid. 'Of all men living', he told a Boston audience at a banquet in 1842, 'I am the greatest loser by [the failure to secure] international copyright'.[112]

A year later, Thomas Norton wrote to *The Times* complaining of 'the damage done to literature' through the lack of controls over British books

---

109 See R. Musgrave, 'Readers in Victoria, 1851-1895' in *Paradigm*, No.26, Oct. 1998. In 1871-4 three out of four schools in Victoria still used them.

110 *Ibid.*, 6 July 1857.

111 For a retrospective assessment of the nineteenth-century struggle see H. Minns, '"Supplying a want long since felt": the Irish Lesson Books and the Promotion of Literacy for the Poor in England' (*Paradigm*, Vol. II, No.1, 2000).

112 See A. Welsh, *From Copyright to Copperfield: The identity of Dickens* (1987), Ch. 3.

published in the United States,[113] and an International Association for the Assimilation of Copyright Laws was formed to keep the subject alive.[114] It was not until 1886, however, that the first International Copyright Convention was signed at Berne. It was ratified by nine participating countries, with Britain, which sent an official representative, signing not on the spot but later in the year.[115] The United States was not a signatory, but in 1891 Congress passed a statute enabling qualified non-resident foreign authors to have their works protected under United States copyright law.

The Times is an invaluable source for the story of the campaign for further copyright reform as it is, more tendentiously, for the argument about book pricing in 1852 in which it was an interested party. Half a century later, it was to reprint its 1852 leaders and correspondence on the subject. It was four years earlier, however, during the autumn of 1848, the autumn when the first volume of Macaulay's *History* appeared, that a Booksellers' Committee (as it then called itself), set out to re-establish the rules of a Bookselling Association which had been formulated in 1828.

The Committee, representing the main metropolitan publisher-booksellers, not a group, drafted new, but basically identical, 'regulations for the guidance of the trade'.[116] It was determined to combat price-cutting of new books by a number of its members' competitors. It declared that its object was to 'entreat undersellers', book dealers who sold books at a lower price than that set by the publisher, to conform.[117] Two years later, when entreaty failed and stringent action was deemed necessary, William Longman became Chairman not only of the 'Association', as by then it called itself, but of a Committee of Nineteen, chosen to enforce price regulations.

The Committee was formed at a meeting of booksellers held in London's great Evangelical rendezvous, Exeter Hall, and well advertised in the *Publishers' Circular*.[118] William believed that he was acting in the interests of 'the general body of the trade'. 'If the Association were to exist, it should

---

113   *The Times*, 30 March 1843.

114   For the background see J.J. Barnes, *Authors, Publishers and Politicians: The Quest for an Anglo-American Copyright Agreement, 1815–1854* (1974). See also Barnes's invaluable *Free Trade in Books: a study of the London book trade since 1800* (1964); W. Briggs, *The Law of International Copyright* (1906); and Bonham-Carter, *op. cit.*

115   See Briggs, *op. cit.*, pp.234ff. and Bonham-Carter, *op. cit.*, p.230.

116   *The Times*, 30 March 1852; Bonham-Carter, *op. cit.*, p.72.

117   A letter was sent on 3 Oct. 1849 to the most prominent underselling firm, Bickers & Bush, requesting them to take up a 'ticket' and 'desist from acting in opposition to the generally expressed opinion of the trade'.

118   PC, 1 July 1850.

be carried on systematically, thoroughly, and completely, and equitably'.[119] Nevertheless, he did not relish the task. Writing later, he claimed that 'he had done his duty firmly, unselfishly, and to the very best of his ability ... at a great sacrifice of time, at a great sacrifice of convenience, at frequently, a great sacrifice of feeling'. The year 1852 when matters came to a head was not for him a year to remember.

Not everyone approved of his leadership, which was moderate in tone and tactically cautious. Indeed, John Murray III, who was at the centre of the stage with him, was said by John Blackwood to be 'disgusted'.[120] Publicity was inevitable once the publisher John Chapman reprinted in April 1852 an article in the *Westminster Review* on 'The Commerce of Literature' along with a collection of letters in *The Times* and a letter of his own, still in proof, to the *Athenaeum*. The principle at stake, he said – and *The Times* agreed with him – was 'the right of the booksellers to sell their own property on such terms as they deem most advantageous to themselves'.

A spirited *Times* leader of 30 March 1852 brought the issues involved into public view, which began not with economics but with politics:

> One of the most quiet and respectable of our national trades is seriously disturbed by commotions within its own body, and it is by no means clear to what result these differences may ultimately tend. The booksellers of the kingdom are at strife among themselves; they are united in combinations and disunited by secessions, while oppression and hardship are respectively practised and endured by those who can exert power and those who are compelled to respect it.

It may well be that this leader was influenced by Chapman. Persistent attempts had been made by other publishers to restrain publishers who felt, like Chapman, that he should not be prevented from selling books 'as cheaply as I had determined to do'.[121] Some of them were adamant. Alongside Chapman, for example, was John Cassell (1817–1865), a self-taught entrepreneur, who had launched his business in 1852 with his *Popular Educator*.

The leader-writer in *The Times*, having started in journalistic vein, found that it was impossible to continue in that vein without focusing on the economics of the book trade which he admitted was not immediately or easily intelligible to the general reader. There were, he pointed out, two groups in the book trade – 'manufacturers' and 'retailers'. The manufacturers, a term hitherto in little use, were the publishers. (There

---

119   *Daily News*, 18 May 1852.

120   Barnes, *Free Trade in Books*, p.136; *Authors, Publishers and Politicians*, p.61.

121   J. Chapman, *Cheap Books and How to Get Them* (1852), Preface. This booklet first appeared under the title 'The Commerce of Literature' in the *Westminster Review*, new series, Vol. I (1852), pp.511–54.

was no reference to wholesalers, who were to figure prominently in practice.) The retailers obtained their books from the publishers and sold them to their customers at a profit.

A book was 'a commodity which, for very obvious reasons always [came] into the market with a fixed and definite price', and the retailer's profit on it lay in the difference between the publication price which he charged and the trade price which he had paid for it. The trade price represented 'the *bona fide* cost of the whole book': it included 'the expenses of printing, binding, and so forth, together with the remuneration of the writer, and when this price [had] been paid by the retail dealer to the publishing house both publisher and writer ought to have received their fair dues as assessed by themselves'.

There followed an apparently authoritative *Times* opinion on the issue of selling price. The trade price was determined, as it had been generations earlier, by a deduction of 25 per cent from the publication price, usually increased through 'customary allowances' to 33 per cent. A book selling at 15s., therefore, would have a trade price of 10s., leaving the bookseller with a profit of 5s. He was not free to vary the prices of his books, however, as it was claimed other 'tradesmen' could do in the light of their knowledge of 'the temper' of their customers or the 'accidental character' of their business. Having paid the trade price, no flexibility was open to him: on the 15s. the most that he could do was to offer a discount of 1s. 6d. to cash customers.

The 'dictates' of the 'Amalgamated Publishers', the author went on, were 'enforced' by 'an organised system of coercion': if a bookseller objected to the system and fixed his own price, he would get no more publications to sell. And now all booksellers operating within twelve miles of the General Post Office in St Martins le Grand were being asked to pledge themselves not to sell books below the publication price (minus, if they wished, the payment-in-cash discount), and only if they did so were they to be granted a 'trade ticket' entitling them to buy further books from the publishers. Those who did not obey were under 'interdict', and their names were 'placarded throughout London'.

The Times described the system as 'imperious' and 'absolute'. It also noted as an aside that since 'the great publishing houses, which were enforcing the policy, were retailers themselves', they were making a double profit. 'We cannot discover any valid reason for this anomalous interference with the free course of competition and the natural operations of trade.' In appealing to 'the verdict of opinion', as it loved to do, *The Times* concluded that 'the remonstrant booksellers' had 'shown a very good case'. Authors were only mentioned *en passant*: 'the remonstrant booksellers' were appealing to the authors 'for the works which the publishers refused to supply'.

Longman and Murray, now operating in common cause, were provoked by *The Times* leader to reply to it immediately in a letter in which they suggested unrhetorically that before taking up the case *The*

Times should have stated that the whole question had been submitted for judgment to Lord Campbell, mentioned earlier in this volume in a quite different context,[122] and that they had promised to implement his ruling whatever it might be. There had been an error, too, they stated, in the account of events set out in the newspaper. The Association to which *The Times* had referred was not a publishers' association, 'but an association of the book trade generally', which had originated (a doubtful statement) with the retail booksellers.

'As publishers', Longman and Murray insisted, 'we are no further interested in it than so far as it has been supposed to promote the solvency of the trade and the prosperity of literary speculations.' As for the imputation of double profit, 'the sale of books by retail' was 'so insignificant a part of a publisher's business' (this was an indication of the extent to which the publisher's role had changed) that it would not determine his support of the Bookselling Association.

Authors, apparently unconsulted at first, did not figure at all in this important letter, which reveals clearly that publishers themselves were now distinguishing their own distinctive role from that of booksellers.[123] But there were 'recalcitrant' publishers besides Chapman, one of whom, Bentley, supported by the influential periodical, the *Athenaeum*,[124] split the Leviathans, immediately challenging the letter written by Longman and Murray. Bentley even went so far as to use the ugly word 'monopoly', which had been employed by Harriet Martineau in relation to publishing in an earlier period and which, thundered from the platforms, had been at the heart of the popular debate on the repeal of the Corn Laws in 1846. Moreover, Chapman focused on, rather than dismissed, the so-called double profit which accrued to Longman and Co., along with other publishers such as J.W. Parker and Hatchard, and referred to 'the wholesale book markets of Paternoster Row'.

Retail booksellers, he claimed, had not founded the Association, which was now being sharply criticised by authors, including Macaulay and Dickens as well as Tennyson and Carlyle. It was Parker, indeed, who printed a pamphlet setting out the views, hostile to the Association, of a hundred authors canvassed on the subject.[125] Some of them had met on 6 May at Chapman's office, where they carried several resolutions, including one proposed by Charles Babbage that 'the principles of free trade having now been established by experience as well as by argument ... they ought

---

122 Longman and Murray did not explain when or why they turned to Campbell.

123 *The Times*, 31 March 1852. Chapman, *loc. cit.*, appended a list of 'the opinions of certain authors' on the question.

124 See L.A. Marchand, *The Athenaeum: A Mirror of Victorian Culture* (1941).

125 *The Opinions of Certain Authors on the Bookselling Question* (1852).

to be applied to books as well as to other articles of commerce'. A further resolution proposed by Knight, so often in alliance in the past with Babbage, included a reference to the Booksellers' Association as 'tyrannical and vexatious'.[126]

The meeting knew that it had the support of W.E. Gladstone, who from the floor of the House of Commons had condemned the book trade as 'a disgrace to the present state of civilisation'. It was not possible to go further than that, and in righteous indignation the authors decided to send a deputation to meet Campbell's committee of three, which had already held one meeting of its own on 14 April. In his letter to *The Times*, one of many, Bentley stated that he had reason to believe that Campbell was 'in favour of free trade in books'.[127]

It was Murray, not William Longman, who replied to Bentley's letter, taking up at once, as he had to do, the emotive phrase 'free trade' which had acquired an aura during debates on other commodities quite different from books, including not only corn but sugar. It had been argued about fiercely during the previous decade, and it was now being proclaimed as a gospel. Small booksellers (and it was they, Murray insisted, who had created the Association) were entitled to the profits that accrued to them under the system. 'The allowance of 25 per cent has been granted by the established custom of, at least, a hundred years.' 'Experience' had shown that it was not too large 'to enable the retailer to display the authors' and publishers' wares in expensive shops, to grant long-term credit, to pay carriage, to keep clerks and porters, and above all, to speculate in the purchase of new books, with the risk of having them left on his shelves unsold.'[128]

Looking to the future of what came to be called 'resale price maintenance', an issue which was to remain alive for more than a hundred years, Murray attacked 'undersellers' who were willing to sell books at 15 or even 10 per cent profit, a margin not sufficient to keep most booksellers in business: 'they are solitary upstarts, who by this means endeavour to filch away the customers from old established houses, and thus carve out for themselves a short road to riches'. If the whole trade were to become undersellers, the result would be the destruction of 'some one hundred existing houses, and the substitution of eight or ten master monopolists, and a very serious disturbance to literature in general'.

---

126 There is an excellent brief summary of the events in H.G. Merriam, *Edward Moxon, Publisher of Poets* (1939), pp.105–9. Moxon aligned himself with Chapman and the 'free traders', although he had been involved in a legal case, subsequently settled out of court, concerning the sale by a London bookseller of a printed edition of his most steadily lucrative book, *Haydn's Dictionary of Dates*. Chapman himself specialised in the sale of American books.

127 *The Times*, 1 April 1852.

128 *Ibid.*, 2 April 1852.

The phrase 'literature in general' recalled the toasts proposed at banquets. The publishers were anxious to appear, at least, to transcend 'interest'. Cultural issues were invoked, similar to those figuring in George Eliot's novels. For William Longman and his closest allies 'the bookselling system' of England (Scotland, with its different history, was not usually brought in) was 'the growth of ages', linking a number of 'beneficent institutions': for *The Times* it was 'an antiquated system' demanding reform, a system under 'the stifling control of a "select" number of monopolists'. And 'the public' was (rhetorically) asked to judge whether 'its own vital interests in literature' should be left to the 'select'. They had appealed to 'an umpire': 'lovers of literature' should be allowed to make up their own minds.[129]

The highly visible and articulate undersellers, Bickers and Bush, who handled Chapman's *Cheap Books and How to Get Them*, replied to Murray, while another 'publisher', anonymous, extended the line taken by Murray and Longman, putting cogently the case for continued retail price maintenance in books much as it would be put during the 1980s. Macmillan played little part in the bookselling argument of the 1850s.[130] Yet, as has been noted, it was a Macmillan, Frederick, and not a Longman, who at the end of the century led the attack on discount selling in the trade and who engineered the Net Book Agreement of 1899.

Meanwhile, in 1852 Murray and Longman, bound by their own promise to accept Campbell's ruling, had to disband their Association after Campbell had concluded after a second meeting that the 'regulations' that it was seeking to impose were '*prima facie* ... indefensible and contrary to the freedom which ought to prevail in commercial transactions'. The other two arbitrators concurred. They were George Grote, prominent Benthamite and historian (and an opponent in Parliament of Talfourd's copyright bills) and H.H. Milman, Dean of St. Paul's, author of many books including a *History of the Jews* (1830) and a *History of Christianity under the Empire* (1840). He was also an editor of Gibbon.[131]

As a result of the adjudicators' ruling the Booksellers Committee resigned, and although a new committee was set up to consider co-operation within the trade, it could not recommend any alternative so that the Association ceased to exist also. Underselling continued, and it was of little consolation to Longman and Murray that the publisher Chapman, who, for all his belief in 'the commerce of literature', went bankrupt in 1854.

---

129 *Ibid.*, 30 March 1852.

130 *Ibid.*, 9, 14 April 1852.

131 A. Milman, *Henry Hart Milman, DD, Dean of St Paul's, A Biographical Sketch* (1900). His monument in St Paul's bore the words *Pastor, Poeta, Historicus, Theologos*. Like William, he was anxious to 'decorate and complete' the interior of St Paul's.

When the issue of underselling became the focus of attention forty years later during the 1890s Frederick Macmillan wrote to a different Thomas Norton, Thomas Norton IV's son, giving his views on what had happened in 1852. His response to a bundle of old newspaper cuttings which Longman had shown him was 'the narrow-minded and selfish position taken up by Campbell and the other authors to whom this matter was referred for arbitration'. 'They appear to have got into their heads that the destruction of the Booksellers' Association and the introduction of unrestricted underselling would result in a pecuniary benefit to themselves [as authors], and they, therefore, took the side of the underseller and contemplated with equanimity the ruin of a large number of undersellers.'

Campbell and 'his friends' had supported their position, he concluded, by 'a number of platitudes which were really quite inapplicable'.[132] He appended a cutting from the *Illustrated London News* which quoted verbatim the then Thomas Norton's closing words before leaving Campbell, Milman and Grote to adjudicate: 'A fixed price for all books, settled by the author and the publisher is desirable for the sake of the public, is essential to the respectability of the trade and conducive to the general interests of literature.' There was a ring about this sentence that was worthy of Frederick Macmillan's father, Daniel.

~

The business of J.W. Parker (1792–1870), who figured prominently in the debates about free trade in books, and who wrote to *The Times* as late as 2 April 1852, dealing with the double-profit argument, raised against publishers, was taken over by Longman in April 1863, the most important take-over of the mid-Victorian years. Parker had had an interesting life. He had been apprenticed to the printer William Clowes, whose pioneering new technology, as we have seen, fascinated contemporaries, but he was no pioneer himself and failed to become a Clowes partner. Instead, he set up business on his own, selling bibles and prayer books published by the Cambridge University Press, and in an independent capacity became the editor of a respectable penny magazine, very different from those described by Wilkie Collins. *The Saturday Magazine* was sponsored by the Society for Promoting Christian Knowledge (SPCK).

A catalogue of books sold by him and their prices included *Cautions for the Times* (3rd edition), *Chance and Choice* and *Essays Written in the Intervals of Business*. No authors' names were given for these titles. There were many famous names, however, among them Charles Kingsley (several books including the novel *Yeast*, a book of poems, a play and five volumes of sermons). Hullah's *History of Modern Music* was on the list, price

*A Record of the Black Prince,*1848 by Henry Noel Humphreys (1807–1859). Longman joined the fashion for elaborate bindings, this one was made of papier mâché and plaster, to resemble carved wood

Longman Archive

---

132   Letter of Frederick Macmillan to Thomas Norton Longman V, 6 June 1894.

4s. 7d. placed immediately before Humboldt's *Life and Travels*, price 1s. 9d. *The Transactions of the Social Science Association* constituted an impressive collection of papers, many of them highly influential.

Among the Longman acquisitions from Parker in 1863 was *Fraser's Magazine*, very different in tone and content from what it had been during the exciting early years after its launching in 1832. Between 1860 and 1867, however, under the editorship of J.A. Froude, it remained as influential as it had been earlier: this was because of the quality of its literary and historical articles. Froude, whose early autobiographical work, *Nemesis of Faith* (1849), had created something of a furore for its candid description of his own part in the Oxford Movement, was in the course of writing his twelve-volume *History of England from the Fall of Wolsey to the Defeat of the Spanish Armada* when the Parker take-over took place. He considered Parker as a 'dear and kind friend', and described his dining room as 'the gathering place of all the clients of the House. Men already famous were to be met there … all good to me, and through them I was introduced to the literary world.' [133] Within that world, his close friend Thomas Carlyle was at the centre, and on Carlyle's death in 1881 Froude became his sole literary executor.

Another Parker author taken over by Longmans in 1863 was Henry Thomas Buckle (1821–1862), a very different kind of historian from Froude (or Macaulay or Carlyle). The idea of writing a *History of Civilization in England* had occurred to Buckle when he was in his late teens, but it was not until 1857 that the first volume of his book with this title, eight hundred pages long, appeared, printed at his own expense, since Parker did not offer him satisfactory terms for future volumes or editions. 'Should the book fail', Buckle told him, 'you will, of course, not be bound to continue your connexion with me after the first edition; and, if on the other hand, it should succeed, it will be for your interest and mine that the connexion should be a permanent one.'

Buckle wanted his book 'to get among the mechanics' institutes and the people', declaring that he would rather be praised 'in popular … vulgar papers than in scholarly publications'.[134] At once, however, he became a celebrity when his ambitious *History* appeared. Darwin was one of his greatest admirers: Chekhov referred to him by name in *The Cherry Orchard*. There were many foreign translations. A second volume appeared in 1861, but the work was far from complete when Buckle died in Damascus in 1862. (On his gravestone the Arabic inscription read 'The writer is resting under the earth, but his works endure.') A third volume was published posthumously by Longmans in 1872.

---

133 Quoted in W.H. Dunn, *James Anthony Froude, A Biography*, Vol. I (1961), pp.175, 199.

134 G. St Aubyn, *A Victorian Eminence* (1958), p.13.

The idea that Buckle's commonplace books should also be published by them was turned down, although it won the support of Mill and his stepdaughter, Helen Taylor, who worked with Buckle while also watching over Mill's posthumous *Autobiography* as it was going through the press.[135] She had edited the three-volume edition of the *Miscellaneous and Posthumous Works of Henry Thomas Buckle* which appeared in 1872. Longmans Green was to produce a three-volume edition of Buckle's *History of Civilization* in 1899.

W.E.H. Lecky (1838–1903), another historian who joined the Longmans list through Parker, had very different opinions of Buckle from those of Mill or Helen Taylor. So too had Froude, who disapproved even of the concept of a one-man history of civilisation, as did the *Edinburgh Review*: Lecky, while realising Buckle's limitations, admired him.[136] Longmans went on to produce many books by Lecky, including one volume of poems and, after his death, *Historical and Political Essays* (1908), which included essays on Reeve, on 'Queen Victoria as a Moral Force', on 'Old-Age Pensions', a topic which gained in importance during the last years of the nineteenth century, and on 'Ireland in the Light of History', a topic at the centre of British politics then as now. In the same year, sustaining its continuing interest in history of all kinds, Longmans Green also published a young J.L. Hammond's magisterial work *Gladstone and the Irish Nation*.

William Longman, who set out to publish readable history, the quality that he prized most in Macaulay, liked to think of himself as an historian, and in 1859, four years before the acquisition of Parker, he published one of a series of lectures on the history of England which he gave at Chorleywood, Hertfordshire. He then lived near to a Chartist settlement there, and his audience consisted of the members of a mutual improvement society, the kind of audience that Samuel Smiles had addressed in the Leeds of the 1840s and that he recalled in *Self-Help* (1859).

This and other lectures of William's were collected in 1863 in a single volume of nearly five hundred pages entitled *History of England to the Close of the Reign of Edward II*; and, having continued his researches, William went on to publish a two-volume *History of the Life and Times of Edward III* in 1869. 'I trust authors will forgive me and not revenge themselves by turning publishers', he explained. 'There is, nevertheless, some advantage in a publisher dabbling in literature, for it shows him the difficulties with which a publisher has to contend ... and ... increases the sympathy which

---

135 *Ibid.*, p.102.

136 J.A. Froude, *Short Studies on Great Subjects*, Vol. I (1894), pp.1–21: *A Memoir of W.E.H. Lecky by his Wife* (1909). For changes in Lecky's views see the chapter on Lecky by C.F. Mullett in H. Ausubel, J.B. Brebner and E.M. Hunt (eds.), *Some Modern Historians of Britain* (1951).

should and in these days does exist between author and publisher.'[137]

~

'Dabbling in literature' was a very different activity from being committed to religion, and the Parker take-over added theologians as well as historians and essayists to the Longman list, including the second editions of Dean Trench's *Commentary on the Epistles to the Seven Churches of Asia* and *Sermons Preached in Westminster Abbey* and Bishop Coplestone's *Remains*, edited by the Archbishop of Dublin. There were to be far more Longman theologians, however, after the acquisition of Rivington in 1890.[138] William Longman himself had religious as well as historical preoccupations. For example, he was closely associated with St. Paul's Cathedral, the first of the Longmans to be so, and he served as Chairman of its Finance Committee for many years. Like other eminent Victorians, he wanted, however dubiously, to improve the ecclesiastical premises for which he was responsible as a businessman. Sir Christopher Wren, also for the first time, was treated with only qualified deference: a new marble reredos, a new pulpit and new stained-glass windows were introduced into the Cathedral, following schemes set out by William in his book, *A History of the Three Cathedrals dedicated to St. Paul in London from the Sixth Century to the Proposals for the Adornment of the Present Cathedral.*

Many of the so-called 'improvements' were to be destroyed during the London Blitz of the Second World War, when Wren's cathedral was saved, it seemed miraculously, unlike the Longman premises in Paternoster Row. There were, of course, many nineteenth-century established Longman authors writing books on theology before 1863. In 1855, for example, Longmans published two books by the Revd. James Taylor, then headmaster of Wakefield Grammar School, one on *The True Doctrine of the Holy Eucharist* and *A Summary of the evidence of the existence of the Deity.* Both were staunchly Protestant, the latter affirming with complete confidence that 'the God of Revelation is identical with the Deity of Nature'.[139]

Parker was also the publisher in 1860 of a highly controversial religious book with a non-committal title, *Essays and Reviews*, which, coming as it did so quickly after Darwin's *Origin of Species*, had what was described as a 'sensational' impact.[140] When its seven authors, all writing from within the Church of England, were condemned in both Houses of Convocation

---

137 Quoted in Curwen, *op. cit.,* pp.108–9. Also see 'A study of Henry Noel Humphreys' (1807–1879) author and designer, by Howard Leathlen is included in *The Book Collector* Vol. 18, No. 2, 1989.

138 See below, p.311.

139 *Notes on Books,* May 1855, pp.7–8.

140 See I. Ellis, *Seven Against Christ* (1980).

for their contributions to the volume, two of them were prosecuted in the ecclesiastical Court of Arches and suspended from their offices for a year. Fortunately for them, after appeal to the Privy Council the judgment was reversed by the Lord Chancellor. This was not the only occasion when there was disagreement between ecclesiastical and secular tribunals.

One contributor to *Essays and Reviews*, Frederick Temple, Headmaster of Rugby, was a future Archbishop of Canterbury. Another was Benjamin Jowett, a future Master of Balliol College, Oxford, as renowned for his social contacts – and his views on education – as for his theology.[141] The authors were all seeking, albeit in different ways, to interpret Biblical texts in a critical fashion, and appealed to a new generation removed from the direct experiences of the early Oxford Movement. For Lecky the publication of *Essays and Reviews* was less the launching of a sensational book than an inspiration for a 'great enlargement of the range of permissible opinions on religious subjects'.[142]

The Longmans became used to sensational controversy themselves as a result of the so-called 'Colenso case', and Lecky mentioned John William Colenso, too, in his study of the history of liberal thought. Born in 1814, Colenso had been appointed to his first living in 1846, and nine years later was named Bishop of Natal. He was a Longman author, although most of the books he had written for the House were on mathematics, not theology. (The liberal theologian F.D. Maurice said of him that his idea of history (he did not say theology) was that it was a branch of arithmetic.[143]) Colenso maintained that the books of the Bible assembled as the *Pentateuch* could not have been in their entirety the work of Moses, for the books were riddled with inconsistencies, and he was daring enough during the debates on *Essays and Reviews* to describe the *Pentateuch* as 'a series of fables – at the most legends – about as reliable as Tennyson's account of the days of the Court of King Arthur'.[144]

When he was appointed to his bishopric in South Africa, Colenso sold all his copyrights to Longman for £2,400, a sum sufficient to pay off his accumulated debts. 'Like Peter in the prison', he wrote, 'my bonds have literally dropped off.' The happiness was short-lived, however, for he ran into immediate ecclesiastical difficulties. Robert Gray, the Tractarian Bishop of

141   See B. Willey, *More Nineteenth Century Studies* (1956), Ch. IV.

142   W.E.H. Lecky, *Democracy and Liberty*, Vol. I (1896), pp.424–5.

143   Quoted in A.O.J. Cockshut, *Religious Controversies of the Nineteenth Century: selected documents* (Johannesburg, 1966), p.217. See also his *Anglican Attitudes: A Study of Victorian religious controversies* (1959) and G. Parsons (ed.), *Religion in Victorian Britain*, 4 vols. (1988).

144   Quoted in J. Guy, *The Heretic: A study of the life of John William Colenso, 1814–1883* (1983).

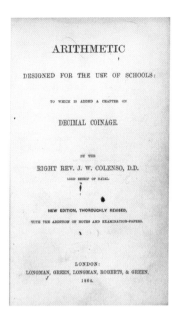

Arithmetic designed for the use of schools to which is added a chapter on Decimal Coinage by the highly controversial bishop, Colenso. New edition 1864

BL 8504.aaaa.33

Cape Town since 1847, who had been appointed Metropolitan of Africa in the year of Colenso's arrival, regarded him as a menace, and eventually deposed him from his see on grounds of heresy in 1863.[145] Colenso, a fighter for his opinions, appealed to the Privy Council which decided in his favour in 1865: his dismissal was deemed illegal. He returned to Natal, therefore, and, although excommunicated by Gray, he continued to preach and publish his views until his death in 1883.

His mathematics books continued to sell when the controversy was at its height. Thus, no fewer than 12,250 copies of his book *The Student's Algebra* were printed in 1853 and another 19,500 in 1856. His views could be controversial even when he was writing as a mathematician. Thus, his *Arithmetic Designed for the Use of Schools* (1862) included a chapter on decimal coinage, which he consistently advocated. His later books included *A Shilling Arithmetic*, which appeared in 1874, and a new edition of *The Student's Algebra* (1878). Meanwhile, his theological works, published by Longmans, in the form of *Lectures*, sold well too, although Longmans demanded amendments when the second and third *Lectures* appeared in 1876. To accept them, Colenso responded, would 'vitiate the whole purpose of his book', and when he offered them a final volume in 1879 he was told that he would have to cover the whole publishing cost himself.[146] Five years later, he produced a *Zulu-English Dictionary*, and in the last years of his life he became as deeply and controversially involved in South African politics as in Old Testament religion.

~

Within a year of the Parker take-over, William had become an active agent in a very different kind of religious controversy. It involved his friend Kingsley, and J.H. Newman, who had been received into the Roman Catholic Church in 1845 and was to become a cardinal in 1879, but in this case William was on the opposite side both to Kingsley and Froude, both of whom had been Longman neighbours as well as Parker authors. After Kingsley had attacked Newman on the grounds of religious casuistry in the pages of *Macmillan's Magazine*, it was to William Longman that a shocked Newman turned for guidance. He contemplated a published response to the charge that he had maintained that 'truth for its own sake need not, and on the whole ought not to be a virtue with the Roman clergy'.

He and William had already been in communication about the publishing implications of Newman's plans for a Roman Catholic

---

145 G.W. Cox, *The Life of John William Colenso* (1888), Vol. I, p.47.

146 Quoted in Guy, *op.cit.*, pp.119, 160. Long before, in 1748, T. Longman and J. Shewell had published along with others, including Rivington, *A Critical and Practical Exposition of the Pentateuch, with notes theological, moral, philosophical, critical and historical.*

University in Ireland of which Newman was Rector,[147] and in 1859 he wanted Longmans, not Burns, another of his publishers – and a Roman Catholic – to publish a new quarterly *The Rambler*, an old Johnson title, with which he was associated. This, he believed, would give it a more 'secular character': 'the less it is theological the better'.[148] At the same time, he intended to offer the copyright of a new English version of Holy Scripture not to a Roman Catholic publisher but to 'the market'.

Newman was a skilled bargainer in his dealings with publishers, choosing which one was the best to approach in any particular situation, and in 1864 he concluded that William Longman was the right publisher to print and distribute two pamphlets in reply to Kingsley and went on to ask William sensible questions about how many copies to print and in what typeface.[149] He was also interested in the destination of review copies. When he wrote his *Apologia* under intense internal pressure in the same year he found that William entirely approved of his plan of publication. 'People wouldn't read a long book.' Nor did they want to wait long to read this particular book. Eight years later he was to write to William that he was glad to learn that 'the *Apologia* still sells, and justifies your recommendation to me, on the second edition, to have it stereotyped. You have taken a great interest in it from the first.'[150]

There was a sequel to the story after Newman had become a cardinal. He carried on a confidential correspondence, amicable throughout, with Charles James Longman about the possibility of Longman paying him a lump sum for all his copyrights. Murray had shown no interest: CJ did. But after he had made careful calculations, offering £2,500 to £3,000, he did not consider it possible to reach an agreement.[151] Later, however, he changed his mind and agreement was reached in 1885. Newman's biographers have shown little interest in this story, but it adds considerably to our knowledge

---

147 C.R. Dessain (ed.), *The Letters and Diaries of John Henry Newman*, Vol. XVII (1967), p.363. For Newman's views on universities see the 1957 version of *The Idea of a University*, published by Longmans Green, and edited by C.F. Harrold. See also F. McGrath, SJ, *Newman's University, Idea and Reality* (1951), also published by Longmans, Green. Longman's interest in Newman extended over a century.

148 Letter of 6 July 1859 in Dessain, *op. cit.*, Vol. XIX (1969). A month earlier, Newman had described his own work as writing. 'I have been writing from morning to night now for ten weeks, or rather months – and my fingers are a-weary, a-weary – and won't make letters.' (*Ibid.*, p.156.)

149 Letter of 30 Jan. 1864, *ibid.*, Vol. XXI (1971), p.33.

150 Letter of 6 July 1872, *ibid.*, Vol. XXVI (1974), p.132.

151 *Ibid.*, Vol. XXX (1976), p.377.

of Newman as a person as well as an apologist or, indeed, as a cardinal.[152] He was negotiating precisely at the time when authors' terms, including royalties, a relatively new mode of payment, were being standardised.

Longmans, winning Newman's complete confidence, went on to publish most of his works, including some of his early works, written before he became a Roman Catholic. 'I find the great London houses', Newman told a friend in 1882, 'are shy, except Longman, of printing the work of a Catholic.'[153] 'They are fair and upright', he told another friend in 1884, 'I don't like a competition with other firms, it would involve the principle of speculation.'[154] After Newman's death Longmans led the way by publishing in 1891 Anne Mozley's two-volume edition of *The Letters and Correspondence of John Henry Newman during his Life in the English Church*, with a brief autobiography. These were the years Newman had covered in his *Apologia*. By a coincidence a publishing merger with Rivington added to the list of Newman titles in the Longman catalogues in the very year of Newman's death. Different Longmans were then in charge.

~

House routines were very much the same, however, as they had been in 1864, and they were followed, it seems, without question, by partners and by staff. Fortunately there are reasonably good records relating both to partners (and the incomes they received from the business) and to clerks, among whom there was an average annual intake of around six. The personal qualities of the partners were well-known outside as well as inside the business. Those of the clerks rest on revealing marginal notes: one could be described as 'a dry old fish' (1848), another as 'a fast dog' (1855) and a third as 'a disagreeable little beast' (1861). To the end of 1850 all entries were set out alphabetically, though no dates of birth were listed. Thereafter, comments seem to have been restricted to clerks with particular problems or of particular interest because of their subsequent careers.

Incomplete figures of arrivals and departures from Paternoster Row from 1851 to 1860 and from 1871 to 1879 suggest that in the first of these periods seventy-six new staff were appointed and in the second, a year shorter in length, fifty-two. In the first period thirteen of these left within a year, in the second eleven. One stayed on until 1916, and one of the partners till 1938. There was a similar pattern in the 1860s when fifty new staff were appointed in the years from 1861 to 1870, with 1865 a peak year (see table).

Four of the people registered in the table died in the service of

---

152 In his meticulous book *John Henry Newman: A Biography* (1988) Ian Kerr makes no mention of publishing.

153 Dessain, *op. cit.*, Vol. XXX (1976), p.69.

154 *Ibid.*, p.363.

the House: only one left on grounds of ill health. Several migrated to Australia, New Zealand, America and South Africa, particularly the first two countries. One 'turned farmer', another 'turned parson'. One man in 1875 was 'discharged in disgrace' on 29 April, 'much too fast'. Some stole cash, one stole stamps from partners' desks. One was said to be 'out of his time'. One man who joined in 1878, W.H. Peet (1849–1916), was in charge of advertising, the publication of *Notes and Queries*, and partners' archives. He was respected for his learning as much as for his diligence and, not

Staff Arrivals and Departures, 1871–79

YEAR	NEW ARRIVALS	LEFT IN THE SAME YEAR	TERMINAL DATE OF LONGEST STAYING STAFF
1871	8	1	1886
1872	9	3	1906
1873	No record		
1874	7	1	1934
1875	6	1	1938
1876	6	2	1894
1877	8	-	1919
1878	2	-	1916
1879	6	2	1883

Partners' Shares, 1867, 1876 and 1879

PARTNER	1867	1876	1879
Thomas Longman	£52,082 18s. 2d	£72,885 2s. 3d	£79,113 8s. 1d
William Longman	£67,737 19s. 4d	£66,546 5s. 11d	£5,960 18s. 7d*
William E. Green	£2,180 14s. 10d	£36,652 7s. 0d	£43,797 2s. 8d
Thomas Reader	£64 17s. 0d	£10,105 10s. 9d	£13,560 4s. 10d
Robert Dyer	£500 0s. 0d	£9,501 14s. 8d	£10,309 3s. 1d
Bevis E. Green	£44,313 7s. 7d	-	-
T. Norton Longman	-	£5,119 7s. 4d	£8,362 4s. 0d
C.J. Longman	-	-	£47,980 8s. 4d

* To executors

'Elf and Owls', an illustration
by Richard Doyle from *In Fairy
Land* by William Allingham,
published by Longmans in
1870. Children's books were
not a large part of Longmans
publishing but this was a good
example of the innovative
nature of illustration at that
time. Edmund Evans, the
engraver, used a number of
wood blocks to create the
illustrations

Bodleian Library, University of Oxford:
[Johnson b.145]

least, for his loyalty.[155]

The reputation of the Partners was not subject to such comment. Yet details were collected of their share in Company profits as recorded in the Partners' Ledger Books which reveal the relative holdings of the five Partners. The accounts were signed by Thomas Longman IV, William Longman, William E. Grcen, Thomas Reader and Robert Dyer. The figures for 1867, 1876 and 1879 are set out in the table on page 277. Given that in each year incomes were offset by 'contra items' and that there were small additional allowances not included in the table, the figures must, therefore, be used with caution.

What is clear from the table, however interpreted, is the dominance of the Longman family interest in the finances of the House. Undoubtedly until his death in 1879 Thomas Norton as the senior Partner was in an extremely strong financial position, although the changes consequent on the deaths of Partners make it difficult to interpret differences from year to year.

Authors shared in the success of the House. During the 1850s and 1860s, when the royalty system of payment was beginning to take over, nearly two-thirds of the House's outlay was on books in which authors shared in the profits. In 1858, for example, of the total outlay on books with a Longman copyright, £47,720, £26,451 was spent on books for which the profits were shared between authors and publishers. By then only £871 was spent on consortia books in which Longmans had a share.[156]

~

The variety of mid-Victorian and late-Victorian publishers' booklists, not only of textbooks, but of books of all kinds, including novels and poems, reveals, to take only Longman, Parker and Murray as examples, the degree of competition within an annual (and by now seasonal) pattern of production, in which, along with Christmas, the start of the school year figured more prominently than it had done in the past. Consortia had little place in the calendar.

Some of the most illuminating individual lists were printed in the back pages of other volumes, and while such pages now tend to survive as

155 'A list of the Names of the Partners and Clerks at Paternoster Row [early names missing] from 1793'. The names were kept by John Lund, head of the Binding Department, and by his successors J. Culliford, Isaac Tyler (until his retirement in 1891), and Robert Taylor. (LA)

156 See C. Blagden, 'Publishing: a historical survey' in *National Provincial Bank Review*, Nov.1960, p.15.

they did not always before the advent of bookbinding, they have seldom been compared in detail by historians of the book. They bear the same relationship to nineteenth-century books as trailers do to twenty-first century radio and television programmes. Their purpose was practical – to provide information to possible readers, including information about prices – not to stimulate, years later, analysis of book-trade trends and the extent of competition within it; but there was not usually a statistical base for what discussion there was at the time, given that statistics, not always consistent, were regularly set out in the *Publishers' Circular* and in other sources, notably *Bent's Monthly Library Advertiser (1802–42)* and *The Bookseller* (for different runs of dates).

The Bookseller, a new monthly, owned by the Whitaker family, was from the start in rivalry with the *Publishers' Circular*, on 25 May 1858, stating its intention 'to supply book-buyers with a complete list of books published or announced during the month, whether issued in Great Britain, the United States or Canada, or on the Continent'. It took over immediately *Bent's Monthly Literary Advertiser (1829–60)*.

The statistics have been subjected to careful analysis following the compilation and publication of the ESTC[157] and the unfolding of a four-year research project, 'Productivity and Profit: a quantitative survey of publishing and authorship, 1830–1939.[158] Simon Eliot has been a pioneer in this field, following initial research on Walter Besant and authorship, revealing how different categories of books, including price as well as subject categories, fared differently at different times. The Survey, which examined changing costs and prices, identified trends,[159] but, to add to the difficulties problems of interpretation arose from the fact that what was included in categories of publications sometimes changed as did the categories themselves. The sources were not always consistent.

What the categories were and what was included in them changed even in the classified lists of books advertised at the end of most published books. In 1877 Longmans separated their lists into no fewer than seventeen categories, which were listed alphabetically at the head of the list, not in the

Thomas Norton IV (1804–1879), portrait painted by W. Reader, in 1879

Thomas IV had joined the partnership in 1832 and became head of the firm when his father died in 1842. He took an especial interest in the *Edinburgh Review*, which Longmans had wholly owned since 1826, and he had particular connections with Macaulay, and Tom Moore

Pearson Education

---

157 See PH, Vol. XXXII (1992), pp.63–6.

158 *Ibid.*, Vol. XXIX (1991), pp.75–6. See also *Book Trade History Group Newsletter*, Jan. 1991.

159 See S. Eliot, 'Some Trends in British Book Production', in J.D. Jordan and R.L. Patton (eds.), *Literature and the Marketplace* (1995), pp.19–43.

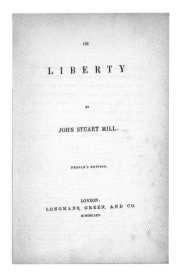

Frontispiece of *On Liberty* showing publication by Longmans, Green & Co in the 'People's edition, 1865'

Longman Archive

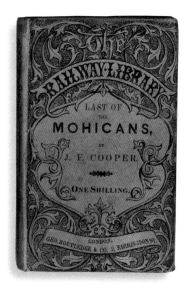

Cheap editions published for the railway traveller; from 1850 onwards Routledge's *Railway Library*, for example, published over forty titles

Bodleian Library, University of Oxford: John Carter Collection

order of the categories listed beneath. Thus, 'Arts, Manufactures &c' came first at the head of the list and not 'History, Politics, Historical Memoirs &c' which figured first in the list itself. 'Mental and Political Philosophy' came second, and 'Miscellaneous and Critical Works' third.

'Historical Knowledge for the Young' was the very last, somewhat surprising, category. It was related to other forms of 'knowledge', and, it was urged, it required to be kept up-to-date. Some titles were described, therefore, as 'in preparation', and not all appeared in the lists. This was even more true of the books announced by the Oxford University Press, whose Clarendon Press Series, announced in 1863, became 'the most heterogeneous series imaginable, divisible eventually into twelve sections', ranging from first 'reading books' to *Irregular Greek Verbs*.[160]

There was no separate section in the 1877 Longman list for works on ancient history or the classics, although a page was devoted to 'ancient historical epochs' opposite the first page of the general list. In that list *The Politics of Aristotle* and his *Ethics* were placed in a 'Mental and Political Philosophy' section which also included Bacon's *Essays* and John Stuart Mill's *On Liberty*. More than a quarter of a century earlier, in 1850, the classical list had included a widely read *Critical History of the Language and Literature of Ancient Greece* by William Mure.

Among the various categories, one genre which remained a staple throughout the period covered in this chapter, as it was to do in the next, was travel literature, which figured eleventh ('Travel, Voyages, &c') in the 1877 Longman list. In 1851, the year of the Great Exhibition, where Longman books were on display, Longmans had launched a *Travellers' Library*, following in the wake of George Routledge (1812–1888). who had begun, like Tegg, by selling remainders, but who in 1848 had launched a *Railway Library*, which offered books of 'valuable information and acknowledged merit': costing a shilling, they were 'in a form adapted for reading while travelling, and also of a character that will render them worthy of preservation'.[161]

The 'railway book' was not necessarily something to be left in the carriage or thrown away, although Bagehot, referring to 'the casual character of contemporary literature', described everything about it as 'temporary and fragmentary'. 'Look at a railway stall; you see books of

---

160 Sutcliffe, *op. cit.*, p.23. No titles appeared until 1866. The first 250 copies of the first of them, A.W. Williamson's *Chemistry for Students*, appeared with fly leaves at the end advertising Macmillan's 'private books'. These were cancelled in later copies and Macmillan was told by the Delegates of the Press not to repeat the practice.

161 For Routledge see F.A. Mumby, *The House of Routledge 1834–1934* (1934), p.141. For a brief reference to other railway libraries see J. Simmons, *The Victorian Railway* (1991), p.246.

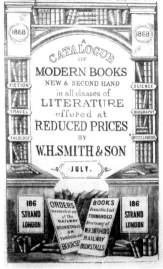

Smith's Station Bookstall at Blackpool North Railway Station in 1896. Punch wrote that 'Messrs Bentley, and Colburn, and Newby will rejoice at this new opening for novels, which had never been connected with railways before, in any other capacity but that of sleepers.'

BL 8054-01

Cover of W.H Smith's catalogue, July 1868

Bodleian Library, University of Oxford: John Johnson Collection

every colour, blue, yellow, crimson ... in every style ... but all small. People take their literature in morsels, as they take sandwiches on a journey. The volumes, at least, you can see clearly, are not intended to be everlasting.'[162]

This was scarcely true of the volumes in the Longman series, each of which cost 2s. 6d. The first volume was *Macaulay's Essays*, and there were two volumes of selections of Sydney Smith's writings. Yet a wide range of travel writings also figured in the first ten, among them *Travels in Tartary and Thibet* (sic) and *African Wanderings*. Less exotic was an anonymously written number sixteen, *Our Coal-fields and Our Coal-Pits*. Another title was *The Electric Telegraph*. So also was *Vestiges of the Natural History of Creation* of 1842, the controversial pre-Darwinian book by Robert Chambers, which had subsequently gone through many editions at various prices.

Longman's *Travellers' Library* was less successful and less comprehensive than Routledge's *Railway Library*, which remained in existence for fifty years and published no fewer than 1,300 titles. Bentley's *Railroad Library*, however, lasted for only three years. If not all the books sold at the new station bookstalls were ephemeral, the most publicised of which, not surprisingly, were those published by W.H. Smith, neither were they all inexpensive: the third and fourth editions of Macaulay's *History of England* were said to have been 'cried up and down the platform at York, like a second edition of *The Times*', when they were newly published, and they then cost thirty-six shillings. Smith had secured his first railway contract to open a bookstall at Euston Station in 1848, and when the first volumes of Longman's *Travellers' Library* first appeared he operated thirty-

---

162 W. Bagehot, 'The First Edinburgh Reviewers', in the *National Review*, Oct. 1855.

five bookstalls. By 1880 he was in charge of 450.[163]

The Longman books read by railway travellers might well include some that did not figure in the Railway Library, but rather dwelt on travel, not usually by trains, to far-off exotic places. The most exciting of them were written by Sir Richard Francis Burton (1821–1890), as valued a Longman author as he was a mysterious and disturbing figure to the Victorian public. In 1855 he 'entrusted' to the House his *Personal Narrative of a Pilgrimage to El Medinah and Mecca* which described how, disguised as a Persian prince, he had embarked at Southampton and how in that disguise he had spent a period in Egypt before proceeding on his pilgrimage.

In the following year Longman published his *First Footsteps in East Africa* in which he described his journey into the interior of the Somali country, reaching Harar, the Somali capital, far less well known to the world than Mecca, which had never before been 'entered by a white man'. Two illustrated volumes of his *The Lake Regions of Central Africa* appeared in 1860, but Longman did not publish *The Kasidah of Haji Abdu-el-Yedzi*, a pseudonym, or Burton's translations of the *Arabian Nights*, a fearlessly explicit version of an old Longman standby.[164] When Burton died, his wife, a Roman Catholic, burnt his last erotic book *The Secret Garden*, 'sorrowfully' and 'reverently', along with his journals. Burton continued to be read long after his death in 1890, and was to be reprinted in a great variety of editions by other publishers.

The Falls, Lakes and Mountains of North Wales ... with illustrations by Thomas and Edward Gilks, from original sketches by D H M'Kewan, by Louisa Costello, Longman, 1845

This kind of travellers' book was published by Longman and other publishers; they included pictures as well as, often, a map

Personal Collection

The travel book that appealed most to the Longman family, however, and to a surprisingly large number of Longman readers, was Lady (Annie) Brassey's *A Voyage in the Sunbeam* (1878). That was the name of a steam yacht, bought and owned by Lord Brassey, son of the great Victorian contractor, one of whose main achievements was managing the building of railways in distant parts of the world. Annie was the first woman (or man) to circumnavigate the world by steam yacht. On her last voyage she contracted malaria en route for Mauritius and died in 1887 at the

---

163 C. Wilson, *First with the News: The History of W.H. Smith, 1792–1972* (1985), p.182.

164 See above, p.67.

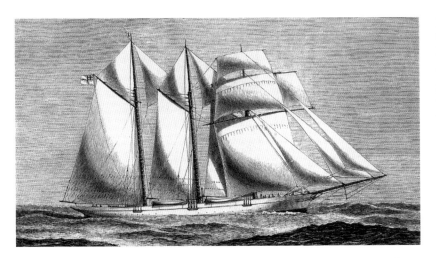

Frontispiece to *A Voyage in the Sunbeam*, by Lady Annie Brassey, 1878

The book's title page told the reader that 'the Sunbeam' was 'our home on the ocean for twelve months'. The General Manager, W.A Kelk remembered that in the 80s Longmans published a sixpenny edition of the title; 'Don't think that we have confined ourselves to theological and intellectual works' he told a reporter on his retirement in 1938

BL W16/1066

age of forty-eight. (Gladstone had sailed on the yacht two years earlier.) Subsequently the *Sunbeam* was presented to the Indian government to be used as a convalescent hospital.[165]

Lady Brassey (1839–1887) was herself surprised at the success of her book, only a thousand copies of which, priced at a guinea, were printed initially. Mudie's promptly subscribed for all of them so that publication had to be delayed until more copies were produced. Eventually a sixpenny edition appeared which sold around a quarter of a million copies. The *Voyage* was translated into seventeen languages, and it is reported that a Finnish reader of the Swedish edition was so impressed by it that he bought an English edition and taught himself English by comparing the two versions. Lady Brassey wrote two other volumes for Longman, both lavishly illustrated, *Sunshine and Storm in the East* and *In the Trades, the Tropics, and the 'Roaring Forties'*.[166]

~

Travel was always as important an element in the Longman lists, therefore, as it was in those of Murray. They were described clearly, and often attractively, not only at the end of other books published by the House but in the distinctive publication, *Notes on Books*, which first appeared in 1855. Some of the books described there had such 'ample' and explicit titles that the editor felt that 'little more [was] needed to convey a notion of [their] contents'. One that he singled out was *The Autobiography of James*

---

165 CC, p.33.

166 Longmans also published Lord Brassey's *Work and Wages* (1872) and *Foreign Work and Wages* (1879), and in 1904 brought out a new composite edition by Sydney Chapman with an introduction by Lord Brassey, who was created a Baron in 1886.

Sir William Herschel
(1792–1871) aged 48,
daguerrotype by Myall

Sir William Herschel,
astronomer and natural
philosopher was regarded by
many of his contemporaries as
England's most distinguished
man of science. He was deeply
interested in early science
publishing. The most well-
known of of his works were the
article on *Preliminary Discourse
on the study of natural philosophy*
for *Lardner's Cyclopedia*, (1830)
which was then published
in a new edition in 1851,and
Outlines of Astronomy (1849)
which went into eleven editions.
Later, in 1857, Longmans
brought together *Essays from
the Edinburgh and the Quarterly
Reviews, with addresses and other
pieces*

The National Portrait Gallery, London
no. P660

Silk Buckingham, including his Voyages, Travels, Adventures, Speculations, Trials, Successes and Failures ... with Characteristic Sketches of Public Men with whom he has had personal intercourse during a Period of more than Fifty Years. Not surprisingly, the autobiography took up two volumes, ending at the point in Buckingham's life when he was on the eve of starting a journey to India as Envoy of the Pasha of Egypt by an overland route through the Middle East. Buckingham's continuing interest to historians lies less in his travels than in his utopian visions of a city of the future which he called Victoria.[167]

Among the other books of exploration on the Longman lists was Huc's *Chinese Empire* (1855), which described the author's journey through 'the heart of China'. Another, felt to be equally absorbing, was an account of the discovery of the North-West Passage made by the *Investigator* in 1850 when its crew were seeking to rescue Sir John Franklin who had sailed from England five years earlier. He had died in 1847 after spending nineteen months caught in ice. A tempting title in the 1899 list was E.F. Knight's *Where Three Empires Meet: A Narrative of Recent Travel in Kashmir, Western Tibet, Baltistan, Ladak and Gilgel*.

Nearer home, there were several books on the Alps, including *Hours of Exercise in the Alps* (1871) by the scientist John Tyndall (1820–1893), author of *The Glaciers of the Alps* (1860). A lecturer much in demand on both sides of the Atlantic as well as a populariser of science, particularly physics, Tyndall, like William Longman, was a keen mountaineer. William was President of the Alpine Club from 1871 to 1874: he had been a founder member. Tyndall, equally enthusiastic, was also a member of the X Club, an influential science group in late-Victorian England. So were William Spottiswoode and Lubbock. As Tyndall's main publisher, Longman kept at the forefront of science popularising. Like Herschel before him – and Tyndall greatly admired Herschel's outlook as well as his output – Tyndall was a key figure in 'scientific evangelism'.[168]

~

There were two Longman books with no geographical or topical dimension which survived the age of Victoria, each with a long life of its own to come – P.M. Roget's *Thesaurus* (1852) and *Gray's Anatomy* (1858). Both, indeed,

167 See L. Mumford, *The Culture of Cities* (1938), p.394 and A. Briggs, *Victorian Cities* (Folio Society edn., 1996), pp.48–9.

168 See A.S. Eve and C.H. Creasey, *Life and Work of John Tyndall* (1945) and W.H. Brock, N.D. McMillan and R.C. Mollan, *John Tyndall, Essays on a Natural Philosopher* (Dublin, 1981).

were to outlive the autonomous Longman Company itself. The first of them was published at a time when, as we have seen, Thomas Norton had many other preoccupations. The second was one of the books acquired through the Parker take-over. *Thesaurus* had taken a lifetime to prepare, although Roget (1779–1869) lived long enough to see a 28th edition: Gray, who was only thirty-one when his *Anatomy* appeared, died young in 1861, having contracted smallpox from his nephew.

As early as 1805, Roget had begun to assemble in neat handwriting a classified 'catalogue of words', which in the midst of a busy and controversial life as Secretary to the Royal Society from 1827 to 1849 he regularly extended and clarified. A physician and a highly versatile scholar – of Huguenot stock – Roget arranged his words 'not in alphabetical order as they are in a Dictionary', but according to the ideas which they express.

Roget was not alone in seeking to tabulate and classify; and for others besides himself, 'ideas' might be divided into 'classes' – abstract relations; space and motion; the material world, a world of things as well as ideas; the intellect; volition; 'the will'; and sentiment and moral powers, not always separated. Yet words could still be treated in different ways from that pursued by Roget. One of Newman's greatest Oxford sermons, 'Unreal Words', was a key text for one of his non-Roman Catholic admirers, the reviewer R.H. Hutton (1826–1897), who abandoned Unitarianism for the Church of England.[169] And in the very decade when *Thesaurus* was published, James Murray, formerly a bank clerk, was collecting slips that made it possible to produce in parts the *Oxford English Dictionary*, which drew on the history of word usage in tracing their derivations and meanings. The first part of the *Dictionary* appeared in 1885.[170]

The *Dictionary* was to trace the word 'thesaurus' back to 1736.[171] That was more than a decade before the appearance of Johnson's *Dictionary* which no longer stood alone or in small privileged company in 1885. Meanwhile, dictionaries had not been neglected in the mid-Victorian years. *Webster's American Dictionary of the English Language*, published in 1828, had been followed up by Ogilvie's *Imperial Dictionary of the English Language*, published by Blackie in Scotland in 1850 and 1854, and in 1858 the Philological Society in London, with F.J. Furnivall as President, had proposed a new *Dictionary of the English Language*, and had set up two committees, one literary and historical, and one etymological, for its preparation.

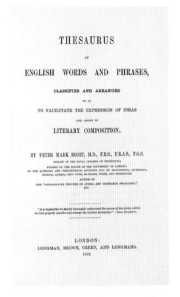

Title page of the *Thesaurus of English Words and Phrases* by Peter Mark Roget (1779–1869). The first edition was published in 1852 and has continued in print ever since

BL 12985.g.5

---

169 See Hutton's review of the eight volumes of Newman's *Parochial and Plain Sermons* (1869 edn.) in *The Spectator*, 5 Dec. 1868. Hutton was assistant editor of the *Economist* from 1858 to 1860 and joint editor and part proprietor of the *Spectator* from 1861 to 1897.

170 Sutcliffe, *op. cit.*, p.93.

171 K.M.E. Murray, *Caught in the Web of Words* (1977), Ch. VII.

A reviewer in the *Quarterly Review* in 1873 proposed as a priority 'a Concise Dictionary in a single volume, neither too heavy nor too costly, close shorn of superfluous detail and speculative fancy'.[172] Longman, committed to Roget, did not then supply one, and both Macmillan and the Cambridge University Press, confronted with an always difficult Furnivall, were not willing to do so. That left the Oxford University Press alone.

Roget had nothing to do with Oxford. Different strands in his life, some of them strands in this History, contributed to the range of his compilation. In his youth he had moved from Edinburgh University, where he studied medicine, to Bristol where he worked alongside Davy and Beddoes, and he had subsequently written a large number of articles for the *Encyclopaedia Britannica* not only on 'physiology' but on such diverse topics as 'ant', 'tree' and 'deaf and dumb'. He had spent four years in Manchester as a doctor – and lecturer – before settling in London, where he concerned himself with public health, a supply of healthy drinkable water, as well as with the development of London University. He was a founder member of the Society for the Diffusion of Useful Knowledge, working alongside Brougham and Knight.

The word 'useful' was often to be applied to the succession of editions of his *Thesaurus* on both sides of the Atlantic. Indeed, for one twentieth-century editor, R.A. Dutch, it was a book that lived 'not by the praises of past generations but by its enduring reputation for usefulness'.[173] Nevertheless, some of its first reviewers treated it, as the *Athenaeum* did, as a 'curious book, novel in its design, most laboriously wrought', rather than one 'likely to be practically useful'. Longman's *Notes on Books* described its 'great object' as comprehensively 'to solve a problem with which every man that has to speak, write, or translate must deal – viz. given an idea, to find the word or phrase by which that idea may be most aptly expressed'.[174]

Roget was as interested in the layout of his *Thesaurus* as in its content, insisting that the text be printed in two columns, with 'positive headings confronting each other'. He thought of his role as that of 'holding out a helping hand' both to native speakers of the English language and to translators: 'the inquirer can readily select out of the ample collection spread out before his eyes ... those expressions which are best suited to his purpose, and which might not have occurred to him without any such assistance'.

The first edition of *Thesaurus*, which appeared in octavo in May 1852,

---

172   QR, Vol. 135, July–Oct. 1873, p.481. See also R.C. Trench, *On Some Deficiencies in our English Dictionaries* (1857).

173   R.A. Dutch, Introduction to the American Book Club Association edition of *Thesaurus*, in conjunction with Longman (1962). Dutch reduced the number of headwords and printed them consecutively rather than in pairs. He also introduced what he called laywords.

174   *Notes on Books*, May 1855, p.11.

cost fourteen shillings. A thousand copies were printed. The work still showed signs of its origins as a private compilation, but a general edition quickly followed in March 1853, and a third edition, duodecimo, 'enlarged' but 'more portable', 'improved' and 'cheaper', was priced at 'half a guinea' in February 1855. By then it had been pirated in the United States. Roget went on adding and correcting his *Thesaurus* until his death in 1869, when his work, now in its 28th edition, was carried on in dynastic fashion by his son, John Lewis Roget, lawyer and printer, who prepared a further new edition (with index and more extended cross references) in 1879.

In the preface to this edition J.L. Roget remarked of his own contribution that it was 'almost entirely of a practical nature, demanding industry and attention, rather than philosophic culture or the learning of a philologist'. By then, the finances of *Thesaurus* had changed substantially. According to the original agreement of 1852, Messrs Longman, Brown, Green and Longmans, as they then were, published 1,000 copies, pricing them at fourteen shillings, and after deducting costs and charging Roget for corrections, they divided profits half-and-half with him. (Roget also received twelve 'free' copies, and as in a twenty-first century contract, he was then charged trade price for additional copies.) When a second edition, which ran to 1,500 copies, appeared in 1853, Roget kept two-thirds of the profits, and for a third, which appeared in 1855, he received a flat £140 with all additional profits going to the House. For the fifth edition in 1855 he received £133 on the day of publication.

The numbers of copies of later editions and the financial relationships involved reveal as much about the success of the venture as the changing content of the contracts does, with revenues continuing to accrue after P.M. Roget's death: J.L. Roget received an annual income of between £300 and £500 for editions issued between 1874 and 1890. Meanwhile, the first pirated American *Thesaurus*, which had appeared in Boston in 1854, ran through a series of printings until in 1886 Thomas Y. Crowell and Co. brought out their first edition, a straight reprint of J.L. Roget's British edition of 1879, to be followed in 1911 by the first standard American edition revised by the American lexicographer, C.O. Sylvester Mawson.[175] There were to be problems concerning international copyright in the twentieth century as so-called 'international editions' of *Thesaurus* appeared. There were also French and German 'synonymies'.

Some of these editions served quite different purposes from those which had originally inspired P.M. He might have been surprised, for example, about the wide-spread appeal of the crossword puzzle during the 1920s and 1930s when turning to the *Thesaurus* for synonyms now became an aid to home entertainment. Longman had to produce no fewer than

---

175 See D.L. Emblen, *Peter Mark Roget: The Word and the Man*, published by Longman in 1971.

five new printings in 1925 when the crossword craze was at its height.[176] But *Thesaurus* long survived the craze. A new 1982 Longman edition, unnumbered, was produced by a Longman Dictionary and Reference Book Department, working on a scale inconceivable even in 1925.

Roget himself would have been unsurprised, however, by the efforts then being made by researchers in an 'age of technology' to explore the possibilities of using his *Thesaurus* in machine translations from one language into another. He had dreamed of a polyglot lexicon conceived on his system, and since for him language was an 'instrument of thought' as well as a medium of communication, he considered that the 'felicitous turns of expression' set out in the volume would 'frequently open to the mind of a reader a whole vista of cultural ideas'.[177]

~

The word 'vista' was well chosen in relation to a decade which opened with the Crystal Palace – Longman displayed several books there as examples of printing – and closed with the publication of Darwin's *Origin of Species*, with its magnificent 'tangled bank' ending, one of many set passages rich in visual imagery.[178] The visual mattered immensely also in *Gray's Anatomy*, the different editions of which reveal as much about the history of illustrations of a medical text as about the history of anatomy. Its author, Henry Gray (1827–1861), was the son of a Court messenger, and unlike P.M. Roget, he had no reputation to protect when the first edition of his book appeared in 1858 costing twenty-eight shillings.

Its immediate reception was unflattering. 'Mr. Gray has published a book that was not wanted', wrote a reviewer in the *Medical Times* in 1858. Gray was a lecturer and demonstrator at St George's Hospital, London, where he had enrolled as a student in 1845. He was not a great anatomist, but he was a good communicator, and his first edition owed much to his illustrator, Henry Vandyke Carter, who provided 363 drawings for a volume running to 750 pages.

'What is so special about this book?', F.N.L. Poynter, a distinguished medical historian, asked in the *British Medical Journal* at the time of the centenary of *Anatomy*, when a special centennial edition, the 32nd, was published. He did not hesitate to answer his own question, drawing on medical imagery: 'Like other centenarians, it owe[d] its survival to the intelligence and skill with which it ha[d] been treated, at critical times, by its medical attendants, in this case a succession of distinguished editors and gifted draughtsmen. They have amputated, excised, grafted and

---

176 See H. Fairlie, 'Years the Crossword Ate' in *The Spectator*, 22 July 1955.

177 P.M. Roget, Introduction to *Thesaurus* (1852).

178 See S.E. Hyams, *The Tangled Bank, Darwin, Marx, Frazer and Freud as Imaginative Writers* (1959).

injected to such effect that Gray himself would regard with amazement the prodigy which has grown from his own modest offspring, although a closer inspection would enable him to recognise its original features.'[179]

The adjective 'modest' seems ill-chosen. And Poynter's further remark that 'biological survival for a hundred years is sufficiently rare to be regarded as a curiosity' now seems as dated as the 1858 reviewer's judgement of Gray's first edition. There was, in fact, something very special not only about the book, but about its origins. Its first publishers, Walton Sons and Maberly, sold it to Parker, but there was no trace in the Longman pre-1914 archives of any formal agreement between the original author and the original publisher.

Thomas Norton had to deal at first with Gray's widow who on the basis of an agreement without a contract put her total faith, as did Gray's later descendants, in the judgement of the House. In Thomas Norton Longman V's words – and he was writing in 1926 – 'the entire business of this very valuable and most successful publication' reflected what he considered to be 'the higher lines of mutual confidence'. And on the part of the House, 'we did all that was possible to secure thoroughly competent editors' so that the sale of the book [in the 1920s] was as large, if not larger, than it has ever been before'.[180]

Gray himself had clearly understood what a successful medical textbook had to be, and already his own second edition, published in 1861, included twenty-seven new drawings by John Guise Westmacott. His first Victorian successor, David Timothy Holmes, understood equally clearly what was required of him, and produced significantly new editions, the 5th in 1869 and the 9th in 1880. Holmes then handed over the succession to Thomas Pickering Pick, a St. George's surgeon who had learnt his anatomy from Gray, and Pick collaborated with his successor, Robert Howden, in preparing the 15th and 16th editions in 1901 and 1905. According to his biographers, he was 'rapid and correct, but not very inspiring, for he followed the lines of Gray's Anatomy so closely that he was popularly reported among his students to know 'that elaborate treatise by heart'.[181]

It was not until 1936, the last edition edited by Howden, that a brief biographical memoir of Gray appeared (along with a portrait) in Anatomy. The centenary edition, costing six guineas, a figure already with a touch of nostalgia to it, consisted of 363 pages of text and 1,329 illustrations, many of them in colour. 'The beautiful electron micrographs in the sections on histology and embryology' had been produced by 'Miss Fitton Jackson, a blood relation of Henry Gray himself'. Referring to this edition,

179 F.N.L. Poynter, 'Gray's Anatomy, the First Hundred Years', British Medical Journal, 6 Sept. 1958.

180 T.N. Longman V, Memories, pp.75-6. (LA)

181 Undated notes for a speech by Mark Longman, 1958. (LA)

the *Observer*, which seldom dealt with medical books, deemed that its 'long span must be a reward for outstanding virtue', a difficult quality to establish. '*Gray's Anatomy*', it concluded 'may be on the threshold of an era of new development which, if properly guided, could lead to another hundred years of useful life.'[182]

When the centenary of *Anatomy* was celebrated at a Longmans' dinner in 1958 Professor Sir Wilfred Le Gros Clark was kinder than Poynter and more in line with the *Observer*. 'I myself was brought up on [it]', he wrote to Mark Longman, 'and I am the proud possessor of a first edition which used to belong to my grandfather when he was President of the Royal College of Surgeons'. Mark had the virtue of the House in mind when he chose the occasion to remind his distinguished audience that in the very first decade of its history the House of Longman had co-published 'at least three works on anatomy', the first of them Cheselden's *Anatomy of the Human Body*, a book also with a long life. It reached a 30th edition in 1792.

The House had also published Sir Richard Quain's *Dictionary of Medicine*, Thomas Norton having signed an agreement in 1874. It was based on an American idea, put forward by Appleton of New York, and although it took years to collect all the contributions, Thomas Norton found Quain so helpful that he turned to him for advice on other questions relating to medical publishing.[183]

~

In ending this chapter with examples of the longevity of books, I have allowed the story at times to stray beyond its closing date of 1879. It is, however, an appropriate date to choose for a chapter ending, for by then the mid-Victorian years were indubitably over. The 1870s had marked a watershed, when new ways of thinking and feeling fascinated intelligent contemporaries, prominent among them the liberal politician and man of letters John Morley (1838–1923), editor of the *Fortnightly Review* during some of its liveliest years, who saw everywhere around him in the 1870s 'doubt, hesitation and shivering expectancy'.

That was not the mood at 39 Paternoster Row, where then and during the following decade of more open conflict, often dramatic,[184] and severe depression Longman profits held up. The House looked secure rather

---

182 The *Observer*, 14 Sept. 1958.

183 *Memories*, pp.78–9. Appleton had put forward the idea of such a dictionary not to Thomas Norton, but to his partner, Dyer, who was visiting New York.

184 The most vivid account of the decade, *England in the Eighteen Eighties: Towards a social basis for freedom* (1945), was written by the American Helen Lynd, and opens with a paragraph by Winston Churchill. See also D.A. Hamer, *John Morley, Liberal Intellectual in Politics* (1968). The phrase quoted from him appears in his brilliant essay 'On Compromise' (1874).

than antiquated, and in 1884 the *Booksellers' Circular*, caught in the spell of longevity, summed up an article on it with a reference back to Scott. It devoted more space to the eighteenth than to the nineteenth century. Nevertheless, the judgements in the article were contemporary in mood:

> Many great changes have taken place in the constitution of the firm since that period, but there has always been a Longman at the head of it, and as publishers they have attained a celebrity within the last fifty years beyond that of other publishing firms. For Longman's to be the publishers of any work is a feather in the cap of an author; if his talent be only mediocre, he may never attain such another compliment, but this is a testimonial that he judiciously preserves … Longman's never publish anything which has not been closely scrutinised and well grounded.

In thus concentrating on authors rather than on booksellers the *Booksellers' Circular* claimed that it had derived its information from many sources, 'published and unpublished, old and new, as well as from personal investigation and inquiry'.

There was little that was new in the article, however, which reproduced a photograph of the cheque paid to Macaulay, then preserved in a frame in Paternoster Row; and although one section of it was headed 'foresight in publishing', its writer had no reason for noting then that in the year 1884, when it appeared, J.W. Allen, who was to transform the educational list of Longman publications, joined the House. He was to do much more organisationally to change the balance and direction of the business than any of the Longmans. None the less, the writer of the article stressed that the presence of four Longmans in the business guaranteed that 'for this generation at least the family will be numerous enough to supply any vacancies'.[185]

He was right, but the writer of an article on Rivington's in 1885 in the American version of *The Critic* was not when he saw no reason for the oldest great publishing family, the Rivingtons, losing their control of their own 'ancient House'. Francis and Septimus Rivington, he observed, were both young men, in charge of a House which 'flourishes and stands high, if not highest of all in the London publishing trade'. There was no foresight there, and the take-over of Rivingtons by Longman in 1890, described in the next chapter, stands out as a far more important date in Longman history than the year 1879. The next two important dates, even more important than 1890, were far in the future – 1968 and 1974.

---

185 *Booksellers' Circular*, Vol. XIII, No.26, 24 December 1884.

LONGMANS'
ILLUSTRATED
FIRST FRENCH
READING
BOOK
AND
GRAMMAR

BIDGOOD & HARBOTTLE

6 Publisher, Readers And Authors, 1879–1918

To move on beyond 1879 is not to sense great change at 39 Paternoster Row. Nor did the change in legal status from Partnership to private Company ten years later make much difference either to established business routines or to the decision-making process. The taking over of Rivingtons in 1890 did make a difference, however: it was described at the time as 'the largest transaction that had ever been carried out in the publishing trade'. These were the words of Thomas Norton V, who succeeded his father as head of the House in 1879. He was speaking at a dinner which Messrs Longman and Co. gave for 'their staff' on 26 July 1890 at the Crystal Palace. Francis Hansard Rivington was also present. The occasion had one 'element of novelty'. Ladies were included in the invitation.

The second toast of the evening after the loyal toast was to 'the firm of Longman & Co.', and the proposer was a director of Messrs Spottiswoode & Co., who began by referring to the more than forty-year old connection of the two firms and who congratulated Longmans on the take-over. He used the ship metaphor when he touched on the recent opening in 1887 of their own binding establishment, the Ship Binding Works at Great Saffron Hill, not far from Paternoster Row, trusting that 'the Ship would not weigh anchor and set sail in the direction of New-street Square', Spottiswoode's own headquarters.[1] His 'cordial' speech did not refer to one of the most striking examples of the power of the Spottiswoode connection. The printers had set and proofed in the utmost secrecy, still a treasured quality in printing and in publishing, the whole of *Endymion* within a fortnight – all setting was then still done by hand – and only ten weeks had elapsed between receipt of the manuscript and publication.[2]

Thomas Norton made what was called a 'very pleasant' reply, recapitulating some of the incidents that had 'distinguished the career of the House' and attributing its success 'mainly to hard work and the strict integrity' with which the firm had always carried out their engagements. A later toast to 'the staff' was proposed by his cousin, CJ, and was more topical and less bland when he began not with 'hard work' but with 'labour

Longmans' Illustrated First French Reading Book and Grammar, 1895

BL 12950.aaa.49

---

1   A record of the speeches was given in the PC, 3 Aug. 1890.

2   My account of Disraeli draws on Annabel Jones's MA Thesis, University of Leicester, 1972, 'Disraeli's *Endymion*: A Case Study in Nineteenth-Century Publishing'.

C. J. Longman (1852–1934)
was a member of the fifth
generation of Longmans,
joining the firm in 1874 and
becoming a Partner three
years later when his father,
William, died. He developed
the Longmans business,
particularly with schools both
here and overseas, and he it
was who appointed three non-
Longman Directors, J. W. Allen,
K.Potter and C.S.S.Higham,
all of whom were to continue
laying the foundations of the
firm for the twentieth century.
He became the first President
of the Publishers Association in
1896, held office for two years
and then served a second term
in 1902–3

Longman Archive

disputes'. These were very topical in the 1890s, particularly in the 'printing industry' as it was now being called.

'Although no difference had ever arisen between this firm [Longmans] and their staff', CJ stated, 'if at any time such an unfortunate thing did occur, it would be because when difficulties arose they were not immediately faced and settled.' He felt optimistically that there were few differences of opinion 'between master and servant which might not be satisfactorily arranged if each had the courage to state his case firmly from the start'. This was still the acceptable language of 'industrial relations', employed not only in parliamentary legislation but even at a private dinner where the House of Longman was hailed for its 'liberality'.

CJ ended his toast to the staff by referring to one non-partner's name, that of J.W. Allen, although years later Allen was belatedly to be made one. CJ described him as 'the principal educational representative of the House, who is starting very soon on a tour round the world in the interests of the firm'.[3] Travelling was as important an aspect of the House's operations as it was an element in the House's publications; and particularly in relation to operations much of it was directly associated with education. Educational representatives, first called 'travellers', were to increase in numbers and importance. In 1879 H.E. Collins, J. Marchant and E.W.B. Chenery were said not only to be highly successful but to have 'a personal charm which added dignity to the positions they occupied'.[4] The lists they were handling included an increasing proportion of educational books, including textbooks. The share of religion declined, and there was now relatively little fiction.

An article on the London publishing houses that appeared in March 1901 in *The Bookman*, a journal founded ten years earlier, was to describe the publication of school books or more strictly speaking, educational works (without mentioning Allen's name), as 'one of the most important, and perhaps [a necessary word, for like Espinasse, the author of the article had no figures to quote] one of the most profitable branches of the business'. According to *The Bookman*, they formed by then nearly a half of the titles in the House catalogue, and they included not only individual books but well-known series of books, also increasingly fashionable, like Hamblin Smith's mathematical series, the *Text Books of Science* series, the Ship series of reading books, and the numerous volumes of 'the very happily conceived

---

3   CJ also mentioned by name (without giving initials) two former chief clerks at Rivington, Moncrieff and Hibberd. The longest serving member of Longman staff taken over from Rivington was W. Jefferay, who joined the New York House in 1893. He was a collector of the portraits of authors of books which bore the Longman imprint (*ibid.*, p.88). His scrapbooks are now in the Longman Archive.

4   CC, p.87.

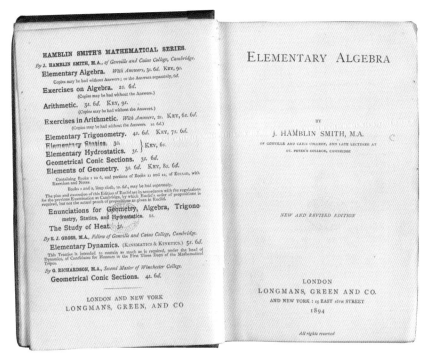

Title pages to Hamblin Smith's *Elementary Algebra*, showing other titles in *The Mathematical Series* published in the 1890s

BL 553.de.44

"Epochs" series – [the first of them] "English History", edited by the late Lord Bishop of London [Mandell Creighton]'.[5] Six years before *The Bookman* article appeared *Longmans' Illustrated First French Reading Book* was published.

Allen's travels around the world were often concerned with textbook enterprises, particularly in India, where a Bombay branch of Longmans, Green was opened in 1895 and a Calcutta branch in 1906, with a branch in Madras to follow. The original purpose behind the travels and the setting up of Longman offices in India had been to promote the sale of books published in Britain. A strategic switch, as it would now be called, came with the recognition by Allen and his colleagues of the huge opportunities opened up by the demand for 'vernacular' textbooks in Indian schools and colleges. The first of Allen's colleagues died of typhoid within a year of his arrival in Bombay, and Robert Taylor, sent out as a traveller in 1899 (from the Advertising Department in Paternoster Row), was appointed Manager in 1904.

---

5   *The Bookman*, March 1901, p.179. In September 1901 the editor, W.R. (later Sir William) Nicoll, claimed that within ten years *The Bookman*, published by Hodder and Stoughton, whose headquarters were at 27 Paternoster Row, had proved useful to 'Bookbuyers, Bookreaders and Booksellers'. Robertson Nicoll was described by Lord Riddell, his journalist friend and proprietor of the *News of the World*, as a 'famous literary gent' with 'great political influence in Liberal circles' (*More Pages from my Diary* (1934), p.1). He remained editor of *The Bookman* until 1923, an outstanding example of editorial longevity.

 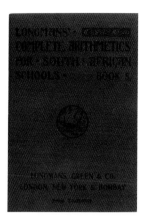 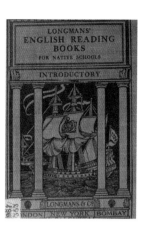 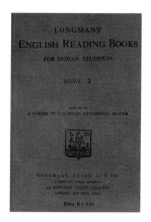

From the beginning of the twentieth century Longman published books for overseas markets:

Longmans' Readers for Burma, 1901

Longmans' Complete Arithmetics for South African Schools, 1915

Longmans' English Reading Books for Native Schools, published between 1915 and 1925

Longmans' English Reading Book for Indian Students, 1910

Longman Archive

By 1914 Longman books were being produced in Urdu, Hindi, Bengali, Marathi, Gujerati, Sindhi, Nepali, Tamil, Telugu, Malay and Kanarese. There was also an extended production of books in Burmese and Thai (Siamese). What was accomplished in Asia continued in South Africa, where books were published in Afrikaans, Kaffir, Zulu and Sesuto. The process, which began with Allen, was of fundamental long-term importance for the House, far outlasting the British Empire and, with it, the unquestioning use of the word 'vernacular'. It also outlasted the disappearance of the Longman Group in 1994. The name Longman remains a familiar one in twenty-first century Asia and Africa.

Allen had no direct influence, however, on the formidable educational output of what was often called the American House of Longman, a House that flourished but did not last.[6] This had its origins in 1875, when C.J. Mills crossed the Atlantic as a 'Yankee traveller', but the word 'House' could not have been used before 1889 when the agency was converted into a New York branch, with Mills now being described, if mainly in New York, as 'Head of the House'. He was a man of enterprise and initiative, who immediately enlisted a number of American authors, including 'literary statesmen', among them Theodore Roosevelt and Henry Cabot Lodge.

Soon there were to be American historical series, including the Harvard professor A.B. Hart's *Epochs of American History*, one volume of which, *Division and Reunion*, was to be written by another future president of the United States, Woodrow Wilson. Hart also edited an *American Citizen* series to which Professor E.R.A. Seligman of Columbia University contributed the volume on *Political Economy* and Professor A. Lawrence Lowell (1856–1943), later to become president of Harvard, *Public Opinion*

---

6   Cassell had opened a single-room New York office in 1860, which closed in 1863, but a new agency was set up on Broadway in 1865. An American manager was appointed in 1876. (S. Nowell-Smith, *The House of Cassell, 1848–1858* (1958), pp.261–3).

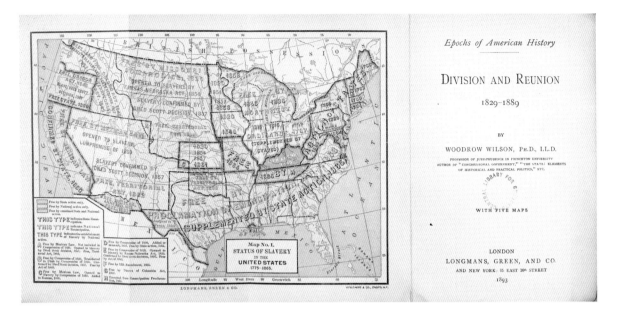

and Party Government.[7] In 1894 a lavishly illustrated series of *College Histories of Art* was launched, edited by the aptly named Professor J.C. Van Dyke of Rutgers University, who also wrote the volume on *Painting.*

While the *Histories of Art* were primarily intended for classroom use, like many Longman books in Britain they were read by large numbers of people who were not specialising in the formal study of the subject. In New York, however, there was an increasing emphasis, as there was in Britain, on class-room teaching both at the school and the university level. Examining was increasingly common as a test of students' ability. G.J. Smith of the Board of Examiners of the New York City Public Schools was the author of an *English Grammar*, which was followed by *A Spelling Book* prepared by Georgia Alexander of the Indianapolis Schools Board. Lindley Murray was now out of fashion on both sides of the Atlantic.

These were also the earliest Longman texts to introduce what was called 'the problem method of teaching reading', the *Horace Mann Readers*, prepared by W.L. Hervey of the Board of Examiners and Melvin Hix, principal of a school in New York City.[8] The use of punch-cards was part of the 'problem method' which was in line with the approach to education of the outspoken philosopher of pragmatism and 'progressive education', Professor John Dewey of Columbia University (1859–1952).

The frontispiece and title page from *Division and Reunion, 1829–1889,* by Woodrow Wilson, published in 1893, in the *Epochs of American History Series*

BL B59.g.22

---

7   See *The Bookseller and Stationery Trades Journal* (Nov. 1924), p.134. A Columbia Professor, Brander Matthews, was Literary Adviser for more than thirty years to Mills and his son, E.S. Mills. (*Booksellers' Record,* 25 Oct. 1924.)

8   Horace Mann (1796–1859) was a greatly admired Massachusetts educator.

His extraordinary influence on American education as a whole has subsequently been recognised, challenged and re-evaluated.[9] Learning by rote was dismissed: students' needs came first.

It is interesting in this connection that another distinguished American pragmatist, the philosopher and psychologist William James (1842–1910), moved to the teaching of psychology and philosophy at Harvard from the teaching of anatomy and physiology. Many of his outstanding books bore Longman imprints, including *The Will to Believe* (1897), *The Varieties of Religious Experience* (1902) and *Pragmatism* (1907). Elder brother of the novelist Henry James, William had all the right qualifications to enter any Temple of Fame.

C.J. Mills, and his son E.S. Mills, were proud of the fact that in 1924, when Longman celebrated its bi-centenary, twelve Longman authors were members of the American Academy of Arts and Letters, founded in 1904 and incorporated by Act of Congress in 1916.[10] They included Roosevelt, Wilson and Lowell. They were proud too that there were then three American Longman offices, in Chicago and Boston as well as New York, and that there was an office, too, in Canada, although this was outside their control. In their anxiety to inform the House of Longman in London of what was going on in New York, the two Millses regularly plied Paternoster Row with news cuttings from even the most obscure American newspapers. There is no evidence, however, that these ever diverted the London Longmans from their course.

~

There were then three Longmans in control of House affairs in Paternoster Row. Thomas Norton, the oldest, eldest son of Thomas IV, never used a dynastic title himself and was most often known as Mr Norton. His father, anxious to retain the favourite name Norton, had called the fourth of his five daughters Alice Norton.[11] Because of ill health he had been at Harrow for one year only, and he never went to university. He started work at Paternoster Row in 1870 when he was twenty years old, and he became a Partner in 1873. After 1879 he shared power in the business with his cousin C.J., who was deeply

9   See J. Dewey, *Psychology* (1887); *The School and Society* (1899); *Lectures in the Philosophy of Education* (1899); and *Democracy and Education* (1916). The *Lectures* were delivered at the University of Chicago, where Dewey had set up a 'laboratory school' in 1896. For an attempt to place the early Dewey in his time, see M.G. White, *Social Thought in America* (1949), esp. Ch.2. 'The primary purpose of the school', Dewey believed, was 'to train children in cooperative and mutually helpful living.'

10   CC, 36–37.

11   Three of the daughters never married. There is a stained glass window in their memory in the Grosvenor Chapel, South Audley Street. In it the Crucifixion in the centre is surrounded by signs of the Ship and of the Black Swan.

interested in the early history of the House: born in 1852, he was endowed with the correct, if now somewhat faded, Whig initials. There was only one non-Longman partner, William Ellerby Green, thirteen years older than Thomas Norton, into whose care his father had passed him over when he arrived at Paternoster Row.

Another partner, already mentioned, Thomas Reader, who had entered the business in 1834 and had taught Thomas Norton how 'to master the mysteries of paper and print', had retired in 1889. Failing eyesight was given as the cause.[12] He had hoped that his son, William, who had entered the House in the 1880s, would succeed him: he had worked in the Paper and Print Department, and had invented a rotary press for printing in several colours, but William was pensioned off on grounds of ill-health. Thomas Reader was not allowed to nominate a successor. Indeed, he was required to withdraw his capital from the business.[13] There was still no doubt as to where power lay at 39 Paternoster Row.

C.J. Longman, like Thomas Norton, was educated at Harrow, although he completed his school years there before moving on to University College, Oxford, where, examinations put on one side, he gained a soccer blue, playing against Cambridge in two successive years, 1872 and 1873. The third Longman, Thomas Norton's younger brother, George Henry, born in 1852, did not retire from the business until 1932, and lived on until 1938. Thomas Norton retired in 1919 and died in 1930. CJ, the most formidable of the Longmans, known as 'black Longman' on account of his square-cut black beard, retired in 1928. These were very long spans of service. Until Mark the Longmans lived long.

In his brief time at Harrow, Thomas Norton had found it extremely difficult to describe to his fellow Harrovians just what his father did. The word 'publisher' seemed to him to be enough, but, if pressed, he would say that he dealt in 'books, of course'. Even to himself the answer seemed inadequate until a 'happy thought' came to him. 'I quite surreptitiously got hold of a dictionary; but alas, on turning up the word "publish" – "to make known" [one of Johnson's old definitions] was all I found, the result being chaos'.[14] It took time for him to learn, Dewey-style, not from a dictionary

---

12   Letter from his great grandson to Cyprian Blagden, 12 July 1950.

13   Thomas invested the capital in an effort to provide an income in retirement. For his obituary see the PC, 6 Jan. 1906. Reader was buried in a part of the churchyard at Abbot's Langley reserved for inhabitants of the Booksellers' Retreat.

14   *Memories, Personal and Various by TNL with Portraits and other Illustrations*, pp.21-2. LA. The first typed page was undated, but the Preface stated explicitly that the date was January 1921. Although Thomas Norton disliked 'machine writing', his handwriting was untidy. He had found it difficult to realise his father's wish that he should write a 'good hand', and, although he obviously enjoyed composing his text, his spelling was bad.

Photograph of Thomas Norton
Longman V (1849–1930)
when young. He joined the
Partnership in 1873.

Longman Archive

but from experience. There is no evidence that he ever knew of the Dewey system of cataloguing books in libraries. Like all the members of his family, he was guided by experience rather than abstract knowledge or imagination. As in other sectors of British industry, it was an inadequate guide in the long period from 1879 to 1926, broken by an unanticipated world war, a terrifying break in human experience that was beyond most people's vision in 1879.[15]

After leaving Harrow, Thomas Norton was put into the hands of a private tutor at St. Leonards, and later he lived in Paris, staying with a Longmans author, Léon Contanseau, whose French *Dictionary* was more useful to Thomas Norton than the English dictionaries which he consulted when at school: it was published in various editions for sixty years. It was while in France that he learned to write good English, and his work as a publisher drew him into theology, history, philosophy and the *Edinburgh Review*, He left to his cousin the editorship of *Longman's Magazine* and the rest of the general list. The division of labour was in no sense absolute, however, and both men had their own sense of what the House of Longman stood for. Thomas Norton wrote eleven chapters of his memories: CJ took up Longman history after his retirement.

For Thomas Norton, who had begun his career in Paternoster Row by serving for a time in all its departments and using his uncle's office as his base, one of the greatest problems a publisher had to solve was 'how best to make his books known'. And that meant paying (with no market research to help him) even more attention to readers than to authors. 'A publisher', he concluded, 'is just a man of business, but he deals in goods literary and no others. His object, therefore, is the same as that of any other man of business, to make as much as he can out of the trade he conducts. That's the whole secret.'

His father (and uncle) had not been so specific. Indeed, Thomas Norton described his father in traditional publishers' language as 'a very genial and popular man; his courtesy and consideration for others, his keen sense of humour, his straightforwardness, and high principles secured him not only the personal friendship of many distinguished authors, but placed him in the position as head of the firm, worthy of his predecessors'.[16]

Revealingly, the founder in 1884 of the Society of Authors, Walter Besant (1836–1901), made exactly the same point about business as Thomas Norton did. On each page of *The Author*, the journal of his Society, which he edited from 1890 to his death, he printed a list of warnings, the fourteenth and last of them reading 'NEVER forget that publishing is a business, like

---

15   Nevertheless, the number of writers forecasting war – and with it invasion – increased greatly between 1879 and 1914. See I.F. Clarke, *Voices Prophesying War* (1992).

16   *Memories*, p.21.

any other business, totally unconnected with philanthropy, charity or pure love of literature. You have to deal with businessmen. Be yourself a businessman.'

Thomas Norton confided to his *Memories* both general observations of this kind and particular secrets that other members of his family did not bother to tell. His text, typed rather than handwritten, divided into eleven chapters and completed only after he had retired from Paternoster Row, nevertheless did not claim to be a 'history of the firm' even in his own lifetime. Privately circulated, it bore 'no sort of resemblance', its author insisted, 'to the various *published* books' which had 'appeared from time to time, connected with the publishing trade'. At best, they expressed 'fragments of thought'.[17]

Yet a number of valid points about publishing were made consistently throughout the whole text, particularly his observations about business. Some observations related specifically to Longmans, Green's business. Thus, he explained that his idea of starting an *Oxford Library of Practical Theology*, which dealt with 'specific theological subjects', like baptism, confirmation or resurrection, was an offshoot of the Badminton series of books on specific sports, and that his choice of an editor, the Revd. Canon Newbolt, rested on the fact that he was a neighbour.[18] Other observations were of a general kind. 'The production of books is a commercial matter and the crux of the whole thing must always be "will it pay?" It is most distressing that so much literary labour shall be thrown away, but I fear the actual fact cannot be denied.'

The expression of regret was real: Thomas Norton's refusal to deny 'the fact' was a recognition of reality. 'As all the world knows, there are many publishing firms and they increase year by year', a fact which meant 'keen competition'. This he considered to be 'of a wholesome kind ... advantageous to the community at large'.[19] It was a generous judgement, shared by most of his own competitors, although there was a huge gap, he felt, between large houses, publishing good, wholesome 'literature' and those dealing in 'poisonous stuff' to which 'hapless purchasers', a less evocative description than 'the unknown public', were condemned. This was a familiar contrast drawn by the *Edinburgh Review*.[20] Meanwhile, CJ, who remained an active partner until 1928, pursued his own historical interests, and devoted much of his time in his last years to compiling a scholarly bibliography of all Longman publications from 1724 to 1800. Sadly he did not live to see its completed version through the Press.

---

17   *Ibid.*, p.164.

18   *Ibid.*, pp.84–5.

19   *Ibid.*, pp.49, 164.

20   See, for example, ER, Vol.165, Jan. 1887, p.63.

William Ellerby Green, (1833–1918) in 1902 , painting by Hayward M Davenport

He was the son of Bevis Green, joining Longmans aged nineteen in 1852. He became a Partner in 1862 and retired in 1916. In his obituary his effects were given as £134,469 9s 10d

Longman Archive

It is difficult from these sources to learn much about CJ's younger brother, Hubert Harry (1856–1940), who had followed him to Harrow and Oxford, and who became a partner in the House in 1880, within six months of joining the business. He took little interest in its daily affairs, but for a time was in charge of the newly opened Ship Binding Works. He retired in 1933. Rather more information is available, however, about the other partner, W.E. Green (1833–1918), who stayed at Paternoster Row for sixty-six years until his death in 1918, two weeks after Armistice Day. This was notable personal longevity.

According to Thomas Norton, Green was 'an excellent all round man of business' who managed the trading side of the House as well as his father had done: he had 'a wonderful gift for organisation and gained for the firm a high reputation for the prompt despatch of all orders'. 'Nothing worried him so much as a rush for any new book, orders for which he could not supply'. There was nevertheless an element of perversity in this. When his colleagues were pleased after the favourable review of a Longman book caused 'a sudden demand for a new publication', Green's reaction was 'unease': he was 'quite unhappy when the orders could not be executed promptly'.[21]

Sport had figured prominently in Green's early life, as it did in that of the Longmans, for he loved rowing, but in later life, when appropriately he lived near the Thames at Teddington, he 'took to the opera'. He also had a beautiful rose garden. He always reached his office in Paternoster Row by nine o'clock in the morning. Enormously stout and with a pointed beard, he wore gaily striped shirts. In his office he sat on a high stool behind a sloping desk on the first floor of 39 Paternoster Row, partitioned off from the country department where his father had preceded him. He would price each book order by pen, issue country booksellers' accounts, and hand them over to Longmans travellers who would present them to booksellers and collect the money. He paid the travellers out of his private account, later being reimbursed by the Company, a curious practice that lasted until his death. Green would also interview leading provincial booksellers himself when they visited London.[22] They treated him as a 'personality'.

∼

Whatever part the three Longmans played in the affairs of the business, they were left with ample time for leisure activities outside. CJ, who knew about most facets of the business, including advertising, spent more of

21   *Memories*, p.12. See Green's obituary in PC, 7 Dec. 1918, where he was described as 'remarkably shrewd in his judgements on men and affairs'. In 1906 he presented a complete X-Ray installation to the Victoria Hospital at Kingston-on-Thames, a borough which conferred its freedom on him.

22   PW, p.43.

his time at Paternoster Row than the other two, although he entertained guests at his Jacobean country home, Upp Hall, Braughing, near Ware in Hertfordshire, and presided over his local bench of magistrates as any country gentleman might still be expected to do.

George Henry, his cousin, educated not at Harrow but at Eton and, after that, at Trinity College, Cambridge, captained the cricket eleven at both places before playing for the Gentlemen versus the Players, was given the responsibility for foreign trade and financial matters as part of a family division of labour. He was happiest, however, moving in society. In 1880 he married Mary Frances, the daughter of Admiral Lord Frederic Herbert Kerr, the brother of the seventh Marquess of Lothian, who held an appointment in the royal household. George Henry also enjoyed the social life of Paternoster Row: he had a good singing voice, and on one occasion he and Thomas Norton played the name parts in *Box and Cox* in a concert for the Longman staff, their families and friends.

Thomas Norton did not live at Farnborough, the place where he was born, for his father did not bequeath it to him (we do not know why), and, as has been noted, it was now occupied by the Empress Eugénie, content to live among the ships and swans. It was not until 1908 that Thomas Norton, who had been chairman of a fund raised by the book trade for the relief of French booksellers during the siege of Paris in 1870–71,[23] acquired a family estate of his own, Shendish in Hertfordshire, which he secured not through the market but through existing family connections.[24] It had been the home of his uncle Charles, the Dickinson Partner, who died in 1873, and he left it to Charles's son, Arthur, another keen sportsman, who from 1873 to 1885 was Master of the Old Berkeley Hounds.

Arthur became a Partner in the Dickinson business in 1886, but the hunt saw more of him than the paper mills.[25] These were years when the paper industry (now, at last, like printing, described as an industry) was undergoing a vast transformation. The processing of chemical wood pulp had been perfected by the time this chapter opened, although it was newspapers, themselves transformed, not least through new printing technology, which tore down foreign forests. 'An area as large as Rhode Island is stripped of its spruce every year to supply the mills that make newspapers alone.'[26] Books

Arthur Longman (1843–1908). Painter and date unknown

The painting shows Nash Mills House in the background, the family home until 1856 when they moved to Shendish

Personal collection

---

23 Eugénie's son, the Prince Imperial, was killed fighting with British soldiers in South Africa.

24 Before moving to Shendish, Thomas Norton spent much time in Derbyshire at Hathersage.

25 PW, p.27. According to Thomas Norton, Arthur was busy nevertheless with 'local business affairs' as a magistrate and as a member of the Board of Guardians (*Memories*, p.130).

26 PC, 26 July 1902.

Shendish Park, Kings Langley,
Hertfordshire 20 July, 1912

By permission of the Hertfordshire
Archives and Local Studies. LRR

and periodicals accounted for a significant share in the increase in demand. Thomas Norton, who left no record of the transformation, took possession of Shendish on Arthur's death in 1908, and it was to Shendish that he retired in 1919, exactly fifty years after he had spent his first day in Paternoster Row.

The political connections of the Longman family were now mixed. Hubert Harry, a Surrey councillor and alderman, stood unsuccessfully for Parliament as a Liberal candidate and was made a baronet in 1909. George Henry, through the Kerrs, moved in Conservative circles: the seventh Marquess of Lothian was Secretary of State for Scotland in Lord Salisbury's Unionist government. Thomas Norton himself, following in his father's footsteps, prided himself on his relationship with Disraeli, who died in the same month as Longman published his novel *Endymion*, April 1881.

~

Endymion figured prominently in Thomas Norton's *Memories*, the second chapter of which concerned those authors whom he came to know personally. Some of the younger among these told him that they would 'far rather sit in the dentist's operating chair than face so terrible a person as a publisher'.[27] There were few professional literary agents as intermediaries during his first twenty years at Paternoster Row, and, as has been noted, there was no Society of Authors until 1884. Publishers' relations with authors, increasingly concerned with their incomes and rights, remained highly personal, not least when there were non-professional intermediaries.

Disraeli was the most important of the authors with whom Thomas Norton, like his father before him, had to deal, and in his personal

---

27   *Memories*, p.20.

relationship with him there was an invaluable intermediary, invaluable that is to Disraeli, his private secretary, Montagu Corry, also raised to the peerage in 1880 as Lord Rowton: 'you are the Magician, best and dearest of friends', Disraeli told him.[28] In July 1880 Thomas Norton saw Rowton twice before he visited Disraeli at his home at Hughenden, the year when Disraeli fell from power, a fall which his victorious rival Gladstone compared with 'the vanishing of some vast magnificent castle in an Italian romance'.[29]

Thomas Norton did not use the language of romance in the chapter that he devoted to *Endymion* in his *Memories* (Chapter V), but Disraeli did when he described in a letter to Rowton how he had sold to Longman the rights to his new novel *Endymion*:

> L[ongman] arrived here yesterday by 5 o'clock train, and proposed that 'our little business' should be transacted before dinner. I was ready: the MS had been carefully revised, and the printer much assisted ... The receipt was ready and the cheque drawn, or else I should have thought it this morning all a dream. I know no magic of the Middle Ages equal to it![30]

There was certainly non-Gladstonian romance, for the sum paid by the House of Longman to Disraeli was £10,000, the first £2,500 paid on the delivery of the manuscript, and the remaining £7,500 on 1 April 1881, less than three weeks before Beaconsfield's death.

This was said to be the largest sum ever offered for a novel, Rowton having pushed up the original Longman bid from £7,500 to £10,000. It was Thomas Norton, however, who had made the first overtures to Disraeli after his electoral defeat. Believing that Disraeli might now have some 'leisure time at his disposal', he suggested that he might prepare a collection of his political speeches.[31] It was then that Rowton told him that Disraeli already had in mind 'a literary project of far greater importance': he had

Benjamin Disraeli, Earl of Beaconsfield (1804–1881)

Photograph by Downey, taken towards the end of Disraeli's life

The Royal Collection © 2008. Her Majesty Queen Elizabeth II

---

28 Letter of 14 Sept. 1880, quoted in W.F. Monypenny and G.E. Buckle, *The Life of Benjamin Disraeli, Earl of Beaconsfield*, Vol. II (1929 ed), p.1424. This monumental Life was published by John Murray. Rowton had become Disraeli's Private Secretary in 1866. Rowton told Disraeli in 1880 about the success of the negotiations with Longman. In *Endymion*, Ch.49, Disraeli stressed the importance of 'the relations between a minister and his secretary', 'among the finest that can exist between two individuals. Except the married state, there is none in which so great a degree of confidence is involved . . .'

29 Letter of 12 April 1880, quoted in J. Morley, *The Life of William Ewart Gladstone* (1908 edn.), Vol. II, p.167.

30 Monypenny and Buckle, *loc. cit.*

31 See A. Jones, *loc. cit.*, in EHP, pp.143–86.

nearly completed 'a new work of the same nature as *Lothair*'.[32] There were complications, Rowton added, because of the interest in it of an American publisher, a 'rival', but at a second meeting Thomas Norton was told that this publisher had now died and that the connection with the House of Longman, which Disraeli appreciated, should continue.

'A good deal of important conversation' then followed, mainly 'on the question of terms', including calculations of past and future American revenues. 'I quite agreed with Lord Rowton', Thomas Norton wrote in his *Memories*, 'that it would be best for the author to sell the Copyright out and out'. The 'grave question' was 'at what price?'. 'Our views differed considerably, so nothing was settled.' Rowton went back to consult Disraeli, and a further meeting between Rowton and Longman took place, this time at Paternoster Row.

Again there was disagreement, but after Rowton had left him, Thomas Norton came to the conclusion that he should accept Disraeli's terms:

> Knowing that the book [which he referred to elsewhere as 'Lothair's brother'] must be worth more to us than to any other firm, since we held the copyright of all his other novels I came to the conclusion that our policy was to take the bull by the horns and *offer* the very large sum expected rather than to place his Lordship in the position of having to say that 'unless you see your way to giving £10,000 I shall feel obliged, most reluctantly, to try my luck in some other quarter'.

It was a conclusion in character.

After Thomas Norton's partners concurred, he met Rowton on the staircase at the Westminster Palace Hotel to settle the deal on Rowton's terms, which Rowton communicated in a note passed to Disraeli on the floor of the House;[33] and as a consequence, Thomas Norton was invited to Hughenden for a long weekend in August 1880, travelling by train to High Wycombe, where he was met by carriage (and by a crowd of onlookers). Almost immediately, he had a *tête-à-tête* conversation with Disraeli who impressed upon him 'the great importance he attached to the matter being kept a strict secret'.

It was in character that when Disraeli showed him the manuscript, which was kept in a red dispatch box, Thomas Norton was struck at once by 'the clearness of the handwriting': 'it really was a remarkable manuscript, so clear and so few corrections'. Knowing even better than Disraeli how to

---

32   Disraeli had started writing *Endymion* soon after the publication of *Lothair*. He had completed over half the book before he became Prime Minister. Rowton did not learn of the existence of the novel until 1878, nor had he read any of it before August 1880. (R. Blake, 'The Dating of *Endymion*', in the RES, new series, Vol. XVII (1966).)

33   'There are things too big to impart in whispers', the note began. (Rowton to Disraeli, 4 Aug. 1880, quoted by Jones, Thesis, p.21.)

keep secrets, he went on to secure Disraeli's autograph, having taken with him a visitors' book which had never previously left 39 Paternoster Row. What he did with it is not known.

The evening ended after dinner, with Rowton reading aloud to Thomas Norton a great deal of the manuscript and telling him 'the real names of many of the characters, which, of course, gave the story a very special interest'. On the Sunday, Longman, having been to church with Disraeli, examined the script himself in the library, saw Rowton catch a fish, heard Disraeli reading Tom Moore – no one would have appreciated that more than Tom Moore himself – and noted the almost total absence of newspapers in the house. All this happened on the 3rd and 4th of August. A few days later, on the 13th, Thomas Norton went back to Hughenden to collect the manuscript, once more staying the night.

On his arrival for the second time, an element of mystery as well as of secrecy was now deliberately introduced. He and Disraeli lit the house candles themselves because, Disraeli explained, he did not want his butler or his servants to know what was afoot. The cheque was then handed over as well as the manuscript. The practical question then was what should be used to carry the manuscript: the bag that Thomas Norton had brought with him had been put on one side by the butler. Thomas Norton was on the point of saying in 'my Gladstone bag', but stopped just in time.

At dinner Disraeli talked of his defeat at the recent election, but again Gladstone's name does not seem to have been mentioned. Instead, the Bible was taken as Disraeli's reference text. 'It was only yesterday', Disraeli said, that 'I was reading *Genesis*, the chapter in which it says that King Pharaoh had two bad harvests, now I had three, and three were too much for me, the elements defeated me.'

Endymion was printed and published remarkably quickly – in ten weeks – in an 'old fashioned' three-volume format of standard length bound in red cloth with silver lettering. News of its impending publication 'leaked' (to Thomas Norton's dismay) in the magazine *Truth*.[34] On its appearance, according to Thomas Norton, 'it created a sensation amongst all classes'. 'The rush at libraries was tremendous', and Mudie's first order, described by Thomas Norton to Disraeli as 'unprecedented', was for three thousand copies.[35] In fact, on this occasion the Library had over-ordered. Borrowing books was cheaper than buying them, and it was still deemed 'a real privilege and a capital return for one's money' to pay a guinea a year

The three-volume edition of *Endymion*. published in 1880, bound in red cloth with silver lettering. Longman had three copies bound in dark green morocco – for the Queen, Disraeli and himself. In Disraeli's copy Longman wrote:

'In pleasant recollection of the personal kindness and consideration received from the author this first copy of "Endymion" is presented to The Right Hon. The Earl of Beaconsfield K.G by the publisher T. Norton Longman, November 1880

Longman Archive

---

34 Nevertheless, news of the publication of *Lothair* had leaked too, and both Thomas IV and Thomas Norton used the same term 'the cat is out of the bag'. (Quoted in Jones, *loc. cit.*, p.33.)

35 Mudie had ordered 2,000 copies of George Eliot's *The Mill on the Floss* (1860) and of Tennyson's *Enoch Arden* (1864), but no fewer than 3,250 of David Livingstone's *Missionary Travels in South Africa* (1857). His Library was by no means tied to fiction.

BENDYMION.

Funny Folks cartoon
4 December 1880

John Bull – "Why Ben! Got to the books again?"

*Ben – "Yes, I couldn't be idle;
and when I lost my situation,
I thought I'd go back to my old
trade. I've something here quite
in my best style, and I hope you'll
give me a good big order."*

BL 122316.k.38.(2)

to Mudie's to borrow one volume;[36] and if Mudie's took out a large number of copies of a three-volume title, as it did on this occasion, it might seem to the author, as it did to Mrs. Oliphant, that it was 'a sort of recognition from heaven'.[37]

In recalling events, Thomas Norton, not surprisingly, did not go on to discuss the question as to whether or not he had struck a good publishing bargain in financial terms. He recorded, however, that four months after publication Rowton summoned him to settle accounts at 19 Curzon Street, the lease of which Disraeli had secured on the basis of the Longman deal. Most settlements were interim. Disraeli was taken ill with bronchitis in March 1881 and died on 19 April: Thomas Norton's last letter to him was dated 24 March.

It was in different places in his *Memories* that Thomas Norton observed that publishers had to be 'men of caution', but that 'the publication of a book, speaking generally, is and always will be a speculative investment'. It might have been John Murray II speaking, and Murray had his own memories of Disraeli (and Disraeli's father, Isaac). 'The subject matter of each particular book', Thomas Norton emphasised, 'brings [to the publisher's mind] a variety and change of thought which is not only welcome, but gives a special and peculiar interest to the routine of business.'[38] *Endymion* was announced, like other Longman books, in the House's own publication, *Notes on Books*, and according to the House's Impression Book, £171 8s. 0d. was spent on advertising.

Notes on Books made the most not of Disraeli's age (and experience) but of his fascination as a novelist with the 'energy of youth'. The novel dealt too – and mainly – with the influence of women in politicians' lives, and had special interest, in that, like Disraeli's other novels, it required a key to identify the real characters behind the fictional. One was printed in *Notes and Queries* the week before Christmas in 1880. *Harper's Magazine* in New York had published another on 26 November 1880. For the character Endymion 'the most powerful men' in the world were not 'public men'. 'A

---

36   The remark was that of the actress Fanny Kemble. For two guineas a year the subscriber could take out as many volumes as he or she wished. (Quoted in A. Cruse, *The Victorians and Their Books* (1935), p.334.)

37   Mrs. Oliphant, *Annals of a Publishing House, William Blackwood and his Sons*, Vol. II (2nd edn., 1897), p.458.

38   *Memories*, pp.182, 73, 52.

public man is responsible, and a responsible man is a slave. It is private life that governs the world.'

There was one particular feature in the story of the publication of *Endymion* that *The Times* claimed might have given it long-term significance in the histories of literature. It might have hastened, it was claimed misleadingly, the demise of the three-decker novel. By the 1880s, however, several publishers were producing novels in single volumes, and the time lag between the publication of a three-volume novel and its publication in a cheaper one-volume edition was shortening. This had begun to happen as early as the 1860s and 1870s.[39] It was undoubtedly a blow to Mudie's, however, when Thomas Norton, with Disraeli's approval, decided, as his father had done in case of *Lothair*, to publish a cheap edition of *Endymion* – he called it, in language of the time, a 'popular edition' – as early as February 1881, not telling the Library about his decision.[40]

Thomas Norton had already been accused, to his annoyance, of narrowing the public for the novel by first printing it in three-decker form; and it was when he realised, as Disraeli himself did, that the demand for the novel in that form and at that price was slackening that he published a one-volume 'cabinet edition', price six shillings,[41] which appeared in March 1881 before Disraeli's death. Other Disraeli novels were soon to be added to the well advertised collection.

Mudie, who lost heavily in consequence of his own over-ordering, wrote to Bentley in 1884, complaining how difficult it was to sustain his business. Indeed, his loss was so great that he reduced his order of novels published by Bentley to keep his accounts 'in trim'.[42] It was no secret that he would 'lose heavily' if he miscalculated the demand for a particular three-decker. 'We are anxious', he went on, 'to minimize *our loss* and wish to do so if possible without materially affecting the interests of Authors or Publishers.'[43] Authors, increasing in numbers in the last decades of the nineteenth century, were appreciating the situation as clearly as publishers, and by 1897 the number of three-deckers had fallen sharply: only four appeared in that year.

---

39 *Birds of Prey* by M.E. Braddon, author of the best-selling *Lady Audley's Secret* (1862), was published by Ward, Lock & Tyler in 1867 at 31s. 6d., but reissued at 6s. six months later and at 2s. five months after that. See R.L. Wolff, *Sensational Victorian: The Life and Fiction of Mary Elizabeth Braddon* (1979).

40 Letter of 9 Feb. 1881. Thomas Norton asked Disraeli to contribute a preface: 'nothing ... would contribute more effectually to increase the popularity of the work'.

41 *The Times*, 17 Dec. 1880.

42 Letter of 13 Jan. 1881, quoted in Gettman, *op. cit.*, p.258.

43 Letter of 20 Sept. 1884, quoted *ibid.*, p.259.

Exchanging books at Mudie's Circulating Library, from *Living London*, 1903 (p.96):

'Altogether no fewer than 400,000 volumes are in circulation at Mudies'

BL q942.1

The exceptionally short interval between the appearances of the three-decker edition and the 'cabinet edition' of *Endymion* was a matter of widespread comment, but this did not mean that this particular short interval, which had a Longman precedent in 1870, killed off the three-decker novel.[44] Longman was not a major publisher of novels, and its influence on a market for fiction that was changing significantly between 1851 and 1901 should not be exaggerated.[45] A new publisher, William Heinemann (1863–1918), who knew how to pick out promising novels, although this was not his main ambition, could claim the credit more convincingly, if it was a credit. In 1890 he published Hall (later Sir Hall) Caine's novel *The Manxman* in an initial 6s. edition, and to his and the author's delight it sold 400,000 copies.[46] The *Publishers' Circular*, discussing Heinemann's action, observed that if it was copied by other publishers the three-decker was doomed. 'The public will forsake the libraries and flock to the

---

44   See S. Eliot, 'The Three-Decker Novel and its First Cheap Imprint, 1862–1894' in TL, Vol. 7, No. 1, March 1985, pp.38–53.

45   See McAleer, *op. cit.*, Ch. 1, 'Popular Reading and Publishing, 1870–1914'.

46   See J. St. John, *William Heinemann, A Century of Publishing, 1890–1990* (1990), pp.25–31, 'Young Heinemann uses Hall Caine to Kill off the Three-Decker'. The gifted Hall Caine went on to write non-fiction as well as novels. His *Life of Samuel Taylor Coleridge* was well reviewed in the QR, Vol.165, July 1887, pp.60 ff.

booksellers.[47] The doom was at hand. By the end of the nineteenth century the three-decker had passed into history.

~

As late as that, Longman was still a publisher of novels, if not a major publisher, but it was in the field of non-fiction, production and marketing (and of publishing organisation) that it had a substantial influence. Indeed, this was considerably strengthened in the spring of 1890 when the purchase of the Rivington business, unanimously agreed upon by the Longman Board, cut through all publishing routines. Thomas Norton devoted the whole of the third chapter of his *Memories* to the purchase, and, as we have seen, it was a main topic at the staff dinner of 1890.

Unlike the earlier acquisition of J.W. Parker in 1863, the purchase was made on the initiative of the seller, Francis Hansard Rivington (1834-1913), who was a guest at the dinner held on 26 July 1890. Thomas Norton confessed in his *Memories* that he was 'never more astonished' in his life than when Rivington came to see him and offered him 'the whole concern en bloc'. As soon as Rivington closed the door Thomas Norton went straight to his cousin CJ's office and told him that he had 'just had the biggest proposal placed before me that has ever been received by the Longman firm'.[48] The two of them hurried to see Rivington at his office in Waterloo Place to report that they both felt favourably about the idea of a purchase – it was in no sense a merger – but that matters could not proceed further until they had seen Rivington's last balance sheet and had been given free access to all his books.

Rivington was 'quite naturally' hesitant about 'divulging his "secrets"', but at last 'gave way', proving 'perfectly fair and reasonable' thereafter. Thomas Norton recalled that he could not recollect 'anything like a difficulty' presenting itself. He noted, however, how difficult it was to transfer Rivington business properties back to Paternoster Row from Waterloo Place, which had started as a branch office in 1819 and had become Rivington's sole headquarters (except for warehousing) in 1853. 'The detail [of the move] was enormous'. The operation took only a week, but work went on each day far into the night, interrupted only by midday lunches of cold beef, pickled onions and beer, sent in from a public house in Warwick Square, and tea at five o'clock.[49]

Thomas Norton had little personally to do with the organisation of the

47 PC, 28 July 1894.

48 *Memories*, p.53.

49 PW, pp.47–8.

move.[50] His and CJ's formidable task was to tackle the Rivington authors, most of them drawn to Rivington under its old eighteenth-century flag, 'Fear God: Honour the King', some recruited late, however, after a Rivington deal with Hatchard in 1889. CJ took in hand the 'educational' authors and Thomas Norton 'the theological'. The former group was numerous, possibly more numerous than expected, for educational publishing had been vigorously pushed by Septimus Rivington (1846–1926), particularly in the field of Latin and Greek textbooks, among them Evelyn Abbott's *Primer of Greek Grammar*. Abbott was an influential Oxford scholar, a colleague of Benjamin Jowett, who published a three-volume *History of Greece* (1888–1900) and a major biography of Pericles, whom he saw, according to a recent scholar, as 'the ancient prototype of Gladstone'.[51]

Rivington's religious list was impressively 'solid', if not comprehensive. According to a family history, 'it had become more and more difficult to obtain a satisfactory circulation for theological books'. 'The habitual reporting of sermons in the newspapers at a fairly full length provided the clergy and laity with nearly all that they [by then] required in the way of sermons.'[52] Half a century before, Rivington had been quasi-official publishers to the Oxford Movement, beginning with the *Tracts* of the 1830s; and after Newman was converted to Roman Catholicism, Rivington continued its connection by publishing the writings of his very different Anglican successor, Canon E.B. Pusey.[53]

In order to make progress after the take-over, therefore, Thomas Norton had to familiarise himself with Oxford, a place relatively unknown to him, and with some of its best-known and most stubborn characters. 'The name of Longman', he wrote, was known there as publishers of '*all* kinds of works', whereas the name of Rivington was 'specially connected with books on theology'. 'The consequence was that some eminent [high] churchmen rather shied at having their publications advertised and mixed

---

50   *Memories*, p.55. For contemporary accounts of the acquisition see *The Bookseller*, 6 June 1890, which reprinted an older account of the Rivington business, and the *Daily Telegraph*, 31 May 1890. For a gossipy American article on 'The Rivingtons' see *The Critic*, 20 Sept. 1883: 'to any but a very wily professor, sleek college fellow, or well-stockinged bishop, the partners' rooms in Waterloo Place must be positively stifling'. The author was too glib when he concluded that clergymen, unlike writers of fiction, were not interested in the financial terms on which their books were published. See also an article by Espinasse in *Harper's Magazine*, Sept. 1885.

51   F.M. Turner, *The Greek Heritage in Victorian Britain* (1981), p.258.

52   See S. Rivington, *The Publishing Family of Rivington* (1919).

53   See R.W. Church, *The Oxford Movement* (1891, reprinted in 1970 with an introduction by Geoffrey Best), and for a scandalous account, W. Walsh, *Secret History of the Oxford Movement* (1897). See also G. Faber, *Oxford Apostles* (1933).

up with those of all sorts and conditions of men.' (This was a phrase borrowed from Besant, whose novel with that title appeared in three-decker form in 1882.[54])

The high church leaders knew too that Longman published theological works of a kind of which they totally disapproved, including some of the non-Trinitarian writings of Dr James Martineau (1805–1900). In an 1877 list Martineau's *Hours of Thought on Sacred Things* appeared immediately after Cardinal Manning's *The Temporal Mission of the Holy Ghost;* and twenty years later four volumes of his *Essays, Reviews and Addresses* – personal, political, ecclesiastical, historical, theological, philosophical and academical – appeared below a Stonyhurst series of six *Manuals of Catholic Philosophy*, among them Charles S. Devas's *Political Economy*.[55] 'Political economy', Devas began, 'is the name commonly given in England to economic science, one of the moral or ethical sciences which have as their subject matter the free actions of man.'[56] The volume was priced at 6*s*. 6*d*.

While Longman maintained its Roman Catholic links, the most eminent of the 'high' Church of England Oxford theologians, Canon H.P. Liddon, born in 1829, 'Pusey's Elisha', for twenty years a Canon of St Paul's and a great preacher there, wished to be assured that the House of Longman would endeavour 'to meet the views of the high church party. 'I do not recollect any case', Thomas Norton recalled, 'in which I was called upon to exercise greater tact or more diplomacy'.[57] And Liddon's early death in 1890, the year of the transfer, added to rather than diminished the strain, for Liddon had not yet finished his massive, scholarly, but inevitably controversial, three-volume *Life of Pusey*.

Liddon's executors, Dr Francis Paget, Dean of Christ Church, the Revd. Charles Gore, then Principal of Pusey House and a future bishop of three dioceses in turn, ending with Oxford, and the Revd. J.O. Johnston, Vicar of All Saints, Oxford, insisted on several volumes of biography. This 'startled' Thomas Norton 'considerably', but he was upset rather than startled when Paget, who took over the Pusey biography, made no progress with its writing. 'Absolutely nothing done by Paget since the autumn',

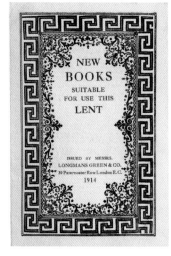

New Books suitable for use in LENT, 1914

Longman Archive

54   See S. Eliot, '"His Generation Read his Stories", Walter Besant, Chatto and Windus and *All Sorts and Conditions of Men*', in PH, Vol. XXI (1987), pp.25–67.

55   For Martineau, who remained closely associated with the Unitarians, although his religious sympathies were exceptionally wide, see 'James Martineau, A Retrospect', in *Transactions of the Unitarian Historical Society*, Vol. XXII (1902). In 1900 a Congregationalist theologian, P.T. Forsyth, placed Martineau in a 'trinity of spiritual powers' with Newman and F.D. Maurice.

56   C.S. Devas, *Political Economy* (1892), p.1.

57   *Memories*, pp.56–7. In 1882 Longman had published Thomas Mozley's *Reminiscences, Chiefly of Oriel College and the Oxford Movement*.

Thomas Norton noted uneasily after a visit to Oxford in May 1892, 'and consequently he has decided to give up the job, as it was simply impossible for him to find the necessary time.'[58]

After no fewer than five or six meetings with Paget in two days, Thomas Norton finally accepted the name of a different author, new to him, the Revd. J. Wilson, Warden of Keble, but only after Johnston, formerly 'Liddon's faithful secretary', agreed to help. Two volumes of the biography of Pusey duly appeared in 1893 and the third volume in 1894, each bearing the names of both Wilson and Johnston, but the fourth did not appear until 1897, the year of Wilson's death. Liddon's original contract with Rivington had been signed thirteen years before, but for Thomas Norton the unlucky figure of thirteen carried with it no significance. His concern was simpler. 'Surely a publisher requires patience.'

Thomas Norton had a moment of true happiness, however, when on one of his 'Oxford trips' he carried a cheque for £1,000 to hand to Liddon's executors.[59] He was happy too, posthumously to publish Liddon's works, beginning with his Bampton Lectures of 1866, still selling and being read in the 1890s. Other works of Liddon published posthumously included *Sermons on Special Occasions* delivered between 1860 and 1889.[60]

The general outcome of the Rivington take-over was a Longman theological list which was not only the most impressive in Britain, but the most diverse, as the twenty-four advertisement pages at the end of J.H. Overton's *The English Church in the Nineteenth Century, 1800–1833* (1894), part of a series, demonstrate. And that advertisement left out many of the Roman Catholic works of Cardinal Newman, which were set out in a separate Longman list, 'available on application'.[61] In his history Overton stopped short of Tract 90 (1841) and of Newman's conversion to Rome, but he mentioned the names of people to whom Newman dedicated his Anglican

---

58   This is not mentioned in the biography by Stephen Paget and J.M. Crum, *Francis Paget* (1912), although in their preface the authors thank Thomas Norton for his help. They also refer (p.149) to a conversation between Thomas Norton and Paget on Froude and to the brochure Paget wrote for Rivington, *Faculties and Difficulties for Belief and Disbelief* (1887).

59   *Ibid.*, p.60.

60   See 'Half-Hours with the Publishers of Church Literature, Messrs. Longmans & Co.', in *Church Bells*, 30 April 1897. For Liddon's place in the Church of England see J.O. Johnston, *Life and Letters of Henry Parry Liddon* (1904); O. Chadwick, *The Victorian Church*, Vol. II (1970); and P.J. Marsh, *The Victorian Church in Decline* (1969).

61   Overton was a Canon of Lincoln Cathedral and Rector of Epworth, the place where John Wesley's father was Rector and John Wesley was born. The first item in the 1894 advertisement was C.J. Abbey and Overton's *The English Church in the Eighteenth Century* (1878). Fifteen titles were listed in the *Epochs of Church History* series, edited by Mandell Creighton, then Bishop of Peterborough.

sermons. Five volumes of these appeared in the 1894 advertisement, three of them edited by the Revd. W.J. Copeland, Rector of Farnham, Essex from 1849 to 1885, a Rivington author, who edited eight volumes of *Parochial and Plain Sermons* in a Cabinet edition, price 5s. each and in a Popular edition, price 3s. 6d.[62]

Copeland, with whom Newman communicated about his publications, was not the only editor or author to figure more than once in the advertisement of 1894, an advertisement in which prices mattered as much as titles. The most successful writers went into different kinds of reprint. Thus, a volume by Edward Bickersteth (1814–1892), appointed Dean of Lichfield in 1875 (and an honorary Canon of Christ Church), *Yesterday, Today and For Ever*, cheap at a shilling, could be bought in a more expensive edition with red borders, part of a 'devotional series', at 2s. 6d., and in a Crown 8vo edition 'still in print' at 5s. A 'classic' like St. Francis de Sales's *The Devout Life* cost 6d. 'limp', 1s. in cloth, 2s. with red borders and 5s. in foolscap. An *Aids to the Inner Life* series, edited by a Yorkshire rector, the Revd. W.H. Hutchings, included editions at 6d. (limp cloth) and 1s. (cloth extra); Hutchings also edited *The Confessions of St. Augustine* in ten books (small 8vo 5s., cheap edition 2s. 6d.).

The range of prices charged for the same title should be compared with the range of prices charged for the tracts of the Society for Promoting Christian Knowledge and for non-theological works, including novels, the category which has received most attention in this connection. So, too, should the standard prices of the volumes in the *Oxford Library of Practical Theology* and the wide-ranging prices of books specially addressed to children, a number of them judged highly suitable as prizes, and a number of them providing links with other Longman lists. For example, the Revd. William Baker, Headmaster of Merchant Taylor's School and Prebendary of St Paul's, had written *A Manual of Devotion for Schoolboys* (cloth limp, 1s. 6d.), and *Daily Prayers for Younger Boys* (8d.). The Headmaster of Rugby, the Revd. J. Percival, formerly Headmaster of Clifton, Bristol, offered *Home Helps for School Life*, following in the wake of his great predecessor at Rugby, Thomas Arnold, whose *Sermons Preached mostly in the Chapel of Rugby School* was still in print in an advertisement of 1894. One of Pusey's books in the advertisement was *Prayers for a Young Schoolboy*. It had a preface by Liddon.

Edward Osborne, Mission Priest of the Society of St. John the Evangelist, Cowley, a part of Oxford to be totally transformed by the automobile in the twentieth century, offered *The Children's Saviour, The Saviour King* and *The Christian Faith*. At the time when Osborne wrote

---

62 For Rivington as Newman's publisher, see L.N. Crumb, 'Publishing the Oxford Movement: Francis Rivington's Letter to Newman', in PH, Vol. XXVIII (1990), pp.5–53.

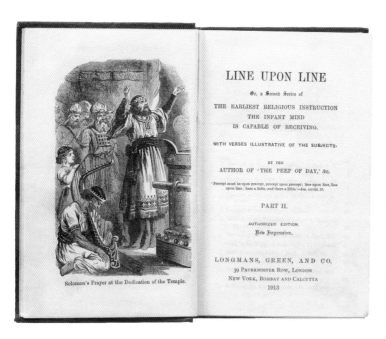

Line upon Line, in *The Peep of Day Series* 'A second series of the earliest religious instruction the infant mind is capable of receiving', Longmans, 1913

Personal collection

there could have been no intimations of the industrial Cowley to come. Nor could there have been to Newman or to Thomas Norton or to those 'Members of the University of Oxford' who wrote *A Series of Papers for Working Men*, prepared for Oxford House, an East End Settlement in London, not far from Toynbee Hall.[63]

Nevertheless, industry figures in the House of Longman vistas of the 1880s and 1890s: in particular it published A.J. Toynbee's posthumous *Lectures on the Industrial Revolution of the 18th Century in England* (1884), a book which established and popularised the term 'industrial revolution'; and the Revd. Ashton Oxenden, the most prolific author in the 1894 advertisement, with more than thirty titles to his name, offered *The Labouring Man's Book* (large type, cloth, 1s. 6d.) along with *Cottage Sermons: or Plain Words to the Poor*.[64] A later book of considerable influence on the evolution of the term 'industrial revolution' was W. (later Sir William) Ashley's *The Economic Organisation of England* (1914) which ended with a chapter on 'the evolution of capitalism'.

Most of the religious titles that entered into this terrain were controversial, and consequentially Thomas Norton could no more avoid religious controversy than his father had done. Charles Gore (1853–1932), although a Liddon executor, was soon engaged in disputes on theological issues, following lines of enquiry that diverged from Liddon's, the last of them, years later, and for a variety of reasons, leading him to resign the

---

63 For the background of the Settlement movement see A. Briggs and A. Macartney, *Toynbee Hall* (1984) and H. McLeod, *Class and Religion in the Late Victorian City* (1974). Longman published few books of social observation, including statistical surveys, many of which made recommendations concerning social policy, but it published the massive work of the Webbs on the history of the labour movement, beginning with *The History of Trade Unionism* (1894) and the two volumes of *Industrial Democracy* (1897).

64 Writing in 'plain and simple language', Oxenden (1808–1892) had established his credentials when he served for nine years as Bishop of Montreal and Metropolitan of Canada from 1869 to 1878.

Bishopric of Oxford in 1919.[65] Meanwhile, he had become a distinctive voice in the Church of England, directing the attention of priests to controversial social issues. Some of the priests were Christian Socialists, like Henry Scott Holland (1847–1918), founder of the Guild of St Matthew, six of whose books figured in the advertisement of 1894. A brilliant lecturer – and wit – he died in 1918.[66] R.H. Tawney's *Religion and the Rise of Capitalism* (1926) was based on Scott Holland Lectures that he had delivered four years earlier and was dedicated to Gore.

~

One writer on the Longman theological list also made his way into the children's lists, as did his wife, and, of greater importance, into the history list. Mandell Creighton (1843–1901), Bishop of Peterborough, who was to become Bishop of London in 1897, was a somewhat enigmatic character, who objected to 'extravagant practices' in church services yet believed in responding to the changing needs of the time.[67] His four-volume *History of the Papacy during the Period of the Reformation*, which he considered his 'great work' and which was sold to Longman on that basis,[68] was one of the most expensive books in the Longman advertisements: the first two volumes cost 32s., the third and fourth 24s.

Creighton had already written many books, some of them published by Longman, beginning with *The Age of Elizabeth* in 1876, one of a series, and while still an Oxford don, he had been approached by Thomas Norton IV in 1874 to edit a series of primers, *Epochs of English History*, the copyright of which he sold to Longman for £100. He also drew in his wife Louise, his future biographer, who long outlived him and was to attend the bicentenary banquet of the House of Longman in 1924, to write *England: A Continental Power, from the Conquest to Magna Carta* (1876). Short of

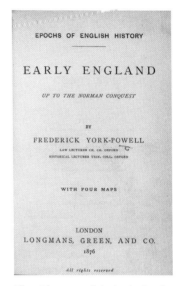

The title page of *Early England* (1876) one of a series of ten primers, written between 1876 and 1895 and edited by Mandell Creighton

BL 9503.b.28

65 Liddon himself had been disturbed not only by a series of essays edited by Gore, *Lux Mundi* (1889), but by Gore's invitations to socialists, among them Ben Tillett, to speak in Pusey House. See S. Mayor, *The Churches and the Labour Movement* (1967), p.217. There were many reasons for Gore's resignation of his bishopric in 1919 twelve years before his death. See his obituary in the first DNB, 1931–1940, by the then Bishop of Durham, A.T.P. Williams. A later Bishop of Oxford, J.C. Carpenter, wrote his biography, *Charles Gore, A Study in Liberal Catholicism* (1949). See also M.B. Reckitt, *Maurice to Temple, A Century of the Social Movement in the Church of England* (1947).

66 See S. Paget (ed.), *Henry Scott Holland: Memoir and Letters* (1921).

67 See L. Creighton, *Life and Letters of Mandell Creighton*, 2 Vols (1904) and J.T. Covert, *A Victorian Marriage, Mandell and Louise Creighton* (2000).

68 Creighton told the Cambridge don, Oscar Browning, that, 'from experience', life was 'not complete unless one has a great work in the stocks' (quoted in Covert, *op. cit.*, p.162). Creighton's 'great work' was never completed.

money, the Creightons proclaimed high moral purposes. The *Epochs*, which 'focused on what young readers needed', Creighton told CJ, would be used in 'all kinds of schools', including 'the broad spectrum of board schools' and would be of particular value in girls' education.

Louise, who shared in this purpose, described her *First History of England* (1881) as babies' history: as she herself put it, she read it to her own babies, who took up so much of her own time that she found it difficult to write.[69] She was contemplating a novel too. Her then close friend Mrs. Humphry Ward (1851–1920), granddaughter of Thomas Arnold of Rugby and Matthew Arnold's niece, was to forestall her in this: her three-volume novel *Robert Elsmere* (1888), which fascinated Gladstone, was to be a bestseller, and between 1890 and 1900 she turned herself into a 'fiction machine'.[70] Louise Creighton followed her own course, and the unpremeditated idea of writing her husband's biography was suggested to her in 1901 by CJ, who by then had become her friend as well as her publisher.

It was CJ who had welcomed the inauguration of the *English Historical Review* in 1886. The idea of such a review, raised nearly twenty years earlier with Alexander Macmillan (and later in 1883, when the Cambridge University Press was considered the likely publisher), had been floated again at a meeting in Cambridge in 1885 soon after Creighton had been appointed first Dixie Professor of Ecclesiastical History there.[71] Apparently all those who were present agreed that Creighton should be first editor, but the idea could not go ahead without assurances from CJ about the willingness of the House of Longman to proceed, and these were duly given.[72]

Creighton was an influential historian, although soon after becoming editor he crossed swords (unwillingly) with Lord Acton (1834–1902), who as a Roman Catholic fiercely disputed Creighton's tolerant attitude towards the medieval Papacy; and it was in a letter to Creighton (3 April 1887) that Acton first used the words 'Power tends to corrupt, and absolute power corrupts

---

69   Quoted in Covert, *op. cit.*, p.158.

70   See J. Sutherland, *Mrs. Humphry Ward, Eminent Victorian, Pre-eminent Edwardian* (1990), Chs. 10, 11, 12.

71   For the earlier efforts involving James Bryce and J.R. Green see D.S. Goldstein, 'The Origins and early years of the *English Historical Review*', in the EHR Centenary Number, CCCXCVIII, Jan. 1986, pp.6-19 and 'The Organization and Development of the British Historical Profession, 1884-1921', in the *Bulletin of the Institute of Historical Research*, Vol. 55 (1982), p.180. See also D. Hay, 'The Historical Periodical', in *History*, Vol. LIV (1969), pp.165–177.

72   L. Creighton, *Life and Letters of M. Creighton*, Vol. I, p.333. In 1872 Henry Sidgwick had made the remarkable admission that he did not believe 'that there is a single man in Cambridge competent to deal with modern history in an intelligent way'. (Letter to Bryce, 19 April 1872. Quoted in Goldstein, *loc. cit.*, p.6.)

absolutely'.[73] Acton was to go on to edit the *Cambridge Modern History*.

In order to impress CJ, Creighton used Acton's name, but early sales of the *English Historical Review* were low, and CJ's continuing support was necessary. He was perhaps more impressed by Gladstone's offer of an article, while realising, as Creighton told him, that 'at present the *Review* is chiefly the organ of historical students and has little attraction for the general public'.[74] In the long run, as the numbers of 'historical students' and their professional teachers and professors grew, the *Review* established itself firmly so that at the time of its centenary its then editors could thank CJ's 'lineal successors': 'editorial relations' had always been close and productive'.[75]

Of the many historians published by Longman, who had been taken into the House after the earlier Parker take-over, some, like Froude, remained controversial to the last, his death in 1894 and even beyond.[76] Yet he made his way without question into the pages of G.P. Gooch's (1873–1968) *History and Historians in the Nineteenth Century*, a new Longman book published in 1913. So, too, did W.H. Lecky (1838–1903), all of whose works figured in the Longman list of 1900, which also included the ten-volume *History of England from the Accession of James I to the Outbreak of the Civil War* by S.R. Gardiner, his four-volume *A History of the Great Civil War* and a two-volume *A History of the Commonwealth and Protectorate*. Gardiner (1829–1902), who succeeded Creighton as editor of the *English Historical Review* in 1891, was the model of an historian for Gooch, who also considered some of Lecky's writings on Ireland similar models, particularly when Lecky was criticising Froude.

Gooch considered that E.A. Freeman (1823–1892), an occasional Longman author, who succeeded William Stubbs as Regius Professor of Modern History at Oxford, when Stubbs moved to a bishopric (Chester) in

---

73 See R. Hill, *Lord Acton* (2000), pp.296–303.

74 Creighton to C.J. Longman, 28 Oct. 1889 in L. Creighton, *op. cit.*, Vol. 1, pp.343–4.

75 *EHR* Centenary Number, p.2. A General Index for the years 1956 to 1985 had been prepared by Angus Macintyre, joint editor from 1978 to 1986. James Bryce (1838–1922), British Ambassador to the United States from 1907 to 1913, who had been involved in the early discussions with Macmillan about a review, wrote a 'prefatory note' in the first number propounding the ideals of 'the scientific spirit', impartiality and cosmopolitanism. He had refused the editorship of the *Review* when it was first mooted.

76 Marshall Kelly, author of *Froude, A Study of His life and Character* (1903), offered the book to Longman, who were in the course of publishing Froude's *My Relations with Carlyle*. For Kelly (pp.125–6) Froude had not been 'without his admirers since his death', but they had been 'almost exclusively of the valet tribe'.

1884, had an assured place in the history of history as a writer and teacher.[77] Yet Henry Liddell, Dean of Christ Church from 1855 to 1891, despised Freeman, and Freeman had no regard for Froude, who was to succeed him in the Regius Chair in 1892.

The Longman history list of 1900 included new titles, including *England in the Age of Wycliffe* by G.M. Trevelyan (1876–1962), the third son of Sir George Otto Trevelyan (1838–1928), biographer of Macaulay. George Otto communicated regularly – and intimately – by letter with Theodore Roosevelt on a variety of subjects, including history itself. Roosevelt, who considered him an 'intellectual playmate', carried with him to Africa in 1908 not only Part III of G.O.'s *History of the American Revolution* but a complete set of the works of Macaulay.[78]

~

As many books by Theodore Roosevelt would have done, *The Story of the Malakand Field Force* (1898), the first book by Winston Churchill (1874–1965), a future Prime Minister as well as an historian, appeared not in the Longman History, Politics, Polity, Political Memoirs, &c list, but in the 'Travel and Adventure' list. And this was its right placing, even though half a century later Churchill's four-volume *History of the English Speaking Peoples* (1956–1958) would vie in popularity with Macaulay and with G.M. Trevelyan's *English Social History* (1940).[79] Gooch, elected to Parliament in 1906, praised Churchill's early books as the 'most delightful' of all his books, but he too had no reason for including Churchill as an historian in *History and Historians in the Nineteenth Century*.

Like Gooch, Churchill, then aged twenty-four, approached Thomas Norton directly with a publishing proposition – in no other respect were their situations alike – in a letter from Bangalore in India in 1898, offering him a novel which did not deal with India. Thomas Norton wrote back a characteristically 'very civil letter' with no conceivable intimation that he was corresponding with a future Prime Minister, professing himself eager to see what Winston had written. In fact, he was already writing on many 'literary subjects', but on this occasion he asked his mother, herself strenuously involved in an ambitious publishing venture, to find

---

77   For Freeman and Froude see J.W. Burrow, *A Liberal Descent, Victorian Historians and the English Past* (1981). Stubbs, described by Acton in a letter to Creighton as 'the angel of Chester', gave no help to the EHR. (Goldstein, *loc. cit.*, pp.8–9.) Reginald Lane Poole, another Oxford don, was joint editor of the EHR (with Gardiner) from 1895 to 1901 and sole editor from 1902 to 1920.

78   See E. Morris, *Theodore Rex* (2001), esp. p.310 and p.540, and H.W. Brunds (ed.), *The Selected Letters of Theodore Roosevelt* (2001), p.348 and p.508.

79   In the winter of 1896 Churchill had 'devoured' Gibbon and Macaulay ('easier reading').

out whether her son might get 'better terms' by offering the story to a magazine in instalments.[80] Lady Churchill was in effect acting as his unpaid agent, and Winston added pertinently that 'the point to insist upon is a real [sic] good proportion on each copy sold – so much in the shilling. I don't ask for more than to stand in well with the publisher.'[81]

Winston always appreciated both the problems and the opportunities of authorship, and he would never have accepted the terms on which Gooch produced his own *History* and his later books, all of them with Longmans, Green. Gooch commissioned the House to publish the book for him at his own risk and expense – this procedure was common for the late-Victorian Longmans – and the House duly paid him what amounted to approximately half of the retail price of every book sold.[82] In pressing successfully for different terms Churchill brought into his picture not an historian but Rudyard Kipling, whose latest book, *The Seven Seas*, was, he felt, 'not up to the standard of his other works', and Rider Haggard, whom he thought was also losing his prowess.

'What happens is this', Churchill generalised, 'an author tails away & and has many failures. Rejected contributions – books which the publishers won't publish accumulate. Money does not. One day he writes a book which makes him famous: *King Solomon's Mines* ... His name now is on everyone's lips – his books are clamoured for by the public. Out come all the familiar productions from their receptacles, and his financial fortune is made ... The author writes no more for fame but for wealth. Consequently his books become inferior. ... I am afraid Kipling is killed.'[83]

Like so much that Churchill was to predict, this prediction was wrong. Yet he did not wait for a novel, as yet unwritten, to be rejected by Longman

---

80 Lady Randolph, recently widowed, was planning a salon quarterly review which was called the *Anglo-Saxon Review* and was published by John Lane. The first number, 230 pages long, appeared in June 1899. See R.G. Martin, *Jennie – the Life of Lady Randolph Churchill: The Dramatic Years, 1895–1901* (1971), p.152.

81 R.S. Churchill, *Winston S. Churchill*, Vol. I, Companion, Part 2 (1967), p.936. Churchill added also that it might make three small volumes. 'The 31s. 6d. edition is of course the only real paying one in these days of circulating libraries.' The 'of course' no longer held.

82 F. Eyck, *G.P. Gooch: a study in history and politics* (1982). Eyck's book was published not by Longmans, but by Macmillan. Some of Gooch's works were published on a royalty basis, for example *The Later Correspondence of Lord John Russell 1840–1878* (1925) and *Historical Surveys and Portraits* (1966). Most of his books were destroyed in the Blitz of 1940 when after the destruction Gooch went to look at the remains of Paternoster Row (Eyck, *op. cit.*, pp.431-2).

83 Letter to his brother, who was then at Harrow, 7 January 1897, reprinted in R.S. Churchill, *op. cit.*, pp.721–2.

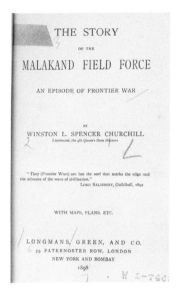

The title page of *The Story of the Malakand Field Force, 1898* by Winston Churchill

At the end of the Preface Churchill wrote: 'I have recorded the facts as they occurred, and the impressions as they arose without attempting to make a case against any person or any policy. Indeed, I fear that assailing none, I may have offended all. Neutrality may degenerate into an ignominious isolation. An honest and unprejudiced attempt to discern the truth, is my sole defence, as the good opinion of the reader has been throughout my chief aspiration, and can be in the end my only support.'

BL W.217443

(or other publishers), but instead, through the professional agent, A.P. Watt, who had been employed by his mother,[84] agreed to publish with Longman his real-life adventure book, *The Story of the Malakand Field Force*. He secured extremely generous terms. Longman would publish it, probably at 6s., a standard price, 'at his own risk and expense' and would pay a royalty of 15 per cent on the first three thousand copies of the English edition and 20 per cent thereafter, 3d. a copy on the Colonial Library edition, 10 per cent on the first thousand copies sold in the United States, and 15 per cent thereafter. He would also receive an advance of £50 on the day of publication. In a letter to Lady Randolph, with the PS quoted at the beginning of this *History*, Watt added 'I have impressed upon Mr. Longman the necessity there is for having the book produced without any delay'.[85]

Topicality, not longevity, was thus at stake. When Churchill received the welcome news from his mother, who sensibly had first approached Algernon (later Sir Algernon) Methuen, the publisher of Kipling's *Barrack Room Ballads*, an overnight success,[86] he replied that he was 'very glad to hear Longmans are publishing – they are a good firm'.[87] He calculated that he would eventually receive about £300. 'I have many literary projects in mind', he also told her. In thinking about terms, his mother added mildly in a later letter, 'you must not be greedy at first'. She had been told (wrongly) that Longman 'as a rule' published only at the cost of the author. 'If your book sells you will make a good deal.' 'I do not quarrel with the bargain', her son replied. 'Every one must begin.'

The beginning was not easy, for when Churchill read the 'revised proof' of *The Story of the Malakand Field Force*, he found it riddled with so many errors that he wired the Indian office of Longman to try to stop publication.[88] They were attributable, he acknowledged, largely to his own handwriting and to what his father would have called 'his slovenly shiftless

84   See J. Hepburn, *The Author's Empty Purse and the Rise of the Literary Agent* (1968), and H. Rubinstein, 'A.P. Watt: the First Hundred Years', in *The Bookseller*, 3 May 1975.

85   R.S. Churchill, *op. cit.*, p.873, Letter of 20 Jan. 1898.

86   Algernon Methuen Marshal Stedman, a former schoolmaster, born in 1856, had changed his surname to Methuen in 1899 when he acquired an office in Essex Street, London. He was later to publish Kenneth Grahame's *The Wind in the Willows* (1908) and Marie Corelli's *The Life Everlasting* (1911).

87   R.S. Churchill, *op. cit.*, p.874. No less a person than A.J. Balfour, the next Prime Minister, had told Lady Randolph that Watt was 'very good at making a bargain and it is a great thing that yr. First book shd be published by such a good firm as Longman [who published him], also that it shd be done at their cost.' (*Ibid.*, p.875.) Lady Randolph also discussed the book with General Lord Roberts, to whom she sent a copy.

88   *Ibid.*, pp.895, 899.

habits'. The spelling of 'vigorously' was one, 'babri' for 'babu' another, and, prophetically, 'causalities' for 'casualties'. An erratum slip appeared in the published edition.

Given this confession, it is testimony to Churchill's remarkable character that after asking his mother to 'imagine my feelings', he told her to read 'Lord Macaulay's essay on Mr. [James] Montgomery's poems. I feel as that wretched man did when he first read it.'[89] Nevertheless, he was not defeated. 'My style is good – and in parts classic' – a statement that he had to qualify in a later letter admitting stylistic blunders, such as reverting on one page from the past tense to the historic present tense. 'No good author that I have ever read changes his tense. Certainly not Gibbon or Addison.'[90]

Churchill was contemplating a second edition and had actually written a preface to it before he wrote again to Longman about a novel, telling his mother soon afterwards to get in touch, if she thought it wise, with Watt or any literary agent. 'I do not think it would be advisable to go to a fresh publisher if Longmans like the book. But, of course [and he returned to his earlier comparison], there is no doubt that Methuen publishes in a better style though they are not so old a firm.' It was neither House, but, instead, Macmillan, who bought the serial rights of the novel *Affairs of State* for *Macmillan's Magazine*, offering him £100. After publication copyright was to return to Churchill who hoped 'to make Longman publish it in book form'.[91]

Fiction moved more slowly than history, however, and the next book of Churchill's that Longman published, dedicated to the Prime Minister, the Marquess of Salisbury, was the two-volume *The River War, An Historical Account of the Reconquest of the Soudan* (1899). This was a vivid account of the country to which Churchill moved from India, being given the opportunity by Salisbury (and others) to take part in the final campaign against the Mahdi. In 1885 Charles George Gordon (1833–1885), who was to provide a subject for Lytton Strachey, had been killed in Khartoum, having been besieged for 317 days by the Mahdi's troops. Thomas Norton Longman had tried to secure the rights of Gordon's 'Last Journals', offering £5,000 to Gordon's brother, who held the manuscript, but was overbid in a curious

---

89 The criticism did Montgomery no harm. The Longman Impression Books show that Montgomery's sales increased.

90 There were 200 misprints in the published edition, leading one reviewer to direct attention to a 'mad printer's reader'. *The Athenaeum*, 16 March 1898, noting and condemning the errors, predicted none the less that 'the author might become as great a soldier as the first Marlborough' and 'a straighter politician'.

91 R.S. Churchill, *op. cit.*, p.1016, Letter to his grandmother, the Duchess of Marlborough, headed Suez, 26 March 1899.

auction held in private by C. Kegan Paul who offered 5,000 guineas. According to Kegan Paul, Thomas Norton is said to have remarked that it was 'those damned shillings that had done it'.[92]

There was no blindfold bidding when Watt again acted as agent for Churchill when Winston was turning his reports on the war to recapture the Sudan into a book.[93] He was then earning five times more by his pen than from his sword, and Watt was good at his job in ensuring a good bargain for his client. Churchill was off to war again, a bigger and more protracted war, in South Africa, before completing the text. In the meantime, however, he had been elected as Conservative MP for Oldham.

Churchill's personal adventures in South Africa made him a more valuable 'literary property' than he had been before,[94] and he did not consult Watt before completing arrangements with Longmans for the publication of two paste-up books of his despatches from South Africa, *Ian Hamilton's March* (1900) and *London to Ladysmith*, which appeared five days before the relief of Mafeking. They sold 22,000 copies in Britain and the United States. They were, however, the last of Churchill's books to be published by Longman, although the partners made an extremely generous offer to him in 1905 (£4,000 on account, with a royalty of 25 per cent, an exceptionally high figure) to publish his *Life of Randolph Churchill*. They even incurred printing costs, having gone so far as to place their imprint on his proofs.

Winston had changed his mind – and his publishers – when in order to get a better bargain he turned, for reasons never fully explained, not to Watt but to an extraordinary mediator, Frank Harris (1856–1931), more often regarded later as an 'advertiser' or, indeed, adventurer than as editor, writer or agent. It may have been a shrewd choice. 'Praise from Harris was never easily won', and Harris 'enjoyed a boom period in his own life in Edwardian England'.[95] Churchill's first letter to Harris was written 'in the train' while a conversation with him was fresh in his mind. 'I authorise you as my friend to talk in confidence & privacy to publishers about my book' and he promised Harris 10 per cent of the excess net profit above £4,000.

Thereafter, while Churchill was writing to Britain's leading politicians to secure letters and other documents relating to his father, Harris was writing to publishers on paper headed 'The Motorist and Traveller'. He began with two of the newest publishers, Heinemann and Methuen, fending off other people who were claiming to be Churchill's

---

92   Thomas Norton told the story in his unpublished *Memories*, p.44; Kegan Paul gave his own account in his published *Memories* in 1899, p.287.

93   For his war despatches see F. Woods (ed.), *Young Winston's Wars* (1972).

94   Letter from Watt to Churchill, 16 Feb. 1900, quoted in R.S. Churchill, *op. cit.*, pp.115–7.

95   F. Swinnerton, *Figures in the Foreground* (1963), p.49.

agents, including William Colles, founder and managing director of an Authors' Syndicate, set up in 1890.[96] Harris himself considered the text of Churchill's biography better than Rosebery's *Pitt* or Morley's *Gladstone*, high praise indeed.

Among the publishers Harris approached, Murray turned it down, and, after meeting Churchill, Macmillan made the successful offer – £8,000, with a payment of £1,000 on receipt of Churchill's acceptance, £1,000 when the proofs had gone to press, and £1,000 when the book appeared.[97] Harris, whose scholarship was praised by Churchill in a letter to Macmillan, quickly revised the proofs, enabling the volumes to appear three days before the general election of 1905. 'You have dared greatly in bringing it out at this time when we are all full of the current fight', Joseph Chamberlain told him.[98]

C. J. Longman handsomely congratulated Churchill on the 'splendid price you have got for your book', adding that he was naturally 'much disappointed that it is not to come out from Paternoster Row'. 'I cannot doubt that you were right to accept the offer', he went on, 'sincerely trust[ing] that we may be associated in some other literary enterprise ... at no very distant date.' This was not to happen, and Macmillan paid the printing expenses Longmans had incurred. Harris told Churchill with obvious satisfaction on 5 February 1906 that *The Times*, then in dispute with publishers about its sale of books, had taken 6,000 more copies and that sales were not far short of 5,000.[99] Meanwhile, in 1904, Churchill had changed not only his publishers but his political party, becoming a Liberal, and he was soon given a prominent place in the new Liberal government which took office in 1906.

~

CJ's and Thomas Norton's dealings with politicians took up considerably less time than their dealings with writers on sport and, indeed, their own diverse sporting activities. It was Thomas Norton who initiated a *Badminton Library* of books on different sports which fascinated the whole Longman family and brought them all together. The sports were no more sports 'for the millions', however, than most of the books that Longman

96 For Harris see his autobiography *My Life* (1930); A.I. Tobin and E. Gertz, *Frank Harris, A Study in Black and White* (1931); and H. Kingsmill, *Frank Harris* (1932). Harris was editor of the *Fortnightly Review* from 1886 to 1894, and in 1894 he bought the *Saturday Review* which he ran until 1898. In 1909 he published *The Man Shakespeare and his tragic life story*.

97 R.S. Churchill, *op. cit.*, pp.476, 478.

98 Letter of 3 Jan. 1906, *ibid.*, p.486.

99 *Ibid.*, p.492.

Graceful Movements, No. 2

A hot return.

An illustration from *The Badminton Library* on 'Dancing' (Graceful Movements, No 2) by Mrs Lilly Grove, 1895

Student's Union Library, University of Oxford: 792.62 GRO

An illustration from *The Badminton Library* on 'Cricket' ('A hot return') by A.G Steel, 1888

The Bodleian Library, University of Oxford: 38454.e.15

published were 'books for the millions'. They were not in competition with newspapers, and were designed in the first instance for active participants in field sports. Thomas Norton drew on his own experience when he wrote 'I placed the Gun second to the Rod, but I have certainly had more Shooting than Fishing.'[100]

Thomas noted that it was CJ who had suggested a sporting series called 'Fur, Feather and Fin': the Fin was added later.[101] The first five were entitled *The Partridge, The Grouse, The Pheasant, The Hare* and *Red Deer. The Salmon* and *The Trout* followed. George Saintsbury, connoisseur of books and of wine, wrote a 'Cookery' section in *The Grouse*. CJ, deeply interested in the Badminton series, wrote a volume, *Archery*, for it. He was the Archery Champion of England in 1883.

The *Badminton Library of Sports and Pastimes* was the most characteristic expression of Longman family tastes at the end of the nineteenth century and the beginning of the twentieth. As early as 1882, the publication of a new edition of Blaine's *Encyclopædia of Rural Sports* was contemplated but quickly rejected on the grounds of its impracticability.[102] Instead, CJ conceived of a sequence of separate volumes dealing with specific sports,

100 Earlier in the century Peter Hawker's *Instructions to young Sportsmen in all that relates to Guns and Shooting*, of which Longman was the sole publisher, had gone through various editions.

101 *Memories*, p.83.

102 In 1901 Heinemann, head of a business not yet in existence in 1882, decided to launch a new *Encyclopaedia of Sports and Games* (published 1911). He chose as its editor a member of the aristocracy who had previously written for Longman, the Earl of Suffolk and Berkshire.

each volume being written by a specialist who could appeal to a distinctive group of devotees to a particular sport. Originally Thomas Norton had no more than seven or eight volumes in mind, all of them following in the tradition of Blaine and of Joseph Strutt's *Sports and Pastimes of the People of England* (1801), but going into far more detail. Eventually, however, thirty volumes were to appear, many of them concerned with non-rural sports at a time when in public schools and universities codified games were gaining in appeal and status, as the Longmans themselves knew, again from their own individual experience.

The great Longmans' coup was to attract as General Editor the eighth Duke of Beaufort, born in 1824, who lived at Badminton.[103] He gave the name of his house to the Library, and his portrait appeared as the frontispiece to *Driving* (1889). He was introduced to Thomas Norton by Tom Paine, ironically named, a keen member of Tattersalls. The Duke's sense of natural authority was well expressed in his chapter on 'Hunt Servants' in the first volume that, very properly, he wrote himself with a co-author, Mowbray Morris. Given the times, however, it was authority that he believed should be curbed by restraint:

> A huntsman, whether he be a gentleman or a professional [then the key distinction in all sports, rural or non-rural], should impress on his whippers-in certain things that they should or should not do. This is better done by quietly talking to them in the kennels or elsewhere than by blowing them up or swearing at them in the hunting field, though it is necessary at times to speak out there.[104]

Deference was taken for granted, and it was through Beaufort's social authority that the series as a whole was dedicated to the Prince of Wales, his 'friend', whom he described generously as 'one of the best and keenest sportsmen of our time'. By way of justification, he added that, 'when the wind had been blowing hard, often have I seen His Royal Highness knocking over driven grouse and partridges and high rocketing pheasants in first-rate workman-like style'.[105]

The adjective 'workman-like', which may catch the feel of Beaufort's

---

103 For the background see J.A. Mangan, *Athleticism in the Victorian and Edwardian Public School* (1981); T. Mason (ed.), *Sport in Britain, a Social History* (1989); J. Lowerson, *Sport and the English Middle Classes 1870–1914* (1993); and W. Vamplew, *Pay Up and Play the Game: professional sport in Britain 1875–1914* (1988).

104 *Hunting* (1885), p.6. See A. Briggs, 'The View from Badminton', in EHP, pp.187–218.

105 Dedication to HRH The Prince of Wales, printed in all the volumes in the series until Queen Victoria's death. Alfred Harmsworth's *Motors and Motoring* (1902) did not include it, but it contained as a frontispiece a picture of Queen Alexandra in a car at Sandringham.

own peer group, might have jarred even at the time to people outside it,[106] while the word 'manly' in the passage about the Prince which followed now sounds heavily dated:

> His encouragement of racing is well-known, and his attendance at the University, Public School and other important Matches testifies to his being like most Englishmen, fond of all manly sports.

'In Badminton country' by John Sturgess. Frontispiece to the *Badminton Library* title on *Hunting* by the Duke of Beaufort and others, 1885

Bodleian Library, University of Oxford: 38445 e.4

It was not only the headmasters of public schools or heads of Oxford and Cambridge colleges who joined the throng.[107] The crowds were turning increasingly to spectator sports during the last decades of the nineteenth century and the first decade of the twentieth.

While the Duke of Beaufort set the tone of the *Badminton Library*, the success of the venture, apart from Longmans' encouragement, depended most on a friend of the Duke, Alfred E.T. Watson (1849–1922), 'a good sportsman, a true gentleman'. It was he who selected the names of the authors of the volumes and submitted them to the Duke for approval after striking out any 'objectionable' elements in the 'schemes' that they had prepared.

---

106 The use of the word 'work' by football managers (and cricket coaches) to describe the performance of their players in the late-twentieth and early-twenty-first centuries was to evoke little surprise. Indeed, the Press could not do without it.

107 See T.J. Chandler, 'Games at Oxbridge and the Public Schools', in *International Journal of the History of Sport*, Vol. 8 (1991). See also M.G. Brock and M.C. Curthoys (eds.), *The History of the University of Oxford*, Vol. VII, Part 2 (2000), Ch. 22 by S.J. Jones, 'University and College Sport'. For a contemporary account see J. Wells, *Oxford and Oxford Life* (2nd edn., 1899).

Watson always took care to interpret and follow the Duke's wishes. After explaining, for example, why he had suggested a book on cycling, which could be deemed a plebeian sport, at times an avowedly socialist one, he contrived to make even cycling sound aristocratic:

> *Shooting* and *Hunting* had appealed chiefly to the 'classes' perhaps but we wished to appeal to the 'masses' also – to adopt Mr. Gladstone's distinction – and at the time never supposed that multitudes outside this latter category would be attracted by such a subject. Still, some persons did ride, the then Lord Bury among them, and he consented to write in conjunction with Mr. Lacy Hillier, who was one of the men who adopted 'the wheel' with distinction.

Lacy Hillier was a stockbroker, former editor of *Bicycling News*.[108] Viscount Bury became the eighth Earl of Albemarle in 1894.

Lord Bury produced some of the excellent illustrations for the volume, including 'Waiting for the Pistol' and 'A Foolhardy Feat'. Watson was delighted with them. He loved illustrations, and these, eclectic in character, were an attractive feature of all the Badminton volumes. When the Library was planned, he explained, no one could have conceivably anticipated drawings of 'what would now be witnessed a dozen times in the course of a very brief journey by road or rail – a party of men and ladies passing along the highway on bicycles, with a little concourse of golf players in the field behind them'.[109]

The volume *Golf* (1890), parts of it written by another aristocrat, Lord Wellwood, included a chapter by A.J. Balfour, golf enthusiast and future Prime Minister, on 'The Humour of Golf'.[110] This was a volume that looked to the future more than to the past: and it revealed a degree of frankness missing from some of the other volumes:

> While the philosopher's views of life are rose-coloured or cynical he

---

108 See his *All About Bicycling* (1896). In that year the weekly periodical *Cycling* sold over 41,000 copies, its peak figure. For the place of cycling in national life see D. Rubinstein, 'Cycling in the 1890s' in *Victorian Studies*, Vol. XX, Autumn 1977. Five editions of the Badminton volume, *Cycling*, sold out by 1895. 'Think of the enormous number of men who now gain their livelihood by the production and repairing and selling of the successors to the once despised velocipede' was one of Watson's comments in 1896 (*loc. cit.*, p.xxi).

109 A.E.T. Watson, 'The Badminton Library', in H. Peek (ed.), *The Poetry of Sport* (1896), p.xiii.

110 The first golf drawing which appeared in *Punch* in 1889, was of the Rt. Hon. Arthur Balfour MP wearing checked knickerbockers, sporting a blazer and a tam o'shanter. Ladies first appeared in a *Punch* drawing dealing with golf two years later. *The Golf Illustrated Weekly* first appeared in 1890 and the *Golf Monthly* in 1911.

will find ample material to interest him while he watches the game. We must warn him, however, that if in the pursuit of his study he insists on accompanying matches, he may find that he proves an excuse for many a miss, and possibly for some bad language. He must certainly be prepared for this.

Unlike team games, covered in many of the other volumes, golf, first reported in the newspaper *The Scotsman*, was described as a 'selfish game in which each man fights with keenness and calculation for his own hand, grasping at every technicality and glorying in the misfortune of his opponents'.[111] Thomas Norton, who loved golf as 'a most refreshing, healthful relaxation', drew attention in his *Memories* to 'nasty, irritating, bothersome, troublesome' bunkers. It was 'consoling' that 'even the best of players' might find it difficult to extricate themselves from them, and he had felt delight to watch and count the strokes of a 'bunkered Bishop' caught in one.[112]

In the case of two of the volumes on team games there was a welcome touch of realism too. Thus, in the pages of Shearman's *Athletics and Football* (1888) which dealt with rugby Shearman challenged the views of the spokesman of the Rugby Union that one of the main tasks of the Union was to 'throttle the hydra' of professionalism. He knew of the moves to create the separate Rugby League. 'Surely if the Yorkshire clubs prefer to play with or against professional teams, they should be at liberty to do so', he maintained.[113] There was realism, too, in a well-written volume on *Cricket* (1888, 2nd edition 1893), co-edited by A.J. Steel and R.J. Lyttelton; although they stated bluntly that 'the more cricket gets into the hands of professional players, the worse it will be for the game and its reputation'.[114] They had some intimations of the long-term future. Shearman could not have predicted it.

In his own contribution to the volume on cricket, Steele, writing more like a sociologist than a philosopher, gave a graphic account of the vicissitudes of a professional's life, idolised in summer, unemployed in winter, and he went on to compare attitudes to the game in different parts of the country. He had no doubt, nevertheless, that it was cricket that was '*the* national game'. Nor had the great cricketer C.B. Fry, when he conceded that football (soccer) was 'more democratic' and already 'had first place in the public heart'.[115]

Many of the points raised in the volumes in the *Library*, like Fry's

111   H.G. Hutchinson (ed.), *Golf* (1890), p.30.

112   *Memories*, p.134.

113   M. Shearman, *Athletics and Football* (1888), p.367.

114   A.J. Steele and C.J. Lyttelton, *Cricket* (1893 edn.), p.7.

115   C.B. Fry, 'Football', in the *Badminton Library*, Vol. I (1895), p.481.

point about 'the national game', were taken up from a variety of angles in the *Badminton Magazine of Sports and Pastimes*, also edited by Watson, which first appeared in 1895. In the notes at the end of its first number, 'Rapier' (Watson) explained that the *Badminton Library* had approached its end 'necessarily': every sport had been treated. This was not quite true. The sport of badminton itself was left out, for example, though it was played by both men and women,[116] while *Sea Fishing*, planned earlier, appeared at the same time as the *Magazine*, along with *Dancing* and *Billiards*. *The Poetry of Sport* and *Motoring* were still to follow.

The Poetry of Sport is disappointing. Its editor, Hedley Peek, found it necessary to begin with what he thought would be a basic question for his readers, 'Is sport a fitting subject for the poet?'[117] Perhaps for reasons of copyright, there were virtually no poems in the volume that dealt with sports as they were being pursued at the time when the *Badminton Library* was being compiled. This was an old problem for makers of anthologies whatever their focus. And the House of Longman, which had largely ceased to publish poetry, had nothing to offer. A few poems from the *Sporting Magazine* went back to the 1830s or earlier. One poem, 'Heredity' (from a manuscript), claimed to be 'after one of Swinburne's Ballads'.[118] Three copyright poems by Charles Kingsley were included 'by permission of Messrs. Macmillan'.

Cover of *The Badminton Magazine*,1895

Bodleian Library, University of Oxford
Per. 3843.d.5

The *Badminton Magazine* made more of the international dimension of sport than the separate volumes had done. There was a greater emphasis also on 'adventure' sports in foreign lands, an overlap with travel literature. The contents of Volume I included 'Hunting in India', 'Sport of the Rajahs', 'Skilörning in Norway' and 'Tarpon Fishing in Florida', with 'On Elephant Back' and 'Sport with the Brigands of Macedonia' to follow in Volume III (1896). Yet the fiction in the *Magazine*, not the most important ingredient, was domestic. The titles in Volume V (1897) included 'Our Day on the Broads', 'A Cricket Tragedy' and 'A Golfing Melodrama'.

In the early-twentieth century the *Badminton Magazine*, which continued in existence until 1923, passed out of Longman hands, but Watson remained as editor. Only one new post-war volume in the series of books appeared, *Cricket, A New Edition*, edited by P.F. (Pelham) Warner in 1920. Its most innovative feature was a wide range of photographs: there had been only one in the first *Cricket* volume. Nevertheless, photography

---

116 Badminton is said to have evolved at Badminton from the children's game of battledore and shuttlecock. The first laws were established at Poona in India in the mid-1870s, and a Badminton Association was founded in 1893.

117 Peek (ed.), *op. cit.*, p.13. Watson in the same volume (p.xxviii) described the difficulties Longmans had had in finding anyone equipped with 'the requisite knowledge where to look' for sporting poems.

118 *Ibid.*, pp.377–8.

had not been ignored in all the earlier volumes. *Mountaineering* had an imposing photograph of Mont Blanc as a frontispiece, and included a whole chapter on photography. Readers were warned that 'with those who carry a camera purely as a plaything ... we have now no concern'.[119] This was not quite the line taken by the editor of *Cycling*, who described every third cyclist as a photographer even if 'they operated chiefly on each other, and on their friends and relations'.[120]

There were photographs on the covers of the late numbers of the *Badminton Magazine*, with the Prince of Wales in one number appearing in an oval above the cricketer Jack Hobbs and opposite the boxing enthusiast Lord Lonsdale.[121] This came out in the year of Watson's death from pneumonia, said to have been brought about by 'a slight chill contracted at Newmarket', where he had been reporting on the Autumn meeting for *The Times*. The Duke of Rutland, who wrote a letter to *The Times*, praising Watson as 'a charming companion and a true friend', stated erroneously that he himself had written an article for the first number of the *Magazine*. That 'honour' went to another aristocrat, the Marquess of Granby, MP, who described in detail 'shooting on a North Derbyshire moor'. More to the point, given the circumstances of his death, Watson himself – often addressed as 'My dear Watson' – wrote an article called 'A Morning at Newmarket'.

The inclusion of the *Dancing* volume in the Badminton Library, the title of which, like *The Poetry of Sport*, raised what its authors thought to be basic questions about the series, was justified on the grounds that 'if Dance cannot be called a sport, it is certainly a pastime'. (All card games, time-consuming passions, had nevertheless been left out of the series.) The editor and main author of *Dancing*, Mrs. Lilly Grove, FRGS (the letters after her name hinted at a qualification), began with 'The Dances of Antiquity', followed by 'Dances of Savages', and only a brief 'retrospect' in the penultimate chapter dealt with dancing as most people then cared for it. 'Dancing as it was practised in 1845 differs greatly from dancing as it is carried on in 1895 in the ballrooms of London society.'

The only concession to current practical interests was a brief final chapter on 'Balls: Hostesses and Guests', written by a member of the aristocracy, the Countess of Ancaster, who affirmed that 'there can be no question that the balls now given in London far excel those of former days in many most important particulars'. One particular was more 'picturesque display', another the presence of 'instrumental bands'. A

119   C.J. Dent, *Mountaineering* (1892), p.403.

120   Bury and Hillier, *op. cit.*, p.51. They referred to advertisements for photographers in the cycling papers. 'The way in which cameras fold up ... and, so speak, almost annihilate space, is among the things no fellow can understand.'

121   *Badminton Magazine*, Vol. LVIII, No. 327 (Oct. 1922).

third was 'the supper and wine'.[122]

The quality of Percy Macquoid's illustrations and of other engravings, prints and photographs was better than the quality of the text, as was the quality of illustrations by J. Sturgess in the Earl of Suffolk's volume, *Racing* (1900). Yet *Dancing* has an extra interest in retrospect in that it was written by women, the only such volume in the series, and that in her last page the Countess of Ancaster described the 1890s as 'an age of women'.[123] Only the *Golf* volume substantiated this claim. 'We do not know that a claim for absolute equality has as yet been made', the editor wrote on her last page, 'but the ladies are advancing in all pursuits with such strides ... that it will not be long before such a claim is formulated. ... Our conscience is clear. We have always advocated a liberal extension of the right of golfing to women.'[124]

~

One of the earliest articles in the *Badminton Magazine*, 'The Old Sportsman', was written by Andrew Lang (1844-1912), a major figure in this *History*, born in Selkirk, who began it with the would-be arresting words 'That Cicero was no sportsman is insisted upon by his enemies and not denied even by his friends'. Despite his reputation for writing sporting ballads among his many other ballads, Lang feared that some of his readers might find what he had to say about sport would stand 'apart from the general purpose of the magazine'. He justified himself, however, by claiming that 'a distant allusion to the classics has always been dear to British sportive [*sic*] writers'.[125]

This particular article was short and lacking in insight, but it played on the associations of many of his readers, some of whom considered it 'not a little bitter', as Lang himself did, 'to find that [with age] one can hardly bowl out an ordinary fourth-form boy'. 'We must grin and bear it', Lang went on, 'or abstain from trying the experiment, which is apt to lower an uncle in the estimation of his nephews.'[126] This article was not Lang's only contribution to the literature of sport, for he contributed to Wellwood's volume on *Golf* a first chapter packed with quotations from diaries, poems and novels. Indeed, he wrote so much elsewhere about golf and other sports, that his well-informed, if uncritical, biographer in the DNB called him 'the

---

122 L. Grove, *Dancing* (1895), pp.1, 401, 411.

123 *Ibid.*, p.428.

124 Hutchinson, *op. cit.*, p.47.

125 Lang also contributed nine pages on 'Classical Sport' to Hedley Peek's *The Poetry of Sport*.

126 A. Lang, 'The Old Sportsman' in the *Badminton Magazine*, Oct. 1895, pp.370–5.

MR. ANDREW LANG AS SEEN BY
MR. MAX BEERBOHM.

'Mr Andrew Lang as seen by
Mr Max Beerbohm' in *The
Academy*, 19 November 1898

Longman Archive Scrapbooks Vol.7

ambassador of all the sporting crafts at the court of letters' (1927). And if only for this reason his place at the court at Paternoster Row was assured.

Yet there were many other reasons. When, after St. Andrews he moved to Merton College, Oxford he had been a friend of CJ's brother, Frederick W. Longman, whose one contribution to Longman publishing history was a book called *Chess Openings*.[127] In complete contrast, Lang made many contributions to Longman history of the most diverse nature. Between 1882, when he began to write for *Longman's Magazine*, until his death in 1912, 'no man alive, who was not a Longman', it was said of him, 'had as much power within the ancient House'. Nor had any newspaper, Grant Richards wrote in his autobiography.[128]

Lang approached 39 Paternoster Row via Fleet Street. Like a number of other Oxford dons, he found literary London a more exciting and rewarding place than the university city.[129] He wrote fluently and attractively for the *Daily News* and other newspapers, and took easily to the discipline of writing 'columns' within set space and time limits, 'wearing his panoply of learning as though it were a garment of iridescent gossamer, turning the driest subject to favour and to prettiness'.[130] His chief interest lay in books, in reading them and writing them, and he stood out then and stands out now as one of the most engaged and most proselytising of 'bookmen' in an age when 'bookmanship' was highly prized.[131]

Eschewing theory, like the Longmans, which he distrusted, Lang made the most of his likes and dislikes, drawn to writers of romance and adventure, like Rider Haggard, rather than to novelists of style or of ideas. 'Thesis novels', as he called them, were an abomination to him, and among these were the novels of Émile Zola. Nevertheless, Lang was the first writer to notice Arthur Conan Doyle's *Study in Scarlet* (1887), and he had words of praise for H.G. Wells's *Love and Mr. Lewisham* and George Gissing's *The Nether World*.[132] Like Conan Doyle, he was interested in spiritualism, and

---

127   Chess was rejected as a title for a Badminton volume (Watson, *loc. cit.*, p.xxvi)).

128   G. Richards, *Memories of a Misspent Youth 1872–1896* (1932), p.119.

129   For the moves to London see C. Harvie, *The Lights of Liberalism, University Liberals and the Challenge of Democracy, 1860–86* (1976) and C. Kent, *Brains and Numbers: Elitism, Comtism and Democracy in Mid-Victorian England* (1978).

130   Richard le Gallienne, *The Romantic Nineties* (1926), p.52.

131   See J. Gross, *The Rise and Fall of the Man of Letters* (1969), pp.132–139, for a dismissive account of Lang. For a favourable scholarly account of him see M. Demoor, 'Andrew Lang Causeries' in *Victorian Periodicals Review* (Spring 1988), pp.15–22. Demoor has written many articles about Lang, all based on meticulous research.

132   See M. Demoor, *loc. cit.*, p.18.

in 1911 he was President of the Society for Psychical Research, of which he had been a co-founder in 1882.

Longman had published eleven of Lang's books by 1895, the first of them a volume of translations and original pieces, *Ballads and Lyrics of Old France* in 1872. The later books ranged from *Custom and Myth* (1884) to *Angling Sketches* (1891). Only three of the pieces in his *Books and Bookmen*, published in New York in 1886, the most representative of all his titles, came from *Longman's Magazine* (1882–1905). The first piece dealt with an older publishing house than Longman, that of Elsevier, founded by a Flemish bookbinder in Leiden in 1580, a house that reappeared in a very different context in late-twentieth-century Longman history.[133] Other Lang pieces in this volume, many of them curiously illustrated, dealt with Japanese 'bogie-books', bibliomania in France, and lady book-lovers. In the same year Lang's *Letters to Dead Authors* appeared.

Lang was still dreaming of becoming a poet, as Macaulay had done, when his *XXII Ballades in Blue China* and *Helen of Troy* were published in 1880 and 1882, but poetry – and fiction – were eventually abandoned. Some of his last books were about Scotland, including a four-volume *History of Scotland from the Roman Occupation to the Suppression of the Last Jacobite Rising* (1900–1907) which was published not by Longman but by Blackwood and which took him ten years to write. In 1912 his *History of English Literature* was published two days after he died. Like Rees, he had returned to his native country, giving orders that all his papers should be destroyed after his death. Throughout his life he had systematically destroyed all his incoming mail.

Even the flattering author of Lang's DNB entry, fellow-Scot George Stewart Gordon, who noted that Lang's father had been a friend of Scott, described his books on books as 'rallies of fugitive, journalistic, prose'. And while the Longmans were anxious to publish any of Lang's books, whatever his subject, it was they too who offered him his favourite platform, a column in *Longman's Magazine*, engagingly described as a *causerie*, 'At the Sign of the Ship'. Preceded by a 'Ballade Introductory' in 1882, in which he described his column as 'our Stall of Bric-à-Brac', it soon became 'the most widely admired and talked about feature of its kind', covering so many subjects that American observers, to his amusement, suggested it was written by a syndicate.[134]

For a time Lang had his own American connection. In 1884 he had been appointed editor of the English edition of *Harpers' Magazine*, although he was 'bowled out of it', as Lang explained in an appropriate metaphor to

---

133 Amsterdam, the most successful bookselling branch of Elsevier, was opened in 1638 by a grandson of the founder. Its motto was *non solus*. See D.W. Davies, *The World of the Elseviers, 1580–1712* (1954).

134 Gross, *op. cit.*, p.137.

The Blue Fairy Book, edited
by Andrew Lang, 1890 (first
published in 1889), the first in a
series of 'colour' fairy-tale books

Personal collection

his friend Edmund Gosse, the following year when W.D. Howells began
his own *Harpers'* column, 'Editor's Study', in the same month as Lang's
'At the Sign of the Ship' in *Longman's*. Thereafter the two men fought
a continuing 'literary duel'. Howells detested 'the sentimental and the
romantic in literature': in opposition, Lang professed that 'if the battle
between the crocodile of Realism and the catawumpus of Romance is to be
fought out to the bitter end' he was 'on the side of the catawumpus'.[135]

In retrospect, such comment has been judged a weakness as has
Lang's versatility. Various critics have treated him as an unfulfilled poet,
an unsuccessful novelist, an over-confident historian, and a ponderous
essayist. Indeed, they never spared him in his lifetime. Thus, a writer in
Blackwood's wrote in 1898 that his writing was often 'snappish' and that
time did not seem to have 'greatly mellowed him'. 'It is not well to have a
dictator of letters, and this one did not (I think) use his power advisedly.'[136]

---

135 For the story see M. Demoor, 'Andrew Lang versus W.D. Howells: a Late-
Victorian Literary Duel', in *Journal of American Studies*, No. 3, Dec. 1987,
pp.416–22. 'From the start it was a polemic', Howells wrote years later.

136 'Some Opinions', in *Blackwood's Edinburgh Magazine*, Vol. CLXIV (1898),
p.595. Yet in the *Magazine's* obituary article on Lang (Sept. 1912, p.425), a
different *Blackwood's* writer stressed that 'beneath all his brilliance was a
foundation of sound learning laid by sheer hard work'. Gosse in his obituary
note, 'Andrew Lang, Some Personal Impressions', in *The Bookman*, Vol.
XXXV (1912), pp.256–9, was coolly critical as was often his wont. But in his
lifetime he had usually appreciated him. See Demoor, 'Andrew Lang's Letters
to Edmund Gosse. The Record of a Fruitful Collaboration as Poets, Critics,
and Biographers', in RES, new series, Vol. XXXVIII (1987), pp.492–509.

The writer used the curiously misleading adjective 'invertebrate'.

Off the scene, Lang was to be remembered as much for his friends as for his writings. Stewart Gordon claimed, indeed, that 'his instinct for friendship became something 'higher and drier', 'an instinct for fraternity'. It was not restrained by literary considerations. He certainly carried friendship with Haggard so far that he could write jointly with him an unsuccessful novel, *The World's Desire*, which Longman published in 1890 and which the poet and editor W.E. Henley, then a friend of both men, described as 'tortuous and ungodly'.[137] The experience daunted Lang who felt that the novel revealed both his faults and Haggard's, but this did not prevent Haggard seeking (in vain) to persuade him to write another joint novel in 1907 and 1911.[138]

Lang made money out of his prose, not least through telling the Longmans, as Henry Reeve had done, what books they ought to publish by other authors, an occupation which was held against him when he was alive. Yet, as early as 1900, he was anxious about whether he would continue to give personal advice to authors. 'Nobody can give to writers "security of tenure".'[139] It is not surprising that Gissing is said to have had Lang in mind when in his *New Grub Street* (1891) he produced his picture of Milvain, one of his unforgettable profiles of authors. Milvain's 'path of success', like Lang's, had led through Fleet Street. 'A journalist', as one of the career guides of the period stated frankly, 'produces work which is eminently marketable; and the more of this quality appears in his writings, the more successful he will be'.[140]

Although Lang hated 'new journalism' and scandal-mongering journalists who pried into authors' private lives, thereby displaying, he thought, 'a base and brazen curiosity ... a quality of savages',[141] he shared the kind of work schedule followed by the fictional Milvain. A fellow writer described the real Lang as 'the quickest writer that I have ever known. I have

---

137 *National Observer*, 13 Dec. 1890.

138 Lang wanted Haggard to produce a 'Zulu novel' which he did in 1892, *Nada the Wily*, which dealt with the rise and fall of Chaka (Cetewayo), the greatest of Zulu kings. There were coincidental links here with a very different Longman author, the much discussed Colenso, who was sympathetic to Zulu ambitions. For Lang and Haggard, see Demoor, 'Andrew Lang's Letters to H. Rider Haggard: The Record of a Harmonious Friendship', in *Etudes Anglaises, Grande Bretagne-Etats Unis*, Vol. XL (1987), pp.313–22. See also W. Katz, *Rider Haggard and the Fiction of Empire: A Critical Study in British Imperial Fiction* (1987).

139 *Longman's Magazine*, Feb. 1900, p.377.

140 John Oldcastle, *Journals and Journalism: with a Guide for Literary Beginners* (1880), pp.39–40.

141 *Longman's Magazine*, Nov. 1889, p.107.

heard him say "Is it humanly possible to write an article before dinner" – taking out his watch – "Twenty minutes before we need go and dress! Yes, I think it just is".[142] Robert Louis Stevenson (1850–1894), a Lang protégé, who called Lang 'garrulous like a brook',[143] agreed to write a monthly *causerie* column for *Scribners' Magazine*, telling Gosse that he only did it for 'lucre' and that he could not hope to emulate 'the Lang business at the Sign of the Ship': 'I could never have managed that: it takes a gift to do it'.[144] And Lang could do more. He wrote *causeries* not only for the Longmans but for the *Illustrated London News*, which from March 1896 to 1897 published a column by him called 'From a Scottish Workshop' and after the demise of *Longman's Magazine* a column called 'At the Sign of St Paul's'.

As a novelist Lang did not care to be remembered, and the fortunes of the one true novelist among Gissing's characters in *New Grub Street*, Edwin Reardon, resembled those not of Lang but of Gissing himself, who up to and including *New Grub Street* had never earned more than £150 a year out of his novels. Lang, who did want to be remembered for his articles and reviews, described himself as 'a dweller in Grub Street', but one fortunate enough not to know anybody resembling the sad failures Gissing described. 'In Grub Street there are many mansions; they are not all full of failure, and envy, and low cunning, and love of money.'[145] 'The author who has wares worth selling', he maintained, 'has only himself to blame if he is so unsuccessful when so many publishers are competing for his business.'

Gissing never felt that many publishers were competing for his business. Indeed, the House of Longman turned down the next novel Gissing wrote after *New Grub Street*, which had been referred to the House by Watt. (Agents did not move easily then or later in Longman circles.) Years later, however, when Gissing was more successful, Lang wrote a 'rave review' of his *Charles Dickens, A Critical Study* (1902) in *Longman's Magazine*.[146] By contrast, Besant never fully appreciated Gissing, and Gissing, who refused to support the Society of Authors' magazine, *The Author*, had no regard for Besant himself. Gissing accused both Besant and Lang, whom he coupled together as 'overworked', of not reading *New Grub Street* 'with close thought'.[147]

---

142 H.G. Hutchinson, *Portraits of the Eighties* (1920), p.10.

143 Quoted in J. Calder, *RLS: A Life Story* (1980), p.118.

144 S. Colvin (ed.), *The Letters of Roberts Louis Stevenson*, Vol. 2 (1911), pp.47–8.

145 *The Author*, 1 July 1891. Lang gave a lecture to adult students on 'How to Fail in Literature'.

146 J. Halperin, *Gissing, A Life in Books* (1982), pp.156–7, 269. For the fortunes and reputation of Gissing, see P. Coustillas and C. Partridge (eds.), *Gissing, The Critical Heritage* (1972).

147 Letter to Edward Bertz, 20 July 1891, printed in A.C. Young (ed.), *The Letters of George Gissing to Edward Bertz, 1887–1903* (1961), p.128.

There were many sides to Lang's achievement which fell outside Besant's and Gissing's chosen territory. Lang was far more than a Milvain. The first side of his versatility was represented best in the sequence of 'colour fairy tale books' that he edited for Longman,[148] beginning with *The Blue Fairy Book* in 1890, written at a time when Longman was not in the lead in developing non-educational books for children.[149] Yet the House converted *The Blue Fairy Book* into a series of class readers for schools, as they did also Besant's *London* (1892), which appeared in this form in September 1893, price 1s 6d (school prize edition, 2s. 6d).

A children's book which stood out in its own right, Stevenson's *A Child's Garden of Verses* was published (unillustrated) by Longmans in 1885, but rights in it were subsequently relinquished to the Bodley Head, a new firm founded by John Lane in 1889, 'more like a club than a place of business'.[150] It was a book which won the praise of William Archer, translator of Ibsen, whom Stevenson thanked, in capital letters, for 'the best criticism I ever had'.[151] One of the last letters Stevenson read before his death far away in the Pacific was from Lang. Stevenson was then living in a newly built island house which he described, with Scott in mind, as his own Abbotsford.

A later children's book published by Longman in 1902 was Walter de la Mare's *Songs of Childhood*, very much at the instigation of C.J. Longman, who after reading the manuscript immediately liked the poems. The fact that they were passed on to him by an agent, in this case J.B. Pinker, did not seem to worry him, and he handed them over to Lang, who read them carefully and made detailed comments on them, most of which (particularly when they referred to de la Mare's rhyming) de la Mare readily accepted. De la Mare agreed too with CJ that his poems, like Stevenson's *A Child's Garden of Verses*, should not be illustrated, going even further, indeed, in arguing that 'if there is any true imagination at all' in writing, 'pictures only confuse and distract the reader's own constantly fleeting pictures'.[152]

Longmans made good use of its titles for additional markets: an advertisement for Longmans' Supplementary Readers, based on the tales in *The Blue Fairy Book*, 1890

Bodleian Library, University of Oxford: 93 C 40

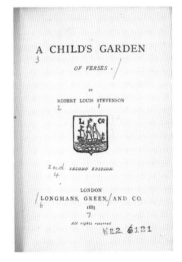

The title page to R.L Stevenson's *A Child's Garden of Verses*, 1885

BL W22/6121

---

148 The point that Lang edited, did not write, the books was stressed in an article 'Two Hundred Years of the House of Longman' in PC, 25 Oct. 1924 (LA Part II/57/225). 'The tales were largely translated by Mrs. Lang and other ladies from foreign sources. Lang wrote the charming prefaces.'

149 See B. Alderson, 'Tracts, Rewards and Fairies, The Victorian Contribution to children's Literature', in EHP, pp.247–82.

150 See the DNB, 1922–1930, obituary of Lane, p, 477, written by J. Lewis May.

151 Colvin, *op. cit.*, Vol. I, p.358. The review was anonymous, and Stevenson had to find the name of its author. 'It's worth writing a book to draw an article like that.'

152 Theresa Whistler, *Imagination of the Heart: The Life of Walter de la Mare* (1993). 'Biography', she rightly observes in her Prologue (p.ix), 'is almost as much an umbrella term as the novel'.

The frontispiece for *Songs of Childhood*, 1902 by Walter Ramal (the pen name for some years used by Walter de la Mare, 1873–1956). 'Under the Dock Leaves', by Richard Doyle, was suggested by CJ Longman.

BL C194.a.240

They were not talking about frontispieces, however, and both wanted an attractive frontispiece for *Songs of Childhood*, an evocative title thought of by CJ, not by de la Mare. It was CJ again who produced the painting. De la Mare had considered a Velasquez, but CJ suggested something very different, a Dickie Doyle watercolour showing fairies playing under dock leaves. CJ asked de la Mare to visit Paternoster Row to see it, and later in life the poet recalled the exact spot on a turkey carpet with a hole in it where the painting was placed. He also recalled 'the kindly bearded face of CJ' as he produced it.[153] Lang would have appreciated this memory, recorded in 1937, but there is no record of what he (or CJ) felt about de la Mare receiving only four shillings in royalties on *Songs of Childhood*, an octavo book, well printed and on good paper, which cost 3*s*. 6*d*. Not surprisingly Longman did not figure among de la Mare's later publishers.

~

Meanwhile, there was yet another side to Lang, also outside the range both of Besant and of Gissing and, indeed, outside the whole miscellaneous field of *belles lettres*, a term then in wide use. Anthropology was still an undeveloped academic discipline in the 1890s when there was increased popular interest in the subject; and before then Lang had already written two books on it. *Custom and Myth* (1884) and *Myth, Ritual and Religion* (1887) were both published by Longman. While they left little impact on

---

153 Quoted *ibid.*, p.99.

the long-term academic development of anthropology, they drew new readers to the subject.

Lang approached anthropology via the classics, the most common approach in Britain at the time. Classical studies were still dominant in the public schools and at Oxford and Cambridge, but among 'general readers' anthropological studies were often stimulated by religious interest – and by visits to museums. Longman entered this field at an early stage, publishing the first book by Edward (later Sir Edward) Burnett Tylor (1832–1917), *Anahuac* (1861), a study of Mexico. (Tylor was appointed Keeper of the University of Oxford Museum in 1883 and a year later the University and the country's first Reader in Anthropology.) In 1907 Longman was also to publish *Anthropological Essays Presented to Edward Burnett Tylor* edited by Sir John Lubbock, whose book *The Origin of Civilisation and the Primitive Condition of Man* had been published by the House in 1870. Lubbock was as keen a bookman as Lang, and in his multi-faceted career many concerns central to the history of publishing converge.[154]

Like Lubbock, Lang never found time amid all his own diverse activities to concentrate on the academic advancement of anthropology,[155] although he had turned to the subject before he read Tylor – or Lubbock. With no false modesty he told the anthropologist R.R. Marett, Oxford correspondent of the *Athenaeum* and a future Rector of Exeter College, Oxford, who was introduced to anthropology through Lang's *Custom and Myth*, that if he, Lang, 'could have made a living out of it', he 'might have been a great anthropologist'.[156] The word 'great' is too strong, but Lang was the author of a much discussed article on 'Mythology' in the ninth edition of the *Encyclopaedia Britannica*,[157] and his *Magic and Religion* (1901) was reviewed in the *Quarterly Review* in the same article as the second edition of J.G. Frazer's *The Golden Bough*, published, like Tylor's two-volume *Primitive Culture* (1871), by Macmillan. Lang did not come out worst.[158]

Lang figured prominently in the late-twentieth century *Dictionary*

154 See H.G. Hutchinson, *The Life of Sir John Lubbock, Lord Avebury*, 2 vols. (1914).

155 See R.R. Marett, *Tylor* (1936) and J.W. Burrow, *Evolution and Society, a Study in Victorian Social Theory* (1966), esp. Ch. 7, 'Tylor and the Growth of Anthropology'.

156 R.R. Marett, *A Journeyman at Oxford* (1941), p.167 and H.J. Rose, 'Arnold Ranulph Marett, 1866–1943', in *Publications of the British Academy*, Vol. XXIX (1943), pp.357–70. See also M. Harris, *The Rise of Anthropological Theory* (1968), esp. pp.142–179; A. Kuper, *Anthropologists and Anthropology, The British School, 1922–1972* (1973); and Brock and Curthoys, *op. cit.*, pp.356–7, 499–503.

157 See R.L. Green, *Andrew Lang, A Critical Biography* (1946) and F.M. Turner, *The Greek Heritage in Victorian Britain* (1981), pp.117–20.

158 QR, Vol. 194 (1902), pp.343–53.

of the History of Ideas, where a section was devoted to him in an article on Myth, singling him out not only as a critic of Tylor and of Friedrich Max Müller (1823-1900), two Oxford scholars in the field, but as an influence on German anthropological writing, particularly Wilhelm Schmidt's twelve-volume *Der Ursprung der Gottesidee* ('The Origin of the Idea of God), the first volume of which was published in 1912.[159] By then German and British anthropology had sharply diverged.

Lang disagreed with Müller's approach and Müller's conclusions in the books on anthropology that he wrote for Longman, in the wake of his *Lectures on the Science of Language* first published in 1864, which had already reached its sixth edition in 1871 (and was a great Longman success).[160] The other books included his *Introduction to the Science of Religion* (1873), his *Natural Religion* (1889) and his *Selected Essays on Language, Mythology and Religion* (1881). Yet whatever the differences between the two men, Lang visited Müller in Oxford, where Müller was a powerful figure, particularly in the Oxford University Press,[161] and Müller later visited Lang in St. Andrews. On Müller's death Lang wrote a touching letter to Mrs. Müller describing her husband as 'a friendly opponent'. Mrs. Müller edited for Longmans her husband's *Life and Letters*.

From inside the Longman House, Lang may well have influenced what the House chose to publish on the classical world which Lang approached less as an historian than as an anthropologist. His own books on the Greeks, like his translations of Homer, were 'full of pictures of archaeological remains, shields, weapons and clothing',[162] and he could appeal through them to the same readership as Rider Haggard engaged. His translation of the *Odyssey* in 1879 (in co-operation with S.H. Butcher, but prefaced by a Lang sonnet) won considerable praise and inspired Stevenson to address him (in various spellings and enunciations) as Odysseus. The translation was published, however, not by Longman but by Macmillan, although Longman published Lang's *Homer and His Age* (1906) and *The World of Homer* (1910).

Some of the books that Longmans published on classical studies linked German and British scholarship, but it was less Longmans in the lead than Macmillan and it always faced strong competition from a number

---

159 See Mircea Eliade, 'Andrew Lang and the Making of Religion' in P.P. Wiener (ed.), *Dictionary of the History of Ideas*, Vol. III (1973), pp.309–10.

160 His *Lectures* included an important letter from Gladstone to Müller, 28 Sept. 1864.

161 See P. Sutcliffe, *The Oxford University Pres: an informal history* (1978), pp.46–7. Müller became a Delegate of the Press in 1870. His public role was important and he became a Privy Councillor.

162 Turner, *op. cit.*, p.183.

of other publishers. As early as 1847 it launched a new edition of (Bishop) Connop Thirlwall's *A History of Greece* in eight volumes, an alternative to William Mitford's *History of Greece* (1824), which was sharply criticised by Macaulay;[163] and in 1850, before Lang had become involved with Longmans, it published William Mure's *Critical History of the Language and Literature of Ancient Greece*. Charles Merivale's *History of the Romans, The Fall of Rome* and *A General History of Rome* figured prominently in their end-of-century list.[164]

In 1870 the House also published George W. Cox's *The Mythology of the Aryan Nations* which was translated into French by Mallarmé.[165] Cox's 'Aryanism' was taken up by Müller, as was his interpretation of the vengeance of Achilles as 'the victory of the sun'. There were dangers in such interpretations. The Aryan myth, an essential element in Nazi ideology, was to prove more dangerous in the twentieth century than any of the myths examined by Lang.[166]

~

Sunshine was given a more innocent place in a quite different sequence of Longman books – those on gardening, a subject of increasing interest to late-Victorian home-owners. Straddling the nineteenth and twentieth centuries, the influential books of Gertrude Jekyll (1843–1932) were at the time associated, in particular, with the buildings of the architect Sir Edwin Lutyens (1869–1944). But they were still being read in the late-twentieth century when Lutyens was out-of-fashion and when gardening became the basis of big business and a favourite subject for radio listeners and television viewers. Indeed, in 1988 the foreword to a new transatlantic book about Jekyll

---

163 Macaulay's review of the book appeared in *Knight's Quarterly*. This was before Macaulay wrote for the ER. (*The Works of Lord Macaulay* (1898), Vol.IX, p.390.) John Clive calls this review Macaulay's enunciation of a new kind of social history. (*Thomas Babington Macaulay* (1973), p.137.)

164 See J.A. Merivale (ed.), *Autobiography of Dean Merivale, with Selections from his Correspondence* (1899). Merivale, educated at Harrow, began his autobiography in 1872 and concluded it in 1880. In a letter of 1848 he had written that if Thirlwall became Archbishop of Canterbury he would expect a history of Rome to elevate Merivale to an Archdeaconry. In fact, Merivale became Dean of Ely in 1863.

165 Longmans published Cox's two-volume *History of Greece* (1874).

166 See L. Poliakov, *The Aryan Myth* (1974), pp.213ff, 260. The great nineteenth-century German historian Theodor Mommsen had been uneasy almost a century earlier. Once, when he visited Oxford he remarked referring to Müller, (Sutcliffe, *op. cit.*, p.47) 'Do you breed no humbugs in your country that you must import them from mine?' Müller's essays included *Chips from a German Workshop* (1867–1870). A collected edition of his works began to appear in 1898.

could describe her star as 'rising for the third time within a century'.[167]

Jekyll's evident commitment to the subject attracted her contemporary readers, who were themselves committed to their gardens whatever their size and their status. For Jekyll herself a garden was 'a grand teacher'. 'It teaches patience and careful watchfulness: it teaches industry and thrift; and, above all ... entire trust.'[168] *Wood and Garden: Notes and Thoughts, Practical and Critical of a Working Amateur*, Jekyll's 'long awaited' first book, was published by Longman in 1899 and went through many editions.[169] It was as remarkable for its photographs as for its words, some of the former having already appeared as engravings in William Robinson's influential *The English Flower Garden* (1883), published by Murray, many of the latter in articles in 1896 and 1897 which were published in *The Guardian*. *Home and Garden: Notes and Thoughts, Practical and Critical of a Worker in Both*, again beautifully illustrated, appeared next in 1900 and was followed in 1904 by two further Longman books – *Old West Surrey: Some Notes and Memories* and the folio-sized, 'sumptuously illustrated', *English Gardens*.

All Jekyll's other books were published by *Country Life*, a new magazine in 1900, for which she wrote a series of articles. She also wrote regularly in a wide range of other publications.[170] Ironically, perhaps, the 1988 book about her had Murray as its British publisher. In perspective Longman had produced gardening books long before Victorian home-owners created their suburban gardens, including some of the most famous books of John Claudius Loudon (1783–1843), whose first essay was *Observations on Laying out the Public Squares of London* (1803). Like Jekyll, Loudon straddled two centuries, and in his planning he brought in buildings as well as gardens.[171]

The title page of *Wood and Garden: notes and thoughts, practical and critical, of a working amateur. ... With illustrations from photographs by the author... etc*, 1899 by Gertrude Jekyll

BL 710*229*

167 J. Brown, Foreword to J.B. Takard and M.R. Valkenburgh, *Gertrude Jekyll, A Vision of Garden and Wood* (1989), p.x.

168 *Wood and Garden*, 2nd edn.(1899), p.6.

169 'There are already many and excellent books about gardening', she told her readers, 'but the love of a garden, already so implanted in the English heart, is so rapidly growing that no excuse is needed for putting forth another.' (Jekyll, *op. cit.*, p.1.)

170 M. Hastings and M. Tooley, 'Bibliography of Gertrude Jekyll's Published Works', in M. Tooley (ed.), *Gertrude Jekyll: artist, gardener, craftswoman* (1984), pp.137–513. See also F. Jekyll, *Gertrude Jekyll: a memoir* (1934) and A. Helmreich, *The English Garden and National Identity: The Competing Styles of Garden Design, 1870–1914* (2002).

171 See M.L. MacDougall (ed.) *John Claudius Loudon and the Early Nineteenth Century in Great Britain* (1980) and M.L. Simo, *Loudon and the Landscape* (1988). There is a full obituary notice of Loudon in *The Athenaeum*, 3 Feb. 1844, p.98, following Loudon's 'sudden death', along with an appeal to subscribers signed, among others, by four dukes and eight earls and by the radical MP Joseph Hume.

Perhaps at first sight surprisingly, he used the word 'suburban' in the title
of his *Encyclopaedia of Plants: The Suburban Gardener and Villa Companion*,
which first appeared in 1829, but it was the building of large new villas on
what was then the periphery of towns and cities that explains his appeal.
His *Encyclopaedia of Trees and Shrubs* was published in the year of his death,
1842. Like Jekyll, he wrote for periodicals as well as books. Nine volumes of
the *Gardeners' Magazine* had publicised his ideas.

In 1863 *The Indoor Gardener* by 'Miss Maling', author of *Indoor
Plants*, was published by Longman with a dazzling chromolithograph by
Noel Humphreys which showed flowers, all of which were well adapted for
growing in a 'windowcase' in April. It paid special attention to those readers
'who are now only beginning to garden'. Some of the material had been
published earlier in *The Gardener's Chronicle*. Yet before Jekyll Longmans
took no special steps to maintain a lead in gardening publications. There
was no special section on gardening in the 1877 list, when Loudon's
Encyclopaedia still figured – and now twice – in the 'Dictionaries' category
and in 'Physical Sciences'. Under the latter, however, Thomas Rivers's
The Rose Amateur's Guide was listed in a new edition together with W.R.
Hemsley's *Hand-book of Hardy Trees, Shrubs and Herbaceous Plants*.
Gardeners were anxious to learn of new named varieties, and at the end of
the century there was a plethora of these.

Gardening was not thought of, however, as part of a 'leisure complex'
either at the beginning nor at the end of the period covered in this chapter,

and it figured less prominently in Longmans' lists than either religion or sport.[172] Cooking too, to be the subject of so many books in the future, was then a preserve for female readers. Eliza Acton's *Modern Cookery* (1845) still figured in the 1900 list, although Mrs. Rundell's 'improved edition' of her *Domestic Cookery* which she had offered to the House of Longman rather than to the House of Murray in 1822, did not.[173] There was a long list of newer books by Mrs. de Salis, however, ranging from *Drinks à la Mode* and *Floral Decorations* to *Tempting Dishes for Small Incomes*. Out of the sixteen de Salis titles, twelve incorporated the words *à la Mode*. Jane Walker contributed two titles – *A Book for Every Woman* and a *Handbook for Mothers*. There was a new reprint of 500 copies of Eliza Acton's *Modern Cookery* in 1905. *The English Bread Book* appeared in 1857, two years before she died.

~

By the mid-1890s the two senior Longmans, Thomas Norton V and CJ, now experienced and confident, were, like their parents before them, being called upon to deal not only with book lists and House affairs but with organisational issues in general publishing similar to those raised during the 1850s. The circumstances, however, had changed. So had attitudes, or at least, publishers' judgements of them. As Frederick Macmillan put it to Thomas Norton:

> The laissez-faire school which was in the ascendant forty years ago, is now very much discredited, and I have not the slightest apprehension that if the matter came before the public now, the undersellers would have the support neither of the newspapers or the authors, as they undoubtedly had in 1852.[174]

Macmillan's main contribution to publishing history was his securing in 1900 of a long-lasting Net Book Agreement. Nine years earlier he had proposed that books should be divided into two classes – 'net books' sold

---

172 Gardeners are given a prominent place in the *New Dictionary of National Biography* (2004). See also Roy Strong, *Garden Party* (2000) where he notes a 'flood of books' about garden design during the 1980s.

173 A short letter from Longman & Co to Murray & Co., dated 29 December 1821, had ended with the words 'Of course you will readily perceive that no Bookseller will refuse the publication of so popular a work when brought to him without solicitation'.

174 Letter from Frederick Macmillan to Thomas Norton, 6 June 1894 (LA Part II 11/14). For a near contemporary view on the end of *laissez faire*, undoubtedly one-sided in its approach, see A.V. Dicey, *Lectures on Law and Opinion* (1905), decades later to be dismissed by historians as an unsatisfactory analysis. See J. Harris, *Private Lives, Public Spirit: a social history of Britain, 1870–1914* (1993), p.12. Books and publishing figure neither in Dicey nor Harris. The only book referred to in the index to Harris is the *Book of Common Prayer*.

strictly at their published prices ('underselling' was not to be permitted) and 'subject books' on which discount might be given to the customer at the discretion of the bookseller – and he invited Cambridge's leading economist Alfred Marshall (1842–1924), to allow him to test his net book proposals with his *Principles of Economics*, which Marshall described as the 'central work of his life'.

Reluctantly and with serious reservations Marshall agreed, and his book was priced at 12s. 6d. net and distributed to booksellers on condition that they traded it at that price and at no less.[175] In sales terms the Macmillan experiment was successful and was copied by other publishers including Longmans and Murray. In 'political' terms the experiment was successful too, and the idea of such a standard agreement was supported by a Council of Associated Booksellers, claiming to 'represent the large majority of booksellers of London and Westminster'. There was still no Publishers Association, however, and that was not formed until March 1896 with C.J. Longman as its first President.

The Booksellers Association had taken the initiative and passed a resolution in 1894, doubtless in complicity with Macmillan and other publishers, 'binding its members not to allow discount on so-called net books', and its Council appealed to the London Publishers to 'assist them in carrying out the resolution by refusing to supply net books to any Bookseller who declines to pledge himself not to give discount'. They should also send a letter to the principal wholesale houses requesting them not to supply net books either.[176]

When the issue had been raised by Macmillan in 1890, he had not only consulted CJ privately but had chosen to put his case in *The Bookseller* and the *Pall Mall Gazette*. Between then and 1900 there were more and more complaints from leading metropolitan booksellers against 'the practice of allowing extravagant discount' – such complaints had never ceased after 1852 – but their Association, 'mindful of the past history of the subject', decided to take legal advice on the last point in their resolution – pressure on the wholesale trade.

Three questions were put to Counsel: 'Is a publisher who advertises a book for sale obliged to supply it to any applicant willing to pay the advertized price?' 'Supposing this to be the case, can this obligation be

175 S. Nowell-Smith (ed.), *Letters to Macmillan* (1967), pp.219–22; C.W. Guillebaud, 'The Marshall-Macmillan Correspondence over the Net Book System' in the *Economic Journal*, Vol. LXXV (1965); R.J.L. Kingsford, *The Publishers Association* (1970), Ch. 1, pp.5-18, with an introduction 'The 1852 verdict'; and Bonham-Carter, *op. cit.*, pp.179–81.

176 Memorandum of March 1894. For Frederick Macmillan's retrospective account of what happened see his *The Net Book Agreement, 1899* (privately printed, 1924).

considered to extend to the supply of a book to a dealer *at trade price?*' 'Can an agreement between Publishers and wholesale Booksellers not to supply Net books to retailers, who decline to pledge themselves not to allow discount, be held to be a conspiracy, or an illegal combination, or other offence against the law?'

The general Net Book Agreement, engineered largely by Macmillan and finalised in 1900, provided an answer to demands for separate booksellers' action, but only after the economic position of the booksellers had in their judgement deteriorated further. 'The book trade is now passing through one of the gravest crises ever known in its history', began an article, 'Authors, Publishers and Booksellers', in the *Fortnightly Review* in the summer of 1898.

> War, famine, epidemics, commercial or financial panics affect even industrial concerns which might be thought well beyond the range of influence. The book trade, curiously enough [and note that participants in it still did not consider the trade to be an industry] is usually the first to feel and the last to recover from the ill effects of any general disturbance. In the present instance, however, the main evil began, where charity should begin, at home.[177]

It was 'directly due to a method of underselling which, pushed to extremes, has reduced booksellers' profits to the vanishing point'.

The booksellers deemed it essential to mobilise authors as well as publishers for support, and it was fortunate for their Association that at the time when the Net Book Agreement was implemented in 1900, the chairman of the Society of Authors for that year was Rider Haggard, who in this, as in farming, about which he wrote a number of books, put his trust in protection.[178] In fact, both in publishing and in farming economic fortunes were neither uniform nor consistent, and some booksellers thrived just as did some publishers.

Other long-term social forces were being brought to bear on publishing too, particularly in 1896, the year when the Publishers Association was founded, designed, like the Society of Authors, to offer collective services to participants in an uncertain trade. This was a remarkable year in social and cultural history, for the historian a vantage point from which to look backwards and forwards. Alfred Harmsworth, later Lord Northcliffe, surprisingly to be a future owner of *The Times* (in 1908), created the *Daily*

---

177 The *Fortnightly Review*, Vol. 31 (18977-8, pp.256–7.

178 In 1902 he published two volumes called *Rural England*, in which he exposed the problems of rural depopulation, and in 1905 he wrote *The Poor and the Land*. He was knighted in 1912.

Interior of Hatchard's bookshop
c. 1900

Longman Archive

Mail in 1896, a cheap morning newspaper aiming at a mass circulation[179]; a young Italian inventor, Guglielmo Marconi (1874–1937), arrived in London to demonstrate a bundle of wireless devices; the first 'moving picture' show was presented in London's West End; and the first motor rally between London and Brighton was organised.[180] This was also the year of the first modern Olympic Games – in Athens.

The deferred long-term significance of a cheap and popular press, of broadcasting, of cinema, of automobiles and of mass international sport, could not be discerned by contemporaries, but the economic and social conditions that accounted for the convergence were clear enough – large, concentrated urban populations; an increase in disposable incomes and a reduction in hours of work and improvements in mass public transport, largely in and around big cities. It was within a context of change that book publishers were now operating, and so, too, were booksellers, whose fortunes were most immediately affected. They could no more take customers for granted than could Mudie's Circulating Library.

There was more than a touch of nostalgia, therefore, in an address of 1900 by Sir George Otto Trevelyan, as there was to be in many of the

179 For an early memoir written just after his death in 1922, Max Pemberton, *Lord Northcliffe, A Memoir* (1922). For a later judgement, based on careful research, see R. Pound, *Northcliffe* (1959).

180 See Briggs, *Collected Essays*, Vol. III, pp.43–4. For Marconi see *inter alia* R.N. Vyvyan, *Marconi and Wireless* (1974).

Photograph of Fleet Street, London at the end of the nineteenth century looking towards St. Paul's and the City

BL YC.2006.a 17844

addresses of later Trevelyans.[181] He was speaking at a dinner of authors, publishers and booksellers, with his address approvingly reprinted in the *Cornhill* magazine. Trevelyan claimed that this was 'the first public dinner, on anything like this scale, of all the three classes in the great hierarchy [that was how he saw it, and not as a network] of book producers and book-distributors'. The idea of the dinner, he added, 'like many other profitable, and some pleasant ideas', had come from America. (He himself had just published the first volume of his *American Revolution*.)

Trevelyan said little about history, except as his nephew might have done, that it should never become an 'arid science', and he refused to comment on the organisation of the book trade. He ended, however, with a declaration of love:

I love book-lists and book-plates and book-covers. But above all I love a bookshop – the interior, if I can find an excuse for entering the shop, or, at the very least, the rows of open volumes displayed in the window. Of all places of business they are the most attractive, and not on account of their shop-wares only. Nowhere does the spirit of courtesy and essential refinement more universally prevail

181   See G.M. Trevelyan, *Sir George Otto Trevelyan, A Memoir* (1932).

than among those who are engaged, in any capacity, in the business
of books.[182]

This must have been a consoling speech for booksellers to hear in the
year when the Net Book Agreement came into operation.[183] Yet even
then not all bookshops, particularly, perhaps, in London, fitted into this
idealized pattern.

There was a slight fall, 211, in the total number of new books published
in the United Kingdom in 1900, 5,760, a fall which the *Publishers' Circular*
attributed to the South African War. The numbers increased in politics and
commerce, however, in voyages and in travels, in history and biography,
and in medicine and surgery, including 'malarial medicine and military
surgery'. Of the total new books, 'theology, sermons, biblical', still the first
category in the list, accounted for 579 – with 129 new editions, but 'novels,
tales and juvenile works' was 1,563 – with 1,546 new editions. The latter
figures were down from 1,825 and 736 in 1889.[184]

~

An unsigned but well-illustrated article in *The Bookman*, published two
months later, headed 'The London Publishing Houses', turned the spotlight
on 'Messrs Longman, Green and Co.', as Espinasse had done in 1860. The
writer drew heavily on the Longmans series of quarterly *Notes on Books*,
which he rightly described as 'no mere trade puff': 23,000 copies of them
were being distributed throughout the world. But he added a paragraph
of his own on 'the past fifteen or twenty years', noting the existence of
Longmans branch establishments in New York and Bombay, which figured
on letterheads.[185] Letters received in London 'often amounted' to 3,000 a
week, while the annual average was 'certainly not less than 60,000'. This
alone demanded 'a very large staff'.

Thomas Norton's *Memories* were to include a whole illustrated
section on the subject of letters, focusing on the unusual rather than

182 Sir George Otto Trevelyan, 'A Bundle of Memories', reprinted in the *Cornhill*,
     Dec. 1900, pp.782–8.

183 Compare his approach with that of J. Shaylor, 'The Evolution of the Bookseller',
     a lecture delivered to the London branch of the National Book Provident
     Company, reprinted in *The Bookseller*, 2 Feb. 1912. In introducing Shaylor to
     his Chairman, R.B. Byles, stated that 'they might as well introduce St Paul's
     Cathedral to the Dean of St Paul's'. Shaylor said in his lecture that 'the art of
     publishing had been elevated almost to a profession'. Shaylor, a lecturer much
     in demand, was a manager in Simpkin, Marshall & Co.

184 PC, 5 Jan. 1901.

185 Macmillan had launched a New York agency in 1869, subsequently a separate
     entity, and opened a Melbourne office in 1904 and a Toronto office in 1905.

on the routine. Many envelopes were addressed to Longmans, London, with no reference to Paternoster Row. One envelope, safely received, had been addressed to 'a good firm of Publishers, Paternoster Row, London'. A third included after the words 'Paternoster Row' all Longman's overseas addresses, ending with Calcutta. An Edwardian envelope read 'Respectable Sir Longman's'. The Post Office was still a respected national institution without which publishing could not function.[186]

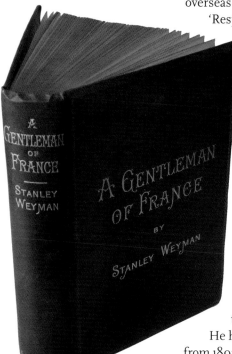

The writer in *The Bookman* respected old institutions. For him old age was 'not always the sign of decay and dissolution, as witness the vigour and activity of Messrs Longman and Co. whose firm is within measurable distance of celebrating its bicentenary'. Its current catalogue ran to 124 double-column pages. 'Numerically', the writer went on, 'the only weak section' was fiction, but what there was in that 'department' he judged, if wrongly, to be 'exceedingly representative' – Rider Haggard, Conan Doyle, Stevenson, Stanley Weyman, Edna Lyall 'and so forth'.

The 'so forth' now stands out more than the names, the three now best-known of whom were by no means 'Longman authors'. Weyman, however, who had a large reading public, was often claimed as one, and his *A Gentleman of France* (1893), first published in *Longman's Magazine*, was generally judged one of the best novels of its type. So too were the novels of James Payn. He had appeared on many publishers' lists before editing the *Cornhill* from 1893 to 1896. The first instalment of his *Thicker than Water* (Chapters 1–4) appeared in the first number of *Longman's Magazine*. His completed book appeared, in three volumes, priced at 21s., on 24 August 1883, with three instalments still to run in the *Magazine*. A one-volume edition at 6s., also published in 1883, was not a success, but 4,000 copies priced at 2s. sold well in 1884.[187]

Binding of *A Gentleman of France*, first published in 1893. Strongly recommended by Andrew Lang, Weyman (1855–1928), who lived in Ruthin, N. Wales, became a very popular novelist, although Longmans was by no means his only publisher

Longman Archive

~

That magazine, a monthly, announced in September 1882 and launched in November, had served as a conduit for a number of authors who were subsequently published in covers. Following the example of *Fraser's Magazine*, fiction was offered to its readers from the start. There would be 'at least one serial tale' in each issue, the prospectus promised, along

---

186 See M.J. Daunton, *Royal Mail: The Post Office since 1840* (1985); and Briggs and Burke, *op. cit.*, pp.139–41.

187 Article on 'Longman's Magazine' by Cyprian Blagden reprinted in A.N. Jeffares (ed.), *A Review of English Literature*, Vol. IV, No. 2, April 1963, p.14.

with 'a plentiful supply of shorter stories by the best novelists'.[188] Along with fiction, the *Magazine* promised 'a full share of that intellectual entertainment which may be obtained in the study of pure literature.

It also promised that one article would generally be devoted to 'physical science or natural history' and that 'field sports and games would form the subject of occasional papers'. Politics, 'which occupy the attention of the daily and weekly press', would be avoided, as would religious subjects 'which are fully dealt with by the organs of the various religious sections and by the graver monthly reviews'. There were to be no illustrations, an omission that limited sales.[189]

One hundred thousand copies of the first issue were printed in two runs, twice as many had originally been decided upon but there were criticisms that the second number was not equal to the first. It included an article by Froude on the Norwegian Fjords and an article by Smiles (anticipating *Longitude*) on John Harrison the chronometer maker. Grant Allen wrote in the third number on 'a mountain tulip' and Richard Jefferies in the fourth on bits of oak bark. That was a number that included Thomas Hardy's 'The Three Strangers'. Rudyard Kipling produced only one story, however, appropriately called *For One Night Only*. Henry James's *The Pupil*, his only contribution, ran over two issues. The non-fiction was more interesting in retrospect than the fiction. Articles in Volume 2 (1888) included R.H. Scott (signed) on 'Is Climate Changing?' and two by William Archer on 'The Anatomy of Acting'.

The *Magazine*, which lacked the allure of the *Cornhill* at its best, made a profit until 1894 (with two numbers exceptionally making a loss), and it had a largely unillustrious but reasonably long life of twenty-three years. By 1905, however, when only 4,000 subscription copies were printed of its last, the 276th issue, CJ, its editor throughout, though never so acknowledged in the pages of the *Magazine*, concluded gloomily that 'the mere endeavour to keep up a high literary standard is not nowadays sufficient'.

There was one non-literary feature of *Longman's Magazine*, doubtless due to the initiative of CJ, who had been impressed by Marion Trench's installation of a food wagon for unemployed dockers, the Don, at the London Docks.[190] CJ installed a wagon himself, the Donna, which was still in use during the dockers' strike of 1889. Readers' contributions to

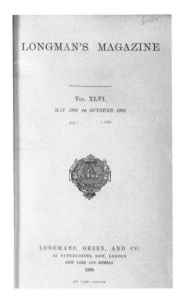

The title page of the last volume of *Longman's Magazine*, 1905, edited by C. J. Longman

Longman Archive

---

188 Prospectus, 1882, quoted by Blagden, 'Longman's Magazine', in *A Review of English Literature*, Vol. IV, No.2, April 1963. See also 'Longman's Magazine' by 'a former contributor' in *The Academy*, 30 Sept. 1905.

189 One American writer has argued that the decision not to include them was an 'anachronism from the beginning' (O. Maurer, 'Andrew Lang and Longman's Magazine, 1882–1905', *Texas Studies in English*, Vol. 34 (1955), p.52).

190 *Longman's Magazine*, Vol. 2, Aug. 1883, pp.416–26.

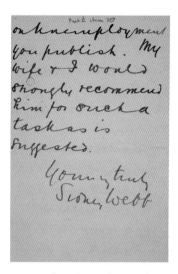

Excerpt from letter from Sidney Webb to Longman:

...The other man, R.H. Tawney of Balliol is very good indeed, and specially qualified to write on Industrial Revolution [sic]. He is perhaps the ablest and more promising of the economists outside professional posts, He is now doing [sic] courses to working men with real success. We know him & like him well. He has, by the way, married a sister of W. H. Beveridge, whose brilliant book on unemployment you publish. My wife and I would strongly recommend him for such a task as is suggested.

Yours truly

Sidney Webb

Longman Archive

its expenses were received and recorded.[191] CJ may have had this in mind when he referred to 'industrial relations' in his speech in 1890 quoted at the beginning of this chapter. Whether he was influenced by Beatrice Webb is not clear, but CJ was aware of the importance of her work before and after her marriage to Sidney in 1892.

Doubtless had Beatrice been a novelist Longman could have published a novel by her as they did a substantial number of late-Victorian and twentieth-century novels written by women. As it was, the House published her autobiographical *My Apprenticeship* (1926) and, much later, *Our Partnership* (1948). Her diaries are moulded as much by literary impulses as by the pressures of life.

Three very different novelists, all friends, Stevenson, Conan Doyle and Rider Haggard, had a prominent place in Longman history for special reasons, a negative one in the case of Conan Doyle because Longman published none of his Sherlock Holmes stories, which began with *A Study in Scarlet*. Stevenson, however, published his most famous book with them, *Dr Jekyll and Mr Hyde*, which had no previous *Magazine* history, brought out by Longman in book form both in cloth and paper wrappers at the end of 1885, the same year as *A Child's Garden of Verses* and *Prince Otto*.[192] Based on a dream, it was more than a 'bogey tale', as Stevenson first described it, largely because he listened to his wife Fanny's advice to re-write his first draft and to turn the novel into an allegory.

According to CJ, who claimed that 'the bookstalls were already full of Christmas numbers, etc., and the trade would not look at it', the book, a quick but not immediate success, entered the shops only in January 1886. Like *Treasure Island*, published by Cassell, who paid only £100 for it,[193] it was to be translated into many languages, and a play, based on the story, the prelude to many plays and films, was staged at London's Lyceum Theatre as early as August 1888. From the start there was a transatlantic dimension to the story. The authorised American edition of *Dr Jekyll*, published by Scribners, appeared four days before the English, and a brief dispute followed between London and New York before Scribners agreed to pay Longmans half the royalties that had accrued to them. In a letter to Stevenson Charles Scribner referred to 'the strange case of Dr Jekyll and Mr Longman'.[194]

---

191 See C.J. Longman, 'The Story of the "Donna" from 1883 to 1897', in *Longman's Magazine*, Vol.31, pp.256–7 (LA).

192 See W.F. Prideaux, *A Bibliography of the Works of Robert Louis Stevenson* (new edn., 1917).

193 Nowell-Smith, *op.cit.*, p.99.

194 Quoted in G.L. McKay, *Some Notes on Robert Louis Stevenson, His Finances, His Agents and Publishers* (1958), p.19. Lang said of the novel, *The World's Desire*, that he wrote with Haggard, 'the hero, having gone to bed with Mrs. Jekyll, wakes up with Mr. Hyde'. (Quoted in Calder, *op. cit.*, p.118.)

Haggard had published his first books, one a history and two of them novels, with a small publisher, Hurst and Blackett, and even after meeting Lang, the start of his friendship with him, he published *King Solomon's Mines* (1885), a book which thrilled Lang, not with Longmans but with Cassells.[195] He moved to Longmans because he knew both CJ and Lang admired his kind of novel. *She* (1887), published in the same year as *Allan Quartermain*, when Haggard was still only 34, was an immediate Longmans success. 'I am glad to tell you', CJ wrote to Haggard when he was in Egypt in 1887, that the book 'keeps on selling capitally. We have printed 25,000 already, and have ordered another 5,000, and I do not think that we shall have many left when the printers deliver them ... Last week we sold over 1,000.'[196]

In his autobiography Haggard discussed his dealings not only with Lang but with CJ to whom he dedicated his *Colonel Quaritch VC*, 'a tale of English country life', a book that Lang thought was the worst that he had ever written. When in 1896 Haggard was worried about reviews of his *Beatrice*, pirated in America, which accused him of offending against morality, CJ assured him that there was nothing that he (Haggard) should regret: 'the idea that the character of Beatrice could lead anyone into vice is preposterous'.[197] Lang was more intimate and direct. 'You confounded ASS, The Thing is Rot [ie the attack on him]. Don't take it *au sérieux*'.[198] After 'dear' Lang's death, Haggard felt nearer to him than he had been for 'many a year'.

Of the letters that Haggard received when *She* was published, one that he particularly treasured came from an electro-chemical factory in Budapest, and was signed by an Englishman, a Scot, a German, a Frenchman, a Swiss and a Hungarian. 'Each of us found in it something that appealed to his sympathies', Haggard was told, 'despite our various tastes, characters and nationalities.'[199] CJ, who was keenly interested in overseas sales of Longmans books, shared the factory's sentiment. He bought the copyright of Haggard's *Cleopatra* for what Haggard called 'a large sum of money' in 1887. Lang did not think so highly of it. 'If I were you I'd put *Cleopatra* away for as long as possible, and then read it as a member of the public.'[200] It was published in 1889.

Arthur Conan Doyle (1859–1930), nephew of Dickie Doyle the artist whom CJ greatly admired, was born, like Stevenson, in Edinburgh. He

Longmans also published novels as 'yellow backs'. *Madam* by Mrs Oliphant was first published in three volumes in 1884, and then as a one volume yellow back in 1885

Bodleian Library, University of Oxford: John Carter Collection

195 *Ibid.*, pp.135-6. Haggard, who changed his mind about the terms, received over £750 after 31,000 copies had been printed by the end of 1886.

196 Letter of 15 March 1887, quoted in Haggard, *The Days of My Life*, Vol. II (1926), p.251.

197 *Ibid.*, p.14.

198 *Ibid.*, p.79.

199 The letter is printed *ibid.*, p.353.

200 *Ibid.*, pp.268, 269.

studied medicine at Edinburgh University, where he observed with interest the diagnostic methods of one of his professors, Joseph Bell. He began to write, however, not from Scotland, but from Southsea where he set up as a doctor in 1882. In retrospect, Conan Doyle stands out, like Haggard, as a 'tale teller', appealing in his case not only to wonder and to curiosity but to ingenuity.[201] But he was not a good judge of his own early work. His early three-decker novel, *Micah Clarke*, rejected by Bentley but accepted by Longman after Lang had praised the text, received such an enthusiastic reception that he contemplated writing a new 'Rider Haggardy kind of book called *The Inca's Eye*, dedicated to all the bad boys of the Empire by one who sympathises with them'.[202]

Instead, his writing career had already taken a very different course. In *A Study in Scarlet* (1887) he had introduced Sherlock Holmes, with at his side or always within call Dr Watson, and although Conan Doyle's *The White Company* (1891) was published by Longman, the House was not involved in *The Memoirs of Sherlock Holmes* (1894). It was not *Longman's Magazine* but the new, well-illustrated and avowedly popular *Strand Magazine*, founded in 1891 by George Newnes, which was the vehicle for the first serial versions of books such as *The Hound of the Baskervilles* (1901–2) and, in different vein, *The Lost World* (1912). Conan Doyle was knighted in 1901: Newnes, whom the Longmans do not seem to have known, had been made a baronet in 1885.

A very different author from Stevenson, Haggard and Conan Doyle, Richard Jefferies (1848–1887), was a naturalist and essayist as well as a novelist, who now stands out as a key figure in any survey of the differences between 'rural', 'urban' and 'metropolitan' or of the ambiguities and contrasts both of agrarian and industrial society.[203] The 'power of thought' behind his writings, including novels, appreciated by CJ Longman as his publisher, grew substantially the more he wrote, so that it is essential to date his writings. *Hodge and His Masters* (1880) is a much-quoted book on the attitudes of farmers and farm workers not only to each other but to religion and politics. *Bevis, the Story of a Boy* (1882) has been described in the *Encyclopaedia Britannica* as 'one of the best boys' books in English', while his own autobiography, *The Story of My Heart* (1883), with a preface

---

201 See J. Barzun, 'The Novel Turns Tale', quoted in Fowles, *loc. cit.*, p.191, and *From Dawn to Decadence* (2001), p.630. See also D. Stashower, *Teller of Tales: The Life of Arthur Conan Doyle* (2000) and D. Barsham, *Arthur Conan Doyle and the Meaning of Masculinity* (2000).

202 John Dickson Carr, a detective novelist, *The Life of Sir Arthur Conan-Doyle* (1949), p.75.

203 P. Ackroyd, *London: the Biography* (2000), quotes Jefferies, p.447. See also E.W. Martin, *The Secret People. English village life after 1750* (1954) and *Where London Ends. English Provincial Life after 1750* (1958).

by CJ, appeared one year before his collected essays, *The Life of the Fields*, and his novel *Dewy Morn*.[204]

In letters to CJ written in 1883 the author stated that he had spent '*seventeen* years' meditating on *The Story of My Heart* and that it was 'a real record – unsparing to myself as to all things – absolutely and unflinchingly true'. CJ sent it to a 'sympathetic critic' and read it himself, concluding that 'the book would please some people very much' but 'would probably excite some adverse criticism'. A royalty arrangement was proposed and later revised – and CJ provided a personal glimpse of his feelings when he told Jefferies that one passage had particularly appealed to him – that where he sang 'the praises of the bow':

> I love the open air and the trees and the birds and the flowers. I love all sports – cricket, fishing, hunting, shooting; but by far the best I love archery.

~

There was a cross-link here with Badminton, and there was a very different cross-link too, that with the classics in the case of another still read and better-known novelist, Samuel Butler (1835–1902), author of *Erehwon* (1901) and of the posthumous *The Way of All Flesh* (1902), who published one edition of *Erehwon*, first published in 1872, with Longmans in 1890. Butler had specific comments to make about the House of Longman in his fascinating *Notebooks*. One note began

> They treat me well at Longmans: everyone is very civil and everything is well done on most reasonable terms. I am in as good hands as can be found in London.[205]

Clearly Longmans, Green as publishers had nothing to do with the unfavourable fictitious sketch in *The Way of All Flesh* of the favourite Longmans author, B.H. Kennedy (1804–1889), headmaster of Shrewsbury School from 1836 to 1866, and Regius Professor of Greek at Cambridge from 1867 to 1889. Kennedy's *Public School Latin Primer* (1866), was a Longmans best-seller,[206] now 'edited with sanction of the Head Masters of

The title page of *The Public School Latin Primer, edited with the sanction of the Head Masters of the Public Schools included in Her Majesty's Commission, 1866, by Benjamin Hall Kennedy*

BL 12934.bb.10

---

204 See S.J. Looker (ed.), *Jefferies' England: Nature Essays by Richard Jefferies* (1937), p.xiii and (ed) *The Story of My Heart* (1947) where Looker quoted hitherto unpublished C.J. letters. Jefferies wrote many of his best pieces for *Longman's Magazine*. Besant wrote a eulogy of him, *The Eulogy of Richard Jefferies* (1888).

205 (LA Part II/27/8)

206 In the August 1866 Monthly Longmans, Green List (LA Part II/110-111) it was 'put forth as a standard grammar for all classes in public schools below the highest'. Priced at 2*s*. 6*d*. (cloth), it was based on an earlier Kennedy grammar of 1847.

the Public Schools included in Her Majesty's Commission'.[207] Frequently revised, for the first time in a major way in 1888, it was still selling 41,000 copies a year in the 1970s.

Curiously, Kennedy had been introduced to Longmans by another Samuel Butler, his own teacher at Shrewsbury, and neither he nor the House were daunted when the *Public School Latin Primer* had a hostile reception when it first appeared in 1866 and when both its contents and terminology were attacked, not least in the letter pages of *The Times*.[208] This had more to do with public school politics than with Latin grammar, although one of his critics was an Oxford Greats don, Henry Roby, who resented the fact that a textbook of his own had not been produced in time by the Oxford University Press, and the initial run of 2,000 was quickly followed up by runs of 5,000 and 10,000. By February 1867 the total print number had reached 32,000.

The younger Samuel Butler's view of Kennedy as a teacher of classics at Shrewsbury was not shared at the time by many of Kennedy's pupils. One of them, Professor Heitland, described vividly a lesson taken by him: 'he is not merely translating Demosthenes: he is Demosthenes speaking *extempore* in English'. This was certainly not teaching by rote. Kennedy, whose approach to the classics has been described as 'far more direct and vital than Lily's', a 'common grammar' long under Longmans' control, always advised his pupils to 'think in Latin, think in Greek.' He also liked to consult headmasters of other schools and university dons, the wisest of them aware of the problems created by their not having a standard Latin grammar, although *King Edward VI's Latin Grammar* by Christopher Wordsworth, the poet's nephew, who became a Bishop, was widely used alongside his brother Charles's *Greek Grammar*. Kennedy completely superseded it.[209]

---

207 The Clarendon Commission of 1861, which dealt with England's nine leading public schools.

208 *The Times*, 20 Aug-9 Nov. 1866. No fewer than thirty-six letters, most of them signed by pseudonyms, appeared in its correspondence columns, one of them by a 'grinder' who compared Kennedy with Bismarck, who had engineered the defeat of the Austrians at the battle of Königgratz on 2 July. See C.A. Stray, 'Kennedy's Latin Primer, A Paradigm', in *Paradigm*, No. 1, Nov. 1989, his 'Grinders and Grammars: A Victorian Controversy' (1995) and his 'Primers, Publishing and Politics: The Classical Textbooks of Benjamin Hall Kennedy', in PBSA, Vol. 90, No. 4 (1996), pp.451–74. Stray, a pioneer in the field of textbook studies, was one of the founders of the Textbook Colloquium which later produced *Paradigm*.

209 There had been an argument between Charles Wordsworth and the House of Murray concerning Charles's decision in 1844 to switch the publisher of his Greek grammar from Murray to the Oxford University Press, and in 1863 the OUP was planning a new Latin primer. It had set up a School-book Committee at the instigation of Alexander Macmillan. See Sutcliffe, *op. cit.*, pp.12, 19ff.

This was because it had the support of the headmasters of nine of Britain's chief public schools, Shrewsbury among them. In 1863 Kennedy, who had been invited to produce both Latin and Greek grammars – he refused the invitation to produce the Greek – had set to work, and two years later he circulated no fewer than two hundred sets of proofs to his colleagues, asking them for their 'opinions'.[210] His colleagues at Harrow, where several Longmans were pupils, did not approve of it, but most public schools did. As a result, the Headmaster's Conference, founded in 1869, was at the centre of continuing debate about the merits of Kennedy, before and after his new *Revised Latin Primer* appeared in June 1888. Yet rival textbooks failed, and the Headmasters' Conference failed also in 1886 to commission a new textbook of their own through a committee. The *Revised Latin Primer*, unlike its 1866 predecessor, bore Kennedy's name. It quickly established itself, however, and subsequently appeared in many twentieth-century editions, the last of them edited by James Mountford, Vice-Chancellor of the University of Liverpool.

After Kennedy's death there were to be well-founded complaints from members of his family that they had not received adequate recognition or rewards for the labours they put into different editions of the *Revised Latin Primer*, including the first. There had, indeed, been a family division of labour. Thus, the wording and arrangement of the accidence throughout the different editions was carried out by Kennedy's two spinster daughters – a third daughter was married – with the correspondence being handled by the eldest, Marion. It was she too who 'read all the latest German and English books for the purpose' of dealing with the syntax. There were other non-family helpers, like Kennedy's ex-pupils, G.R. Hallam and T.E. Page, but taken as a whole the *Revised Latin Primer*, the daughters insisted, was a family enterprise.[211] Having been treated generously by Longman in 1888, when they secured 60 per cent of the profits on sales, the House retaining 40 per cent, the daughters secured the valuable copyright in 1914.[212] It did not run out until 1992.

~

Although this chapter is entitled 'Publisher, Readers and Authors' for reasons associated with the history of publishing in general – the rise, or so it was claimed, of a new reading public or publics to whom publishers were responding – authors must still figure prominently in it. They were just as heterogeneous a group as they had been at the beginning of the

---

210 There were different 'opinions' on its merits. Harrow did not adopt it. (Note by Kennedy in the Longman archives.)

211 Note of 7 Dec. 1914 (LA Part II/111/18).

212 (LA Part II/111/34-37)

nineteenth century, and the position of an author like Kennedy, whether or not he was supported by his family, was very different from the position of Haggard or of Stevenson. The judgement of school teachers mattered as much to him as the judgement of adult readers mattered to novelists. Reviewers, except in specialised educational journals, mattered less than they did in criticising novels and all types of *belles lettres*.

Nevertheless, there were obvious and interconnected moves towards professionalisation in both educational and literary circles, with a number of authors identifying themselves during the 1880s as 'authors by profession' if not as 'professional authors'. The Society of Authors which by twelve years preceded the Publishers Association purported to represent all authors, but the twelve men who met to found it in 1883/4 included barristers – for centuries highly professional in education and outlook, but not primarily authors – and journalists who were claiming to be professionals only in the face of persistent opposition. As early as 1862 Fitzjames Stephen, Leslie Stephen's brother, had written in the *Cornhill* that 'journalism will no doubt, occupy the first place or one of the first places in the literary history of the present times'[213] but there was to be no National Union of Journalists until 1907, and even then it was not to be fully representative of the profession.

The Society of Authors' first Council of eighteen, which met in February 1884 to set up the new society, included the novelist Charles Reade, who as we have seen had strong views on publishing,[214] and G.A. Sala, most famous of Victorian journalists. The span, therefore, was wide, and the 'literary men' who joined the Society included Edward Lytton, son of Bulwer Lytton, and Matthew Arnold, John Ruskin, Cardinal Manning, James Martineau, Richard Burton, Wilkie Collins, Charlotte M. Yonge, Thomas Huxley and W.S. Gilbert. The crowning triumph came when Besant, prominent Chairman of a small Committee of Management, who was indefatigable in his organisational energies, persuaded Tennyson, Poet Laureate, to become President.[215] Clearly, unlike Besant, most of the 'literary men' did not depend on their pens. But more of them were now beginning to be paid on a royalty basis, on sales, and this could transform their livelihoods.

A new standard royalty agreement was printed for Longmans, Green in 1887, leaving the amount of royalties to be filled in. It covered translations and 'all Copyright, Foreign and other Rights, under existing or future Treaties or Conventions with American or other Foreign Countries'.

---

213 *Cornhill*, July 1862, quoted by M.M. Bevington, *The Saturday Review* (New York, 1941), p.1.

214 See above, p.240.

215 Bonham Carter, *op. cit.*, pp.118-22.

Two years earlier there is a note of 8 July 1885 in ink on the first Longman printed contract – 'Agreed by Mr CJL inserting words in America and elsewhere'.[216]

The context of book publishing was changing, as were perceptions of 'bookmanship' and some novelists felt increasingly isolated, alienated, even, from the currents of social and cultural change[217] as was William Morris (1834-1896), who identified himself with manual workers rather than with collar-and-tie professionals and was busy with his Kelmscott Press in the last years of his life.[218] The Society of Authors was rooted in Victorian England but one of the authors invited to join it in 1884, Cardinal Manning, was to be one of Lytton Strachey's *Eminent Victorians*, and Matthew Arnold (1917) was the son of another.

~

How was culture to be related to commerce? Would the market prevail in literature as in the retail trade? None of the Longmans were interested in producing best-sellers with a topical twist, although they were soon bound to take account of new ventures in publishing 'the classics' such as J.M. Dent's *Everyman's Library* or the *World's Classics*, ultimately acquired by the Oxford University Press, or, indeed, of Arthur Mee's *Children's Encyclopaedia* in 1907. It was not, however, through another new encyclopaedia of their own that Longmans Green moved into the world of children. They published the two sisters' Bertha and Florence Upton's *The Adventures of Two Dutch Dolls* in 1895, the first of a series, in which a new creature, the golliwogg, so spelt, was introduced to child readers. The series included *Golliwogg's Christmas*, *Golliwogg's Circus* and *Golliwogg's Desert Island*.

The House of Longman provided a steady income to the two sisters, but neither it nor the authors derived any financial benefit from the appearance of golliwogs on china and on chintz in Edwardian England. There was a separation between the market for books and the market for pottery or textiles. There was an awkward tension, however, between bookselling and the selling of one particular newspaper, *The Times*, most famous of all newspapers, between 1905 and 1908. Indeed, the tension spilled over into bitter warfare, a 'Book War', fought between the Publishers Association and *The Times*.

The manager of *The Times*, Moberly Bell (1847–1911), short of funds

MRS. BERTHA UPTON.

MISS FLORENCE K. UPTON.

Photographs of the authors of *The Adventures of Two Dutch Dolls* from the Longman Scrapbooks

Longman Archive

---

216 (LA Part II/61/No. 3)

217 See P. Keating, *The Haunted Study* (1989).

218 Morris fits appropriately into Longman history not through royalties that he received but through the labours of his daughter May, who edited twenty-four volumes of his collected works between 1910 and 1915 (she frequently went to work at 39 Paternoster Row).

and guided by two energetic American booksellers, Horace Hooper and W.M. Jackson, had created a Times Book Club in 1905 in an effort to increase annual subscriptions to the newspaper. The Club lent new books to subscribers and then proceeded to sell them at second-hand prices when still relatively new (having been taken out by borrowers only two or three times). For the Publishers Association this was a new version of traditional 'underselling', which the Net Book Agreement (signed by *The Times*) had been framed to prevent, and the process was even more disturbing to the Booksellers Association whose members were continuing to go through a difficult period of adaptation. A new book trade agreement was drawn up, therefore, binding on publishers and booksellers, laying down that no book should be sold second-hand until after six months following its publication.

The initiative in the subsequent phases of the 'Book War' was taken neither by the publishers nor by the booksellers but by *The Times* itself which printed not only aggressive leaders on the subject but conspicuous advertisements, deviating totally from the old advertising 'smalls' on which it, like all provincial newspapers, had for decades depended. It meanwhile kept its correspondence columns open to every point of view, including those of vociferous 'literary' supporters of the line it was taking led by George Bernard Shaw.[219] Attempts at mediation on the part of other authors failed. Many, like Kipling, for example, were on the book publishers' side – and it required a legal action to terminate the 'War'.

The Longmans, who had originally supplied copies of some of their books to the Times Book Club before hostilities began, did not play a major part in the 'War', although CJ was a Vice-President of the Publishers Association from 1906 to 1909 and had been approached by Moberly Bell telling him about his plans before any other publisher.[220] Moberly Bell had made an attempt to approach John Murray also, and the Book War ended in the courts after Murray figured as plaintiff in a successful libel suit against *The Times*, which had published a letter accusing him of extortion as a publisher. In response he claimed that the appeal of *The Times* was to 'the instinct of greed' and observed that there was 'no business in London (except, perhaps, the management of a great newspaper) which calls for so much constant labour, so much alertness of mind and so much attention to infinite detail as that of a publisher'.

The observation soon had a twist to it, for while Moberly Bell was seeking energetically to protect the interest of the newspaper, as he saw it,

---

219 A narrative of the 'Book War', written by Edward Bell in 1912, was appended to Macmillan's book on the Net Book Agreement. F. Harcourt Kitchin in *Moberly Bell and his Times* (1925) unconvincingly claimed (pp.188–9) that 'The Times, which was discredited by the Book War, was not really a belligerent at all'. Throughout the 'war' there were echoes of 1852.

220 E.H.C. Moberly Bell, *The Life and Letters of C.F. Moberly Bell* (1927), p.259.

The Times acquired a new proprietor, at first anonymous, Lord Northcliffe, who was soon pressing Moberly Bell to improve *The Times* system of accounting, if it could be called a system.[221] 'What I personally want with all my numerous responsibilities', Northcliffe told Moberly Bell (p.359) are 'accounts that I can look at as a barometer. What I have never been able to obtain from *The Times* is how much money we have made this week, how much money we made last year and the year before, and what *The Times* made since the beginning of the financial year.'[222] Longman and Murray could not have provided such information about book publishing.

No one was happier about the outcome of the Book War than Frederick Macmillan. 'Failure', he wrote later, 'would have endangered and probably broken down the Net Book System.'[223] Yet the 'Book War', coming half way between the South African War and the Great War, did not figure prominently in Longman accounts of the history of the House, as set out, for example, in a set of notes made in the 1950s by William, the elder son of CJ, born in 1882,[224] and educated, like his father, at Harrow and University College; he was always known in Paternoster Row – and usually outside it – as 'Mr Willie'.

~

The notes made by William make it clear that in his view Longmans was virtually a tied house. He did not use the word 'integrated'. All Longmans paper, he noted, was bought from Dickinson, with whom the family connection was strong, strengthened, indeed, through recent marriages, and almost all binding was done at the Longman Binding Works – the Ship. The advantage of the latter arrangement was that output could be controlled, preference could be given to any books urgently wanted, and work could be spread 'to keep the factory on an even keel', but the disadvantage was higher costs. All binding was done at London prices. There could be no shopping around. William saw all the economic implications. As familiar with Longmans' finances as any professional accountant could have been, he kept a close watch on Longmans, Green finances before and after taking over the control of accounts in 1914 from his uncle George, who was left

---

221 See Pound, *op. cit.*, Ch.13, 'A Climacteric Year'.

222 *Ibid.*, p.359.

223 Macmillan, *op. cit.*, p.77. When Macmillan received his knighthood in 1909 (for hospital work) Moberly Bell wrote him a letter of congratulations and assured him that during the Book War he had never had feelings of personal animosity against him or any other publisher.

224 William's notes, undated and entirely factual, are called 'Random Notes of Changes in Longman, Green and Co. during the Last Fifty Years'. The text suggests that the notes were compiled in 1956 (LA Part II/A2, LA Part II/42/3). The Bell letter is quoted in E.H.C. Moberley Bell *op. cit.* p.278.

with staff organisation and salaries.

William and Robert Longman joined the House together, each aged twenty-four, on the Tuesday after Easter in 1906, a date they never forgot, a few weeks after the return of a Liberal government to power with a great majority. Seventy-five people were then employed in 1906 (none of them women) and eighteen of them warehousemen. What William and Robert took most pride in was the fact that they were representatives of a sixth Longman generation, and when they became Partners three years later they were largely content to stick to 'tradition'. The private Company which they were called upon to help direct produced no annual profit-and-loss account or annual balance sheet, there was no audit, and no chartered accountants were employed. Every third year, the Partners drew up a valuation of the business, as they had done in mid-Victorian years, and the resulting profit or loss, based on the estimated proceeds of the next three years, was added to or deducted from the individual Partners' capital. Each Partner was entitled to draw 5 per cent per annum from his capital until the next triennial valuation. He was also entitled to receive an annual salary of £600, an increase on the mid-Victorian figure. Each Partner's individual income tax (the rate in 1906 was 1s. 2d. in the £) was paid by the firm, and at the triennial valuation was charged against the sum allotted to the Partner. No provision was made by a sinking fund or by creating reserves to deal with the retirement or death of a Partner.

The 'system', which would have shocked Northcliffe as much as the system he found in *The Times*, persisted until 1914, with the curious mode of paying country travellers through W.E. Green's personal account. The outbreak of war, however, was followed by the passing of a new Companies Act, which required Longmans, Green as a private company to produce an annual audited balance sheet and profit-and-loss account. A table, prepared later and typed, gave uncorroborated details, down to a penny, of profits between 1910 and 1923 before and after Directors' fees, interest and the writing off of goodwill had been allowed for.[225] Figures for some items in some years were missing, and the table as a whole showed that it was not only the mode of payment of country travellers which was curious and cumbrous. Partners themselves did not know clearly just how they were faring, and the Companies Act of 1914 did not seem to have made any difference to their knowledge.

Many other items in the table on page 365 were at best conventional. The figures that mattered were not Directors' fees but Partners' profits.

What the table revealed plainly was that there were good years (e.g. 1912) and bad years. Since, however, the table took the value of the pound as constant, it did not chart general rises and falls in the price level or in the prices of books. The general price level had fallen between 1870 and 1895

---

225 (LA Part II, 319/162)

Longmans profits, 1910–23

Year	Profit before charges	Income tax	Directors' fees	Goodwill written off	Profit, including interest on partners capital
1910	£34,502 7s. 10d.	£1,510 7s. 11d.	£3,000	£1,656 13s. 4d.	£18,157 11s. 11d.
1911	£34,200 3s. 9d.	£582 6s. 10d.	£3,000	£1,656 13s. 4d.	£18,783 8s. 11d.
1912	£38,417 8s. 4d.	£582 6s. 10d.	£3,000	£1,666 13s. 4d.	£23,000 13s. 6d.
1913	£33,063 1s. 1d.	£582 6s. 10d.	£3,000	£1,666 13s. 4d.	£17,630 0s. 5d.
1914	£33,379 17s. 11d.	£1,403 17s. 11d.	£3,000	£1,666 13s. 4d.	£17,125 6s. 2d.
1915	£22,382 12s. 4d.	£1,987 5s. 9d.	£3,000	£1,666 13s. 4d.	£15,444 12s. 9d.
1916	£39,227 6s. 0d.	£1,724 8s. 10d.	£2,700	£1,333 6s. 8d.	£24,134 5s. 6d.
1917	£41,829 17s. 4d.	£1,552 16s. 3d.	£3,000	£1,333 6s. 8d.	£26,461 4s. 5d.
1918	£51,192 8s. 11d.	£1,565 14s. 6d.	£3,000	£1,333 6s. 8d.	£35,780 17s. 9d.
1919	£61,391 17s. 0d.	not given	£2,850	–	£48,395 11s. 9d.
1920	£56,314 17s. 0d.	£3,015 6s. 5d.	£4,350	–	£40,103 2s. 11d.
1921	£19,275 8s. 8d.	£3,973 9s. 10d.	£4,112 10s. 0d.	–	−£5,607 2s. 1d. loss
1922	£34,294 9s. 5d.	£1,763 10s. 11d.	£6,050	–	£9,953 17s 6d.
1923	£43,727 0s. 3d.	£1,001 0s. 4d.	£5,550	–	£20,594 6s. 11d.

and risen again after that, but the pricing of books followed a somewhat different pattern. Their movement reflected differences within the price range. By 1895 the number of middle-priced books (5s. to 7s. 6d.) had already reached 15.7 per cent of the total number of books produced, and by the First World War reached 19.8 per cent (roughly the same proportion as that for books priced between 2s. and 3s. 6d.).

Longmans Green still did not publish as high a proportion of low-priced books as some other publishers. Nor did the total number of their titles expand as fast as the number of all publishers' titles. Between 1901 and 1914 there was a steady expansion of reading in quantitative terms and the number of totally new book titles, which had been 6,102 in 1890 (with 1,311 new editions), totalled 6,044. By 1913 it had more than doubled to 12,379.[226]

Within this context William's final judgement on the finances of the House of Longman as a whole was that after 1906 the business was expanding only slowly. (The terminal date he chose for comparison with 1906 was not 1918 or 1923 or indeed 1947, when Longmans became a limited liability company, but 1955.) The growth, moreover, was almost entirely

226 S. Eliot, *Some Patterns and Trends in British Publishing, 1800–1919* (1994).

overseas. None the less he noted substantial changes in the scale of the business between the first and the fifth decades of the twentieth century, for example in staffing. There was relative stability in staffing before 1914, although there had been one other major innovation before then according to the staff records, which William did not discuss. In June 1910 for the first time five women were taken on at Paternoster Row. Two stayed until 1919, seeing through the War when other women were employed in the absence of men. One left in 1911, two in 1913.

Meanwhile, staff records for new entries of clerks (and Partners) during the three decades 1881–90, 1891–1900 and 1901–10 showed an increase in the new century, with a further increase to follow in the 1920s:

New Arrivals, 1881–1910

Year	No.	Year	No.	Year	No.
1881	2	1891	5	1901	4
1882	4	1892	2	1902	10
1883	6	1893	0	1903	5
1884	3	1894	2	1904	9
1885	1	1895	9	1905	12
1886	1	1896	3	1906	5
1887	3	1897	5	1907	4
1888	7	1898	7	1908	4
1889	5	1899	8	1909	1
1890	4	1900	4	1910	7*
Total	**36**	**Total**	**45**	**Total**	**56**

Includes the five female workers mentioned in the text.

The figures do not include workers taken on from Rivington. In 1890 there were twelve of these. Of those entering in the 1880s, three stayed on until 1933 and one until 1938; of those in the 1890s one stayed on until 1945, one until 1947, one until 1953 and one until 1955. The last of these was not a totally new entrant: he was promoted from his position as a packer, the only such promotion registered in the table. Of the Edwardian intake one stayed on until 1916.

The total intake for the decade 1921 to 1930 was eighty-two, and in two years, 1925 and 1927, was as high as fifteen. At the time Mr Willie was making his calculations and writing his 'Random Notes' during the 1950s Longmans were employing 273 people – 12 travellers, 80 male clerical staff and 188 female staff, 26 porters and warehousemen, 1 male canteen employee and 8 female canteen staff, cleaners and a housekeeper. This was a huge increase in scale, and in consequence the financial accounts also looked quite different.

Longmans Finances, 1906 and 1955

	1906(£)		1955(£)
Cash in hand	10,511		163,139
With Brokers	10,000		14,600
Debtors	33,158		296,992
Trade Creditors	?9,896		292,974
Paper in stock	8,340		128,528
Reserves	Nil	*General*	300,000
		Stock	30,000
		Sinking Fund	18,980
		Profit and Loss	114,632
		Capital	32,241
		Income Tax	123,000

In 1906 £12,331 was spent on salaries and wages, in 1955 £145,421, with the average payment rising from £166 to £532.

William's 'Random Notes' did not touch on quality of output, although they gave the names of the 'four literary advisers' employed in 1906 and of the income they received. Religion still came first, now only because of the alphabetical order of their names. The Revd. H.N. Bate was given an annual honorarium of £100, Professor A.W. Reinold, a scientist, received £100 also, as did the Hon. A. Elliot, who also received £400 for help with the editing of the *Edinburgh Review*. Once again the outstanding name was that of Lang, who received £400. When he died no one could replace him.

~

From 1906 or, indeed, a little earlier, it is possible to use oral history and private memoirs, such as Mr Willie's, to describe what was happening at Paternoster Row in non-quantitative terms. One unpublished volume of 'Memoirs [not 'memories'] of the House of Longmans' (*sic*), completed in 1972, fifty years after Thomas Norton's *Memories*, with which it overlaps, supplements 'Random Notes'. It was written by E.W. Parker, who 'early in the reign of George V', his words, joined the firm in November 1911 with an active career ahead of him which began not with people but with premises, or rather with now forgotten people in premises that have long since disappeared.

When in 1911 Parker had opened the 'massive front door' of 39 Paternoster Row, what he called 'one of the most elegant and functional book publishing buildings in London', he found in front of him

> a large hall, with high ceilings: to the right of this hall was a staircase
> leading to the first floor. Facing me was a glass partitioned room
> [occupied by A. Brettell, the chief cashier, who had joined Longman
> in 1874] who was sitting on a round topped high stool facing a sloping
> desk [the kind of stool behind which William Ellerby Green had sat
> when Thomas Norton arrived in 1869]. Opposite him was his chief
> assistant, [A.R.] Scarfe [who had joined Longman in 1889], and in the
> background at another desk was [A.L.] Sherwood.[227]

Parker had to wait in this room until the arrival of Richard Bartram, the
Head of the Country Department, as it was still called.

He was then introduced to George Longman, 'an active man in his
fifties',[228] who was sitting in a smaller glass partitioned room on the same
sort of high stool. Bartram's father, William (1835–1926), had preceded
Richard in the same job, and having retired in December 1910 after fifty-
three years' service, he lived long enough to take part in the bicentenary
celebrations in 1924 at the age of eighty-nine. Parker himself was not to
retire until 1962 after what he called fifty-one years of 'fascinating slavery'.

When Bartram read Parker's school report, which he had not seen
before, he swiftly transferred him on his first afternoon from the 'titles'
section to the Publishing Department, where he met and was placed under
the care of the white-haired W.A. Kelk, whom Parker described as 'the willing
slave of his master', CJ. According to Parker, Kelk also had 'willing slaves'.
He could 'at times roar like a lion', but he was by nature 'a kind man'.

Clearly the slavery image appealed to Parker, who as a 'junior' moved
from department to department, 'learning the inner working of one of the
most fascinating branches of commerce' and in the process meeting all the
partners. They too had all moved around, in their case starting in 'titles'
where they learned to prove themselves manually adept in handling newly
published books.[229]

Kelk, usually known by his initials, WAF, was a man on whom the
partners had come to rely. He had joined the firm in 1882 at the age of
fifteen, one of the four staff members recorded as joining in that year in
the table on p.366 (the other three had all gone by 1890), and in 1902 he
had taken the place of Reuben Ling as head of the Publishing Department,
known then at 39 Paternoster Row as the House of Lords. Ling had been

---

227 E.W. Parker, 'Memoirs of the House of Longmans' (1972) unpublished, p.7.
   (LA Part II/43/1-2)

228 *Ibid.*

229 In the 'Titles' section small bags of books were held in sixes and sevens
   depending on the size of the binding. Bulk stock was held on the upper
   floors.

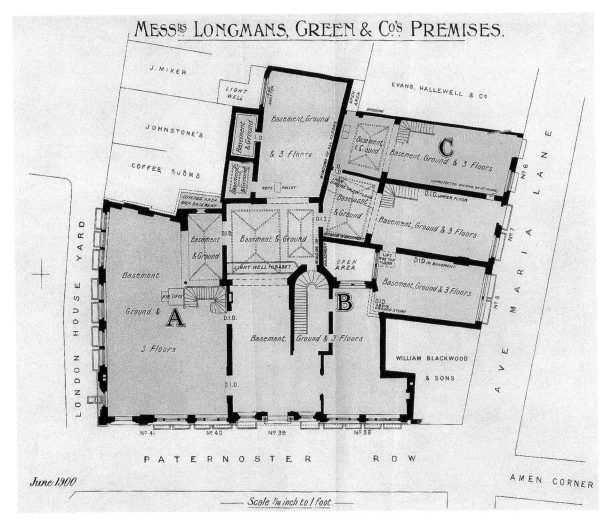

A Plan of Messrs Longmans, Green & Co.'s Premises, June 1900

Longman Archive

in the post since 1889, having joined the House in 1855. Kelk did not retire until 1938 when he was seventy-two. Parker got to like and to trust him, but he was aware of how intimidating he could be. 'Accuracy is of the first importance' was one of Kelk's mottos. Another was 'always date your memorandums', advice which sadly was sometimes to be forgotten in the twentieth century – even at the highest Board level – after Longman had moved from Paternoster Row to Harlow.

The shape of Paternoster Row dictated its pattern of activity as much as the orders given within it. The Publishing Department, 'the hub of the whole business', faced Paternoster Row. On the north side its large windows looked into the smaller windows of two other publishers, Nelsons and Hutchinsons, very different kinds of businesses from Longmans, the former founded in Edinburgh in 1798 and handsomely housed in Paternoster Row since 1870, the latter, supervised by George Hutchinson,

A photograph of Longmans'
Publishing Department in the
early twentieth century

Longman Archive

who had started his career as a traveller with Hodder and
Stoughton, less grandly moved into 34 Paternoster Square
in a basement office in 1880.

Their staffs did not appreciate the facts of corporate
difference, for they were carrying out the same tasks as the
workers in Number 39, and 'could be seen moving about
and doing things which were exactly similar to our own
operations'. Kelk put it in verse:

Here we suffer grief and pain.
Over the way they do the same.
Come let us be joyful.

On the side of the Publishing Department that
was opposite to Paternoster Row, there was another glass
partition which separated it from a long corridor from
which the partners' rooms opened out. They scarcely
opened out into the world:

Opposite Bartram's high stool and sloping desk was a
parcel lift and a staircase with access to the busy ground
floor where vans gathered outside to collect books and
deliver books. In the largest room on the first floor there
were massive tables 'around which a number of packers
were engaged in packing up the books ordered by the Country
House ('Home' department). (Kensington still perversely counted
as 'country'.) The packers called on the services of 'the titles' for
'handling the orders which came in from the country booksellers in
the early morning post'.

There was daily bustle here, as there had been since 1861. Yet Parker
described the Paternoster Row premises as a 'country house', a term often
applied also to the British Museum, and picked out for special mention 'the
library', from which the staff could borrow books, noting that it was lined
with bookshelves containing Longmans' own past publications. Sadly, and
unforgivably, the collection was to be dispersed after the First World War.

The ground floor was not to change much between 1911 and the
Second World War when the premises were destroyed. In a small office
Arthur Cutbush, head of the warehouse since 1907, who served the firm
from 1895 to 1945, and who was to help Brack after the 1940 disaster,
looked out over the huge green ledgers dealing with current books in the
warehouse. Cutbush communicated with the warehousemen by speaking
tube, asking them when necessary to count books for stocktaking.[230] Some

---

230 Parker noted that one of them, C.F. Grogan, who worked alongside Cutbush,
    had worked earlier with Rivingtons. He did not retire until 1937.

of the warehousemen themselves could tell at once how many copies of any particular book were binding, and they were in close touch with the Ship Binding Works. There were large bins containing fast-selling titles in the warehouse, and Parker named the two people handling them. One of them, G. Gale, had worked with Rivingtons. His salary (£200 a year) was twice that of his colleague A.W. Walker.

Next to the warehouse was the Foreign Department, headed by H.G. Collins, one of the two sons of Longmans country traveller H.E. Collins, another example of generational continuity. H,W died in 1905, H.G. left for Australia in 1918 The Foreign Department looked after the whole of the world as knowledgeably as the Country Department looked after the whole of Britain. It distributed books abroad, including some bearing the imprint of the neighbouring publisher, Edward Arnold, as well as school stationery and even school furniture for India. Between the Foreign Department, facing Ave Maria Lane, where horses and carts came and went, and Paternoster Row there were the Education offices occupied by J.W. Allen, one of his sons, P.H. Allen, and their zealous assistant, S.E. Root, who was also responsible for keeping stock of the educational material which was being sent to India.

J.W. Allen had the largest annual salary of any Longman employee, £1,500. His son, P.H. Allen, just appointed, received £70. Another son, J.C. Allen, appointed in 1897, had moved to India in 1805. The trade travellers ('reps'), working closely with Allen, were headed by E.W.B. Chenery, who had joined Longman in 1874 and received the large wage of £900 a year. One of the travellers, H. Kelly, had worked earlier with Rivington.

All large and some small publishers employed 'reps', and an Association of Publishers' Educational Representatives (APER) was founded in 1898 at the Castle Hotel in Swansea. One of its purposes was 'to overcome ill-feeling and unnecessary rivalry' but this was difficult to achieve. Meetings could be fractious. There were sharp divisions not only between 'reps' of different publishers but geographically between 'reps' working in the north and the south. There were, indeed, two separate associations of 'reps', not united until 1945, with a Longman trade representative, Cornelius Bennett, as leading organiser in the north.[231]

Trade representatives had to know about books and how to describe them as well as how to sell them: they contributed to *Notes on Books* and they attended teachers' conferences in their spare time. They had to be knowledgeable not only about individual books but about series. A good example of the kind of Longman book they had to know about was A.W. Poyser's well illustrated *Magnetism and Electricity* (1889) which reached

---

231 See APER, *Fifty Years of Progress* (1948). Keighley was a leading northern centre of the union. At a Leeds conference in 1910, a group of representatives met a committee of the Publishers Association.

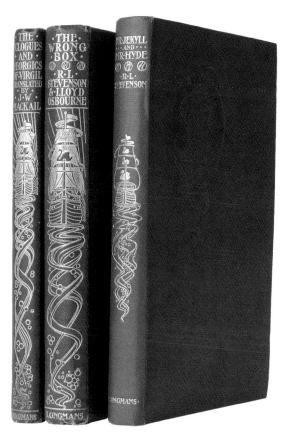

Between 1907 and 1913 Longmans published some thirty titles in the *Longmans' Pocket Library* with its own distinctive green and gold binding

Personal collection

its fourth edition in 1892. Poyser had been assistant master in the Wyggeston and Queen Elizabeth School in Leicester (a school with a remarkable record that persisted deep into the twentieth century), before becoming headmaster of Wisbech Grammar School. His book was designed primarily for 'those who are reading for the South Kensington Elementary Examination in Magnetism and Electricity'.

Members of the Longmans staff, not only reps, read books at very different levels, and they could all buy copies of Longmans books at trade prices. William Bartram, Head of the Country Department before his son, was a classical scholar who is said to have had a working knowledge of fourteen languages[232]: he spent part of each week at the British Museum. One of Parker's first purchases was a two-volume popular edition of Macaulay's *History of England* for which he paid 4s. 2d. Later in life, after having been switched over to educational publishing and allowed exceptional freedom as an initiator of new titles, he read Trevelyan's *History of England* (1926) with equal delight and wrote the blurb for its dust jacket. He also persuaded the Company to issue in a separate volume the social history chapters in Trevelyan's *Blenheim* under the title *The England of Queen Anne*, and this was one of the first volumes, priced 3s. 6d., to appear in what was called the *Swan Library*.[233] I received it as a school prize.

Long before Parker, in no doubt about his own importance, left Paternoster Row, he had acquired an obvious influence in the House. Before 1914, however, he had little. He noted in his 'Memoirs' how in the Publishing Department there was a safe which contained a folder of envelopes 'called, "for some strange reason", caps'. 'They were arranged in alphabetical order and contained the essential documents relating to forthcoming publications of all types and there were 'scarcely one hundred in all'. 'The fact is', he judged in retrospect, 'all inspiration, all searching for new books, indeed all new ideas, had dried up.' And even during the last years of his life at Paternoster Row Parker was disturbed not only about the lack of ideas for new books but about the careless way in which records relating to very old books could be handled. One of his colleagues 'found by accident a loose receipt for £35 from Oliver Goldsmith for the next novel

---

232 See PW, p.47.

233 See Parker, *op. cit.*, p.12.

he was to write but never did'.[234]

Parker devoted two paragraphs to J.E. Chandler, 'the soul of kindness in all advertising matters'. He was more than that. He had joined the House in 1889 on the recommendation of H.E. Collins, having served his apprenticeship with a bookseller in Bedford. He started in the Country Department, and made his mark after he moved to the Publishing Department in a section called 'manufacturing'. Like Parker, he left a brief memoir,[235] but unlike him, he left the House for a time, having assisted Thomas Norton with the *Badminton Magazine*. On his return he was joint author with Harold Cox of the Longman bi-centenary volume, *The House of Longman, 1724–1924*, and he completed CJ's bibliography of Longman books from 1724 to 1800. His knowledge of Longman history was substantial, but in his judgements of people or of issues he was not as critical as Parker.

Another person of a very different kind whom Parker did not mention was Joseph Ridgewell, the 'Dickensian' Head Porter at No. 39, 'an old retainer' who wore a frock coat. He not only saw visitors on and off the premises, but served the Partners by bringing in a menu daily from a nearby restaurant from which they ordered what they wanted to eat in at 1 p.m. Ridgewell was so 'autocratic' that even the Partners gave way to him.[236] In most staff matters, however, the Partners could be as autocratic as their Head Porter, for status mattered profoundly in Paternoster Row as it had done earlier and as it still did in almost all publishers' offices.

Long hours were kept by workers – 9 a.m. to 7 p.m. in 1900 with an hour for lunch and 9 a.m. to 2 p.m. on Saturdays; 9 a.m. to 6p.m. in 1906 and 9 a.m. to 1 p.m. on Saturdays. Cleaners arrived at 8 a.m. The Partners' luncheon room was 'used in the normal way only by Thomas Norton and C.J. Longman'. Ironically when the latter retired in 1928 lunch was no longer ordered or served and the luncheon room was converted to house a switchboard. In 1906 the telephone had only recently been installed and there were no telephone extensions to Partners' rooms or to the various departments. CJ still did not have a telephone in his room when he retired. Throughout his long years of authority CJ could never talk at a distance with any of his employees.

There were two Remington typewriters on the premises before 1914, the one used by J.W. Allen's assistant, Root, and the other by Tommy Nutt, the shared secretary of Thomas Norton and CJ. All the invoices and ledgers were, however, written by hand. Invoicing was complicated by the fact that most books were still sold subject to the 'traditional system' of counting – 13 books as 12, 7 as 6½, in some cases 25 as 24. Thus, seven copies of a book priced at 3s. 6d. might be invoiced as 6½ at 2s. 7½d. Even before the age of

Thomas Norton Longman V and his wife, Florence, outside their home at Shendish Park, 1917. When Thomas Norton died in 1931 he left £93,812 (a considerable fortune at that time)

Longman Archive

---

234 *Ibid.*, p.4.

235 PW, pp.47-8.

236 PW, p.48. Ridgewell was succeeded by Albert Penn, a 'lugubrious character'.

decimalisation, which did not begin until 1972, the meticulous invoicing of halfpennies – and in 1906 there were farthings too – looked completely archaic.

So, even more, did the rites which went with employment at Paternoster Row, forbidding rites that interrupted regular routines. J.W. Reynolds, who joined the business in 1899, described them in a series of vivid reminiscences published in *The Log* magazine of July 1975.[237] Such a magazine would have been unthinkable in 1899 or 1906. One particularly disagreeable rite consisted of standing any newcomer upside down in a lavatory basin full of water and then transferring him to a huge bin of sawdust to dry off. The language itself was archaic.

Reynolds had become an employee at a 'salary' of £1 13s. a month, after an interview with George Longman at which Reynolds's father was present. This consisted, as far as he could remember seventy years later, of a long discussion on fox hunting and horse breeding between his father and Longman. Once in the care of William Bartram, who, in his memory at least, 'ruled the younger staff with a grip of iron' (other members of staff remembered Bartram mainly as being absent-minded), he too was 'broken in' as Parker would have been had he not at once been moved up. Reynolds started as 'Title Boy' under the control of the warehouse, worked for a time in Education, the job he preferred, and after an interview with CJ, which he requested, was placed in the Country Department, which he intensely disliked. Like others, he came to appreciate that being 'Title Boy' was the right start: it taught a newcomer all about the stock of the House.

~

This was the view from below, a view in which intermediaries, such as Kelk and Bartram were more prominent to employees than the partners were. In the view from above, there was more to see, with other publishers in the picture as well as House employees, and this chapter ends, as it began, with a speech by CJ, this time to a meeting of the Publishers Association held in the Stationers' Hall after the outbreak of the First World War. Alec Waugh, with hindsight, called it 'a wise and temperate speech'. Nobody knew, CJ said, what was going to happen to the book trade. 'Whatever happened', however, he supposed, 'the children would have their usual Christmas, and the firm would go forward with "juveniles" and books of that kind, but would walk warily at first in more speculative ventures.' Not quite 'Business as Usual', and a significant

---

237 *The Log*, pp.8–10 1975. He or his editor called the reminiscences 'I would rather have been an Engine Driver but father thought otherwise'. Reynolds, who called his piece 'Longman of Paternoster Row', did not give his own name. He described himself as 'a not very important Member of Staff' in the Paternoster Row of the early-twentieth century. (LA Part II/213-214)

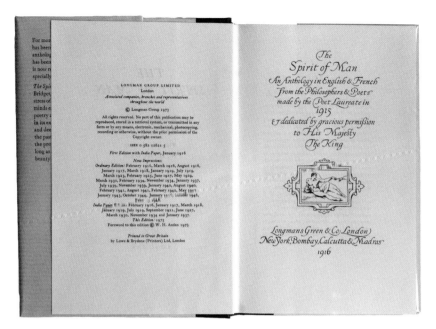

The Sprit of Man, an anthology in English and French, from the philosophers and poets, made in 1915 by Robert Bridges, the Poet Laureate. The book was published by Longmans in 1916 and presented to the King. It went into twenty-nine impressions between 1916 and 1948, and was re-published in 1973, with an introduction by W. H Auden

Personal collection

change in the metaphor of motion, 'walk', not 'sail'.[238]

The war years from 1914 to 1918 changed little in the routines of Paternoster Row, except that many people were serving in the Forces, and that the *Publishers Circular* added a new category, 'Military and Naval', to its categories of published books. In its first year it accounted for 3.5 per cent of books published, and at its wartime peak, 1916, 5.4 per cent. When the War ended and surviving servicemen returned to Paternoster Row all the same 'top people' were in control in an undamaged Paternoster Row as had been there when the War began. There was a contrast, therefore, between the Great War and the Second World War. Only after 1939 did 'the Great War' begin to move back into memory, and with the passage of time to become known eventually after 1945 as the First World War. The day might come, historians were to fear, when the two wars, different though they were in their causes and in their consequences, might, if unwisely, come be considered as one. There were some Longman employees, including Parker, who were involved in both.

---

238 For an interesting American forecast of the effect of war on the book trade, see G.H. Doran's comments in the PC, 26 Nov. 1914. He considered that 'a reaction back to book reading' was likely, but that there would be no boom in religious books' as there might have been twenty-five to thirty years before.

G·M·TREVELYAN·O·M

Illustrated
English Social History

VOLUME FOUR

The Nineteenth Century

7   Continuity and Change, 1918–1968

There was more continuity than change in the story of Longman between the end of the First World War and 1926, the year when Longman was incorporated as a Private Limited Company: the change of designation made no more difference to daily patterns of work or to family relationships within the business than the creation of a private unlimited company in 1889. There was likewise more continuity than change in the twenty-one years between 1926 and 1947, when the Company, named as before Longmans, Green, went public in December.

Its share capital of £177,902, consisting almost entirely of cumulative preference shares of various classes, seemed safe in family hands. Class A ordinary shares, 40 per cent of the total, were held by Directors, Trustees of family settlements, ex-Directors and members of the Longman family. These assured them control of the business: each share carried two votes. The settlement seemed to need little monitoring. 'Seven share 31,000 per cent bonus', wrote one city editor of the 1947 conversion. He noted at the same time that some of the shares were being disposed of by three of the seven Longmans, Green directors, William Longman, Robert Guy Longman and K.B. Potter, were selling £125,000 of a new category of Class B Ordinary shares to James Capel and Co., stockbrokers, who were setting a quotation price of 30s. a share. These shares carried one vote.

Two years later, on 16 December 1949, a staff party was held at 1 Elverton Street, the headquarters of the Westminster Dragoons, to celebrate the 225th anniversary of the foundation of the Longman business, when the first speaker was William Longman. Why, he asked, had Longmans, Green & Co. been so successful? Part of the success, he concluded, had been 'due to luck', and it was family luck to which he referred: 'there had always been sons and nephews'. Nonetheless he recognised that 'team work' too had always been important.

The Longman family, he admitted, had not been 'a great one at producing stars', but, like successful football managers, they had known how to select, with the help in his own lifetime of Allen, Potter and Higham. They had also known how to foster the necessary 'team spirit'. The team they had selected, which was then performing effectively, was 'the best team in the publishing trade'. 'The world is at our feet'. William might have quoted the words of a song, 'The Good Old Thirty Nine', written by T.H.H. Barnard in 1907. (Perhaps it was sung that evening):

The cover of Volume Four of the *Illustrated English Social History* by G.M Trevelyan O.M., 1944. Robert Longman wrote that he had 'received a letter (10th November 1943) from the Master of Trinity to R.G. Longman in which the Master expressed his happiness at the Company's decision somehow or other to find sufficient paper for the publication of his *English Social History*'. An American Edition had been published in the Autumn of 1942, but lack of paper had made it impossible to produce and publish in England.

R. G. Longman replied that, 'by order of the Company the print and his inscription was to be framed and kept as a permanent record of how delightful the relations between Author and Publisher could be.' RGL 15 November 1943. 'The above' refers to a sketch entitled 'Publisher and Author' showing a humble, scrawny author offering a ms. to a supercilious well fed publisher in a booklined room and underneath Trevelyan has written 'GMT beseeching R.L. to publish his Social History.'

Personal collection

William Longman (1882–1967)
was the elder son of C. J.
Longman, one of the sixth
generation of Longmans to
enter the firm, which he did
in 1906 and then with his
cousin, Robert, became a junior
Partner in 1909. Responsible
for much of Longmans'
expansion overseas, he was
also ultimately in charge of
replacing Longmans stock
when it was reduced overnight
from 5,000–6,000 titles to 12
when the building was bombed
during Christmas week, 1940;
within a week the first orders
for reprints were with the
printers and an emergency
trade counter had been opened

Longman Archive

Happy is our service,
With the Firm that treats us well.
We are proud of their heritage
Which age upon ages well,
We'll do our very best,
To make our record brightly shine,
To win more fame and fresh laurels gain
For the dear old Thirty Nine.

William himself chose to look forward. He believed,
he said, that 'in 1974, when the 250th Anniversary ...
will be celebrated, not only will the younger ones of you
celebrate that event with your friends John, Michael and
Mark [the still young Longmans] but that you will also be
celebrating a very largely increased turnover.' And with
that he ended his 'welcome'.

It fell to the lot of N.D.J. Brack, 'General Manager
of Longmans', to reply, and he began by stating with
feeling that 'surely at no previous time did the staff hold
such a genuine affection for those who control the House
of Longman as they do today ... The war years and the
changing times have helped to strengthen a personal bond, which [had]
in no way been weakened by the rapid expansion of the staff.' Numbers of
London staff had doubled since the 200th anniversary celebrations. Then,
twelve women had been employed. Now there were seventy.

The last speaker on the occasion of the 225th, George Frisby, who
had joined Longmans, Green in 1897 and had gone on to become head of
the Production Department, handed a book to 'Mr Willie' at the end of the
evening, quoting as he did so 'the booksellers' slogan' that 'A Book is the
Best Gift'. The book was a new edition of Mumby's History of Publishing,
and Brack was given a copy too. 'Mr Willie' described himself as 'touched
beyond measure'. It would be one of his 'greatest possessions'. Yet it
would also remind him of the saying of 'one of the great men of literature
associated with the firm' – Andrew Lang, still lingering on the stage,
though now only a ghost, in 1949: 'Whenever a new book is published,
read an old one!'[1]

~

Longmans, Green produced a substantial list of new books while William
was a partner and, later, after 1932 Chairman, and the authors, most of
them 'handled' by Robert, included Noël Annan, Hector Bolitho, Elizabeth
Bowen, David Garnett, Christopher Hibbert, Edward Hyams, Brian Inglis,

---

1   A House account of the Staff Party, 16 Dec. 1949.

James Kennaway, Francis King, Gavin Maxwell, John Julius Norwich, Sean O'Faolain, David Storey, Evelyn Waugh and Antonia White.[2] It is a not unimpressive list, although most of the authors figuring on it published most of their books with other publishers, a few with more than one of them.

This was perhaps symptomatic of the whole post-war history of Longman's 'general' publishing. Despite Mark's efforts and the considerable skills of John Guest, his friend and war-time fellow officer, it was not a list which ever stood out in the fiction publishing scene, especially when compared with the lists of a major publisher such as Collins and of smaller publishers such as Jonathan Cape and André Deutsch. And some quite poor titles (for example *Big River, Big Man* (1960)) were published in order to 'bulk out' the list. As John Chapple, who joined the business in 1956, noted later, fiction was 'a weakness for many years'. It was transferred to Penguin in 1972, where it joined Allen Lane, still one of Penguin's hardback imprints.

The fact that the authors were not tied to the House of Longman mattered less to Robert and his advisers than it would have done to many other highly competitive publishers, but a few successful authors, such as the American playwright Thornton Wilder (1897-1975), were particularly treasured. Wilder's first novel, *The Cobola* (1926), published in America, was recommended by the first and most sought after of Robert's readers and literary advisers, J.C. (later Sir John) Squire (1884–1958), editor of the *London Mercury* from 1919 to 1934, a man with many friends and some enemies, often accused of founding a 'squirearchy'. Wilder's next novel, a short bestseller, *The Bridge of San Luis Rey*, was published in London by Longmans a year later.

CJ could make neither head nor tail of the new novel, but his sister-in-law Dr Joan Evans, great-niece of the paper-maker John Dickinson, was so fascinated by it that she told him that Longmans *must* publish it.[3]

John Guest (*right*) with Maurice Edelman, M.P. photographed for the Longman House Magazine *Sixes and Sevens*, Summer, 1960

Longman Archive

---

2   Bolitho, a regular Longman author, published his *A Biographer's Notebook* in 1950. That year he was invited to give one of a series of staff talks on publishing, describing it from an author's point of view. In Brack's opinion, the lecture was 'short and very poor', contrasting conspicuously with a brilliant talk by J.G. Wilson, 'doyen of booksellers', then Manager of Bumpus's bookshop. Wilson, who had sixty-two years' experience of bookselling, brought with him J.M. Barrie's personal copy of the first small edition of T.E. Lawrence's *Seven Pillars of Wisdom*.

3   PW, p.69.

Robert Longman responded willingly. He was the most receptive of the Longmans described in this chapter, an agreeably civilised publisher who was even more interested in music than in books. He married a violinist, was a member of the Bach Choir, and fostered folk dancing not only at his home but at the Ship Binding Works.

Guest, brought into the House by Mark, had a bigger list than the substantial one set out above. It included the Duke of Edinburgh, Basil Davidson, a left-wing historian of Africa, who was talked of as a possible editor of the *New Statesman* and who felt that reviewers never did justice to his work, the theatre critic Harold Hobson, who was felt to influence the size and shape of London audiences, the art connoisseur and dealer, J.H. (later Lord) Duveen and Lord Eccles (1904–1999), Conservative Minister of Education in a critical period of educational expansion from 1959 to 1962 and Chairman of the British Library Board from 1973 to 1978. In this last role he was largely responsible for the initiation of the building of the new national library (not to be completed for another twenty-five years).

Many of these authors had no agents. Indeed, those who depended heavily upon them were still admitted only reluctantly to the House of Longman. One agent with the firm of Curtis Brown, David Higham, who started working for them in 1925,[4] was so unimpressed by the chilly attitudes of the Longmans to agents that he did not give Longmans a place in the index to his autobiography. He was content to mention them melodramatically in the text, where he described them as 'dingily embalmed' in a 'literally (not – oh God not – metaphorically) smutty old office' in Paternoster Row, still 'known then to journalists as the Mecca of Publishing'. On a visit there in the mid-1920s on behalf of an author who wished to be freed from a Longmans option, he was received by an elderly messenger, dressed for the part in appropriate black, who conducted him through 'a catacomb of musty corridors' where he was received by 'the ancient head of the firm' (Mr Willie), the 'tendrils' of 'whose white beard lay spread over the table'. His answer was 'No'.[5]

Higham, no relative of the Longman Highams, had a beard of his own which was not his most beautiful feature. He reported the rumour, without questioning it, that up to the Second World War 'Longman were really broke' (they were not), noting, however, that when Longmans, Green 'went public' in 1947 *The Times* 'printed a full-page advertisement setting out every fascinating (to me) detail of a firm's business – assets, liabilities, shareholdings, directors' salaries, above all, the balance-sheet'. Longmans in 1946 had made a net profit before tax of some £227,000.

---

4   Albert Curtis Brown had become an agent just before the beginning of the twentieth century.

5   D. Higham, *Literary Gent* (1978), pp.161–2.

In fact, the crowded advertisement appeared in *The Times* on 5 January 1948, stating under its heading that it was 'not an invitation to the public to subscribe' but a statement 'in compliance with Stock Exchange rules'. Current assets were set at £260,913. Profit after tax in 1947 was given as £129,502 as compared with £25,387 in 1938 and £31,500 in 1945. Such a profit would have seemed unlikely during the pre-Second World War years when it was possible that rumours were then circulating as Higham reported. Indeed, during the early 1920s, owing to trading difficulties, there were cuts in salaries and wages in Longmans, Green, as there were in many different kinds of business.

In this case, they were cuts of 5 per cent for those with more than twenty years' service and 10 per cent for those with less. By 1925 the cuts had been restored, and during the 1930s the new non-Longman partner, Kenneth Boyd Potter (1897–1962), the youngest member of a shipping family, who entered the House in 1921 and was made a Director in 1926, tapped in necessary funds when the limited liability company was set up. His father went on to provide £25,000 at a crucial moment in 1932 when Longman's bankers were unwilling to provide them.[6]

The 1930s remained difficult times, not just for Longmans, Green but for many other publishers, and an interesting memorandum, drafted by Brack in 1968, the terminal date of this chapter, explains how shortage of funds encouraged the first attempts at business forecasting. In order to print new titles – and an increasing number of these were published on commission from their authors or from institutions, in publishing terms a retrograde step – it was necessary to estimate what size of funds would be available. There was no surplus capital to employ. Overheads were straightforward to calculate, and the size and total remuneration of staff barely altered. It was known too what sum would be necessary to pay half-yearly royalties, now the basic form of payment to authors.

Three kinds of revenue forecast were devised in the Company's Record Office by E.J. Coombs. The first, 'RO1', was based on the provisional forecasts of the publishers, 'always well in excess of their actual needs'. The second, 'RO2', was a precise forecast of expenditure on all books, both new and reprints, which were in active production. The third, 'RO3', was conjectural, a monthly forecast of the sums which would have to be spent on the reprinting of books not yet requested within the House. Coloured tabs were used to identify each kind of new title or reprint. The system was time-consuming, but it enabled the directors to allot any identified available funds to the Publishing Department, which they could then employ 'as

---

6   The offer of help is substantiated in a letter from John Butler to Brack, 2 Jan. 1983 (personal archives). Butler joined Longman in 1914 and was given the information by two friends in the Cash Department.

they thought best'. 'Had we had a computer then', Brack concluded, 'the whole thing would have been simple.'[7]

~

There was no hint of any past financial difficulties in the speeches made at the 225th celebration of the House in 1949. They were all cheerful in tone, with no speaker echoing CJ's ominous words at the bi-centennial. Nevertheless, during the brief post-First World War epilogue which precedes the two periods covered in this chapter, each of twenty-one years, it was industrial unrest which stood out as a major theme. In 1925 there was the first long printers' strike in the industry and in Longmans and publishing history, fully reported in the Labour Party and Trades Union Congress's *Daily Herald* as well as in *The Times*.[8] It lasted for twelve weeks and affected those warehousemen, packers and porters who had joined a union, the National Union of Printing, Bookbinding, Machine Rolling and Paper Workers, and were demanding an advance in wages. More than a thousand men were involved, only four of them at Paternoster Row, all of whom were back at work after two weeks.

The publishers were linked in the Book Trade Employers' Federation, and while it was newsagents rather than book publishers and booksellers who were most affected, Longmans, Green, Murray, Macmillan and Pitman were among the sixty publishers of books whose names appeared in advertisements, pledging themselves to resist union demands.[9] All the packers, porters and warehousemen working for Longmans, Green had joined the Union except for Albert Penn, the head packer.[10]

The fact that the strike collapsed probably meant that the General Strike of 1926 had less serious effects on publishing than it might otherwise have had. And thereafter there was no more industrial action within the House of Longman until after the end of the Second World War. Moreover, the fact that 1926 was also the year of the creation of Longmans, Green and Co. Ltd, brought this prelude to a close.

~

During the two periods of twenty-one years between 1926 and 1968, in many ways contrasting periods, other themes stood out in the history of

---

7   N. Brack, 'Financing New Books in the Slump of the 1930s', June 1968 (personal archives). Brack showed this memorandum to Wallis, who was then examining the forecasting problems of the 1960s.

8   *Daily Herald*, 7, 11, 24, 30 Nov. 1925, 23 Jan. 1926. *The Times*, 31 Oct., 3, 5, 14, 16, 19 Nov. 1925. The fact that the Oxford University Press was hit in itself made headlines (*Morning Post*, 9 Nov. 1925).

9   *Daily Telegraph*, 20 Nov. 1925, *Daily Herald*, 21 Nov. 1925.

10 Letter from John Butler to Brack, 1 Jan. 1983 (personal archives).

Longmans, Green, and of publishing as a whole. During the first twenty-one years, broken by war and depression, careers in publishing still remained open mainly to 'gentlemen' who expected no great financial rewards from it. London was still the centre of the book trade, and London clubs were still the favourite rendezvous for publishers and their authors. There was abundant life in Paternoster Row, and most publishers with headquarters there kept their warehouses in the Row as well as their offices.

There were some new initiatives in publishing, however, notably the creation of book clubs, the most famous of them Victor Gollancz's Left Book Club, founded in 1937; book tokens, devised in 1933 by a well-known publisher, Harold Raymond, senior partner of Chatto and Windus; the spread of paperbacks, particularly Penguins; and the intrusion of new names on the list of publishers, some of whom showed little interest in the Publishers Association.[11] The Association continued to win wholehearted support from Longmans, Green and Co., however, as it had done from its foundation in 1896.

Longmans, Green could have had few more unlikely neighbours in Paternoster Row than Hutchinson, established there before 1914. Walter Hutchinson (1887–1950), who in 1925 took over the business founded by his father, George, was described by the writer of an unusually vitriolic obituary of him in *The Bookseller*, as having an 'uninhibited capacity for self-glorification'; he had worked during the First World War as 'Hon. Private Secretary to the Secretary of the War Office'.[12] During the course of the Second World War, having earlier acquired through take-overs a cluster of surviving Victorian and older publishing houses, diverse in tradition and output, he withdrew his business from the Publishers Association, to which his company did not return until after his death. Walter was an irascible character, capable of offending his own employees at the highest level, yet he made money and attracted a few highly profitable authors to his House.

It is interesting to note that in a most successful Hutchinson book, undated, by Michael Joseph, a literary agent with Curtis Brown before he

---

11   For Book Clubs, see J. Baker, 'British Book Clubs – A Growing Market', in *The Author*, Vol. LXV, No. 3, pp.56–9. (In the same number G. Wagner described American book clubs as an 'overgrown market'.) See also J. Lewis, *The Left Book Club, An Historical Record* (1977). For Book Tokens, which celebrated their silver jubilee in 1958, see *The Bookseller*, Dec. 1957 and April 1958. In the year ending 31 March 1933, 32,050 book tokens were issued: in the year ending 31 March 1936, 200,383.

12   The obituary, by the editor of *The Bookseller*, is quoted in M, p.124. In *Who's Who* Hutchinson listed a number of books edited by him, including *Wonderful Things, Beautiful Birds of our Country, A Pictorial History of the War* and *Hutchinson's Encyclopaedia*. He listed as his recreations fishing, riding, racing, yachting, motoring and tennis.

" Sea-nymphs hourly ring his knell ;
Hark ! now I hear them,—ding-dong, bell."

The Book of Fairy Poetry, published by Longmans in 1920. The illustration comes from one of Ariel's songs from *The Tempest*. The book, edited by Dora Owen, included sixteen coloured plates by Warwick Noble

Personal collection

became a publisher in his own right in 1938 (David Higham's first job was that of his assistant), Longmans, Green did not figure in a chapter on 'What Publishers Want'. The book included publishers' statements, often by their chairmen or directors, on behalf of a group of publishers old and new and disparate in their motivations: Murray, Blackwood, Chapman and Hall, Collins, Cassell, Cape, Allen and Unwin, the Bodley Head, Heinemann, Secker, Ernest Benn, Harrap, Mills and Boon – and even the Religious Tract Society.

The Hutchinson statement began 'Messrs Hutchinson & Co., are ready to consider works of every description': that of Murray began 'Of course, every publisher wants to bring out books that pay their way – and something more – but like all who desire to uphold the dignity and good name of our craft – I want to bring out books which have a permanent value and are of use to mankind'.[13] Michael Joseph's own publishing business in Bloomsbury was managed from 1935 to 1956 by Robert (later Sir Robert) Lusty, who was never short of words. He had worked 'below' Walter Hutchinson and was to return to direct the Hutchinson business from 1956 to 1973.

Lusty was Chairman of the National Book League from 1949 to 1951, and went on to become Vice-Chairman and for a time a highly articulate Chairman of the Board of Governors of the BBC from 1966 to 1968.[14] The best contemporary profile of him appeared in W.H. Smith's *Trade News*.[15] Meanwhile, Joseph had sold out his publishing business to Illustrated Newspapers, later acquired by Roy Thomson (later Lord Thomson of Fleet) (1894–1976), a Canadian tycoon.

Much media history, as it now must be called, is incorporated in the above short paragraph, for Thomson became the builder of a huge conglomerate, not then so described, which included the *Scotsman*, purchased in 1953, Scottish Television, 'a licence to print money', a franchise acquired in 1959, and, a year later, the *Sunday Times* which in 1962 printed Britain's first colour supplement. Thomson also had interests in a newspaper chain in Nigeria and moved as a major player into the travel business, which became his main preoccupation. He himself drew a distinction between television and radio and newspapers. 'You can own newspapers but not

13   M. Joseph, *The Commercial Side of Literature* (n.d. but 1925), p.24, p.243.

14   See A. Briggs, *Governing the BBC* (1974), pp.128–9, p.162.

15   *Smiths' Trade News*, 13 July 1963. See also R. Lusty, *Bound to be Read* (1975).

television or radio ... You cannot neglect majorities or minorities.'[16]

These changes in ownership, to be followed in 1968 by another tycoon, Australian-born Rupert Murdoch's acquisition of the *News of the World* and a year later of the *Sun*, ushered in what at the time was beginning to be called a 'communications revolution', a term which preceded radical breakthroughs in the application of electronic technology, to which the word 'revolution' was not applied at the time.[17] Yet Thomson and Murdoch, who were to move into the book trade, were different kinds of people driven by different ambitions. Moreover, the word 'revolution', soon to be overworked, had already been applied in the 1930s to the advent of Penguin paperbacks, a concern with the destinies of which Longmans was later to be closely associated.[18] The word had also been occasionally employed during the 1930s in discussions of educational change, sometimes with the adjective 'silent' placed in front of it.[19]

The second edition of a Longmans, Green textbook widely used in teachers' training colleges, A.G. and H.E. Hughes's *Learning and Teaching: an introduction to psychology and teaching*, first published in 1937, recognised the extent of the educational changes since the 1920s, including those made during the Second World War, without using the adjective 'revolutionary':

The Education Act, 1944, is evidence that the public conscience has been awakened, and it has made possible a number of welcome changes in the text of the previous edition. For example, it is no longer necessary to write as if the normal size

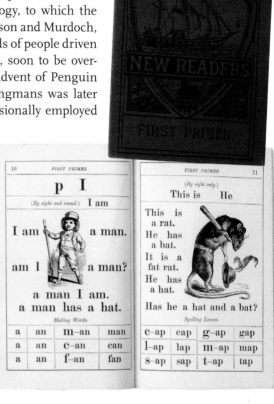

Longmans published a series of *New Readers* in 1938, which used 'a combination of the Alphabetic and Look and Say methods' of teaching reading

Personal collection

16 Quoted in C. Jenkins, *Power Behind the Screen* (1961), p.181. For Thomson's ownership of *The Times*, which he acquired in 1966, and for a comparison with Northcliffe see S. Jenkins, *The Market for Glory: Fleet Street ownership in the twentieth century* (1986), pp.114-16. The *Economist* (quoted *ibid.*, p.55) described the purchase of *The Times* as a licence to lose money.

17 Texas Instruments in the United States began to sell tiny silicon chips in 1954, but neither their sale nor the development of the integrated circuit created immediate excitement. It was not until 1977 that the word 'revolution' was used in a special issue of the *Scientific American* on microelectronics. See A. Briggs and P. Burke, *A Social History of the Media* (2002), p.282. Two years later, Gollancz published in London a book by C. Evans (1931-1979), *The Mighty Micro: the impact of the computer revolution*.

18 Membership of the Publishers Association increased from 124 to 214. See also H. Schmoller, 'The Paperback Revolution' in EHP, pp.283–319.

19 See G.A.N. Lowndes, *The Silent Social Revolution* (1937).

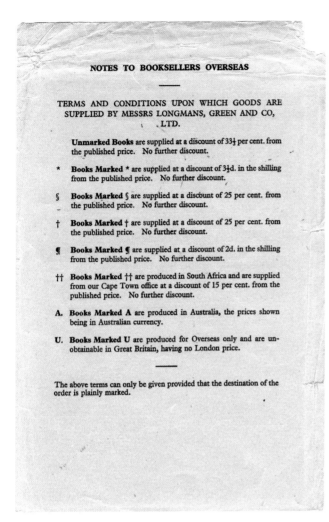

NOTES TO BOOKSELLERS OVERSEAS

———

TERMS AND CONDITIONS UPON WHICH GOODS ARE SUPPLIED BY MESSRS LONGMANS, GREEN AND CO, LTD.

Unmarked Books are supplied at a discount of 33⅓ per cent. from the published price. No further discount.

* **Books Marked *** are supplied at a discount of 3½d. in the shilling from the published price. No further discount.

§ **Books Marked §** are supplied at a discount of 25 per cent. from the published price. No further discount.

† **Books Marked †** are supplied at a discount of 25 per cent. from the published price. No further discount.

¶ **Books Marked ¶** are supplied at a discount of 2d. in the shilling from the published price. No further discount.

†† **Books Marked ††** are produced in South Africa and are supplied from our Cape Town office at a discount of 15 per cent. from the published price. No further discount.

A. **Books Marked A** are produced in Australia, the prices shown being in Australian currency.

U. **Books Marked U** are produced for Overseas only and are unobtainable in Great Britain, having no London price.

———

The above terms can only be given provided that the destination of the order is plainly marked.

Between the wars the overseas market was increasingly important to Longmans (and to British publishers generally). This advertisement shows Longmans' terms to overseas booksellers

Personal colection

of a class in school is forty, or of secondary education as if it were a privilege for a selected few.

These words appeared in the Preface to the second edition. There was nothing in the text, however, to suggest that everything had changed, and the Preface began with the words, 'this post-war edition is not substantially different from the first edition, for even a great social revolution such as we are now experiencing does not change the fundamental needs and nature of children'.[20]

Genuinely new significant technological change in communications had already taken place during the 1920s with the advent of wireless broadcasting, and this had affected children in the classroom as well as the home. In Britain, unlike the United States, radio (at that time seldom so called in Britain) was not allowed to develop as a market force resting on advertising for its revenues. In 1927, five years after regular wireless broadcasting in Britain had been inaugurated under the direction of a commercially-based but dividend-restricted British Broadcasting Company, the British Broadcasting Corporation, a public corporation, was founded by Royal Charter. The Corporation was required to educate as well as to inform and to entertain, and very quickly it became an institution. A Central Council for School Broadcasting was formed in 1929, and Mary Somerville directed it with a strong sense of commitment until 1947.[21]

There seemed to be a logic – even at the time – in the step-by-step extension of broadcasting from sound into television, the first new stage in the communications revolution, which was to affect children's behaviour far more; and how to finance television, a more expensive medium than sound (or book publishing) once again raised old issues of commerce

---

20   Preface to A.G. Hughes and E.H. Hughes, *Learning and Teaching: An Introduction to Psychology and Education* (1941 edn.).

21   See R. Palmer, *School Broadcasting in Britain* (1947) and A. Briggs, *The Birth of Broadcasting* (1995 edn.), p.23 and *The Golden Age of Wireless* (1995 edn.), pp.172–210.

versus culture, never to be absent in media history.[22] Book publishing was affected by the changes, but to a minor extent before the 1960s. Indeed, it was in relation solely to publishing and not to the media as a whole, still rarely thought of as such, that two articles appeared in the *Times Literary Supplement* in August 1938, as war clouds were gathering, complaining in the words of an un-named foreign author that 'One no longer knows what to do. . . It seems that poetry and literature are losing some of their old enchantment and value, for us [authors] and the public.'

Later in the article *belles lettres* were mentioned, and certainly, although the term was still in use, these were less prized than they had been before 1914. So too were what the author of the *TLS* article – all such *TLS* authors were then un-named – called 'the more delicate forms of literary art' – 'essays, causeries, non-mystical fantasies, witty and elusive satire'. Education was beyond the frontiers of concern of the author, and with it every kind of textbook and work of reference, a profoundly serious omission. More generally the *TLS* author's interpretation was untrustworthy. Despite his sense of disenchantment, there were essays and fantasies galore during the 1920s and 1930s and much else in, for example, Aldous Huxley, while during the 1930s Evelyn Waugh was producing superb satires that are still read and still live.

In retrospect, the reviewer's comment that 'Mammon has succeeded the Muses as the fountain of literature' – Gissing might have made the same point – appears misplaced and mistimed.[23] Sometimes such articles illuminate perceptions of contemporary culture as they had done in the early-eighteenth century on the eve of 'the rise of the novel'. These articles did not. In other circumstances their title might well have been 'The Death of Lang', but his name had virtually disappeared from print or conversation during the 1930s.

As it was, a livelier and more balanced picture of the state of the book trade was provided in a fascinating small shelf of eight *J.M Dent Memorial Lectures*, delivered eloquently and published attractively between 1931 and 1937. These surveyed current practices and problems in the British book trade, described by Basil Blackwell in the first of the lectures, 'The World of Books', as a trade 'full of incalculable hazards': 'he who plays for safety

---

22   See A. Briggs, 'The Communications Revolution', a lecture of 1966 reprinted in *Collected Essays*, Vol. 3 (1991), pp.62–76, and Briggs and Burke, *op. cit.*, pp.160–3.

23   *TLS*, 6, 13, 20 Aug. 1938; Blackwell, *op. cit.* p.50. In S. Unwin, *Authors and Publishers* (1926) he referred to fifty-three years of 'unbroken association with authors of all ranks and all qualities'.

plays also for defeat'.[24] Blackwell, like John Johnson after him,[25] Printer to the University of Oxford since 1925, went on to deal with all the players in what neither of them called 'the game of publishing', drawing on his experience as the most famous of Oxford booksellers, where he had been Chairman ('the Gaffer') of B.H. Blackwell Ltd since the death of his father in 1924.

Born in 1889, Blackwell had been – and was – a publisher as well as a bookseller. But he refused to believe that the Net Book Agreement, as it was then interpreted, marked the last word in the relationship between booksellers and publishers. In a privately printed article of 1933 called 'The Nemesis of the Net Book Agreement' he recognised that the Agreement was 'the Magna Carta of the book trade, the rock on which we are founded' but he pondered long on the implications of the emergence of what he called, as had done many others before him, 'The New Reading Public'. His was an independent voice, and in reaching his conclusions he paid attention to the form that the relationship between booksellers and publishers had taken in other countries, particularly Germany. Blackwell was interested in the work of the Joint Advisory Committee of the Publishers Association and the Associated Booksellers, set up in 1928. William Longman was a member.[26]

None of the Dent Memorial lecturers mentioned Longmans, Green, although Harold Raymond, born in 1885 and in the 1930s senior Partner in Chatto and Windus, dwelt at some length – if uneasily – on the advent of sixpenny Penguins, later to be within the range of Longmans, Green vision, which he described as a bigger 'portent' than twopenny libraries or Book Clubs.[27] Could the book trade afford 'to cut its profits to the fine point which a sixpenny novel nowadays involves'? There was a touch of now somewhat disagreeable sarcasm in Raymond's picture of the future. If 'the book' took rank with 'the magazine' and became 'a thing to be bought, used quickly then thrown away', a further portent might be an *Ostrich Weekly*, so attractive to advertisers that it could be priced at threepence or even fourpence, and would offer its readers a full-length novel, biography or book of travel. 'Other birds of the same feather would appear' and 'before long library subscriptions would dwindle rapidly', and authors would have

---

24 B. Blackwell, *The World of Books, A Panorama* (1932), p.11. The volumes cost 1s. 6d. each, and J.M. Dent's son, H.R. Dent, who had consulted his friend J.G. Wilson, wrote a foreword to the series. The lectures were delivered in the Stationers' Hall.

25 J. Johnson, *The Printer: his Customers and his Men* (1933). Another lecturer, Michael Sadleir (formerly Sadler), historian of publishing, explored *Authors and Publishers. A Study in Mutual Esteem* (1932).

26 *The Publisher and Bookseller*, 3 July 1929; Kingsford, *op. cit.*, pp.102–4.

27 For Penguin see Chapter 8.

to be satisfied with 'lump-sum payments ... for an ephemeral trade'.

Raymond was not alone in putting first the 'stability of our trade and a reasonable remuneration for author, publisher and bookseller', a priority that could only be preserved by 'maintaining a fairly high initial price for general literature and avoiding too rapid and too steep a reduction in price in a subsequent cheap edition. He was seeking the kind of stability provided in the nineteenth century by the three-decker novel, and described the book trade of the 1930s as 'threatened as never before by the commercial and political tendencies of the day'.[28] The 'advent of the Penguins', sold outside bookshops, was for Raymond a 'veritable bombshell'.[29]

One publisher, knowledgeable but humourless, was mentioned more than once in the booklets based on the Dent Lectures – Stanley Unwin (1884-1968), a founder member (1921) of The Society of Bookmen. So was his book, *The Truth About Publishing*, which had first appeared in 1926, and was to go through seven editions and a world war between then and 1960.[30] Described by another publisher, Jonathan Cape, as 'the publisher's Bible', it kept Unwin in the forefront of publishing politics. He went on to become President of the Publishers Association from 1933 to 1935. (William Longman had been President from 1929 to 1931, in Unwin's opinion the best President the Association ever had.[31]) Blackwell made gentle fun of Unwin. The 'impulse towards construction', or purposive collaboration between publishers, international as well as national, would provide a subject for 'a most interesting Dent Memorial Lecture in years to come, and the lecturer would have to seek much of his information in 'a book not yet written – is it necessary to tell you its title? – *The Truth About Stanley Unwin*'.[32]

Unwin wrote the introduction to another compilation of essays on the book trade, *The Book World*, published by Nelson in 1935, along with a chapter on 'English Books Abroad'. It was the by-product of a conference of publishers and booksellers called together by Unwin and Blackwell, then President of the Booksellers Association. 'That this book should be published, and furthermore be certain of a warm welcome and careful study' was 'evidence', Unwin suggested, 'of a marked change in the book trade'. 'There have been histories of bookselling and many of publishing houses, but as recently as twenty years ago there were few books in English dealing with current book trade problems and practice.'[33]

---

28 Blackwell, *op. cit.*, p.50.

29 H. Raymond, *Publishing and Bookselling* (1938), p.27.

30 An eighth edition in 1975 was partly re-written by Philip Unwin, his nephew. Philip also wrote *Book Publishing as a Career* (1965).

31 PW, p.24.

32 Blackwell, *op. cit.*, p.50.

33 *The Book World* (1935), p.1.

How 'marked' the change was seems less clear in retrospect than it was at the time. Certainly technology was almost completely left out of the discussion. And for Unwin the main sign of change had had nothing to do either with the content of books or their styles of presentation. It concerned what Blackwell called 'the impulse towards construction' within the world of the publishers. In the past there had been a lack of 'active organisation' – already Germany was offering the right model – and the lack had led to 'an absence of recognition accorded to the book trade'. Nazi Germany, where books were burnt, was scarcely a model, but pre-Nazi Leipzig, where Unwin had worked for a time, lingered in his memory.

Unwin survived the defeat of Nazi Germany in the Second World War and lived to the age of eighty-four, by which time British publishing was on the eve of greater changes than he could have envisaged, some of which were the very reverse of what he had hoped for. In 1935 he unequivocally condemned, as did Frank Swinnerton, 'the increasing commercialization of literature'.[34] Both men were suspicious of topicality. Thus, in the course of condemning equally both 'dilettantism' and 'academic priggishness', Swinnerton complained that contemporary authors now tended to be 'as topical as newspapers, and very nearly as ephemeral in their themes'.[35] 'Stunt books' were 'prevalent': 'they made news'. But in Unwin's opinion it was not upon 'such foundations that the stable publishing houses are built'. The adjective 'stable' still stands out.

No one at 39 Paternoster Row was interested in articulating a philosophy of the book trade, although the House of Longman rested on more stable (and far older) foundations than Allen and Unwin or Chatto and Windus where Swinnerton had worked. Indeed, George Allen, a friend of Ruskin, who founded the Unwin business, had gone bankrupt in 1913 after merging his business with that of Swan Sonnenschein, the son of a Moravian immigrant, who had set up his business in Paternoster Square in 1878.[36]

During the 1930s, when the Dent Lectures were being delivered, the one highly successful novel which Longmans, Green published was *Cold Comfort Farm* (1932), a brilliant parody of the novels of Mary Webb by Stella Gibbons (1902–1989). From its publication date it was a best-seller. (Coincidentally Stella's husband was called Webb.) Much of the book was written on scraps of paper while its author travelled on the tube between her home in Hampstead and Fleet Street.[37] *Cold Comfort Farm* appeared

---

34   *Ibid.*, p.10. Swinnerton in an essay on 'Authorship' was most concerned about 'the frantic busy-ness of the age'.

35   *Ibid.*, p.31.

36   See F.A. Mumby and F.I.S. Stallybrass, *From Swan Sonnenschein to George Allen and Unwin* (1955).

37   Obituary in *The Times*, 20 Dec. 1989.

in a year of depression which, as we have seen, affected Longmans more seriously and more immediately than switches in cultural trends. Stella Gibbons produced no fewer than forty-five other novels in the following forty years, but none of them made much mark.

~

There was a sharp contrast between this first period of twenty-one years in the history of the House and the second twenty-one years covered in this chapter, the years from 1947 to 1968, when Britain moved from austerity to what was called at the time affluence. These were years when the word 'revolution' was being freely applied, at least from the late 1950s onwards, to the controversial social and political changes which accompanied increasing wealth and leisure. This was an unprecedented phenomenon. There were significant signs of change in the mid and late 1950s, but the climax came during the 1960s in both national and international history, a watershed decade, as controversial in retrospect as it was at the time.[38]

During these years, when there was much talk of a generation gap, students, who never attracted much attention during the 1920s and early 1930s, were seldom out of the news. Their activities, often dubbed revolutionary, were shown on television screens and reported everywhere in the media (a recent term) as they took to the barricades in Paris in 1968 while across the Atlantic American students were marching in support of civil rights. Although the political scenario (and mood) in Britain was different from that in France, Germany or the United States, there were always echoes in Britain of what was happening outside it.

There was a sound accompaniment too to historical change – that of the heady noise of rock music, much of the loudest of it crossing frontiers. It was soon to have its own history, economic as well as cultural. In cultural circles there was talk already of 'the death of the author', as there was to be later of 'the death of the book'. Philosophers were to make the most of both 'deaths' and, indeed, of the 'death of God'. These were stirring times for publishers, whatever their problems, and revolutionary students were among their most eager customers. They knew what kind of books they wanted to read.

In its functioning as an educational publisher, concerned with students of all ages and persuasions, Longmans, Green, if it were to remain successful, was bound to respond to educational and social change, whatever forms it took and whatever the theories being advanced, some of them contradictory, to justify it. This it did pragmatically and highly successfully by further increasing its business involvement in education

---

38   See M. Sissons and P. French (eds.), *The Age of Austerity, 1941–1951* (1963); V. Bogdanor and R. Skidelsky (eds.), *The Age of Affluence* (1970); and A. Marwick, *The Sixties* (1998).

E.W. Parker holding *Europe since Napoleon,* innovative in its approach for its time. Parker was very influential in both schools and academic publishing in the UK market

Longman Archive

at all levels. E.W. Parker took the initiative in the 'home market' as C.S.S. Higham did for the 'overseas market'.

Parker helped to build up a formidable list of textbooks for the secondary school (chiefly grammar and independent schools) covering virtually every subject; and while the names of his schoolbook authors were not of international renown, they were certainly familiar to generations of schoolchildren (just as Kennedy and Ritchie had been to earlier generations). E.H. Dance had a distinguished career ahead of him; Denis Richards was to make large sums of money out of his school books, but also to write the wartime history of the Royal Air Force.[39] R.H. Rayner, a prolific Longman writer, had led the way. He prepared 'notes' for every historical 'period' that he covered: they were based on notes which he had used in his own classroom teaching, as were 'typical examination questions' that he appended. Yet he wrote books for other publishers besides Longman. His *A Middle School History of England* in three volumes was published by Murray, and his *A Public School Manual of Rugby Football* by Andrew Melrose.

A very special case was W.F.H. Whitmarsh's *A School Certificate French Course* (1935) which dominated the field in that subject for many years. Whitmarsh was a former student of Professor F.C. Roe, one of the many readers that Parker employed – he attached great importance to scholarly opinions – and he had published two anthologies with Longmans. Another regular reader did not approve of Whitmarsh's approach, but Parker went ahead notwithstanding, happy that the published course went on to form 'the prototype of many schoolbooks at that level in three languages'.[40] Another of Roe's pupils, C.D. Jukes, wrote jointly with Whitmarsh an *Advanced French Course* (1940)and a *New Advanced French Course* (1971).

There were many other Longman courses that involved completely original approaches and new authors. Indeed, the rise of series publishing, with a long history behind it, was even more crucial to twentieth-century educational publishing than the rise of serial publishing had been for the fortunes of the Victorian novel. Meanwhile, old authors' books often survived their authors. For example, J.W. Mellor's *A Comprehensive Treatise on Inorganic and Theoretical Chemistry*, first published in 1924, sold 10,000 copies in a new edition of 1951, revised by G.D. Parkes, and another 10,000 in 1961. It had a Longmans competitor, P.J. Durrant's *General and Inorganic Chemistry* (1939).

An independent writer in 1924 observed that a 'casual inspection of a few hundred chemical books leads us to estimate that Longmans have published more chemical books that we should care to have on our shelves than any other firm', although curiously perhaps he began his list not with chemistry but with 'monographs on physics', including Lymans'

39   See below, p.531.

40   E.W. Parker, 'Memoirs of the House of Longman' (1972), p.28.

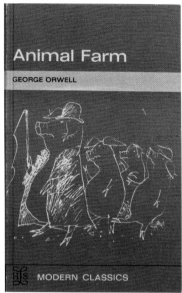
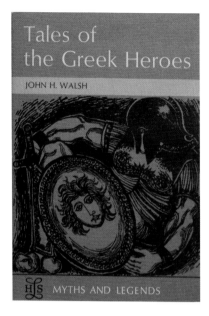

Spectroscopy of the Ultra Violet and J.J. Thomson's *Rays of Positive Electricity*. His list ended with 'several books fit to be in every gentleman's library, among them Mellor and Thorpe's *Dictionary of Applied Chemistry*. If you know your way about Thorpe and Mellor – and Mellor's path is not everybody's path – you can for a long while fare as if you were a chemist.'[41] Some specialised science series were directed at target readerships, among them R.C. Wallwork's *Physical Chemistry for Students of Pharmacy* (1956) and Pointon and Elwell's *Physics for Electrical Engineers* (1970).

Parker himself created a very special sort of series as far back as 1934. The *Heritage of Literature Series* (known inside the House, inevitably, as *HLS*) started with four titles in that year and grew steadily. Twenty-five years of its existence was marked by an article by Parker in the *Longmans House Journal* for Spring 1959: 'I made up my mind that a first-rate series of English readers might very well form the keystone of a successful educational list.' And so it did. The range was wide from *As You Like It* and Elizabeth Gaskell's *Cranford* to George Orwell's *Animal Farm* and Evelyn Waugh's *Brideshead Revisited*.

Even the teaching of English to foreigners, or English language teaching (*ELT*) publishing, which was to become a rich jewel in the Longmans crown, began with Parker himself, according to his account, as well as with C.S.S. Higham and Michael West. He claimed that it started in the Regent Street Polytechnic when he talked to the Head of the English Department and was told of the 'extraordinary development in the

The *Heritage of Literature Series (HLS)* was started and edited by E.W.Parker, to provide 'interesting reading matter for children' at school; there were different formats for different ages and it was said that if all the books sold in the Series were placed end to end they would stretch from London to Glasgow

Personal collection

---

41   *Chemistry and Industry*, 28 Nov. 1924, p.1178.

teaching of English to foreigners' of whom there were about 1,000 in his department. One of his assistants C.E. Eckersley was anxious to write a book for students. The book was *England and the English* and 'we felt that a first printing of 3,000 was a reasonable speculation for this little book priced at 3/6'.

Eckersley went on to write *A Concise English Grammar for Foreign Students* (1935), *Modern English Course* (1933), *Essential English* (1938), *Brighter English* (1937) and many other books, some of which sold hundreds of thousands of copies all over the world. They built on the work of Michael West, who founded Longmans' tremendous success in *ELT* publishing. West, MA, DPhil, who made his name in Bengal, had originally approached the Oxford University Press in India with a proposal for a series of 'experimental readers' but had been turned down.[42] He went on to produce an 'Alternative Series' of his *New Method Readers* for schools where a change was required from the first *Readers*.[43]

Adult general readers could get pleasure as well as information or education out of some Longmans, Green books labelled 'educational', and throughout the period covered in this chapter, the House never ceased to regard itself as a general rather than a specialist publisher. In particular, Mark Longman, who entered the business in 1938, nearly three years before the destruction of 39 Paternoster Row, believed that 'only firms with wide foundations' were likely to prove 'viable' (a more appealing word than stable).[44] It was under his chairmanship that John Guest, who had served with him in North Africa and Italy during the Second World War, became literary adviser from 1949–1972. One of their writers was Gavin Maxwell, author of *The Otter's Tale, A Reed Shaken by the Wind, Harpoon At a Venture, Lords of the Atlas* and *Raven Seek Thy Brother*. Maxwell employed an agent, but this was no longer any impediment to a happy publisher-author relationship with the House of Longman.

Long before, Robert Longman, always looking out for new authors, had taken up another still much-read novelist, Mary Renault (1905–1983). Her first book, *Purposes of Love* (1939), immediately appealed to him, although Eric Gillett, another experienced Longmans reader, suggested

---

42   Sutcliffe, *op. cit.*, p.214. In turn, Longman, more than content with West, turned down Laurence Faucett, who followed a similar approach, and Faucett went on to help E.C. Parnwell to launch *The Oxford English Course* published by Oxford University Press. Longman retained the competitive advantage.

43   *The New Method Composition, Alternative Edition* (1938). A paperback edition of 1944 showed a picture of an aeroplane on its paper cover. The Preliminary Exercise to be learnt was 'I'm a boy. [I'm not a girl]' or 'I'm a girl. I'm not a boy.'

44   Profile by Dudley Barker in *Trade News*, 19 Oct. 1963, pp.23–5.

cuts.[45] Robert invited her to his office on a wet day, welcoming her with exactly the right words for her, 'so this is the 200,000 word author'.[46] Their subsequent relationship, avuncular in character, was close, and during the Second World War, when Renault received Robert's messages, she is said to have 'glowed with pleasure'. Mark's relationship with her was less close, but it was he who published her book *The Charioteer* (1953) at a time when American publishers were daunted by the homosexual element in it – to be followed by her other novels, all of them edited by Guest.

Later, Mark recalled what Paternoster Row had been like around the time when Renault, then aged 34, first visited it. 'Working conditions in the warehouse', he stated in 1963 in characteristically light-hearted fashion, 'were such as would not be tolerated today for a moment', but they were 'fine for games of cribbage behind the bookstacks'.[47]

~

Like almost all reasonably educated recruits, Mark, who had been educated at Eton and Cambridge, was first consigned to 'Titles', the traditional way of learning the Longmans, Green catalogue by heart where (as Parker had been) he was under the scrutiny of Kelk, then on the eve of his retirement at the age of 72. Mark later served for a time as a salesman, and, in his own later, not light-hearted, words, 'loathed' it. In many towns, he learned, it was impossible to sell a book at all. 'It gave me an appreciation of what salesmen have to put up with' and 'a deep sympathy with them' which he continued to feel after he had become Chairman in 1964 on the retirement of William. Robert, who survived 'Mr Willie' by four years, had retired long before in 1948.

On the same day as Mark arrived at Paternoster Row in 1938, another Longman, Thomas Michael (1916–1978), Robert's son, had arrived there too – via Marlborough and Cambridge. Like Mark, he was commissioned in the Army, having just had time, as Mark did, to capture the sense of a Longmans, Green *ancien régime*. Unlike Mark, however, he developed a particular interest in theology, coincidentally one of Kelk's major interests;[48] and after he became a Director in 1947, he set out to develop energetically the then relatively unprofitable theological side of the business more

Robert Guy Longman (1882–1971) by Bernard Dunstan R.A. (n.d.). Robert joined Longman at the same time as his brother William and published particularly theology and literature. P.C.B. Wallis (who knew him) wrote that, in his opinion, he was one of the outstanding publishers of his day 'with a real feeling for literary merit, and flair combined with judgement, in his search for authors'

Pearson Education

---

45   Gillett, born in 1893, an Oxford graduate, who lived in Hove, had served in the Second World War. In 1947 he edited a *Junior Film Annual* and published *Eric Gillett's Film Book*.

46   For Renault, see D. Sweetman, *Mary Renault, a Biography* (1993).

47   *Trade News*, 19 Oct. 1963, p.24.

48   Two years after retiring in 1938 Kelk was ordained and edited the Church of England newspaper, *The Record*. He preached at evensong in Westminster Abbey only four months before he died, aged 82, in 1948.

Thomas Michael Longman
(1916–1978), portrait by David
Trindle c. 1958

Pearson Education

actively than his fellow Directors, including Mark, wished.

Like many of his Longman predecessors, Michael ran into controversy with one book, *The Rise of Christianity* (1947), by E.W. Barnes, controversial Bishop of Birmingham since 1924. The book had been offered to Longman in 1944, but it was judged one-sided. Michael accepted it in 1945 but it was not published until two years later. Priced high at 15 shillings, it went through five impressions in little over a year and by July 1948 had sold over 18,000 copies. According to Barnes's son and biographer, 'the wish to discover the truth' shone 'through every page'. Yet his father showed 'impatience', not for the first time, with 'contrary opinions'.[49] The book was referred to the Convocation of Canterbury, and it did not help when the *Sunday Pictorial* decided to serialise it.

Michael tried to tone down the foreword, but failed, and the commercial success of the book did not save Michael from criticism in the House. In 1959 Michael left the Board and started his own business, the first of the Longmans ever to do so, taking with him G.C. ('Tim') Darton, his Anglican editor, who had previously run the South African branch of Longman, and John Todd, his Roman Catholic editor, who was a theologian in his own right. The imprint of the new firm was (and still remains) Darton, Longman and Todd, and it was from new headquarters that the new Jerusalem Bible (1966) was planned. As early as 1948 Brack and Higham (at Michael's request?) had been to see officers of the Society for Promoting Christian Knowledge about publishing a new translation of the New Testament 'in simple English'.[50] There were echoes of Rivington in this.

Potter, by then the most active partner in the daily operations of the business, felt it necessary to send a statement to the staff in the spring of 1959 about Michael's departure. The other directors had considered that the large number of religious titles which he was proposing 'tended to unbalance the general list', and a limit had been set which he was not prepared to accept. The parting had been amicable, and the care of books other than religious books for which Michael had been responsible, including Roget's *Thesaurus* and *The Annual Register*, would be handed over to Mark. It would not be the policy of the firm in future to seek new books for religious markets.[51]

A third young Longman, John Cecil (1912–1965), son of George Henry Longman, joined the House in 1944 on a temporary war-time basis, having been invalided out of the Forces. He had never intended to be a

49   See J. Barnes, *Ahead of His Age, Bishop Barnes of Birmingham* (1979), a biography published by Collins, esp. pp.405–17.

50   Brack, *Diary*, 11 Nov. 1948 (personal archive).

51   K.B. Potter, 'Notes for a Statement to the Staff', 13 April 1959.

publisher, but he became a Director in 1947 at the same time as Mark, and was designated Company Secretary. Interested less in ledgers than in the mechanical arts, including model building, he was forced to resign his Directorship on grounds of chronic ill-health in 1956 and died seven years before Mark who now became the sole Longman left in the business.

By 1956 Mark had taken over general publishing (*belles lettres*, a term then still in use, fiction and non-fiction), becoming Vice-Chairman of the Company in 1962, two years before he succeeded 'Mr Willie', who by then had become something of a recluse, travelling to the office each day but lunching in silence in the canteen and saying very little at the lunch-time meetings of the Directors. Nevertheless, in 1956 he was sent a remarkable letter by Potter, 'writing on behalf of all his colleagues', on the occasion of his jubilee 'in the service of the Company'. It began 'My dear Willie', and went on

'Fifty years is a considerable period in the life of any man and in your case the experience has been, I imagine, as varied as that of anyone. For it stretches from the days before the first war, when life was so different, through two wars, two slumps – one the most severe ever known – and two periods of inflation, with the second of which the country is still grappling.'

Potter's own role during the slump of the 1930s has already been described. Now he referred to 'Mr Willie's steady control' after 1932 as his 'greatest contribution to the Company'. His eyes had been 'firmly fixed on the goal' – survival? – 'without on any occasion failing to consider sympathetically the effect of policy on the fortunes of individual members of the staff'. Longmans, Green had, 'of course', 'for very many years been a leading publishing house, but it must be a source of great satisfaction and pride to you to see it ... as firmly established as ever as one of the most profitable [by now an acceptable key adjective] and [Potter believed] most enterprising companies in the trade, pre-eminent in its own special fields and with that priceless asset of a publisher, namely a staff capable of carrying it on and developing it in an era of expansion.'

In his last paragraph Potter added that 'the problems of an expanding business are almost as difficult as those of a contracting one'. Willie had had experience of both, the two contrasting periods identified in this chapter. His office at Grosvenor Street was sparsely furnished,[52] but it contained a bookcase and a deed box, the latter containing the secrets of the House. These were never to be revealed to the world by him.

Mark, not mentioned specifically in Potter's letter, provided a complete contrast. Charming, ambitious, an excellent ambassador, he appreciated the need for change. 'There might well come a time', he told an interviewer

---

52   Longman moved to 48 Grosvenor Street in 1961.

A photograph of Mark Frederic
Kerr Longman (1916–72), the
last Longman to join the firm,
the youngest son of Henry
Longman and brother of J.C.
Longman. Both joined the
Company in 1947 and Mark
became Chairman in 1964,
and then President of the
Publishers' Association from
1969–71.In charge of what was
called by then the 'general' side
of publishing, he also travelled
widely, supporting the younger
publishers whom he brought in
to the House. In his final years
he negotiated the acquisition
of the firm by a subsidiary of S
Pearson and Son

Longman Archive

in 1963, 'when control should pass to some talented young man growing up in the firm, who is not a member of the family.' The interviewer 'had the feeling all the same' that after a quarter of a millennium 'tradition is unlikely to be broken'. But that time was only ten years ahead.[53] Necessity dictated the outcome. Mark had discernment, tact and charisma, and it was difficult for him to contemplate a House of Longman without Longmans in charge of it. Yet in 1972 there was no other Longman left to take over.

~

A flashback is necessary. It was during the years leading up to the Second World War that the two non-Longmans, K.B. Potter and C.S.S. Higham, had become indispensable to the running of the business. Potter was only twenty-four when he arrived at Longman. He arrived at Paternoster Row with Winchester and New College, Oxford, where he read classics, behind him, and a brilliant First World War record, which had been followed by a brief period studying accountancy. He had interesting personal connections. Beatrix Potter, thirty years older than him, was a close relative. His older sister, Shena, closely involved in local government and in the Workers' Educational Association, married Ernest Simon, later Lord Simon of Wythenshawe, Chairman of the BBC from 1947 to 1952 and subsequently a pioneering advocate of new Council housing estates.[54]

As has been noted, it was not so much Potter's connections or his knowledge of accountancy – or, indeed, his financial acumen that went with it – that counted for most when he entered the House of Longman, but his capital. Yet by the time that he died he had offered much else. After the Second World War, in which he served again, he was largely responsible for the arrangement to convert Longmans, Green into a public company. The word 'public' mattered to him, for while he was quick-tempered and always unwilling to suffer fools gladly, he reigned supreme over the telephone switchboard, with which William persistently refused to connect. William lived on to be very old: by contrast, as Philip Wallis noted, 'Potter was not born to be an old man'.

One month after Potter was made a Director in 1926, C.S.S. Higham (1890–1958), with academic, not family connections, entered the House. Born seven years before Potter, he had been a history scholar at Trinity College, Cambridge before becoming a lecturer in history at Manchester University, under the professorial leadership of T.F. Tout, a revered figure at 39 Paternoster Row. If Potter brought money into Paternoster Row,

53   Parker, *loc. cit.*, p.25.

54   See E.D. Simon, *A Century of City Government* (1938), dedicated to Mrs. Sidney Webb, and Lord Simon of Wythenshawe, *The BBC from Within* (1953). The Simons' son Brian devoted his career as an historian to the history of British education.

Higham brought in brains and academic experience, along with an often related delight in travel, which became extremely valuable to his colleagues. He was equally interested in the Middle East, Africa and Asia.

Higham did not become a Director of Longmans, Green until 1940 when the Longmans, Green Board had been temporarily reduced to two. Nevertheless, before the Depression he had been building up a strong list of titles, and it was after the production of new books and the reprint of old books had been curtailed during the Depression that he persuaded the Directors to allow him to travel to Egypt – at his own expense – to push overseas sales. This was the first of many overseas trips, and the immediate purpose of his visit was to encourage the sale of West's *New Method Readers*. He always had such purposes in mind, for, as the distinguished geographer, Sir Dudley Stamp, a prolific Longmans, Green author, put it in an obituary of Higham in 1958: 'He wanted to be a missionary and his journeys were missionary journeys ... He followed the great tradition of J.W. Allen of Longmans, whose simple method of costing, usually successful, was to say: "This book is needed, it must not cost more than 5s. We will publish it".'[55] Allen had died in 1932. Higham raised the money for his Egyptian tour from the proceeds of his own book *Pioneers of Progress*, based on bedtime stories he had told his children.

West's pioneering series had been launched in India by W.E. Candy, who successfully managed the Indian business of Longmans for nearly twenty years, but during the Second World War the ship, in which he was returning to India in March 1941, was sunk by enemy action in the Indian Ocean, and in consequence a relatively young newcomer to 39 Paternoster Row, Cyprian Blagden (1906–1962), was sent out to Calcutta to take his place. He had entered the House, which he was to study as well as to inhabit, just before the Second World War, having previously been for a short time a history master at Uppingham and an HM Inspector of Schools.

Blagden's gifts were highly distinctive, and I myself have benefited directly from them in writing this *History*. It was history that most interested him, not least the history of Longman and of publishing in general, a rare interest in his time; and both in India and back at home in Britain after 1948 he not only wrote much about publishing (including a valuable history of the Stationers' Company) but 'sponsored' – to employ what had become the in-House term – an attractive history list. This continued the Longman tradition in both general and academic history publishing which had most recently been expressed by Robert Longman in his cooperation with G.M Trevelyan and was later to be further secured by Andrew MacLennan, a publisher with distinctive qualities of his own. Longman owed much to Blagden. He was on the best of terms both with schoolmasters and university professors, some of whom, to their surprise,

Portrait of K. B. Potter (1897–1962) by Bernard Dunstan R.A. (n.d.). Potter had joined Longmans aged twenty-one and in January, 1926 when Longmans became a limited company, was made a Director, (as were all the other Partners). His own money brought financial stability during the slump, and Potter brought his financial understanding to Longman as well as his staunch support for the book trade. The day before he died, preparing for a public speech, he told a colleague 'I know; they should know; I'll tell them!' He died suddenly, aged sixty-four in 'what would have been perfect circumstances, with a salmon on the hook and his gilly by his side.' (Note to all staff by Noël Brack)

Pearson Education

---

55   Quoted in PW, p.54.

he asked to read manuscripts, and with authors, whom he always tried to introduce to each other.[56]

It is somewhat surprising that Blagden never became a Director. The man to whom he reported was Brack, a Cambridge graduate, who served Longmans, Green loyally, keeping it on an even keel from his arrival in the spring of 1928 – before the Depression – to his departure in 1968. Before joining the House Brack had worked with Crosby Lockwood, technical publishers, and during the last ten years of the Kelk régime he cooperated closely with him, taking over the publishing department when Kelk left.

Brack's greatest strength was his ability to cope in all situations, setting an example to others. This was revealed abundantly during the Second World War, a devastating and visible break in the history of Longman, which makes the word 'continuity' seem completely inappropriate as part of the heading of this chapter. Yet, to a great extent due to him, Longman not only survived fire and water once more, but, with a depleted staff, kept its identity while embarking on new ventures.

~

The indispensable source not only for the War years but for the years of austerity that followed it is Brack's detailed diary, its value enhanced by comments that he added (for my benefit) in 1982 and 1983. It is not, however, the only source for the War years. Chapter 1 survives of what is called 'Longman's Own War Story', written from Ambleside, 43 Albert Drive, Wimbledon, as early as October 1939; and there is a fascinating Louis McNeice-like script for a play or broadcast called 'The Burning of the Books' which relates the destruction of Paternoster Row not only to the Nazi burning of books before the War, where the script starts, but to the Great Fire of 1666 which destroyed old St Paul's and many of the shops of the booksellers who lived nearby.[57] There are also several letters written at the time to Longmans, Green employees abroad.

Before the War, in the spring of 1939, the Company had wisely secured on a rental basis Ambleside, home of a school, Beltane, as a centre to which staff could be evacuated. It had been discovered by Bernard Workman, who had joined the House from Collins in 1937 and was responsible *inter alia* for a series of atlases published jointly with his previous publishers.

Cover of the *History of the British Empire* by C.S.S Higham, 1947. Higham also wrote the titles in *Pioneers of Progress: Stories of Social History, 1750–1920* to finance his own trip to Egypt (re-paid later by the directors), the first of his many journeys abroad on behalf of Longmans, and from 1937 he wrote the series *Discovering History*

BL W2/2248

56 There is a brief obituary of Blagden in the *Longman House Magazine*, Autumn 1963. LA Part II 209

57 The script, which includes various voices and many sound effects, is called 'Destruction of Paternoster Row: The Burning of the Books'. See also in very different style but carrying the same message, an article by Stanley Unwin in the *Spectator* 10 Jan. 1941, 'The Bombed Book Trade'. Unwin also compared the bonfires of 'the best of their own German literature' and their 'attack upon the British book trade'.

The destruction of the Longmans building in January 1941. It had already been bombed on the night of 29 December 1940 during the London Blitz

Photograph by Cecil Beaton in the Longman Archive

The decision to seek a site outside central London, which Mr Willie did not favour, was to prove crucial. Beltane contained many rooms of varying sizes which overlooked Wimbledon Park and the All England Lawn Tennis Club. Its pupils were duly evacuated to Wiltshire just before the beginning of the War, and on Friday 1 September 1939 Longmans staff arrived to dig slit trenches in its spacious garden: Blagden, 'a fine figure of a man without his shirt', was one of the diggers. Later two steel air-raid shelters were added.

The first complement of sales staff, twenty-eight of them women, moved in three days later, on Monday 4 September, and began work immediately, with the staff sitting on school chairs in front of folding school desks. Other furniture arrived by night in 'Ship' vans. Two days later a canteen was opened. Meanwhile, twenty-eight staff remained in Paternoster Row, and they in turn were to be evacuated to Wimbledon only after the total destruction of Paternoster Row on the terrible night of Sunday 29/30 December 1940, one of the worst nights of the Blitz, when

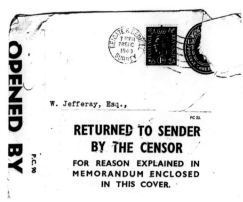

The Censor's envelope

Longman Archive

'the hub of the English book trade' was left 'in ruins'.[58] On 28 December Longmans, Green had been in a position to supply between five and six thousand titles: on the following Monday it was left with just twelve.

The Ministry of Information released the story, naturally without revealing such fascinating personal details as the fact that 29 December was Brack's 38th birthday or the fact that he was in charge on that day only because Willie and Robert Longman were taking their Christmas holiday. Brack had his own secrets. It was public information, not private information, however, that he wrote about in a letter to the Longman agent in New York, Walter Jefferay: 'Although we had endeavoured to spread our stocks by getting printers to hold small quantities of sheet stock, nearly the whole of our bound books, and a very large proportion of quires were destroyed, for our other big London warehouse was also burnt out that night.' An earlier letter, written on 23 December, had been 'returned to sender by the Postal Censor'. Brack was warned 'to be more careful in the future', for he was said to have breached defence regulations.

Brack's letter ended with a description of Kelk striding into the middle of the debris. As a colleague of Brack put it, 'he always had a nose for trouble'. Brack told Jefferay that he 'looked as fit and cheerful as ever'. He added that valuable current business records had been safely moved to Ambleside during the next few days, along with the tin box of 'secrets', 'Mr Willie's secrets' they were sometimes called, kept in the strong room, the only part of Paternoster Row which survived.[59] Everywhere else 'a vast quantity of material of historic and literary interest ha[d] perished'. 'It will mean', Brack added, 'that a great number of books will have to go out of print – many dear old friends, slow, steady sellers – but not commercial propositions as reprints.'[60]

By what seemed a miracle, 613 copies of *Cold Comfort Farm* were saved, a detail that survives not because of Brack's efforts but because of a letter from Stella Gibbons to Robert Longman. She told Robert that she could not love that part of London which had been destroyed, but she knew how much it meant to him. 'When buildings are destroyed, especially old

---

58   *The Bookseller*, 2 Jan. 1941, which appeared just as usual, included a memorable description of the Blitz by a City bookseller, Hubert Wilson, who after the war ran a small chain of retail shops in the City and a busy export department.

59   Letter to Miss Esther Tait Reid, 21 Feb. 1941. 'The contents were untouched', the letter writer (Brack?) went on, 'which speaks well for the way they built such places in the 1880s.'

60   Letter from Brack to Jefferay, 8 Jan. 1941.

buildings, thousands of moods and memories are lost.'[61] More than old buildings had gone, including details of their acquisition and occupation.

There were other firms among Longman's neighbours in Paternoster Row, who fared far less well than Longman did after the Blitz. Indeed, some of them never recovered. In particular, the distribution business of Simpkin Marshall, just opposite Longmans, Green, the product of many past mergers, with its origins in 1814, lost all the stocks on which it completely depended, four million books in all.[62] It had published some books itself, but made its profits by handling books of all publishers through an intricate distribution system, national and international. Now a new business concern would have to be created from the wreck.

A group of publishers, headed by Sir James Pitman, in the kind of collective move that might have been made in the eighteenth century, took over the distributive business from the Miles family that then owned Simpkin Marshall after the family decided to liquidate it. Thereafter, in difficult war-time conditions a new non-profit-making concern ran the distributive business for a time from Book Centre, a Pitman subsidiary in London's North Circular Road. The trade, however, no longer had a 'hub'. Nor did it after a newcomer to the business and to the country, Robert Maxwell, known then as Captain Robert Maxwell, MC, refloated the wholesaler Simpkin Marshall in 1951. Maxwell, a Czech immigrant though he did not give his place or date of birth in *Who's Who*, was to come to represent a very different kind of publisher from the Longmans, but this, the first of his commercial ventures, failed within three years.

There is no record of any discussion in 1940 or 1941 between Pitman and any member of the Longman family. Nor was there the slightest intimation then that in the period covered in the next chapter of this *History* the Pitman firm, which had a completely different history and business culture from Longmans, Green, would be acquired in 1985 by what was by then a very different House of Longman from that of 1940 or 1960. In 1940 Longmans had seldom published a book on business or on management, not surprisingly, given that those members of the family who were in charge of its operations still thought of themselves as partners, not as managers.

At Ambleside, far from the City, a sense, not merely a semblance, of order was quickly restored. Joyce Nairn, who had joined Longman in 1931 as a shorthand typist in days of deep economic depression, when there were at least two salary cuts, and who was to go on to become Personnel Manager, has vividly recalled how after one of the grimmest nights of the Blitz, Higham and Brack spent a weekend at Brack's home going through

---

61 Letter from Stella Gibbons to Robert Longman, 15 Jan. 1941.

62 Simpkin, Marshall had been a main target in the labour disturbance of the 1920s. See Kingsford, *op. cit.*, pp.88–90.

Ambleside. 'Hitler invaded Poland and... Longmans advance parties were on the premises and a member of staff sign-painted the names of Directors and the names of Departments outside their allotted doors' (*Three Addresses*, Cyprian Blagden, 1947)

Longman Archive

all the stock record cards, dividing the titles into four categories – the 'urgent urgents' for reprinting; the next, the most urgent; the third, those to reprint when there was paper available; and the fourth, an interesting category (how big?), those which 'you were thankful to lose'. Nairn, kept busy typing list two, noted that among those in its last category were 'all the Westminster versions of the Sacred Scriptures'.

That was only the beginning of a huge task which involved problems on the warehousing side as great as on the producing side. Nairn, who left Ambleside for a different war-time job (as did Workman), had to confront an incendiary bomb in her own small first-floor flat in Earls Court in February 1944. Single-handed she saved her own and her neighbour's property.[63] From her dangerous vantage point she believed that as far as control and planning were concerned, 'the whole working pattern' of Longmans, Green, if not its structure or its identity, changed completely during the War. Higham and Brack took all the key decisions. Nevertheless, Willie and Robert Longman were there, too, Willie living in a leased flat next door, more than nominally in charge, and Robert kept in close touch with his authors as the complicated background story of *English Social History* reveals.

Life at Ambleside, where no two days were the same, is vividly described in Brack's diaries which catch moods as well as tell stories, first of improvisation and then of attempts, belated in Brack's opinion,

---

63   Brack, *Diary*, 20 Feb. 1944 and a later note of 1982.

to plan. Danger was almost taken for granted, as fire-watching and the Home Guard were, and on one occasion Ambleside was hit by incendiary bombs, one of which pierced the roof cavity.[64] Most serious of all was the destruction of the Ship Binding Works in an air attack of April 1941. In such circumstances the weather itself was never taken for granted. Nor was illness. 'People were constantly away ill', including Willie for four months in 1941 and Higham for over two months in 1943, 'and this added stress, at any time, for those fit to carry on.'[65] One employee 'got the sack' after he had been ill for several months.[66]

'Discipline' was maintained, but there were quarrels, even among seniors, some of them arising from what Brack called 'bloody mindedness', many provoked by the insensitivities of E.V.B. Smith, the Company Secretary. 'Bright and fine', Brack began his daily diary entry on 19 September 1944, 'but WL upset things by telling me that GW had complained of Smith's rudeness to her and to the staff and of the very rude way in which he treated me.'[67] When Brack, more liberal than some of his colleagues, suggested in the same year that staff should be paid individually and not forced to queue up in the hall, Smith told him that he would 'fight any alteration to the last ditch'.

Quarrels were overshadowed in Brack's mind by the failure to prepare for the future. 'I am very worried', he wrote in September 1944, 'that all my efforts, going back over a year, have failed to get the Company moving in regard to post-war reconstruction except insofar as new offices and educational books is [sic] concerned ... What we are going to print and with whom should have been settled months ago.'[68] On the very week of the bombing of Paternoster Row Brack had been optimistic about the future. He felt that 'the disaster ha[d] thrown open the door to great possibilities ... We can also look forward maybe to fine, well-planned offices, instead of the dear old Row, with its many snags and inconveniences, though we must wait until we have smashed Hitler and his Nazis.'[69]

~

64   Letter (from Brack?) to Miss Jean Hunnisett in the Longman Toronto Office, 29 Jan. 1941.

65   Note by Brack, 2 Feb. 1984.

66   *Diary*, 27, 31 Oct. 1941.

67   *Ibid.*, 28 Feb. 1944.

68   *Ibid.*, 5 Sept. 1944. In 1982 Brack wrote to me after re-reading his diary that this 'note of myself to myself is interesting'.

69   Letter to Jefferay, 8 Jan. 1941.

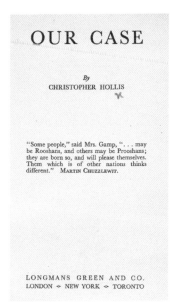

OUR CASE

By
CHRISTOPHER HOLLIS

"Some people," said Mrs. Gamp, ". . . may be Rooshans, and others may be Prooshans; they are born so, and will please themselves. Them which is of other nations thinks different." MARTIN CHUZZLEWIT.

LONGMANS GREEN AND CO.
LONDON ❖ NEW YORK ❖ TORONTO

Our Case, by Christopher Hollis. The first 'wholly war-time' book published by Longmans Green & Co. in 1939

BL 08028.bb.28

Brack always had 'Hitler and his Nazis' in mind, as did many, but by no means all, of the authors responsible after 1940 for new titles emanating from Wimbledon. Education had a priority. Yet the first 'wholly war-time' book, 'planned, written and produced' after 3 September 1939, had been published on 9 October, during the 'phoney war' and before the destruction of Paternoster Row, and was called *Our Case*. Christopher Hollis, a Conservative MP, was the author. Another very early war-time book, *England*, with a foreword by Lord Halifax, was commissioned from E.H. Carr, who was to become one of the most cogent advocates in *The Times* and elsewhere of a policy of 'radical social reconstruction'.[70] Unlikely later titles were *The Average Man Broadcast Addresses by The Radio Padre*, The Rev. Ronald Selby Wright (three impressions, 1942); Wright recorded his thanks to R.G. Longman. Even more unlikely was *First Aid Through Photographs* (two impressions, 1941).

The War was a period when, in the words of Harold Raymond, the book trade swam along with its head just under water.[71] It was only after Churchill became Prime Minister in May 1940 that he claimed in three most difficult days that 'books are one of the most vital services in war'. Raymond, himself never short of words – or judgements – remained pessimistic about the effects of war on the British book trade,[72] but the facts were against him. From the start the war-time demand for books was to be far greater than the supply, and the 'book trade' was always on the offensive. This was to be a war with very different cultural consequences from those of the First World War or the Boer War before it.

Even before Churchill became Prime Minister, Geoffrey Faber, then President of the Publishers Association, fought successfully a 'battle of the books', backed by the National Book Council which organised a meeting in the Stationers' Hall to protest against proposals to levy purchase tax, a new tax as VAT might have been, on books.[73] Faber, aware of all the likely problems for publishers in war-time conditions, including paper rationing, introduced in April 1940, believed that 'all kinds of books would be in demand, not only books on the future reconstruction of the world'. The demand for crime novels might fall, but if it did not, 'fiction of all kinds should begin to see better days'.[74]

---

70   See E.H. Carr, *Conditions of Peace* (1942) and *Nationalism and After* (1944). His role on *The Times* is charted in D. McLachlan, *In the Chair, Barrington Ward of The Times, 1927–1948* (1971).

71   Letter to Mrs. Patmore, 14 Nov. 1939 (Chatto and Windus Papers, f.2021).

72   H. Raymond, 'The Effect of War on the British Book Trade', Dec. 1939, *ibid.*, f.2917.

73   National Book Council, 'News Sheet', No. 131, Aug. 1940.

74   G. Faber, 'Publishing and the War', in *The Spectator*, 15 Sept. 1939.

Faber was broadly right, but within the context of the phoney war it was economic considerations that were always stressed by publishers. Curiously, in November 1939, Potter was in the Chair at a Group II meeting of the Publishers Association, concerned with fiction, outside his own main range of interest, when a resolution was carried that until inflation reached a point which made it impossible to maintain prices of novels 'anywhere near their present level', prices should be increased 'by no more' than was necessary to cover the bare increase of costs and that 'trade discounts and royalties [should] be calculated upon the pre-war published prices'. It was reported that the Juvenile Group of the Association was making the same recommendation. Among those present at this meeting were Faber himself, A.S. Frere of Heinemann, Raymond and, now returned to the fray, Walter Hutchinson.[75]

The photographs for *First Aid* were by Vera Elkan, the short text by L.A.Michaelis, Longmans 1941

Personal collection

More battles of the books had to be fought in the perilous summer of 1940, when it was proposed to halve the paper ration and to impose purchase tax on books, and in 1941, when restrictions on printing were being demanded and essential workers in the book trade were losing their already carefully restricted exemptions from call-up.[76] Faber was no longer President of the Publishers Association, however, in August 1941, when another committee of the Association, described as Technical Advisory, which included no representative of any of the firms present at the Potter meeting, met to discuss a scheme of economy in book production that would be acceptable to the newly-founded Ministry of Supply.

This time there was near-consensus, and after complex negotiations

---

75 Report of a Publishers Association Meeting at the Stationers' Hall, 24 Nov. 1939. The Report was marked 'Private and Confidential'.

76 G. Faber, 'The New Threat to Books: Imperilling a Principle of High Policy', in the *TLS*, 18 April 1941.

a Book Production War Economy Agreement came into force on 1 January 1942, which dealt with both new books and reprints, as well as 'general literature' and educational books, but which exempted lectern and school Bibles. The Agreement set out detailed specifications not only for paper and binding but for page lengths, chapter headings, paragraph breaks and even colophons, which could not be used 'in any unauthorized manner'. There was to be no 'extravagant display'. Books produced only for export were exempt from all restrictions, but their publishers were 'expected to observe all possible and reasonable economies'.[77]

Physical restraints were not relaxed until the autumn of 1945, and then only slightly. A book could from then onwards be 'set to any measure, provided the type area (including headlines, if any, but excluding folios) is not less than 55% of the area of the untrimmed page. The type (or types) used in books produced to this Standard must keep within the maximum size and degree of leading.'[78] The quality of paper was poor, and paper rationing remained in operation until 1949. Apart from controls, there were many other production problems. In the spring of 1946 Brack wrote in his diary 'Very busy day. Printers have delivered over 2,000,000 books to our binders in the last 6 months (500,000 in last month alone) but the binders in the same six months have only sent us 1,500,000 bound books.'[79]

~

It was within a framework of restriction that the major war-time glory of the Longman House, G.M. Trevelyan's *English Social History*, was published. Planned before the War, and based, as we have seen, on a suggestion by Robert Longman, it appeared in 1944 two years after it had been printed in the United States, and the 15,000 printed copies were sold out before publication day. By then the Blitz had already turned into both history and myth, although German rocket attacks had now started. *English Social History* was well timed. As the historian Herbert Butterfield, a Cambridge critic of Whig history, put it, during the War England was throwing out ropes 'to the preceding generations as though in time of danger it was a good thing [an historical cliché deliberately chosen] not to lose touch with the rest of the convoy'.[80]

---

77 The Publishers Association, 'The War Production War Economy Agreement, The Schedule with an Introduction and Some Notes on Interpretation' (1942).

78 Note by F.D. Sanders, Secretary of the Publishers' Association, 1 Oct. 1945, 'Amendments, Book Production War Economy Agreement'.

79 *Diary*, 6 May 1946.

80 H. Butterfield, *The Englishman and His History* (1944), p.v. Compare Butterfield's very different essay *The Whig Interpretation of History* (1931).

Trevelyan's cheque, May 1946

Longman Archive

Trevelyan, who was deeply conscious of the war-time break in historical continuity, made a large sum of money from his volume, and when Robert sent him a royalty cheque for £14,589 11s. 4d. in May 1946, one in a sequence, he reminded him of the famous £20,000 cheque sent to his great uncle Macaulay, leaving out how much tax he, Trevelyan, unlike Macaulay, would have to pay from it. There was to be continuing income as new reprints appeared, and by 1949 400,000 copies had been sold.

When Robert Longman asked Trevelyan to write a social history Trevelyan had asked him what social history meant. Unlike many later social historians, he did not see social history as unifying history. Nor did he believe that it incorporated politics. Moreover, the Second World War scarcely figured in his *Social History*, and there was only one sentence in it on the consequences of war which included the qualifying clause 'unless we become a Totalitarian State and forget our Englishry'. 'What will happen to England in peace and war', Trevelyan wrote in his last pages, 'the historian is no better able to guess than any one else.' The kind of social history which became acceptable during the 1950s and 1960s was very different from Trevelyan's. The politics was then put in, and an attempt was made – it still continues – to explain what 'Englishry' implied than to take it for granted.

Nevertheless, in an interesting footnote in *English Social History*, the last, Trevelyan noted the importance of education. The fighter pilots of 1940, Churchill's 'few' to whom the many owed so much, were the products, Trevelyan conceded not of public schools, but of primary and secondary schools, and it was for pupils in those schools that Longmans, Green was to cater not only during the difficult post-war years but during the War itself. Within three weeks of the destruction of Paternoster Row, a new catalogue of secondary school books was published.

Normally a schools catalogue included 'very many books which are slow sellers'. This one did not. It contained no book that would not sell quickly. And, unlike previous catalogues, it added the words 'of Paternoster Row' to the name of the House.[81] The catalogue also included a photograph of an emergency trade counter opened a week after the destruction and a section of the first catalogue of books published in 1656 at the Sign of the Ship by John Crooke, 'our forerunner'. 'Cromwell ruled England'.

~

The sense of emergency had not disappeared by the time that Longmans, Green moved from Wimbledon back into central London, meeting only some of Brack's aspirations, in 1944 and 1945. Two moves led directly back into the eighteenth century. Numbers 6 and 7 Clifford Street, occupied in 1947, off Old Bond Street in the West End,[82] were described by John Summerson, the historian of architecture, as characteristic of the best type of town house of 'about 1720';[83] and the rate books for the property reveal that they were first occupied in 1721, three years before the first Thomas Longman arrived in London. One of their late-eighteenth-century occupants had been Lord Sidmouth, formerly Christopher Addington, the Home Secretary responsible for the Six Acts of 1819 which restricted freedom of speech.

The façades remained there in 1947, but there had been many changes in interiors and use, with the two houses being amalgamated in the mid-nineteenth century to become a family hotel, Almonds. In the late Second World War they were used as an American Red Cross Hotel for officers, the Reindeer. Nonetheless, when Longmans acquired the property their request for them to be used for non-residential purposes was at first turned down, and it was only after an appeal to the Ministry of Health, then in charge of housing and planning, that, after substantial alterations, Longmans could move in.[84] Brack was disappointed that the architects Henry Dawson & Co. Ltd., who had been responsible for the new Paternoster Row building of 1863, were not given the contract to restore the premises: they had been helpful during the War, and they were familiar with Longman history. Instead, an architect friend of Robert Longman, D.L. Bridgwater, was selected in April 1946. He did his work so well, however, that Brack thought the new premises 'wonderful'.

They certainly attracted many visitors who wished to be shown round

---

81   Reprint of the Introduction to 'Messrs Longmans' Catalogue of Educational Works', Jan. 1941.

82   The nearby Coach and Horses Yard was also occupied.

83   J. Summerson, *Georgian London* (1945).

84   The winning of the appeal was announced in a letter to Messrs Longmans, Green & Co by the Cromwell Road regional office of the Ministry of Health on 23 Feb. 1946.

– authors, among them Thornton Wilder, other publishers, and, not least, relatives and friends. Few of them, however, saw the Coach and Horses Yard, where the Warehouse and Packing Department moved in June 1948. It was an invaluable acquisition, for lorries were able to load or unload stock in the very heart of the West End, and a ground-floor way was opened up between Clifford Street and the Yard. (The only other way to get from one to the other was via The Coach and Horses public house and New Street police station.)

The second move in 1961, when Clifford Street proved too small, creating, in Brack's words 'a real problem',[85] was to No. 48 Grosvenor Street, not far away. This was a simpler move, and it inspired verse:

> The Ship that Hitler's bombs burned down
> In Clifford Street gained fresh renown,
> It anchors now near Grosvenor Square ...

The new premises were opened by Eccles, and the most distinguished visitor was the Duke of Edinburgh. This was soon after Longmans, Green had published the Duke's *Birds from Britannia*, a book of photographs for which he had written a substantial text. 'Having been met by Mr Mark at the front door', the Duke looked around the showroom and signed the visitors' book before meeting about forty people, including the President of the Booksellers Association, in Mark's room.

A third move was to take Longmans, Green out of London to Harlow, designated a post-war 'new town', one of a cluster of planned such towns. It was a move made in parts, the first, that of warehousing, taking place in 1959. A site was acquired at the Pinnacles Estate with packaging and despatching facilities on a lease which would not expire until 1981. Pinnacles was in full swing when the first new office accommodation, acquired on a 99-year lease, was occupied in 1968. Gibberd's now demolished new building was planned, an undated Longman brochure put it, 'to provide a working environment which is both effective and attractive', the latter a controversial claim.[86] Brack left Longman just before this move, the importance of which he fully recognised. It provides the conclusion to this chapter.

～

Whatever changes there were in Britain during the twenty-one years from 1947 to 1968, there were even bigger changes abroad. Heavily tied

---

85 Notes on Longman, 1948, 7 March 1985. Brack visited Ambleside for the last time on 18 March 1948. Oaklands nearby was still being used for warehousing.

86 *Longmans in Harlow*, p.9. See also the *Architectural Review*, 'Publisher's Office, Harlow, Oct. 1968, pp.251ff., with sketches of the exterior and interior.

A stamp designed for the
British Empire Exhibition of
1924

The British Library Philatelic Collection

as Longmans, Green then was to the colonial book trade, it was faced with new, unprecedented situations as it confronted the post-war transformation of the colonies into new independent countries, a protracted and complex process, with no two colonial situations quite the same. The year 1924 had been that of a great Empire Exhibition, opened (with a broadcast) by King George V. The twenty-one years from 1947 to 1968 saw the dissolution of empire.

In changing circumstances, English language teaching (*ELT*) publishing, already mentioned, stands out as the great link between pre- and post-war Longman history; and it was through its imaginative enterprise as a producer of textbooks for the teaching and learning of English as a foreign and second language that Longmans, Green, with *ELT* as its 'powerhouse division', moved with the changing times into European and Latin American markets and into the Anglophone countries of what quickly came to be called 'the developing' or 'third' world.[87]

To back its overseas enterprise, Longmans, Green, faced with strong competition, particularly from Macmillan and the Oxford University Press, needed to be influential in English language studies in Britain itself and in the preparation of dictionaries and of reference works. In the 1960s it also developed a strong list of titles in Linguistics and Applied Linguistics, with distinguished books appearing in the *Longman Linguistics Library* and the *English Language Series*. Its strength in these fields was of immense importance, for as the British Empire dwindled, it left behind a shared language which itself, as Longman lexicographers were the first to realise, had never ceased to change. Longmans, Green was helped in its task by the British Council, founded in 1934 but not given a Royal Charter of Incorporation until 1940.

Without the Second World War it is doubtful whether the Council's deeply committed Chairman, Lord Lloyd, with the support of Sir Rex Leeper at the Foreign Office, could have persuaded the Government to provide funds for language development, and the Council was often to be subjected to arbitrary government cuts in the future. Motives for supporting (or attacking) it varied. Leeper, head of the Political Intelligence Department of the Foreign Office, was one of the first officials in Britain to interest himself in propaganda, a word which acquired new force during the Second World War and, even more, during the Cold War which followed it. Yet propaganda was an unpopular word in Whitehall, and during the 1950s and 1960s there was no talk of propaganda when the teaching of English as a foreign language became one of the Council's key priorities in

87 See A. Pettigrew and R. Whipp, *Managing Change for Competitive Success* (1991), p.153.

one of the most lively periods in its history. Its motto then, wrote Bernard Levin, the talkative and controversial music-loving reviewer and columnist, might well have been one of Samuel Johnson's definitions of publishing – 'spreading the word'.[88]

'The English Language Abroad' was the title of a special article in the Council's Report for 1960. Concerned as it was – more broadly – with the future of the written word and with the 'culture of the book', as it was now beginning to be called, the Council staged no fewer than 143 book exhibitions in 1968 and issued five and a half million books from its scattered libraries to 300,000 registered readers from a stock of two million. Many of them were learning English from Longman textbooks, and Longmans, Green were the publishers of the Council's own series *Writers and their Work*. Five years later, the Council's annual report devoted a whole section to *ELT*, now so-named, and British education overseas. Thirty *ELT* experts had joined the Council's staff between 1962 and 1965, and at the third Commonwealth Education Conference in 1964 Britain's offer to provide a further thirty posts by 1970 was accepted.[89]

John Chapple and the young Tom Openda in Nairobi. Openda went on to become Managing Director of Longman Kenya, having joined Longman in 1967

Longman Archive

The creation of a Longman *ELT* section was a climax, therefore, as much as a beginning. Since the time of J.W. Allen, Longman agents, still not called managers, were active on the periphery – or rather the peripheries (no two were alike) – of the Empire, not usually called the Commonwealth until after the end of the Second World War. It was then, in 1948, that Higham and Chapple, who figure prominently in this and the next chapter, set out on a world tour to Australia and New Zealand via the Middle East, Singapore and Malaya, returning via Fiji, Central America, including Mexico and Venezuela, California, New York and Toronto. Wherever they went, they made contact both with their agents or managers and with booksellers, assisted throughout by the British Council, which everywhere entertained them. It was a source of satisfaction and a challenge that everywhere, as Higham put it, the demand for books seemed 'insatiable'.[90]

~

88 F. Donaldson, *The British Council: The First Fifty Years* (1984): review of Donaldson's book in *The Observer*, 9 Dec. 1984.

89 The British Council, *Annual Report, 1964–1965* (1966), p.17.

90 'Round the World, April 7th 1948 – September 25th 1948', an account by Higham in the Longman Archive, 27 Oct. 1948.

A Higham survey of overseas business, dated 6 September, 1957, told the story in some detail of what had happened in Africa since 1935, the year of the last of the periodic visits there of Allen, who had always relied on influential advisers on the spot. Higham was keen to establish permanent agents, the first of them G.C. Darton, 'educational traveller', already mentioned in a different context, who in the midst of the upheavals of 1940 was sent out to Africa to look for markets and to establish new contacts. He stayed on as manager, now described as such, of a largely autonomous Longman business in Cape Town with its own profit-and-loss-account, seeing through a policy of decentralisation in Africa. He visited Nyasaland, as Malawi then was, and Northern and Southern Rhodesia as Zambia and Zimbabwe then were, and started a new *Pathfinder* series which he hoped to market throughout the whole of Africa.

Another of Darton's initiatives, introduced years earlier in India, was to float local editions and to produce far more books in vernacular languages. Back in London, his tactics were considered wise. 'We have an expensive establishment in South Africa', Higham wrote, 'but it must be remembered that they are relieving us of a vast programme of production work.' That was a way of putting it that would have sounded odd ten years later, but Higham clearly had his fellow Directors in mind: they were deeply concerned with the difficult conditions of post-war publishing in Britain as long as paper rationing survived and, with it, restrictive practices in printing.

Higham was interested in West Africa also in 1957, recognising Longman's 'very great potentialities'. When Longman's *New Method Readers*, already mentioned, were introduced from India *via* London, they had been very successful there; and although they were now being 'ousted' by an OUP series, that was a challenge rather than an obstacle for Higham:

'The very large number of the population, the comparative wealth of the area (oil palm, cocoa, etc) and the policy of mass literacy, promise a great development of potential business. We must do all we can to keep in the forefront of business here, and especially today when we have many rivals.'

Allen had visited West Africa in 1930 and appointed a respected local adviser, and Higham had followed this visit up five years later. Meanwhile, turnover had risen from £2,740 in 1930 to £7,345 in 1935 and £16,528 in 1945. By 1948 the figure was £68,512. Turnover for Nigeria, without oil, was then only just ahead of the Gold Coast. The main distributors were missionary bookshops.

Political change was rapid, particularly in the Gold Coast, which became independent and acquired a new name, Ghana, in 1957, and the speed of change and the political thrust behind it created a situation which favoured Macmillan and Co., still family run, which had in Harold Macmillan a publisher who was also a leading politician. In consequence, issues that had been raised in Ireland in the nineteenth century were raised afresh – state sponsorship of publishing and printing; the effects of monopoly on the planning of the curriculum; and the power of politicians to influence the actions of publishers.

Until 1962, when Longman set up a company in Ghana, Wilma Gladstone, a civil servant with an educational background, had been responsible inside the Ghanaian Ministry of Education for the preparation of primary and middle-school syllabuses and the chairmanship of a Textbook Committee. She was now replaced by Service Addo, a change that was accompanied by a complete revision in official procedures. Until 1962 all publishers had always been notified of government intentions to change syllabuses: now they were not. Only Macmillan knew what was happening, and the authors it employed to produce new national textbooks were largely drawn from the Ministry of Education.

A year later a State Publishing Corporation was proposed 'with the supply of the country's textbook needs as its main purpose', but Longmans, Green, who had offered help with training and in other matters, was not consulted. Its company in Ghana had never been allowed to trade under its own name, and it now had to close down its warehouse. Meanwhile, the State Publishing Company was 'rendered almost completely impotent' in 1964 after Harold Macmillan, then Prime Minister, met the Ghanaian President Kwame Nkrumah at a Commonwealth Conference, and put forward alternative publishing proposals to him, ensuring its grip on the lucrative primary-school textbook market for the next five years.

'Had the State monopoly in book supply not been set up', Longmans, Green concluded, 'there is no doubt that by now publishers would have introduced a [warehousing] system similar to that pertaining in Nigeria, where supply problems do not exist.' Nigeria now became a model for

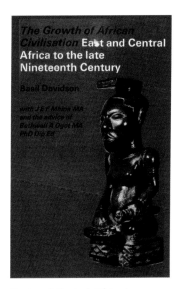

*East and Central Africa to
the Late Nineteenth Century,*
Basil Davidson, with J.E.F
Minha, and Bethwell A. Ogot,
published by Longmans
Nairobi, 1967

BL x 709/6183

Longmans, Green, who praised its leaders for 'eschewing' the idea of state publishing. They operated there as an indigenous company, which in the first nine years of its existence contributed £250,000 in taxes to the Nigerian government.[91]

In East Africa, where for many reasons political progress was slower than in West Africa, missionary shops remained the distributors of Longmans, Green and other books. Turnover in Longmans, Green books rose from £399 in 1930 to £1,688 in 1935, £3,655 in 1945 and £20,955 in 1948 and even under this régime books were published locally in the Swahili and Luganda languages, with the co-operation of the Society for Promoting Christian Knowledge, the old Rivington ally. In Nairobi there was a separate arrangement with the Church Missionary Society, by which the Society commissioned books with a guaranteed first order for East Africa, and Longmans, with its imprints, paid a royalty on all sums received from sales outside East Africa. The series included along with Swahili readers, *Highway Guides*, in English and Swahili, a *Highway Nature Guide*, and a *Geography of East Africa*, also in English and Swahili.

Higham concluded his 1957 survey of overseas business by giving gross turnover figures in 'overseas trade', not categorized, for selective years only: £52,000 in 1930, £251,000 in 1946 and £437,000 in 1948. These figures, he rightly stated, despite changes in the value of money and concomitant rises in prices, meant 'a very real increase in overseas business'. He provided no more up-to-date figures, however, although he was writing in 1957.[92] Nor did he focus on Europe or the United States.

The position in the United States was unsatisfactory. During the depressed 1930s Longman had cut down its distinctively American enterprise, settling in 1932 for an operating arrangement with Coward-McCann, a four-year-old business, at 55 Fifth Avenue. All shipping, billing and general office services of the two businesses were handled jointly. Not surprisingly, therefore, a generation later, in 1953, a letter signed by Blagden, possibly prompted by Longman authors, raised the question as to why Longmans, Green did not sell more specialist books in the United States and Canada. 'We publish a large number of books which our New York and Toronto Houses automatically order in small quantities as *wholesaling importers* would order.' If wholesalers in Britain were to be used and advertising done through Blackwells in Oxford 'we would certainly increase our sales in this market: we cannot, any how, do worse than we have with a *General Service List'.*[93]

Blagden stated that he was writing with the support of colleagues in

---

91   'Publishing in Ghana', an unsigned memorandum, April 1969.

92   'A Survey of Overseas Business', 6 Sept. 1957.

93   Note, 'The American and Canadian Market', 14 Dec. 1953.

Australia and India, and early in 1954 Potter wrote to Mills, still operating in New York, passing on these worries. 'If we had no New York house, we should of course circularise all our important books to potential customers on our side. It looks, then, as if the fact that we have a house in America, so far from being a bull point, from the view of an author may in fact be a bear point.'[94] In retrospect, it seems curious that there was so little interest in American opportunities when the sense of an African opportunity was so strong. In fact, it was a major failing at this period in Longman history, and Blagden's letter was much to the point, as Potter had realised. When Longmans, Green Inc. was wound up in the early 1960s Longmans, Green then sold all the rights in its books to American publishers until a new Longman Inc. was incorporated within the USA in April 1973. From that time development in America became a high priority for Longman as is described in the following two chapters.

~

It was on the African periphery that some of the most interesting Longman figures emerged in the 1950s and 1960s. Some had their own origins in education.

They found a model in W.P. (Bill) Kerr, an extrovert Scot who had joined Longmans, Green after Oxford in 1948. He left an indelible mark in Africa, where he began by managing, with great success, Longmans South Africa Pty Ltd, by then a wholly owned subsidiary, returning to London as head of the African and Caribbean operations of Longmans, Green in 1961, and joining the Longmans, Green Board three years later. This was a position which gave him ample scope to move from one African country to another during the 1960s, meeting people and setting up a cluster of new companies.

The warmth of Kerr's personality and his publishing drive inspired many other Longmans, Green managers, yet his drive was sometimes stronger than his judgement. As Colin Hayes, another recruit to the House, who met him at Grosvenor Street, wrote, 'his [Kerr's] approach to people on first acquaintance was always full-frontal'. It was not a coincidence that as a schoolboy he had decided to become a publisher after reading James Agate's *Ego*.[95]

One of the most remarkable men inspired by him was Julian Rea, who started his career with Longman in 1961 as representative in Nigeria, having been an Education Officer and an Inspector of Schools in Ghana. He became a Director of the recently founded 'local company', Longman Nigeria, in 1965, three years before returning to Britain to become Joint Managing Director of a new Africa and Caribbean Division alongside

94 Letter from K.B. Potter to E.E. Mills, 1 Feb. 1954.

95 For his later career, below, p.453.

Henry McWilliam ('Mac'), a highly gifted publisher, who also produced a scholarly history of technical colleges in Ghana. David Mortimer, who had joined Longmans as a trainee, had briefly preceded Rea in Nigeria before returning to Britain in 1964 in the *ELT* section of the business, becoming its Senior Publisher and later Divisional Managing Director.

On a different point on the periphery, Derek Adkins took charge of Longmans, Far East, the first new Longmans company, established 'from scratch' in Hong Kong. In October 1957 he had produced for the Board an extremely interesting two-page 'Memorandum on Organisation with Particular Reference to Overseas Sales' described by him as an 'objective interim report on the need for reorganisation'. The sale of Longmans books abroad depended, his memorandum stated, on 'an efficient and aggressive selling organisation'. It would have to concern itself (a) with 'getting orders' (promotion) and (b) with executing them (trade), and it would have to cover booksellers, schools, colleges, universities, teacher training establishments and their libraries, and 'educational specialists, including departments of education, literary bureaus [*sic*], etc'.

There was something of a gap at that time and later, as there had been for generations, between production and sales, but Adkins clearly recognised the need to coordinate them. The activities associated with promotion, his memorandum suggested, should be the responsibility of an area manager and those under trade should be the responsibility of an export sales manager, and it would always be necessary to ensure that there was effective coordination between the two. There would also have to be export trade managers in London, dealing operationally with all orders and trade queries.

The memorandum also made more detailed practical recommendations, based on experience, relating to the supply of credit facilities – and on what terms – to booksellers, to invoices (there should be tally cards with invoice numbers), and to ledger accounts using the same number. The booksellers' tally cards should be returned to the area manager after the records section had dealt with them so that the names of booksellers ordering in sufficient numbers to justify their turnover being regularly recorded could be identified. The Mailing Department, 'the life-blood of the ... business', should be divorced from advertising and become a separate department with a trained executive in charge. It was 'so supremely important that it deserve[d] the most careful supervision and attention to detail[96].

~

---

96 Memorandum, 10 Oct. 1957. Adkins quoted *The Bookseller*, 5 Oct. 1957, where there were requests from booksellers in Copenhagen, Bulawayo, Tel Aviv, London, Perth and Lucknow to be added to publishers' mailing lists. The publishing of these requests may have stimulated Adkins's memorandum.

The year 1957 assumes importance in retrospect not only because it was the year when John Newsom joined Longmans, Green, but because of this and other memoranda including a document prepared by Higham for Potter, an 'educational budget', so headed, for 1957/8, which provides a fascinating insight into the economics and procedures of Longmans at the time when Newsom, commissioned by the Board, was setting out to reform them.

Covering new books and new editions, Higham's budget projected the gross total of expenditures at £219,000, an increase of £18,000 (9 per cent) on the total for 1956/7 in view of the increase in sales. This did not seem 'excessive', yet, as in the previous year, Higham doubted whether 'we could actually succeed in spending this total'. He was 'very worried' about the 'large amount of money' being 'locked up' in the editorial side of one venture, but in general, he concluded, there had been 'a more realistic approach to budgeting than usual'.

The document is interesting not only because of its references to budgeting or the guarded way in which the forecasts, initialled by Willie and Mark Longman, were set out but because it gave precise comparative figures of estimates made in the previous five years. Further figures related to increases or reductions for 'categories' of publications for 1957-8 (see table).

Longmans' Educational budgets,1953–8 (£)

Year	Estimate
1953-4	121,794
1954-5	134,608
1955-6	176,379
1956-7	201,623
1957-8	219,363

Longmans' Educational Categories, 1958 (£)

Changes	+	−
Primary	-	5,200
Category 6 (Secondary Modern)	12,055	-
Category 7 (Overseas trade)	14,485	-
Category 8	-	3,700
Category 9	100	-
Totals	26,640	8,900

Category 7 covered overseas books, and what Higham said about them went beyond budgetary figures. He noted, for example, that the people concerned with 'the large production programme' were 'reorganising' the

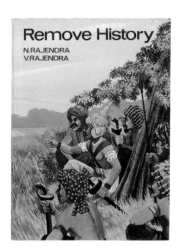

Lively secondary school publishing for Malaysia, 1969, following a new syllabus. In the *Longman House Magazine* (Spring 1964) the recently-returned Tim Rix wrote a description of the early years of Longman Malaysia. He recorded that fifty-one new titles had been published, with a very small staff, since the Company's registration in 1961

Personal collection

production process, and Malaya, later to be called Malaysia, was picked out as the country where there had been most progress: 'we now have a balanced publishing programme which covers the whole of the local (schools) syllabus'. The most important single series in the overseas list was a new three-year *Foundations of English* course (1956, by D. Hicks), in three volumes, an alternative to 'the ever-successful Eckersley'.

Among the home 'categories' listed in his table 'primary education' was distinguished from 'secondary modern' education (Category 6), the latter in the course of total reconstruction. The primary education budget was reduced, Higham stated, not because of any falling off in our 'planning', a word still not defined, but because it reflected the longer time necessary for editing and producing 'this type of book'. Work was 'actively proceeding on [a] fundamental reading scheme', but nothing would be completed in the budgetary period 1957/8. The upturn would come in the autumn of 1958. In secondary modern education, C.M. Bennett's *You and Your World* (1958), 'the first straightforward course' in this field, would be completed.

During this period the interests of those involved in schools publishing were concentrated on developing the newly created secondary market, and there was little new publishing for the primary market, but the arrival of Newsom, introduced to Potter by Basil Blackwell, in 1957 suggested in itself that the balance might change. With his distinguished educational and administrative experience, Newsom was now put in charge of Longmans educational publishing in the United Kingdom.[97]

There are other reasons too for the historian to focus on 1957. That was the year when Higham retired from the House, leaving a multitude of memories behind him. His great empire was now divided. John Chapple, briefly an assistant to Higham and thought of at first as his understudy, was now appointed as the Director responsible for overseas education, called upon to carry on the same basic policy as Higham had done, that of extending Longmans' publishing activities throughout the Commonwealth and the Third World. He was to do something far more than carrying on. For Philip Wallis, writing in 1974, he converted an evolutionary into a revolutionary process, making regular overseas visits, and working out[98] detailed arrangements for setting up local companies, sometimes before former colonial territories received their independence.

One part of the world where Chapple travelled regularly was the Middle East, especially to Egypt, which at one point, before Suez, accounted for 10 per cent of Longmans' total sales, and the Lebanon where Beirut was home to the headquarters of the Sayegh organisation, the Longmans agent in the Arab world, strong on the ground, and through its marketing dominant in *ELT* throughout the Arab World. Since 1945, when Khalil Sayegh, sensing,

97   Board of Directors, Minutes, 30 Oct. 1962. LA.

98   PW p.57.

without the help of formal education, the future importance of English in the Arab World, had written to Longmans, Green with proposals for expanding Longmans' sales in Lebanon, Syria, Jordan and Iraq, a remarkable partnership had flourished and there were significant new titles, starting with *New Method English for the Arab World* (1951). The most famous was *Living English for the Arab World* (1961) by Ralph Cooke and W. Stannard Allen (the latter the author of *Living English Structure* (1947), one of the top selling books in the whole of Longman history).

Khalil Sayegh's commitment to Longmans, Green was wholehearted, as was his commitment to Chapple personally, and in 1972, the twenty-fifth anniversary of the signing of the partnership agreement, the John Chapple Hall, a substantial expansion of the Librarie du Liban (the great Sayegh bookshop in Beirut), was named in his honour. Sadly it was to be destroyed during the Lebanon civil war when everything else, and not just publishing and bookselling, was under threat.

There was a direct link between Chapple and Potter, who stayed on the Board, a key figure, until his death in 1962. Chapple had served in the artillery under Potter during the Second World War. Before the War he had been a demonstrator at the Department of Botany in Oxford, and he was an expert on orchids. He was, indeed, the first member of the Longman Board to have taken a science degree, and to his death he remained an expert gardener. Once on the Board, Chapple, a powerful force, was committed to the growth of Longmans, Green, to the production of high quality books and, above all, to wide international (post-colonial) distribution.

Perhaps most important of all, he believed in training young graduate entrants to publishing. Two graduates a year were selected for a two-year period, with Roger Watson, David Mortimer, Jeremy Osborne and Andrew MacLennan conspicuous among the 'chosen few'. (A bright young Oxford graduate, James Kennaway, had been appointed earlier, and when he was forced to retire through ill health he was succeeded by Jocelyn Baines, a lively author, like Kennaway, who left the House to join the Thomson Group, afterwards soon becoming Managing Director of Nelsons.) Of the new recruits who stayed with the House, Watson was to become Managing Director of the UK Schools Division; Mortimer Managing Director of the *ELT* Division; Osborne, an Oxford history graduate, first employed in Uganda, International Sales Director of what had by then become the Longman Group; and MacLennan, who was anxious to avoid administrative entanglements, an outstanding history publisher, following in the wake of Blagden.

Chapple, watching over the individual fortunes of his new recruits, was concerned for the future of a business which had been changing hands while he was rising within it. There was a change of name to Longman too in 1969; from 1969 'Longmans, Green' became 'Longman'. Gruff and at times abrasive on the surface, in the words of his obituary

Tim Rix, Khalil Sayegh, and John Chapple in Egypt in the early 1970s

Sayegh, was a Christian Syrian who had started with less than nothing, but had an idea about which he wrote to a number of British publishers. Most did not reply. He was proposing to stock books for the teaching of English, and only Longmans offered him credit. In 1947 Chapple's assistant, Thomas Gill, went out to make contact and draw up agreements. The plane crashed, Gill was killed and all records were lost. Longmans honoured all the agreements on Sayegh's word, which Sayegh never forgot. The business grew until, around the 1970s, it was worth around £1m.

Personal collection

writer in *The Bookseller*, he was by temperament modest, even shy.[99] His role in the business after 1968 is described in the next chapter. It was a very different role from that of Newsom, who was never gruff or abrasive, but whose publishing career was only one strand in his remarkable life. It was from the heights – he would never have been an understudy – that he supervised the dramatic, but for many Longman employees traumatic, move of the Longman business in 1968 from Central London to Harlow New Town in Essex,[100] a move smoothly made in instalments. It was others who guaranteed the smoothness, but Newsom, like Gibberd, its architect, had a particular interest in Harlow. For him personally the move was a natural one. Neighbouring Hertfordshire was the county where he had been Chief Education Officer, appointed at the extraordinarily young age of twenty-nine.

Already before that he had been a regular army officer, a social worker and a publican, and it was in his position as Chief Education Officer that he had established a national reputation not only as an 'educationist', a word then coming into fashion, but as the man who commissioned architecturally modern school buildings that won worldwide acclaim. He is said to have travelled round Hertfordshire with a trumpet in one hand and a trowel in the other.[101] It was on the basis of this record that he was drawn not only into Longmans, Green but into national educational policy making. His name had been given to the official report on secondary education for the 'less able', *Half Our Future* (1968). It was one of the most widely read reports of its time.

There was a network of organisational as well as personal interconnections when Newsom became involved in the Longman story. Both the educational policies of the 1950s and 1960s and the idea of building (almost) completely 'new towns' – there was an 'Old Harlow' – were by-products of a post-war effort to make the country and, indeed, the world a better place than it had been before the Second World War. While the War lasted – and for a long time it never seemed likely to be about to end – there had been more than intimations that the post-war world would be very different from the pre-war (or inter-war) world, when the dynasty of Longman had established its twentieth-century reputation in the aftermath of the celebrations of its bi-centennial in 1924. With the

---

99 *The Bookseller*, 1990.

100 For plans and pictures of Harlow New Town see G.E. Cherry, *Urban Change and Planning* (1972), pp.166-70. See also *The Architectural Review*, Oct. 1968, 'Publishers' Office Harlow', pp.251ff., and Gibberd, 'The Master Design; Landscape; Housing; the Town Centres', in *New Towns, The British Experience* (Town and Country Planning Association, 1972), pp.88-102.

101 E. Boyle, *The Politics of Education: Edward Boyle and Anthony Crosland in Conversation with Maurice Kogan* (1971), p.24.

experiences of the Second World War in the background, the First World War, the 'Great War', faded into memory. And by the end of the 1970s the Second World War was fading into the memory also, or would have been had it not been kept alive by the media, particularly the BBC.

~

Changes in the vocabulary of the media, including the Press and broadcasting as well as book publishing, are interesting and revealing whether they relate to structures or procedures, and it is pertinent, therefore, that during the Newsom years, which ended with his relatively early death in 1971, the word 'policy' rather than the word 'strategy' was used to describe business moves in Longmans, Green as it was in the country. Four policy objectives were being identified in clear-cut language after 1962. They were 'to obtain a larger share of the British market', in which competition was stiffest, by 'widening the range of products, supported by better marketing and selling'; to create a 'new generation' of book titles for diversified overseas markets, including books in English and books by 'indigenous authors' writing in their own languages; to expand and develop materials for the teaching of English as a foreign language; and, not least important, 'to employ indigenous staff however and whenever possible in all overseas establishments'.

There were financial implications at every point in the implementation of such a policy, and some of them were set out, again in 1957, before Adkins produced his memorandum, by F.W. Tiller, the then Company Secretary, who proposed changes in the organisation of the Accounts Department, adding that he had discussed them previously with Potter. Subsidiary companies or 'branches' should regularly submit to the Board in London details of sales, production costs and overhead expenses and produce their own 'budgets' which the Board could then scrutinise. All Longmans, Green Directors 'should be given information on the financial and/or taxation implications of any proposal to be considered by the Board'.[102] A *qualified* deputy finance director (Tiller himself underlined the word) should be appointed to ensure that the Directors could be given the information required, and a more 'mechanised system' to present it in an accessible form should be introduced.[103] Through these moves the Company was

Catalogue cover of Longmans at the British Industrial Exhibition in Peking, 1964

Longman Archive

---

102 Accounts Department, Note by Tiller, 26 Aug. 1957.

103 Note of 4 Nov. 1957.

already preparing the way for the introduction of what would come to be called a 'corporate plan'.

In November 1957 Newsom himself prepared, as he had been asked to do, a 'preliminary survey' of 'administration' – the word 'management' was still used far less often then than it was to be later in publishing or in education – 'with special reference to the relationship between the Directors and the senior executives', promising more papers to come.[104] He started with an historical survey:

> The over-all picture seems to me to be of a small firm which, until the War, employed about ninety people with three Directors and a static or only slowly rising turnover which has become, in post-war years, a very much larger undertaking both in terms of turnover and, consequently, in terms of staff. Indeed, the growth has been so phenomenal – even allowing for the depreciation of the £ ... that a quite drastic change in the method by which the firm conducts its business is needed.

For Newsom, who did not use the word 'family', 'drastic change' depended above all on the role of the Directors. For him it was an 'occupational disease' of Directors to interfere with matters properly delegated to executives, and while the Directors of Longmans, Green and Co. were 'not aloof from detail, ... they must avoid at all costs getting bogged down in it'.

Familiar as he was with educational administration, Newsom believed also that it was wrong of directors to become involved in the details of business assigned to their other directorial colleagues. They should work 'as a group and accept a group responsibility', and here he looked upwards 'rather in the same way as the Cabinet [did]'. Newsom doubtless had the higher Civil Service in mind when he added that individual executives possessed 'a technical or professional skill not necessarily possessed by the Board', although he recognised that there were many exceptions to this generalisation.

Newsom's point of view was always closer to that of a higher civil servant than to that of a businessman. For all his value to the House of Longman, he never understood the financial routines of business – for example, the basic difference between cash flow and profit. Moreover, while he could and did handle individual authors he took little interest in the non-educational side of publishing; and 'Books for Schools', an educational venture of his own, operating through a consortium, not instigated by Longmans, Green staff, but made possible only by assistance from them, quickly faded away. Perhaps most seriously, he did not appreciate the immense opportunities in publishing for universities, which were undergoing great changes at the very time when he was concerned with change at the secondary-school level.

6 & 7 Clifford Street taken from the cover of the Longmans Catalogue for 1960. The Clifford Street lease became available when the building's use as a hostel for American Officers came to an end. The building work took three years to complete and Longmans moved in in 1947. This catalogue cover was designed by Tim Jaques, who later designed the new colophon

Longman Archive

---

104 Note of 4 Nov. 1957.

The two, indeed, were interconnected. The Robbins Report on the future of higher education appeared in the same year as *Half Our Future*.[105] In consequence, the entrepreneurial drive of Longmans, Green & Co. – the Green was now completely silent – came, as we have seen, not from the centre but from the periphery.

From a British vantage point 'the present Board', Newsom argued, 'did not fulfil the classic role' that he had outlined, but this, he felt, was 'not necessarily a bad thing in itself': 'disaster not infrequently follows any attempt to make tidiness of administrators the dominant factor in the organisation of an undertaking'. The 'only thing' that mattered was that 'we should be as efficient as we can'. The Longmans, Green business was not. There was duplication at the top. The fact that Mark and Michael Longman, the latter soon to leave the Company, although no one then foresaw this,[106] combined executive and directorial responsibilities disturbed their staff. It also provided them with 'heavier guns' than they should have had as publishers within their own business. There was a puckish note here, as there often was in what Newsom said or wrote, even a hint of indiscretion.

W. Stannard Allen's *Living English Structure* was an enormously successful practice book for foreign students. It was first published in 1947 and the fifth edition was published in 1974

BL 12987.aa.17

Meanwhile, according to Newsom, Potter by reason of his seniority was involving himself in matters that did not lie within his particular purview, and Brack was performing functions as a Director which should properly have been discharged by an executive. It was 'of paramount importance that staff should not trot around from one Director to another to find one who will support their course of action'. Chapple and he himself were still 'too newly fledged to have acquired any sins (or virtues)', although this might not be generally agreed.

Newsom was 'pulling no punches', he went on, as he suggested an alternative, if not a very different and a far from radical, distribution of responsibilities. William from his 'accumulated wisdom and experience' should handle any problem he wished: he should stay just as he was. (What else could Newsom have written?) Potter by reason of his seniority should deal with 'general issues of policy', while concerning himself specifically with broad financial issues and public relations. Michael Longman should stick to religious publications and try to establish European links. (This was a rare reference to Europe, which, of course, had always been a centre of theological studies.)

Mark Longman, guardian of the future of the family, should understudy Potter on finance and act as a 'fire brigade in emergencies', for example in Hong Kong, the one outpost which Newsom mentioned up to

---

105 In a four-page supplement, which included a report of the Newsom Press Conference on the report, *The Times Educational Supplement*, 18 Dec. 1963, headed the first page 'A longer school life and a longer school day'.

106 See above, p.396.

this point, and the outpost where Adkins, the first Longman 'Mandarin of the East',[107] made his mark. He, Mark, should then spend a smaller proportion of his time on general publishing, which he liked best, while continuing to devote most time to 'the wide field of public relations'.

Chapple should be in charge of production and distribution in all foreign territories, with specific areas excluded, notably Australia and New Zealand, and Newsom himself should deal with home education and 'general administration', the latter inextricably interlocked with the duties of the Personnel Director. Newsom was the first person in the House to use the word 'personnel' rather than 'staff', as Brack, now so scheduled, noted with some distaste. In Brack's newly defined post he should 'leave more' to Joyce Nairn, Newsom urged, and she should be given a title, which she eventually was, that of Assistant Personnel Manager.

Adrian Beckett, not Brack, should be responsible for Clifford Street and for the move of the warehousing to Harlow, including the allocation of space there and the purchase and distribution of equipment. Somewhat surprisingly, however, Beckett was also to be responsible for 'all cars owned by the firm and for the problems connected with their use' – Brack was deeply interested in cars! – and was to have access to the Board: no proposals for new procedures or for structural re-organisation should be pursued until his views had been taken into account. He should 'know something of the whole picture', at least concerning the Company's policy in terms of 'publishing, production, advertising, etc.'. Among his colleagues he should be *primus inter pares*.

Newsom did not suggest that Beckett should be their 'boss', but even in the one area, personnel, where the General Manager was himself responsible to someone else, it would nevertheless be Beckett's responsibility to deal with all matters of testimonials, references, arrangements for and follow-up of interviews; and he, and no one 'above him', should be responsible for appointments of, say, below £600 a year. Newsom went further. While not being burdened with publishing policy, Beckett should preside at meetings responsible for publication dates, and, along with Potter, supervise any new system of budgetary control, at the same time measuring and defining the scale and quality of services to be provided.

This long list of varied duties prescribed by Newsom, which included 'sorting out muddles with other departments', including warehousing, incorporated some duties which Newsom should have allotted to himself had he re-examined his own role as carefully as he did the roles of his colleagues. He felt bound to end it with a plea that the General Manager should not be overwhelmed by regular, routine work. Consequently, he should have at his disposal 'a small and highly competent staff'. This was a doubtful recommendation. Beckett was being given a place which he

---

107 *The Log*, No.3 (1975). For *The Log*, a house journal. (LA Part II 213)

scarcely deserved, and it was not certain how he would handle it. He was a delightful person to know, with obvious intellectual talent and cultured tastes – he had previously worked for the publisher John Lehmann – but he did not find it easy to make up his mind about crucial issues. He procrastinated. He dealt badly, as Newsom himself did, with the warehousing side of the business, especially with industrial relations at the 'Distribution Centre' at Pinnacles in Harlow.

~

Newsom concluded his memorandum not with personalities but with procedures, going into considerable detail. The procedure for signing cheques, for example, was 'archaic by the standards of modern enterprise': and it should certainly not form part of financial control. The 'letter book' should be purely functional and be treated as a departmental record and seen only by the Director ultimately responsible for the affairs of the department. There was a place there and elsewhere for 'substitute Directors' who could serve in the Director's absence for whatever reason, but their role should cease as soon as the Director concerned returned.

A handbook of procedures, the last in a long series going back into the nineteenth century, signed by Beckett but not written by him, survives from 1959. Working hours were now from 9 a.m. to 5.30 p.m. and 'sickness' and 'accidents' were dealt with in separate memoranda. The routines memorandum was divided into five parts, the first dealing with House regulations, the second with general office routines (this included a sub-section called 'Common Sense'), the third with 'the routine of seeing books through the Press', the fourth with sales promotion routine, and the fifth with 'reprinting and record cards'. Beckett emphasised in his introduction that 'at every level' in publishing 'small details' had to be 'watched with the greatest care'. This was particularly true of Longmans, Green 'because there are so many people in the firm doing different jobs rather than a lot of people doing the same job'. Instructions were necessary. 'People have put flower pots on the window sill [!]; notes and memoranda are only too often unsigned and undated [an old complaint that the historian more than anyone would stress]; and the filing system is from time to time grossly abused.'

All incoming mail had to have a date stamp on it as soon as it arrived. Outgoing mail with an enclosure in it had to be marked 'enclosure'. Internal post from 'department to department' – the term used – would be collected regularly several times a day. For senior staff initials could be used. (This was a privilege.) Every letter sent out internally or externally should have at least one carbon copy. Papers for filing should be marked in blue pencil. Cables and telegrams should be typed in triplicate, two copies for the Central Services Department who would send them. 'When answering the telephone, always give your name. NEVER NEVER lift the receiver and say "hallo"[*sic*].'

There was no hint of computing in the whole set of instructions.

The need for 'economy' was recognised but not emphasised. Within the building electric light had to be switched off unless needed and taps turned off after use. The lift could be used only for journeys of more than three floors. The most contentious set of instructions related to authors, and the surviving copy of the memorandum shows that changes had been made in the section headed 'charging'. 'A free specimen copy of a book being sent to a representative or an inquirer for sales promotion purposes should be CHARGED TO WORK ... If you want to give someone a book as a gift because they have helped Longmans in some way, type a slip to duplicate in the same way, but CHARGE TO PRESENTATION.' In the first draft the words THE HOUSE were used, not PRESENTATION.[108]

Longmans House Magazine
spring 1964

The happiest link with the past read: 'You may buy Longmans' Books at a Discount by asking for and paying for them in the Showroom. You may also buy other publishers' books at a discount through Trade Department.' These 'arrangements', it was added, perhaps gratuitously, 'are a privilege [the second time that the word was used] and are meant for your own benefit: they are NOT to be used as a means of getting books cheaply for a large circle of friends and relations.' No evidence is easily available as to how many employees took advantage of the opportunity.

~

In 1959 a House magazine, apparently the first in Longmans history, planned at first to appear twice a year, provides evidence of a different kind about the daily life of Longmans employees before the move to Harlow. It was called at first *Sixes and Sevens* and in 1961, after the move to Grosvenor Street, *Longmanship*, 'by divine inspiration of John Guest'. Its first editors, D. Bristow (Social Activities), L.A. Carter (Publishing Matters) and Miss P. Craft (Staff Matters), noted how the Longmans Directors demurred at the title *Sixes and Sevens*. 'Would it not give the impression', they asked, 'that we concentrated exclusively on the books in the categories so numbered – Home and Overseas Educational Books – and [an alternative question] that we admitted to an habitual state of chaos?'

There was, in fact, another reason, and the editors stood firm by their own intentions. 'Subversive mutterings to the effect that neither inference could properly be classified as fictional have now been silenced by managerial squads, and the title has been agreed on, *strictly* because of its

---

108 Royalties were paid to the author if a book was given away (Presentation); if it was 'Charged to Work', for promotion purposes, the author was not paid.

allusion to the address of Clifford Street headquarters.' It was '*not* another catalogue', they went on. Their assumption was 'that most people in the widely scattered and ever-growing Longmans organization are interested in what other fellows [*sic*] are doing... .'[109]

When the name of the magazine was changed to *Longmanship*, its first editor complained of 'apathy at home' – his magazine did not seem to have 'annoyed anyone' – but he was delighted that it was welcomed overseas. It had also won the praise of *Smith's Trade News*. In the fourth number an evocative article, taken from *The Bookseller*, was published describing the official opening by Eccles of 48 Grosvenor Street.[110] It was Eccles himself, not Longmans, Green, who in his speech provided the relevant statistics. From selling 2¼ million books in 1945 Longman had raised the figure to 15 million. Exports to the East had increased thirty-five times and to the Middle East six times.

Eccles added that although he knew that it was not easy to get people to read books, he did not share the pessimistic views sometimes attributed to the Publishers' Association. 'The desire for knowledge was far greater than it used to be, as were the means by which knowledge could be acquired.' Within a few years 'the book trade would come very much into its own again'. Another speech at the opening was made by Blackwell, speaking as a bookseller and publisher, who described Longman's 'resurgence' after 1945 as 'one of the wonders of the post-war book trade'. The opening ceremony ended with Mark presenting the two speakers with copies of the recent and sumptuous Longmans' production, *The Orchard and Fruit Garden*.

In the same number of *Longmanship* Virginia Carrick described 'scouting for Longmans', revealing how well she knew how to deal with agents and how to deal equally well with Mark. There was also a section called 'News from Overseas' which started with Kuala Lumpur and with the arrival there in March 1961 of Tim Rix who had 'come to stay'. Among the photographs – and *Longmanship* was a costly production – was a picture of Lady Elizabeth Longman taken at Grosvenor Street with a group of staff who had already moved out to Harlow. No fewer than 120 of them had attended a Grosvenor Street party.

Covers of *Longmanship* (Spring and Autumn 1962) and *Sixes and Sevens* (Spring 1959) and the *Longman House Magazine*, (Spring 1964). Leo Cooper and Tim Rix were editors at different times

Longman Archive

---

109 *Sixes & Sevens*, Longmans' House Journal, Spring 1959, p.1. (LA Part II/206)

110 *Longmanship*, No.4, Longman's House Magazine, Spring 1962; *The Bookseller*, 6 May 1961. (LA Part II/207)

In 1958 Longmans celebrated
the centenary of the first
publication of *Gray's Anatomy*,
at the Stationers' Hall. In
this photograph from *Sixes
and Sevens* (Spring 1959) the
Chairman of Longmans, Mr.
W. Longman has, on his right
Professor Johnston, editor of
Gray since 1930, and on his left
is Professor Vaughan Davies,
who collaborated in preparing
the new 32nd edition

Longman Archive

Longmanship always found a prominent place for parties and for
visitors. It also described many visits overseas, like one by Philip Wallis,
then Production Manager, whose flight to Hong Kong took seventeen hours.
Wallis had also written an article, 'The Publisher's Year' in the first number
of *Sixes and Sevens* which included an account of the official opening of the
Hong Kong branch in July 1958. From the start the branch had an entirely
Chinese staff apart from Adkins, the 'local manager', who introduced Wallis
on his arrival to the 'three young men who were under Derek's supervision
in his Production Department'. The literal translation of Longman as
pronounced in Cantonese meant 'Bright-as-the-moon literature'.[111]

There were then about five hundred printers in Hong Kong, only half-
a-dozen of them book printers, but they were already working on a shift
system and turning out millions of copies of bound books. New plant and
machinery were being installed. New technology and lower costs were giving
Hong Kong a differential advantage over older printing centres. Yet it was
not only Hong Kong that impressed Wallis. On his brief stops at Singapore
and Kuala Lumpur on his return, he had interesting conversations with
David Yeoman, installed in a bungalow as first resident representative in
the Far East in 1952 before moving to Singapore in September 1955, where
a new office was opened. (Potter had been an earlier visitor, spending three
weeks in Malaysia and Singapore before going on to Australia.)

Wallis's return trip included Beirut, where he met Khalil Sayegh,
and he arrived back in Britain feeling that he could appreciate more clearly
some of the problems with which 'our Houses overseas' are beset, but
feeling too that although London was everywhere 'held in high regard',
there was no doubt that 'London has a lot to learn from them'.[112]

~

There were many comings and goings between 1957 and 1962, but it was
not until 1962 that the first real reorganisation of the business took place.
In October of that year Newsom and Chapple, having asked sensibly for
explicit 'service agreements' relating to themselves, were made Joint
Managing Directors, the former to serve until the age of 65, the latter to the
age of 67; and the tenure of Brack, assisted by Joyce Nairn, was extended
to the age of 69.

Service arrangements were also made for forty-three employees

111 *Ibid.*, p.16.

112 This number of *Longmanship*, Autumn 1962, pp.2, 4, 8, also included two
     pages on the successions of imprints of the House of Longman and an
     article on 'The Burning of the Row', consisting of extracts from the Brack
     diaries. *Sixes and Sevens* included an article on 'Longmans in Ghana', where
     there was a 'permanent rep', George Preston, and on Pakistan, where S.G.
     Clutton had established an office and showroom in Lahore in July 1957. (LA
     Part II/206 and 207)

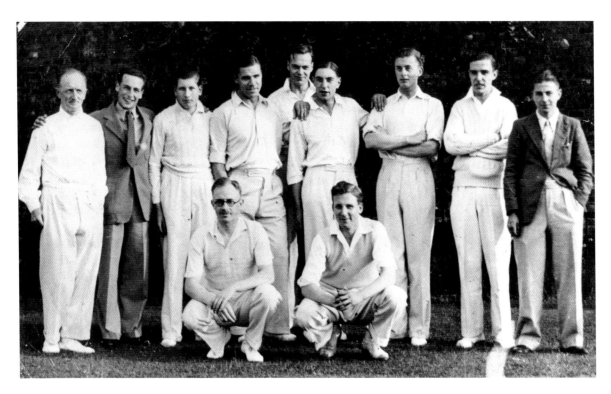

working at Grosvenor Street, including Beckett, Nairn, Wallis and J.R.C. Yglesias (1914–1998). The most recently appointed of them was Yglesias, who had been brought into the business by Newsom mainly to supervise publishing for the expanding secondary modern school market. Wallis, whose memories went back furthest, had joined the House in 1929, when the staff at Paternoster Row numbered around a hundred, many of whom had served with Kelk and Frisby. Authors' accounts were then handled by five members of staff, and trade ledger accounts by E.V.B. Smith, who proved so difficult – as Company Secretary – during the Second World War years at Wimbledon.

Nine members of staff and as many packers as were necessary had then handled country sales. For London sales, booksellers' 'bag men' would call at the counter to collect their books in sacks as they had done in the nineteenth century, paying cash if they did not have an account. Stock control was still in the hands of A.R. Cutbush: it was the subject of two extremely meticulous memoranda of 1961 by an unidentified trainee. This first memorandum, dated February 1961, began with the words 'So many people and departments nibble away the mound of stock of a new book that it would seem an impossible task to integrate these diverse uses into a polished essay'.[113] It was.

The pre-war Longmans cricket team, which included Mark Longman (standing third from the right)

Longman Archive

---

113   Memorandum sent to Brack by F.E. Atkinson, years later in June 1968.

Both the trainee and Wallis referred admiringly to Arthur Stanton, the Sales Director who had been picked out by Brack during the Second World War when Stanton was a provincial sales representative. A considerable figure in the wider publishing world, he had a remit which included educational books, later to involve his son Dennis.

It was a formidable woman, however, Pam Troughton, who then decided which books educational representatives should carry around with them. The 'reps', with a long history behind them, remained an indispensable element in the Longmans 'labour force': they were not allowed to sell books, although they might offer teachers a 'free' sample copy ('Charge to Work') which the teacher could keep if the title was ordered as a class set. This prevented the educational publishers' representatives from harassing teachers. Teachers sent their order in to their supplier. 'Trade' books, i.e. those sold through Trade 'reps', on the other hand did take orders from booksellers.(Bookshops did not then generally stock school books.) No two 'reps' were quite the same, but they were conscious of a group identity.

Six out of the forty-three employees identified by Wallis in 1961 went on to work at Harlow, and seventeen of them, including Adkins and Rix, worked overseas, with Rix returning to London at the end of 1963, later to become Joint Managing Director in Harlow (with Yglesias) in 1972. A short 'special list' of six included Blagden. Each of the full-time Directors was now given charge of 'a particular section of the Company's activities', with named 'administrative heads' responsible to them – M.J.A. Hoare to Mark Longman in General Publishing, Yglesias to Newsom for Home Educational Publishing; Kerr and J.A.E. Higham, Overseas Manager, to Chapple. The younger Higham was the son of Charles and had joined the House in 1956. He left it in 1975 to join the venerable American House of Wiley.

In his role as the Director in charge of General Administration, Newsom, whose many outside commitments entailed that he should be given the strongest possible support, had by his side Beckett and P.B. Hepburn, a recently appointed Sales Manager, who had worked for the Booksellers Association and had been sales director at Allen Lane's Penguin. His role at Longmans was ill-defined and in 1975 he was to take early retirement. Wallis was Production Manager, with a substantial degree of control, and P. Meade, the Chief Accountant, was responsible to Newsom and not to Godfrey Phillips, a managing director of Lazards and a man of exceptional talents, who had just joined the Board as a non-executive financial adviser. He had secured first class honours in the Cambridge Law Tripos and had been President of the Union. He was part author of the standard law textbook (E.C.S.) Wade and Phillips, *Constitutional Law* (1931) that was published by Longmans. He died in 1965 and was succeeded on the Longman Board by a Lazards Partner, Daniel Meinertzhagen.

Four area sales executives, dealing with specified overseas areas, were responsible to Hepburn, though with considerable freedom to act on their

own, with a 'punch card' system for sales statistics and analyses, but as yet
no computerisation. It was difficult, therefore, to estimate profit month
by month. There were other gaps too in providing the Board with better
and quicker management information. Hepburn himself was responsible
for overall control of advertising, assisted by an advertising manager, at
a time when publishers' advertising policies varied considerably. The
Longmans budget was not high. Nor was it then exceptional in this: as J.A.
Sutherland observed in his book *Fiction and the Fiction Industry* (1978), in
1974 the book trade spent on advertising only one-sixth of what the record
industry spent.

Soon, however, the modes of book advertising, some of it dubbed
'American', were to vary as much as the modes of printing, which were
handled by Wallis with a staff organised in sections, including Design
and Copyright, which dealt not only with printing and binding but with
purchases of paper and the scheduling of publications. The Department,
well run, also supervised overseas publications. It had already begun to
place printing orders in Hong Kong, where educational books could be
produced most cheaply: even after shipping costs had been taken into
account, there were savings on home printing. This had a direct influence
on the price of books, and that in turn had a direct influence on both
turnover and profits.

Before the changes of 1962, more complicated and involving more
devolution than Newsom had suggested in 1957, turnover and profits had
already risen substantially in the intervening five years (see table below).[114]

Turnover And Gross Profits, 1958–62 (Year ended 31 May)

YEAR	TURNOVER £	GROSS PROFITS £	GROSS PROFIT AS A PERCENTAGE OF SALES
1958	2,222,563	1,015,244	45.7%
1959	2,557,042	1,162,113	45.5%
1960	2,975,568	1,370,247	46.1%
1961	3,329,321	1,633,263	49.1%
1962	3,563,500	1,703,832	47.8%

Gross profits represented the difference between revenue from turnover
and the net manufacturing cost of sales and payments to authors. The
percentage of gross profits on sales was affected, inevitably, by the volume
of publications that were considered as surplus to demand at annual
stocktakings. Judgement on this varied from year to year, but from this
period onwards more attention than ever before was paid to controlling

114 Report to the Board Appended to the Accounts, Oct. 1962.

Portrait of William Longman
(1882–1967), 1958, by Ruskin
Spear R.A.

Towards the end of an era:
William Longman had been
the Chairman for nearly thirty
years, retiring in 1964

Pearson Education

gross overheads as far as possible. Just as the shelf-life of books in booksellers' shops was shortening, so too was the duration of the period of publishers holding books in print. These were significant moves in the history of publishing.

The financial situation within the House of Longman was to change completely during the next six years, largely as a result of heavy once-and-for-all development expenditures, financed not by outside borrowing but from the operational revenues of the business, and while these costs were covered from inside the business during the five years from 1963 to 1968, retained profits were exceptionally low. There was an obvious need in such circumstances for an injection of new capital, if the Longman Group, as it was called after 1966, were to be strong enough to cope with the threat of takeover, most likely American, although the feared Cecil King, maverick member of the Harmsworth family was lurking in the wings also.

There was an obvious need too for a comprehensive change in operational structure to improve efficiency, and this took place in steps from 1966 onwards. Until then there had been three 'Departments', which Newsom, unaware as he was of earlier Company history, none the less identified clearly – Production, Publishing and Sales. Now the 'Departments' were replaced by publishing 'Divisions', which were set out in numerical order from A onwards. The move was intended to achieve a more effective span of business control while compartmentalising editorial responsibilities. Wallis devised the original scheme, which had the strong backing of Rix. Ironically he had learnt much from observing the structure of McGraw-Hill, an American company which was on the lookout for British acquisitions. At least on paper, the Divisions were based not on one single criterion but on either geography or on category of publication.

Some of the new Divisions were far more significant in terms of business operations and profits than others. The first of them (A) dealt with general and juvenile publishing, the second (B) with university and technical publishing, and the third (C) with school publishing. Then came three geographical Divisions, with *ELT* sandwiched between them, (D) African and Caribbean publishing, (E) Australasian and Far East publishing, (F) English language teaching and audio-visual aids, and (G) Arab World publishing, oddly linked with Collins/Longman atlases.

～

Further changes in Divisional structures followed (in steps) the incorporation of the Longman Group into the Pearson organisation in 1968, a momentous change in ownership, carried out in the first instance through Finprov, Financial and Provincial Publishing Company, an amalgam of Pearson publishing interests, including the *Financial Times* and the Westminster Press chain of provincial newspapers.

For Mark Longman, who took the initiative in proposing the incorporation, the move was logical for both sides, since Lord Cowdray, a Pearson, whose family fortune had been built up through earlier ventures entirely outside publishing, had been responsible the year before for the merger talks which led to the formation of Finprov. Pearson owned directly and indirectly 64.3 per cent of its capital: only 28 per cent of Longman equity was in family hands.

This was a time when mergers were in the air. For example, the newly founded International Publishing Company, IPC, had taken over the prestigious legal publishing House of Butterworth, founded in 1818, after a battle in which Robert Maxwell, best known at this stage as the owner of the Pergamon Press, was involved. And there were to be far more mergers to follow in the years that lay ahead. Ironically, not long before, Mark had discussed with a divided Butterworth Board the idea that Longman might take it over.[115]

The Pearson/Longman deal of 1968, announced in the *Financial Times* as a merger, immediately provided Longman with £1.5 million in cash to help to finance its continuing expansion plans.[116] In the opinion of the *Economist*, also partially owned by Pearson, the deal was generous on Pearson's part. Shares, loan stock and cash amounted to over twenty-five times the Longman Group's estimated profits for 1968.[117]

If the deal had not taken place, Longman would have urgently needed other outside funds. The Harlow move had cost more than £1 million. Yet there were also advantages for Finprov, capitalised at £22 million, a figure not significantly larger than the Longman £17 million. Moreover, the Finprov subsidiary, Bracken House Publications, with its headquarters in Bracken House, the offices of the *Financial Times*, at the centre of the Pearson publishing business, had a profit record that was less impressive than that of Longman. There was uncertainty too about the future. Whatever happened to book publishing, the newspaper industry

---

115   H. Kay Jones, *Butterworths, History of a Publishing House* (1980), p.222.

116   *Financial Times*, 3 Feb. 1968. See also *Daily Telegraph*, 3 Feb. 1968: *Financial Times*, 3 Feb. 1968. Full details were given in both these newspapers of the implications of the merger for Longman A and B shareholders and of an accompanying rights issue.

117   The *Economist*, 10 Feb. 1968.

was undergoing great changes, and there were even bigger ones around the corner.[118] Estimated profits for Longman and Bracken House together were £1,965,000 in 1970, compared with £1,631,000 in 1969.[119]

Pre-Tax Profits, 1963–68 (£ ooos)

YEAR	LONGMAN	BRACKEN HOUSE
1963	913	234
1964	1,170	282
1965	1,258	179
1966	1,353	252
1967	1,374	279
1968	1,100	281

Already Bracken House had moved into book publishing, having acquired Oliver and Boyd, an old established firm in Edinburgh, which had started as a partnership in 1808, securing it a foothold in educational publishing, and E. and S. Livingstone and J. and A. Churchill establishing a very strong position in medical publishing. All three firms had fascinating histories of their own. Livingstone, for example, founded by two brothers, had celebrated its centenary in 1964:[120] and Churchill had published anonymously in 1844 Robert Chambers's *Vestiges of Creation* which had a sensational success when it stirred up debate on evolution fifteen years before Darwin. All three firms were to be transferred to Longman, resulting in the transformation of its medical publishing and providing an interesting addition to its own schools publishing.

Oliver and Boyd had not been performing well financially (its children's books were acquired separately by Chatto and Windus) and it was now incorporated in the Longman schools publishing division (while remaining in Scotland). It had some important schools' titles, however, all

---

118 See A. Smith, *Goodbye Gutenberg: The Newspaper Revolution of the 1980s* (1980).

119 *Financial Times*, 3 Feb. 1968. See J.A. Secord *Victorian sensation: the extraordinary publication, reception, and secret authorship of Vestiges of the natural history of creation*, 2000, which illuminates and relates publishing to the sciences; J. Rivers, 'Fifty Years of Medical Publishing' in *The Practitioner*, August 1957. As publishers of the pioneering *Medical Directory* (1845–) and later the *Medical Intelligencer* (1883), John Churchill (1801–1875) claimed that he was publishing a 'larger number of Medical Works than are issued by all the other publishing houses'.

120 *Footprints in Time* (1964); *The Scotsman*, 3 June 1963. The two brothers had started as booksellers on South Bridge in Edinburgh in 1863.

of which were incorporated in the Longman lists. For Longman, Edinburgh would now be added to its list of British addresses, figuring again as it had done in the days of Constable when the *Edinburgh Review* was founded.

Lists were not then computerised, but the Pearson 'merger' coincided with the introduction of computerisation into the Harlow business. Between November 1969 and April 1970 the sales invoicing and stock control systems were handled in parallel by 'traditional' methods and by computer, but in April 1970 there was a complete switch-over to the computer, remarkably free from start-up problems. Considerable benefits were promised, including the reduction of inventories. Computerisation was to become an increasingly important element not only in the routine operations of the firm but in the development of its list of publications.

~

It would be impossible to close this long account of the years from 1918 to 1968 without moving away from Harlow and returning to overseas developments which accounted for a large share of profits, for, as has been shown, it had been in the light of the peripheral, rather than central, enterprise, that it was possible in face of pressures at the periphery, successfully to set up local companies, a necessary step for political reasons in some of the countries concerned. Their status and relationship to Harlow varied.

In 1962 there were three Longman overseas companies – Longmans, Green (Far East) Ltd, Longmans of Malaya Ltd and Longmans of Nigeria Ltd, the trio forming part of Longmans, Green (Overseas Holdings) Ltd which handled the entire capital of all three. Assets, liabilities and trading results were incorporated in a consolidated balance sheet and profit-and-loss account. In four other overseas companies Longmans, Green had a share, including 33 per cent of Orient Longmans Ltd, registered in India, now a well established and prestigious (if financially precarious) business, and 35 per cent of Longmans Canada Ltd: the other 65 per cent was owned by Harcourt Brace. The other two companies were Thibault House (Pty) Ltd, South Africa, a company formed to take over the property occupied by Longmans South Africa, and Angus and Robertson, an Australian retail bookselling company in which Longman owned 50,000 third preference shares.

In 1967 there was a further significant extension of Longman interests in Australia when a new subsidiary, Longman Australia Pty Ltd, was set up, and a 14 per cent interest was acquired in a South Australian publishing company, Rigby Ltd, which became the exclusive distributor (though not for long) of Longman and Oliver and Boyd titles in Australia. A 10 per cent stake was also acquired in Bakers Bookstore Holdings (Brisbane). In 1969 the book publishing side of Halls Bookstore Ltd in Melbourne was purchased. A New Zealand textbook and academic publishing firm was acquired in 1968 and re-named Longman Paul Ltd. The word 'globalisation' might well have been used to describe this pattern of activity, for there were also Longman resident representatives in the

Argentine, Brazil, Egypt, Ghana, Japan, Pakistan and Thailand.

In Europe, which was soon to play a bigger part in what was then beginning to be called a Longman strategy, Longman joined in a 50/50 deal of 1967 with Browne and Nolan Ltd, a Dublin based firm of educational and school contractors, to form Longman, Browne and Nolan; and, as described in the next chapter, even before Britain joined what was then the Common Market Longman had made moves in the Netherlands, Germany and France which were recognised at the time as being part of a new strategy. It had also become involved in a joint venture with the well-known language school operator, International House, and had established a language school in Paris, but it did not prosper and Longman extricated itself from the Joint Venture as it did from other language school ventures in Japan and Hong Kong.

It was in the light of such enterprise outside Britain that in 1966,

The Burnt Mill building at Harlow, into which Longman moved in 1968

Longman Archive

after outside advice had been taken, the name of Longmans, Green & Co. had been changed to the Longman Group of Publishing Companies, and that had been two years before its 'merger' with Pearson. In the years that followed, the Group, impressive in its range of enterprises and less vulnerable to take-over, remained subject to competition, now intensified, from other publishers, including Macmillan and the Oxford University Press, both of which were now consciously following global strategies.

~

This chapter ends not with Nigeria or Hong Kong but with the move of Longman UK and of the Longman Group to Harlow in the early summer of the momentous year, 1968. Brack continued his diary until 31 May 1968, a few weeks before the final move took place. He was an observer only on this occasion, therefore, not in the thick of the fray. There were some young employees with a future ahead of them in the House, like Michael Wymer, who had been interviewed by Brack before joining Longman, who at first did not like the thought of the move; and to the very last rumours were in the air that Harlow might not be the destination. Even Bristol, where everything had begun, was mentioned.

Nairn found the move to Harlow 'one of the most punishing times' she had lived through: some of her friends told her cheerfully that she would be 'back in London in two years'. It was her responsibility, however, at a time when television was the glamour industry, to attract new staff as well as to persuade old staff to move, and a brochure in colour, almost a necessary dimension of communication, 'Longmans in Harlow', was intended 'to help young men and women, who were starting a career, and who may be drawn into the strange and fascinating world of books'.

There was a wide range of jobs on offer, ranging from picture editors to progress control assistants, men and women who were expected to be 'practical and imaginative'. Moreover, with the future of Europe in the news as well as in the business pages of newspapers, European sales promotion assistants were specifically mentioned, not only with languages that they could read and write, if not speak, but 'with a Common Market mentality'.

Before long, Burnt Mill, Harlow, seemed as natural a setting for Longman headquarters as 39 Paternoster Row had been for more than two centuries. The Harlow story, however, was to be far shorter. It is told in the remaining chapters of this History.

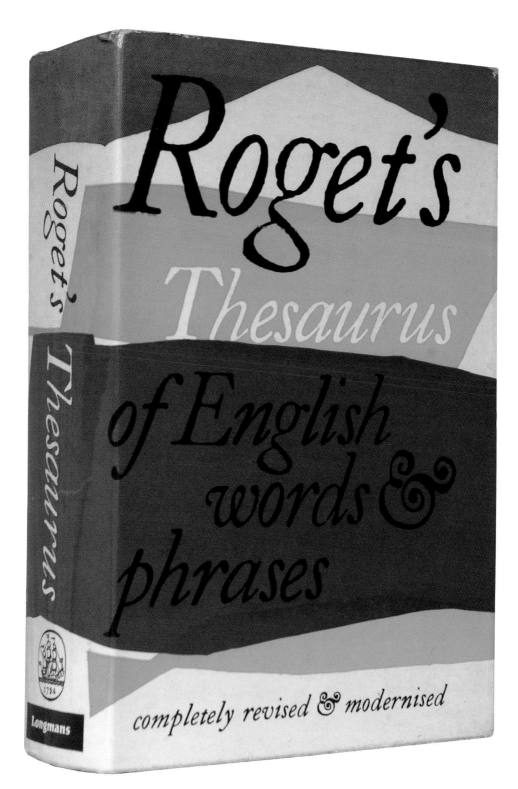

8 Recalling Yet Re-structuring, 1968–1976

The eight years between 1968, when the Longman Group became part of S. Pearson and Son Ltd. and 1976, when Rix, who had joined Longman in 1958, became its Chief Executive, stand out as hinge years in the history of Longman even more than they do in the as yet unwritten history of Pearson. It was important in the history of Longman that the initiative for the Pearson/Longman deal, a gentlemanly deal, described in the last chapter and at the time called by the *Economist* a 'natural' deal, had been taken not by Pearson but by Mark Longman[1]. He died at the early age of 55 two years before the House of Longman, proud of its longevity, celebrated in style its 250th anniversary in 1974.

There was less re-structuring at the time of the Longman anniversary in 1974, a year of celebration, comparable with 1924, than there was recalling. Nevertheless, the years from 1972 to 1976 marked the beginning of a period when Pearson/Longman business priorities were more clearly defined on paper than ever before. Indeed, a corporate plan – so designated for the first time and probably one of the first for a publishing house – was produced (and signed by Chapple), that covered the years from 1973 to 1976, complete with business and profit forecasts.[2] It involved the effective end of Division A, the University and General List, in the latter part of which Mark had taken particular interest, but which Chapple now stated frankly had been 'a weakness for many years'. The Group's 'tertiary publishing' was now to be handled by Division B: 'Tertiary' was the critical word. A new division J (journals) included *The English Historical Review* and *The Practitioner*, the latter a journal which was then very widely read by general medical practitioners.[3] Division M dealt with medical publishing, and Division O with Oliver and Boyd.

Changes in strategic planning, accompanied by such structural changes, are fully described in the next chapter. The first of them, before Rix became Chief Executive in 1976, were partly forced on the business, which Rix believed should finally cease to be thought of as a family concern. If it

This 1962 edition of Roget's Thesaurus used a new cover design by Tim Jaques, one of a new 'family' of reference book designs. In 1982 a completely revised edition used the computer to sort and order the meanings of words

Personal collection

---

1   *Economist*, 10 Feb. 1968.

2   Longman Holdings Ltd and Subsidiary Companies, Corporate Plan, 1973–1976. (LA files from the Office of the Chief Executive 408-638)

3   Founded in 1868, *The Practitioner* was sold in 1976 to Morgan-Grampian Ltd.

A book needs

The Publishing Department

1 AN IDEA: whether from author or publisher: subject, level, length have to be considered.

2 A WRITER: many of our books are for students in schools and colleges, so teachers have to be found to write our books.

3 A CONTRACT: so that author and publisher know the legal and financial arrangements.

4 AN EDITOR: who will turn the typescript into a clear, neat document ready for . . .

The Production Department

1 PLANNING: the production controller makes sure that the book is designed, its type chosen, its pages clear but attractive.

2 THE PICTURES, diagrams, etc., have to be drawn or photographed.

3 A suitable printer has to be chosen, his costs worked out.

4 PAPER must be bought, printing ordered, binding chosen.

Long before the book is a finished product it is . . .

The Sales Department

1 PROMOTED by Representatives calling on schools and bookshops, and by the distribution of prospectuses and catalogues.

2 ADVERTISED through newspapers, journals, etc., on publication.

All these Departments rely on

1 *The Secretarial Service*: where Audio and Copy Typists produce letters to authors, printers, booksellers, schools, colleges and all, from Tooting Bec to Timbuktu.

2 *The Trade Department*: which receives orders from our customers, invoices them and handles all correspondence concerning the supply of our publications.

3 *The Warehouse*: in which all the books are stored, packed and distributed to booksellers and contractors all over the world, so that in their turn they can pass it on to the reader.

4 *The Accounts Department*: which pays bills and salaries, royalties to authors, and collects money from booksellers and contractors.

5 *Administrative and Personnel Department*: since Longmans is a worldwide organisation, employing over 700 people (and not a few machines) it needs an Administrative and Personnel Department that takes on and looks after staff. This is where we hope you will first meet us.

In 1968 Longman had moved to Harlow. The House published a 'recruiting' brochure, *Longmans in Harlow*, explaining what Longman did, and the main processes (as they then were) of publishing

Longman Archive

was to remain competitive, he insisted, it had to become more deliberately 'professional'. The business challenges to be met – and they were not unique to publishing – were related to the economic circumstances of the country, including a combination of unprecedented inflation coupled with unemployment, 'stagflation', a phenomenon which contemporaries found difficult to understand.

For publishers the rising cost of print was the most serious problem. The price of print materials rose by 29 per cent between 1970 and 1974. In order to cope with this inflationary situation print-buying operations had to become more centralised, and competitive tender arrangements for supply had to become 'established', a hazardous word to use in a period of uncertainty. In the circumstances Chapple realised, as Adkins had done, how important Hong Kong was as a printing centre, and his willingness to print there, resented by highly unionised British printers but widely copied, had a profound influence on the economics of book publishing.

There were, in fact, far-reaching changes without precedent in the British printing industry during the 1970s and 1980s, particularly in the printing of newspapers. 'A technical industry', wrote Raymond Snoddy in a letter printed late in 1989 in the *Financial Times*, 'is in the grip of rapid technological change and dramatic restructuring. Some think the changes to come in the next decade will be more fundamental than in the 500 years since Caxton.'[4]

In Britain problems in industrial relations affected the business as well as the country, and they hit the headlines even more than inflation or technology did. At Harlow they deteriorated so much that when Rix became Joint Managing Director he regarded their improvement as an 'input priority'. It was not until 1972 that a Joint Consultative Committee was set up there, and its constitution had to be re-examined at the end of the

---

4   *Financial Times*, 23 Oct. 1989.

decade in 1978/9, the year of the 'winter of discontent'. By then the Company had granted negotiating rights to four trade unions, ASTMS, the Association of Scientific, Technical and Managerial Staffs (for the majority of Longman employees), SOGAT, the Society of Graphic and Allied Trades, NUJ, the National Union of Journalists, and NGA, the National Graphical Association. They were to deal with matters affecting terms and conditions of employment for the groups of workers they represented.[5]

There was one other national change, political as well as economic, which affected the economy and the business – the entry of Britain into the Common Market, engineered by Edward Heath, who had led the British negotiations to join it during the previous decade. In 1970, Harold Wilson's Labour government (1964–70) fell from office after the general election of March, and it was Heath, who came to power as Prime Minister of the new Conservative government, who took the historic decision. The mood then was optimistic, despite some opposition to joining even in his own party, but the international oil crisis in 1973, which raised the price of oil fourfold, changed the national mood completely.

John Chapple, who became the Director responsible for 'overseas education' in 1957 and was Chairman from 1972–1976

Longman Archive

The year 1974 was one of the bleakest in British history, and there were two general elections, both of which Heath lost. As a result, Wilson returned to power, promising the electorate a referendum on Britain's entry into the European Common Market. A large majority favoured entry in June 1975, but national economic difficulties worsened further, and in 1978 Britain had to apply to the International Monetary Fund for financial support, the most unprecedented of all the events.

At the time of the Pearson deal it had not been apparent how many economic difficulties for book publishers lay just around the corner or how different the moods of the 1970s would be from those of the 1960s. And there were to be even bigger changes of mood during the 1980s. After the 'winter of discontent' in 1978/9 the general election of May 1979 was won

5   Joint Consultative Committee, Statement by W.F.K. Barnett, Director of Personnel Services, 3 Feb. 1978. (LA)

by the Conservatives, led by Margaret Thatcher, so that for the first time in British history a woman became Prime Minister. Before she took over, the recent past had become more confusing to contemporaries than the distant past, but Thatcher knew clearly what she wished to do – to stay 'in Europe' but to repudiate all talk of European federalism and independently through privatisation to redress all Britain's economic policies. Willing, even eager, to abandon consensus politics, she remained in power for eleven years, with publishers, like other businessmen, now operating within a Common Market. Her interest in books, like her interest in the arts, was strictly limited, but, having been Secretary of State for Education, she was fully aware of the importance of the book trade to the economy.

In the brief period between 1968 and Britain's acceptance of the Treaty of Brussels in 1972 Longman made its first important new moves in Europe. Indeed, in the week of the Treaty being signed it announced that it too had signed a contract with Langenscheidt of Munich for the formation and operation from 1 January 1972 of a joint subsidiary company, Langenscheidt-Longman GmbH which would stock and distribute, with sole rights, a large part of the Longman *ELT* list in West Germany, Austria and Switzerland. (The last two countries were outside the Common Market). It would go on to publish books, along with audio-visual and other material, for the teaching of English in the German-speaking market. Tielebier Langenscheidt and Rix, who signed the contract, were to be joint *Geschäftsführer* of the new company. This was the first time that Rix had assumed not only such a new name but such a new role. The contract was signed beneath a portrait of the Tielebier Langenscheidt who had founded the German family business in 1856.

In France agreement was reached and contracts prepared with the prestigious Librairie Armand Colin of 103 Boulevard Saint-Germain for the formation and operation from 1 February 1972 of a joint subsidiary company, Armand Colin-Longman SA. This would stock and distribute *ELT* books and materials in France and other parts of the French-speaking Community, including Africa. The Chairman (*Président-Directeur-Général*) would be French, and Rix, Rea and Mortimer would be Directors. Armand Colin had been founded in 1870, and *The Bookseller*, reporting the signings (with a photograph), made the most of history as well as of new European prospects.[6]

The model for these European joint companies had been established two years earlier, with the formation in Holland of Wolters Noordhoff Longman with similar *ELT* objectives. This came about because the distinguished Dutch publishing firms of J.B. Wolters and Noordhoff had recently merged (not least by knocking through the wall separating their two offices in Groningen, North Holland) and the newly joined-up Board

---

6 'Longman and the Common Market', in *The Bookseller*, 22 Jan. 1972.

had visited London in search of publishing acquisitions. Talks with Chapple and Rix led not to an acquisition but to the formation of a joint company.

It was at this time too that Longman, at last, revived a real interest in the American market. Longman Inc. was incorporated in April 1973 and a New York office was established under Lothar Simon. At first, the staff were guests in the Penguin offices at 72 Fifth Avenue, but in the same year Longman's own small office was set up in the same building. A move to larger offices in West 44th Street followed in March 1976. The initial task was to import, promote and distribute books published in the United Kingdom. But a publishing programme soon followed, greatly helped by the acquisition of the David McKay Company in 1978.

After its return to the USA Longman, with Pearson support, had been looking out for possible acquisitions of relevant American publishers and with the help of a specialist broker had identified Wadsworth, a highly successful and attractive West Coast college publisher, as an ideal target. Excellent relations were established, an offer was made, and a letter of intent was signed. But International Thomson got wind of the deal and with the help of a dissident shareholder 'gazumped' the offer at a very high price, the first of many such outcomes. This was a major disappointment for Longman. Had the deal gone through, it would have completely changed the history of Longman in the USA and probably the history of the Longman Group as a whole.

~

In 1974, the year when the House of Longman celebrated its 250th anniversary, it published the handsomely produced *Essays in the History of Publishing*, referred to in the first Chapter, and P.J. Wallis, who had joined the House in 1929, wrote after his retirement a short history, *At the Sign of the Ship, 1924–1974* (1974), printed for private circulation, which supplements *Essays*. Given access not only to business records but, through Lady Elizabeth Longman, to family papers, he emphasised not the need for increased professionalisation, as Rix did, but the importance of family inheritance and tradition. Longman, he insisted, had been 'most fortunate in having a family of absolute integrity at its head for all but two of the two hundred and fifty years'. And as he reached towards the present Wallis mentioned only briefly Pearson's acquisition of the firm, describing it, none the less, as 'perhaps Mark's major contribution to the fortunes of Longman'.[7]

In writing his still useful and much quoted book Wallis drew not only on his own memory but on the memories of other former Longman employees, particularly J.E. Chandler, who had moved from the handling of stock to the production of books, and E.W. Parker, whose Memoirs have

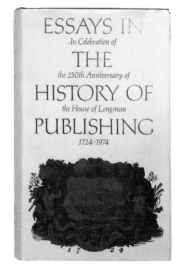

Essays in the History of Publishing, in celebration of the 250th Anniversary of the House of Longman 1724–1974. The illustrated volume included twelve essays on aspects of the history of the book trade, edited by Asa Briggs

Personal collection

---

7   PW, pp.v, 38.

In 1968 Longman was acquired by S. Pearson & Son. It was a good home for Longman, Pearson's culture then being similar, and longevity (although not as long as Longman's) a feature of its history. Samuel Pearson became a partner, in 1844, in a small building firm. The firm grew as it moved into and out of different areas of industry, reflecting their growth or decline. In 1979 Pearson's Report pointed out that 'the pattern' that is 'followed today' was to 'acquire only quality companies, select good management and allow it to manage. Each component part has a high degree of autonomy, and yet has access, in principle, to the capital resources of the whole'

Longman Archive

already been drawn upon in this *History*. He referred too to Brack who had been a close colleague. Chandler, who had written a memoir of his early days in Paternoster Row and had been an unacknowledged part-author of Harold Cox's adulatory and uncritical *The House of Longman, 1724–1924*, published in 1925,[8] had also edited CJ's Longman bibliography covering the 'lost years' from 1724 to 1800.

As we have seen, Parker was far more critical than Wallis was to be. He had formed what he called 'a magnificent team' with Higham, whose enterprise he greatly admired, but, in retrospect, after fifty years' dedicated service he had come to discern lack of enterprise in many sections of the House, particularly when compared with its competitors. Parker was not interested in the young 'new men' who were to transform the business. Nor was he particularly knowledgeable about them. But in his last years he declared respect for Newsom whose 'quick mind … caused him to ask many pertinent questions', mainly about domestic trade, the questions which he himself was asking. One, which related directly to education, was 'why [should] a business vaunting itself as the biggest educational publishers be relying on only 5% of the school population for selling its wares?'[9]

Essays in the History of Publishing, written after Parker's manuscript but before Wallis's book appeared, did not draw on any such memoirs, but it broke different ground in securing contributors to the volume from other and newer publishers, willing to join in the preparation of the volume as well as in the celebrations. Thus, Hans Schmoller, Penguin's distinguished chief designer, contributed an essay on 'The Paperback Revolution'. The first essay in the volume – on copyright, an old and a new

8 'Memoirs of the House of Longman', 1972, p.48. (LA Part II 43/1-2)

9 'Memoirs', p.42.

issue – was written by Ian Parsons, Chairman of Chatto and Windus, most professional of publishers, who had been involved in a merger of his own with Jonathan Cape (1969) and later with Bodley Head (1973), mergers designed in part, like the Longman merger, to forestall an American take-over. Later, however, a merged Chatto/Cape/Bodley Head combination was to be taken over by Random House.[10]

In 1968, the year of the Pearson deal, Murray, Longman's oldest rival and oldest ally, who, like Macmillan, did not figure prominently in the *Essays*, celebrated its own bi-centennial one year after the death of its Chairman, Sir John Murray V. The House of Murray had already become a limited company in 1951, but it was moving differently through the twentieth century before being taken over in the spring of 2002, as we have seen, by Hodder Headline, itself the product of a reverse take-over, later acquired by W.H. Smith. There were no intimations of this in 1974, nor of the fate of Macmillan, which was soon to cease to be a family business,[11] and John Murray VI ('Jock') was among the first publishers to congratulate Longmans on their 250th anniversary. He spoke of the past not only of the Longmans but of British publishing as a whole.

One of the most satisfying was Gibson's statement to the annual meeting of S. Pearson Publishers Ltd. in 1970 that his Board was recommending that the name of the Company should be changed to Pearson Longman; and while Gibson explained that the main reason for this was 'confusion of names' since the take-over deal, he added that the Board was 'particularly happy to be able to link the famous name of Longman with that of Pearson in the new title'. Again there was an historical dimension.

Even more satisfying was that in the same report Gibson was happy too to announce a 'remarkable buoyancy of profits' in 1968, adding that after the take-over took place, 1969 Longman profits (over £2 million) had been slightly higher still and had 'substantially exceeded expectations'. In the home market there had been 'a satisfactory increase' in turnover despite 'restrictions in grants to schools', with a consequent impact on the purchase of books and other materials, but it was the overseas market that had provided the greater part (again an increased part) of the turnover, over £34 million in all. While saying little about Europe – or the United States, Gibson picked out Africa and within it Nigeria, in particular, as the most promising market now that the Biafran War in Nigeria (1967–70) had ended.

Nevertheless, the profits of the Rhodesian market had been blocked after Ian Smith had declared unilateral independence, and there had been problems too for Longman South Africa (Pty) in a country which faced the

---

10   E.D. Bellaigue, *British Publishing as a Business since the 1960s* (2004).

11   Holzbrinck took control of Macmillan London in two stages during the 1990s, 71 per cent in 1995 and the balance in 1999.

Longman Young Books was
set up when Constable's
children's list (Constable
Young Books) was sold to
Longman and Patrick Hardy,
its publisher, continued to run
it. Leon Garfield was one of
its major authors, and both
The Drummer Boy and other
titles were included in the
Pleasure in Reading series for
schools, which therefore bought
multiple copies

Personal collection

threat of sanctions because of its toughened policy of apartheid. Furthest
north in Africa, however, there had been negotiations to reopen the
Egyptian market, and the Far Eastern companies in the Longman Group
had all registered gains in sales.

In line with Pearson history, Gibson dwelt in the first part of his
speech on newspapers, the Westminster Press chain rather than with
Longman, noting that it had acquired two further provincial newspapers,
and it was only when he came to that point in his statement where he dealt
with the then best-known newspaper in the Pearson empire, the *Financial
Times*, that he introduced the House of Longman into his speech. Literature
did not provide the link. Longman was collaborating with the newspaper,
he said, 'in the field of business and management publications'.

The first fruit of the collaboration had been the publication of the
Financial Times Year Book at the end of 1969, but Gibson referred explicitly
to *Financial Times* support for the first National Management Game,
devised in association with the Institute of Chartered Accountants and
International Computers Ltd. There was to be no shortage of management
games – or other games – during the 1970s and 1980s as management
jargon came to dominate almost all aspects of British life. It was a favourite
subject for books – and broadcasts, and Longman itself, which took over
the business of Pitman in 1985, was to produce many books on different
aspects of it.

There had been collaboration also, Gibson went on, in 'audio-
visual aids', the awkward and ugly term still in regular use before a new
information vocabulary developed. The first official report on the subject,
prepared under the chairmanship of Brynmor Jones, Vice-Chancellor
of Hull University, a chemist, was called 'Audio-Visual Aids in Higher
Scientific Education' (1965).[12] Gibson did not mention technology as such,
although the adjective 'educational' had already been attached to it and as
early as the summer of 1968, when the merger took place, Nigel Calder
had written in *The Author* that 'even authors whose interests lie far from
science and technology will be aware of some stir in the communications
world'.[13] Over the next quarter of a century there was to be a protracted
stir, culminating with the Internet and the 'World Wide Web'.[14] Yet as
early as 1972 *Longman Young Books* had published a *Worldbook* called *The
World Communicates*, written by Maurice Rickards, who among his other

---

12   For school-level visual aids the small National Organisation for Audio Visual
     Aids in Education (NOAVE) was modestly supported by local education
     authorities.

13   *The Author*, Vol. LXXVI, No. 2, Summer 1968, p.57.

14   In 1993 the Society of Authors launched *The Electronic Author* which printed
     articles by M. McGrath, 'Information Superhighway, the Mysteries of
     Cyberspace' in Summer 1994 and 'The Internet for Authors' by J. Schofield in
     Winter 1995.

pioneering activities was to found the Ephemera Society. The chapters included 'Post Box or Head Set: the Electronic Way from A to B' and 'Now, Facsimile and Video, Visions by Wire, Tape and Disc'.[15]

When Gibson came to the brief passages in his Annual Report where he focused entirely on Longman, he paid particular attention to periodicals in the Longman list. He also referred not only to the enlarged Medical Division, which had had 'an exceptionally good year' and to the 'highly specialised and successful publishing of English language teaching books', ELT, a field in which American publishers then showed relatively little business interest, but to the preparation and launching of Breakthrough to Literacy (1970), a new reading scheme for primary schools which had been initiated by the recently founded Schools Council.[16] Literacy at that time had not yet been widely identified as an adult problem, as soon it was to be.[17]

Longman was sensitive to such shifts of concern, including the Schools Council's concern for new teaching methods, including the use of 'audio-visual aids', strongly advocated too by the Nuffield Foundation; and in 1970 it acquired Common Ground Ltd., a company set up in 1951

there are lots of things to read at school.
14

there are lots of things to read at home.
15

Breakthrough to Literacy was one of the earliest, and most successful, projects developed by the Schools Council, the new curriculum development body. Published for it in 1970 by Longman, the aim was to make direct contact with children, putting the emphasis on using their natural language and interests

Personal collection

---

15   Longman Young books also included Rickards's The World Fights Crime, which he pointed out, was becoming a major 'subject which touched everyone's life'. Other very different titles in this wide-ranging series were The History of the Common Market, Away in a Manger, The National Youth Theatre, What a Boy Should Know about Sex, What a Girl Should Know about Sex and 150 Careers in Advertising (cased £1.95: paper 95p net). The prices in this series were as varied as the titles.

16   This constitutionally cumbrous representative body, which nevertheless was prepared to take initiatives, had been set up in 1964, just before Harold Wilson, eloquent about the claims of technology, became Prime Minister. It was the brainchild of the Conservative Secretary of State for Education, Sir Edward (later Lord) Boyle (1923-1981).

17   The Uses of Literacy, the title of Richard Hoggart's widely read and admired book of 1957, received more attention than illiteracy. For a subsequent change of stress in Britain see the Report of the Bullock Committee on Reading and other Uses of the English Language, A Language for Life (1975). For illiteracy and literacy campaigns outside Europe, which were of special interest to Longman, see UNESCO, Literacy 1967–1969, September 1970.

to produce educational film strips which would supplement the activity of the expanding Audio-Visual Section. The use of film strips was then regarded as an adventurous new departure in education, and there was increasing talk too on both sides of the Atlantic about 'teaching machines' and 'programmed learning'.[18]

As early as 1964 Longman had used records to teach pronunciation to accompany Eckersley's *Essential English* course, and in 1965 it created an audio-visual (A/V) production unit to serve all departments wishing to use its services. After the move to Harlow an A/V room, designed by Rix and Judy Little and their colleagues in *ELT*, was opened, fitted with recording and playback systems, screens, slides, film strips, some of them in regular use in history and geography teaching, and film projectors. Particular attention was paid to feedback.[19]

The term 'audio-visual aids' was at last beginning to be superseded by the terms 'new technology' and 'new educational technologies'. The thrust to develop them through 'convergence', a favourite noun of the 1980s, was common both to Pearson and Longman and to the merged Pearson Longman enterprise. There were always risks involved in the process, however, as there were in film production, in which Pearson, through Goldcrest, became deeply involved in 1980.[20] Already in 1970 Gibson had to announce losses through investment in 'a new process called Technical Information on Microfilm, designed to provide a new system of information retrieval to enable suppliers to present their technical data in a revolutionary new way to enquirers'. As was frequently to be the case later, the development costs had been far higher than anticipated.

~

Gibson's 1970 statement left much out. There had obviously been behind-the-scenes discussions in 1969 when Gibson and Mark Longman agreed on the change of name to Pearson Longman, helped by the fact that the two men had been at Eton together and knew each other well, but it would have been wrong for Gibson to look back to these given Mark's painful

---

18   See the pioneering study by Richard Goodman, *Programmed Learning and Teaching Methods* (English Universities Press, 1962). The first *Annual Review of Information and Science Technology*, edited by Carlos A. Quadra, had been published in New York in 1966. Three years later an international conference was organised in London by the Association for Programmed Learning and Educational Technology. It resulted in a Pitman publication, *Aspects of Educational Technology*, edited by A.P. Mann and C.P. Brunstrom.

19   Three of the ten papers in Mann and Brunstrom were on 'programmed instruction', 'the use of audio-visual aids in programmed learning' and 'feedback classrooms'.

20   See below, p.462.

illness. Mark had joined the S. Pearson Publishers Board as a Director and later the Board of Pearson Longman, and he remained as active as he could in Longman affairs until his death.[21] Nevertheless, in 1969, when Alex Hamilton wrote two largely factual articles for *The Author* on Britain's top twenty publishers, he did not describe Longman as a family business as he did Macmillan and, of course, Murray. (The publishers were listed in alphabetical order so that the Longman Group came immediately before Macmillan.)

Each article included a section called 'personality' –soon afterwards it would have been called 'corporate culture'[22]   in which the main features of the business were picked out. In the case of the Longman Group – and this was before the linking of the names of Pearson and Longman – it was not 'family' that was identified as its main personality trait but a 'constant stream of new projects at a serious level'. 'Heavy investment, particularly in education and scientific textbooks for emerging countries' was another main trait. Newsom was noted by name among directors, but at the end of the entry Chapple was singled out as 'Group Publisher = Editorial Director'. The number of Longman UK personnel was then given as 650, and the number of books published with a Longman imprint in 1968 as 750.[23] The comparable figure for books with a Macmillan imprint was 538, and that of Penguin 450, including 213 originals.

~

The comparison with Penguin had more immediate point in 1970 than it had in 1969, for the announcement of the change of nomenclature to Pearson Longman was quickly followed by the further announcement in July of a

---

21   After his death a Mark Longman Library was opened at the headquarters of the National Book League. It concentrated on 'books on books'. An appeal committee, headed by Robert Lusty and with Lady Elizabeth Longman and Martyn Goff amongst its members, had raised more than £30,000. Mark's portrait by Graham Sutherland was loaned indefinitely to the Library, but later Rix felt that the original portrait should hang in Longman House and arranged for a handsome copy to be given to the National Book League. The Library is now located within the Archives at Reading University Library. See the Report on the library and its opening in *The Log* No. 3, July 1975. (LA Part II 213)

22   Roger Harrison, a social psychologist, working on both sides of the Atlantic, emphasised the importance of 'understanding your organisation's character' in 1972 (*Harvard Business Review*, Vol. 50 (1972), pp.119–128). 'Perceptions change even in dealing with an organisation's character.' At the end of the millennium a writer could claim that 'corporate identity simply doesn't matter any more' (*RSA Journal*, 4 April 2000, p.4), an issue that is undated on its cover and on its contents page.

23   *The Author*, Vol. LXXX, Autumn 1969, pp.79–80.

Mark Longman, painting by
Graham Sutherland, 1970.
Chairman of Longman 1964–72

Pearson Education

merger of Penguin with Pearson Longman, a merger that was described in financial circles as a 'good fit'. The deal took the form of a reverse take-over, as did some of the other publishing deals at the time.[24] It had the effect of making the Penguin Publishing Company, a company set up in 1961, the holding company for both Longman and Penguin and, indeed, for the whole of Pearson Longman's book publishing interests. These were to be profitably extended a year later with the purchase of all the shares in Wills & Hepworth, the publishers of *Ladybird Books*, a highly enterprising business described more fully below.[25]

In July 1970, as part of the new deal, the Penguin Publishing Company, which had appointed Mark Longman as its Vice-Chairman, acquired the whole of the share capital of Longman Holdings, wholly owned by Pearson Longman, and through a new issue of 6¼ million shares the total issued capital was brought up to 10 million shares.[26] On the day when the news of the merger was announced Penguin shares shot up by 3s. 3d. to 46s. 3d., valuing the company at £8.7 million.[27] To complete the Penguin deal, a significant minority interest in the firm was bought out. Before the merger, McGraw-Hill, as interested in Penguin as it had been in Longman, had built up a holding of 17.3 per cent in Penguin (649,000 shares). These were now sold, a move that led to a shilling fall of Penguin shares to 45s. 3d.

The *Economist*, in which Pearson had a direct interest, asked why Penguin had not sought to become an international company in its own right: it had 'the prestige, the products and the profits'. Of its total sales of 31 million books in 1969, the four million which had been sold in the United States accounted for 22 per cent of its revenues. It had the capital to have taken over a modestly based American company and 'possibly one

24   *The Bookseller*, 30 April 1974, 'City listens to publishing heads'.

25   See below, p.464.

26   See the report of the stockbrokers Buckmaster and Moore, *Penguin Publishing* (Feb. 1971).

27   *Economist*, 11 July 1970.

even larger than itself'. Instead, it was as afraid of an American take-over as Mark Longman had been.[28]

There were positive reasons for the new merger also, as there had been for the 'merger' between Pearson and Longman. Three-quarters of the new total combined turnover of Longman Holdings and Penguin Books was described as 'educational in character', and the merger of the two was said to offer possibilities of 'coordinated publishing' in other fields, too, 'notably juveniles and general hardbacks'. Longman had a very small paperback involvement, Penguin had a small but specialised hardback business.[29] There could be 'some joint purchasing of raw materials and print', both of which, as we have seen, had already increased in price. Most important, 'the ultimate backing of the main Pearson interests' would 'in itself create openings from which Penguin as an independent firm could not have profited'.[30]

At that time, exports and overseas sales accounted for 76.7 per cent of Longman sales and 56 per cent of Penguin sales, the latter chiefly in North America, still not a main Longman market, and in Australasia, which already was. And Gibson had added in his 1968 Report on the Pearson/Longman merger that 'we have sent a Longman Director, Mr. W.P. Kerr, to Australia to take charge of our operations in the whole of Australasia and the Far East'.[31] One of the last moves in the interim period covered in this chapter was the acquisition in 1976 of the Cheshire Publishing Company in Melbourne. This led to Longman Cheshire becoming Australia's leading educational publisher.

The *Economist* in pointing to the economic logic behind a merger between Longman and Penguin did not pay adequate attention to the comparative strength of Longman in relation to Penguin:

W.P. ('Bill') Kerr left running the Africa operations to go to Australia in 1968 as Managing Director E (Australia and the Far East). He remained there until his early death in 1981.

Personal collection

Longman and Penguin

	LONGMAN	PENGUIN
Number of employees	1,250	650
Capital employed	£7,631,000	£3,290,000
Sales	£10,377,000	£6,748,000
Pre-tax profits	£1,945,000	£900,000

Not only were the two companies very different in size, but, equally

---

28   *Ibid.*, 15 Aug. 1970.

29   *Economist*, 11 July 1970.

30   Buckmaster and Moore, *loc. cit.*, p.3.

31   *Annual Report*, 1968 p.7. (LA)

important, they had very different 'corporate cultures', to use the term of the future, as well as different histories, and the differences – some related to age as well as scale – were accentuated in 1970 by a planned, if undeclared, Pearson intention through Gibson to give the then Managing Director of Penguin, Christopher Dolley, executive power over the Longman Group too. Dolley, a Unilever-trained manager, had made a considerable success of the Penguin business in the United States, but there were doubts, not only in Harlow, about whether he was the right man with the right temperament and character to be given one of the potentially most important and interesting jobs in publishing.

~

At this point in the Longman story a flashback is justifiable in order to introduce one of the most imaginative publishers of the mid-twentieth century. Allen Lane (1902–1970), the founder of Penguin, was neither a manager nor thought of himself as one, and he died in the week that the merger between Pearson Longman and Penguin was announced. He had publishing links with the past, however, for he was the nephew of the nineteenth-century *fin-de-siècle* publisher, John Lane (1854–1925), who 'At the Sign of the Bodley Head' had published Oscar Wilde and Anatole France.

Having no son, John had passed over his business to his nephew, then called Alan Williams, who was born in Bristol, a Longman echo, and who moved to London at the age of sixteen.[32] There was little in common, however, between 'At the Bodley Head' and 'At the Sign of the Ship'. Nor was there any link between the House of Longman and Penguin during the highly innovatory first decades of Penguin history.

Allen Lane had brought to birth the first of his ten Penguins, 'conceived on a railway platform', on 3 July 1935 in the crypt of Holy Trinity Church in Euston Road. They appeared At the Bodley Head. All of them reprints, they were well-designed as well as cheap (sixpence), a price said to have been decided upon because of the Woolworths slogan, 'Nothing over sixpence'. Woolworths did, in fact, stock them, and ten more of them were promised every three months, a promise fulfilled. By the spring of 1937 there were more than a hundred, and Penguin Books, incorporated in 1936, had established itself as a successful independent company.

Its colophon, as unforgettable as the Longman ship, had been designed by a member of the Bodley Head staff, Edward Young, who in 1954 was to be the author of Penguin Number 1,000, *One of Our Submarines*. By then there were many Penguin originals as well as reprints, including non-fiction Pelicans and Penguin Specials which had followed in the wake

---

32   J.E. Morpurgo, *Allen Lane, King Penguin* (1979), p.12 and Jeremy Lewis, *Penguin Special* (2005).

of the Penguins, after Lane had moved his premises to Harmondsworth, a new place on the publishing map, not far from what was to become Heathrow Airport. The Specials dealt, as did many other publishers, particularly Gollancz, with topical issues in world politics: some of them sold more than a quarter of a million copies. Few of the titles would ever have been published by Longmans, Green. Nor would Longmans, Green have matched the speed of Penguin Special production. The first Penguin Special, *Searchlight on Spain*, by 'the red Duchess' of Atholl, MP, was brought out only eleven weeks after she finished writing it.[33]

The first Pelican had been edited by an Indian, Krishna Menon (1896–1974), who after Indian Independence in 1947 was to become a highly ideological Indian High Commissioner in London; and a third person involved in the early selection of titles and in the first editing was the social historian H.L. Beales (1889–1988), then and throughout his academic career a lecturer at the London School of Economics. Beales was a very different kind of social historian from G.M. Trevelyan, and in 1976 became the first President of the new Social History Society. He wrote little himself, but he knew a great deal about what almost every other social historian had written. He also knew more about the secrets of Lane and the early history of Penguin than any competing publisher.

The early Penguin bias was social, not academic, and the desire on Lane's part to make money was strong. His fiction list was managed by Eunice Frost, who had begun life as his assistant, and it was after a visit to Agatha Christie that he first dreamed of a series of Bodley Head paperbacks: he had been short of anything to read on the train. Instead, 'Green Penguins', easily identified by their colour, took their place, detective stories then in fashion, with Agatha Christie prominent among his authors. Lane knew how to sell them. Indeed, the 'peculiarity of Penguin', it was claimed in 1937, was that it had 'put the selling into bookselling'.[34] But there was a sense of style too, along with a strong element of innovation at Harmondsworth.

During the Second World War the paper rationing system favoured Penguin – allocations were based on pre-war sales – and after the end of the War, which had popularised Penguins in barracks, aerodromes and ships, including submarines, Penguin Classics attracted a wide readership. The 1950s was their golden age: *The Odyssey*, translated by E.V. Rieu, sold a million copies by 1960, a figure that would have amazed Andrew Lang. So, too, would the range of novels included in Penguin Modern Classics, novels

---

33 *Fifty Penguin Years* (1985), p.29. 'The maps ... needed continual revision as the situation changed' (*Liverpool Daily Post*, 10 June 1938).

34 *Shelf Appeal*, Aug. 1937, quoted in *Fifty Penguin Years*, p.21. The book was designed to accompany an exhibition held in the autumn of 1985 in the Royal Festival Hall. It had an introduction by the novelist Malcolm Bradbury.

The first Penguin

BL YK 2006.a.17447

with grey spines and provocative pictorial covers. When the Company went public in 1961, the issue was heavily over-subscribed, and the share price for the thirty per cent of issued capital on offer rose by 43 per cent on the day of issue. Lane became a paper millionaire.

By the mid-1960s, when Penguin had competitors – Pan Books was launched in 1946 and Fontana in 1952, each with hardback affiliations – there were more than 3,000 Penguin titles in print, a remarkable backlist, and a *New Penguin Shakespeare* was appearing in regular instalments. In 1964 there were 363 new titles, more than a quarter of them 'originals', books published for the first time in any form, and in 1966, the year of the publication of *The Penguin John Lennon*, an Education Division of Penguin was launched, directed by Charles Clark, a move into the specifically school textbook field where Longmans, Green was so strong.

When the Company published three Nuffield Foundation projects associated with curricular reform, in two cases it was as a co-publisher with Longmans, Green, the first convergence in the history of the two businesses. Not surprisingly, this was a point seized upon by the *Economist* – and others – when the Penguin/Longman merger was announced in 1970.[35] The Education Division of Penguin was not financially successful, however, and later the schools market was left entirely to Longman, who became sole publishers of the Nuffield Projects. For the *ELT* market, in which Longman was so well-established, a new Penguin course 'Success with English' offered readers tapes and wall charts as well as books and this was successful, for despite having to compete directly with Longman courses, it was in use by 1970 in no fewer than thirty-two countries. All in all, new titles in education rose to fifty in 1968, seventy-five in 1969 and ninety in 1970, by which time there were around 214 titles.

Lane had been knighted in 1962, was made a Companion of Honour in 1969, and in the same year had been awarded the Albert Gold Medal of the Royal Society of Arts 'for his contribution to publishing and education'. Moreover, although he himself had no experience of higher education, such was the reputation of Penguin that there were serious discussions about the setting up of a university-based trust to acquire Lane's personal shares in the Penguin business at two-thirds of their market value. The most experienced educationist to emerge from the difficult discussions, guided by Lord Goodman, trusted adviser to Harold Wilson, was Boyle, who moved from politics to become Vice-Chancellor of the University of Leeds in 1970, but who, like Mark Longman, died young, in 1981. He had joined the Penguin Board in 1965, and in 1970 had been its Acting Chairman before Gibson took over.

The person who made Gibson change his mind about Christopher Dolley's suitability to run a combined Penguin/Longman business was Robert Allan (1914–1979), who, after Mark's death, had been brought into

35   *Economist*, 11 July 1970.

the affairs of Longman by Pearson Longman. Allan, to be created a Life Peer in 1974, was a politician with a distinguished naval war record, who had served successive Conservative Prime Ministers, beginning with Macmillan. Before joining Longman, he had been responsible inside Pearson for handling Bracken House's publishing acquisitions. He was, indeed, far better known outside Harlow in 1970 than the people with whom he had to work closely.

In order to make Gibson appreciate the difficulties in the way of making Dolley overall Managing Director, Allan invited Gibson to Harlow to meet the Longman Advisory Board. It was a crucial meeting. Had the appointment of Dolley been pushed through from Bracken House, there would have been intolerable strains at Harlow, and Rix, who was to play the central executive role in Longman in the future, would probably not have stayed there.

Thereafter there was considerable turbulence in Penguin during the five years between 1973 and 1978, when re-shaped Longman followed its own course, although new birds were regularly brought into the Harmondsworth aviary, some, like Peregrines, to languish, others, like Puffins, to fly.[36] In 1973 Gibson was succeeded as Chairman of Penguin by Jim Rose, his 63-year-old brother-in-law, who chose a war-time colleague

An early Picture Puffin of 1963

Personal collection

at Bletchley Park, Peter Calvocoressi, as Publisher and Chief Executive. Before joining Penguin, Calvocoressi had been a Reader in International Relations at Sussex University and a Director of Chatto and Windus. He made it clear in 1972 that he was being contracted for only a limited period of five years.

Rose and Calvocoressi made their first major decision very quickly. They dissolved the Education Division of Penguin, incorporating many of its titles in their general list and handing others over to Longman.[37] Meanwhile, Charles Clark had left the Educational Division of Penguin to

---

36 The Puffins were under the care of Kaye Webb from 1961, who took charge also of a hard-back Kestrel collection, originally Longman Young Books. She stayed on until her retirement in 1979.

37 The *TES*, 1 March 1974, had praised Penguin Education's 'freshness of approach and design' and the way in which it had 'developed a personality for [its] imprint which contrasted usefully with those of [its] more staid seniors'.

join Hutchinson, of which he later became Chief Executive. He was not the only senior employee to leave. Even before the brief Penguin-Longman merger Tony Godwin, a possible heir-apparent to Lane and a Penguin chief editor greatly admired by his authors, brought in, with no previous editorial experience, by Lane in 1958, had left the firm (a departure engineered by Lane), although he believed in a bigger Penguin business as a liberating influence on publishing policies.

There was one experienced survivor of the Lane régime, however, who survived all the changes of the 1970s: Ronald Blass, who had started by driving a Penguin van before being called up. He had returned to Penguin after the war and had risen steadily upwards in the organisation, becoming Sales Director in 1962 and later Executive Vice-Chairman. Now, working closely with Rix, he was instrumental in keeping the relationship between Longman and Penguin stable and amicable, in particular resolving the very difficult relationship which developed between Longman and Penguin in Australia. Relations were far better in Japan and South Africa.

~

At Harlow, Chapple (far more experienced than Rose), continued to play a major part in the development of Longman's overseas business. He carried immense weight, having further increased his hold over the business as a whole and of its daily operations after Mark's death in 1972. Indeed, a year before that, Newsom's death had meant that Chapple had no longer had to pay attention to his most prestigious colleague's activities inside and outside Harlow. He fully appreciated, however, that he had to depend on new men within the Longman Group, and in May 1972 as part of a bigger re-organisation he made Rix and Yglesias Joint Managing Directors and members of a Group Executive Committee with Chapple as Chairman and Beckett as Vice-Chairman and Finance Director.[38] At the same time, there was a 'sales re-organisation' and a separation out of the Accounts Department from other services.

The new Group Executive Committee replaced the previous top management trio of Allan, Beckett and Chapple himself, which had scarcely been a dynamic combination. Its managerial skills were limited. Beckett's weaknesses have been noted: Allan's gifts were those of a politician and a mediator, not of a 'developer'. By contrast, Rix was a developer by instinct, who had used his position as Divisional Head of *ELT* since 1968, when the divisional structure was introduced, as a base from which to galvanise the Longman business as a whole, and he was ready to take over. Nevertheless, his progress to the position of Chief Executive in 1976 after Chapple's retirement, which in retrospect seems as 'natural' as the Longman Penguin merger, was not entirely straightforward.

---

38   Note of 31 May 1972. See also Chapple, Note to Staff, 7 Dec. 1972. (LA)

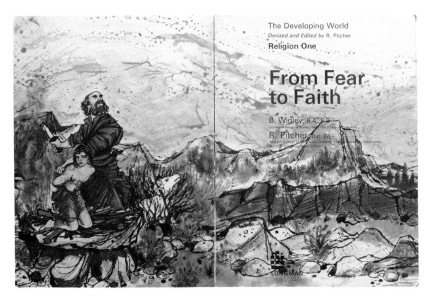

The Developing World
Devised and Edited by R. Pitcher
Religion One

**From Fear
to Faith**

B. Wigley, B.A., D.D.

R. Pitcher, Dip. Ed.

LONGMAN

Roy Yglesias was instrumental in publishing a co-ordinated series, *The Developing World*, 1969, which covered geography, history, religion and science, and reflected the approach of many secondary schools

Personal collection

In particular, his joint managing directorship with Yglesias was frustrating to him, for the two men were temperamentally different. Yglesias seemed to Rix 'rather lackadaisical', and Yglesias may have found Rix 'rather pushing'. There was a far bigger immediate difference, however, in attitudes and aspirations than there was in temperament. Yglesias remained seriously interested only in the secondary-school business which Newsom had brought him in to develop: Rix had a sense of the business as a whole, centre and periphery, and he not only knew what he wanted it to become, but was confident that he could make it become so.

His vision was apparent at a series of planning conferences which were held in 1973, 1974 and 1976, the records of which fortunately still exist in the Longman Archive at Reading. The papers prepared for them and the discussions of the conferences themselves covered not only the current situation and hopes for the future, but the fate of individual titles of current and possible Longman books.[39] Longman's directors always recognised that, in a sense, a publishing house is nothing but the specific titles it publishes.

In dealing with the *ELT* Division, therefore, it was not only noted that total turnover had risen from £750,000 in 1961 to £3m in 1973, but that new courses were successfully replacing the old faithfuls: L.G. Alexander's *New Concept English* (1967–73) now accounted for 16.3 per cent of the turnover, W. Stannard Allen's single title *Living English Structure* accounted for 5 per

---

39 Records of: 'Long-range Planning Conferences' November 1973 and November 1974; 'Management Conference' October 1974 and 'Senior Management Planning Conference' July 1976. (LA files from the Office of the Chief Executive 408-638)

cent and the various series of readers 18.8 per cent. And *ELT* as a whole was providing 20.6 per cent of total Group sales. Periodicals too were an increasing source of revenue, and the need for a 'strategic drive' into publishing dictionaries and reference books was agreed upon at a planning conference and is covered later in this chapter.

Just as Gibson in his 1970 annual report had referred particularly to Longman's enlarged Medical Division and to periodical publishing, so the 1973 planning conferences noted with satisfaction that the Journals Division, formed, as we have seen, in 1970, now published thirty-nine journals, of which nineteen were medical and paramedical, co-existing comfortably alongside the medical book publishing. The merger of J. & A. Churchill and E. & S. Livingstone within the Longman frame had created a medical publishing operation with a well-balanced list of 850 titles. As well as the flagship titles (the *Medical Directory* and *Gray's Anatomy*[40] which Longman had published for over a hundred years), the list included textbooks, high-level monographs on medical practice, and books on nursing. Some of them had a transatlantic appeal. Indeed, medical publishing was to be a key component in the development of Longman's United States publishing.

The conferences also kept a careful watch on the activities and progress of key competitors, and the conference records include the following table comparing four of them:

Longman and Its Competitors

COMPETITORS	1969		1973	
	Sales (£000s)	Profits (%)	Sales (£000s)	Profits (%)
Longman	9,131	17.9	14,026	24.5
Macmillan	7,237	3.1	11,114	6.5
ABP	7,402	8.4	12,631	10.3
Heinemann	4,007	12.9	7,533	15.4

Minutes of Board Planning Conference (LA).

The extraordinarily high Longman profit margins, not to be maintained in later years, were mainly attributable to the African (and

---

40 Susan Alan, described as a visual text analyst, prepared for Churchill Livingstone International an undated account of 'three centuries of the publishers' trade' called *Archives of the Corporate Dance Card*. It began with an 1837 illustration of an advertisement of John Churchill's Medical Books 'published during the current year. Mr. Churchill was described as 'the successor to Messrs Callow and Wilson'. Callow had begun publishing in 1784.

especially to the Nigerian) business and to *ELT* publishing. The House was in a dominant position, now comparable to its position in the first decades of the nineteenth century, but its dominance was not to survive in its entirety the collapse of the Nigerian market eight years later.

In looking to the future Rix was not always happy to find himself in a quartet which included as well as Yglesias both Beckett and Chapple. He sometimes found that Chapple, the man of power but, in his opinion, a leader with little vision of the future, could be difficult. The result was that both men spent rather more time in tricky discussion than either of them wished and less on the affairs of business which Chapple had always put first and which Rix was consistently to put first then and in the future. Yet it is important not to exaggerate. Despite tension within the quartet, it was Chapple within it – and he had the necessary authority – who encouraged Yglesias to seek early retirement in 1975, leaving Rix in charge of all of the daily operations of the House, excluding finance.

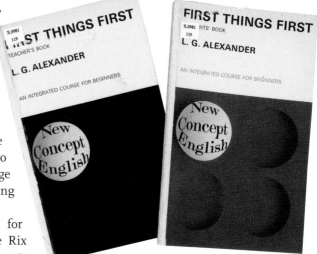

There was, however, another frustration for Rix. Finance was Beckett's domain, and while Rix appreciated Beckett's intellectual (and literary) interests, he did not consider that his financial control was decisive enough. Nor did he judge him sufficiently 'dynamic', an adjective that regularly recurs in this *History* (see Chapter 3), to make necessary managerial changes. Nevertheless, in 1976, when Chapple retired, Beckett accepted with grace the promotion of Rix to the post of Chief Executive, which he might have sought for himself, and he worked loyally with him until his death in 1979. In the same year Allan died in Australia, having retired early from Pearson Longman to pursue his outside interests and having ventured on a deserved farewell round-the-world trip arranged by Pearson.

The final handover by Chapple, who was to visit Harlow many times after his retirement, was a happy occasion, as his later visits were to be. At a farewell ceremony at Brown's Hotel, London, captured in photographs, Chapple reverted to the old familiar metaphor, choosing as his last words:

> May Ship and Swan and all the crew
> Accomplish what they try to do.

In an account of a retirement party held for him in Harlow written around this time, Chapple was described as the Captain, and Roger Brooke, who had joined Pearson in 1971 and was to become non-executive Chairman

By 1979 about a quarter of Longman's turnover came from the teaching of English as a foreign language (ELT). Louis Alexander was one of the best-selling authors in the English language selling over two million copies a year – far more than any popular novelist! *New Concept English* was published between 1967 and 1973. Alexander also published *Look, Listen and Learn* 1971, *Follow Me* 1980, *Direct English* 1993–1998, as well as practice books and the *Longman English Grammar*

BL X.0981/119.

of Longman, as the Admiral.[41] The Admiral was in fact less important than the Captain, and the next issue of *The Log*, now the House journal, devoted two pages with photographs to what it called 'The Captain's Table', a new table with a few old faces still around it.[42]

Brooke remained non-executive Chairman of Longman from 1976 to 1979, leaving Pearson in 1979 to become Managing Director of EMI, at that time and later at the centre of the entertainment business. It says more about *Who's Who* as it was then composed than it does about Brooke that his name was not in it (although it was to appear afterwards). Yet Brooke had had an interesting career before he joined Pearson, working first at the Foreign Office, then as second-in-command to Ronald (later Sir Ronald) Grierson in the Industrial Reorganisation Corporation. He apparently was the first person to commit Pearson funds to Jake Eberts, founder of what became Goldcrest, for the making of the film of *Watership Down*, based on the highly successful novel by Richard Adams, which appeared in Penguin in 1974 (having been first published in 1972).

The interplay of Pearson personalities was even more intricate than that of Longman personalities, for the multi-faceted Pearson business, which did not always consider itself as a conglomerate, incorporated such a diversity of parts and of personalities that it was difficult for the men of Millbank Tower to formulate or implement a common strategy.[43] Individual units were left to themselves, in the same way that its Board seemed willing to leave Longman. This was the policy not only under Gibson but under his successor, Michael Hare, the second Viscount Blakenham, four years younger than Rix, who succeeded Gibson as Chairman of Pearson PLC in 1983, having been its Chief Executive since 1978. He remained Chairman until 1997.

Rix did not meet him until 1976, and their subsequent relationship, though largely amicable, was not to be an easy one. With the death of Mark, any family ties in Longman were broken, but there was still a strong family strain in the Pearson business. Like Gibson, whose son briefly joined Rix's new Captain's table in 1976, Blakenham had a Cowdray connection. His mother was the daughter of the second Viscount Cowdray. One of Blakenham's closest business associates, however, Frank (later, 1998, Sir Frank) Barlow, had no such family ties. Ironically, his career as a newspaper manager had begun in 1960 in Nigeria, where Longman interests were so strong. He was to go on into the 1990s as a key figure in

---

41 *The Log* No. 6, May 1977, p.10. (LA Part II/214A)

42 *Ibid.*, No. 7, March 1978, pp.2–3.

43 Until 1975 S. Pearson Publishers and Pearson Longman held their annual meetings at Bracken House. Starting in 1975, however, they were held in Millbank Tower.

Pearson management, serving as Pearson Plc's Managing Director from 1990–1996.

In 1979, however, all this was in the future, and when Brooke left Pearson for EMI he was succeeded by a Scot, James Lee, who, after attending school at Glenalmond, had studied at the Harvard Business School before joining McKinseys, the business consultants. He was the first man with a professional business training to lead Pearson Longman, and he was granted the title of Chief Executive also. His head-hunter told him that Blakenham wanted a Chief Executive of Pearson Longman who would help him to develop a long-term strategy for Pearson as a whole, guiding him as to where they should place Pearson capital.[44]

Lee stayed on until 1984, by which time Rix was well established in the post of Chief Executive at Harlow. Strategist rather than operational manager, Lee introduced, with the wholehearted encouragement of Rix, more sophisticated strategic planning procedures at Harlow. He was also highly supportive of the acquisition in 1980 of Oyez Publishing, the first in a sequence of strategic acquisitions. When the announcement was made that Longman had purchased the publishing business of the Solicitors' Law Stationery Society, he was quoted as saying: 'We paid £1.7 million for goodwill which gives you an indication of how much we wanted to buy this. If we had not done this deal we could virtually have kissed goodbye to getting into the legal publishing field in the United Kingdom because it is controlled by so few people.' Soon afterwards Lee himself faced problems inside Pearson. He was caught up in the problems of the ill-omened Goldcrest film business, to which he moved over full-time in 1983.[45]

~

At a launch party for the new acquisition at Lincoln's Inn in March 1980 Rix jokingly said that Longman was such a dynamic company that it had only taken it 258 years to get into law publishing. For both Rix and Lee this was a real milestone, giving Longman a much-desired strength in 'professional' publishing. It could now compete with established law publishers in publications aimed at practising lawyers as well as at accountants and tax specialists. A flagship was the *Solicitors' Journal*, and a large proportion of income was derived from subscriptions to it. Some of Oyez's book titles

---

44   See J. Eberts and J. Illat, *My Indecision is Final: the Rise and Fall of Goldcrest Films* (1990), p.49. Chapter 5, consisting largely of personal statements, is called 'The Pearson Connection'.

45   The film industry had not been mentioned to him by his head-hunter, and Lee thought that the business was solely that of a newspaper and book company. It was only after he took on the post that he learnt from Blakenham of Pearson's desire to get into film and television. See *ibid.*, p.53, and for some of the complications in the story pp.285ff.

were 'mouth-watering' to Rix and his colleagues, titles such as *Tax Forms Manual* and *Profitable Management of a Solicitor's Practice*. Two major legal works on conveyancing, a major preserve of solicitors, and on road traffic offences were almost as well-known as the *Hambro Tax Guide*, 'certainly the most highly regarded consumer tax publication on the market'.

If the takeover of Oyez was seen as a milestone, there were two other earlier acquisitions, completely different from each other, which were important to the House – *Keesing's Contemporary Archive* and Ladybird. The former was a well-established weekly news reference service containing detailed factual and objective reports on all major national and international political, economic and social developments throughout the world. The publication averaged twelve pages and over 20,000 words per issue. The distinctive binders were a familiar sight on library reference shelves. It had administrative headquarters in Bristol and editorial offices in Bath[46].

Printing continued in the West Country, and all the existing staff were retained, but there had been some changes in the Board of Directors, which was joined by Allan, Beckett, Chapple and P.J. Munday, Divisional Managing Director in charge of the Longman Journals Division at Harlow.[47]

The second acquisition in December 1971, that of Ladybird, arranged like the acquisition of *Keesing's* on the initiative of Pearson, was an exceptionally shrewd move. All the shares in Wills & Hepworth, Ladybird's owners, were bought, so that there was no minority interest to consider, and in 1974 there were to be record Ladybird sales of 24 million books, one in five of them exported. By then, Ladybirds had been translated into around fifty languages, including Arabic and Japanese.

As in the case of Penguin, a flashback is necessary. In 1904 William Hepworth of Kidderminster had entered into a partnership with Harry Wills, owner of a bookshop in Loughborough. Wills produced his own *Almanac*, an old way into publishing, and ran his own library (again back in spirit to the eighteenth century) while

The Ladybird list ranged widely, introducing young readers to all kinds of new subjects, including computers, producing over fifty titles a year and many being translated into over sixty languages. The Key Words Reading Scheme was one of the most widely used in the UK, and Ladybird also produced, from 1976, with Longman Caribbean, The Ladybird Sunstart Reading Scheme by William Murray

BL X.0900/455

---

46   For a short account of Keesing's see *The Log* Dec. 1974 pp.13–14, 'Keesing's Contemporary Archives 1931-74 Just Giving the Facts', by A. Day. (LA Part II 213)

47   Munday had joined the *Financial Times* in 1964. In 1969 he had been appointed Managing Director of *The Practitioner* and in 1970 Managing Director of the newly formed Journals Division.

carrying out 'every description of printing' in his Angel Press. The partnership was well-timed, and by the end of the decade it had begun printing children's books for other publishers, one of the first of them a collection of Bible stories with hand-coloured illustrations, 'pure and healthy literature' in which both men put their trust. It was during the First World War, which raised problems for most publishers, that the two men decided to print and publish books themselves under the imprint Ladybird, the logo for which was registered in 1915. (No one recalled in the 1970s just how the name was chosen.)

During the Second World War Wills and Hepworth began to produce their books in a reduced 'pocket-size'. Until then all of them had dustcovers and miniature cover pictures hand-pasted on to the bound cover. Print runs of at most a few thousand just made this feasible. Yet after 1945 sales increased greatly when James Shield Clegg, who had joined the business as a Director before the War, was Company Accountant and Douglas Keen editor; and although the Company continued to carry out general printing on commission, the range of their own titles was greatly extended. One of them in 1945 was by Uncle Mac, Derek McCulloch, of the BBC, who had regularly presented *Children's Hour*.[48]

During the 1960s, when the royal children, Charles and Anne, were among Ladybird readers, the crucial decision was taken to abandon general commercial printing, but that was not the only change. As in the case of Longman, there was an increasing bias towards educational publishing. Thirty-six carefully graded, illustrated and integrated Ladybird reading books were launched in 1964, making the name *Ladybird* almost synonymous with early reading. The textual pattern, based exclusively on the use of the key words most frequently used in the English language, 'one quarter of all those we read and write', was devised – after research – by William Murray, an experienced headmaster, and Joe McNally, an educational psychologist.[49] 'The first books that a child looks at', Ladybird proclaimed, 'are as important as any he will ever have. If they delight and satisfy, then it is certain that a solid foundation is being laid for a love of books.'[50]

Thomas the Tank Engine and Ladybird readers

Personal collection

---

48   See S. Briggs, *Those Radio Times* (1981), Ch.4, 'Hullo children'.

49   Their *Keywords to Literacy*, 'a teachers' book', was published by the Schoolmaster Publishing Company.

50   There is an interesting article on Ladybird by P. Medlicott, 'A 52 page package', in *New Society*, 13 Feb. 1975.

This was a universal proposition, and, as in the case of the Longman Group, successful attempts were made to expand it overseas as well as in Britain. The consequences were Ladybird moves overseas into continental Europe and the Third World. Overseas translations, the first of them in Swedish, with two African texts to follow, made the Ladybird name known across the continents. This too was what was to come to be called 'globalisation', not a Ladybird key word.

The word 'education' was interpreted broadly and imaginatively, and there were *Read-it-Yourself* fairy tales and *Storyboard* books. *Thomas the Tank Engine* was a universal success. Not surprisingly, therefore, after the take-over by Pearson Longman the Ladybird premises were moved in 1972 from Loughborough marketplace to a new three-and-a-half acre site where operations in publishing, printing, binding and warehousing could all be integrated. Such integration was becoming a feature of business operations during the 1970s. There was to be integration of a different kind too. At first Ladybird reported directly to Pearson which had bought it in 1971; but it was deemed too small a unit for that to be appropriate, and later it became a Division of Longman with its Managing Director, Malcolm Kelley, formerly a sales director of Penguin, joining the Board of the Longman Group.

~

Ladybird regularly raised questions of editorial policy. So also did emphasis within Longman itself on the importance of publishing more dictionaries and reference books, treated as a priority even before Rix took over as Chief Executive. Rix himself emphasised its importance in a note to all Divisional Managing Directors which had been approved by the Publishing Advisory Committee;[51] at that point a key committee for him in pushing his own priorities. From 1 January 1973, therefore, a new Dictionaries and Reference Book Department was formed within the *ELT* Division (F). Its designated responsibilities included managing *Roget's Thesaurus* and a *Longman English Larousse*, keeping under review opportunities for new dictionaries, English and foreign, and planning reference books, including reference books for the 'non-professional readers'.[52]

Further attention was to be paid to marketing, and as far as dictionaries were concerned, it was recognised from the start that American lexicographers should be involved and that Commonwealth and Third World needs should be met. Charles McGregor, then Longman Publisher of Dictionaries and Reference Books, stressed that as the use of the English language throughout the world had increased, one element of globalisation,

51   *The Log* 1985, p.8 'The Ladybird story'. Note circulated by Rix, 6 Dec. 1972. (LA Part II 213)

52   *Ibid.*

attention would have to be paid to 'common-core English', that portion of the language which was common to all varieties of English wherever it was spoken and written as a first language. In other words, the role of the new department was directly related to overseas expansion, particularly in the United States, which for Rix was an equally important priority.

For guidance and for action the Longman Group was able to draw on a British linguistician of genius, Randolph Quirk, brought up in a farming family on the Isle of Man and educated at University College, London, to which he returned as a Professor in 1959, subsequently becoming Rector and Vice-Chancellor of London University from 1981 to 1985. He was knighted in 1983 and became a peer in 1994. Quirk, introduced to Longman by Chapple, was described by a learned American colleague as 'probably the finest student of the English language since Harry Sweet', the original of Professor Higgins in G.B. Shaw's *Pygmalion* and the musical *My Fair Lady*. Quirk himself, who dabbled in Welsh while he was a student evacuated to Wales, stressed in recollections years later how he became 'obsessively sceptical about orthodoxies, religious or political'.[53] In particular, he did not believe in 'the decadence of the language', a topic of conversation on both sides of the Atlantic, or in one 'single standard of acceptability'.[54]

Quirk had initiated a detailed survey of contemporary English usage, blessed by the BBC, which gave him a desk and, still more important, access to all its tapes. Chapple and Rix helped him too with Longman financial support as he turned to computational analysis, made possible by a 'vast and clumsy' Atlas machine in Gordon Square, the kind of computer that was before long to make its way into a museum. His main helpers were Professor Geoffrey Leech, Professor of Linguistics and Modern English Language, at the University of Lancaster, Sid Greenbaum, later to succeed Quirk as Quain Professor of English Language and Literature at University College, London, and Professor Jan Svartvik, initially Assistant Director of the Survey. They were also co-authors of Quirk's great book *A Grammar of Contemporary English* which Longman published in 1972. It was followed shortly afterwards by two shorter books, *A Communicative Grammar of English* and *A University Grammar of English,* and then in 1985 by *A Comprehensive Grammar of the English Language* described in the *Preface* as 'a culmination of our joint work' resulting 'in a grammar that is considerably larger and richer than *A Grammar of Contemporary English*'.

The remarkable capacity of Quirk to attract collaborative finance was as

A
COMPREHENSIVE
GRAMMAR
OF THE
ENGLISH
LANGUAGE

Randolph Quirk
Sidney Greenbaum
Geoffrey Leech
Jan Svartvik

Longman

Published in 1985, this *Grammar* was the culmination of the joint work of Quirk and his co-authors

Personal collection

---

53 Interview with K. Brown, Feb. 2001, published in K. Brown and V. Law, *Linguistics in Britain: Personal Histories* (2002), a Philological Society volume.

54 See a brilliant broadcast talk that Quirk gave on 'Our Changing Language', printed in *The Listener,* 2 Jan. 1984. He quoted critically a correspondent in *The Times* who had warned that 'the prospect for the communication of ideas is bleak'.

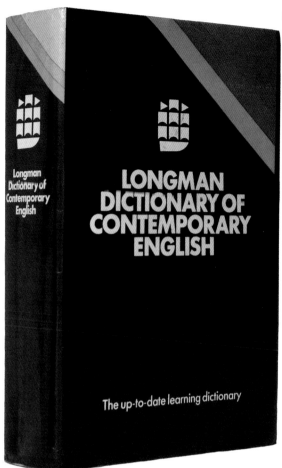

*Longman Dictionary of
Contemporary English*, first
published in 1978

Personal collection

striking as his delight in 'collaborative writing'. It was one of his outstanding qualities that he could raise money for fellowships, persuading the Ford Foundation, for example, to send to his College American scholars and the Leverhulme Foundation to 'bail out' his survey when it faced financial problems. Subsequently the Longman Group was to set up a Longman Fellowship that funded postgraduate students from the Third World so that they could use the survey materials in the publication of English teaching materials in their own countries. The Longman relationship was mutually rewarding. 'Dr. Johnson's publishers back in dictionaries' was a headline in *The Bookseller* in August 1976.[55]

An early demonstration of this was the publication in 1978 of the *Longman Dictionary of Contemporary English*, edited in-house by Paul Procter, a distinguished lexicographer himself and an excellent manager of lexicographers and of the dictionary-making process. Described as 'the up-to-date learning Dictionary', it incorporated 55,000 entries with 69,000 examples of word usage in sentences. Designed to be read by anyone who turned to English as the living 'world language', it owed an immense debt to Quirk who again assembled a somewhat unruly team of distinguished non-lexicographers to advise him on new contemporary words in their own fields.

Their names, with a few changes, appeared too in the *Longman New Universal Dictionary* in 1982, 'specially designed for that most unspecialised readership, the family'. They included among others (they did not all attend) Germaine Greer, R.D. Laing, John Gross, Clive Jenkins, Melvyn Bragg, George Melly, Clement Freud, Anthony Hopkins, Billy Wright, Dipak Nandy, Janet Street-Porter and myself as Chairman. Their meetings took place in the deliberately, if inappropriately, grand setting of the Athenaeum Club. For Quirk and for John Ayto, who worked closely with him, language was always 'one jump ahead of lexicography'. The *Dictionary* claimed to be – and was – 'non-sexist': 'chairperson' appeared as well as chairman. As Chairman I was not always addressed as such. Nor as 'Chair'.

New words figured as well as new meanings. 'Teen-ager' was one of the former: 'acrobatic' one of the latter. 'When I use a word', said Humpty Dumpty in *Through the Looking Glass*, 'it means no more and no less than

---

55   *The Bookseller*, 21 Aug. 1976.

I want it to mean.' His words seemed to apply more generally in the late-twentieth than in the late-nineteenth-century context. There were other relevant aspects of dictionaries too, as there were of encyclopaedias, and a second group of advisers to Quirk and his colleagues included consultants who covered 'Canadian English', 'New Zealand English' and 'South African English'. It was strictly relevant too that some words came into the language from slang, including American slang, words like 'budget' which meant 'poor quality', and 'regulate', meaning 'to enforce rules', 'to keep people in line'. The media were another major source.

One of the in house team professionally developing the Dictionaries project was Ken Moore, computer systems manager; and in one of the issues of the Longmans house journal, *The Log*, the question was asked 'did the computer really write the dictionary?'[56]

~

Similar but broader questions were asked in 1974, the year of the 250th Anniversary celebrations, in a leading article in the *Times Educational Supplement* by Brian Alderson. It was called 'At the Sign of the Ship'. On its front page the *TES* reproduced an illustration of Paternoster Row in the mid-nineteenth century.

Alderson in a so-called review of *Essays in the History of Publishing* – he was one of the contributors to it – ended in both dubious metaphor and dubious fact:

> As it now stands, 250 years on, the Longman Group has exchanged the florid confidence of its first ship for a smoothly styled vessel whose [design suggests] that it may have been worked to final precision with the aid of the ubiquitous computer.

The Longman vessel was not then 'smoothly styled'. Tim Jaques, its designer, had produced his colophon entirely by hand with meticulous care and imagination. The computer was then far from being ubiquitous. Cecil Beaton's photograph of Paternoster Row after the Blitz, well reproduced, was memorable, but an article by John Skillen, dealing with current bookselling trends, 'The Net and all that Jazz', was not: it was not referring, of course, to the Internet, not yet developed, but to the Net Book Agreement, then being challenged by a number of booksellers, particularly Pentos, after being upheld by the Restrictive Practices Court in 1962.

---

56   See an interesting account of Quirk's work by Philip Howard in an article on 'Data' in *The Saturday Book* (1979) pp.45–8.

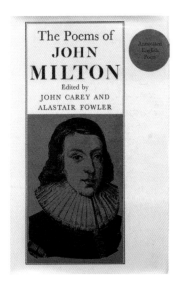

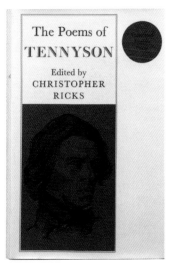

The academic publishing flourished in the 1970s and beyond. It was exemplified by the magisterial series *The Annotated English Poets*. Each title took the editor years to complete and was intended to be definitive

Personal collection

The debate continued.[57] Meanwhile, computerisation proceeded at Harlow as elsewhere, with more and more authors taking it up. Between the late 1980s and the end of the period covered in this *History,* as with other publishers there was a steady extension of the use of computers throughout the business of the House. Accounting, stock control, royalty calculations and payments were all affected. There was a steady expansion too in the computer power available. Rix, who avoided the word 'transformation', used the adjective 'steady' twice in dealing with Longman computer history. Mini-computers and later personal computers transformed the conditions of development, but it was not until the late 1970s that the full implications of computerisation began to be appreciated.

In 1976 it was announced that after eighteen months of planning a new 'phase in computerisation', 'the first stage in the planned employment of systems', had begun at Pinnacles with the arrival in May of an IBM 370 computer, a replacement for the existing Honeywell machine. The second number of *The Log* in December was to describe its 'teething troubles'. It was only after 'one false start and a few sleepless nights' that the main invoicing and stock system were transferred to the new computer. 'Far superior in power' to the discarded computers, it reduced the invoicing cycle from 10½ to 5½ hours.

Anthony Hyman in *The Author* in 1980 described the silicon chip as being like 'a fantasy which has suddenly materialised from science fiction',[58] and a pioneering seminar on 'authors, publishers and the microchip' was organised by the Educational Writers' Group of the Society of Authors in spring 1981, one of several such groups within the Society. Gordon Graham, the Chairman of a new Publishers Association Multi-Media Committee, delivered the opening address in which he urged 'a new treaty between authors and publishers, adapted to the electronic age, [in order to] reaffirm the creative elements in authorship and publishing'. 'In the busy street of hurrying futurists the philosophical descendants of Gutenberg should say hello to one another'. Authors and publishers were partners in the diffusion of ideas. 'The author originates. The publisher disseminates.'[59]

57   *The Times,* 8 June 1995 described how 'book price fixing' had survived intact after a two-month enquiry by the Commons Heritage Select Committee. Authors quoted in support of its retention included Jilly Cooper, Mary Wesley and Joanna Trollope.

58   A. Hyman, 'Living with the Chip' in *The Author,* Vol. XCI, No. 2, Summer 1980, p.71. Hyman, the author of a biography of Babbage, had just published *The Coming of the Chip.* As early as the spring of 1971, before cassette players had become available in Britain, *The Author* had stated that 'cassettes or, more comprehensively, Audio Visual Recording and Presentation Systems (AVRP) have given rise to a fever of speculation and investment'.

59   *Ibid.,* Vol. XCII, No. 1, Spring 1981, pp.6–8.

A new quarterly journal appeared in 1977 called *The Media Reporter*, edited by a former staff journalist on the *Guardian*, and while it was not until after 1981 that the pace of technical change began to be fully appreciated in Britain and its implications assessed, the increasing use of the word 'multi-media' prepared the way. Both hope and fear were elements in the response, and when the example of the United States was cited, what was happening there was seen, as in the early years of broadcasting, as much as a warning as a model. Big publishers across the Atlantic, it seemed were getting bigger and bigger, and the bigger they got the more they were driven by the desire to boost best-sellers. The gap between best-selling authors and other authors was opening up dramatically.

The 'conglomerates' – the word was still placed between inverted commas in Britain in 1977 – were 'inter-media' in character. Thus, in the mid-1970s, RCA, the Radio Corporation of America acquired Random House, which then acquired Ballantine Books (300 titles), while CBS, the Columbia Broadcasting System bought Holt, Rinehart and Winston and Popular Library. An international dimension – it was still not called global – was evident when the Bertelsmann Group in Germany, in the future to become immensely powerful in world publishing, bought Bantam Books for a reported $70 million. Another merger was that between Penguin and Viking.[60]

~

As always when a sense of hope and a sense of threat co-mingled in British responses to technological change, the temptation to recall rather than to forecast was irresistible, and during the 1970s the recalling was not restricted to the House of Longman. Within the Pearson cluster of companies the *Financial Times* gave a dinner in November 1969 to celebrate its 25,000th issue, and in the following year the *Northern Echo*, the oldest newspaper in the Westminster Press, celebrated its 150th birthday. In 1972, when the BBC had celebrated its 50th anniversary, the final sentences in a brochure 'Profile of Fifty Years' expressed 'a modest sense of pride' in its record of having responded to 'the challenge of constant change'.[61]

On the front page of the *TES* 'extra' on Longman, where Alderson's 'review' appeared, the illustration of Paternoster Row appeared alongside an advertisement for John Murray books, mainly educational. The only 'non-educational' items listed were the first three volumes of Marchand's *Byron's Letters and Journals*. On the next page a full-page Longman advertisement was headed 'the 250 years Voyage': it referred both to the *Essays* and to an exhibition, 'The First 250 Years of the House of Longman', to be held at

---

60 See H. Moorepark, 'American Vistas' in *The Author*, Vol. LXXXVIII, No. 4, Winter 1977, pp.141–43.

61 A. Briggs, *The BBC, The First Fifty Years* (1985), p.36.

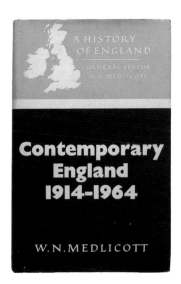

Longman, as well as the Oxford
and Cambridge University
Presses, was concerned with
history at every level. Edited
by W.N. Medlicott, *A History
of England* planned in ten
volumes (including *The Age
of Improvement* by Asa Briggs,
1959) was published by
Longman from 1953. Although
there was to be no uniformity
of treatment, Medlicott pointed
out that the authors had been
asked to give attention to various
aspects of national life and
achievement dominant at each
period – 'political, constitutional,
economic, social, religious,
military, foreign, or cultural'

Personal collection

the National Book League in Albemarle Street (Murray's street) and later
at Longman House in Harlow. It was subsequently to be shown at Heffers
Bookshop in Cambridge, still then a thriving institution, almost as well-
known outside Cambridge as Blackwell's (to which it now belongs) outside
Oxford.[62]

Alderson did not note that two of the essays in the volume, which
was beautifully bound and illustrated, a triumph of old technology, were
written by the then Joint Managing Directors of the Longman Group –
Yglesias and Rix. The former, who wrote on 'Education and Publishing
in Transition', did not mention Newsom, who had drawn him into the
business. The latter, aware of technological change, wrote 'Beyond the
Book' with Susan Holmes, who had worked with him at Longman on audio-
visual developments. Theirs was an essay which looked to the possibilities
inherent in new electronic technology.

The final chapter of *Essays*, called 'Planning for Change', was written
by two people outside Longman who were practically concerned with
the implications of the issues raised by Yglesias and Rix. Tony Becher,
who had guided an enthusiastic Nuffield Foundation in its projects in
educational technology,[63] was to be appointed Professor of Education at
Sussex University, and Brian (soon to become Sir Brian) Young, formerly
Headmaster of Charterhouse, a classicist by origin, had already become
Director-General of the Independent Broadcasting Authority in 1970.[64] His
direct switch from education to the media would have been inconceivable
when the debates on commercial television took place during the early
1950s. But so, too, would have been the advent of the Open University,
a favourite project of Harold Wilson. Inspired by Jennie Lee, Aneurin
Bevan's widow, it took in its first students a year later.[65]

One remarkable Longman writer and editor of educational books, who
was deeply interested in the Open University – and in 'lifelong learning'
– but who did not herself rely on new technologies was Marjorie Reeves
(1905–2003), an Oxford medievalist who was History Tutor at St. Anne's

62   *TES*, 14 May 1974.

63   See R.A. Becher, 'University Innovators' in the *British Journal of Educational
     Technology* (1979). This valuable journal was launched in 1965.

64   See B. Sendall, *Independent Television in Britain*, Vols. I and II (1982, 1983) and
     A. Briggs, *The History of Broadcasting in the United Kingdom*, Vol. V (1995). For
     Young's views on continuity and change in broadcasting see 'The Paternal
     Tradition in British Broadcasting', Watt Club Lecture (1983). See also G.
     Wedell, *Broadcasting and Public Policy* (1968).

65   See W. Perry, *Open University* (1976).

College and for a time its Vice-Principal.[66] During the late 1940s she had become deeply concerned about ways of teaching history in schools, and inspired by a fellow teacher, who years before had discussed her ideas with Nelson, she persuaded B.A. Workman, then Educational Adviser to Longmans, Green, to launch a new *Then and There* 'junior' series in 1951, each booklet, well illustrated, covering 'a patch' of history, a 'topic', with herself as general editor.

The first titles in 1954 included *The Medieval Village* and *The Medieval Town*, to be followed by *The Medieval Castle* and *A Medieval King Governs*, but all periods of history, including the most recent, were to be dealt with later, each requiring the young reader to carry out research on a particular aspect of the topic. The material was to be 'as concrete and detailed as possible, abstract terms and generalisations being eliminated'. In each booklet there was a 'How do we Know?' section and a glossary.[67]

Reeves, 'inner-directed', guided her publishers Longmans, Green rather than being guided by them, and over the years exercised a seminal influence on history teaching. Meanwhile, other historians were 'searched out' by the Company, which, like other educational publishers, spent a great deal of time – and money – on visits to universities. The countryside remained a favourite field of study. Lord Ernle's *English Farming Past and Present* had been published as long ago as 1912 and still sold; C.S. Orwin and A.E.H. Whetam's *History of British Agriculture, 1846–1914*, was a new book of 1964, as was G.E. Mingay's *The Gentry, The Rise and Fall of a Ruling Class* in 1976. Long before that a new historian had entered the field of European history – David Thomson, Master of Sidney Sussex College, Cambridge, recommended to Parker by Professor Lilian Penson, who, with her London College, Bedford, had been evacuated to Cambridge during the War. Thomson had arranged to publish his *Europe since Napoleon* with Alfred Knopf in the United States, but Mark Longman, a friend of Knopf, arranged for a joint publication which covered not only the nineteenth century but the years from 1789–1815.[68]

The *Then and There* series was revolutionary in its 'patch' approach to history. Edited by Marjorie Reeves FBA, herself a mediaevalist at St Anne's Oxford, she had started her adult life as a teacher in south-east London. When the 100th title was published, she described in *The Log* (No.8 October 1978) the criteria for choosing topics, which included the readers' experience for them to be able to 'stand in these new shoes'

Personal collection

---

66   See M. Reeves, 'A Love Affair with the Past' in the *TES*, 5 Dec. 1980 and J. Saraga, 'The History Woman' in *ibid*, 12 July 1985. In 1981 Longman published Reeves's Festschrift, edited by Ann Williams, *Prophecy and Millenarianism: Essays in Honour of Marjorie Reeves*.

67   Reeves kept the bundle of papers relating to her plans, including letters to Margaret Sutton of Longmans, Green, the first dated 29 June 1949, which by courtesy of Annabel Jones, I have been able to see.

68   Parker, 'Memoirs', p.37.

Thomson, who was to die young and to have many competitors, did not entirely supplant a far older book on the same subject, A.J. Grant and H. Temperley's *History of Europe*. Oddly enough, Russian censors ordered it to be removed from display at a Moscow exhibition:[69] it was, in fact, a very safe text. After Britain joined the Common Market there was scope for books on European history of a very different kind. They were not immediately forthcoming.

~

To catch the mood of the 1970s, when nothing at home as well as abroad could be left out of the reckoning, least of all relationships and memories, it is illuminating to leave the *Essays on the History of Publishing* behind and to examine in some detail the first two numbers of the new Longman house journal, *The Log*, the first numbers of which were published in July and December 1974. They begin with classified 'personal' advertisements of the kind that had until recently been printed on the first page of *The Times*: 'To all my friends to whom I have not been able to speak in person before my departure – Martin Marix Evans.' This implied that if Longman was no longer a family business, Longman House, Burnt Mill, Harlow, was a place where friends worked together. Some of them felt like members of a family and some, at least, were deeply aware of family history.

One of the photographs in the first issue was that of eighteen Longman pensioners, representing 555 years of service, who were present at a 250th anniversary lunch in July. There were new links, too, with the bigger Pearson Group. Twelve members of the Longman Journals Division had paid a visit to Bracken House in London to see the *Financial Times* put to bed, and a photograph of the opening of the Longman Exhibition showed Young and Wallis chatting amiably with Blass, then Vice-Chairman of the Penguin Board.

The first number of *The Log*, printed in England by Nicholson and Jermayne, Hertford, quite deliberately did not have an editorial. It was published from Room E201, and fourteen people, members of 'an editorial team', were picked out for special thanks. This was not the only team mentioned. The last pages, like the last pages of a newspaper, were devoted to sport, as we have seen an old Longman family preoccupation; and in addition to details of the soccer team, founded in 1970, for which a young Glenn Hoddle, whose father worked with Longmans, played on several occasions, there were references too to cricket, table tennis and squash teams and to the Sports and Social Club, nearing completion at the Pinnacles.

Scotland, so prominent in publishing history, now described as Longman North, a poor label, also had all its sporting activities reported.

---

69   *Grapevine*, Autumn 1985. (LA Part II 213)

Yet the time and space vistas of *The Log* were universally acceptable. Much of the first number was devoted to the 250th Anniversary, to *Essays in the History of Publishing*, and to the Exhibition mounted at the National Book League. *The Log* was 'enthusiastic about the Anniversary, emphasising [as it did] the continuity and depth of tradition in British publishing'. The continuity was well brought out in a photograph of the presentation to Longman of a silver salver by the Westminster Bank, which since the eighteenth century had been involved in even more mergers than Longman itself

Thomas Longman II had opened his first account with Smith, Payne and Smith of Lombard Street, which had remained independent from 1758 to 1902: he was one of its first customers. Another example of continuity involved the nineteenth century and the role of Longman as a giver rather than a receiver. When Chapple presented £5,000 to the Book Trade Benevolent Society, he reminded its President, Thomas Joy, that Thomas Norton Longman, William Longman and Cosmo Orme had been founder members of the Booksellers' Provident Institution from which the Benevolent Society had descended. He also referred back to the £10,000 benefaction of Thomas Brown.

The Log for July 1974 gave a stimulus to all senior and retiring staff to contribute to the process of recalling. Yet it is necessary to emphasize that the new was given as much importance as the old. On the same page in which it was announced that the unique but 'uneven' Longman Archive was to be 'placed on permanent loan' at the Library of the University of Reading,[70] it was also announced that the IBM 370 computer had been installed.

Felix Iwerebon joined Longman in 1961, and became the Managing Director of Longman Nigeria Ltd. Before joining Longman he had held several important civil service positions

Longman Archive

Much space in the first issue of *The Log* was devoted to another new venture, 'the first ever' conference of African managers, convened by Julian Rea and held at Harlow, in June, which included lectures on finance and personnel, and was opened by Chapple. Photographs of all the principal participants were shown, and brief biographies were placed beside them. Felix Iwerebon from Nigeria had worked with Longman for the longest time, since 1961, and he was to remain with Longman in frequently changing national circumstances after 1980.

Ben Moshi from Tanzania had worked with Longman since 1962 before the name Tanzania was given to his country; Alex Malinki from Malawi had been a Longman employee since 1964 and Mustafa Mutyaba from Uganda since 1965; and Stephen Tembo from Zambia joined Longman in May 1965 and Trix Johnson from Sierra Leone in 1966, Thomas Openda from Kenya in 1965, and Kwami Segbawu from Ghana in 1969. The last of these had taken over as Manager in 1971, responsible for Sierra Leone,

70 The Penguin Archive passed to the University of Bristol, Special Collections Section.

Examples of overseas educational publishing:

The *Target Course* was first published in 1977

Caribbean Lands A geography textbook first published in 1963 with the fifth edition in 1990

New Biology for Tropical Schools was originally published in 1958, followed by this new edition in 1969 and a third edition in 1981

The Lands and Peoples of East Africa This school certificate geography had its first edition in 1960, its second in 1973 and the third in 1986

Longman Archive

Liberia, Cameroon and Gambia as well as his own country.

The conference, leaving history behind, was 'particularly concerned with planning all aspects of company developments up to 1980, and in some cases beyond that date'. In African terms this was a long vista, and much was to happen to Longman in the continent before 1976, the terminal date of this chapter. More still was to happen to Hong Kong (and to Africa) by the end of the century, and in the second issue of *The Log* there was a photograph of seventy-two members of the staff of Longman Group (Far East) Ltd *en route* for Macao, which was (just) to outlive Hong Kong as a colonial territory.

In central Africa much had happened during the 1960s following Ian Smith's declaration of unilateral independence in Rhodesia in November 1965, and in 1970 he proclaimed an independent republic. Faced with sanctions, it too was short-lived, and the treaty was signed in 1979 with elections in 1980 bringing a new state of Zimbabwe into existence. The story of Longman first in Rhodesia and then in Zimbabwe, told in part in *The Log*, in itself reveals the intricacies of publishing in Africa. No manager for Rhodesia was present at the Harlow conference of African managers in 1974, yet in 1964 Longman Rhodesia had been brought into existence. Ben Gingell, who became its first Managing Director, had been appointed Manager for Central Africa in 1959, two years after arriving at Longman in Clifford Street. Sam Mpofu, a teacher, joined Longman Rhodesia in February 1967 and was appointed Marketing Manager in 1976 when a new two-storey office block was built to house the company. David Mackenzie was General Manager and Company Secretary. *The Log* devoted two pages to the staff in 1977.[71]

During the next three years, when an intransigent Smith lost control of the situation and Robert Mugabe, from a Marxist background, rose rapidly to power, the scenario completely changed, but Longman Zimbabwe with Mpofu as Managing Director recognised that at the point of change it was possible to take new initiatives. Thus, Joanna Sibanda, who had been Resident Representative for Longman in Matabeleland, was appointed to a new post as Area Manager, Southern Area, extending beyond Matabeleland to Victoria Province and Midlands. An expert in infant education, she was the first Zimbabwean woman to be appointed headmistress of a large school. As an author she had worked in the mid-1960s with Dr. Hemming on the original Longman *Day-by-Day English Course* for primary schools.

Rhodesia/Zimbabwe was in various respects a special case. Yet by 1976 every country in Africa, for all the diversity of the continent, sharing common problems and opportunities, was a special case. South of Zimbabwe, South Africa, which had become a republic in 1961 and left the Commonwealth, was ostracised in Britain and large parts of Africa for

---

71   *The Log*, No. 6, May 1977, pp.8–9. (LA Part II 213)

its apartheid policies. But on the spot Rob Francis, Publishing Manager in South Africa in 1976, carried out operational research and recruited new staff, capable of writing for black African schools. There was strong competition from Macmillan South Africa, which appointed Luchi Balarin, formerly of College Press, Zimbabwe, to pursue publishing and marketing development in black education throughout southern Africa. His approach was similar to that followed by the Macmillan Company in West Africa during the 1960s: he accepted state publishing as a natural development from which Macmillan could benefit.

In Kenya, Longman Kenya Ltd., incorporated as a private company in May 1965, specialised during the 1970s in the commissioning, editing, design, production and marketing of books for which there was a ready market in Kenya, sub-contracting its printing to Kenyan printers. It concentrated on the provision of up-to-date materials for use within Kenyan schools and employed a high proportion of Kenyan nationals as authors. In 1977 40 per cent of its shares were held by Kenyans, its Managing Director was a Kenyan, T.J. Openda, and of the fifty-eight staff employed only two were from Britain, one on a short-term basis. There were three British Directors, however, Rix, Rea and Williamson. The Company owned the leasehold of warehouse property and rented office accommodation in Nairobi. Trading profits rose threefold in 1975 from the 1974 figure, but there had been substantial losses in 1972 and very small losses in 1973. Turnover almost doubled between 1972 and 1975, but profits were affected by the need to make provision against amounts owing from Uganda and Tanzania.[72]

Such details, crucial to business success, do not do justice to the 'adventure' of publishing in Kenya and, indeed, elsewhere in Africa, a continent 'thrillingly' described in a 1961 Ladybird *Flight Five* by David Scott Daniell. An article 'Longman Kenya, Sales Safari' in a 1978 issue of *The Log*, replete with photographs, did not claim to be thrilling, but it was. In the first of eleven photographs Charles Mumanyi, a sales representative, was shown trying to climb up a steep rocky hill during the dry season: he and his safari boy had to unload the books in the attempt. The third photograph showed Titus Kamuyu, the Company's sales manager, on his way to a secondary school in a different part of Kenya: 'he is going to follow up the work of the reps, for he cannot just sit in his office while they do all the travelling'. The 'reps', sales representatives, played a major role in the dynamics of the African book trade as they had done in the dynamics of the book trade in Britain in the late-nineteenth century.

The most interesting photographs, numbers 7 and 9, showed Titus listening to the geography teacher at Mbugiti secondary school pointing out weaknesses in the old edition of *Map Reading for East Africa* that the

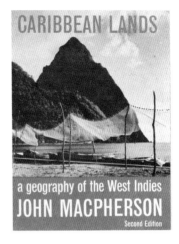

72   Draft letter, undated, written by Rea in 1978.

school was using and Frank Njuji, a 'rep', standing over a typical display of books in the staff room in which 'every teacher' was said to be interested. In number 7 the headmaster of the school is following the discussion with 'particular interest', doubtless reassured to learn that *Map Reading* had been revised and that new copies would soon be available.

Publicity was as important to educational publishing in Africa as it was to best-seller promotion in the United States, and in photograph number 9 Njuji is making sure that all the teachers in the staff room are involved in the photograph. The eleventh photograph in what was effectively a storyboard showed Njuji handling an Oliver and Boyd Craigie Kit which he had been taught to demonstrate by a representative from Britain. 'The physics teachers became so interested that they recommended the school to buy three kits. In one month Njuji sold twenty of them.'[73]

This article was completed with a Longman map of Africa showing Kenya, Uganda, Tanzania, Zambia, Malawi, Rhodesia (Zimbabwe), Botswana, Swaziland, Namibia, Lesotho and South Africa on the east, and Liberia, Sierra Leone, Ghana, Nigeria and Cameroon on the west. There were few statistics, but, in statistical terms it was plain that Nigeria, impelled by the presence of oil, was the great success story not only in Africa but in the world. 'Not surprisingly, in a country which is still some 75 per cent illiterate', wrote Rea, 'the oil revenues which formed the basis of the Development Plan were seen as an opportunity to provide both basic education for the total population and to tackle the problem of technical and managerial skills associated with rapid development from a primarily peasant base.' Consequentially Nigeria had 'by far the largest book requirement in black Africa, perhaps six times as large as Kenya, her nearest rival',[74] and in an outstanding year, which deserves to be picked out and remembered, 1976, Longman's Nigerian sales, which had almost doubled in a year, even exceeded its sales in Britain.

The Log reported very fully on other parts of the world, particularly the Far East, Singapore, Malaysia and Australia. The Arab world, centre of many of the tensions, was never neglected although it was impossible to treat book publishing there as a routine economic activity. Indeed, there were few places in the world where the political dimension could be ignored. 'I am sorry that politics impinge so much on the job', Adrian Higham wrote to Robert Duncan in Kuala Lumpur in 1968, 'but it always was so.'[75] Undoubtedly the changing political relationship between Malaysia and Singapore dictated many publishing decisions, and possible 'integration'

Black Orpheus was a magazine, published by Longman in the 1960s, containing African and Afro-American prose. The Magazine was sponsored by the Nigerian Western Region Ministry of Education

Longman Archive

---

73   *The Log*, No. 8, Oct. 1978, pp.14–16. (LA Part II 213)

74   C.J. Rea, memorandum of 11 Aug, 1978.

75   Letter of 7 Feb. 1968.

affected Hong Kong too – and, further away, Australia.[76]

In Japan representation was shared with Penguin as it had been since 1959 before there was any talk of a Longman-Penguin merger. The Longman Penguin office (LOPLO) situated in the heart of the Kanda district of Tokyo, the centre of Tokyo's bookselling and publishing area, employed a staff of five in 1977. The Director was Tadao Sakai.

~

High (and low) politics figured less in *The Log* than reminiscence. In its first year, the year of the 250th anniversary celebrations, the pattern was set by Joyce Nairn, who before retiring stayed on at Harlow just long enough to take part in them. She had begun working at Paternoster Row in a year of economic depression, 1931, when as a shorthand typist she acquired an inside knowledge of the business of the kind that only shorthand typists do. It was Josh Reynolds, Frisby's deputy, however, who taught her new things, for example, book design. (There was no resident designer then.)

One of her tasks was to test the strength of paper, and she was the first woman in the firm to be allowed to order this essential commodity. Choosing the right paper for the right book was an art. As Richard de la Mare had put it in the Sixth Dent Memorial Lecture in 1936, the choice of paper was an 'all important factor' in book production. 'Let it not be thought that, if the actual typographical arrangement of the page is well done, the question of paper may be allowed to settle itself. ... The appearance of more books is spoilt by the use of paper unsuitable to the type that is printed upon it than by almost any other single cause.'[77]

Books posed other challenges for the young Joyce Nairn. There was doubt about the propriety of her seeing the illustrations in *Gray's Anatomy* when she joined the firm. Yet she was to stay on in the House throughout the argument about *Lady Chatterley's Lover*, the *cause célèbre* of the post-war years which involved Penguin. In August 1960 the police asked for a copy of the unexpurgated edition which Penguin planned to publish, and on 8 September Penguin Books were committed to trial at the Central Criminal Court from Bow Street Magistrates Court charged with publishing an obscene book. Penguin in a rare moment of total triumph was acquitted. This was a 'landmark verdict' in the history of censorship, and it was registered in business success. The print order for the paperback novel rose to 500,000 within three days of the verdict.

Nairn worked with Longman long enough to see women managing men. After becoming Assistant Personnel Manager, she had been provided with a Personnel Manager, John Quash, who worked alongside Brack

76 Letters from Duncan to Higham, 2 Sept. 1968 and Higham to Duncan, 25 July 1968.

77 R. de la Mare, *A Publisher on Book Production* (1936), p.21.

until Brack retired, but Quash retired early in 1973 to become Bursar of Durham School. After his departure she was briefly in full charge until the appointment of a new personnel director.

In 1975 J.H. Adam, who retired after forty-four years of service, and who had started in 'Titles', as Mark and so many other Longman employees had done, had his memoirs edited by Nairn, who wrote about his extremely varied career in *The Log* under the title 'Retirement of a Longmaniac'.[78] His path had crossed with hers when he worked in the Art Department, part of the old Production Department. After the Second World War, when he was mentioned in despatches, he became Deputy General Manager of Longman, India, and later the first Director of Orient Longmans. He returned to Britain in 1961 where he was appointed Deputy Head of Division G after the divisional reorganisation. In 1974 he was its Acting Director.

Longman's primary school list continued to grow in the late seventies and the Monster series was extremely popular with children.

Monster looks for a friend, 1973 and *Monster goes to the circus* – the sixteenth adventure of Monster

Personal collection

Nairn had left Harlow by the time that 'a humble member of staff' at that time published his memoirs, which stretched back to the Paternoster Row of October 1899. In the same issue of *The Log* in which he reminisced contentedly there were photographs of thirteen home sales 'reps', together known as Dad's Army. As well as topping up bookshops with stock replacements from a large back-list, they took subscriptions for forthcoming books, organised exhibitions and advised on marketing for new trade publishing projects such as the Reference Book list. They were all members of the British Publishers' Representatives Association, brought into existence in 1924 after years of factional argument, and two of them served as its Presidents after the Second World War – Charles Webster in 1945 and Frank Dixon in 1972.

Retired employees of firms acquired by Longman received as much attention in *The Log* as Longmaniacs. Thus, a report headed '75 Years with Oliver and Boyd', described with a photograph the retirement of Bob Robertson after forty-six years service and William MacDonald ('Mac') after twenty-five years. Robertson had joined the warehouse staff in 1929 having been asked at his interview only one question, 'Are you strong and fit and do you have good feet?' He ended his career as Assistant Warehouse Manager in charge of the Company's packing and distribution. Macdonald was a cashier.[79]

The pages of *The Log* that reveal the delight in recalling did not end

---

78   *The Log*, No. 3, July 1975. (LA Part II 213)

79   *The Log*, No.4, Dec. 1975. (LA Part II 213)

Randolph Quirk and Tim Rix at the launch in 1984 of the *Longman Dictionary of the English Language*, completing the series of dictionaries, which had been planned since the early 1960s

Personal collection

in 1974. The words 'in print', always welcome to authors, appeared in the title of many later reminiscences such as those of John Dracott in 1983 and 'Johnny' Johnson in 1984. Dracott, a salesman, who began working with Longman at Wimbledon in 1943, merited an article also in *Publishing News*. Its editor, Fred Newman, chose him as the subject of an interview: the Longman Group gave him a retirement party, planned in secret, at the Sir Christopher Wren Inn in London near the original Longman site of 1724. Over 150 booksellers and publishing colleagues were present.

Edgar Richard Johnson, known to his colleagues as Johnny and to Mark Longman as 'Doc', had joined Longman in 1935 at the age of fifteen as a 'looker out', a term for 'order picker' or office boy that subsequently dropped out of use. He earned £1 a week and his season ticket for travel across London alone cost him 3s 6d. The book trade was familiar to him through his father, who had worked for the Cambridge University Press, and his brother who worked for Rivington. After war-time service with the RAF, Johnson returned to Longmans, where, having joined the Sales Department, he was 'allowed to go out on the road', serving as a 'rep' at first in the provinces but then in London. His mentor was Arthur Stanton, but his career took a new twist in 1959 when he moved as part of the first advance party to Harlow.

Eventually Johnson spent much of his time with the Data Processing Department, and there was yet another new twist when he moved after 1970 to Edinburgh to help move Oliver and Boyd books and papers. In 1976 he acted as Computer Services Manager, combining the role with other jobs, until a new appointment was made. He even had one trip to Nigeria, where new offices were in the course of construction. Johnson also noted in his account that he was present at the wedding of Mark and

Lady Elizabeth Longman without mentioning that Princess Elizabeth and Princess Margaret were present too.

There was nostalgia in everything that Johnson wrote. He lamented the 'old times' and regarded trade unions as hostile to progress. Nevertheless, not all employees felt like him. Dracott, who moved from being a 'rep' to being Home Sales Trade Manager in 1966 and Director in 1978, had a somewhat different credo:

> A good rep has to be prepared to battle with his sales manager if he believes it is in the interest of the customer. He has to try and influence and advise editors, have a view on things like the look of a book and print runs, and he has to be prepared to accept the ill will of colleagues if he believes he is acting in the best interests of his customers and long-term sales.

Dracott wrote these words after he had been appointed Home Sales Trade Director.

In 1976, as Wymer recalled, there was still a status gap, noted earlier in this book, between selling and publishing, and changes in attitudes inside the House of Longman, although not throughout publishing, belonged to the future not to the past. Meanwhile, there was little place in *The Log* for authors. Yet this was a period when many of them felt as 'loyal' to the House as its full-time employees did, and some of them recalled their publishing careers in non-House publications. For example, S.H. Burton set out 'some birthday thoughts' in *The Author* in 1980 when he recalled the first book that he had written, *The Criticism of Poetry*, published by Longmans, Green in 1950. Subsequently he had published over fifty books with nine different publishers, three of whom had been 'swept away by the economic storms through which publishers and authors ha[d] lived – or died since I wrote my first book'. He now had fourteen royalty-earning books in print, bringing him in an income of about £3,000 a year, and Longman was his biggest source of livelihood.

For Burton 'the rapid increase in the expenses of authorship' had not been 'balanced by an increase in rewards', and the rewards on a book were not commensurate with the amount of work put into it. From June 1978 to May 1979 he had worked 'at a big book for anything up to 14 hours every day – yes, seven days a week for twelve months – at my desk at 9 a.m. every day.' 'To live' he had to write three books a year, and that was a 'cracking pace' because some of his work was 'very demanding'. His *ELT* readers, for example, were written 'within rigid linguistic constraints'. There were days when 250 words was a difficult target to achieve'.[80]

A few months earlier, *The Author* had published a personal note in which Burton gave the titles of two Longman books that he had just

---

80   *The Author*, Vol. XCI, Spring 1980, pp.6–9.

finished – *People and Communication*, a book of 160,000 words, and *Eight Ghost Stories*. He was now 'well on' with two titles for Longman Cheshire's *Question and Answer* series. The London House had kept his *Criticism of Poetry* continuously in print since 1950.[81] Burton was more interested in particularities than in generalities, and he would have had little sympathy with 'the challenge to the concept of the author as source and centre of the text' which was said to have been 'decisive in contemporary criticism and aesthetic theory'.[82]

The details in these last few paragraphs carry the reader beyond 1976 where this chapter ends. Yet there was no great break in publishing and selling then. There had been a slight (and rare) drop in the total number of book titles in 1976, as there had been in 1971 and 1974, the latter 'a year of shortages and tribulation for publishers', but in 1975 yet another record for the number of new titles had been set.

As far as authors were concerned, the undoubted new national landmark was 1979 when a Public Lending Right Bill was passed in March in the House of Lords. 'Now is not the moment to regret that it took so long to achieve this simple measure of plain justice for authors', *The Bookseller* stated. 'It is rather the moment to look back with pride at the long battle now crowned with success.'[83] Recalling and re-structuring were still to go together.

---

81 *Ibid.*, Vol. XC, No.5, Autumn 1979, p.131.

82 J. Caughie (ed.), *Theories of Authorship* (1981), p.1.

83 *The Bookseller*, March 1979, quoted *ibid.*, 24 and 31 Dec. 1983, p.2543.

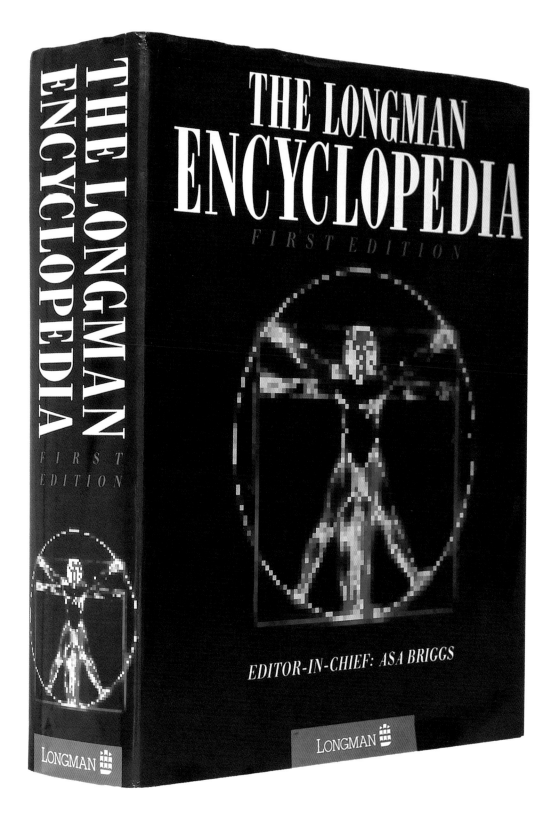

THE LONGMAN
ENCYCLOPEDIA
FIRST EDITION

EDITOR-IN-CHIEF: ASA BRIGGS

LONGMAN

9   *Profile of an Enterprise,*
1976–1990

The substantial part of the story of Longman has now been told from its beginnings in the year 1724 to the year 1976 when Rix became Chief Executive, going on to add the title of Chairman in 1984. This final narrative chapter is, however, among the most important both in the business history of the House and in the history of the economic, social and cultural context of publishing. Both kinds of history, as has been shown, were then in the course of transformation on both sides of the Atlantic.

The final date in the chapter is precise, for it was on 31 March 1990 that Rix, after over thirty-one years in the business, retired. He had circulated a note on 17 July 1989 telling staff that he was to retire on that date.[1] In the same number of *Publishing News* which announced Rix's carefully timed retirement, a deal between the booksellers W.H. Smith and Waterstone provided the headline on the front page. For once bookselling, not publishing, seemed, as in 1724, to be at the centre of the story of the book, and soon new links between bookselling and publishing, unfamiliar since the period covered in Chapter 2 of this *History*, were to be forged.

The continuing argument about the Net Book Agreement linked the two, with a number of bookselling firms, particularly the Pentos Group, led aggressively by Terry Maher, seeking in the name of competition and in confrontation with the Publishers Association to get rid of the Agreement through militant campaigning.[2] Meanwhile, publishing – and media –

The Longman Encyclopedia,
1989

Personal collection

---

1   A Note to the Staff, 17 July 1989. Rix had written to inform me of what was happening 'in advance of other channels' on 14 July 1989, Bastille Day. He added that he had no 'health problem' and that he was in no sense retiring from publishing. He had not and did not.

2   For the profitability of Pentos, which was involved not only in bookselling but in postcard and greetings cards publishing, the making of office furniture and property development, see *Publishing News*, 13 March 1987. For the Net Book Agreement, which Pentos argued should be abrogated, in the light of changes in the retail business since 1962, see P.J. Curwen, *The UK Publishing Industry* (1981), Ch. 3. For a defence of it in the context of the early 1980s see C. Bradley, Secretary and Chief Executive of the Publishers Association, 'Publishing: A Vital National and International Asset' in *Journal of the Proceedings of the Royal Society of Arts*, June 1982, p.5. The House of Commons Heritage Select Committee recommended its continued maintenance in 1995 (*The Times*, 8 June 1995), although by then several publishers, including Hodder Headline, had withdrawn from it.

Born in 1934, Tim Rix worked
for Longman for over thirty-one
years and in 1976 became Chief
Executive. In 1984 he added
the title of Chairman. He was
President of the Publishers
Association from 1981–83, and
also chaired Book Trust and
was on the Boards of the British
Council and British Library

Personal collection

mergers continued to capture space in newspapers
and more specialised publications;[3] and publishing
mergers, like other mergers, continued to capture
attention, sometimes outside the business pages
of newspapers. In the same number of *Publishing
News* questions were being raised in other pages
about the long-term profitability of the take-over by
Random House of Century Hutchinson.

These were years which two business
analysts of the Longman business, R. Whipp and
A. Pettigrew, concerned as they were with the
complex processes involved in the formulation of
organisational 'strategies', called 'post-colonial and
post-modern', the latter the most fashionable, if the
vaguest, of adjectives[4]. Yet neither adjective was
adequate. A writer in *British Book News* in March
1988, Vivienne Menkes, chose to return to the oldest
metaphors. 'It is hard', she wrote, 'when studying the
history of Longman, the world's oldest commercial
publisher, to avoid using the sailing metaphors that
have been associated with the business ever since
the first Longman launched a seven-generation
bookselling and publishing business at the Sign of the Ship.'

'Navigating', like 'surfing', was to acquire a new association during the
1990s with the advent of the Internet and the 'World Wide Web'. Already,
however, in the 1980s it seemed apt that one eighteenth and nineteenth-
century maritime theme, piracy, was still alive. Taking advantage of
new printing technologies which made book reproduction easy, pirates
operating in Taiwan and other places outside the English-speaking world
were publishing copyright titles, including novels and encyclopaedias, at
low cost. One consignment of Longman titles, printed in Taiwan, made
its way to Nigeria. Not surprisingly, the Publishers Association began

---

3   See, for example, N. Stacey, 'Making the Most of Mergers' in *Investment
     Management*, Feb. 1991, p.54 and F. Newman, 'The secret of conglomerate
     publishing' in *Publishing News*, 5 July 1991. For later writing on this subject
     during the 1990s, including books, see N. Clee, editor of *The Bookseller*, 'Eating
     Wildebeest' in *The Author*, Summer 2001, pp.57–8.

4   A.M. Pettigrew and R. Whipp, 'Competition and Management of Change in
     Book Publishing: Longman' (1988), p.9. This invaluable analysis, started at the
     end of 1985, was produced by the Centre for Corporate Strategy and Change
     at the University of Warwick. For the approach see Pettigrew, 'On Studying
     Organizational Structures' in the *Administrative Services Quarterly*, Vol. 24, Dec.
     1979, pp.570–81 and *The Politics of Organizational Decision-making* (1973).

a campaign against piracy in 1983 and issued an 'Anti-Piracy Kit'.[5] The campaign was led by Rix, then President of the Association, who with Nicolas Thompson of Pitman, the chairman of the Suppression of Piracy and Protection of Copyright Committee, wrote to heads of member houses urging them to support the campaign and pledge funds.[6]

Vivienne Menkes abandoned the old metaphor as early as the end of her first paragraph, when she introduced, as Whipp and Pettigrew did, the ugly but by then essential word 'conglomerate'. Distinctions were not always drawn between different kinds of 'conglomerate', for the word was still in the making as well as the institutional form itself. Indeed, while the words 'conglomerate' and 'conglomeration' appeared in the third edition of the *Shorter Oxford English Dictionary* in 1973, there was no reference to business or to economics. It was in the *Longman Dictionary of Contemporary English* of 1978 that a third meaning of the word 'conglomerate' was given – 'a large business firm that controls production of goods of very different kinds' – and in 1984 the *Longman Dictionary of the English Language* made this definition more concise as well as more accurate when 'conglomerate' was defined simply as 'a widely diversified business company'.

In the winter issue of *The Author* in 1989, the year when Rix announced his retirement from Longman, the publishing director of Viking, now part of an American Pearson group of companies called Penguin USA, defended 'conglomerations' against those critics who believed that 'only small is beautiful'. Meanwhile, Vivienne Menkes had bypassed controversy by praising the Pearson Group on the grounds that it had 'successfully trimmed its sails to adapt the old-established company to new developments in the publishing industry and to changing markets'.

Before Menkes mentioned Rix, 'the navigator' – and there were no intimations then of his leaving the business – she concluded confidently that

> with a host of overseas companies, a world turnover in 1986 of £142 million, 3,325 people employed *in toto*, a backlist of more than 25,000 titles in print and publishing over 1,500 new titles a year in the UK alone, the sturdy old Longman ship, wearing its 264-year history remarkably lightly, is looking a reassuringly seaworthy vessel as the eighties draw to a close.

The second of her two articles, which was called 'The centuries-old ship embarks on a new voyage', mentioned various unlikely new Longman titles, such as Wilkinson's *Road Traffic Offences* (which had come to

---

5   See the Publishers Association pamphlet *The Economic Importance of Piracy* (1985). In 1991 China became a signatory to the Berne Convention, largely closing that source of piracy.

6   *The Bookseller*, 2 March, 2 April 1983.

Longman with the acquisition of Oyez Publishing).[7] Coincidentally for sailors, on the next page of *British Book News* there was a review of *Lloyd's Nautical Yearbook, 1988*.[8]

~

This chapter ends, fittingly, with particular books, but it considers them within their business context. Just after Rix took over, the Longman Board at its planning conference in July 1977, made a financial appraisal of each of the publishing divisions and of lists of its top-selling twenty titles. Then the top twenty-five titles or series for the whole Group were listed. This intriguing list showed the importance (as already described)

of *ELT* publishing: W.S. Allen's *Progressive Living English for the Arab World*; L.G. Alexander's *New Concept English*; O'Neill's *Kernel Lessons*; the *New Method Supplementary Readers*; and in the African market Channon and Smith's *New General Maths* (African edition); *Day by Day English* (Nigerian edition); *New Biology for West African Schools*; and in Yoruba, *Longman Language Texts*.

The list reveals both the impressive breadth and scope of Longman's publishing for Anglophone African countries and its financial importance at that time for the Longman business. There are only three entries in the list for the UK schools market: *Longman Audio-Visual French* (the much-needed successor to Whitmarsh),[9] *Breakthrough to Literacy*,[10] and F.J. Schonell's well-known *Wide Range* and *Happy Venture* series which had come to Longman with Oliver and Boyd. There were no academic or higher education titles in the list and no 'general' titles. But there were two medical titles— Murray's *Radiology of Skeletal Disorders* from Churchill-Livingstone and from older Longman lists the flagship *Gray's Anatomy*. Many of these titles were to fuel the ship's voyage in the closing phase of this *History*.

Part of Longman's strategy was the continued growth of the Primary school list. As well as main Reading and Maths schemes it added popular series of readers, for example the *Whizz Bang Series*

Personal collection

---

7   There was an inset, p.171, to the first of the two articles by Vivienne Menkes, 'A New Voyage'. 'As this issue went to press, it had just been announced that Longman's parent, Pearson, had acquired the American educational publishing group, Addison-Wesley.' For this acquisition and its consequences, see below, pp. 521 ff.

8   *British Book News*, March, April 1988.

9   See above, p.392.

10   See above, p.449.

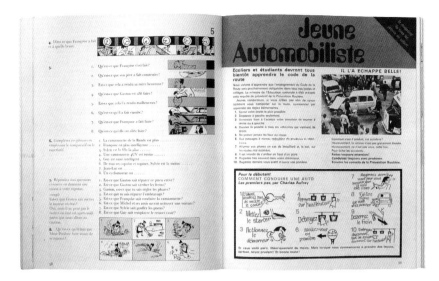

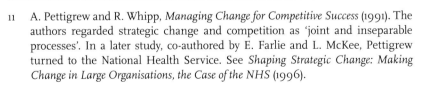

Longman Audio-Visual French was the new main secondary school course, the successor to W.F.H.Whitmarsh's *Complete French Course*, first published in 1935, (which remained in print, with others of Whitmarsh's titles). Moore and Antrobus's new course included tapes, worksheets and filmstrips

Personal collection

Much had changed in the course of the voyage by 1991 when Pettigrew and Whipp incorporated in book form their sharply pointed case study of Longman within a general context, drawing comparisons and contrasts not only with other publishing businesses, but with businesses in other sectors, including merchant banking, life assurance and automobiles.[11] The authors clearly recognised – and stated explicitly – that the market for books, which had rightly been likened by others to a honeycomb, a very different non-nautical metaphor, continued to have distinctive features.[12] Even in the short run, publishing history, treated as a case study, raised cultural as well as financial questions, as it always had done. The content of books could not be ignored. And in the long run, as Pettigrew and Whipp observed, 'the industry's smallness', with or without conglomerates, concealed its cultural importance.

While paying little attention to the publishing of fiction, which for most journalists – with 'bestsellers' and 'celebrity authors' in mind – was the main centre of interest (they themselves considered it a 'separate' case[13]),

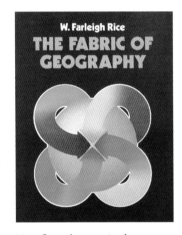

To reflect changes in the curriculum, Longman chose a well-known author, W. Farleigh Rice, to write *The Fabric of Geography* published in 1983 for secondary schools

Personal collection

11   A. Pettigrew and R. Whipp, *Managing Change for Competitive Success* (1991). The authors regarded strategic change and competition as 'joint and inseparable processes'. In a later study, co-authored by E. Farlie and L. McKee, Pettigrew turned to the National Health Service. See *Shaping Strategic Change: Making Change in Large Organisations, the Case of the NHS* (1996).

12   *Ibid.*, p.43.

13   Pettigrew and Whipp, *op. cit.*, 'Competition and the Management of Change in Book Publishing', p.3. They believed that Longman demonstrated that 'there was more to publishing than just the trade or fiction areas that had received most attention in the financial and commercial press' (p.4).

they did not foresee that within the next decade fears would be expressed
that with the increased scale of multi-national, multi-media corporate
business 'book culture' as a whole, and not merely 'quality' fiction, would
be threatened not only from without but from within.[14] The 'culture of
print', it would be argued, would no longer be the dominant culture.

Within the book publishing 'industry' of the 1980s there was a strong
awareness, even within merged structures, of increased competition for
markets, and it was within what he believed rightly to be an unprecedented
competitive context that Longman under Rix followed a conscious business
'strategy' within a conglomerate in which Pearson ultimately set the
financial terms. 'Strategy' was still a new term in Longman history, and
while the strategy, incremental in its scope and timing and seldom set
out in formal mission statements, passed through a number of different
phases, it was always 'market-led' and it was always international in its
orientation.

'All Longman Companies throughout the world', Rix insisted, should
ensure that their publishing was market-led in order to provide the best
possible *service* to the 'consumers of our books, periodicals, audio-visual
aids [the term was still not dead], electronic products [unmentioned in
1976], training, examinations and seminars'. They should set out to be
'market leaders or major players in all their chosen areas of publishing'.
'Chosen areas' should have been printed in italics. At the same time –
and this was in line with what had come to be thought of, not only by
Rix, as 'traditional' publishing – they should provide 'the best possible
service and care to authors and contributors, recognising their essential
part in the publishing process'. The *'highest possible quality'* was the object
most stressed, but quality was now directly related to 'market needs for
all our products'. Companies were required to 'provide the most effective
possible marketing in the interest as much of customers and consumers
as of their own sales' and to 'respond effectively in relation to *changes* in
markets and technologies while remaining *market* not *technology* driven'.
There would be a need for proper monitoring and controls to ensure that
this requirement was being met within the Longman Group as a whole.

To achieve these objectives, all Longman companies, whatever their
regional location, had to be 'profit-driven'. 'Good profits' would make
possible expansion and development, and the offer of an 'even better
service to our authors, customers and consumers'. (This was a new trilogy.)
Staff also had to have access to 'excellent financial information' and be
'motivated' in all jobs to be 'as efficient and productive as possible through
good communications, clear objectives, performance appraisal, effective

14   See T. Daniel, 'Facts about Fiction' in *The Author*, Vol. LXXXIX, No. 2,
Summer 1978, pp.73–76. Daniel was reviewing J. Sutherland, *Fiction and the
Fiction Industry* (1978).

training provision and management development', while recognising and responding to their 'social and community responsibilities'.[15] In a multi-national business the last of these words had special force in countries as far apart geographically and culturally as Nigeria and Malaysia, and they were to acquire new force in Europe with the collapse of the Soviet Union and the ascent of nationalism after 1989.

For Pettigrew and Whipp the enunciation of this strategy implied, inevitably, a concomitant shift of emphasis from editorial to marketing priorities. The heads of the different Longman divisions, reorganised more than once since Rix took over, knew consequentially that they were required to pay increasing attention to financial resources and to sales requirements. Any residual status differences between publishers and salespeople were eliminated, therefore, and while it was Rix's Finance Committee, a small team, that worked out Company strategy, other sector leaders were fully involved. There was always what Robert Duncan called 'two-way movement'. Duncan was head of the Longman division (Churchill Livingstone) that was concerned with medical books. It inherited an impressive list, but it was always keen to extend it.

All the above concerns are well illustrated in the corporate plans produced each year through the seventies and eighties and in the records of the board's conferences (already referred to in the previous chapter).[16] Although publishing planning was obviously a central concern, they dealt with every possible aspect of running and developing a publishing business. Thus, the Conference held in October 1978 included sessions on 'Group production; computer services; stock control; global distribution strategy; and personnel and IR policies'. There was much agonising over the balance of Longman's business between the 'safe' and 'unsafe' geographical areas of the world and the urgent need to shift the balance. And so there was when corporate plans were drafted for 1980-82 and 1981-83 which had to deal with 'a very high level of uncertainty' following the collapse of the Nigerian market in 1980. As a result, in the latter plan the 'overriding and critical objective' was 'to reverse the trend of falling profits and cash drain of the last two years'.

More positively, there was much emphasis on 'development' and especially development in the USA. As recorded in the last chapter, Longman returned to New York in 1973 with the incorporation of Longman Inc., initially as an import company, but it was in the following fifteen years that there was to be substantial publishing development and many acquisitions. The strategy was successful and resulted in a huge increase in American

15   These details are taken from the Introduction by the Chief Executive from *The Log: Report to Employees, International Results for the year ending 1986.* (LA Part II/213-213B)

16   Conference minutes and Corporate Plans held in the Longman Archive.

sales from 2.7 per cent of total sales in 1973 to 30.2 per cent in 1987.

Longman Inc. quickly developed its own college publishing programme (based on the acquisition of the college division of the David McKay Company) with a special emphasis on medical publishing (using the Churchill Livingstone imprint). Duncan, responsible for all the Group's medical publishing, so much shared Rix's enthusiasm for expansion in the USA that he described it as a 'joint vision'.[17] In order to implement it Tim Hailstone, seconded from Churchill Livingstone in Edinburgh, energetically devised a new American medical list. The first title published, still in heavy demand ten years later, was the *Atlas of Gray Scale Ultrasonography* (1978), and two successful series were also quickly launched: *Contemporary Issues in Nephrology* 30 Vols. 1978-95 and *Clinics in Diagnostic Ultrasound*. Hailstone was succeeded by Lew Reines, who assured Churchill Livingstone's future with the publication in 1981 of the monumental *Anaesthesia*, edited by Ronald D. Miller in two volumes. This rapidly established itself as a standard work. The list was further strengthened in 1987 by the acquisition of the medical reference books published by John Wiley & Sons.

In a quite different field another important step forward in the USA was taken with the acquisition in April 1982 of Development Systems Corporation which, despite its name, was actually a business publishing house. It had been founded in 1967 by Robert C. Kyle, who was to become the key figure in Longman's progress in the USA up to the end of this *History*. It maintained around one hundred titles in print and it had a flagship in *Modern Real Estate Practice*, a book co-authored by Kyle himself. From the now-established base of Longman Inc., Longman Group USA, which combined those two and many subsequent acquisitions, was built up by Kyle, who became its President, working closely with Michael Wymer and John Williamson in Harlow.

By 1987 the Longman Financial Services Institute in the United States, publishing and providing training in the fields of insurance, securities, real estate and other finance had sales of £15.6 million. Its fortunes were devastated, however, by the stock market crash in the autumn of 1987 so that the Institute made a loss in the following year of £2.8 million. As always in publishing history, such crashes had wide ramifications, changing attitudes, if not ambitions.

Longman's total sales of £36.8 million in the USA fell by £1.1 million until the major acquisition by Pearson of Addison-Wesley in 1988 changed the picture yet again. Longman Inc. was now 'backed' into Addison-Wesley; Federal and Capitol Publications (specialist legal publishers acquired earlier) were transferred to Pearson; and, under Pearson pressure, Longman Financial Services Institute, subsequently to prove extremely

---

17   Pettigrew and Whipp, *op. cit.*, p.153.

successful, was bought out by Kyle. All that remained to Longman of its USA interests was now Churchill Livingstone.

~

This was an entirely new picture, but before it was framed by Pearson, the American developments described above had completely altered the regional division of Longman Group sales and the balance of Longman business between 'safe' and 'unsafe' areas of the world. The following table illustrates the regional balance of the Longman business in 1988:

Longman Group Sales by Region, 1988

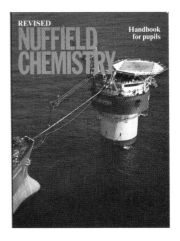

REGION	£m	%
North America	44.2	29.2
Latin America	1.9	1.2
Caribbean	2.0	1.3
UK	44.1	29.1
Europe	16.3	10.8
Arab World	3.9	2.6
Africa	10.4	6.9
Asia	15.3	10.1
Australia/NZ	13.3	8.8
Total	151.4	100.0

The Log and Report to Employees; International Results for the year, ending December 1989, p.5. (LA Part II 213)

These figures show how much had been achieved, although Rix and his colleagues no doubt wished that the outcome had been achieved positively instead of to some extent negatively through the reduction in sales in Africa and elsewhere in the Third World in the wake especially of the Nigerian market collapse in 1980.

It had, of course, also been the aim over the same fifteen years to diversify and extend Longman Group's range of publishing. It is difficult to give precise figures for shifts in different kinds of publishing because of the different mix of publishing in the companies outside the United Kingdom, but the following table giving details for the UK Company shows that by 1988 real balance had been achieved 'at home':

Longman developed a strong relationship with the Nuffield Foundation in science publishing; these two titles were published in the late 1970s when Nuffield was in the forefront of science curriculum development

The Nuffield Foundation

Longman UK Company, 1988 World Sales by Publishing Field

	£m	%
ELT	13.5	19.5
UK Schools	12.1	17.4
'Overseas Educational'	5.6	8.0
Medical	10.9	15.7
Academic, Scientific, Technical	5.5	7.9
'General'	1.5	2.2
Dictionaries	2.8	4.0
Business and Management	6.6	9.5
Law, Tax and Finance	6.7	9.7
Industry and Public Service Management	4.2	6.1
Total	69.4	100.0

UK Report to Employees, 1988 p.8. (LA Part II 213)

~

The 1988 sales figures included many new titles, among them in *ELT* a new *Longman English Grammar* (1988), the first student grammar to be published by Longman for twenty years. Its author, L.G. Alexander (1932-2002), whose *ELT* books had been Longman best-sellers for years (*New Concept English* (1967–73), for adults, *Look, Listen and Learn* (1971), for children), now became one of the best-selling authors of all time (as recorded in the *Guinness Book of Records*). In schools publishing the most spectacular success was *Nuffield Co-ordinated Sciences* (1988), 'a new GCSE scheme for balanced science'. Other successes included S. Hammond's *Business Studies* (1988) for A level students and F. Palmer's *Themes and Projects in Art and Design* (1988).

The year 1988 saw the publication of the government's long awaited first National Curriculum proposals which had far-reaching implications for all schools publishers, and Longman UK was in a favourable position to take advantage of them. The idea behind the proposals implied a major change in the approach to school education, for since the Education Act of 1870 Britain had regarded curricular guidance from above as a 'continental' malady. Local authorities, universities and schools made their own choices. Now there was to be guidance from above. Yet in the near future the new National Curriculum was to prove no more safe than university student grants, long thought of as the foundation of a British tradition in higher education.

There were other major changes of approach – for example the education of doctors and nurses where British and continental practice had always diverged, and following a new pattern in 1988, Longman was once more ready to cope with change. The cluster of medical publishers now incorporated within the House were responsible for many new key titles, including a reference manual for pathologists, D.L. Page and T.J. Anderson's *Diagnostic Histopathology of the Breast* (1987), priced at £60, and 'a new kind of nursing course' linking a theoretical model with practical nursing, E.M. Jamieson's *Guidelines for Clinical Nursing Practices* (1988), which was described by *The Nursing Times* as 'an absolute must' for all nursing schools.

In the Academic, Scientific and Technical Division new editions were as prominent as new titles, among them the eleventh edition of *Russell's Soil Conditions and Plant Growth*, edited by Alan Wild (1988), and the third edition of John Briston's *Plastics Films* (1988). There was one major new textbook in electronics, however, R.J. Maddock and D.M. Calcutt's *Electronics: a course for engineers* (1988) which was as well-received as, in a very different and also changing field, the novelist David Lodge's anthology *Modern Criticism and Theory*.

The creation of a Dictionaries and Reference Books Department was recorded in the previous chapter, and in 1988 a new edition of the *Longman Dictionary of Contemporary English* was published. Since its first publication in 1977 it had sold in huge numbers all over the world. So too had other DRBD publications, from the flagship *Longman Dictionary of the English Language* to the *Longman Crossword Key*. The Department had its own in-house computerised system for generating titles and published whole series of pocket dictionaries. A revised edition of *Roget's Thesaurus* incorporated a massive cross-reference and index system that was computer checked.

One of the most ambitious ventures was a new single-volume Longman Penguin *Encyclopaedia* (although Penguin dropped its interest in the project before publication), incorporating entries from the 1983 edition of the much admired *Columbia Concise Encyclopedia*. There had been sparse coverage of European topics in the *Encyclopedia*, however, and substantial re-planning even of general articles was essential. The first meeting to plan the new *Encyclopedia* was held under my chairmanship in October 1986,[18] and the editorial team included Sir Herman Bondi, A.S. Byatt, John Ashworth, Mary (later Baroness) Warnock and Stuart Hall. The complete work, completed on schedule and incorporating 18,000 entries, appeared – to favourable reviews – in 1989.[19]

---

18   *Minutes*, 27 Oct. 1986. (Personal Archives) The first Managing Editor, Anna Hodson, left Longman before writing began. When the *Encyclopaedia* appeared the internal House control of the project was under the supervision of Peter Zombory-Moldovan.

19   See, for example, *Daily Telegraph*, 19 Oct 1989; *Books*, Nov. 1989; *New Scientist*, 2 Feb. 1991.

Big projects were becoming difficult to implement. Thus an even more ambitious *Video Encyclopaedia*, which could have brought in the BBC, never saw the light. A preliminary memorandum (undated) was exciting. It stated that a 'video encyclopaedia should be to television documentaries, current affairs and features what a book encyclopaedia is to printed non-fiction, fiction and newspapers'. [20] This was a project far removed in scale and design from 'visual-aids' or film strips. The word 'global' was not employed in relation to it, but to meet its objectives it would have required global, not national coverage.

~

The range of other projects and shifts of publishing strategy in the various regions of the Longman Group expressed more, however, than geographical coverage. There was also what Pettigrew and Whipp described as a shift from 'transactional leadership' to 'transformational leadership'. [21] It was a description which would never have been put in these terms by Rix himself – or by Duncan – for it might have implied a minimisation of the continuing importance of 'traditional' editorial activities in all fields of educational publishing, including categories as different as medicine, already mentioned, and history, in which Longman was anxious to retain – and did effectively retain – a position of leadership. It was particularly important in *ELT* which, as we have seen, was Rix's own lead-in to the business (as it was to be the lead-in of his successor as Chief Executive, Paula Kahn), not to rely too much on 'old faithfuls'. Finding new authors, including local authors in the developing world, and preparing new titles were essential aspects of publishing, 'transactional' or 'transformational'. 'Language teaching is changing – and so are we.'

Experience, individual and corporate, rather than management theory provided Rix's motivation whatever decisions he took. He had read English at Cambridge after leaving Radley and completing National Service in the Royal Navy, and as his career progressed, he became more interested in the cultural history of books and their contents than probably any other contemporary publisher in Britain. Yet he saw nothing incompatible between this interest and publishing professionalism. Current business operations had always stimulated him. After leaving Cambridge, he had spent a year at Yale as a Mellon Fellow, writing a thesis on 'Attitudes of American Private Bankers, 1925-1935'. By the time he became Chief Executive of the Longman Group, he knew through his own experience that publishing had many facets. The editorial was not the least important, but marketing was indispensable.

---

20   Meetings took place with Grolier, but while key questions of timing and staging were posed and tabulated they were not answered.

21   Pettigrew and Whipp, *op. cit.*, p.152.

It was personal experience that gave him a grasp of the international dimension of publishing. He began his career in publishing with Longman after three months as a proof reader and three months as a schools representative, following this through by working on what was described in the last chapter as 'the periphery' of the Longman business, as had most of the other members of the team that he assembled. His first post in London in 1959 was that of Publishing Executive (sponsor) for the Caribbean and Latin America, and his first overseas post was that of Publishing Manager, Far East, based in Kuala Lumpur and responsible for all publishing for South East Asia but especially for Malaya, Singapore and Hong Kong. He travelled extensively during his three years in Kuala Lumpur on sales visits to Brunei, Sarawak, Thailand and South Vietnam, and in 1962 he set up the local publishing company, Longman, Malaya Ltd., later after a change in the name of the country, to be called Longman, Malaysia. On his return to Britain in 1963 via Australia and the United States, a business trip, he was appointed Head of *ELT* in 1964.

When he took over as Chief Executive of the Longman Group in July 1976, the editor of *The Log*, as has been noted, described the Directors that he inherited, or chose for himself, not as a Board of Directors but as 'The Captain's Table'. (The editor rejected as an alternative title 'Tim's Flying Circus'.) Three nominees of Pearson joined the Table as non-executive Directors, but it was the executive Directors who were the main people sitting at it. Beckett was Vice-Chairman, as he had been at the Chapple table, and Williamson, the Group Finance Director, who had been appointed Chief Accountant in 1968, served also as Company Secretary. He had succeeded Frank Tiller in 1971. One member, Kerr, whose personality and achievements have been described earlier, now based in Australia, had the title of Divisional Managing Director, Division (E), Australia and the Far East. In different circumstances either he or Beckett might have been the Captain at the table. No one else could have taken up that position.

Four of the others around the table in 1976 were still to be members of the Longman Group Board ten years later, and that was after Rix had modified the divisional structure and in an important structural change which affected the whole dynamics of the business had created 'sectors' as well as divisions. The 'divisional structure' had served the Group well,

The Longman English-Chinese Dictionary of Contemporary English, 1988

Personal collection

Rix said in a note placed on 'all UK Notice Boards' in 1983, and it was 'by no means being completely abandoned', but there would now be 'sectors', each the responsibility of a Group Executive Director. 'The organisation structure within each sector will then be appropriate to the nature and extent of the markets served and particular media or publishing operations' requirements'.[22]

Rix was using the word 'sector', familiar to economists, but a new concept within the House of Longman, just as the word 'division' so recently had been. Moreover, he was deliberately using it in a quite different sense from economists in order to refer to planned devolution in which he put his trust, believing, perhaps too trustingly, that Pearsons shared his belief. In his announcement he used the word 'structure' more often than the word 'sector', stating specifically that there were no changes in the Management Committee of the Board.

There were seven sectors operating in 1989, each with its own Head and its own code number. Four of the Heads, all of them members of the UK Board, were concerned with different branches of publishing. Three formed part of the services division. All were directly responsible to Rix as Chief Executive. There was also a three-member Finance Committee, responsible for the overall and day-to-day management of the Group. Rix, who chaired it, had no doubt about the three members' knowledge and commitment. He believed too that they could and would work closely together.

The Board member with the longest service, Michael Wymer, had been made Deputy Chief Executive in 1986 and a member of the Finance Committee. He had joined Longman straight from National Service in 1957, originally working, at first on a temporary basis, in what was called before the introduction of divisions the Trade Department.[23] This was a more hazardous way into business leadership than through 'Production'. In 1973, however, Wymer had already become Group Sales Director, having been made Overseas Sales Manager in 1967 at a time when 'there was a 'very poor atmosphere between publishers and selling'.

Not only did he help to improve it – within a new set-up – but he was directly involved in Rix's American strategy. He told an interviewer in 1982 that he wanted Longman in the United States to be regarded as an American

---

22   Note of 17 Oct. 1983.

23   Wymer had been given his temporary job before his National Service after an interview with Noël Brack, who had made it clear that there would be no prospects of any long-term employment in the House. (*The Log*, new series (not so specified) No. 3, March 1982, p.7.) It was Beckett who took him back, and it was Chapple who sent him out to Hong Kong. (In his interview Chapple had asked him whether he could type, and he went on to learn.) After his return in 1961 he took over for six years Rix's job as the person responsible at Clifford Street for the Caribbean and Latin America. He then replaced Ian Millar as resident representative in the Caribbean, combining publishing and selling.

publishing house, not just as a top British publisher selling there. This was a vision shared, as we have seen, with Duncan, who in 1976 was Divisional Managing Director (Division M), dealing with medical publishing with a strong American thrust. He had joined Longman in 1961, having previously worked as a journalist, and in 1986 he was Managing Director of Sector 7, which included the Academic, Scientific and Medical Divisions.

Like Wymer, who was familiar with all aspects of the global business, Duncan knew as much about life on the Longman periphery as Rix himself did. He had been responsible for Far East liaison between 1961 and 1963, had followed in Rix's footsteps to Kuala Lumpur in 1964, and had then served as Deputy Managing Director to Kerr in Sydney. He was recalled by Chapple in 1973 to take over the Divisional Managing Directorship of Churchill-Livingstone, returning with enthusiasm to his native Edinburgh. Until 1981 there had been many Longman offices there, open-planned like Croythorn House on the fringe of Edinburgh New Town or a maze of stairs and corridors like Annandale Street. Duncan's secretary, Catherine Grubb, had worked for thirty-eight years in Edinburgh first with Oliver and Boyd and then with Churchill-Livingstone.

The third member of the Finance Committee, John Williamson, the Group's Finance and Planning Director, who had taken over these responsibilities on Beckett's death in 1979, had an intuitive grasp of what was and was not possible, and, almost as important, carried a sense of natural authority. Moreover, he had other valuable gifts, not always found in a Finance and Planning Director, particularly a highly professional one. He saw the limitations of an exclusively accounting approach to the targeting and monitoring of improved performance. He got on well with the managing directors of Longman's overseas companies and helped them, often informally, to achieve successful results.

Roger Watson had joined Longman in 1962 straight from University as a Management Trainee, one of only two people sitting round the Captain's Table in 1976 to have done so, and he had become a Publisher in the Schools Division and succeeded Yglesias as Divisional Managing Director in 1972. In 1986 he was Head of Sector 6, the UK Schools sector, with responsibility, too, as in 1976, for Oliver and Boyd. He visited Edinburgh regularly. The General Manager and Production Director there was Alec Dunnett, who had worked for thirty years with Oliver and Boyd. But in 1988 Oliver and Boyd transferred to Harlow, bringing to an end its long Edinburgh history.

Pat Munday who, as has been noted, was a relative newcomer, having arrived in Harlow via Bracken House, was still at the Captain's Table in 1986 as Managing Director of the Business and Professional Services sector. In 1976 his Longman responsibilities included not only journals but oversight of *Keesing's Publications*. He had never worked overseas. In 1986, echoing Rix, he was emphasising the 'multi-media and multi-format' scope of his business operations, 'characterised by the interlinked publishing of books,

A promotional brochure put together in 1984, to mark Longman's 260th year. The publisher acknowledged its debt to history in the main fields in which it published, but it could now divide those into academic, science, schools, medical, professional and law, children's books (including Ladybird), ELT, and dictionaries and reference publishing. Its main emphasis was on the future and the publisher's internationalism, pointing out that approximately 70% of Longman's business was then outside the UK

Longman Archive

directories, journals, loose-leaf services and newsletters'.[24]

Among the others who had sat around the Captain's Table in 1976 but, for whatever reason, did not sit on the 1986 Board, was Ron Hobbs, who had joined Longman from United Biscuits in 1969, one of the most daring cross-business moves in the history of the House, where he made his mark as Divisional Director of the Distribution and Computer Services Division. In 1974 he had become Managing Director of a new Longman Distribution, Computer and Production Services Division (LDCPS) within which the Group Administration Department and Group Production Services were merged – a domestic use of the verb. By then Hobbs's specialist knowledge had proved invaluable in Harlow, and in 1976 his responsibilities were extended to include Group Personnel Services too.

David Mortimer, in 1976 Divisional Managing Director of the *ELT*, Dictionaries and Reference Books Division, had followed a very different career. He had joined Longman straight from university as an 'official executive trainee' in 1960 and, as has been noted, had spent part of 1961 in

---

24 Menkes, *loc.cit.*, Part I.

Nigeria before returning to London to edit and publish in the *ELT* section. In 1972 he succeeded Rix as Managing Director of the *ELT* Division, adding the Arab world to his responsibilities two years later and in 1976 the new Dictionary and Reference Book Department. He left the House in 1985.

Robert Welham, who had joined Longman in 1969 as Science Publisher in Division B, had previously been with Chapman & Hall Ltd., and E. and F. Spon Ltd., companies operating within Associated Book Publishers Ltd., a business which was compared at some length with Longman by Pettigrew and Whipp.[25] In 1976, after succeeding Adrian Higham as Divisional Managing Director of the Academic, Science and Technical Division, his span of oversight included one of the newest Longman acquisitions, Construction Press Ltd.[26] He left the House in 1984 on becoming Publishing Director of the Royal Society of Chemistry, his own subject area.

In presenting the people sitting round the Captain's Table in 1976, the editor of *The Log* offered individual photographs in the hope that employees of the Longman Group might become acquainted with them, and it was doubtless with the same intention that the editor of *Grapevine* produced in 1988 a chart which also included individual photographs.[27] By then there were the two women members of the Board, each with substantial power. Judy Little, Director of Personnel and Administration, had entered Longman in 1963 as a copywriter, and in an unusual transition had become Personnel Manager after working as an *ELT* editor and an audio-visual production controller and manager. Hers was an outstanding career progression which qualified her admirably for dealing with personnel (including their training) and 'administration services'. (The word 'administration' was still used in this context.)

Meanwhile, Paula Kahn, who had been interviewed by Rix personally when she joined the House in 1965 and had followed Mortimer in directing *ELT*, was in charge not only of *ELT* but, as he had been, of Dictionaries and Reference Books, and after 1986 of a new International Education Division. Ambitious and determined, she was to take over the Chief Executiveship (Publishing) in October 1988 with all publishing divisions reporting to her, and she was to succeed Rix as overall Chief Executive in October 1989.

Both in 1976 and in 1986 all Board members were expected to be fully professional in their approach to House business. But Longman was not exceptional in this. Professionalism was pronounced the one necessary ingredient in the media system of the 1980s, not least in the BBC, ITV and the advertising agencies, and it had its own values. The most essential of

THE FRANKISH KINGDOMS UNDER THE CAROLINGIANS

751-987

ROSAMOND MCKITTERICK

The 1984 promotion brochure put emphasis on Longman's own history of University and College publishing: 'Longman's history authors are heirs to an enviable tradition of excellence in history publishing that goes back over 150 years, and which links them to such names as Lord Macaulay in the nineteenth century and G.M. Trevelyan in the early part of our own'. *The Frankish Kingdoms Under the Carolingians 751-987* by Rosamond McKitterick, 1983, was only one of many examples

Personal collection

25   Pettigrew and Whipp, *op. cit.*

26   See below, p.528.

27   The *Grapevine*, Spring 1988, pp.10-11. (LA Part II/213)

them was that of relating 'output' to 'resources', financial and physical; and with Rix in charge at the top of the Longman Group it was Wymer who professionalised sales management, oversaw UK distribution operations and 'modernised' the increasingly indispensable information system.[28] He also played a major role, very close to Rix, in the implementation of the acquisitions strategy from the research stage through, if successful, to the particular acquisition.[29]

Another key Sector Director was Julian Rea, almost as familiar with the Arab world and with South East Asia as he was with Africa, where, unlike many native-born Africans, he was equally at home in Ghana and Nigeria. The African situation was always changing, and Rea saw it in the broadest of contexts. In a memorandum written in 1984 he asked what could be done with Third World countries in difficulties where 'the requirement for books and related materials is higher than ever before'. Would their inability to pay for them be permanent? What could be done about it 'within our normal trading procedures'?[30]

Rea dealt as effectively as possible with the collapse of the dominant Nigerian market, which he had helped to build up, and went on to arrange and supervise the merger of Longman Southern Africa with Maskew-Miller, a highly respected educational publishing company and subsidiary of the *Argus* newspaper group, turning it into a highly enterprising and profitable business. He was encouraged to learn from Nigeria in 1986 that Chief F.A. Iwerebon believed that despite the ending of 'the days of oil boom', 'the initial momentum of growth in the educational sector' had not been completely lost.[31] In Britain Rea shared Rix's enthusiasm for the Publishers Association – Chapple had chosen to play comparatively little part in it – and, as Mark Longman and Rix before him, was Chairman of

---

28   It was announced in 1988 at the time of Kahn's appointment as Chief Executive (Publishing) that Longman Distribution, Computer and Production Services would report to Wymer. The Finance Division would continue to report to Williamson. (*UK Report to Employees, Results for the Year Ending December 1988*, p.2, p.3 (LA Part II 213). In this *Report* the page on finance (p.19) was divided into two – the UK Finance Department at the Pinnacles and Group Finance at Burnt Mill.)

29   See an interview with Wymer, then in charge of overseas sales, in *The Log*, March 1982.

30   J. Rea, 'Third World Publishing 1984', Memorandum of 2 May 1984.

31   Paper delivered at the International Managing Directors' Conference, 18–20 June 1986 (LA). With a staff of around 200, including 21 sales representatives, Longman Nigeria had 1,500 titles on file.

the Book Development Council, the Association's international division.[32]

The other new Sector Directors on the Longman UK Board in 1986 were Paul Blackburn and Jeremy Osborne. Blackburn, who had risen inside the House from Divisional Production Controller to Production Director, reporting to Hobbs, had replaced Hobbs when Hobbs left Longman in 1982 and was now Managing Director of the first of the three Longman services divisions, Longman Distribution, Computer and Production Services (LDCPS). Osborne, Group Sales Director within the same Services Management grouping, had wide-ranging overseas experience in Africa and Asia and was to continue to play an important part in the affairs of the House after Rix left Harlow.[33]

Blackburn's place in the structure, and that of his staff, some appointed from outside the publishing industry, was important. Computing and production services at Harlow needed to be efficient. This meant direct discussions about working practices with the relevant trade unions, not only SOGAT, the NUJ and NGA, but ASTMS, led in its golden years by the most voluble of trade unionists, Clive Jenkins, a 'master of the mass media'.[34] At least two of the members of the Longman UK Board had been active members of ASTMS, although they did not play a leading part in local union activities.

~

Rix's introduction of a sector approach was subject to continuous review. From the start he had emphasised that the 'structures [of 1983] may be expected to change from time to time as market, or publishing operational requirements, change'.[35] Yet, while it was a strategy that worked, just because the structures were subject to such review, there could sometimes

Cartoon of Tim Rix and Julian Rea, from the House Magazine of Longman Penguin, Southern Africa (Pty) Ltd, June 1982 No 4

Longman Archive

---

32   Under Bradley there were four divisions in the Association – the Book Marketing Council (Home); the Book Development Council (International); the Education Publishers Council responsible for schools; and the University, College and Professional Publishing Council. In 1983 Publishers' Databases Limited was inaugurated as a 'cooperative vehicle for publishers planning to engage in electronic publishing'. (Bradley, *loc. cit.*, p.8.)

33   The *Grapevine*, Spring 1986, pp.10–11. (LA Part II 213)

34   A. Sampson, *The New Anatomy of Britain* (1971), p.637.

35   Note of 17 Oct. 1983. (LA)

be uneasiness among UK Longman employees.[36] When changes of organisation were proposed both within and between sectors and in the names of 'departments', a word that did not disappear from the House vocabulary were spelt out, but their personal impact was bound to differ. The attention that Rix also paid (and rightly) to quasi-autonomous 'publishing cells', located not in Harlow but throughout the country, might involve necessary shifts of location which could provoke more than uneasiness unless they could be justified in terms of new growth.

Such new growth could often be singled out. Thus, the first location of one such 'publishing cell' was a Resources Unit set up in 1971 in York at a medieval house in the Shambles, initially created to design, edit, print and promote the materials of the Schools Council's General Studies Programme that were published by Longman. Its work expanded greatly under Roger Watson's guidance and over a million General Studies project units were sold between 1971 and 1977.

A central Longman point socially – and in business terms – was Number 5 Bentinck Street, in London's West End, where a variety of activities flourished. It was now far more than the showroom and registered office of Longman UK. It was the place which Longman staff working abroad visited when they were in Britain, and formal as well as informal meetings (and interviews) were held there. It was obviously an attractive location and in 1986 the building was given a face-lift.[37] It was a location that survived.

Rix, who frequently entertained employees and visitors at 5 Bentinck Street, was always at the centre of the stage. On 4 January 1984 his fiftieth birthday was celebrated with a surprise party in a different setting, the Senate House of the University of London. It was given by Quirk, who

---

36 See for an example of change, set out in a memorandum by Diana Scholefield, 'Reorganisation', 16 May 1985, dealing with LDCPS (initials only given), Longman Distribution, Computer and Production Services. A chart was attached. One of the changes of name was from UK Customer Services Department to UK Trade Services Department. The change, it was said, was 'to clearly identify the servicing of UK Trade customers', but it involved the appointment of a new post of UK Trade Services Manager. There were further major changes in 1988. Thus, in the Administration Department the Sales Administration Section met weekly in 1985 at 10 a.m. on Fridays for several months 'to enable us to constantly monitor [scheduled] changes in responsibilities' (Undated note, 'The Reorganisation of the Division D Sales Department' LA).

37 So too improvements for the Pinnacles and Bentinck Street properties were announced in the *Grapevine*, Spring 1986. 'Those of you who have had the occasion to visit either the Pinnacles ... or Bentinck Street in London may be curious about the forbidding signs – "Do not enter" – [and] the festoons of plastic curtain and tarpaulin concealing hordes of workmen hammering and singing!' (LA Part II 213)

was now its Vice-Chancellor: he called it 'a sort of *Festschrift*'. In line with tradition, the occasion, long prepared and designed to coincide with the bicentenary of Samuel Johnson's birth, was celebrated in a poem, a sonnet, which referred indirectly to Orwell ('There was no double-speak when Tim was born') but looked back to the beginnings:

> There was a long man long ago
> Who garnered Fortune from the store of words,
> The Words that Johnson listed row by row.
> The Long men came and went. The words still flow.

~

Open-ness was prized by Rix in all his activities inside and outside the House of Longman. He had settled the pattern from the very beginning of his spell as Chief Executive, and it is illuminating to consider the sequence of new-style 'confidential reports' that he produced for staff as Chief Executive and later also as Chairman. The first of them was in 1976: the last to be introduced by him was in 1988, but they were to be continued by Kahn. Each began with a statement by Rix, re-named 'Introduction' in 1979. There was a clear purpose behind all of them – that of inviting employees to compare the business performance of one year with that of another, while taking a longer five-year period into account. At least in retrospect, however, there were interesting differences between them. They evolved. The first reports were contained in plain white covers: the last were in colour throughout, incorporating photographs as well as diagrams and charts and giving details of outstanding new publications as well as of profits and losses. There was by then a glossy touch to them as there was in other House 'literature', which often contained the same information differently handled. No employees of any business could have been better informed. In 1986, in order to reflect 'corporate identity', new Longman colours were introduced, dark blue, dark red and light grey in place of orange and grey, and a new layout was devised for stationery and, less ubiquitous, for the name 'Longman' on Group vans.[38]

The earliest Rix Report (Rix had taken over as Chief Executive in 1976), simple in form, included a statement by the then Chairman, Roger Brooke, who referred to other branches of Pearson business as well as to Longman Group figures, noting that 'our parent company', Pearson Longman, had produced an 'illustrated brochure' describing in words and pictures the activities of the Group's companies, including Longman's [*sic*], copies of which were available for 'any of you who may be interested'. In his own statement, which appeared on the next page, Rix, introduced by

Examples of the annual confidential reports to Longman employees

Longman Archive

38   *The Log*, n.d. (1986), p.8. Unfortunately *The Log* was unable (no reason given) to print the new colours on its cover or in the column describing them.

Brooke, made it clear that he wanted this Report to be seen by everyone, whether interested or not!

After consultations with the Staff Committee and representatives of ASTMS, the relevant union, Rix had concluded rightly that this was the kind of report that they wanted, more informative than a balance sheet and profit-and-loss account. Those still could be seen by anyone who wished to do so, but Rix added that he hoped to be talking to 'all of you' not through printed words and figures but through divisional or departmental meetings. The year 1976 had been a 'very good year' when 'profits were much higher than expected and we improved our financial (cash) resources quite considerably'. There were none the less qualifications to note. The figures did not take account of the adjustments which needed to be made to reflect the effects of exceptionally high inflation. More specifically, the size of the profits had depended to a substantial extent on 'the tremendous expansion of our business in Nigeria', as was demonstrated in the last chapter, and Rix made it clear that it was necessary for Pearson Longman to acknowledge that 'there were risks for us in the structure of our business abroad'. The Longman Group was an international company. Of its 1,375 employees 468 worked outside the United Kingdom. 'The fact that as a company we did well in 1975 and 1976 was thanks to the contribution of all our employees round the world'.[39]

From the very start Rix was stressing that conditions and results in different years (and in different places) might be very different. It was necessary for employees to be able to compare one year with another. It was also equally necessary for them to take a long-term view. In the short run, the prospects for the next year, 1977, were only 'middling', a word Rix was to use often: 'it seems quite possible at the moment that we shall not achieve the sales and profits we had budgeted for in 1977'. Eleven years later, he could report 'the best financial performance for several years': the 13.8 per cent profit margin was 'even better than budgeted'. The background of both statements is important. Budgeting and longer-term planning had begun to be an accepted part of Longman procedures before Rix became Chief Executive. Now forecasting had become increasingly awkward. There would be 'very great difficulty in planning ahead in terms of sales and profits for the next few years'.

The longer-term period Rix had in mind was three years, the period he thought necessary to employ in all corporate planning, and in this first report he gave details of turnover and other indices for the years between 1972 and 1976. The last column was important given the national and international economic situation:

---

39   *A Confidential Report to employees of Longman Group ... for the year ending 31 December 1976.* (LA Part II 213)

Longman Group Turnover, 1972–76 (million £)

YEAR	TOTAL	INDEXED	UK RETAIL PRICES
1972	13.9	100	100
1973	14.8	106	109
1974	18.4	132	127
1975	23.1	166	157
1976	32.5	234	183

In later reports Rix was able to make the longer-term contrasts he wished employees also to be able to make. He was also able to emphasise that 15 per cent was a target trading profit that had to be aimed for. With that margin, the business would have 'a more appropriate cash position from which we can continue to finance ... growth and development'.[40]

It was not until 1981 that for the first time in five years a 'real' increase in both turnover (now £63.6 million) and profits (now £11.5 million) was achieved, although there had been few signs that this result would be reached. From the January of 1979 it had been possible to pass over only 40 per cent of Nigerian profits to Harlow, and there had been considerable difficulties in the Nigerian market; the result was that in real terms, 'taking the inflation rate into account ... profits [had] fallen quite dramatically since 1978', which Rix had described as 'a reasonable year'.[41] The actual profits, too, were lower than had been forecast.

As always in publishing, there were good and bad years. 'Hard going for publishers', the literary editor of the *Financial Times*, Anthony Curtis, headed an article on business performance and prospects in 1979.[42] He pointed out correctly that the 'present ills' were directly related to 'the underlying problems of the economy as a whole' – in particular higher costs and the strength of sterling against the dollar. For Rix

> that we did not do worse is a measure of our strength as an international company and our ability (which I am confident we shall maintain, though doing so will get more difficult) to keep up our "gross" profitability, that is, our ability to buy our printing, binding and paper more effectively (more cheaply!) than our competitors and to publish and price our books more skilfully.[43]

---

40 *A Confidential Report to Employees, UK Report 31 Dec. 1988.* (LA Part II/213)

41 *A Confidential Report ... 31 Dec. 1979.* (LA Part II/213)

42 *Financial Times*, 16 Oct. 1979.

43 *A Confidential Report ... 31 Dec. 1979*, p.3. (LA Part II/213)

It was with all this in mind that in 1980, in the midst of a deep international recession, Rix introduced a section in his introduction to his annual report 'What do lesser profits mean?' He also introduced then the concept of 'cash drain'. Within each year there were significant changes in cash flow so that it was necessary to look for patterns within years as well as between them.[44]

It was equally necessary, he told his colleagues, to examine the fortunes of each national and regional market within what was an international concern. For example, profits accruing from Nigeria, whatever the problems that it had faced, had made it possible for the Group's financial position at the end of the year to be better than had earlier been expected. Longman had 'deliberately planned and built up [its] financial strength to cope with new developments'. For other markets there had to be particular financial provisions. Rix was optimistic in 1981 when he pointed not only to the effects of development in the Arab world and Australia but to the need for 'good operating' in production, distribution and cost control.[45]

In 1982, however, the situation had completely changed in the light of the continuing international economic recession and, within that context, of unpaid Nigerian debt that was owed to the Group, accompanied by likely further delays in its collection:

> As a Company we have less financial security than in the past – we have at the moment little "cushion" if [Longman results] go wrong in some unexpected way. That is still the situation despite taking action to cut back operations in those areas of the Company most directly affected by difficult trading conditions.

Rix, who never liked to be on the defensive, was always uneasy at times when there were 'cuts', but he insisted then – and correctly – that publishing programmes had not been cut back, except in relation to Nigeria, and that, with 'the help, hard work and, indeed, dedication of staff' necessary development would be resumed. He added that, as in the previous year, he had asked Divisional Managing Directors to 'talk to their Divisions after the issue of ... final results of 1982 ... and about how things seemed to be going in the early part of 1983'.

In fact, 1983 was a 'bad year', and Rix found it important to point out that the Longman Group had reached its 'borrowing limits', and that this implied that 'if anything further were to go wrong with our expected sales income or cash position, we would have to make sudden and extensive cuts in our operating costs right through the Group'.[46]

44   *A Confidential Report ... 31 Dec. 1980*, p.3. (LA Part II/213)

45   *A Confidential Report ... 31 Dec.1981.* (LA Part II/213)

46   *Confidential Report to Members of Staff at Longman Group Limited*, 12 Jan. 1983, following a letter from Rix of 22 Dec. (Eve of Christmas) 1982. (LA Part II/213)

It had been a matter of great pride in 1979 that Longman had won one of the Queen's Awards for Export Achievement, presented to Rix by the Lord Lieutenant of Essex in the presence of six hundred Longman employees, for this gave a boost to morale. It was of more general importance, too, in that this was the first time that a publishing house had been so honoured. The award was referred to in the report of that year by Brookc, on the eve of leaving Pearson Longman, as evidence that the Longman Group was 'an enterprising and efficient business'.[47]

Thereafter, from 1980 onwards only Rix's name as Chief Executive (and later also as Chairman) appeared in the reports, which by 1987 were not merely statistical, although the statistics were set out colourfully with the aid of modern graphics (sometimes, sadly, not as easily accessible as the traditional tables), but full of photographs. The issue of that year began with a page 'Formula for Success: the Kind of Publishing Group We Want to Be'. It not only looked forward, but summed up much which had already happened or was happening to Longman strategy. What had once been called 'policy' was now unequivocally 'strategy'.

~

The well-produced 1988 Report is particularly interesting because of its richness of content and, not least, because it presents a full picture of Longman UK immediately before the acquisition of Addison-Wesley changed the framework of reference. It picked out a 'number of firsts', which included a joint venture with the BBC for the development of course materials for primary and secondary schools; the first bilingual 'learners' dictionary for 11 to 14 year-olds published by Longman Dictionaries for Longman Italia; and the appointment of the first Managing Director of Longman France, Tim Horsler, who had previously worked in the former Africa and Caribbean Division at Harlow and in Nigeria. The other 'firsts'

Tim Rix receives the Queen's Award for Export Achievement from the Lord Lieutenant of Essex, 11 September 1979

Longman Archive

---

47   *A Confidential Report ... 31 Dec. 1978*, p.2. On the cover of this report a Longman ship logo was shown side by side with the design of the Award. (LA Part II/213)

included an unprecedented new major course contracted after tender with the People's Education Press, China; and details of the enrolment from the staff of the first MBA student. There had been earlier reports of the first Open University graduates from Longman UK.

A 'review by division' began with *ELT*, where Tim Hunt admitted that 'we did not quite make our ambitious sales budget', but pointed out that 'we managed to achieve a record level of profitability in 1988'. In dealing with Education Watson had to report a decline 'with unexpected severity' in the schools publishing market in Britain, but he too could point to a small increase in net profit margins. In International Education Rob Francis could take pride in 'sales being better than budget'. Longman Dictionaries could proclaim itself 'global market leader in *ELT* dictionaries overcoming stiff, often cut-throat, competition from OUP and Collins'. Longman Industry and Public Service Management Division achieved a growth rate in excess of 18 per cent and a near quadruple trading profit compared with that of 1987.

The diversity of opportunities and problems faced by a global business was apparent in Kahn's report on the European Companies. Longman Italia and Longman España had been bedevilled by strikes in the educational system, but had achieved significantly higher sales. Churchill Livingstone, flourishing, had worked out business deals with Ciba-Geigy, Glaxo and ICI and had registered a 37 per cent increase in advertising revenue from its journals. Longman Academic, Scientific and Technical had enjoyed an excellent year, 'exceeding its sales budget and its profit budget for the second year in succession'. Architecture, Design and Technology Press, established in August 1988 as a new division with only five people working in it, had recruited four of them from Architectural Press Books when it was sold in 1987.

General Books had had a great success with its *Chronicle of the 20th Century* which sold out its initial print run within a month and sold 160,000 copies by Christmas: it reached the top of the best-seller lists. It was a chronicle that had little to report about publishing in its pages. Nor did *Keesing's Record of World Events*, the writing, editorial and origination of which was transferred at the end of the year to a new company established by former Longman staff. The *Record* covered the particularly dramatic world events of 1989, leaving unrecorded for the world the 'full establishment' of Longman France with headquarters in the Boulevard St. Michel, the appointment of Jeff Andrew to the new post of Development Director for Europe, and the winning of a World Bank tender in Uganda.

There were many other publishing events to record in the 1988 Report. The most important retirement to be announced from Harlow in that year was that of Roger Watson, while there was a singling out of the name of Michael Johnson, who had been appointed as Managing Director of Longman, Academic, Scientific and Technical. Great care was being taken at Harlow to make the VISTA computer system work. It had been

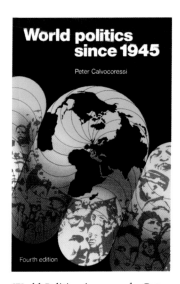

World politics since 1945

Peter Calvocoressi

Fourth edition

World Politics since 1945 by Peter Calvocoressi was first published in 1968, a second edition in 1971 and thereafter went into eight editions. It was an example of how Longman paid attention to backlist publishing (for all markets) as well as developing new titles, series and courses

Personal collection

recommended by a Working Party which identified the advantages of VISTA to publishers, and a high-level steering group was attempting to resolve issues as they arose at Harlow following devolution of computer usage to publishing staff so that they could combine publishing and marketing approaches. The first organisational change in the process had been a merger of the Cashiers' Department with the Wages Department, as a result of which the preparation of royalty contract forms was fully transferred to the Contracts Department, headed by David Lea, a devoted and loyal employee of Longman UK who had been with the House for forty years.

As well as his long service and his great knowledge, crucial to Longman, of contracts and copyright, a changing field, Lea had another role, crucial to the historian of Longman. He was the link man to Reading University Library where as part of the 250th anniversary celebrations the Longman archives had been deposited. Lea was responsible in particular for ensuring that current archive material continued to be handed over to Dr. Jim Edwards and to his successor Michael Bott. Between them they built up the leading archive of British publishing, an invaluable resource for scholars. Lea was himself a skilled collector of Longman first editions. It is sad that he has not written an account of his life in the House to compare with that of E.W. Parker.

Lea's service was to extend to fifty years as he continued to assist Lynette Owen, who had joined Longman in 1976 as a foreign rights executive and who had gone on to acquire responsibility for all rights, contracts and copyright matters. Longman (and subsequently Pearson Education) were fortunate because she became a leading authority on copyright and the sale of rights business throughout the world. She became the editor of the standard work *Clark's Publishing Agreements: a book of precedents*.

～

Precedents still counted in the practices as well as the law of publishing. But so, too, increasingly, as we have seen, did statistics. In the late 1980s, for the first time in publishing history, book trade statistics were abundant, although there were many complaints about their reliability. 'The air resounds with the thud of volumes of statistics on the book industry', a relatively new way of describing it, Ion Trewin had already written in *The Author* in the autumn of 1979.[48] There was still no single statistical source in 1988, but three fascinating Book Trade Year Books, brought out by the Publishers Association, broke new ground. They showed that in 1987 the total value of book sales, including reprints, had grown in constant prices

---

48   *The Author*, Vol. XC, No. 3, Autumn 1979, p.119.

by more than a third over a nine-year period.[49] It remained difficult to make comparisons on a statistical basis between one publishing house and another of the kind that Pettigrew and Whipp were looking for: 'we are not as keenly aware as we should be of the performance of our competitors', one of the Longman staff whom they interviewed told them.[50] He was aware that market share did not always fully indicate fully comparative strength. The overhead costs of different publishers varied significantly: no-one knew just how much.

Nevertheless, the total turnover figures for the Longman Group as a whole (Longman Holdings) and for the Longman Group UK, the largest company in the Longman Group, for the four years leading up to 1988 reveal much in themselves. Longman Group UK's sales, as presented in the Table, were of books published in the UK and sold within the UK or exported.

Longman Group and Longman UK sales and trading profits, 1985–1988 (£ million)

Year	Group total sales	Group trading profit	Group trading profit as a % of sales	Longman Group UK: total sales	Longman Group UK: trading profit	Longman Group UK: trading profit as % of sales (Target 15%)
1985	122.9	15.1	12.3	54.4	4.1	7.6
1986	142.3	14.2	10.0	60.2	6.6	11.0
1987	151.2	18.9	12.5	70.0	8.6	12.2
1988	151.4	16.2	10.7	69.4	8.5	13.8

Targets were always set, including an ultimate, if elusive, target of 15 per cent, both for the whole Group and for Longman Group UK, a target which adds significance to the fourth and last columns in the Table. Rix accounted for the improved 1988 target percentage figures for Longman Group UK in terms of better production and materials purchasing, printing the right quantities of new books and imprints, and, not least, controlling overhead costs. The lower target percentages for the Group as a whole in 1988 reflected the economic and financial problems of the United States.

---

49 Publishers Association Statistics Collection, PASCS, for the years 1981 to 1986 showed a decreasing share for school publications (18.6 : 14.6 per cent) and an increasing share for 'university professional' (22.6 : 25.3 per cent).

50 Pettigrew and Whipp, *op. cit.* See also Curwen, *op. cit.*, Ch. 1, 'Statistical Overview'. In Chapters 9, 10 and 11 Alan Singleton examined the publishing of journals, a field in which Longman was actively engaged. The chapters covered range, size and price, but Singleton acknowledged (p.134) that his enquiries throughout had been 'bedevilled by problems of definition'.

~

The openness apparent in all Rix's published statistical tables and in all his internal reports, was apparent too in the House magazines *The Log* and *Grapevine*, the former revived in 1981 to cover international issues, the latter launched in 1984 for Longman's UK staff. *The Log* for 1984 had an appropriate science-fiction style coloured cover and referred to a new edition of Orwell's *1984*, 'complete with introduction and glossary'. 'Buy your copy now for only 73 pence (UK staff discounted price)'.

One of the articles in the first issue of *Grapevine* dealt with the transfer of the Keesing's business from Bath to Westgate House in Harlow, 'just up the hill from both Burnt Mill and the Pinnacles'. It was called 'Diary of a Relocator', which sounded like 'newspeak', and in tone it could not have been described as cheerful. 'The attractions of Harlow proved sufficient to lure only four of the dozen Keesing's staff from Bath', the Relocator wrote. One of them was Alan Day, the Relocator himself.[51] *The Log* reminded the four of them that the only reason *Keesing's* had been in Bath since 1940 was that German bombers were perceived as a threat to editorial concentration at its previous offices in central London.[52]

In the new-style *Log*, there was an element of nostalgia, never to be entirely abandoned in subsequent numbers, for example, in the presence on the first page of a photograph of Rix on a visit to Kuala Lumpur being presented with a salver almost exactly twenty years after he arrived there to 'look after' Longman operations in Malaya. As has been noted, he had started Longman Malaya (later Longman Malaysia) in 1962. Times had often been troubled in Kuala Lumpur – and they were to remain so: on one occasion in 1970, when Duncan had been in charge, it had been reported that 'we are almost the only expatriate publishers to have weathered the political changes'.[53] There was no nostalgia on the spot.

There was no nostalgia either in the fact that the new *Log*, planned for July and December each year, was printed in Malaysia. Procedures – and motivations – were thoroughly up-to-date. The editor in Harlow sent final copy to the Longman office in Malaysia by air courier, where setting was done 'free of charge'. Galleys were then returned to London, and the final proofs travelled east again to be printed and bound.[54] An article in

---

51   While at Bath, Day had written an article in *The Log* in 1977, 'New Technology comes to Keesing's' in which he described the first steps towards computerisation. He noted then that there was 'some inevitable nostalgia at Keesing's for the old letter-press system'. (LA Part II/212/3)

52   *Ibid.*, No. 6, March 1984, p.11.

53   Letter to Potter, 5 Jan. 1970. (LA)

54   *The Log*, No. 2, July 1981, p.1. (LA Part II 213)

the second issue of *The Log* by David Powell, 'Database publishing – A concept for the 1980s', looked without alarm to the future – 'the perpetual progression of the so-called electronic revolution'.[55] Powell, who joined the Journals Division in July 1979, had just been appointed Publishing Director – Reference Publishing with the remit to 'weld' together the various pieces of Division J's reference publishing.

The contents of *The Log* did not follow a route: they moved freely across space. 'As our constituent parts increase', one of its editors explained, 'it becomes ever more likely that someone working in one part of the Group may have little idea about what goes on in another. So *The Log*, which is helping to bridge the great geographical distances, becomes more and more important'. For the historian it helps to bridge time differences too, since there is much information in it which is not available elsewhere. Time, too, has many surprises. In the same issue that featured Rix with his Malaysian salver another photograph showed him presenting a cheque for $100,000 in December 1981 to the Minister of Education and Culture of Zimbabwe. Earlier in the year, Longman Zimbabwe had donated £150,000 to the Zimbabwean government to assist the reconstruction of rural areas damaged during the Rhodesian War.[56]

Also in the same issue was an account of a Longman television commercial, the first of its kind, for the new *Longman New Generation Dictionary*, which was being handled as a certain best-seller. It appeared at a time when steps were being taken to attract unprecedented attention in the media, a process which was to call for an exceptionally large expenditure on advertising. Since it involved concentration on a particular product, the impact of this advertisement, which had as its 'punch line' 'Explanations you can understand for words you can't' was being 'closely monitored' by other publishers.[57] The *Dictionary*, which appeared in 1983, went straight into the *Sunday Times* best-seller lists. Appropriately, it included more scientific terms than any of its competitors and introduced a number of what soon became familiar new terms like 'rate capping', 'nuclear-free zone' and 'user-friendly'.

There were two continuing emphases in the various numbers of *The Log* – on overseas personalities and activities in the Longman Group and on 'Longmaniacs', people who had spent twenty-one years or more working with Longman. Interviews brought out both continuity and change. So, too, did a number of articles, such as one by Louis Alexander, describing

---

55   *Ibid.*, p.14.

56   *The Log*, No. 3, March 1982, p.2. It quoted the *Zimbabwe Herald*, 2 Nov. 1981 for a favourable response. (LA Part II 213)

57   *Ibid*, p.3.

a visit to China which he called 'The China Experience'.[58] The 1976 issue which announced the appointment of Rix as Chief Executive: 'Change at the Top – Acquisition down Under', also recorded in verse, on the same opening page, the departure of Adrian Higham (to John Wiley):

> Farewell, a large but gentle man,
> No more to tread the hallowed halls,
> To sit at tables high and be
> A Longman man for all to see.[59]

The young Willie Shen as a production controller in Hong Kong in 1960

Longman Archive

Higham, son of C.S.S. Higham, had joined the 'overseas educational department of Longmans' during the 1950s and had been instrumental in arranging Rix's appointment to Kuala Lumpur in 1961. He, with Kerr, had joined the Board of Longman in 1964.

An issue of *The Log* in 1985 reported a 'hearty welcome in Hong Kong for Tim Rix', who had been received there by Willie Shen, since 1975 Managing Director of Longman Group (Far East) Ltd., and by Alex Wu, a Director of the Group and of much else in Hong Kong besides. Shen holds a very special place in the history of Longman not least because from 1975 he managed the Hong Kong operation not only as a publishing house in its own right and sales agent for the rest of Longman, but as a production powerhouse for the whole Longman Group. He had joined the company in

58 *The Log*, No. 3, March 1982, p.19. (LA Part II 213)

59 *Ibid.*, *The Log*, No. 5 July 1976, p.1. The acquisition was of Cheshire in Australia. (LA Part II 213)

Using computer technology, the *Longman New Generation Dictionary* was published in 1981

Personal collection

1959 as a clerk (a post which he did not enjoy) but moved on to production under Adkins. Between 1961 and 1963, as production controller, he worked very closely with Rix who was publishing educational books for Malaya, Singapore and Hong Kong.

Shen became Production Manager in 1967, and eight years later Kerr told him that he was to succeed Adkins as Managing Director. He later wrote (in *The Log* for December, 1982) that his appointment had come as a shock, 'as I felt at that time it seemed a very brave move appointing a local Chinese to be responsible for an English branch company'. Thereafter Longman publishing for Hong Kong schools flourished, and Shen developed, with remarkable skill and tenacity (he was fluent in Mandarin as well as Cantonese and Shanghaiese) Longman's publishing and rights business in mainland China. He had travelled to Beijing in 1964 with Adkins and with Mark and Lady Elizabeth Longman, for the British Industrial Exhibition at which Longman was the only publisher represented, and in 1985 he accompanied Rix and Osborne, then Group International Sales Director, on a trip to Beijing for ten days of 'intensive talks with top Chinese government officials'.

In Britain itself links with government were sometimes described, as for example, when Longman acquired Councils and Education Press in 1977. The Press had had 'a somewhat chequered history' which went back to 1903, the year after the passing of a new Education Act which in effect created the system of local education authorities in England and Wales. From then onwards, the Press, a private company, had published a weekly journal, *Education*, which was largely devoted to the interests and activities of local education authorities, and in the 1920s it was acquired by the powerful Association of Education Committees. By 1977, when it had long been drawn into more general educational debate, the Association had ceased to function.

The Longman acquisition, along with two important directories, *The Education Committees Year Book* and the *Social Services Year Book* was highly appropriate for a leading educational publisher, while it also boosted Longman's growing publishing of directories and its publishing of books on educational administration. *Education*, edited by Tudor David a distinguished educational journalist, remained influential: it was known to be read carefully every week by at least one Permanent Secretary in the Department for Education and Science.

~

If *The Log* is a necessary source for the detailed history of Longman, another less serious, gossipy house journal for all UK staff, *Grapevine*, is rich in detail, concentrating on social activities and events, location by location, and revealing as much about the private activities of Longman employees as about their contributions to the business. Members of staff who won prizes and awards, a relatively new publicity feature of the time, were given special attention, and those who had travelled on company business described their visits abroad, revealing in the process the global scope of the Longman business. There were farewells to Longmaniacs, as in other House journals, and welcomes to 'new starters' and reminiscences that might not have appeared elsewhere.

Publicity was given to new books which might interest Longman staff, and these ranged from N. and S. Allison's *Drinks A-Z* (1985) and Rosemary George's *The Wine Dictionary* (1989) to Simon Majaro's *The Creative Gap* (1988), 'a revolutionary new book for business today', and Richard Dawkins's brilliantly witty *The Blind Watchmaker* (1986) which won the Royal Society of Literature Award (a Heinemann bequest), the first time that a science book had been awarded this distinction.[60]

Most important of all, there were *Grapevine* pieces by Rix on Longman Group UK results, for the quarter not for the year, pieces which combined explanation and exhortation. In January 1987, for instance, he described how in January the Group's budget had been 'suspended and completely reworked to reduce our 1987 sales budget to a more realistic figure because we did not achieve our 1986 targets'. By the end of March sales were £1.2 million behind the original budget figure, but in line with that reached in the re-worked budget. This, he pointed out, 'clearly demonstrate[d] why the exercise was necessary'.[61]

~

Rix also used House journals to describe new business acquisitions. The first major British acquisition with which Rix was directly associated was that of Oyez Publishing in 1981 (as described in the previous chapter). Pitman followed in 1985. In its time it was as important an acquisition as that of Rivington in 1890.

Each acquisition depended on approval and financial support from Pearson and for Rix it was the acquisition of Pitman in 1985 which showed the relationship between Longman and Pearson at its best. He had asked the Pearson Executive Committee for what was called 'a hunting licence' seriously to pursue the possibility of acquiring Pitman, about which he and his colleagues had been collecting a substantial body of information; and he knew that this acquisition had special attraction for that Committee as it did for himself. Pitman business publications, along with vocational and secretarial (shorthand) books, their historical lead-in to their business, had the highest of reputations, although the financial return on them was not currently outstanding, and Rix wished to make the Longman business list as impressive as its medical list.

There was an extra and very strong attraction. Copp Clark Pitman,

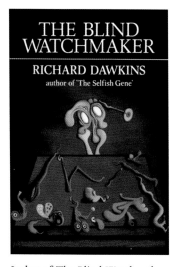

Jacket of *The Blind Watchmaker* by Richard Dawkins, 1986. Published in the Longman Scientific & Technical list, it was one of the key popular science books of recent times

Personal collection

60   *Grapevine*, Late Summer 1987. (LA Part II 213)

61   *Ibid.*, Summer 1987.

a Canadian educational and vocational publishing house, would give Longman a strong base in Canada. The attraction was so strong because since 1979 Longman had had no presence in Canada at all. There had originally been a Longmans, Toronto, but it had been turned into a partnership with the US publisher Harcourt, Brace in which Longman was the minority partner. And then in 1979 that minority stake had also been sold to Harcourt. For Australia too, Pitman's Australian business, launched in 1914, fitted in naturally with Longman's extensive operations there.

After the purchase in 1976 of the Cheshire Publishing Company in the face of heavy pressure from American publishers on the then owners of Cheshire, the Xerox Corporation, Longman was interested in further expanding its Australian business, and it was Kerr from his base there who foresaw that what became Longman Cheshire could become the leading and the largest educational publisher in Australia. The deal with Cheshire was not easy, and it might have fallen through had not Nigel Farrow, who handled the publishing interests of Xerox outside the United States, stood by it. By comparison Pitman, Australia was straightforward.

By then Longman had become a leading educational publisher in New Zealand through the acquisition of a respected local publishing house, Blackwood and Janet Paul (to form Longman Paul), and later the acquisition of three local publishing lists – Reed Education, Nexus and Methuen New Zealand. Under Kerr's guidance, two exceptionally able women, Rosemary Stagg, Publishing Director and Liz Nelson, Sales Manager, had taken full advantage of new openings.

The code-name for the Pitman project was P-Z, and as in the Australian case there were other parties who were interested, particularly in Copp Clark Pitman. High prices were being paid for such publishing concerns, and Lazards who led the negotiations – as was normal in Pearson acquisitions – were fully aware of the extent of the competition from, in particular, American and Dutch bidders. The Longman Group, however, because of the complementarity of its business with that of Pitman could predict a greater rate of return than its competitors could. It estimated that Pitman profits would rise from £956,000 in 1984 to £2,828,000 by 1989.[62] In 1979 they had been £1.2 million.

The Pearson representative in the negotiations was J.A.B. Joll, with whom Rix had to work closely. He was in charge of all Pearson's financial moves, and in particular, with all its book publishing activities. A journalist by background, one of the highly successful *Financial Times* team, he was for Rix easier to deal with, at least at this stage, than John Hale, who had joined Pearson, 'head-hunted' from Alcan, the Aluminium Company of Canada,

---

62 Possible Acquisition of Pitman Publishing and Examinations Institute (n.d.). (LA)

completely outside the publishing world. At the very last moment, however, Rix had to telephone Lord Blakenham, at the very top, with a request from the Pitman side for a final increase in the price. He gave his agreement.

~

A flashback is once again both interesting and necessary. Pitman history went back to the very beginning of Queen Victoria's reign, when in 1837 Isaac Pitman (1813–1897), born in Trowbridge, Wiltshire, the son of a handloom weaver, then a young Gloucestershire schoolmaster, invented a new and rapid shorthand system following a pattern devised by Samuel Taylor. This was an interesting coincidence of names across time.[63] Isaac prepared an edition of *Stenographic Soundhand* (1837) setting out details of his system for a London publisher, Samuel Bagster, who took half the copies for sale in his own shop, but it was Isaac's unremitting entrepreneurial drive that guaranteed the business success of the system.

On the first day of Rowland Hill's new penny post, 10 January 1840, Isaac issued a 'Penny Plate', offering tuition based on *Phonography or Writing by Sound* to any person who wrote back to him, and in less than five years 10,000 people scattered throughout the country were learning shorthand from him. This was practical education at its best. 'Time saved is life gained' was Isaac's motto. With business secured, he moved his business to Bath, where he established a 'Phonetic Institute'; and it was from his Bath headquarters, not from London, that he published in his lifetime around twenty editions, most of them meticulously revised, of his *Phonography or Writing by Sound, Being Also a New and Natural System of Short-Hand*.

His was a genuinely universal system, for it could be used, whatever the language, in all parts of the world. It also lent itself to diffusion as office management was transformed with the growth of business; and Isaac took advantage of the development of the typewriter, largely a Victorian invention, to make his shorthand an office necessity. *The Office*, 'a penny journal for office men', which advertised typewriters alongside fountain pens, did not immediately recognise that it was office women who would soon become typists, a word not then invented. They, and not the machines, were at first called 'typewriters'.[64]

Pitman's Metropolitan School of Shorthand in Chancery Lane, near the Law Courts, soon to be called not a school but a College, offered equal access from 1870 onwards not only to men but to all women who could read – a not unimportant date in women's history – and its syllabus included 'office routine', accounting and law as well as shorthand and typing.

---

63 *Essay intended to establish a standard for an Universal System of Stenography* (1786).

64 See A. Briggs, *Victorian Things* (1996 edn.), pp.365–8.

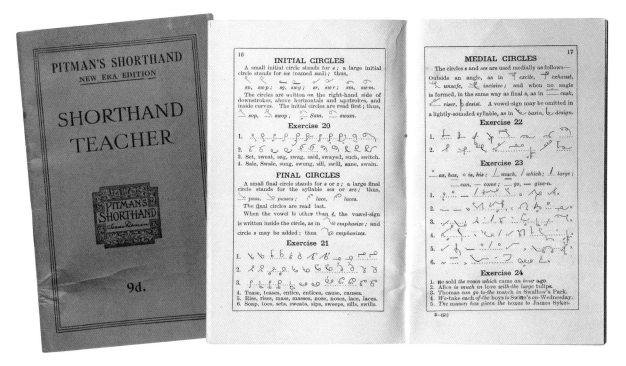

Two pages from The New Era edition of *The Shorthand Teacher,* 1943, showing the science of shorthand

Personal collection

Remarkably quickly there were hundreds of other colleges, scattered throughout Britain and the Commonwealth, 'from Australia to Africa, Canada and Ceylon', that were teaching Pitman shorthand. (Soon Japan was on the map.) Through vocational examinations, at first organised in 1864 by the Royal Society of Arts and the London Chamber of Commerce, they relied on Pitman textbooks.

Isaac Pitman & Sons Ltd was set up as a company in 1886, eight years before Isaac was awarded a knighthood; two years later the Pitman Press began to publish from Bath. In 1892 *Pitman's Shorthand Weekly* began to appear. London premises were also acquired at No.1 Amen Corner, not far from Longmans, Green, and when Isaac died in 1897, the year of the Queen's Diamond Jubilee, his two sons, Alfred and Ernest, took over. In 1920 they moved their London office from Amen Corner to Pitman House in Kingsway.

Ernest Pitman's son, I.J., later Sir James Pitman (1901–1985), politician as well as publisher, who joined the Board in 1924, was educated at Eton, where in one day – it would have endeared him to Thomas Norton and C.J. Longman – he won the hundred yards, the hurdles, the quarter mile and the long jump. He was far more than a 'boy wonder', however, and under his control the scope of the Pitman firm was broadened to cover all aspects of business, now organised in three departments, commercial, technical and educational.

James deemed it essential to keep abreast of educational developments. Yet shorthand was never neglected, and in 1974, looking to the future, a modified system was introduced called Pitman 2000. By the year 2000, of course, the typewriter was to become an almost obsolete object, but answerphones and laptop computers, all in action by 1990, needed the same kind of imaginative instruction that the Pitmans knew how to provide. The death of Sir James Pitman in 1985 forced the family into difficult domestic discussions, a necessary prelude to the Longman take-over.[65]

In 1985 the future of the Examinations Institute figured prominently in the discussions about the take-over, and Rix had to lobby hard with the Pitman family to persuade them it had a future within the Longman Group. After the acquisition Giles Pitman became Chairman of the Institute. Meanwhile, Mark Pitman, Joint Group Managing Director of Pitman PLC, who was anxious to dispose of the whole business, including the Institute, agreed to a reorganisation before the final merger, himself becoming the owner of Pitman Training. After the merger Ian Pringle, who had joined Pitman in 1976, took over the Managing Directorship.[66] There was still one Pitman involved in the new venture, James, Isaac's great great grandson, who had joined the Company in 1983 as a Publishing Executive.

Changes had already been made in the Institute. Rix took over the Chairmanship of the Institute, appreciating that it was an integral part of the Pitman enterprise, and Janet Elliot became Director-General in 1986. Between them they kept the Institute financially viable, providing a service in seventy countries, facing the same problems in some countries, such as Nigeria, as the Longman Group as a whole was facing. They initiated PEI prizes, which attracted world-wide interest.[67] So did an advanced word processing examination in 1989 and the issue of a new group certificate in business information processing.[68]

~

The acquisition of Pitman, followed by that of Macdonald and Evans (whose list fitted well with that of Pitman), and the complex story of the subsequent acquisition of the American publisher, Addison-Wesley, announced in a London press release of February 1988, continued Pearson's supportive

---

65   *The Log*, Nov. 1987, pp.10-13, 'Pitman ... the short story of a long tradition'. (LA Part II 213)

66   See I. Pringle, 'Fifty Years of Business Education' in *Business Education*, published by Pitman, Jan. 1987.

67   *Pitman Examinations Institute, 1988, an Annual Report*. A link was made with the *Financial Times* and the *Investors' Chronicle*. There is an interesting well-illustrated 'company profile' in *The Log*, Nov. 1987, pp.10–12 which ends with a page on 'Pitman People'. The Pitman books chosen among the illustrations include *The Electronic Office* and *Digital Communication Switching*.

68   PEI letter from Mrs. Elliott, May 1989. See also *PEI Progress Report*, a newsletter, Spring 1989. (LA)

approach to Rix's régime at Longman. However, after that merger, relations between Longman and Pearson became more difficult. So did the relationship between Rix and Blakenham which was to lead to Rix's early retirement in March 1990.

The word Pearson was used in the heading of the 1988 announcement of the Addison-Wesley acquisition, not the Longman Group, and the press release began with a statement that a successful 283 million dollar cash bid had been made by Pearson's United States holding company, Pearson Inc. It added that the acquisition 'continues Pearson's strategy of building strong international groups in its core business areas'. The Addison-Wesley Publishing Company was described as the sixth largest college publisher in the United States, and the ninth largest school publisher. The 'merger with Longman', therefore, would, as the announcement put it, 'create a new global force in educational publishing with combined sales of £250 million'.

Four people were named from whom further enquiries were now to be made – Joll as Finance Director of Pearson in London, David Veit, then President of Pearson Inc., Rix, who fully appreciated the potential in a merger, and Donald Hammonds, the Chairman and Chief Executive of Addison-Wesley. The acquisition, it was stated, was to be financed from 'Pearson's [substantial] cash reserves and existing borrowing facilities'.[69] A later press release of 16 March 1988 announced the acceptance of the deal. Enquiries were now to be made to Joll, who dealt directly with Blakenham.

From the mid-1970s Longman, supported by Pearson, had been keen to acquire an American business, and in 1974, as already described, it had believed that it was on the point of acquiring Wadsworth, the right kind of firm. It had even secured a 'letter of intent' before being 'gazumped' by Thomson. In the autumn of 1987, when Addison-Wesley revealed that it was 'up for sale', an acquisition once again seemed just right, and from the start Pearson was the favoured bidder. There was an element of irony in the fact that in 1986 Addison-Wesley had set up an 'English Language Publishing Center', based in the United Kingdom, to 'contract the production and publication of all English language titles from our overseas companies in Australia, Singapore, Hong Kong, Amsterdam and London'.[70]

A large part of the issue of *The Log*, which incorporated in 1988 Rix's 'Confidential Report to Employees on the International Results for 1987', was devoted not so much to the Pearson purchase of Addison-Wesley, but to an account of Addison-Wesley as a publisher and to the implications for Longman employees of the creation of a new Addison-Wesley-Longman Group Ltd. The 'fit', it was said – and 'fit' was again the favoured word –

69   For Immediate Release, 15 Feb. 1988. (LA)

70   Addison-Wesley Publishing Company, Annual Report, 1986. (LA)

was 'excellent'. Addison-Wesley, employees were told, had been founded by Melbourne Wesley Cummings in 1942, and since then the Company had won 'remarkable international acclaim'. It had 1,255 employees world-wide and had become a world leader in the fields of mathematics, life and physical sciences, computer sciences and engineering.

Addison-Wesley authors included forty-three Nobel Prize winners, and among its best-selling books were *University Physics* by Professor Francis Sears and *Calculus* by George Thomas: both were in their sixth editions. *Addison-Wesley Mathematics*, a complete programme for schools, had been a market leader since its first appearance in the 1960s. *New Horizons in English*, 'an American-English product' – and these were now in increased demand – had sold over thirteen million copies world-wide. *And Take Care of Yourself*, 'a general interest trade book', had sold more than four million.

In the computer sciences field Addison-Wesley had exclusive agreements with Apple Computer Inc. and Lotus Development Corporation to publish books proposed by them, and among related items it held exclusive marketing rights to an educational version of what was described as 'the world's most popular software program', Lotus 1-2-3.

One of its two higher education divisions was centred in Menlo Park, California, as was its school division. Its other higher education division was located in Reading, Massachusetts, as was its General Publishing Group which incorporated a General Books Division, Consumer Software and Addison-Wesley Training Systems, with offices in Massachusetts and New York City. In consumer software Addison-Wesley had published in 1986 a computer software game, J.R.R. Tolkien's *Fellowship of the Ring* (what hidden treasures there were there!), and its Training Systems Division had introduced course training in artificial intelligence.

Before this information was being given to employees, talks were held at Harlow at which Rix, Wymer and Williamson met Donald Hammonds. The first of them dealt with the clearing up of operational questions following the merger and with the creation of a joint executive committee which, it was agreed, would meet at least six times a year in the United States or in Britain. A strategic review was planned for May and approval of budgets in November. There was discussion, too, detailed enough to cover letter heads and colophons, and the meeting ended with Rix explaining how *The Log* operated on a three-issue a year basis. It was agreed that 'once the merger was complete it would be turned into an Addison-Wesley-Longman journal.[71]

This was more than a promising start, and while he was in Britain Hammonds met key Longman employees, helping thereby, it was reported,

---

71   Minutes of the first meeting of the Addison-Wesley Longman Executive Committee held at Longman House, Burnt Mill, 25 Feb. 1988. (LA)

to lay a sound foundation for the future of Addison-Wesley Longman.[72] Further executive meetings proceeded until in the autumn of 1988 a business plan for 1989 to 1991 was drafted jointly by Rix and Hammonds, along with a mission statement, the kind of statement then *de rigueur* in transatlantic business operations. There were two important preliminary meetings in May at which only Longman representatives were present, and at the second of them Rix reported that announcements had now been made in the USA, the UK and internationally concerning the change of name and membership of the Addison-Wesley Longman Board.

At the same meeting 'the Committee ratified with pleasure' the appointment of Warren Stone as a member of the Addison-Wesley Longman Executive Committee.[73] Stone was President of the Addison-Wesley International Division, and he now became also Vice-Chairman of Addison-Wesley USA. On behalf of Pearson, Joll gave his approval to this and other changes, the most significant of which, perhaps, was the abandonment of the name Longman Holdings Ltd.[74]

Joll and his colleague Veit had joined Rix and Wymer on a visit to the Californian headquarters of Addison-Wesley in April, where they were given special presentations which 'developed [their] knowledge of A-W operations', and Hammonds re-visited Harlow in May. Meanwhile, one other new Addison-Wesley name emerged, that of the man who was to be in charge of Addison-Wesley after Hammonds and Stone – Larry Jones, then Director of its Educational Publishing Group. The previous Addison-Wesley Chief Operating Officer, Wayne Oler, had resigned, and Jones now became a main reference point, far less knowledgeable about Longman or international publishing than Hammonds.[75]

The mission statement of November 1988, which accompanied the three-year plan, is of more interest in retrospect than the plan itself which was never to be implemented. It began with the pledge that A-W-L, as it now was usually called, would be 'market-leaders or major players in all our selected markets world-wide'. This was familiar Longman language, and the section in the plan on 'strategies and action' marked no change in previous Longman Holdings procedures. 'The planning processes and structures' hitherto employed would be followed. Business plans, to be submitted annually to Pearson, would not deal in 'major analyses of markets, competitive advantage, longer-term strategies, etc.' but would 'summarise' key issues from the period under review within the longer

---

72   Minutes, 29 Feb. 1988. Only Rix, Williamson and the Secretary, J.E. Mollison, were present at this meeting.

73   Minutes, 16 May 1988.

74   Minutes ... 27 April 1988: [Private Collection]

75   Minutes ... 28 March 1988.

three-year period and the key 'input developments' required. The plans would be accompanied by a 'full financial commentary' and full 'financial schedules and notes'. These would go to Joll and through him to Blakenham and to the Pearson Board.[76]

All seemed on the surface to be relatively straightforward, but at the end of January 1989 Rix wrote defensively to Joll after a difficult meeting in New York with Blakenham, Hammonds and Joll himself that 'had we not taken the merger approach and post-merger strategy which we did, we would have had considerable difficulty getting, and might well not have obtained, the quite substantial merger benefits which have been achieved'. Nevertheless, Rix hinted at present and future difficulties: the personalities involved were so different in their temperaments and in the corporate structures to which they belonged. He might have added 'cultures', very much to the point.

Another complication was that Blakenham had been pursuing parallel discussions in Europe with the ancient firm of Elsevier. In fact, the difficult meeting in New York between Blakenham, Joll, Hammonds and Rix (at which it became clear to Rix that the progress of the merger was no longer 'straightforward' within A-W) followed a larger meeting between representatives of Elsevier and Pearson. There was a share swap between Elsevier and Pearson (described in the Press as 'an engagement leading to a marriage') but the relationship was later severed and Elsevier merged instead with Reed.

Rix continued to defend to Joll the strategic value of the merger and what had been achieved as a result ($3 million had been added to profits through the immediate absorption of Longman Inc. into A-W) but whatever Joll's own views may or may not have been, by March 1989 Blakenham had decreed that Longman and Addison-Wesley should now operate as separate 'sister' companies, each reporting direct to Pearson. At the same time, he suggested to Rix that he should 'stand down' as Chief Executive of Longman on the grounds that the Chairmanship of Addison-Wesley Longman, which he had so briefly held, had been disbanded.

At first Rix demurred, arguing that it would not be wise to link such a move with the separation of Addison-Wesley and Longman after so much effort had been made, at Harlow in particular, to publicise the importance of the merger. The timing was wrong for him also. Indeed, the situation was more than difficult. He was not unwilling to leave Harlow, however, after more than thirty years of service to the House of Longman, now no longer so called, for he no longer found it congenial to work within Pearson plc. Recalling, as he did, the original terms of the Pearson-Longman association when Mark Longman and Gibson had agreed that there would be effective operational autonomy, he grasped the nettle that autonomy

---

76 Business Plan and Mission Statement, 7 Nov. 1988.

was now being lost. In subsequent talks with Joll, therefore, agreement was reached amicably that he would retire on 31 March 1990.

~

At that point, 31 March 1990, this chapter began. There was no sense then, however, of 'at the end of the day', already the most hackneyed of clichés. Nor was the handover from Rix to Kahn as sharp a break for either of them as it might have been. She had already been acting as Chief Executive since October 1989, when Rix spent a period in hospital, and before that Rix himself had promised to do his best 'to ensure an effective hand-over and transition'.[77] The issue of *The Log* reporting on the international results for the year ending December 1989 carried photographs of both of them, and the accompanying text was a farewell to Rix and a welcome to Kahn.

The Log itself gave every sign of continuity, providing, for example, details of the acquisition by Longman España in June 1989 of Editorial Alhambra, a well-established name in Spanish educational publishing, and of the enterprise of Longman Group, Far East, which after Tiananmen Square had published the biography of Deng Xiao-ping by David Bonavia and a guide in Chinese to *World Democracy Movements* as well as the fourth edition of *The China Investment Guide*. Ironically, the only sign of discontinuity was the inclusion of an announcement of a management buy-out of the Longman Financial Services Institute in the USA.[78]

There were interesting pages in the same number of *The Log* on Longman Group UK's attitudes to European expansion (an interview with Jeff Andrew, Development Director, Europe), on Longman Nigeria, which in the course of 'propelling itself [a jarring non-nautical image] into the 'computer age', had acquired a desktop publishing system, and on Longman Zimbabwe, Longman Kenya, Maskew Miller Longman and Longman-Penguin, Japan. Looking ahead in Europe to 1992, Andrew stressed the need for new thinking as well as for coordinated effort: 'we know very little of the market seen from *within* Europe. This has now become our home market.'

The same could not have been said about the African markets, where there was ample political discontinuity. In Zimbabwe, with far more political troubles ahead, there had been a gift, funded by the British Overseas Development Agency, of 181,000 books, air freighted to Harare, and a new initiative of the British Council which had supplied 1,200 club 'libraries' to the most disadvantaged rural secondary schools. In Kenya, where the government was encouraging parents to buy their children's books rather than leave it to the government to buy them, there had been a strong Longman presence at the much publicised Nairobi Book Fair and at

---

77   Announcement of 17 July 1989.

78   See *The Log*, December 1989. (LA Part II 213)

a National Book Exhibition. In Nigeria the Board of Directors of Longman Nigeria had been re-structured. Iwerebon, who had been Managing Director/Chief Executive since 1972, became Chairman/Chief Executive, and Abiodun Olowaniyi was promoted from Finance Director to become Operations Director. In Lesotho there were tenth anniversary celebrations of Longman Lesotho, and in South Africa, the opening of the new premises in Johannesburg had been celebrated.

From Japan Jeremy Osborne, Longman Group Sales Director, reported sales in 1989 of 84,000 copies of the *Longman Dictionary of Contemporary English* and a move to new offices, opened by Blakenham, who was photographed with Shinsuke Suzuki, Managing Director of Longman *ELT* Japan and T. Sakai, Managing Director, Japan, who was celebrating his thirtieth year with Longman in Japan. Blakenham also met a new accountant who had only been with Longman for ten days, and visited a newly-opened Pearson Corporate Office in Tokyo, a city where there were separate Addison-Wesley offices but where Penguin as well as Ladybird was represented by Longmans.

~

At the end of the 1980s Longman was a diversified publishing house active (Rix's ambition for it) in a range of markets – educational, academic, scientific and technical, medical, business and professional and, of course, the important and profitable *ELT*. The orientation was more clear now than it had been in 1974, and the House was making a substantial contribution to the revenues of Pearson. Out of Pearson's total sales of £1,459 million in 1989 book publishing contributed £611.1 million, 26 per cent more than in the previous year. Longman's trading profit was up by 43 per cent to £23.1 million, while Penguin dropped by 9 per cent to £18.8 million.[79]

Longman's publishing lists were lively, and there were interesting new ventures, like Denis Gifford's *Encyclopaedia of Comic Characters* (1987) and in 1990-91 a Peter Maxwell Davies music course for schools.[80] Two Oliver and Boyd series, one in primary sciences and the other in the secondary sector, *Modular Courses in Technology* in association with the National Centre for School Technology (1980–83), were highly successful. A long-awaited publication was the *Historical Atlas of Africa* (1985) edited by J.F. Ade Ajahi and M. Crowder, ten years in the making and rescued from an early death by a Nigerian private subsidy, as rare an event in twentieth-century publishing history as the appearance of the *Atlas* itself.

Perhaps most characteristic of the time was Longman Scientific and Technical, designed to provide what was called 'sharper focus'. It

---

79 These figures were conveniently published in *The Author*, Vol. CI, No. 2, Summer 1990.

80 *The Log*, Nov. 1987, p.6–7. (LA Part II 213)

was conceived of as more than a division, more, indeed, than a sector. It brought together – 'embraced' was the chosen word – all Longman's international publishing activities in science and technology, abandoning all the old imprints, which included Pitman and other recent acquisitions, Macdonald and Evans, George Godwin and Construction Press, the last of which had brought into the Longman field the remunerative *Sunday Times Book of Do-it-Yourself* (1975), now disappeared.

The motto on a late-1980s publicity brochure was 'The New Imprint for the Future Building on Great Names of the Past'. Again, therefore, in the midst of all the excitement of change there was a recognition of continuity expressed forcefully by Peter Warwick, who was Joint Managing Director, along with Michael Johnson, of Longman Academic, Scientific and Technical. In a paper on the new imprint he stressed that he and his colleagues were 'placing some emphasis upon Longman's heritage of scientific publishing'.[81] In a backlist of more than a thousand books, some of them, like Peter Sykes's *A Guidebook to Mechanism in Organic Chemistry* (6th ed. 1976), described as 'the bible of mechanistic organic chemistry for thousands of undergraduates', several of them had been through many editions. (*Kaye and Laby's Tables of Physical and Chemical Constants*, first published in 1911, was in its fiftieth.) There were seven journals, among them *Tissue and Cell* and *Heredity*, an international journal of genetics, the latter published on behalf of the Genetical Society.

~

It was never the intention of this *History* to cover the period from 1990 to 1994 following Rix's retirement. That task must await the attention of another historian (perhaps of Pearson with its continuing history). Under Kahn, after Rix the Chairman and Chief Executive of Longman, there was nothing defensive either in the rhetoric of Harlow or in the operations of the business. The end of Longman was certainly not foreseen, as 1994 progressed, by any of its employees. Major initiatives were still in train or were imminent. Employees in Harlow were looking forward to the opening of a larger new building, 'environmentally friendly', having participated actively in its planning. It had cost £21 million, and according to local opinion Bryant Construction had 'scored top marks' for its still incomplete achievement.[82] Given Longman history, its address was apt – Edinburgh Way.

Very ambitious plans for the future under the title 'Longman 2000' were appearing ('proclaiming as our goal a £500 million company with profits of £100 million'). Longman had had a 'good year' in 1993 with

---

81   Background Paper of 6 June 1986.

82   *Harlow Star*, 17 Feb. 1994. Wearing a tin hat and Wellington boots I explored the unfinished building on 23/24 June 1994.

operating profit up by 23 per cent to £29 million on sales up 15 per cent to £202 million.[83]

All seemed set fair yet on 20 September 1994 employees learned, attending a (by any standards) extraordinary event, that the history of a 'great British and international publishing company'[84] was being brought to an end by its parent. They were told in the morning to gather in Harlow's cinema (and London based employees were bussed there). Once assembled, Kahn introduced the proceedings with what was, in the event, a brave farewell address. She was followed by Frank Barlow, Managing Director of Pearson, who described ('falteringly' according to one witness) what was about to happen (effectively from 1 January 1995).

Churchill Livingstone, Pitman Publishing and Longman's other professional publishing operations were to join Financial Times Business Information to form a new company, Pearson Professional, with Peter

The aftermath of the demolition of the Longman Building

The architect's drawing of the new building, in the end not called Longman House. Longman moved into the new building in Edinburgh Gate in 1996

Longman Archive / Personal collection

---

83   *The Bookseller*, 1 April 1994.

84   See Pearson News Release 20 Sept. 1994. 'Jobs go as Pearson dismembers Longman', *The Bookseller* 23 Sept. 1994. Rix letter to *The Bookseller*, 7 October 1994.

Warwick as its Chief Executive. Educational and *ELT* publishing were to be placed under American management in the form of Addison-Wesley and, more particularly, under Larry Jones, its only recently appointed Chief Executive Officer, a manager with (as already noted) no international publishing experience.

At the end of Barlow's address the shell-shocked employees were split into two groups (itself a deeply disturbing experience), those to go into Pearson Professional, to be addressed by Warwick, and those remaining with 'Longman', to become part of 'Pearson Education', to be addressed (with Kahn present) by Larry Jones. This was indeed the real end of the day for Longman and for this *History*. The traditional Longman Christmas party that December (attended by Rix and again bravely and stirringly addressed by Kahn) was a wake. There was still, three months after the news of the de-construction of Longman, among those present, a sense of bewilderment and of sadness. Longevity was no more. I myself felt as sad – and confused – as any full-time employee.

~

Despite the drama which attended the end of Longman, it seems fitting that this chapter – indeed, this whole volume of Longman history – should end not dramatically but quietly with books. On the cover of the 380-page *Complete Catalogue* of Longman UK books, published in 1989, the last of the Rix years, there was a large ship colophon in red which contrasted sharply with the dark blue around it. Although it dealt only with Longman UK books, it provided for booksellers a list of seven Longman UK addresses and included a page of 'special notes' for booksellers overseas. There was a brief reference to Addison-Wesley in the introduction to the Catalogue, but none to Pearson:

> Following the recent merger between Longman and Addison-Wesley Addison-Wesley titles should be ordered from Southport Book Distributors [acquired as part of Pitman and based at Southport on Merseyside, a place far from Harlow or London] with effect from 1 January 1989. However, the Addison-Wesley UK Computing for Schools list has been transferred to Longman, and all orders for books on that list should be sent to Longman in Harlow, and for software to Longman Resources Unit, York.

Times were soon to change.

The *Complete Catalogue* was carefully coded with cross references to the initials of the various Longman divisions. There was no P for Pitman, however, although the address of Pitman Publishing was given (since 1982, 128 Long Acre). The letter P in the catalogue entries, important for booksellers, stood not for Pitman but for titles supplied at a discount of 30 per cent off the published price. Among all the titles there were twenty-two that incorporated the word 'computer', in the *Complete Catalogue*, two that incorporated the word 'computational', and seven that incorporated the word 'computed'. They covered most 'Longman subjects'. Medicine was obviously one, for both research and teaching of the subject now depended on the computer. Less obvious was the use of the computer in English, although one book, dated as far back as 1966, before Longman itself was computerised, was called *Computers in English Language Teaching and Research*. Four books were concerned, as their titles explained, with 'computer literacy'. One included a computer pack which was linked to BBC course programmes. Two memorable titles were *Computer Power for Your Accounting Office* and *Computer Power for Your Law Office*, both dated 1985. Whatever else the *Complete Catalogue* demonstrated, it was the presence of computer power, sometimes hidden behind initials and acronyms like CICT, FEW and LSR. Acronyms were multiplying every year.

There was no separate history list in the *Complete Catalogue*; different disciplines were not separated out from each other. Nevertheless, many distinguished historians figured unobtrusively in the alphabetical list of authors, while prominence was given to an index of historical series, now more publicised than single monographs in Longman academic publications in relation to most disciplines and at every level of learning. Most other publishers, including the Oxford and Cambridge University Presses, favoured series also. The market for them was competitive.

Several historians who were writing for Longman moved easily and with enthusiasm back from university to school and from monographs to series, chief among them the learned Oxford medievalist, Dr. Marjorie Reeves, as active and 'creative' as ever, who was keenly interested in the educational changes of the period and was always prepared to ask provocative general questions, as, for example, in her *Why History?*. *The American West* by R.A. Rees and S.J. Styles, won the History School Book Award in face of strong competition from the Oxford University Press, Macmillan and Blackwell. It was praised by the judges both for dealing fairly with 'the Indian as well as the immigrant experience' and for its 'clear links between text and illustration'. At a celebratory party the host was the *Times Educational Supplement*.[85]

At least one pre-eminently successful Longman history writer for schools, Denis Richards, who had initially been encouraged by E.W. Parker, moved in the reverse direction from Reeves, sometimes working with co-authors. He was given a Longman Fellowship at Sussex University in 1965, having been Principal of Morley College since 1950. In 1953 he had written an authoritative monograph, *Royal Air Force*. The sales of his school textbooks, the first of them *An Illustrated History of Modern Europe Since 1789*, first published in 1938, had reached over two million by 1986.

---

85 *Grapevine*, Feb. 1988, p.1. (LA Part II 212)

By then in a seventh edition it took the story down to 1984.[86] In 1986 Longman gave a dinner for him at the Garrick Club which was attended by, among others, Rix, Roger Watson, then Divisional Managing Director, UK Schools Division, Anthony Wood, Longman author and formerly history master at Winchester, and Stuart McClure, then editor of the *Times Educational Supplement*.[87]

The various Longman history series were advertised in a separate brochure of 1989 and included a new series of *Studies in Modern History*, edited by John Morrill and David Cannadine, the latter to be biographer of G.M. Trevelyan and, later, Director of the Institute for Historical Research in London; *Themes in Social History*, edited by John Stevenson; and two series edited by Professor Denys Hay (1915–1994), author of *A General History of Europe* (1961) and author of two volumes in the Longman *History of Italy*. Hay edited the *English Historical Review* from 1958 to 1965. The Longman editor largely responsible for the management of these series was Andrew MacLennan, a brilliant commissioning editor but who was as careful as he could possibly be to keep out of the management and politics of publishing described in this *History*. He stayed on in Harlow after 1994. It was doubtless due to him that the words 'A Tradition in its own Right' appeared on the cover of the 1989 history brochure. He was even contemplating 'a set of history textbooks for the American market'.[88]

In ending this chapter and the main part of this *History* with books on history I am not only paying tribute to a tradition but seeking final symmetries. An able and exceptionally enterprising historian concerned with history as taught in schools, John Robottom, born in 1934 and a graduate of Birmingham University, had no fewer than six history books listed in the *Complete Catalogue*, including two on Russian history. The first of them, *Modern China* (1967), in the *Modern Times* series, was the first school textbook on the subject since the setting up of the People's Republic.

During the 1980s Robottom co-authored with W. Claypole a two-volume textbook on Caribbean history for use in courses leading to a new

---

86   Richards and Quick, *Tudors and Stuarts* (1965) had sold 37,393 copies by 1986. Details of 'all time sales' had only been easily accessible since 1965 when the Longman computer 'went live'. They could, of course, be derived more laboriously from royalty accounts.

87   A special 1985 edition of the *TES* celebrated the 75 years of its history. McClure chose as its title 'High Hopes and Low Spirits – an education system in the making'. The edition appeared in the middle of a protracted teachers' pay dispute. 'Who can doubt', McClure asked, 'that the time will come, not too long hence, when the expansion of educational opportunity will again be a prime aim of public policy?'

88   Undated memorandum on his proposals for university history books.

West Indies-based Caribbean Examinations Council Certificate. In 1974 he became an Education Officer with the BBC's Broadcasting Council. His *Social and Economic History of Industrial Britain* (1986), a lively book for 14-16-year-olds, began with a description of Daniel Defoe's *A Tour Through the Whole Island of Britain*, a book which had first appeared in 1724, the year when this *History* starts. Yet while in the later chapters of his book broadcasting, cinemas and teletext were featured, at no point in the story was publishing introduced. He did not even mention, therefore, that the House of Longman was founded in 1724. Authors even as devoted to Longman as Robottom – and they included biographers as well as writers of textbooks – often neglected the role of their publishers.

It has been one of the main objects of this *History* to demonstrate that for historical as well as for bibliographical reasons the history of publishing should be integrated into general history. And no one believed in that proposition more profoundly than Tim Rix.

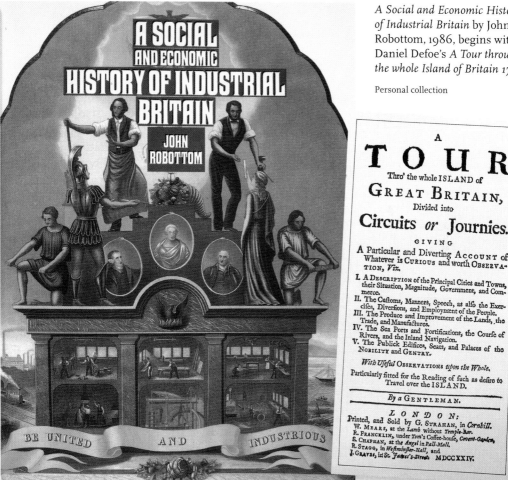

A Social and Economic History of Industrial Britain by John Robottom, 1986, begins with Daniel Defoe's *A Tour through the whole Island of Britain* 1724

Personal collection

10 Epilogue: Posterity

This Epilogue, which refers back to the longer Prologue of this *History*, is at the same time a prologue in itself. 'What's Past is Prologue' were the opening words of a brilliant lecture by D.F. McKenzie, delivered, sadly in his absence through illness, to the Bibliographical Society on the occasion of its centenary in 1992. His concluding words were that while the Society could look back at what's past (our last century) 'with considerable pride': what happened then was a 'prologue to a new dispensation, one in which the *programme* becomes the text and *hard* bibliographical evidence is metamorphosed into *software*'.

Within three years of McKenzie's address it had become clear that internet technology, first introduced on a limited scale for military – and later academic – purposes in 1973, was there to stay. Turned over to the private sector in 1984, within little more than a decade it offered access in 180 countries, with more than 30 million users. The 'World Wide Web', devised from Europe by Tim Berners-Lee in 1989, a year before this *History* ends, set the terms of 'globalisation'. Nothing, however, was superseded or totally transformed. In what was sometimes called a 'media-sphere' books survived all predictions of their eclipse.

The timespan of this *History* is far longer than a century, but this is not as long as the time span of printing, already established when Thomas Longman I arrived in London in 1724. Some of the features of the period between Gutenberg and the advent of Thomas Longman as a bookseller have been touched upon in these chapters. There remains far more of relevance to say, however, about that interim period – for so it appears to be within the perspectives of this *History* – than historians of the book, growing in numbers, have already said. Their perspectives change, but they still use words like 'era' and 'moment' as well as 'century' and 'decade'.

As for the period from 1724 to 1990 or to 1994, when the House of Longman finally ceased to exist, what French historians would call *une longue durée*, there was so much change that for decades within it change seemed, if misleadingly, to be constant. Yet as late as 1983 the founder of a new printing company, Bookprint Ltd., could claim that Caxton, who died in 1491, 'would be perfectly at home in the average book-printing works [in Britain] today'; and six years later a writer in the centre page of *The Times*, dealing with publishing rather than with printing, directed attention to a new American vogue for reprinting (down to the misprints) the first editions of famous books. 'We appear to be entering the era of the reproduction book.' The adjective 'retro' was then coming into use.

At the end of the period covered in this *History*, following the

Some of the devices and colophons used by Longmans, mostly in the nineteenth century

Longman Archive

rapid development of electronic communications, including desk-top publishing, old and new technologies co-existed, there was a sense that there was an element of 'trendiness'. It had been possible in 1982 for UNESCO to choose 'Towards a Reading Society' as the theme of a World Congress on Books held in London. Its *News Bulletin* did, however, refer to the need for the 'integration of new technologies into the book chain so as to take advantage of the opportunities they offer in every phase of book production and distribution'. There was a growing sense of a continuing communications revolution that would move on past the millennium, and there were some cultural critics, not for the first time, for whom the death of reading seemed imminent. 'Book trade faces electronic future' was a headline in *Publishing News* in May 1984.

Within the period 1724 to 1994 books, not individuals, spanned the centuries, and some had long lives of their own, many of them prolonged beyond the life of the publishing house that first produced them. Indeed, of the vastly increased number of books printed in the twentieth century, many were still alive in the twenty-first century, long out of copyright, published by scores of publishers, old and new, and read in both cheap and expensive editions – the range widened – by more people than ever before.

Books printed long before 1724 had, as we have seen, been treated as 'classics' in the nineteenth century. For three generations or more they came to constitute a canon, with publishers determining what it should include before professors of English literature, a new university subject in the late-nineteenth century, took over – or helped to take over – the task. Books which subsequently stood up to 'the test of time' were books not just for the limited number of readers who read them when they first appeared, but books for posterity. This was a grander noun than survival or even longevity, and in the twentieth century such books were not only being re-read, re-examined and re-interpreted (with every kind of hidden meaning drawn out of them), but transmitted through other media, including television and film. One of the most memorable of twenty-first century books – and sub-titles – Nicholas Basbanes's *A Splendour of Letters: the Permanence of Books in an Impermanent World* (2003) starts with a quotation from Emerson, spanning space and time, and was reprinted in 2004 in a paperback edition with an appropriately named 'Perennial' imprint.

There are, of course, thousands of books that enjoyed lives shorter even than their author's – annuals not perennials – while there are some authors, quoted in this *History*, who span whole chapters even if in the constraining biological circumstances that limited the human life span, they could not span centuries. As authors they hoped still to live. As the twentieth-century novelist Vera Brittain put it in *The Author* in 1964, 'The majority of authors, unless their incentive is purely commercial, write in the hope that their work will outlast their vulnerable lives.' Some authors, particularly poets, felt in their own lifetime that they were writing as much for posterity as for their contemporaries, whether or not they succeeded in doing so. Some of them thought that they would be better appreciated in the future than they were in their own time.

The sifting processes which have determined whether particular books survive are complex, and had started before 1724 with Congreve and Dryden. It was already clear by then that books which had not survived could be 're-discovered' and 'revived'. It was clear too, as the whole of this *History* has demonstrated, that booksellers or (later) publishers played a bigger part in the processes than authors before and after the introduction of English literature into schools and universities. How large the first print runs were, how many editions there were and in what formats, and what the prices were, always demand attention. It was already clear too before 1724 that some books were considered, almost necessarily, as ephemeral, as were newspapers and most magazines. The same was even more true in the nineteenth century when the number and circulation of newspapers, periodicals and magazines surged. (The word 'exploded' has frequently been used.) 'An old bookseller' wrote in 1837 in the very short-lived *Aldine Magazine*, (referred to in an earlier chapter) that of a thousand books published in 1820 750 were 'forgotten within the year, 100 in two years and 150 in three': only 50 survived for seven years.

The fact that the *European Magazine*, also mentioned in this *History*, a periodical long neglected by historians, lasted through 89 volumes and spanned forty-five years, was unusual. So, too, was the far longer life of the *Edinburgh Review* and of *Blackwoods*. But it does not seem surprising that *The Spectator*, founded in 1711, was printed in book form by symposia of publishers throughout the eighteenth century and was an extremely profitable commercial proposition. It was to contribute to posterity.

The title of the old bookseller's reminiscences was 'The Fate of Books', and 'Fate' or 'Destiny' was a concept dear to many novelists and dramatists. Yet there is little about Fate in Anthony Rota's *Books in the Blood* (2002), 'the memoirs of a fourth-generation bookseller'. His third chapter is headed 'The Customer is Always Right – Well Almost Always' and his thirty-fifth is on 'The Ones that Got Away'. The motto of the League of Antiquarian Booksellers, which Rota chaired from 1988 to 1991 – and which Basil Blackwell had chaired long before him – is '*amor librorum nos unit*'; and while the relations between Amor and Fate are entangled in history, as are the relationships between authors, readers and publishers, most lovers of books, looking backwards and forwards, choose a different language of reference, frequently falling back on the language of romance.

Nevertheless, a sense of romance usually did not imply the absence of a sense of purpose. 'The founding of a Library is one of the greatest things we can do' wrote Thomas Carlyle, and he put his belief into practice when he was the main influence behind the founding of the London Library in 1840. 'In Books lies the *soul* of the whole Past Time', he declared, 'all that Mankind has done [and] thought' was 'preserved', 'as in magic', in the pages of books. This 'high view' of books conferred 'immortality' on them, or at least on those which made their way into libraries, and the concept of immortality is related to, while different from, the concepts of 'survival' or of 'longevity', the title of my Prologue, which dealt mainly with publishers, and 'posterity', the title of this chapter, a grander title than longevity, which covers authors, agents, readers, publishers and booksellers alike.

In setting out to examine this cluster of concepts and relationships I turned back to the great Longman book often mentioned in this *History*, Roget's *Thesaurus*, an invaluable book of reference. In a 1966 edition 'longevity' was placed in Section 6, 'Time', under 'Diuternity, long duration', appearing just after 'length of days' and 'cat's nine lives' and just before 'Age', the subject of a separate heading, under 'Diuternity', as was 'Survival', which was treated quite differently and placed under the very first general heading in the *Thesaurus*, 'Existence'. There was a strong commitment to posterity in the nineteenth century, and Roget's *Thesaurus* itself, as was explained earlier in this *History*, had a complicated history of its own, involving several generations of the Roget family and several generations of Longmans. So too had other Longman textbooks that were rewritten and often re-illustrated for different generations. It has been part of my own purpose in writing this *History* to integrate within book trade history that of textbooks and works of reference. Longman specialised in both.

It was a welcome recognition of their significance when in November 1989 the first newsletter of the Colloquium on Textbooks, Schools and Society, *Paradigm*, a key word of the 1970s and 1980s, first appeared. The Colloquium was the brainchild of Chris Stray and Iain Michael, who recognised clearly and early that their study was both historically illuminating, sociologically central and currently relevant. They appreciated the difficulties too. The processes of 'transmission' of knowledge were as complex as the ensuring 'survival' for 'posterity' of a small group of 'creative' literary texts.

The creation of the Colloquium itself was part of a bigger pattern of research, for studies of the history of the book trade multiplied in unprecedented fashion during the 1980s and 1990s precisely during a period when 'the death of the book' was being threatened or even acclaimed. A valuable summary of developments down to 1994 and of plans for future research was published in 1993 in *Logos*, 'the professional journal of the book world', where an article, written jointly by Tim Rix and Ian Willison, then Senior Research fellow of the Centre for English Studies at the University of London, was called 'Remembrance of things past; worldwide activity on book and book trade history'.

In 1985 a Book Trade History Group had been founded in London, and by 1990 it had more than a hundred members. In his editorial for the first number of its *Newsletter* in February 1986 Simon Eliot, a pioneer of laborious and difficult quantitative studies, described the Group in language which would have appealed to Johnson when he wrote of 'diffusing the word'. It was to be 'a broad church' . ... not established to promote one idea or advance a single set of related projects'. 'Its interests', Eliot rightly stated, 'are the sum of its members' interests, and thus are as wide and open as book trade history itself.'

As was suggested at the beginning of this Epilogue, the role of D.F. McKenzie was of strategic scholarly importance in inspiring such a Broad Church. As a New Zealander by birth, he looked beyond Europe, and long before he acquired a British academic base he looked at globalisation, a word he never used, and other aspects of the book trade, from a New Zealand vantage point. He pondered not only on the relationship of the oral to the written and printed but on the relationship, present and future, of the visual to the verbal, of print and electronics. It is pertinent to note that within less than a decade organised book trade studies had begun to take shape in almost every country where over the centuries Longman, under whatever name, had built up its global business, some of them drawing the distinction between 'centre' and periphery' which I have drawn in this *History*.

However many uncertainties there may be concerning the future activities of great conglomerates, largely, if not entirely, determining the future of the book trade – and they have been created through uncertainty as much as through enterprise – 'a future for book trade history' seems assured. Both institutions and individuals are seeking with imagination and enthusiasm to guarantee it for posterity. Happily there are and have been ample new initiatives. Thus, the National Life Story Collection, a pioneering venture in institutionalised oral history, with ample experience behind it, has recorded interviews with people from all areas of the book trade, including both production and distribution. Tim Rix is one of them. They will all be accessible at the British Library's National Sound Archive. It is an archive that will grow, housed in the new building of an old institution.

'Longevity' was deliberately picked out not only as the title of the Prologue to this *History* but also as part of its title, for it raises both curious and searching questions about both human and institutional longevity and points to the biggest of all the social changes since 1724, those associated with demography. Perennially curious questions were the subject of books like Eugenius Philalethes's *Long Livers: a curious history of such persons of both sexes, who have liv'd several ages, and grown young again*, published in 1722, and the serious subject of articles such as one in 1888 in *Longman's Magazine* by public health pioneer, Benjamin Ward Richardson. His preoccupations were very different, however, from mine in this *History* or from those of Age Concern, of the Open University's course of the 1990s, K256, 'An Ageing Society', and the All Party Parliamentary Group on Ageing and Older People.

Interest in the subject of ageing, like interest in book trade history, is now common to many countries. There are International Longevity Centres in London, Paris and New York with their own publication, *Health in the Future*, an 'interpretative voice', setting out the conclusions of 'policy-orientated research into the role of health and ageing in overall social well-being'; and in all three capital cities twenty-first century newspapers frequently employ headlines like 'Living to be 100 will be routine by next century'. Answers to the question concerning what the consequences will be are even more controversial than answers to the question 'will books survive?'. The word 'greying' has been introduced into the discussion. There was more 'greying' in the nineteenth-century history of Longman, however, than there was in its history in the late-twentieth century.

It is plain that policy-oriented research on both subjects, individual and institutional, must be interdisciplinary, for a multitude of issues converge in any discussions on the extension of the life expectancy of human beings as they do on the shortening of the shelf life of books. Nevertheless, economic aspects are fundamental in both cases, and in the economic circumstances of the 1980s, described in the previous chapter, when book prices rose twice as quickly as the rate of inflation – and printing costs soared – booksellers set out deliberately for economic reasons to reduce stocks and publishers to destroy back lists. Meanwhile, as politicians were caught up in 'the political economy of demographic change', particularly when they wrestled with issues relating to pensions – as they now do more than ever – so public libraries were – and still are – deeply involved both in economics and in technology. Their responses were as varied as the responses of publishers, some discovering niches, others broadening outreach.

Spending on books fell between 1981–2 and 1991–2. Yet, there were far more books in circulation in 1990 than there were in 1724 or 1824 or 1924, just as there were far more people. According to *The Bookseller* a total number of 95,064 titles were published in the UK in 1995. The range of books was wide. Books on computer software were much in demand, but so were other areas, including 'Mind, Body and Spirit'. Meanwhile, book selling chains concentrated, as big publishers did, on likely bestsellers, for which authors through their agents secured unprecedented advances. Success depended more on pre-launch publicity than on reviews in newspapers or periodicals.

Large numbers of published books had often been thought to constitute a threat to the future of 'the book'. Indeed, as long ago as 1740, before the great increase in the number of books and readers (the latter limited by the high costs of books), a French writer, M.L.S. Mercier, in his book, *L'An 2440*, described a future world when 'the lumber of letters' had perished and 'the sages of the political millennium' exhibited their stores of 'useful learning' in a cabinet containing a few hundred volumes. He had no intimations of how 'literature', always making special claims in the period covered in this *History*, would expand in scale and in scope even in his own lifetime. In 1930 the *Spectator*, only in name the descendant of the eighteenth-century *Spectator*, talked of books rather than of people in Malthusian terms. 'Nowhere could the principle of Malthus be applied with such beneficial effect as in the world of books. In no other sphere do we suffer so much from the discomfort of over-population.' Far from publishing books for posterity, they were producing 'unwanted foundlings within six months of their publication'.

Around a generation earlier, in 1890, a century before the point where this *History* ends, the aged W.E. Gladstone, who read an immense number of books, old and new – and took them very seriously indeed – meditated in an article in *The Nineteenth Century* on the pressure of human numbers on food supplies and of the number of books on space. 'A book, even Audubon, I believe the biggest known, is smaller than a man, but in relation to space, I entertain more proximate apprehension of pressure upon available space for the book population than from the numbers of mankind.' And in as melancholy a mood as Malthus had been he was even prepared to contemplate 'book cemeteries'. He also used the word 'repositories', but his 'cemeteries' were more than that. They would not have guaranteed immortality, but they would have recorded longevity. And Posterity could draw upon them.

At least from the eighteenth century onwards cemeteries have been associated – through the poet Gray – with elegies, and among the books published on books and their future during the last decade of the twentieth century was Sven Birkert's *The Gutenberg Elegies* (1994). The *Washington Post* review of it was headed 'Closing the Book on Books'. In Britain the response to it was negative. A cluster of letters to the *Independent* was headed 'Too soon to write off books and switch on the Internet'. Argument continues as I conclude this *History*. It will doubtless continue after the publication (date unknown) of the last volume in the seven-volume *History of the Book in Britain*, a huge scholarly enterprise of the Cambridge University Press on which work began during the late-1980s, my own *History's* terminal date.

Appendix 1

A Note on Sources

This note in no sense constitutes a bibliography. That would be a separate venture which in itself would require the space of a book. It sets out, however, details of the Longman Archive at the University of Reading and other archives which I have used. The footnote references to books and articles in each of the chapters bring out the wide range of published sources, literary, historical, economic and social. It was the great physician Sir William Osler, a collector of books, who wrote that 'there is no better float through posterity than to be the author of a good bibliography'.

In 1973 Robin Myers, dedicated guardian of the archives of the Stationers' Company, produced an invaluable illustrated bibliographical guide to *The British Book Trade from Caxton to the Present Day*, based on the Libraries of the National Book League, which sponsored the project, and of the St. Bride Institute. The *Guide* covered authorship, bookbinding, bookselling, book design and production, book illustration, the history of the book trade, children's books, the law relating to the book trade, the Net Book Agreement, paper for book work, printing ink, the printing of books, private presses, the history of publishing and private publishing. Among her other books Myers co-edited with M. Harris *Development of the English Book Trade, 1700–1899* (1981) and *Spreading the Word: The Distribution Networks of Print, 1550–1850* (1990). See also M. Plant, *The English Book Trade* (3rd edition, 1974), I. Maxted, *The London Book Trade, 1775–1800* (1977) and P.D. McDonald and M. Suarez (eds.), *Making Meaning: Printers of the Mind and other Essays by D.F. McKenzie* (2002).

For other studies, their origins and orientation, and for the *Cambridge History of the Book* project, launched in 1987, see this Appendix and I.R. Willison, 'Remarks on the History of the Book in Britain as a Field of Study within the Humanities, with a synopsis and Select List of Current Literature' printed in W. Barnes *et al* (eds.), *Essays in Honor of W.B. Todd* (1991). See also S. Eliot, *Some Patterns and Trends in British Publishing, 1800–1919* (1994) and P. Kaufman, *Libraries and their Users, Collected Papers in Library History* (1969). *Publishing History*, launched in 1977 by Chadwyck-Healey Ltd is the most important periodical source, containing articles based on detailed archival research. Chadwyck-Healey also launched in 1989 a CD-ROM version of the British Library General Catalogue of Printed Books to 1975.

For the way in which they had been arranged earlier in the Library see F.J. Hill, *Shelving and Classification of Printed Books in the British Museum, 1753–1953* (1953), an essay for the Library Association. The eighteenth century ESTC (English Short Title Catalogue) is fully described in this History. The first volume of the *Nineteenth Century Short Title Catalogue* appeared in 1984. Robin Alston described the cataloguing project, launched at a reception in Oxford's ancient Bodleian Library, as an 'odyssey'. He observed that 'scholarship thrives on books not heard of', and the subsequent bout of library cataloguing, drawing for its production and diffusion on new technologies, has made possible further advances in the developing (and more sophisticated) study of the history of the book trade. See his *The Nineteenth Century Subject Scope and Principles of Selection* (1986). Four Specialist Collections were planned, one of which was *Publishing, the Book Trade and the Diffusion of Knowledge*. See *A Sample Short-Title List* (1987).

The more sophisticated – and analytical – history of the book trade has had an international dimension, and the overseas contribution to the development, which preceded the British, is covered briefly in the *Epilogue*. A rapidly expanding list of volumes includes H.J Martin, R. Chartier and J-P Vivet (eds.), *Histoire de l'édition française*, 4 vols (1982–1986); D.H. Borchardt and W. Kirsop (eds.), *The Book in Australia, Essays towards a Cultural and Social History* (1988); J. Tebbel, *A History of Book Publishing in the United States*, 4 vols. (1972–1981); L.A. Coser, C. Kadushin and W.W. Powell, *Books: The Culture and Commerce of Publishing* (1983); J. Epstein, *Book Business: Publishing Past, Present and Future* (2001); and A.G. Hopkins (ed.), *Globalization in World History* (2000). An important study by W. St. Clair, *The Reading Nation in the Romantic Period* (2004) includes 270 pages of appendices, some based on the Longman Archive, and forty-eight pages of bibliography, including a list of manuscript archives of publishers, printers and booksellers.

Detailed studies of individual publishers – and of individual books – depend, as this *History* does, on access to primary archives, written and when available audio and visual. Learned libraries in Scotland have been collecting publishers' archives since the 1920s, and the National Library of Scotland holds the archives, well-catalogued, of materials relating to Oliver and Boyd, drawn into the Pearson Group and subsequently absorbed in Longman. So, too, was J. and A. Churchill, whose archives are held as part of the main Longman Archive at the University of Reading, which has become a centre for book trade archives. J.A. Edwards, first archivist in charge of them, wrote *A Brief Guide to Archives and Manuscripts* (1980), and subsequently A. Ingram produced an *Index to the Archives of the House of Longman, 1794-1914* (1981). Chadwyck-Healey placed it on microfilm.

Many other publishers' collections are housed at Reading, including those of the House of Chatto and Windus. Michael Bott, who succeeded Edwards as their keeper, produced along with Alexis Weedon an invaluable *Location Register of British Book Trade Archives, 1830–1939*. It was published by two of the pioneers of book trade history, Simon Eliot and Michael Turner, editors of *Publishing History*, as part of a History of the Book-On-Demand (HOBODS) series. The interest of the University of Reading went back to the 1930s when Robert Gibbings, for some years owner of the Golden Cockerel Press, taught typography and book production in the University. His pioneering work led to the establishment in the University of a unique Department of Typography and Graphic Communication.

The Longman Archive (Ms.1393), depleted by fire and flood, first transferred to Reading in 1974, is divided into three parts – Part I ledgers, registers, letter books and other bound records; Part II documents, papers and photographs; and Part III books published by Longman. When transferred the contents of Part I originally comprised 20 sets of items and Part II 171. Listed first in Part I were the Divide Ledgers, 1797–1913 (1-18) and the Commission Ledgers, 1807–1908 (19-43). These record income and expenditure on books published, with the Divide entries referring to books published on the basis of a division of profits between author and publisher and the Commission entries referring to books published at the author's expense. The former set out essential details of paper, printing, advertising and distribution costs and the latter accounts of financial arrangements with other booksellers. Both types of ledger include alphabetical name indexes. It was not until the 1880s that the royalty system of payment to authors came into regular use, not supplanting the Commission system, and a few Royalty Ledgers, 1884–1908 (60-67) figure in Part I. They also incorporate alphabetic indexes.

Other records in Part I include Statement Books, 1902–1931 (68-81), covering sales, but restricted to certain areas and, like other records, including Letter Books, 1811–1837, 1881-1940 (97-133), with obvious gaps. Transcripts were made of entries in the Letter Books from 1811 to 1837. Copyright Ledgers (277-85) show the shares held by Longmans in books published by them and the number of copies printed; Chronological Registers, 1843–1933 (82-86) record dates of publication and of deposit copies sent as a legal requirement to the British Museum Library; and Impression Books, 1794–1963 (137-276) give details for 1823-1873 of printing costs and numbers of copies printed of individual books in which Longmans were not sole copyright owners and for 1794–1963 information, unfortunately not complete or continuous, of individual books in which Longmans had acquired the copyright.

All these Ledgers and Books constitute what remained of the core records of the House of Longman. Also in Part I were printed Monthly Lists, 1872–1917 (324-340), New Book Lists, 1932–1966 (89-96), and of Notes on Books, 1855–1903 (341-368). There was more continuity in the Catalogues of Antiquarian Books, 1814–46 (293-323), the 'old rare books' in which Longmans then dealt, and in the J. and A. Churchill archive, 1829–1959 (369-400A), which were acquired in 1968 when the business, already taken over by Pearson, was merged with Longman. They include Authors' Ledgers from 1829 to 1934 and deeds, press cuttings and photographs. The records of other firms taken over earlier by Longmans include Ledgers relating to Sir Richard Phillips, 1812–1836 (53-56), to A.J. Valpy, 1838–1865, and the Paper and Print Records of J.W. Parker, 1833–1862 (51-52). There are other items relating to the take-overs in Part II, which begin with Trade Catalogues, 1704–1768 (1-4), Photostats of Title Pages, 1641–1719 (5-9), and Stationers' Hall Dividends, 1690–1737 (10). These are among the oldest surviving records.

For the historian the naming of the very miscellaneous range of items included in Part II suggested many treasures, although singly they were often disappointing in their range, as were the Papers collected by Cyprian Blagden (18, 147), Photostats and Newspapers 'of Longman interest' (28, 31) and Andrew Lang (115). Taken together they demanded careful scrutiny. Fortunately I had built up my personal Longman Archive, which included many Blagden papers, before I started working on the History. Some Part II items were as valuable historically, however, as the items in Part I, and there were some overlaps between them. Among these were Partners and Staff Ledgers (133), Partnership Agreements and Papers (134) and Directors' Minute Books and Papers (135). Sadly the last of these only cover, and then patchily, the years 1926–1946. Minutes at the highest level were not regularly taken until late in the history of the House. The 'Second World War' section (145-146) was far less valuable as a source than Noël Brack's Diaries (which he handed over to me), and James Raven's studies of Paternoster Row are far more comprehensive than the three Longman files on Paternoster Row (128-130). There is important material in Part II, however, which relates (if selectively) to the overseas expansion of Longman business – in India (139), the United States (195, 198, 361), the Caribbean (331), the Arab World (214), Africa (332, 348, 357) and Asia (144).

The further development of Longmans' global activities is well covered in the many files of archival material, which became continuous after 1974 and which led to a reorganisation of the Reading Archive. Part II now includes an 'item', so-called, on Information Technology (661). Among the 17 headings covered, microcomputers figure prominently and there is an interesting self study – 'Project Colditz' (13). Studies carried out by people outside the House include three Reports by the London Business School (10, 11, 12), a Report of 1982 by A.D. Little on New Technologies (9), and a Report 'The Impact of Electronics on Consumer Publications' (15), a 1984 Report by BIS Marketing Research Ltd. Item No 7/6 refers to the VISTA Computer System, described in the text.

The material that came from the office of the Chief Executive, Tim Rix, after 1983 is listed under 'boxes'. They include Minutes of the Board, and relate to business acquisitions as well as with new technologies. The arrangements for the Pitman deal is traced in Box 5 (856, background: 857, current). Item 359 deals with Lord Allan's obituary as well as S. Pearson's Reports and accounts 1975, 1976, 1977, and 860 with Chapple's retirement. Item 861 covers the 250th Anniversary. In Part II, Item 1144 is described as 'Longman 2000 – Our Vision, Our Mission, Our Goal'. It consists of papers to managers by Paula Kahn, dated 7 Feb. 1994.

Appendix 2

Succession of imprints of The House of Longman 1724–1990

1724	T.Longman
1725	J.Osborn and T.Longman
1734	T.Longman
1745	T.Longman and T.Shewell
1747	T.Longman
1753	T. and T.Longman
1755	M. and T.Longman
1755	T.Longman
1793	T.N.Longman. Also T.Longman
1797	Messrs. Longman and Rees
1799	T.N.Longman and O.Rees
1800	Longman and Rees
1804	Longman, Hurst, Rees and Orme
1811	Longman, Hurst, Rees, Orme and Brown
1823	Longman, Hurst, Rees, Orme, Brown and Green
1825	Longman, Rees, Orme, Brown and Green
1832	Longman, Rees, Orme, Brown, Green and Longman
1838	Longman, Orme, Brown, Green and Longmans
1840	Longman, Orme & Co.
1841	Longman, Brown & Co.
1842	Longman, Brown, Green and Longmans
1856	Longman, Brown, Green, Longmans and Roberts
1859	Longman, Green, Longman and Roberts
1862	Longman, Green, Longman, Roberts and Green
1865	Longmans, Green, Reader and Dyer
1889	Longmans, Green & Co.
1926	Longmans, Green & Co. (Ltd.)
1959	Longmans
1969	Longman

Appendix 3

Note: The dates in red show the year of ownership and then entry into Partnership.

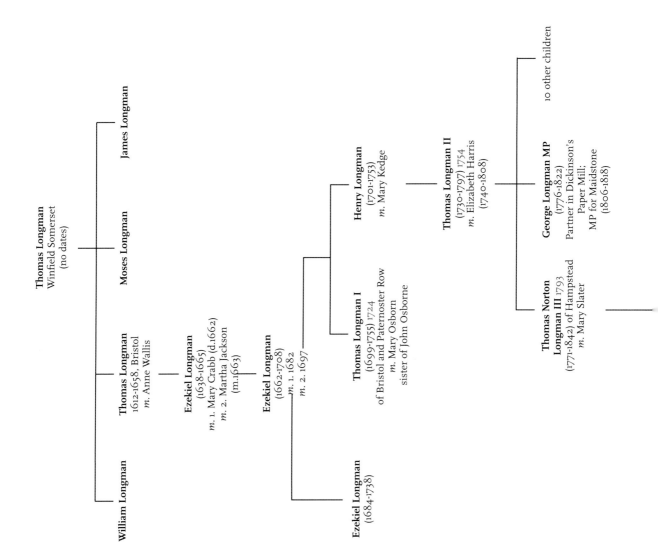

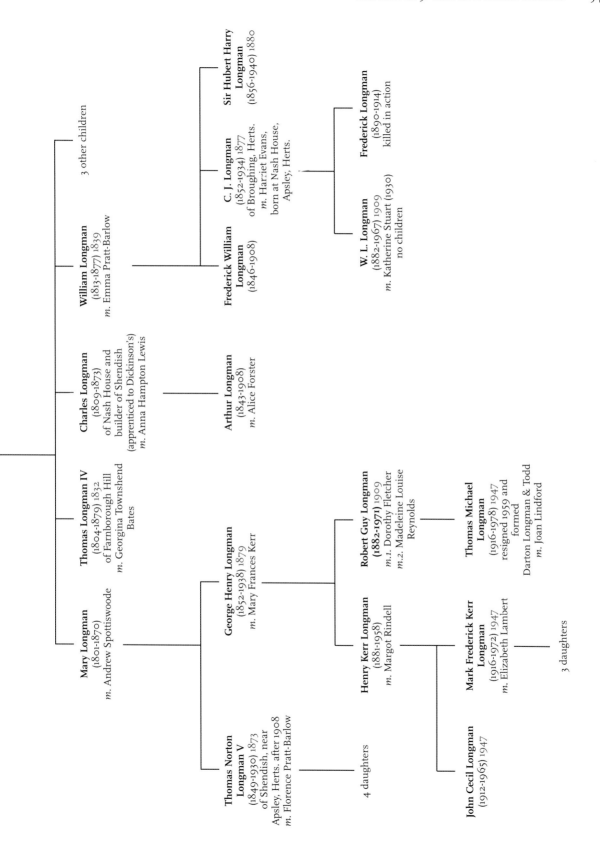

3 other children

William Longman
(1813-1877) 1839
m. Emma Pratt-Barlow

Sir Hubert Harry Longman
(1856-1940) 1880

Charles Longman
(1809-1873)
of Nash House and
builder of Shendish
(apprenticed to Dickinson's)
m. Anna Hampton Lewis

Frederick William Longman
(1846-1908)

C. J. Longman
(1852-1934) 1877
of Broughing, Herts.
m. Harriet Evans,
born at Nash House,
Apsley, Herts.

Arthur Longman
(1843-1908)
m. Alice Forster

W. L. Longman
(1882-1967) 1909
m. Katherine Stuart (1930)
no children

Frederick Longman
(1890-1914)
killed in action

Thomas Longman IV 1832
(1804-1879)
of Farnborough Hill
m. Georgina Townshend Bates

Mary Longman
(1801-1870)
m. Andrew Spottiswoode

George Henry Longman
(1852-1938) 1879
m. Mary Frances Kerr

Robert Guy Longman
(1882-1971) 1909
m.1. Dorothy Fletcher
m.2. Madeleine Louise Reynolds

Thomas Michael Longman
(1916-1978) 1947
resigned 1959 and
formed
Darton Longman & Todd
m. Joan Lindford

Henry Kerr Longman
(1881-1958)
m. Margot Rindell

Thomas Norton Longman V
(1849-1930) 1873
of Shendish, near
Apsley, Herts. after 1908
m. Florence Pratt-Barlow

4 daughters

Mark Frederick Kerr Longman
(1916-1972) 1947
m. Elizabeth Lambert

John Cecil Longman
(1912-1965) 1947

3 daughters

Appendix 4

Time span 1724–1990

The list of dates and items below is highly selective.
For authors only one work, the first of importance, is usually cited.

LONGMAN AS A PUBLISHER	THE CONTEXT
1724 Thomas I forms partnership with John Osborn. Publishes titles in consortia from this date	
1725 J. Osborn and T. Longman imprint. *The Works of Robert Boyle*	
	1727 *The Craftsman*
1728 Ephraim Chambers, *Cyclopaedia or an universal dictionary of arts and sciences*	
	1730 *The Grub Street Journal*
	1731 *Gentleman's Magazine*
	1732 Covent Garden Opera House opens. *The London Magazine* prints thinly disguised parliamentary debates.
1734 Death of Osborn. T. Longman imprint	
1736 Thomas I and Samuel Buckley acquire the privilege of printing Lily's *Latin Grammar*. Ainsworth's *Latin Dictionary*	
	1740 Bath Subscription Library. Richardson *Pamela*
	1741 Thomas Wright's Entertaining Universal Circulating Library
	1742 Fielding *Joseph Andrews*
1745 T. Longman and T. Shewell imprint	
	1747 Johnson *Plan of a Dictionary of the English Language*
	1748 Smollett *Roderick Random*
	1749 Griffiths begins the *Monthly Review*
	1751 First volume of French *Encyclopédie*
1753 Thomas II becomes a partner. T. and T. Longman imprint	1753 Founding of the British Museum
1755 Longman a co-publisher of Johnson's *The Dictionary of the English Language*. Death of Thomas I. Mary Longman, Thomas I's widow, senior partner with Thomas II: M. and T. Longman imprint. Mary dies, Thomas II sole partner: T. Longman imprint	
	1756 Smollett launches the *Critical Review*
	1758 *Annual Register* founded
1760 Thomas II marries Elizabeth Harris	1760 Death of George II, accession of George III. Sterne *Tristram Shandy*

LONGMAN AS A PUBLISHER	THE CONTEXT
	1764 The Literary Club founded. Hargreaves's Spinning Jenny
	1765 Stamp Act imposed on the American colonies
	1768 The *Morning Chronicle*
	1769 Arkwright's spinning machine
	1770 Death of Thomas Chatterton
	1771 First edition of the *Encyclopaedia Britannica*
1772 Thomas II starts American correspondence with Henry Knox of Boston	
	1774 House of Lords rules that perpetual copyright had been illegal in England since 1710
	1775 Beginning of American War. Watt's steam engine
	1776 American Declaration of Independence. Smith *Wealth of Nations*. Gibbon *Decline and Fall of the Roman Empire*, Vol.1
1778 Folio edition of A. Rees *Cyclopaedia*	
	1780 First British Sunday newspaper. First steel pens
1782 Isaac Watts *The Improvement of the Mind*	1782 *The European Magazine*
	1783 *The English Review*. Bell's copper cylinder for calico printing
	1784 Death of Johnson. Cort's puddling process
	1785 Pendred *The London and Country Printers, Booksellers and Stationers Vade Mecum*. Rotary motion steam engine
	1786 R. Burns *Poems*
1788 S. Trimmer *The Sunday School Catechism*	1788 *The Analytical Review*
	1789 The French Revolution. Blake *Songs of Innocence*
	1790 First steam rolling mill in England
1791 S. Johnson *The Lives of the Most Eminent Poets*	1791 Boswell *Life of Johnson*. Ordnance Survey established
1793 Thomas Norton III becomes a partner. T. N. Longman imprint also T. Longman	1793 Britain goes to war with France. Chappe's semaphore system
	1794 Ratcliffe *The Mysteries of Udolpho*
	1795 Archibald Constable sets up business. Hydraulic press
1796 T. Rees *A New System of Stenography*	1796 Coleridge and Southey profess Pantisocracy and are first published by Joseph Cottle. Richard Phillips launches the *Monthly Magazine*
1797 Owen Rees becomes Thomas Norton's partner. Messr. Longman and Rees imprint. Death of Thomas II	1797 Bewick *British Birds*
1798 Cottle's copyrights acquired. Lindley Murray's copyrights acquired.	1798 Senefelder invents lithography. First paper making machine. Cottle publishes the *Lyrical Ballads*. Stamp tax on newspapers raised, Oliver and Boyd founded.
1799 T.N. Longman and O. Rees imprint. Lindley Murray *English Grammar*	

LONGMAN AS A PUBLISHER	THE CONTEXT
1800 New Longman/Rees edition of the *Lyrical Ballads*. Longman and Rees imprint	1800 Stanhope's iron printing press. Trevithick's high pressure steam engine
1801 Southey *Thalaba*	
1802 *The Edinburgh Review* launched	
1804 Longman, Hurst, Rees & Orme imprint	
1805 W. Scott *Lay of the Last Minstrel*. Wordsworth completes *The Prelude*	1805 The *Eclectic Review* launched
	1807 Britain abolishes the slave trade
	1808 Copyright extended
	1809 Founding of *The Quarterly Review*. Byron *English Bards and Scots Reviewers*
1811 Thomas Brown becomes a partner: Longman, Hurst, Rees, Orme and Brown imprint	1811 Founding of the *British Review*. Koenig's patent for a Cylinder Printing Machine
1812 Longman acquires Mavor *English Spelling Book*	1812 United States declare war on Britain. Main streets of London lit by gas
	1813 Southey becomes Poet Laureate. Austen *Pride and Prejudice*
	1814 Treaty of Ghent ends the British-American War. The Times printed by steam power. Copyright extended
	1815 Increase in stamp duties
	1816 Cobbett *Political Register*
1817 T. Moore *Lalla Rookh*. Bowdler's *Family Shakespeare*	1817 *Blackwood's Magazine*. Coleridge *Biographia Litteraria*. Keats *Poems*. Colburn launches the *Literary Gazette*
	1818 Select Committee on Copyright
	1819 Six Acts. New stamp duties
	1820 Death of George III. First steamship crosses the Atlantic. First iron steamship. The *Retrospective Review* is established to review older works. *John Bull* launched
	1821 The *Manchester Guardian* founded
1822 W.E. Green becomes a partner	1822 Launching of the *Mirror* and the *Sunday Times*
1823 Longman, Hurst, Rees, Orme, Brown and Green imprint	1823 Babbage starts building his mechanical computer. *The Lancet*. The *Forget-me-not*, the first English illustrated annual
1824 J. Johnson *Typographia, or the Printer's Instructor*	
1825 Longman, Rees, Orme, Brown & Green imprint. Macaulay's first contribution to *The Edinburgh Review*	1825 T.C. Hansard *Typographia*. Hazlitt *The Spirit of the Age*
	1826 Financial crisis. Collapse of Constable & Company. W. Clowes acquires Appleyard's printing business
	1827 Chromolithography. The *Evening Standard*. The *Foreign Quarterly Review*
	1828 The *Literary Chronicle* merges into the *Athenaeum*. Roman Catholic Emancipation Act
1829 Lardner's *Cabinet Cyclopaedia* started	1829 Liverpool and Manchester railway
	1830 Death of George IV: accession of William IV. The Whigs return to power

LONGMAN AS A PUBLISHER	THE CONTEXT
	1831 Founding of the British Association for the Advancement of Knowledge
1832 Longman, Rees, Orme, Brown, Green & Longman imprint. Thomas Longman IV becomes a partner	1832 Great Reform Bill. *Fraser's Magazine* launched. C. Knight launches *Penny Magazine*. J. & A. Churchill founded
1833 Printed paper jacket for *Keepsake*	
	1834 Invention of Braille
	1836 First phasing out of the Stamp Act. Dickens *Pickwick Papers*.
1837 Death of Owen Rees	1837 Accession of Queen Victoria. Electric telegraph. Pitman's shorthand. Carlyle *The French Revolution*. *Publishers' Circular*. The People's Charter
1838 Longman, Orme, Brown, Green & Longman imprint	1838 Bruce's typecasting machine
1839 William Longman becomes a partner	1839 Fox Talbot and Louis Daguerre announce photography. Faraday *Researches in Electricity*. Timperley *A Dictionary of Printers and Printing*. First steam hammer. Darwin *Voyage of the Beagle*
1840 Longman, Orme & Co imprint	1840 Penny post. Wood pulp used in Germany to make paper. Opening of Kew botanical garden
1841 Longman, Brown & Co imprint	1841 Tract 90. Bradshaw's *Railway Guide*. *Punch*. London Library opened
1842 Death of Thomas Norton III. Longman, Brown, Green & Longmans imprint. Macaulay *Lays of Ancient Rome*	1842 British Copyright Act. Mudie starts his circulating library. *Illustrated London News*. Bibliographical Society founded
	1843 Death of Southey: Wordsworth becomes Poet Laureate. Ruskin *Modern Painters, Vol.1*
1844 B.H. Kennedy *Progressive Latin Grammar*. Fox Talbot *The Pencil of Nature*	1844 Morse code sends message in Morse. Macmillans found Cambridge business.
1845 E. Acton *Modern Cookery*	1845 Newman converts to Roman Catholicism. First cable across English Channel. *Vestiges of the Natural History of Creation*
	1846 Repeal of the Corn Laws. Rotating cylinder press. Howe's sewing machine. *The Economist*
	1847 C. Bronte *Jane Eyre*. E. Bronte *Wuthering Heights*. Thackeray *Vanity Fair*. Chloroform
1848 Thomas IV acquires Farnborough estate. Macaulay *History of England*, Vol.1	1848 European revolutions. Chartists gather at Kennington Common
1849 End of Second Hand Book Department	1849 Froude *Nemesis of Faith*. *Notes and Queries* launched
	1850 The Public Libraries Act. *Household Words*. Wordsworth dies: Tennyson becomes Poet Laureate
1851 Travellers' Library	1851 Great Exhibition in the Crystal Palace. Launching of *New York Times*. Tenniel draws for *Punch*
1852 Roget *Thesaurus*	

LONGMAN AS A PUBLISHER

1853 M. Arnold *Poems*

1855 *Notes on Books*. Burton *Personal Narrative of a Pilgrimage to El-Medinah and Meccah*

1856 Thomas Roberts becomes a partner: Longman, Brown, Green, Longmans and Roberts imprint

1857 Trollope *Barchester Towers*. Buckle *History of Civilisation in England*, Vol.1

1859 Longman Green and Roberts imprint

1860 Gas first used in Paternoster Row. F. Espinasse articles on the House of Longman

1861 Fire at 39 Paternoster Row

1862 Longman, Green, Longman, Roberts & Green. Colenso *The Pentateuch Examined.*

1863 Take-over of J.W. Parker. New building completed at 39 Paternoster Row. Colenso deposed and reinstated on appeal

1864 Newman *Apologia pro Vita Sua*

1865 Robert Dyer becomes a partner: Longmans, Green, Reader & Dyer. H. Spencer *The Principles of Psychology* Longmans, Green, Reader and Dyer imprint

1866 *Complete Works of Macaulay*. *Public School Latin Primer*

1868 Imperial Quarto edition of the New Testament

1870 Disraeli, *Lothair*. G.O. Trevelyan *Life and Letters*

1871 William Longman elected President of the Alpine Club

THE CONTEXT

1853 Repeal of advertisement tax

1854 Crimean War (ended 1856). Northcote/Trevelyan report leads to founding of the Civil Service Commission

1855 *Daily Telegraph*. *Saturday Review*

1856 Burton and Speke discover Lakes Tanganyika and Victoria. Samuel Pearson founds his Bradford business

1858 Barry's Covent Garden Opera House

1859 Darwin *Origin of Species*. Smiles *Self-Help*. Eliot *Adam Bede*. Meredith *The Ordeal of Richard Feverel*, *The Rubaiyat of Omar Khayyam*. J.S. Mill *On Liberty*, Tennyson *Idylls of the King*. Dickens *A Tale of Two Cities*. *All the Year Round*

1860 Italian unification. *The Cornhill*. *Essays and Reviews*. *Hymns Ancient and Modern*. *Golden Treasury*

1861 Reade, *The Cloister and the Hearth*

1862 Mrs Braddon *Lady Audley's Secret*. English cricket team tours Australia

1863 Football Association founded

1864 E. & S. Livingstone founded. Knight *Passages of a Working Life*

1865 M. Arnold *Essays in Criticism*. President Lincoln assassinated. First successful transatlantic cable. *Pall Mall Gazette*. *Fortnightly Review*

1866 *Contemporary Review*. Swinburne *Poems and Ballads*. Nobel invents dynamite

1867 Second Reform Act. Typewriter comes into more general use

1868 Public executions abolished. First American newspapers to use wood pulp paper. Hodder and Stoughton founded. Morris *Earthly Paradise*

1869 Girton College, Cambridge founded. Suez Canal opened. M. Arnold *Culture and Anarchy*

1870 Death of Dickens. Franco-Prussian War. Papal Infallibility decreed. First national Education Act. Royal Commission on Science

1871 Religious Tests abolished at Oxford and Cambridge. Stanley meets Livingstone. FA Cup established

1872 Edison's 'duplex' telegraph. Hardy *Under the Greenwood Tree*

LONGMAN AS A PUBLISHER	THE CONTEXT
	1873 Hoe's web-fed rotary press. First oil well sunk in Baku, Azerbaijan
1874 Greville *Diaries*	1874 Trollope *The Way We Live Now*
1875 Death of Thomas IV	1875 Theosophical Society founded
1876 G.W. Trevelyan *Life of Macaulay*	1876 Bell's telephone. Edison's phonograph
1877 Death of William Longman	1877 Prototype of Remington typewriter. First Wimbledon tennis championship. *The Nineteenth Century* launched
1878 Lecky *History of England*, Vols 1 and 2	1878 Victoria declared Empress of India. Salvation Army founded. Electric light bulb. Invention of microphone
	1879 London's first telephone exchange
1880 Disraeli *Endymion*	1880 James *The Portrait of a Lady*. Hutchinson sets up publishing business
	1881 Stevenson *Treasure Island*. Opening of Natural History Museum
1882 *Longman's Magazine* launched: Lang column 'At the Sign of the Ship'	1882 Besant *All Sorts and Conditions of Men*. Society for Psychical Research founded. Regent Street Polytechnic opened
1883 End of Retail Department. Jefferies *Story of My Heart*	
1884 J.W. Allen joins business	1884 Third Reform Act. Parson's steam turbine for making electricity
1885 *Badminton Library*, Vol.1. Stevenson *Child's Garden of Verses*	1885 Beginning of *Dictionary of National Biography*
1886 *English Historical Review* founded. Stevenson *Dr. Jekyll and Mr. Hyde*	1886 Defeat of Irish Home Rule Bill. Berne Copyright Convention. Gas mantle invented. Amateur golf championship
1887 Haggard *She*. Opening of the Ship Binding Works	1887 'Bloody Sunday': Trafalgar Square riots. Queen Victoria's Golden Jubilee
1888 The Silver Library started	1888 Accession of Wilhelm II as German emperor. Hertz verified existence of radio waves. Pneumatic tyre. 'Kodak' camera
1889 Longmans, Green & Co. imprint. Thomas Norton Longman pays his first visit to America. New York Agency, 55 Firth Avenue. Lang *Blue Fairy Book*	1889 London Dock strike. Eiffel Tower. Daimler's first 4-wheeled motor vehicle
1890 Take-over of Rivingtons. Longmans, Green become sole publisher of the *Annual Register*	1890 W. Booth *In Darkest England*. Frazer *The Golden Bough*. William Heinemann founded. Marshall *Principles of Economics*. First London 'tube'. First corridor train. County cricket clubs classified
1891 First Longman cricket club	1891 United States accedes to international copyright treaties. C. Booth *Life and Labour of the People of London*, Vol.1. Gissing *New Grub Street*
1893 Weyman *Gentleman of France*	1893 *McClure's* Magazine
1894 S. and B. Webb *History of Trade Unionism*	1894 *The Yellow Book* launched. Kipling *The Jungle Book*
1895 *Badminton Magazine* founded. Death of Henry Reeve. F. and B. Upton *Two Dutch Dolls*	1895 Wells *The Time Machine*. Oscar Wilde trial. *The Ballad of Reading Gaol*. Hardy *Jude the Obscure*

LONGMAN AS A PUBLISHER	THE CONTEXT
	1896 Marconi arrives in London with radio patents. *Daily Mail* founded: costs 1/2d. First Olympics in Athens. Cinema displays in London. Macmillan becomes a private limited liability company. First Nobel Prizes
	1897 Queen Victoria's Diamond Jubilee. Monotype setting machine
1898 Churchill *Story of the Malakand Field Force*	1898 Discovery of Radium. First Zeppelin airship
1899 Trevelyan *England in the Age of Wycliffe*	1899 Board of Education. Aspirin invented. Magnetic recording of sound. Net book agreement
	1900 *Daily Express*. Freud *The Interpretation of Dreams*
	1901 Death of Queen Victoria. Accession of Edward VII. Marconi transmits messages across the Atlantic
1902 Walter de la Mare *Songs of Childhood*	1902 *Times Literary Supplement*
1903 Max Planck *Treatise on Thermodynamics*	1903 The Wright brothers fly
	1904 Workers' Educational Association founded. Safety razor blades
1905 Longman's *Political History of England* begun	1905 Automobile Association founded. Einstein propounds his first theory of relativity
1906 Branch opened in Calcutta	1906 R.A. Fessenden transmits words and music by radio. Book war with *The Times*
1907 Longman's Pocket Library	1907 Boy Scouts founded
	1908 Berlin Copyright Convention
	1909 Blériot crosses the Channel by air
	1910 Death of Edward VII and accession of George V
	1911 Ford's Model T. New Copyright Act. First studio in Hollywood. Britain joins Berne Convention
	1912 Invention of cellophane and stainless steel
1914 Opening of Madras Office	1914 Outbreak of the Great (First World) War
1916 *The Spirit of Man* anthology ed. R. Bridges	
1918 J.W. Allen becomes a partner	1918 Votes for women over 30. Pearson acquires Westminster Press
	1919 Mee's *Children's Newspaper*. Transatlantic flights. First successful helicopter flight. First motor scooter
	1920 Royal Institute of International Affairs founded. First public broadcasting station opened by Marconi Company at Writtle. British Board of Film Censors established.
	1921 Institute of Historical Research founded.
1922 Branch opened in Toronto	1922 British Broadcasting Company founded. Society of Bookmen formed. Joyce *Ulysses*
1924 Bicentenary celebrations. .	1924 British Empire Exhibition at Wembley
1925 Cox and Chandler *The House of Longman*. Printers' strike	1925 National Book Council

LONGMAN AS A PUBLISHER

1926 Longmans, Green and Co. becomes a private limited liability company. K.B. Potter becomes a Director. C.S.S. Higham joins the business. M. West *New Method Readers Handbook*

1927 Wilder *The Bridge of San Luis Rey*

1929 Dudley Stamp *The World*

1931 Potter provides financial backing

1932 Gibbons *Cold Comfort Farm*

1934 First title in *Heritage of Literature* series

1935 West *New Method English Dictionary*. Whitmarsh *Complete French Course*

1937 R.M. Rayner *A Concise History of Britain*

1938 D. Richards *History of Modern Europe*. Eckersley *Essential English*

1939 Collins-Longman *Study Atlas*

1940 Destruction of 39 Paternoster Row. Move to Wimbledon. Miall *New Dictionary of Chemistry*

1944 G.M. Trevelyan *English Social History* pub. in UK

1946 Chapple joins business

1947 Longman becomes a public limited liability company. 6/7 Clifford Street acquired. Allen *Living English Structure*

1948 Chapple/Higham world tour

1949 225th anniversary celebrations

1950 Burton *The Criticism of Poetry*

1951 Vogel *Textbook of Organic Chemistry*

1952 Kuala Lumpur offices opened

1953 M. Renault *The Charioteer*. Stonier and Hague *Textbook of Economic Theory*

1954 First titles in *Then & There* series

THE CONTEXT

1927 British Broadcasting Corporation: first Charter. United States Federal Radio Commission. Book Trade Joint Advisory Committee

1929 Wall Street crash. Central Council for School Broadcasting

1930 F. Mumby *Publishing and Bookselling*

1932 Book tokens scheme. Q.D. Leavis *Fiction and the Reading Public*

1934 British Council founded. Federal Communications Commission (USA)

1935 George V's Silver Jubilee. First Penguin paperbacks

1936 First BBC television

1938 Munich crisis

1939 Outbreak of Second World War

1940 Blitz. Destruction of premises of Simpkin Marshall, wholesalers

1941 First RAF planes fly with Whittle jet engines

1944 Education Act

1946 Regular BBC television service reinstated

1947 First supersonic air flight. Invention of transistor

1948 National Health Service. First long playing record. University Copyright Convention, Brussels Convention. First Reith Lecture. N. Wiener *Cybernetics*

1949 People's Republic of China proclaimed

1950 First cable systems

1951 Festival of Britain

1952 Death of George VI

1953 DNA: double helix model announced. Coronation of Queen Elizabeth II televised. Press Council set up

1955 First independent television programmes in UK

1956 Suez crisis. Revolt in Hungary. Transatlantic telephone service

LONGMAN AS A PUBLISHER

1957 John Newsom joins Longman Board

1958 Hong Kong branch opened. Mary Renault *The King Must Die*. Stone and Cozen *Biology for Tropical Schools*. Longman imprint. Tim Rix joins business

1959 Thomas Michael Longman leaves the business. Thesiger *Arabian Sands*. *The Annual Register 1958* - Bicentenary volume. *Day by Day English*

1960 D. Storey *This Sporting Life*. Maxwell *Ring of Bright Water*. Gray *Dictionary of Physics*
1961 48 Grosvenor Street acquired
1962 Longman, Ghana created and Longman Malaya. *Roget's Thesaurus* (latest rev. ed.)

1964 Orwin & Whetum *History of British Agriculture, 1846-1914*

1965 Pinnacles property acquired at Harlow. Longman Nigeria and Longman Kenya incorporated

1966 Longman Group created
1967 Blagden *Fire More Than Water*. Robottom *Modern China*. Alexander *New Concept English*

1968 Move to Harlow. The Longman Group becomes part of S. Pearson & Son Ltd. Divisional structure introduced. Tim Rix becomes Head of English Language Teaching (ELT)
1969 Longman imprint

1970 Pearson/Longman inaugurated. Pearson acquires Penguin. Brief Penguin/Longman merger. Switch to computers. *Breakthrough to Literacy* (Reading Scheme)
1971 *Keesing's* and *Ladybird* acquired. O'Neill *Kernel Lessons*
1972 Death of Mark Longman. Re-organisation of Longman Group Board. Robert Allan joins Board. Rix and Yglesias Joint Managing Directors in new Executive Committee. Joint Consultative Committee set up for labour relations

THE CONTEXT

1957 Russia launches Sputnik. Pearson acquires the *Financial Times*. Altick *The English Common Reader ... 1800-1900*
1958 USA launches Explorer I. Stereophonic gramophone records. USA establishes ARPA (Advanced Research Projects Agency). Penguin publish first British book without the use of metal type
1959 Integrated circuit patent applied for. First stretch of British motorway. Hovercraft. First attempt to pass a Libraries Public Lending Right Bill. Printers' strike lasts nearly seven weeks
1960 *Lady Chatterley's Lover* law case

1961 University of Sussex
1962 Telstar communications satellite launched. Net Book Agreement ruled valid by Restrictive Practices Court. McLuhan *Gutenberg Galaxy*. *Private Eye* launched
1963 The Newsom Report *Half Our Future*
1964 Schools Council set up. Labour government under Harold Wilson. World Book Fair. McLuhan *Understanding Media*
1965 Early Bird communications satellite. First walk in space. First novel in Europe produced type-set by computer
1966 First National Library Week
1967 Biafran War in Nigeria (ended 1970). Financial, Provincial and Overseas(Finprov) formed by Pearson. British colour television
1968 Student disturbances in Europe and United States. John Murray's bi-centenary. Demonstration of Online system in San Francisco. Restrictive Practices Court ratifies Net Book Agreement. Booker Prize founded
1969 25,000th issue of *Financial Times*. First moon landing. ARPANET begins in California. Sony launches video-tape cassettes. Murdoch acquires the *Sun*
1970 End of Labour government: Edward Heath succeeds Wilson. A. Toffler *Future Shock*

1971 Open University admits first students. Microprocessor devised
1972 Britain joins Common Market. Videocassettes on sale. E-mail developed within ARPANET. Fiftieth anniversary of BBC. UNESCO World Book Year: slogan 'Books for All'. British Library established by Act of Parliament

LONGMAN AS A PUBLISHER

1973 Dictionaries and Reference Book Department created. Quirk, *Grammar of Contemporary English*. Longman Inc., New York set up

1974 250th Anniversary celebrations: *Essays in the History of Publishing*. Wallis *At the Sign of the Ship*. House magazine, *The Log* launched. First conference of African managers

1975 *New Biology for West African Schools*

1976 Chapple retires; Rix becomes Chief Executive. Roger Brooke is non-executive chairman. Cheshire Publishing Company, Australia acquired. Freezing of prices of book titles in stock. Allen & Cooke *Living English for the Arab World*

1978 Longman *Dictionary of Contemporary English*. Award for Export Achievement. Channon *New General Maths for West Africa*

1979 Brooke leaves: succeeded by James Lee

1980 Oyez acquired

1981 Miller *Anaesthesia*

1982 Launch of video range. *Longman New Universal Dictionary*

1983 Blakenham becomes Chairman of Pearson. Lee moves to Goldcrest.

1984 Channon *New General Maths for West Africa* 2nd ed.

1985 House magazine the *Grapevine* launched. Longman Espana set up. Acquisition of Pitman. *New Biology for West African Schools* 2nd ed.

1986 R. Dawkins, *The Blind Watchmaker*. Longman Scientific and Technical established

1987 150th anniversary of Pitman

1988 Merger with Addison-Wesley. Russell *Soil Conditions and Plant Growth*. Alexander *Longman English Grammar*. Nuffield *Co-ordinated Science*

1989 Rix tells staff of his impending departure

1990 Departure of Rix as Chairman; succession of Paula Kahn

1994 A re-positioned Longman ceases to exist

THE CONTEXT

1973 Oil crisis. Value Added Tax not applied to books and newspapers

1974 Two general elections in a year: Heath loses both. Annan Committee on Broadcasting

1975 Referendum on Britain joining the Common Market: majority in favour

1976 United States Copyright Law. Apple 1 launched. Microcomputers

1977 Mobile telephones. Optic fibre installed in California

1978 Britain applies for financial support to the International Monetary Fund. First Publishers' Delegation to Chinese People's Republic

1978/9 'Winter of discontent'

1979 Public Lending Right Act. Margaret Thatcher becomes Britain's first woman prime minister

1980 Pearson involvement in Goldcrest

1981 Murdoch acquires *The Times*

1982 Falklands War. First UNESCO World Congress on Books. Opening of Public Lending Right Register. Publishers' Data Base Ltd

1984 Videocameras and compact discs. CISCO Systems established

1985 Founding of Book Trade History Group

1986 Microsoft becomes a public company. *The Times* moves to Wapping

1987 Stock Market crash

1988 Share swap between Pearson and Elsevier. British Copyright Act

1989 Fall of the Berlin Wall. Collapse of Soviet power. Berners-Lee devises the World Wide Web

1990 Radio and Television Act. BSkyB formed by merger

1993 Privatisation of British Rail. Clinton administration in US proclaims 'information superhighway'. Society for the History of Authorship Reading and Publishing (SHARP) set up

Appendix 5

Life span, an autobiographical note

My own life span has covered the important changes in communications and in communications technologies described in Chapters 7, 8 and 9. I was born in 1921, the year before the foundation of the BBC, the history of which I began to write on invitation – it was not an official history – in 1958. Subsequently I wrote five volumes on broadcasting in the United Kingdom, the last of them, *Competition*, published in 1995. All the earlier volumes, the first of which, *The Birth of Broadcasting*, had first appeared in 1961, were then revised to appear in parallel in a new edition. I also wrote *The BBC, The First Fifty Years*, which appeared in 1985, *Governing the BBC* (1979), and, with Joanna Spicer, *The Franchise Affair: Creating Fortunes and Failure in Independent Television* (1986). For more than a decade, from 1966 to 1981, I had been a Director of Southern Television, one of the franchise holders which lost its franchise in 1981 as part of 'the Affair'.

I would not have been invited to write the history of the BBC in 1958 had I not already had wide-ranging experience as a broadcaster: I first broadcast in 1944, while in uniform, before the end of the War. I had also been deeply involved by 1958 in research on the evolution of the printed media, particularly newspapers: a lecture to the Dugdale Society, 'Press and Public in Early Nineteenth-century Birmingham', was published in 1948. The Birmingham Collection, then housed in the Birmingham Reference Library, was the first archive that I explored. My *History of Birmngham 1865–1938* (1952) brought me – and still brings me – into the life of the city. Leeds figured too on my communications map. It was as Professor of History at Leeds University from 1955 to 1961 that I was deeply involved in the pioneering Communications programme financed by Granada Television and directed by Joseph Trenaman: Sir Gerald Barry became a friend as later did Sir Denis Forman and Lord (Sidney) Bernstein. In 1966, five years after I left Leeds, I delivered the third Mansbridge Memorial Lecture in the University on 'The Communications Revolution', and in 1971 I wrote a chapter on the Manuscripts Department of the British Museum in *Treasures of the British Museum*, based on a series of Thames Television programmes.

My first association with Longman – through Cyprian Blagden, who, again, became a close friend – began while I was at Leeds when I was beginning work on *The Age of Improvement* (1959), a book that was written, like some of my later books, on both sides of the Atlantic. I had a much treasured room to myself in Harvard's Widener Library. I subsequently edited the Longman history series *The Economic and Social History of*

England, working closely with Professor W.N. Medlicott, who edited the parallel *Political History* series in which *The Age of Improvement* appeared. From 1950 to 1970 I did a lot of publishers' reading for Longman and for other publishers, and in 1978 I wrote an introduction to a new illustrated edition of G.M. Trevelyan's *Social History*. Meanwhile, I had been approached by Lord Goodman to join a small group considering a different future for Penguin from that which was actually to be followed.

It was in the light of such experiences that I was invited to edit for the 250th Anniversary of the House of Longman *Essays in the History of Publishing*, choosing my own authors and discussing with them the subject matter of their essays. The first essay writer was a Sussex neighbour, Ian Parsons of Chatto and Windus, who greatly helped in the founding of a short-lived University of Sussex Press. By a curious twist of history, as early as 1963 I had been introduced to the early history of Pearson, which acquired Longman in 1968, when I wrote a foreword to Keith Middlemass's *The Master Builder* which dealt with the pre-publishing Pearson business. Indeed, I already knew something of that early history from my childhood days in Keighley long before Keighley was incorporated into Bradford.

While a Fellow of Worcester College, Oxford from 1945 to 1955 I had been appointed Reader in Recent Social and Economic History in Oxford University in 1950. This was a new post, specially created for me: the 'recent' was a not uncontentious adjective chosen by G.D.H.Cole, to whom I owe a great debt. While holding it I described my *History of Birmingham, 1865-1938* as 'total history', explaining why without at that time having any acquaintance with the *Annales School*, but it was not until more than thirty years later that I began to think of myself as I now do, as a cultural rather than as a political, economic or social historian. In 1976 I became President of the Social History Society, and the Society itself has moved in the same direction. As I was finishing this *History* the Society was in the process of launching a new periodical *Cultural and Social History*. In 1983 I wrote the first edition of my *Social History of England*, published not by Longman but by Weidenfeld. George Weidenfeld personally encouraged me to write it. Then the book followed on with a series of programmes on English social history that I wrote and delivered for the Chinese Service of the BBC.

I was well acquainted with the *Annales School* across the Channel long before I returned from Sussex University, where I was Vice-Chancellor from 1967 to 1976, to Worcester College, Oxford, where I was Provost from 1976 to 1991, but I was not so well acquainted with French studies of the history of the book. It was while at Worcester – at the invitation and with the financial support of Tim Rix and the Longman Group – that I began to direct a series of seminars in the College on the history of the book in 1983. These brought together in agreeable surroundings scholars of various disciplines concerned with book trade history, including from Oxford itself Michael Turner from the Bodleian Library and Giles Barber from the Taylorian Library.

My interest in libraries had grown over the years, beginning in the period of nine years from 1956 to 1965 when I was President of the Workers' Educational Association; and as Vice-Chancellor of Sussex I was for a time Chairman of the Vice-Chancellors' Library Committee. In 1992 I gave the Inaugural Lecture, 'Books and Bookmanship: Changing Perspectives' in the new Public Library in Chicago. I had strong links with Chicago where I had twice been a visiting professor, and with American publishing.

The Worcester College seminars laid the foundations of this *History*. Annabel Jones of Longman helped me indefatigably at every stage with their organisation, as did Susan Hard. There are reasonably full records of the meetings, although we deliberately did not use tapes. I had become interested in the use of tapes when I was writing my history of the BBC, and it was through oral history that I met Paul Thompson and subsequently became Chairman of the National Real Lives Collection which took up book trade lives in 2000 as a special project. When the *History of the Book in Britain* was launched in Cambridge I became Chairman of the Advisory Group of the Cambridge University Press to supervise all seven volumes, and I organised links with foreign scholars involved, mainly but not exclusively, in their own book trade history. I also became involved with an entirely separate venture, The Cambridge Project for the Book. Through this I came to know and to appreciate the work of James Raven.

While Provost, I supervised a number of post-graduate students from several Oxford Colleges who were researching on communications history, and, with two exceptions, such students, along with students in other fields of interest to me, were the authors of the *Festschrift volume, Cities, Class and Communications*, edited by Derek Fraser in 1990 and published by Harvester/Wheatsheaf. The Harvester Press, launched by an old Sussex pupil, John Spiers, had published the first two volumes of my *Collected Essays* in 1985, with the University of Illinois Press publishing them in parallel across the Atlantic, to be followed by a third volume, *Serious Pursuits: Communications and Education*, in 1991, the year that I left Oxford.

The third volume included many of my essays on communications with some new ones added. In it I tried to bring together education, information and entertainment. While in Australia in 1960, when I was Visiting Professor at the Australian National University, I had delivered the Joseph Fisher Lecture in Commerce at Adelaide University on 'Mass Entertainment, the Origins of a Modern Industry' which, along with my essays on 'The Welfare State in Historical Perspective' (1961) and on 'The Language of Class in Nineteenth-Century England' (1979), have become seminal university studies. My book *Victorian Things* (1988), which along with *Victorian People* and *Victorian Cities* I regard as a trio, re-published by the Folio Society, is my most original contribution to the study of history.

Much of my writing had its origins in lectures, including the James Thin Lecture in Edinburgh University on the history of books in November

1999. With this *History* in mind, I chose as its title 'Shelf Life: the Limits to Longevity in Publishing'. I did not publish two sets of T.S. Eliot Lectures which I gave in the University of Kent and the University of Virginia, but go back to them frequently. The most prestigious of my London lectures was 'Good Times, Bad Times', a Livery Lecture delivered in Stationers Hall in London in 1996 on the occasion of the centenary of the Publishers Association. I was proud that it was printed by the London College of Printing. As Honorary President of the Ephemera Society since 1984 I have treasured my close association with Michael Twyman, an expert in printing history and a winner of the Society's Pepys Medal and before that with Maurice Rickards, the Founder (he deserves a capital letter) of the Society. I have also gained much through my Honorary Presidency since 1983 of the Victorian Society. I gave one of the three addresses at the symposium *Do Books Matter?*, presided over by the Duke of Edinburgh and held appropriately at the National Film Theatre. George Steiner gave another of them.

I was a Governor of the British Film Institute from 1970 to 1976 and from 1968 to 1986 a Trustee (and for a time Research Chairman) of the International Institute of Communications, originally called the International Broadcast Institute. And that took me to Japan on several occasions. In Britain I was a member of the Planning Committee of the Open University during the 1960s and its Chancellor from 1977 to 1994, and unlike any other Chancellor I took part in the preparation and broadcasting of some of its course units. I was drawn from the start to the idea of the Open University which drew on the convergence of twentieth-century educational opportunities and communications technologies. It seemed a necessary extension of the idea when in 1988 I became for five years Chairman of the Commonwealth of Learning, with its headquarters in Vancouver. In 2003 I was made a Distinguished Fellow of COL at a meeting in South Africa, my first visit there since the ending of Apartheid. On the invitation of Sonny Ramphal I had been Chairman of the Commonwealth Secretary General's Advisory Committee, which led to the setting up of COL, directly concerned, as is Britain's Open University, with distance learning.

Since I am by conviction an historian who tries to encompass literature as well as the social sciences, I revel in time travel and detest being tied to one period of history. Yet I have focused increasingly during the last fifteen years on the history of communications. In 1992 I delivered the Ellen McArthur Lectures in Cambridge on *Commerce and Culture: The Publishing Business in Britain*, the first time that such a subject had been chosen for these Lectures. Nevertheless, to demonstrate that a personal life span is a cycle not a sequence I was encouraged to feel that I was lecturing in the same lecture room where as an undergraduate I had listened to G.M. Trevelyan.

In 1991, my last year as Provost of Worcester College, I delivered the Ford Lectures in the Oxford Examination Schools on *Culture and Communications in Victorian Britain*, which I hope will soon be published by Oxford University Press. This, too, was a first occasion, for there had been no previous Ford Lecture on such a topic. The bibliographical tradition in Britain, which I greatly respect – and which in recent years has benefited from new insights – has contributed less to their development than the work of historians and anthropologists. While the subject of communications had never figured previously in Ford Lectures, I am sure that mine will not be the last lectures to do so. Media studies now figure more prominently in some universities than the study of history as a whole. Their proneness to jargon – and to duplicated or derivative research – has not restricted their appeal, and there are scholars of distinction associated with them.

The Ford Lectures were specifically confined to English history when I delivered them, but through my travels as much as through my researches I have always been drawn to the comparative and global history of communications. I contributed an essay to *La consommation culturelle dans le monde anglophone* (2000, eds., L. Kerjan and R. Dickason) on 'The Culture of the BBC', a subject on which I have often lectured in France, and I have spent two spells in New York, the last of them in 1995, with the Communications Institute, later called Freedom Forum, financed by the Gannett Foundation and now sadly dissolved. During my first visit it was directed with distinction by Everett Dennis, who became a cherished friend. He is now deeply concerned with human longevity and has launched *Health and the Future*, the journal of the International Longevity Centre.

On both my visits to New York I was examining the relationships between forecasts and outcomes in communications history, a subject which I took up years ago (and have subsequently by no means exhausted) after I was awarded the Marconi Medal for my work on broadcasting history in 1975. I have worked then and later at the Aspen Institute in Colorado, and have taken part in the stimulating seminars on communications organised by Charlie Firestone, where I have met distinguished practitioners in the field of communications and have been able to keep in touch with rapidly changing technologies. I owe a great debt to Charlie Firestone who knows almost instinctively how important it is to bring together 'academics' and practitioners.

In 2002 I was invited to become a Kluge Distinguished Senior Fellow at the Library of Congress, an honour which I deeply appreciate. After a serious illness I could not take it up in 2003 or in 2004, but I did so in 2005. I carried out research then on the history of radio in Britain and the United States in the formative years from 1921 to 1927, asking myself how and why two quite different broadcasting systems developed given the same new technology. I hope to produce a short book on the subject. Fortunately, as I write, my own story continues.

Index